Novels by Melvyn Bragg

For Want of a Nail
The Second Inheritance
Without a City Wall
The Hired Man
A Place in England
The Nerve
Josh Lawton
The Silken Net

SPEAK FOR
ENGLAND

SPEAK FOR
ENGLAND

An Oral History of England:
1900-1975
based on interviews
with inhabitants of
Wigton, Cumberland

Alfred A. Knopf, New York

1977

This is a Borzoi Book
published by Alfred A. Knopf, Inc.

Library of Congress Cataloging in Publication Data
Main entry under title:
Speak for England.
1. Wigton, Eng. (Cumberland)—Social life
and customs. 2. Wigton, Eng. (Cumberland)—
Biography. I. Bragg, Melvin, [date]
DA690.W599S7   1976b   942.7'87
76–48172   ISBN 0–394–40855–1

Manufactured in the United States of America

FIRST AMERICAN EDITION

TO DAVID FARRER
for his friendship
and with thanks for his skill
in editing this book

But we are the people of England; and we have not spoken yet.
Smile at us, pay us, pass us. But do not quite forget.

from "The Secret People" by G. K. Chesterton

CONTENTS

Illustration inserts follow page 52 and page 212

Map I (Wigton and the North-East) is on page 494

Map II (Wigton in 1901) is on page 499

ACKNOWLEDGEMENT OF ILLUSTRATIONS

Again John Higham has to be thanked for making so freely available the collection of photographs
he has built up for the school archives. Bill Walker,
Cumberland News Photographer, has been invalu-
able in taking portraits of contributors, reproduc-
ing old photographs and doing the major part of
the assembly. To him, particular thanks.

Many people have been most generous in lending
photographs, among them, the Fell family, John
Holdsworth, Mrs. Kerr, Dr. Loveday, Donald
McNeil, Christine Scott, Miss Snaith, Miss Todd,
Cumberland Newspapers Group Ltd., Skyviews &
General Ltd. I would like to thank especially
Donald Penrice, whose shop and character stand
firmly in the middle of the town.

Map II by Cartographic Enterprises.

SPEAK FOR
ENGLAND

INTRODUCTION

If we want a new start we must look to the past. The present is too occupied, the future too obscure.

I believe this to be true, both for countries and individuals. When my first wife died I found that one of the courses of action I eventually took was to bring our daughter back to the place where I was born. For better or worse I wanted to root her into a part of the world and a family of relationships I knew. My present wife and I found a place which looked north to the sea and south to the hills. And the three of us dug in.

While we were there I began working on this book which reaches back in order to go forward as I did. I began to interview people, make notes, find out about life this century as experienced by the people of that district. As the number of interviews grew over the next two or three years I saw that the material was not so much a cross-section of local history as a representative record of English life during this century. Indeed one could see where the material outreached not only local but national boundaries: accounts of trench-life in World War One are common to the histories of many nations, and poverty, the fading of religion and the rise of affluence are similar in kind and in degree, in many countries. But to find out about England was enough.

When a book gets going inside a writer's head it is because in some way an idea magnetises his mind and all sorts of notions, ambitions and facts suddenly find a location where they can cluster. That is what happened here. I started the interviews out of curiosity, out of a need to find a strategy which would not leave me too much alone at that time and out of a continuing affection for the place in which I had my childhood and adolescence and to which I shall always return. I had set much of my fiction there; I had made various investigations into aspects of its history. But as the project grew so did a number of different considerations which for years had been idle or dormant. The most important of these concerned the nature of history and the fate of this country.

I read History at Oxford University and though it was called Modern History I never reached the twentieth century. What was called History, though, was really Politics and Economics. It could scarcely be otherwise if you were determined to use the best available evidence, to cover a great number of years and to play the game. I enjoyed playing it: to invoke, re-order and, best of all, dispose of the destinies of dead events is no small thrill and it is no surprise that so many kings and emperors have loved History – the past can be as real as Napoleon's new map of Europe. The past, that is, which is the record and almost the preserve of great men and great occurrences; the past, in brief, which is the testament of what the leaders of society have ordered to be done. Similarly, and in parallel, if you wished to know the way in which nature had made its mark, then you needed to know about prevailing economic conditions. But between these two, between politics which described life at the top and economics which described life at the foundation, there was what could be called no-man's land: this book aims to occupy that territory.

For what Politics and Economics did not tell us was what people thought of their lives, how they saw it, how they had passed from one unknown to another. At Oxford I learnt something of the way in which people were told to live their lives and something of the way in which they were compelled to lead their lives; but what they made of it and what they thought they made of it was almost entirely unknown. Most of the dead are buried without leaving any trace. My own family, for example, which has been in Cumberland as far back as one can go – a few hundred years – has entered history as part of a number. "Soldiers – 14", "labourers – 12", and so on. At Oxford there was neither the inclination nor the room for ordinary people to tell their own version: now there is both.

This is not to say that I have been assembling a work of propaganda. It is only to point out that here, as, happily, in many other contemporary histories, we discover the voice of the people. The new idea of history is that everyone has played a part.

But before this century the way in which many people fleshed and blooded the past was through works of art. Paintings, buildings and particularly imaginative literature told us what it was *like* to be alive in times past. Mayhew's *London Labour and the London Poor*, though entirely sympathetic to my own feelings in its intentions, was, nevertheless, clearly dealing with one section of society only and looking for evidence which would scandalise and stir the Victorian conscience. For a picture of social life with some sense of comprehensiveness we turn to the fiction of Dickens and George Eliot.

This book attempts to be comprehensive; it deals with all sorts of people, all classes, all ages, all conditions. In that sense it might appear to take over the job of fiction. I can report that, whatever its merits or demerits, it is essentially different from a novel. Two of my novels cover roughly the same time-scale as this book: they concern themselves with people who live in the area which is inhabited by the contributors to this book: their work, leisure, behaviour and habits are necessarily like those of the "real" people who speak for themselves here. Yet these two books are different from this – better or worse, richer or thinner depending on your opinion of fiction in general and these novels in particular – and different in so many ways that it would take another essay to detail them. Their differences, though, raise one important matter which needs to be underlined before going any further: everything quoted in this book is directly quoted and, as far as is humanly possible, accurately quoted from the person stated. No lines are switched from one person to another for effect. No lines are added by me. What is said is said by the people as they said it – and that fact can illustrate one of the differences between documentary history and fiction. For I longed to switch lines: I itched to embroider and take off and elaborate on innuendoes and use the hints and gossip I remembered from childhood or picked up along the way. In short I was tugged in the direction of fiction: resisting that pressure brought home one of the many distinctions between imagined life and life recalled. It might be better to adopt a "hearing mode" when reading.

It is difficult, even embarrassing nowadays, to talk about "the fate of this country". Patriotism is seen not only as the last refuge of the scoundrel but as the first bolt-hole of the hypocrite. As the twentieth century has proceeded, "England" – the word – has appeared to some observers to be as bled of meaning as it has been of men and possessions. I don't share this view. I have a great curiosity and concern about the future of this place.

It is easy to respect the suspicions of those who distrust all calls of "England". England this, England that – far too often, the name of the country has been used as the trump in a pack of lies. Far too often it has been brandished by the powerful to subdue the restless or hoisted by the strong to force a salute from the weak. And, fortunately, our age distrusts denominations which denote complacency: "an Englishman's word ..." "An Englishman would never ..." "An Englishman always ..." All these clichés we have seen turned to easy profit or exploited in order to achieve shameful superiority. We have every right to beware of those who talk of England's heritage while their companies batter down its great buildings; who boast of English virtues while evading English taxes; and a duty to prevent the world being tribalised in such a petty way. For when they boast of an Englishman doing this or that, it is almost always in order to show how much better or sounder or wittier he is than an American or a Dutchman or an African: it is important to confuse that issue as much as possible – national caricatures soon become a disability.

That is what has happened here, I think. England has become fixed in a past which can no longer be placed. Like an actor who has played one character for so long that every other rôle he plays resembles the rôle for which he is famous, England has stuck in a part which is less and less meaningful: the play has moved on. For though cheap and easy tags about England and the English must be shown for what they are, there *is* in any country with a tradition, a culture and energy, a recognisable face. The one we had no longer fits; it is my hope that in the mirror of this book we can discover the outlines of a new appearance.

It is when you go abroad that you see your home most keenly and when I first went abroad, just after the mid-century, the notion and the image of an Englishman was still clear. He could be found in the City and in the Clubs, in the pages of Somerset Maugham and in the films made at Ealing; he had a stiff upper lip and yet a sense of humour, a sense of honour and yet an opportunistic, even perfidious, determination, good taste, good clothes, firm prejudices, good manners and so on and so on. Although I had personally never met anyone like that – not even among the teachers at the local grammar school – and although behind this image was the brutal fact that such poise relied and depended upon the service and subservience not only of colonies overseas but of classes within the land itself, classes which included my own, yet I recognised this type and saw it as a standard. An Englishman was a gentleman – that could be the summary. Very well, if you had no money, no privileges, no luck and no taste at least you could end up "not-a-gentleman". You could be on the way to being a gentleman, almost a gentleman, not quite a gentleman, no longer a gentleman, a failed gentleman, a little gentleman, an old gentleman, a gentleman at last and, of course, a real gentleman. Where are they now?

Who has replaced the gentleman? It's still unclear.

That is why we must speak up. Not boastfully – though if we wanted to boast there is plenty to boast of in this country: our sins might be great but so are our achievements; for a small nation we have survived, recovered and conquered too often to be scared for long – but straightforwardly and simply we must, as Orwell urged, "tell it like it is".

This, then, is not the voice of Elizabethan England, though it continues Shakespeare's language; it is not the voice of Johnson's England, nor have we the tones of the great Victorians; even Churchill's England is past. But none of these – nor all the others – are lost as long as we choose to speak at all. They are the past which we can claim and use for present and future progress. And as a type of Englishman has emerged again and again over the centuries, each time distinctly different but each time recognisably the same, so we can look out for the new type who will surely emerge now.

Yet to hare up and down the countryside looking for him would be foolish, I think. Moreover, I am sufficiently superstitious to believe that there is something so delicate and complicated in all this that it is best left mysterious – and so to look at all directly would be a mistake – like staring at the sun to learn about light. The purpose of this book is for those who contributed to tell their history of England from the end of the nineteenth century to the present day. Whatever else comes out will reveal itself by chance.

To find the world in a grain of sand has been a sound method in science and art since men started looking for answers. And so it seemed to me a good idea to settle on one place for this book. Wigton is fully and statistically described in the appendixes, as are all the contributors, but a few general remarks about both are needed here.

I would claim that Wigton is a representative town: or, rather, that out of it I have been able to gather as representative a sample as is consistent with the resources of an essay such as this. Like most places, not only in England, but in North America, Europe and other parts of the world, its great twentieth-century markers were the First World War, a depression, the Second World War, and increased affluence. Like most places in the Western World, those older people who live there look back to a world in domestic comforts so bleak that their grandchildren have great difficulty in comprehending it. Of course there are deprived minorities and continuing incrops of obstinate wretchedness, but overall, the people of Wigton, like those elsewhere, have taken part in a revolution in life-style and in expectation.

Wigton is in the northern part of Cumberland, on the border with Scotland, geographically about the middle of the British Isles. It has always been a market town and still the farmers come in on Tuesdays and Thursdays. Naturally, it has experienced the general drift from the land, compounded by the drift from such counties as Cumberland to the large cities. However, since the beginning of the century and more important since the 1930s, Wigton itself has been a "city-force": a factory, now entering a boom-stage, has drawn in the men from the villages and held onto some of the men from the town. There is also a clothing factory which has employed a considerable number of women throughout the century: these two industries and the former possibilities of the nearby pits make Wigton more Town than Country despite its rural location. It is a centre for schools, from a Quaker school to a Roman Catholic school, with national schools of all stages in the educational process between: there are minor industries, banks and churches and pubs in rich supply, there once was a Great House and, like its twin across the bowl in which the town is set, there once was a Workhouse – now both changed, one into luxury flats, the other into a hospital. Throughout the century the population has risen slowly – very closely in line with the national figure, about twenty-five percent – near 4,000 people in 1900, about 5,000 now.

It is not the static, homespun little place the postcards portray. A very substantial number commute from Wigton every day: an almost exactly equal number commute to Wigton. New estates stand where even I can remember green fields. Like many places, the centre has been scooped out for a car-park: again like many places, just about enough has been retained to keep the town's identity. The old fee-paying grammar school became a state grammar school and is now part of a comprehensive. There is street lighting everywhere it is needed and musak in the younger pubs. These notes are enough, I hope, with the further details at the end of the book, to substantiate the claim that Wigton can be described as a representative setting for a book on England which aims to let it speak for itself.

I spoke to people of all ages. The oldest, a woman in her eighties; the youngest, a girl then eight. People of all classes, from a woman whose chief occupation in the winter is fox-hunting, to farm labourers and ex-miners worn out with toil. To men in the professions and men in the factory, to Tories, Labour and Liberals, to Catholics and Protestants and atheists, to the highly educated and the poorly educated, to people whose tastes are as different as it is possible to imagine, and the balance I tried to strike was, again, a representative one. I gave a preponderance to ordinary people because there are more of them. Though proper acknowledgment is made later, I want to thank everyone for the time and pains they took to answer my questions: I have material for ten books. It was a help that I had been born there, that my parents and grandparents and many uncles and aunts still lived there and thereabouts; but when the tape-recorder was running it still

6

took patience and generosity to speak up.

It was not my intention to ask about local history and there is scarcely anything of that here. At one stage I did try to make links with events in our national history: with particular Acts of Parliament, with specific strikes or international events. This did not get very far. I discovered that the history people wanted to talk about, that which they wanted to record and remember, was human history. So a man will talk of the Second World War, not in terms of Rommel or Montgomery or Eisenhower, but in a way in which everyone who served under those generals would understand. And poverty in the Thirties to a woman with six children would not be in terms of coalition governments and social legislation and trade union demands, but soup-kitchens, shoes for the family, the memory of a day's outing to the seaside – the common body of daily life.

This book carries the voices of those who contribute to it. Whatever may be the strength of my arguments or intentions I wanted to make as sure as I could that what people have said would not be used for my own private purposes. So I devised a double-barrelled system: half of the book – almost alternate chapters – consists of a collection of evidence around a particular event or period – a war, education, religion, etc. This enables the reader to get an idea of the range of society, the differences, the similarities – gives weight, I believe, to the basic, invariably simple, chapter title. Between these I have placed what I called to myself "portraits": that is, a chapter entirely devoted to a single person speaking at some length about his or her life, sometimes from birth to the present day. Thus, just as the "theme" chapters generally take the book forward from the end of the nineteenth century to the present day, these "portraits" sometimes themselves span the entire period, giving individual voices a chance to be heard without the constraints of my system. Above all I was pleased that people talked most strongly about what most mattered to them – and it is these strengths which I have followed in putting the book together, believing that what people thought to be important *was* important – and external events, however significant, had, in this case, to be played out like the battles and alarums in a Greek tragedy: off-stage.

Not very long ago it was quite fashionable and acceptable for young people to write their autobiographies. I cannot think of one of my contemporaries who would dream of doing that today. It is as if we are over-awed by the past. No wonder. Only three-quarters of the way through the century, and England has fought two world wars, ceded the biggest empire known, achieved an incomplete but remarkable social revolution, and produced more than its fair share of scientists, scholars, artists, soldiers and men of affairs; and so far contained the most relentless urban guerrilla challenge in the world. Not so much awe as fatigue, perhaps: but we feel, rightly, that to sit down and have a rest, however well deserved, simply would not do. There is too much enjoyment in the contest to throw it away. I am thirty-six, about half-way through the Biblical span, born after the start of Hitler's war and brought up close to a grandfather who was a man before Queen Victoria's death; and *his* grandfather had stories of Napoleon. My daughter, D.V., will spend much of her life in the twenty-first century, her granddaughter could conceivably see the twenty-second. Three, four, even five centuries, then, within reach on either side. It is a good position in which to gather up these stories, modest, unassertive, kindly and good humoured on the whole; but in their serious plainness, and in their persistence there is, for me, an authentic human history of twentieth-century England. An England which, at present, needs to speak out.

On 2nd September 1939, England was in danger. The danger, which is again with us now, consisted chiefly in not speaking out when we needed to, not standing up for what we believed in, not being prepared to fight for the values and, above all, the liberties which still make this country unique and potentially a world influence. In short, we were still vacillating before Hitler. The war in Poland had begun almost two days earlier. Chamberlain was not providing the leadership which the Commons and the country in its sense of outrage and justice wanted and demanded. At Westminster Arthur Greenwood got up to reply for the Labour Party. From the Conservative benches Leo Amery expressed the will of the people who were uniting in a late but strong determination to throw this country against the forces of totalitarianism. Amery called out "Speak for England, Arthur!" Greenwood did what he could, and so do those who make up this book.

CHAPTER ONE
The Big House (1900-1914)

Three generations ago, England bristled with big houses. Ancient and aristocratic castles, halls and manors in the countryside; enormous dwellings of local magnificence in small and larger villages; big houses for doctors, big houses for vicars, big terraced blocks for young professionals and tradesmen, enormous town houses for the rich, new town squares for the nouveaux riches, ton on ton of brick and stone from kiln and quarry, furnished with the wealth and style of centuries, bloated by unseen sacrifices in the colonies and staffed by the barely acknowledged poor of the land, these monuments to energy, skill, privilege and brutality seemed to represent and summarise all that was most powerful about England for a thousand years. Inside those big houses, at the end of the nineteenth century, imperial England could wander in safety and at will. Point to those houses, the history they supported, the invention they nurtured, the limitless zeal and ease they contained, the suppression they continued and you would point to much that Englishmen thought best and worst in their country then.

Wigton had its big houses, the doctor's, the vicar's and some tradesmen's and industrialists', but the biggest house was on a hill overlooking the town. Georgian, with an odd tower more striking than the factory chimney and on higher ground, seen for miles. Highmoor House, owned in 1900 by a bachelor, Mr. Banks.

Mrs. Carrick remembered it clearly in its heyday – indeed she, like all the others who spoke of it, saw that heyday before World War One as a golden age. They were young then, of course, but the nostalgia was full of longing for grandeur and a sense of settlement. Mrs. Carrick was a widow, lived alone in a small terrace in the middle of the town between a school and the auction. We talked for some nights in winter, in her parlour with a coal fire and a clock on the mantlepiece, photographs of herself and her husband on the wall. There had been no children. She was full of an earnest and eager innocence, perched excitedly on the edge of her chair, strong grey hair, still fresh-faced, a brooch at her throat which she touched or clutched now and then, full of gaiety and questions about London and my daughter and books. She was reading her favourite, Quiller-Couch, for, as she said, "the last time".

"It was a beautiful mansion, Highmoor House, beautifully furnished inside, and there were two brothers and once they were on their holiday in Italy – that was before the tower was built and they saw a tower identical with the one at the end of Highmoor. So they came back and had one built at Highmoor. Then a big firm who makes bells, they fitted it up with a huge bell and you could hear it if the wind was in the right direction, you could hear it when it struck the hours at Carlisle – eleven miles off – and heaven help you if you were up in the tower when the clock struck! Then there was a carillon of bells played tunes and you could be in the tower then, and there was a clock.

Ethel Ivinson – she's been dead many years but she and I were friends, and her mother was housekeeper at Mr. Banks' with a lot of servants under her, but she was the housekeeper because she was a widow when she was very young. So Ethel and I had a pretty fair run of Highmoor when we were young and Mr. Banks would take us up into the tower to hear the bells going and so forth and the clock strike but as I say you hadn't to be up when the big bell went. And in the summertime the Sunday School scholars used to march up, when we got the Parish Rooms, we used to march up with banners flying and the Wigton Town Band, which is now non-existent, playing and it had a particular tune of its own – someone local composed this tune – and if you could get a tassel to carry up off one of the banners, oh, you wouldn't have called the Queen your aunt! And the little girls had a little bunch of flowers and we used to march up and, do you know – I suppose you can hardly credit it – but I never knew it be a wet day? And I went to that party for many many years. And we used to march up that West Avenue and it's three-quarters of a mile long and on the front they had tables set – you had to take your own mug. And we used to have our tea. The tea was cleared away and there were games and then Mr. Banks would come out on the front-doorstep with a huge bag of mixed sweets and used to throw them out and the kiddies would shout This way Mr. Banks, this way Mr. Banks, this way, you know, wanting him to throw them to them. And then at night there was the most beautiful display of fireworks at dusk and that went on for years and years. I have a photograph somewhere of one of them. And he was such a kindly man, Mr. Banks, so gentle and kindly.

Do you know where Lowmoor Cottage is down Lowmoor? Well, that was all the park, beautifully kept – the railings are all bashed now, but it was in beautiful order. And there were llamas in the park and they used to come if you stood at the railings, they'd come and spit at you through the railings. That's perfectly true, and all sorts of deer and on the north side there was a pond, the remnants are still there, with all sorts of fancy ducks on it. It was lovely, and one of the inhabitants of one of the bungalows up there at the moment saying, she says do you know there's still some lovely ducks come in the summer period and she says I feed them. Mrs. Wallace, her husband was a barber but she says they're threatening to fill that in when they make it into luxury flats. They are going to make it into luxury flats, Highmoor, for about seven pounds a week so I'm afraid I won't get one of those!

Oh it was beautiful. There wasn't the vandalism then. It was a usual thing for families to go round Highmoor on Sundays as a family would – the father and the mother and take the children – Come on now, we'll just go round Highmoor and the gardens and maybe the peacock would be on the terrace. The peacock was called Solomon. And you could go round and sit down. There were seats all over the place. But nobody, they didn't even pick a flower. They never touched anything.

There were people who had factories – Pattinsons and them, but they didn't live in anything like the House ... well, Mr. Pattinson lived at the bottom of King Street, you know, just before you turn down to Market Hill. I believe he lived in one of those houses and there were different ones but they just lived – maybe up Station Hill in a good house you know but nothing like Highmoor. Highmoor was the only mansion, the only one. And do you know Mr. Banks had most of his money in shipping. Now I had an uncle in shipping, Mr. Kennar, he lived in Whitehaven for many years but then the shipping practically left Whitehaven and he moved to Liverpool, he and his wife and family. They're all dead now, every one of them. And he progressed in Liverpool and he had boats of his own, you know trading boats, you know merchant boats, and he said if people in Wigton had left Mr. Banks alone till after the First World War he would have been a millionaire. Shipping had gone down a lot just before the 1914–1918 War but it picked up again and he said if they had only let him be.

People in Wigton you see they closed on him. A lot of people would maybe give him a pound or two to invest. You know wages were maybe eighteen shillings a week then. You can't understand that, but they'd scrape and screw and put a few pounds for Mr. Banks alright. We'll give it to Mr. Banks and he would put it into shipping shares and I don't know how much it was now, I couldn't say what the whole thing amounted to. But they suddenly got a bit wheezy about it and they closed on him and he couldn't pay it not just at that moment but eventually everyone got every penny but they'd sold and pulled the house to pieces and sold everything and he went down and he died in some sort of club in London. His ashes are in the cemetery in the mausoleum but he died down in London, and as my uncle said if they'd left him alone and been patient until after the 1914–1918 War he would have been a millionaire.

Oh, you just had to ask Mr. Banks for anything and Mr. Banks gave it. He gave the pulpit in the Church and oh all sorts of things, the Swimming Baths, and the Parish Rooms and now his pew is where our Lady Chapel is in the Church. It was Mr. Banks' private pew and of course it has got dilapidated now after he went and that and eventually they did it up and made it into a Lady Chapel.

There was no pride about him, he wasn't a bumptious man, he was a gentle man in the true sense of the word. He was a lovely man. He was too gentle, but none of them could come up to Mr. Banks, and the charities he gave out at Christmas and all that sort of thing. People just had to ask him for anything and he would give it.

Mr. Banks never married, nor did his brother, there were two brothers – what did they call the other one? I've forgotten at the moment, but these two brothers they never married and the mother died just at the turn of the century. There were two or three people died in Wigton, rather important people, they were all lying dead together just at the turn of the century, 1901, the old Queen, old Queen Victoria and Mrs. Banks and one or two noted people in the town, they all died about the same time."

Highmoor House was recollected by others in similar rhapsodic sentences. Even a wary farmer whose small acreage had bordered the railed-in parklands of the big house spoke of it only with admiration.

The staff at Highmoor House, inside and out, ran into double figures. What is difficult to credit today is how widespread was the keeping of servants then. There is, for example, in Wigton, a terrace of eight four-storeyed houses built towards the end of the nineteenth century. Typical of tens of thousands. Mrs. Parker Moore left the jam factory ("I was on topping, labels and tops on. Run by price. The more you did the more you made. I can't tell you the wage") to go to live in and work with Miss Twentyman at No. 4. In every house there was at least one maid and Mrs. Parker Moore rhymed off all the owners in one row. About her own work, Mrs. Parker Moore was laconic.

"You'd just get up in the morning and do the cleaning up, and put the fire on, make the breakfast and do the general housework, that's all. But naturally you had your work cut out for every day. There was a bedroom day and there was a washing day, and a cleaning day and things like that. Then there would be silver to clean certain days and more or less just general work. Naturally if you had an hour or two in the afternoon you would have tea to make, and at night you would have supper to make and that and then of course you had your time off. You had your days off and that – your evenings off rather.

I never thought it was very easy, because in those days naturally there weren't sweepers and all this sort of thing. It was all brush and dust-pans and things like that. I always remember – if there was any floors, I can remember at the doctor's – where I went later – there used to be a mop and this bucket with holes in, the same as there are now, but I was never keen on that. I liked to be down on my knees. I used to think it was only half-done if it was done with a mop. I never did like mops."

Women live longer than men and if this opening chapter is over-balanced on the feminine side, it is chiefly because of that simple truth. I was looking for those who could clearly remember life before 1914 and of all the childhoods I recorded, the childhood of Miss Snaith contains most of the characteristics which made Victorian England so rich.

It is not an "average" childhood. The Snaiths had a small shop and were definitely what Mrs. Carrick would call "Betterme folk": on the other hand, as Mrs. Parker Moore pointed out to me, several supposedly well-off families to her certain knowledge "employed" their daughters as unpaid servants – though the lines were clear, the work was common. There will be a great deal in this book of the deprivations and struggles of early life: here, to open, is, in sentiment and fact, a picture-book family.

Miss Snaith, in her eighties now, lives in a bungalow on the West Road, the rooms full of her father's clocks and ships, and photographs of her parents and three sisters. She still sings in a choir and catches a bus to go eight miles to an evening class and, lately, she has taken to travelling further. She had just come back from Israel when I spoke to her and the photographs were dealt from her hands to mine as she showed me the "Holy Places". Eventually we started to talk about her own life – like most of the older people I talked to, she was so shy and modest about her life that it took time to reassure her that I really was interested, but finally she spoke of her early life, in the last decade of the nineteenth century, in a small shop in the High Street.

"I was born in that house in 1889. We were all born there, four sisters. I was the third. Fanny was the eldest. She was eighty-six when she died. Well you see my father was well over forty before he was married. Of course that's pushed us, either younger or older than we would have been, I don't know how it is, but our cousins are younger than we are – their parents were young too. Anyway, Alice was the second one. She died ten years ago. She was only seventy-five when she died. Well I'm the third. Jessie was the youngest. You won't remember her. She died when she was nineteen. That's her, George Scott took that photograph. That was taken when she was ill. She somehow or other developed St Vitus' Dance at that age, and then the doctor said it's to be hoped rheumatic fever doesn't follow in seven years, because he said if it does it's practically hopeless. And that's just what happened. But I think she overstrained her heart, going to the baths so much and swimming. She went in for life-saving, and she just about lived in the baths. And I'm sure she strained her heart a bit. But she was a very clever girl was Jessie. That was the first break. 1913 when she died – before my father died.

My father came along to this shop after he had left school. It was a John Telford who had the business then. Father must have been about fourteen. Well before he was nineteen he made that beam engine model. I think it was wonderful. It shows what he had in him. Now it's in the Museum at Carlisle, in Tullie House.

He was absolutely devoted to his craft. Clockmaking and watch-making.

And music. He was just as great with music. Wonderful. He used to play the organ at church. And I had some music in there that he used to play. Mozart's Twelfth Mass was one of them. I never heard anything more beautiful than listening to him playing that on the piano. He had a most wonderful touch. Well you see in some cases engineering flair does go with music. They get both. Well it did with him. He was a wonderful man. I fairly adored him. I was only about thirty when he died. I feel as if the longer I live the more he seems to mean to me because of the music primarily, I think. I'm awfully mad on it.

14

We seemed to live for one another. We really did. We were always going in the country. My father was very fond of walking. We had bicycles, but my father couldn't ride one. No, but he was very great on country walks. The longest walk we had was twenty miles. We went round by Mealsgate and Ireby, past High Ireby Grange, all round there. I don't know how we did it. But my father he would walk like billyo. Then another time we went up Skiddaw and he went with us. He got to be rather giddy in the head and he couldn't climb to the top but we all went up to the top, with this Thomas Davidson, the man that worked for us. That was a wonderful day's outing. We went with a horse-drawn thing. Something like a wagonette, and two horses.

Well then Fanny and Alice went to a private school in George Street, a Mrs. Bell, and then my father had helped his relations on both sides so much that when I came along they couldn't afford to send me to this school. So Fanny taught me till I was eight at home. She was clever. I did adore her. Well I went to the National School here when I was eight and I stayed there till I was fourteen. That was where I got an awful grounding in singing. They had a modulator and learnt all the tonic solfa there. They were very great on singing. And grammar. They were good at grammar. And arithmetic. Sometimes it seemed a treat of a job just to have great long tots to add up and do all that. It was like a pastime. But there was the arithmetic and the singing and they were good at scripture too. It was quite good. I quite enjoyed it, and the mistresses were very nice. There was only Miss Ivison that took this singing. She was awfully good, the singing and scripture she took. Yes, it was quite good. And we did needlework, that sort of thing as well. And we used to do parsing and analysis and all that.

When I wrote that account of my trip to Israel I was staying with Olive – Collie, this time last year. I didn't write it to have it printed. I never thought of it. I said I must write an account of my tours. I said I just want to put it down while it's in my mind. I didn't take any notes at all. I said it made such an impression. But I can just sit and write it all from day to day. And she was sitting beside me. And day after day went on while I did this and then when I'd finished she said she says you'll have to read it all over. Oh, she says, this is wonderful. And she wept bits over it. And she said I'm thrilled to bits over it. She says where did you learn your English? I said I didn't learn any, not as such. I said I only went to the National School. I said if I learnt it off anybody I learnt it off my father. He was a wonderful letter-writer and he hadn't any education really. He had it in him though.

Well you see his father, Williamson, he died when he was about thirty. He was what they call a cabinet-maker, and I think he must have made a lot of the cases. But it was all done before he was married, so I wasn't on the spot, and he never would talk about himself. Anything but boast at all. He hadn't that in him. But his work showed what he was like – what he could do. He showed such ability in this that by the time he was twenty or just a bit over he got this business, this John Telford, he saw what he was and what he was like and he went back to Maryport and left my father in charge with this. That was years before he was married.

We had a very good Wigton Choral Society. Miss Kentish who lives at Wigton Hall there. She was very good. She was Superintendent of the Sunday School and she took what we called scripture union classes. We went to those. And then she got the idea she would like to take us to the Carlisle Festival. And she got us on the go for that. They were wonderful days those, but she wasn't very good at it. She just thought she was, but we never did very much. Till a Mr. Reed came from Carlisle and took us and his son is Vicar of Caldbeck now. He was wonderful, Mr. Reed. He used to come and train our church choir so she got him to take us and after that we used to come out first and before that we were always at the bottom. We went there for years, then of course we got into going into the grown-up ones after we got into our teens. I was about sixteen I think. And Barbara Wilson there, of Kirkland House, her mother went to these before her mother was married and I got friendly with her. Amy Storey. She used to talk about those days quite a lot. I liked her very much. We had very good choral classes.

They were mostly in the winter because the festivals were in the spring – March or April. Every week anyway, then nearer the time it would be two or three times. I sang in solo class once over, in that children's day do. My mother used to say I used to sing songs after her when I was two years old. Anyhow I got that from my father, and he was so proud and so pleased that one of us could sort of follow him in that sort of way.

He was awfully keen on music. Fanny was more like him. The mechanical part of it. She was a marvellous sight-reader. She could sit down and read anything. Well, I couldn't. Not like she could. And then we would have musical dos at home. We would sing and she would play. Alice would sing a bit but it was natural to me and with her and I together it was wonderful. And friends came in.

The Wallace family lived next door to us. Lizzie Wallace. They came there when Lizzie was two and the eldest one, they called her Nellie, well she was my age exactly and had a lovely voice that girl. She was really splendid. Well we used to get her in and we'd sing these part-songs – 'The Flowers of the Forest' and 'Oh the summer', and 'Sleep Holy Babe'. We had such stacks of songs. And we'd sing the lot, after midnight a good long time. And their mother used to be in the bedroom right near, sort of just as it might be there and she'd hear us carrying on, singing and playing, and she would go knocking on the wall. Tell our Nellie to come in she says, we've had enough of this. Nellie didn't take any notice at all. She had a lovely voice though that girl. But she and I you see we were keen on it together and we'd sing in the back yard and have little dos. Just very homely affairs on our own but what we could enjoy. She had a wonderful voice. Well she developed some sort of rheumatism and she died in 1953. She was exactly my age. And a wonderful girl.

And I went into the shop and did the book-keeping and there was one salesman, they called him Jacobs and he did for my father watch-work, and he was a Jew, and he asked my father to go over and see them once in Birmingham. My father said what a marvellous home he had and what a place he had and then he came ever so often – he sold watches mostly, but really he developed more into a friend than anything. It's a funny thing, he came just the day before my sister Jessie died. And he went upstairs to see her and he said well she's very ill I know but I do know many cases where they've recovered, and I hope you have better news tomorrow. And the doctor was getting a specialist from Carlisle but however it wasn't much use. She died at midnight the next day.

He was a wonderful man, Mr. Jacobs, and even yet, till now, we deal with that firm after all these years. And they did watch-repairs. I could send them now if I wanted to. But oh I haven't, with losing Fanny and all that went on over that, everything seemed to go from me completely. I followed her into the valley of the shadow. I could hardly get back. We were indivisible. And she seemed to depend on me so much because I knew that she was weak in some ways. They said her heart wasn't very good, but it must have been for the length of time she lived, but I did any amount of things for her to make it easier for her. Alice used to say you spoil her. I said well I'm not going to do anything else. She had a lovely nature.

That's the grandfather striking. Father made that. I just got it – well it was before Fanny died. Before that we had a very old one. It had George Snaith round the dial instead of figures. It had these letters George Snaith. It was very unusual. Well this cousin we want him to have it, because he had two sons and he had two little boys, so it should go down to them. The other brother's married but hasn't any family. It should go where it can be handed down so that's what

I hope will happen to that.

We didn't go to Sunday School, I don't know why, but we went to St. Mary's Church. My father went regularly every Sunday night and I sit in the seat now where he used to sit, and sometimes when he had to deputise for the organ he would do that. Yes we went to church all our lives, then we got into Sunday School teaching. And Fanny and Alice both taught at the girls' school for years and I got into the boys' school under George Scott. He was a wonderful Superintendent too. I stayed there till my mother died then I came home to work. Alice kept on with hers. But I never would leave Fanny at nights. That's when I gave up the Choral Classes after Alice died. I wouldn't leave Fanny whatever. She would be nervous and didn't like to be alone. You wouldn't think it but that was what she was like. She didn't like to be alone, especially at night.

We did learn dancing. I went once or twice to dances, but I don't think Fanny ever did. We learnt dancing though down Union Street where they have that Mission place. Used to be the Oddfellows Hall. Well anyway we learnt the foundation of waltzes and that sort of thing, polka and lancers and what was on the go in those days. We went to a few but not like the others used to.

Fanny, I don't think she would have been strong enough really to go about for that. No, we didn't seem as if we got into that. I was more in the singing and choral classes and that went on until just now, just after Alice has died, and now they want me to join them again this winter. I don't know whether I will or not. They still have them. They have a Rural Choirs Concert in the Assembly Hall in Carlisle every spring. It's a wonderful do that. But I don't know whether to or not. I go to a class at Aspatria in the winter now. They call Musical Appreciation Classes. They're grand. They do Beethoven and Schubert. Mr. Nuttley takes them. He lectures. And he has a gramophone and he has this – he gives excerpts on the gramophone. A whole symphony he gives sometimes. I met some people a bit ago – Todhunters, Mrs. Todhunter was in the Labour Exchange in Wigton, and I got to know her, I don't know how but I did, and I liked her very much. Oh, she said, will you come to our musical class at Aspatria? Anybody else you can get. I mentioned it to one or two but they didn't come so I didn't bother, but I go every Monday night. In the winter. It's wonderful.

After my father died we managed to keep the shop going. These commercial travellers, they were very helpful. They were wonderful. They seemed more like friends really, and they understood the position. But I liked it, and if you like a thing it goes with your mind. It isn't irksome.

We often used to have a carnival week in Wigton. They don't have that now. And they had shop-window dressing competitions. Well we won that first prize – twice over. And another year we didn't enter it, and the judge said Why didn't you enter that window of yours? It looked wonderful. And I said, Oh I don't know. I think my mother was alive then. She was rather diffident. I said we didn't seem to go quite that far. He said, Well if you'd entered it I would have given it first prize. He said it was lovely. But the next year we did enter it and it got first, and the next year, and the next year we got – no, after the second year we got first. They didn't have any more of these carnival weeks so we couldn't compete any more but I loved that sort of thing. It was wonderful. And we had to enter it in the Class – Things to Use. There was Things to Wear, Things to Eat and Things to Use. Of course ours was Things to Use. Everything put in the window was what you could use. Watches, and things for the table, and all that sort of thing. We didn't put a tremendous lot in but we dressed up in the sort of colours sweet peas are, and we had a crepe coloured paper in the bottom all round it in that shape and everything more or less to tone. I don't know how many votes we didn't get for that. It was done by public voting. Then we heard some people talking about it. It was great fun and everybody was on the go about it when the judging day came on the Saturday. One woman was looking at the window, Oh I'd just give that first prize she said. I wouldn't look at others. We got first prize too.

But it was a lovely line to be in. It was all sparkle and attractive somehow. Oh, I liked it awfully and I think it's because we liked it we didn't seem to want anything else. And then Fanny had her piano-teaching. A wonderful business she had. And after my father died, oh she says we're going to see if we can pull this together. We found books where he'd given so much money to this uncle Paul, he married my father's sister, and he was a sea captain. But oh he was a wild fellow. Very very pompous and all that. He was a rotter really. And my father helped him out over and over again. Well, then we thought we'd lost so much through that. Fanny says, We'll see what we can do. We'll see if we can pull it round and I have my teaching, she said. Well together we worked at it and of course there was always housework to do. That was a full-time job for one.

Alice and I between us did that but of course I did so much of this shop work. She was very good at minding the shop, going in the shop. We did that sort of thing together. Then I went to cookery classes. I liked that. It was lovely. It was fun. And then Rita Fenwick, she took them one year. She was very good. We did enjoy them, and all the recipes, and we used to have to taste all the stuff she made and then we could make some ourselves and bring them back for inspection and all that. Oh, I liked the cookery classes.

And then one year when we had an agricultural show, we used to have that for years in Wigton, they had bread-baking competitions so I thought, I was very friendly with a farmer family at Aikbank, the Barnes of Aikbank. Emily went to this private school that I went to and I got very friendly with her. I went there an awful lot. Well, they got me to go in for this bread-baking competition and Mrs. Barnes said I'm going to try so you'd better try your hand too. Well I won a prize for that bread-baking and she didn't.

Then of course I had four girls that I was very very friendly indeed with. This Nellie Wallace was one, Emily Barnes was another, and Jean Arnison, very friendly with her and Janie Backhouse, she lived in Station Road. She went to school when I did. But all those four have died – everyone of them. They didn't die of old age either. So that was a tremendous loss to me but there always seemed to be somebody else to take their place, and get on with others. I was fond of life, very, and I am yet."

A few shops up the street, born just after the turn of the century, was Willie Johnston, one of a family of six living in the small premises above his father's grocer's shop and butching house.

"Got to stun them first with an implement – hit them on the head. This thing about so long, like a mallet. Expert fellows could do it better, a fellow who wasn't so good at the job, they used to have one fixed to a handle, they used to put that on the head where he wanted it and they hit that with a mell. And then you were sure you were on the place, but I've seen fellows trying to kill them – some horrible sights – missing completely and maybe going through its eye and what have you. Terrible cruel. Shocking. Then of course start on Thursday and all these pigs had to be cut up and used to cure bacon, hams and then sell it.

Nothing but pure pork went into the sausages. Not another thing. Well, I'm perfectly convinced you can't buy good Cumberland sausage today. It isn't there, because the type of pig that you would require to make them, it still isn't there today. I've seen pigs when I go up to the auction mart now, I've seen my father wouldn't have them given. They hadn't a pickle of fat on them, and you can't make good Cumberland sausage without fat. And that is correct."

We were talking in the back room of his house, overlooking a small garden which, though this was in the middle of the town, led onto fields. Throughout the afternoon, Mr. Johnston paused to point out the birds, all favourites, which came and went in the garden. This interest had begun in his childhood.

"I've always been fond of birds and at this time of the year in particular, bird-nesting was a great job. Always used to go bird-nesting. I could take you even today where we used to go looking for certain types of nests. Not particularly to take their eggs but we used to like to go and find them and then go back and see them when they were hatched.

There were thrushes, blackbirds, but of course when you got those were too common, we used to try to find – I used to know a place where the owls – in a rock-face, wingchats and birds like that. And then later on we used to go down onto the marshes to look for what we call peewits and gulls. I was very fond of that. I still am as a matter of fact.

I'll tell you this much. There's a terrible shortage of birds to what I remember. About three years ago, the poor fellow's dead now who used to go walking with me sometimes, and we both noticed that there are very very few thrushes. In fact you could hardly find a thrush. But they seem to have picked up again now. There are more now than there used to be. I understand that it's through these chemicals – is it dexidrine? that the birds are picking this up off dressed corn. Insecticides. There's no doubt about it in my opinion. It's definitely played a part – there's not the birds there was here. There's not the variety either. I'm absolutely certain. I used to see a lot of goldfinches. I see very few now. Moorfinches I used to see quite a lot of. I have seen an odd one. Up the lonnings there at the moment and has been for the last few years, there's been a flock of linnets. They're still there but not in profusion. Not the way they used to be. You couldn't go wrong with them once over but you would have to look hard nowadays to find them.

I tell you what's getting scarce around here, you can believe it or not, I've never heard a cuckoo for two years. I could if I really set myself out. If I went four miles out of the town I could hear one when they're here but once upon a time you could walk to the top of the road up there and you would hear a cuckoo any time of day. You never hear one now – very rarely. I've seen me thirty odd years ago here with that window open you could hear a cuckoo over there. Any morning.

There were two naturalists in my youth I looked up to. Father Kerr, he was the Roman Catholic father, and there was, of course, and he's still alive, Charlie Ritson. A great fellow. He used to give me eggs, very scarce ones that you couldn't find round here. Oh, he used to go up away into the wilds of Scotland looking for these scarce birds. I once remember I had heard a corn bunting and the next time I met him I'd said I'd heard a corn bunting the other night and he said Whereabouts did you hear it, Billy? And I told him. It took him a week but he found it. Very shy bird and very bad to find their nests. He was the town solicitor. He used to collect eggs and nests. I don't know what's got it in the back of my mind but I believe he used to sell them to Americans. I may be wrong but I've still got a vague recollection. But Father Kerr had a wonderful selection of eggs. Marvellous. I seen them when I was a youth anyways.

At the height of my own collection, it's difficult to say but I would have easy fifty to a hundred different species. Most of the scarce ones given from Mr. Ritson. But a lot collected round here. You see I could have taken you twenty years ago on to a certain stretch where I could have guaranteed I could have found a yellow-hammer's nest. Well you hardly ever see them nowadays. Very, very rarely. I don't get out as much as I used to do but old Stanley Dixon, he was a great naturalist, and he died two years ago, and he said many times, it's all changing. The birds aren't there, that used to be. I'm listening every morning now to hear my first willow-warbler and there's a few fly-catchers used to come and nest over there.

But the birds out there in the garden are the same. More or less. I still feed tits till the beginning of March and then I stop it because Mr. Ritson again told me that it was a silly thing to do to feed them after March, because you feed them on either a piece of fat hanging or you buy nuts and of course they're oily fatty too. We were talking one day, he does the same thing, but he never – he stops it because he reckons that it's the fat, if you feed them like that, they become that they can't breed, they're too fat, their eggs aren't fertile and ever since Mr. Ritson told me that I always stop say the end of February unless they're very very hard then I put some out but now I stop it.

There's the blackbird, an odd thrush, I have a little robin's nest at the back, starlings in profusion. In very hard weather, gulls. I've had wagtails, pied wagtails and chaffinches. And wrens, and about three or four types of finches. We get the coal-tit, the ordinary little small tit, there's about three or four different breeds. My wife knows them now because we can see out of the window. They're very beautiful to look at. I love them. Actually I love watching them. The antics they put on. You see the starlings come and they're dying to get at it and I've seen them dive at that fat to get a bit off it. Of course they can't stop on the string. The only way they can get it is to make one dive and hope that they knock a bit off and then get down on the ground to pick it up."

We went on to talk about the look of the town when he was a boy: like all the others, the quaintness and the fondness of the memory finally outweighed any residual traces of disadvantage and the town emerged from the past as a peaceful familiar place.

"The High Street was cobbled. I remember many many the time if you lived on the main street and someone in your family was very ill they used to put bark down on the street so that you couldn't hear the horses. Thick bark. I remember that very very well indeed.

Every Tuesday it was just a procession with the horses. Coming and going. On market days they all came in by horses. I think the first motor-car I remember belonged to the Rev. John Terris from Waverton Vicarage. It was a sort of a two-seater affair, sat at the back and somebody could sit in the chair at the front. I think that was about the first one. I can remember when there were hardly any motor-cars at all. I think every butcher in the town would have a butcher cart as they called them. Made to put in his joints of meat and what have you. They all did.

I like to look back on these old places. Poor people who are dead and gone. Little wee tiny places there was in Water Street. There was Nancy Spencer's, where you could go and buy a haporth of Woodbines – one and a half for a halfpenny. And she used to break one in two and give you the half. Not that I was buying them then but I remember people buying a haporth of Woodbines and I remember when we had the shop too. There was an awful lot of tramps on the go then. Roadsters. And eveningtime they used to come in the shop and what they could get for sixpence was nobody's business. You could get half a loaf of bread, a pair of kippers, a haporth of tea and sugar, mixed in a bag – the sugar and the tea together – and a clay pipe and a haporth of tobacco in small pieces, you know twist tobacco, cut into little pieces that were left over. It was amazing what they could get for sixpence.

It's changed completely as far as living's concerned. I haven't any doubt about that. You very rarely saw any trouble in Wigton – maybe on a Saturday night when a few of the old stagers got to fighting but not often. You didn't see any of the carries-on you see today. People had to make their own pleasures."

The claim that people were happier then and better then was almost unanimous. "People had to make their own pleasures then" was a litany, word for word, from all the older people I spoke to. People were, of course, forced to be self-reliant because, compared with today, there was so very little they could get from the state or their employers. This self-reliance was emphasised in Dr. Dolan's description of his father's practice. His father came to Wigton as a doctor before the First World War. They lived in the middle of the town: two parents, two children, one cook, one housemaid.

"It was a country practice – a rural practice, and the people were not well off. They were what you call low paid people. It wasn't what you called a money-making practice. You could survive on it. Reasonably.

When he first came he had a Wetherall motor-cycle which had a strap belt instead of a chain, and when you went up hills you had to get off and change the belt. After that he got a Ford car. I think the work would be very arduous then because the distances were the same but the mode of transport wasn't quite so easy. The farm lanes were not so well kept and the weather at that time as far as I remember it was a lot worse than it is now, so in the summertime it was quite good but in the wintertime you were off in floods and stuck in snow-drifts. And of course the lamps for the car were carbide-lamps. You had a little carbide-cylinder in the car which you put water in, mixed the carbide, light your front lamps, your side lamps were oil-lamps.

The doctoring he'd have done then was really more a family confidant than anything else and he would have more clinical experience without the necessary technical and laboratory aids which we have now. And the patients would do an awful lot more for themselves than they would now, and they wouldn't call you out so often as they do now. I mean they wouldn't call you out for a sore throat. They wouldn't call you out for a septic finger or something like that unless it was really bad.

I think the older people had more knowledge, whereas at present, today, they're a younger generation and you find the younger generation are more what you might call frightened or timid as it were. They don't know as much as the older people did. The older people would apply poultices and all sorts of things, bacon round your neck for sore throats and – I forget that oil they rubbed on their chests – cod-liver oil or castor oil mixed with mustard, something like that, for a poultice, or they put a bread poultice on. They'd use vinegar for sprains and things like that. Now they come to surgery to have a look at it. The older people seemed to be more stable with a better idea of how to treat these little ailments that came along. Whereas the present generation, they come up for even aspirins sometimes. Well they used to put a small roasted onion in your ear if you had an earache. They used to use glycerine for bad throats or blackcurrant tea for sore throats which are quite good now. They used to put iodine on cuts or salt on them and then just bandage them up. Or if they were very bad they used to put a piece of lint on, that's all. Some of them used to put docking leaves on for stings, and things like that.

The patients didn't only come for ailments. They maybe wanted to know what they should do if there was a squabble in the family or if they wanted a divorce or if somebody was going to die, what about their will and could he sort of tactfully mention it or something like that to say the husband should make a will before he died or something like that. Or he used to help about in various ways – the poorer lot they never got a bill at all. But those that could pay they maybe paid just a little bit more than normal. But the charges then were very small. They were, what, two and six for a bottle of medicine and five shillings for a visit. If you got a visit it was seven and six. The poorer people very rarely got a bill, but those who could afford it, they did probably pay instead of five shillings maybe ten."

The generosity of "Old Doctor Tom" was confirmed on all sides.

But the cosy picture so far sketched in was only part of that past and foreign world. The majority were bent to a struggle to survive or, at best, to meet the most modest expectations – food, clothing, a roof, an occasional treat. This will come out clearly as people tell their own stories. Simply as a foretaste, here is a reference to the life of a farm labourer then.

"Anyway, at the age of fourteen my father had to go to farm work, which was sort of the accepted thing of the day. And he moved into the Keswick area and also into the Longtown area. The only two sort of things of comment that I might mention is I remember him telling me how, when he was working in Keswick, he had to start work at quarter past five in the morning, and of course in the summertime and that sort of thing, they had to work until ten, half-past tennish at night; in fact, until dark, when they came out of the hayfield, and that sort of thing. And opposite the farm there was living a – an accountant-type; he was a city type who had retired; my father recalls him as being very much of a gentleman. And he used to give my father – by the way, his wage at that time was two pounds ten for the half-year. And of course he got his keep with that – and so, this fellow that used to live opposite the farm used to give him two shillings for cutting his lawn, which he thought was absolutely fantastic. And this fellow, having nothing to do, took it upon himself, this accountant type, to calculate – he told him, quite out of the blue one day. He says, Do you realise how much you're earning per hour? And he said, I have no idea. He said, I know what I earn for the six months and I'm working hellish long hours some days. And he said, I've worked it out; I've tried to keep a record of it; and you're earning something like an eighth of a penny an hour.

The farmers were extremely hard task-masters. He recalls how they had a maid who – one of the sons of the farmer had been doing some shooting, and he spilled some gunpowder in some way or another on the floor of the bedroom. And when the girl was doing out the bedroom (I'm not sure how it happened) but there was a bit of an explosion – and he recalls how it sort of blew the skin off her hands. But she more or less had to continue working. Now, out in Longtown, again he says that they were quite good, but they didn't give them much food. And he recalls how he used to walk from Longtown to his aunt Mary's, and the most attractive thing – the reason why he used to walk, apart from obviously wanting to see his aunt, was that she used to give him a sandwich and a piece of apple cake."

Billy Lowther talking about his father: this will be taken up in the chapter on farms, just as the theme of very hard, very lowly paid labour is the constant desert under the mirage of the past. There was exploitation but on the land it was poor pickings all round: many of the farmers had only a few acres and their lives would be no easier and a little more comfortable than that of their hired men.

The obvious is too often overlooked and it would be foolish not to mention that in most parts of England outside the emerging militant nucleus in the coalfields, there was "a lot of difference between the classes", as Mrs. Carrick said, alert to the fun of making fine distinctions.

"There was a lot of difference but you knew your differences – you didn't intrude or impinge on anybody else's toes. There was a lot of respect given to people who deserved it; really, you know, as I say eighteen shillings a week was a usual wage and anybody with anything higher, well you looked up to them. I wasn't – we never had a lot, my mother and my granny. There was a paint-shop we had – Carrick. My mother was a Carrick, do you understand, and she married a man called Samson, a Cornish man, and did I loathe that name? I'm rather reconciled now because there's a saint, Samson. I thought oh well that puts me in the upper ten. The Saint Samson. But I never liked the name Samson. And when I grew up Willie's Carricks [her husband's] came from Dalston (six miles off). They were not Wigton people really but my great-grandfather, Edward Carrick, was the first postmaster in Wigton. But we weren't quality, we were just ordinary, you know. But in that churchyard dozens of the Carricks are buried. I used to say Alright, you know, just teasing him – I only married you for one thing. Oh, I know exactly what that was, he'd say. You wanted my name – Carrick. I said I always wanted to be called Carrick so I got my wish but we were no relation and, no, my mother's people were just respectable tradespeople – nobody of any importance.

No, you knew where you stopped. The tradespeople – you were tradespeople amongst tradespeople but anybody high-living – you didn't know what they did really – if they did anything you wouldn't have thought of mixing with them you know. And the Sunday School – I went till I was nineteen to Sunday School and I had a Bible when I was eighteen. Miss Kentish of Wigton Hall, she was another. Her grandfather was a Dean of Carlisle, Dean Close. There's still a Dean Close ward in the Infirmary. Unfortunately I've sampled that Dean Close ward two or three times. They were quality but you wouldn't have thought of mixing with them you know. They patronised such as we scholars you know. There were Humphries at the Grammar School and different ones. Riggs, they lived at Grange Bank, they were solicitors, and other different ones like that. The Duddings of Green Hill – and when they first came to Wigton they hadn't a halfpenny, but they got on. They built Greenhill, a beautiful house. The corridor upstairs is the same length as Wigton Church aisle."

And then there were the "Betterme" tradespeople and then there were the shopkeepers and way above them were the teachers and way below them were the labourers and in between them were the nice ordinary people: Mrs. Carrick knew them all by name, street and ultimate relation.

Around the town there are many villages, all but two – which have become dormitory suburbs – smaller than they were at the turn of the century. Coal-mining villages, a fishing village, a village where there were once lead-mines and woollen mills and nine pubs with a brewery – all of which are now gone but for one pub. In that particular village, Caldbeck, Mrs. Scott was brought up, partly at the house of her grandfather, who was born in 1822 and employed his son on his farm.

"We never saw Father in the morning and we didn't always see him at night but if he had Sunday afternoon he would be up at Knocker House with us, and then after tea we had our hands and faces washed and our hair straightened up and went with Father into Grandfather's house and sometimes we got a ride on the old pony in the yard for a treat. And then he used to ask us about what we had learned at school and what we had been doing. How many hens and how many ducks. He was a great hand at asking questions, Grandfather.

He had the farm and the woollen mill, what everybody called the factory, and he used to go round with the old pony and trap and gather up wool, clippings of wool, and then he used to make – some people wanted a pair of blankets, some people wanted some rough stuff and he spun wool for knitting men's stockings and made this Skiddaw Grey, the tailor made it into coats and trousers, but mostly coats, and then when the cry out was about John Peel's coat whether it was red or grey, it was rather disputed about it, but we had an old coat of Father's, and Mother – when it was done for working in, Mother made two or three pin-cushions and tea-cosies and chair-cushions, every scrap was used, except where it had been worn under the arms and at the elbows. It was just used up. In fact I still have a little bit somewhere. And that was Skiddaw Grey.

We used to go to church with Father on Sunday mornings and then after dinner we went to Sunday School, then when we came home we had to go upstairs and take our Sunday clothes off. And Rector Simpson was great on the Fourth Commandment. Remember the Sabbath day to keep it holy. Six days shalt thou labour and do all the necessary work. Yes, he often preached from that text. On the Monday he used to go to people's houses to see why they hadn't been to church on the Sunday.

Mother had said reading was a waste of time but we had a few old-fashioned ones, *The Boy makes the Man* and Mrs. Henry Woods, as we grew older. Then I joined the G.F.S., The Girls' Friendly Society, which Mrs. Simpson ran. And then the choir. And I helped in the Sunday School, but as I grew older and after I left school I had to turn in and help with the farm work, milking and feeding the calves. Instead of learning at school I had to learn on the farm. Of course it was hard work some days and not others.

When Mother was younger she could do most of the housework herself. She washed the dishes on the table and we had a tray and she lifted them out and I had to dry them with a towel and put them away. We worked long hard hours. We thought nothing about it because everybody else did. Monday was washing day, Tuesday was ironing day and patching if you hadn't got ironed the night before, Wednesday was – maybe a room you didn't use very much got a good dust-out. Then Thursday was churning day and Friday was baking day and Saturday was scrubbing-out day, the kitchen and the kitchen – well, what we called pot houses in those days. Where they set pots – you call them coppers now, put a fire on underneath.

On baking day, after everything had been fed and the dishes washed and the milk things washed up and then the oven – the plate was taken out and this all under the oven, where you put some sticks and extra coal and it gradually heated while the bread – white and brown – the yeast was rising. And while it was rising there would be scones and maybe teacakes and slab cakes. You put it on a tin the size of the oven then Mother used to cut it out in squares. When we were working in the field, we got ten o'clocks brought to the field and we came to the house for our dinners, then we got our teas brought about three or half past three in a basket, and everybody had a half-pint pot. Well there was always plenty to eat but it was plain fare. There was no cream cakes those days."

Caldbeck is a beautiful village, a place for tourists now. Only half a dozen miles away is another village, Fletchertown, which is never likely to attract a single holidaymaker – except for those returning to this pit village, those who were born there and find in the few rows of back-to-back terraced cottages thrown up to shelter the men who would go down for coal an irreplaceable sense of community. In the middle of nowhere, it stands, the pits around it all closed down, a few score buildings in brick left behind like an industrial fossil. Sammy Tate was born there in the 1890s.

"We lived on Allhallows Terrace then. And there was only two bedrooms. There was nine of us, and Mam and Dad was eleven. So in wintertime it was a case of two or three washing in the same water, because you had all your water to boil in those days. And instead of hot-water bottles in those days it was a case of either heating bricks in the oven or warming salt on the fire-shovel over the fire and putting it into a stocking.

Well you had to live careful. You had to live careful with everything because there wasn't the money. Of course in my younger days Dad used to work down the colliery and then his health broke down and then he had a pony and cart, and you could go to Allhallows Colliery then, buy ten hundredweight of coal for five shillings and it was one and six for leading it from the colliery to Fletchertown for a man and a horse and cart."

The mines and those who work in them will recur in this book.

Just as people "knew their place" – though this simple declaration is contradicted by what many of them say – so too, in that glowing time, after a century without fear of invasion or conquest, "the Majesty of the Law" was unmistakable. Joseph Barnes, born in the tiny village of Micklethwaite:

"Somehow or other we knew we had to behave ourselves – I don't know that they were exceptionally strict. I don't know if I was a terribly good boy, if it comes to the point, but you got a knock if you'd done something really bad. But I think somehow or other we were brought up to understand we had to behave ourselves. I think that was the whole point. And then of course the police at Micklethwaite, our local constable, come from Thursby on a push-bike and he carried a walking-stick and I knew about that walking-stick because we had our own fruit trees but not far away, in fact one field-length away, there was a lovely orchard; and somehow or other those apples were nicer than ours. There was also some nice greengage and Victoria plums. Well, this particular night I'd had another raid. I never got a lot, just two or three in me pockets and away. But when I was coming out the policeman was just there. I just got that stick right over me backside and I honestly think myself that did more good than all the juvenile courts today. Like I honestly think that. He didn't say anything to me parents about it or anything like that. I don't know whether he told the owner of the orchard that he'd caught me. But I knew he'd caught me.

Well you see we saw quite a bit of the police every Monday there because a sergeant used to come out from Wigton and the Aikton policeman used to come and the Thursby one and Micklethwaite was just the place where they met. Whether the sergeant took any reports there was back into Wigton, most likely I would think, but on the other hand like we were scared of the police. Like, you know, it's maybe wrong to say scared but as soon as we saw the man in blue we automatically went on to our best behaviour. Of course that's another thing that's changed now."

Wigton, when he was a boy, was his metropolis.

"Before the First War, I was young and really it did seem grand. Of course, one of the things when I came in was to go up to Lily Smith's, near the Church. Course you were in clogs and you sat on a chair while Lily threw your clogs down to her Uncle Joe down in the cellar and put new corkers on. Then you were fit for the road again.

And of course it was always upon the agenda that we called at Mary Ann Martin's, fish and chip shop; that's where the Throstle is now, like on that block. And you know a haporth of chips they used to last me out till Spittal Cottage, walking home and eating them out of the paper all the way, and that was, you looked forward to that.

Once in a while Mother would go on a spending spree and they were always bought at Miss Little's. That's opposite corner to Mrs. Lund's, at this corner. And I always remember going in there. And Johnston's, like for clogs, I always got clogs at Johnston's.

Now then when I was young the working class, they like sort of dressed plain and that as you might say. Of course they hadn't the money to do anything else. And on the other hand the posh-like –

31

Park Square and Station Hill – they were poles apart. And I know like going back say into the Twenties I could go up the street, Hello Joe, Good morning Joe, How do Joe, What fettle Joe, you know. I could walk up the street now and see hardly anyone that I know. Of course there're more families in Wigton, even though the size of the family is less. The population really, it hasn't gone up, not in proportion to the way Wigton's expanded. And like nowadays when you come across single women going into a three-bedroomed house up on the new housing estate there, I know that – I know two that have moved in just recently. Well, what I mean to say, a house of that size in the olden days, there would have been the parents and four or five kiddies at least in that house."

The big families, mentioned by Joseph Barnes, were, in a sense, the complement to the big houses. Neither could have existed without the other. Primitive sanitation – the slop bucket, the waste-, excrement-bucket, to be dug into the ground every morning. "You either did it before your breakfast and then you couldn't eat: or you did it after and you brought your breakfast back up again" – wood and coal heating – fires to be made – no electrical appliances and so on: the big working-class families provided the motor power for those innumerable big houses.

It is dangerous to say of anyone that they are "typical": and after these interviews the first and least of the facts you learn is that whatever limitations are imposed, the variety of response is astounding. However, let the last interview be with Mrs. Dixon, whose memory of the early years of this century is vivid and whose father, Bob Monkhouse, was a porter on the railways.

Like Mrs. Carrick, Mrs. Scott and Mrs. Parker Moore, Mrs. Dixon is a widow. She lives a couple of miles outside Wigton in a cottage abutting the farm which she and her husband built up and her son now works. The sitting-room was dominated by photographs of her late husband and she was more eager to talk about him than about herself. Their struggle to farm is told later. She looks much younger than her years, dressing in what might be called "the modern style" – that is to say, not surrendering to the uniform and restrictions of old age at the age of fifty as women used to do in the recent past. She was one of a family of ten. They lived in Railway Terrace.

"There was a living-room, sitting-room, we'd have all these aspidistras and the lot and the antimacassars, the holy of holies that, kitchen, no back kitchen but a shed as such, separate washhouses, coalhouse. Bath day was a weekly affair with the old set pot on and the girls first and the boys after – and two bedrooms and two attic rooms.

They were mostly big families in the cottages. Pearsons you know, the rugby lads. Their grandparents lived next door and there was a big family of them. I was born there and eventually the family all went and married. Didn't always seem to be full because there were some of them married, and one working away and such like.

My mother lived till she was eighty-eight. Father was seventy-eight. You know when you're kids it takes so little to keep you happy. If you have a good home and we always had plenty to eat. My dad was a shooting man and a fishing man. Big garden and orchard. He could grow everything. Potatoes, gooseberries, apples, everything. We kept hens. He always had his licence. I don't know whether there was a game licence or not then. I suppose there would be. He had a poacher's pocket in the back of his coat. And then the river was worth fishing then because it was before the effluent out of the paper mill went into it. You see at the bottom of this farm, the Wiza joins the Wampool there, and there's good lots of fish there. Sea-trout used to come up because it's semi-tidal.

Mother baked everything. Bread, teacakes – she baked nearly every other day. Smashing bread, I can smell it yet. Brown bread, oatcakes, great big long tins – one of my brothers, my second brother, Tom, was a plumber with Aird's – plumber and tinsmith – copper-smith – and he made her huge bread-tins where she made three loaves into one, and the oven held two – two big long tins, that was six loaves and that came out and they were big two-pound loaves. So that was six loaves every other day. Teacakes opposite days – she baked every day but Sunday. A big pan of broth with dumplings. Smashing. Not jam or treacle though. They were plain suet ones.

Clothes – one of my elder sisters was a dressmaker – tailoress and dressmaker. She served her time at a Miss Pearson's in New Street opposite where Harry Moore's was. Served her time there and sewed at home. She had one of the little attic rooms was closed off – it was her bedroom and her sewing-room. She done most of her sewing for people and kept the family clothes going as well. She could make anything. And they, I think we were all sort of keen on sewing and Mother was a housewife and washing days, the old poss tub. In fact I've got the old poss yet. Just keep it. When my mother died and she was lying there, her work-worn hands I just thought, poor old woman, she had slaved and brought us all up. That was what hurt me when I saw her hands. And she died as peaceful as a baby. She used to say every day when we used to go and see her, I would say, Are you tired? 'Oh, very tired. But the Lord's given me another day.' She always said the Lord gave her another day. And her memorable saying was 'Life's sweet at any age'; so you see she was a grand living woman.

There were quite a lot of vagrants and tramps round in those days. An old man used to come every Sunday morning and play his tin whistle – 'My own Sweet Emily' he used to play, and he used to get a halfpenny and a can of tea. Every Sunday morning. He came from Highfield House – from the Workhouse. Just across the road.

And there was another old chap called ... we called him Jack the Giant but Mother and Father said that he was a schoolmaster at Gilcrux or somewhere and he was very clever, but he'd been a drunkard. Well he was a pack-man, he went round with a pack during the summer. He sold bootlaces, anything that was needed on the out-lying districts. And threads, buttons, anything like that – needles, anything that they could sell like that. And then in the winter he used to leave his pack with Mother in the shed and he went into the Workhouse for the winter.

We never thought the Workhouse was grim. It used to look very nice. They always looked a lot cleaner and better fed when they came out. They used to go up there daily, some of them used to walk across the bridge that came across the water from Scotland. They used to seem to walk the roads like that. Settle there for the night – they'd chop sticks for their keep. But it seemed to be the dread of old Wigton people that they would finish in the Workhouse. Mine didn't. With being a big family they looked after them.

I remember the winter nights. On a bright starry night we used to play between the lamp-posts with a ball and marbles, skipping, and I used to often think it would be hard frost and we would be really warm. Clogs used to make sparks, gallop up and down, round the top and back what we called Pump Lane. Pump Lane came through opposite Highfield. But we were warned we hadn't to run up and down there so much. These old roadsters. So that was a risk. We were doing that when we shouldn't have been. Galloping up and down there. Then there was three ponds on the top and they used to freeze over. But they were just like hollowed bits, and we used to clog-skate across them. The whole way round the three ponds, back by the top of Standingstone and there was one there, but now they're all levelled. Round there, back down by the old water fountain at the bridge. Often slippy there where the water had been coming over, and right back, and the two big walls of Station Hill were dark places and we scuttered up there very quick. And then we were home.

Of course we knew the stars. Yes, the Plough and the Great Bear. We used to watch them, and the Evening Star and we used to know all the names then, and make them out. I think one of my brothers was keen, and my sisters used to teach us, and then I used to like to read. I used to read everything like that. I still watch the stars, but I don't know them as well. But it's surprising; if I pick it up again and I read I can see it all from then. Me dad used to show us them.

He was a musician. The old concertina and the violin, fiddle hung up on the wall. Sunday nights we had a harmonium and that's why I've got a little electric organ now. We used to sing. All the old Sankey Sunday nights. It's one night he was never out. 'Pull for the shore, sailors' and 'I have a Saviour'. They were real Sankeys. He was the composer of most of these old hymns. Not so much Church as Salvation Army type and they always went with a swing. But that was Mother's night out. She went to either Church or Mission or something, whatever it was. I just don't know. I think it would be the Mission – the Salvation Army Mission, and we stayed in and we had all these hymns and supper.

Then of course there was the horse sales which was a terrific three days. I used to be terrified. I used to get behind those railings at the station bridge. I was petrified. Between those two big walls there was hundreds of horses. You daren't walk on the footpath. Galloping along. That's one of my big impressions of it.

Then there was also cows and sheep. Pigs, but they seemed to drive those in those flat wood carts. I always remember Scott's – Town End Scott's as we used to call them – they had a horse-drawn thing for pigs, so they came here. And then they started off with a car then as well. Motor-car and trailer. But the horse-drawn one was the one that I remember then – for pigs and a few sheep or anything like that.

Well you don't think of yourself as being badly off then. We had a good home and good loving parents, you see. I suppose we would be – I never remember being hungry or anything like that. Might remember needing shoes, but we wore clogs and shoes were for Sundays only. But we always had nice clothes, even if they were just made up. Cut-me-downs or hand-me-downs, whatever they were, but they were always very nice.

Well there were lots of big families and there would be quite a lot wouldn't be as well off as we were. Maybe the house wasn't big enough by these standards, you know, no bathroom but that didn't keep us from being clean and well scrubbed. We were only threatened with Father. Wait till your dad comes in – that was sufficient.

I left school at fourteen. There wasn't scholarships or such then. No, you'd got to get working. Started off with office work during the War on the railway. It wasn't very long and the War finished and that was finished. And then I went as a nursemaid. That was about all I done. Well, it was sort of mother's help you know. And that's about all. Just done housework till I married.

The biggest threat was to be put onto a farm. And then I married a farmer!"

It has been impossible in this chapter to avoid sentimentality and that is no surprise: people at the end of their lives looking back on when they started out, remembering parents and family and friends – the sense of loss must be stirred, it would be strange if it were not so.

The last time I saw Mrs. Carrick was on a bitter spring day. She was resting on a bench outside the church, looking across at some demolition work which the local council, like most others all over England, had eventually undertaken and not yet repaired. What had once been stables – derelict, slummy though they were – had been full of quaintness and charm for Mrs. Carrick. Soon there would be new buildings. But she would not live to see that. Now there was rubble.

She had broken her hip and moved into an old people's home but she would not be confined and she had got herself a walking aid, a small construction like a fireguard which she leaned on and pushed in front of her. She looked cold and gaunt and had about her that sense of loneliness which is easily and conveniently mistaken for a desired solitude. We talked a little and I remembered how in one breath she had said of the councillors that they had "ruined" the town and in the next admired the bungalows they had built for old age pensioners. They were grand, she said, all you could wish for. Wonderful.

When she set off on the painful slow walk to the home the street was completely empty although it was just after six o'clock. In her day it would have teemed with children.

As she went on what might have been her last walk her head pecked the air, for sight of them. But they were on the housing estates which whitely encircled the outskirts of the town like the large settlements of a new people, come to rest. These were the feature of the place now as once the big houses had been: the descendants of those whose big families had staffed and served the big houses were in those centrally heated, hot and cold, roomy, subsidised dwellings, each with its garden; and the large homes they used to sustain were now flats, hospitals, firms, schools, institutions or abandoned. Occasionally, still, the home of a single family. But in all the town that day there was only one family with a maid; and she came in the morning and returned in the evening on a bus.

CHAPTER TWO
Elizabeth Armstrong

She was born in 1898 in a pit town a few miles to the west of Wigton. The family was large – ten children – and she herself was to manage a family almost as big.

We talked in the small living-room of the council bungalow in which she lives with her only unmarried son, now aged fifty. A few yards up the avenue her youngest daughter has a private bungalow and she comes down to visit and help her mother at least once a day. Not that Elizabeth Armstrong gives the appearance of being someone who needs assistance. She has a mixture of busyness and tranquillity: the house is not only clean and tidy but fresh from recent re-painting and re-decorating: she bakes, looks after all the flowers in the garden, gets up to see her son off to work and is always pleased to see the living-room full of people sitting about talking. And when she herself joins the company and sits down, there is no fussing or agitation in her gestures – she relaxes into the enjoyment and you notice the extraordinary freshness of her skin, the gentleness of the features, above all the seeking out of things to laugh over.

Yet in some ways the only present comparison for the life she has led would be with poor people in, say, India. At the beginning of this century there were great numbers of the working class – industrial and rural (both of which she sampled) – whose daily round and expectation were far closer to those of the deprived in the Third World than to their own lives today. It's an interesting aspect of our history that the same men, literally, could at one stage in their careers be responsible for the administration of a large chunk of the colonial globe and, at another, for the employment of their own countrymen in conditions not very dissimilar to those they found in the "backward" countries overseas. If this is thought to be exaggerated, then all I can urge is a careful reading of Elizabeth Armstrong's life-story.

It is no complaint, her story. Indeed it was difficult for her to dwell on the painful part of her past – the humiliations and the distress had been too sharp and anyway she is a "cheerful body"; her disposition warded off self-pity. Moreover, her life is the song of a woman who has come through. Like millions of "ordinary people" (she often referred to herself in that phrase), she, and the class she belongs to, have inherited this century in the West. No matter that the wails of the disinherited aristocrats and the sneers and forebodings of the old middle class have tried to diminish the achievement by saying that the world is no longer worth inheriting, the truth is that the over-whelming social movement in this century has been the rise in fortune and comforts of the "masses". Their ascent has been accompanied by cries of snobbish contempt by those who thought they were better served when the meek and lowly merely cultivated the earth. But there is no denying that Elizabeth Armstrong is one of millions who can look back and both wonder at and take pride in the distance she has travelled since her birth.

We talked a long afternoon and into the evening. Her bungalow is just opposite Highmoor House – now luxury flats. There are several of these old person's bungalows, well placed in a cul-de-sac – a friendly little community. Beyond these bungalows, in what was the Deer Park, a new private housing estate is going up where the llamas once walked and even Solomon the peacock.

"Father was on farm work until he married and for a year or two then, and ever since I can remember, he was a collier all the time. He worked at No. 3 – No. 1, No. 3 and No. 4 Brayton Pits. But he didn't work below ground. He worked in what they call the pit fire-places for to get up steam for the engines to pump air into the pits and anything of that sort, and then as time went on he was made electrical engineer. That was for pumping air and water out of the pit.

We had a rather nice house but very small. Only two bedrooms and it was three storeys, so you went through one bedroom up the attic stairs to the top one. So of course you couldn't have an adult family growing up so as soon as we were fourteen and left school, we had to get out and make room for the younger ones as you might say. All the children slept in the attic. It was a good big one. It had two beds in but it only did while we were young. And it was about two and six a week – the rent. It used to be an old lodging-house, you see, and they re-conditioned it, as they did in those days, and made it into two. Well it was really too small. They should have made it into one big house, but of course people wouldn't pay the rent

39

them days. It was only two and six a week.

We were really part country and part town. We knew about farming as well as mining. My brothers went into farm service first and finished up mining when they got married. They went into farm service first because there was no room at home for sleeping accommodation and such as that, and I think it was the easiest way to get into any job and a bed. It was just sort of natural that you went on to farm work. Same as myself when I left school at fourteen I had to get away. I was fourteen one week and I was in service the next week. Three pounds for the half year. I went to a little place called East End at Hayton, the other side of Aspatria, just going into Hayton, and they called them Miller's.

I had to get up and put the fire on first thing in the morning, and I'd never put a fire on in me life, I had to learn. And then I had to put the porridge pan on. You put it on the side of the fireplace and brought it up to the boil with the oatmeal and such as that in, then you pulled it forward and put the lid on just so it would simmer and then took a bucket and went out to milk the cows. So while you were milking the cows the porridge was boiling and then the mistress didn't get up first thing. She used to get up when we were nearly ready for coming in. She used to dish the breakfast up. There was porridge and a cup of tea and bread and butter. And there was a lot of scrubbing to do and washing milk-cans and such as that. And these separators, they were very complicated; a lot of bits and pieces, and they were all to wash separately and scald with boiling water. It was a miserable job doing that in a morning. You were either red raw or chapped up with the frost in winter.

I had quite a nice room at my first place. I've never really had a bad bedroom. It's been fairly decent and of course cold in winter and red hot in summer. There was just one farmer that we didn't have our meals with, and they sat at one end of the kitchen and we sat at the other. I sat with the farm lads, and they sat up at the other end, and that was when I was at Westfield House here, out Wigton way. Miller's was a small farm; he just had three cows. Willie Miller, they called him, and he married a woman called Slack from Threapland. He was what they called a hine for his dad. His dad had the big farm at Whiteleas. His father farmed that place and he had bought this little place for his son so he was just sort of renting it. It didn't belong to him. And they were called hines in them days. He was hine on the farm. I was the only person on the farm apart from him and his wife. But I didn't work out in the fields

40

at that place. With him not having any land. But I had to help at haytime and that.

When I was a girl at home there wasn't a lot to do, just being two rooms up and a kitchen and a back kitchen and back yard. I had to dust and such as that and wash dishes, things that lasses have never liked, and do a bit of knitting and that. We played in the street. We had a grand place beside the church at Aspatria, and we used to play on there. We would all get together of a night but, mind, we weren't allowed to play out late. We were in by seven o'clock and in bed, regular. Of course you see my father and mother they had to be up early because he had to be at the pit by six o'clock so of course they wanted to go to bed early.

In wintertime – we had a good wide street always at Aspatria and it had a gentle slope down. And when the frost and snow was on we used to have a lovely slide down there. And our old landlady lived on the main street. She used to go and put ashes on. Every night; we used to be fair crazy.

My father was always jobbing about the house and he was able – you know, if the fireplace wasn't right, he was able to do them sort of jobs and he kept everything tidy. When he got his coals, he always stacked them up tidy, just like down the brick wall. And then the mush and such as that he put that where he would be able to get it when he wanted to build up, and his sticks were all put in a tidy heap. He was a tidy fellow, you know.

But he never did any washing-up. That was below him, such as that. But he cleaned the shoes every Sunday morning – no, every Monday morning after the Sunday. They were set aside and they were cleaned on the Monday morning and they were put up onto a shelf out of sight and they weren't down again till next Sunday morning. Yes, he always cleaned our shoes for us but we had to clean our own clogs for school so they were cleaned every morning before we went to school, in the back yard, not in the kitchen. And I've known some gey frosty mornings as well, and it was the old fashioned blacking then. It was made with water. It took you a long time to get a polish on them. But we hadn't to go with them dirty. And Mother wouldn't let you go to school with holes in your stockings or anything. Course she used to knit for us all. She was always knitting.

We only had meat once a week. We only got it on Sundays when we had a hot dinner with Father and Mother. The rest of the week, what meat was left was left for my Father because he needed good feed because of his hard job. He was shovelling these coals into these big fireplaces all day long from six to six at night and sometimes he would have a long weekend and he would go out on a Saturday morning and he wasn't back till the Monday morning, and he was shovelling all that time. And cleaning them out. While one was out the other was on. Two big furnaces. Or three. Just like the coke ovens, you know, only these weren't for coke because it was all clinkers that came out. It was all to make steam.

We had bread and butter and jam and porridge and such as that and we got taties every day. Maybe bacon and something of that sort. Very often not any bacon or meat either, just taties and pudding – mostly rice pudding. We didn't like bread pudding. Sometimes we got them but you know milk was only a penny halfpenny a pint in them days. So we got a canny sup of milk. And in those days when I was a kiddie there wasn't any separators for to separate the cream from the milk. So the milk was set up in bowls, then it had to stand twenty-four hours, then the farmers used to go round the bowl like that and just tip it and it all fell off, all the cream fell away. And this milk that was left was very blue because there was no cream. It was sold as blown milk and you got it an awful lot cheaper. You could get a big tinful like that for a penny. And that's what we got. And I tell you what Mother made a lot of, pea soups and such as that. She used to make good broth. Used to put a big boiler – you know, the washing boiler – and that would be full of broth. But all the neighbours got, you see. All the neighbours round about all got what would do the kiddies' dinners of a dinnertime, and then maybe another week another neighbour would boil it and it was returned. And there was always a dumpling in and a big bag of split peas, all sort of things in, as well as the broth. So we got good stuff but it was very plain. And we got kippers and maybe an egg. Sometimes we got the top off the egg and that was all.

We never wanted for a slice of bread. I can never remember ever being hungry but we maybe have been at times but you forget these things. But we were never refused any bread. There was always bread and butter till margarine came on the market. As things were improving, margarine came onto the market and oh I hated that. Mother got it because it was cheap. But my father hadn't to eat it. He had to have the best of everything because of his hard work and we had to make do. But I hated margarine and I do today. He had to have the best, you see, because they couldn't afford much really. They weren't making a big wage.

He used to like to drink and once every three weeks he used to get tight, 'cos that was his weekend when he hadn't to go to work on the Sunday morning. So he used to just get drunk and he just had one door to pass and then the pub. It was the Fox and Hounds, and we lived up that road called North Road in the two cottages. But they're very dilapidated now.

I think that women were more against drink then than what they ever were today. It was – although it was cheap, they just couldn't afford it, to be drinking their money. And they had to save for their old age. There was no pensions or anything. And I've often thought, I just used to think they were a bit mean over giving us a penny now and again, or anything of that sort. But when you realise they were just going to have ten shillings a week to live on, if they'd lived that long . . . But women never went into the pubs the way they do today. Maybe an odd gin drinker did, that type of people.

A lot of women worked on the screes in the pits and that as well. They had to help out. Very often it was a widow, maybe been left with a young family, and they used to turn out to work the same time as the men. And they screed the coal, got all the bad coal out as it went along. The coal that we burn today, they would have been fined in them days. When my brothers worked down the pit, if there was any stone found in their wagon when it came up, there was a token on that tub and they knew exactly who had sent that dirty tub up. It was knocked off their wages. They had to get clean coal up and get the old rubbish thrown at the side. And these women used to stand and pick all the coal out, summer and winter, and they were just in open sheds. And yet they used to go with white aprons on and they were clean and particular. And they all wore caps like a man. But they had a bun at the back. I never did but I can remember them going. The bun was at the back of their hair and the cap just rested on the back and the neb was here. But they were always tidy. Grand clean workers. Their houses were spotless; steps were scrubbed. Everybody took a terrific pride in being clean in them days. And there was only the ordinary hard soap, no toilet soap or anything of that sort in them days. It was one to try and beat another. And if somebody hadn't got their steps washed by dinnertime, it was a crime.

We had a woman lived next door, related to Billy Dodd. She was as easy as me old shoe, she didn't care. She wasn't a bad sort, but she didn't fuss herself. She didn't bother. We thought she was lazy. It was a crime if you were lazy in them days. Something you couldn't live down.

My mother didn't work at the pits but when they were younger she used to work out in the fields. This was when they lived at Westnewton before I was born. They lived in a little place called the Mill Fold and it was just going into Westnewton. My father them days was working at No. 3 pit and he used to walk from there to No. 3 pit every morning and he put in twelve hours a day. And yet he would come back and him and me mother would go and harvest in the harvest field. What they called gleaning and such as that. And make up the sheaves as they cut because all the stuff was to bind in them days before the combine things came into being. So many made bands and so many were going on and putting it into sheaves, and another lot following and tying these bands round the sheaves. And then it was all set up before they went out of that field that night because it would have soaked easier if it had poured down, so it was all put into stooks. I never had to do such as that. I have had to work in the fields but not to that extent.

They used to say they couldn't afford this and they couldn't afford that and they were always tired. No wonder they wanted to go to bed early because they had to be up early. When you didn't want to go to bed; come on now, we've got to be up early in the morning. We've had a hard day. We've been up from so and so. Well, when father was walking from Westnewton, they were both up at four o'clock in the morning. It's two miles from Westnewton to Aspatria; it would be about three miles. And you see there was no gas or anything. The fire was to kindle and to get going to boil the kettle for them first and to make their porridge. So they had to be up to get something to eat before they went. Of course they always had their breakfast, as far as we know. Some may not have had it but my father always had his breakfast. But you see they made porridge for the colliers with bread in them days, and they poured boiling milk on it and sugar and they got the goodness of the milk and the bread. And that's all they had – and a cup of tea in the same basin. The basin was rinsed out and the tea was poured in. They economised that way as regards washing up.

I can always remember him being in the Foresters' Club. There would be sick clubs them days but I can't remember – unless he was in the Union later on in life when I got up into my twenties and that. There wasn't as much Union carry-on then anyhow. I remember a strike. It was during summer. I remember the 1926 strike because I was older then. I remember we couldn't get any coals and we were burning anything we could get hold of. I was at Flimby. I'd married Dad then. And Dad had just started a butching business up as well and of course everybody was out of work and they brought him to the door, as you might say. They wouldn't pay for the meat and stuff. Well, we had to get rid of it. I didn't like it all the same. I didn't

44

like Flimby. I hated it. I don't like west. I would rather go east than west. [The coalfields and iron ore mines are to the west.] I was there a year and I was glad to get out as well.

Then we came onto farm work. That was because we hadn't any money. Nobody would pay back their debts so we just had to leave it, and we went onto farm work then. That was with Dixon's of Bank Head. And we had twenty-three shillings a week and there was four bairns. And I can always remember, they were in very tight circumstances. They couldn't afford to pay me, they were that poor. Mind, I really believe at that time farmers were poor. They were just having as big a struggle as we were. It would be about 1926–7. And I remember one Christmas we didn't get any wages for three weeks. We hadn't a penny. They couldn't afford to give us our wages. I don't know whether they couldn't afford it or what it was. I had to borrow off my mother and I hated borrowing because it's always to pay back. But we were awfully poor there. There were four bairns. Stanley, Mary, Elsie and John.

Of course things were cheaper but after all that was a poor wage. I know I did go out to work once to get myself a pair of shoes so I could go home now and again to see my mother and father. So I went and thinned turnips for these shoes and it took them weeks to pay me that money. And when I got the money Mary was wanting shoes so I had to buy Mary shoes and I had to do without myself. And I didn't get any for a long time. I used to walk to the bus in my clogs till Waverton Church, and the vicar's wife used to be good with us and told me to leave the pram there. And I used to change out of my clogs into me shoes so as I just used me shoes on the bus and didn't walk in them. Just to spare them. I left my clogs in the pram. And Fred would be a baby then. And I would leave the pram there because the bus stopped there just at the end of the road and bring Fred out, and I would put me shoes on and leave me clogs in the pram for to come back home again. No, it was just a sort of respectability that you really couldn't afford.

I liked Aspatria but I don't like it now. I liked it while I was a kiddie. And there was always a lot going on in the church and we were always acting in concerts or something of that sort. Church of England. Father went to church and Mother as well. Father not as much as Mother. And we had to sit still as well. But you know my father couldn't read or write. He left school when he was about ten or eleven and he lived down by Mawbray way, down Silloth way. And when he was a lad he used to go out and get that sea coal. He used to gather that. And no shoes or stockings on. When I'm

45

sitting down, as a rule, I never have my shoes on. I say it must be with me father. And he wouldn't go to school. My mother was a good scholar, but they had to pay for her going. And she was a marvellous writer, up till she died; all that old-fashioned – it was like an f for an s and such as that. She was a lovely writer. And so she used to read the papers to him every Saturday morning so that he knew the news and was able to converse even though he couldn't read or write. You got used with it – always knowing he couldn't read or write. Yet we never said anything to anybody about it.

He was an uneasy fellow. He couldn't sit still very long. He was always on the go. Always finding a job of some sort.

School – our Irwin [her son] often said that we'd been taught far better than what they learned at the town school. Irwin – when he used to be studying and he would ask something, I was able to tell him and he was really surprised. Such as square root and all that. We had been taught that up in the 5th Standard in them days. Not that I was brilliant at it but I'd a bit of an idea about it. But you see we left school at fourteen, just when you were beginning to take an interest in things, and it was all lost that. You didn't get any further because you had to go right out to service and you never saw a paper or anything. You weren't allowed to read at the farm. Not of a night when you were finished. The men could maybe read but there was only one paper, the *West Cumberland Times*, that was all the week. It was scandalous. And they used to sit on it on Sundays so that you couldn't get it. That's true. Either the boss or the mistress did. I don't know whether it was because they didn't want us to read or because they were religious. Sort of religious. I think it was a bit mean of them. No, we never saw a paper or anything so when you left school at fourteen you were stuck.

There was one or two nice books I got a read at and then this place I was with them two years and a half and as time went on they gradually bought me a book when they saw I was a reader. They bought me an authoress called Annie Swann. She was very Scotch and very pathetic. No, there was no reading in them days. They bought me three books altogether, I think, in the two year and a half. I was as proud as Punch. Even at home girls weren't allowed to read. You should have some knitting in your hands or something of that sort. It's just a waste of time, reading. So we weren't encouraged to advance in any way. You just had to work.

The boys got away with a lot more than we girls did. The girls used to do the washing-up and you had to have some knitting in your hand or something. The boys had comics. *Chips* they used to call it.

It was a little pink paper called *Chips* and they used to swop with one another. We had many a bit of fun of a night in the house and Mother and Father would sit watching us. And then we would fall out and there was a scuffle on the floor, and they were them red and blue tiled floors. Cold – you didn't sit on them, mind. Just had a rug in front of the fireplace. There wasn't any lino down or anything of that. It was scrubbed out every day. I can remember there was a settee. Well, it wasn't a settee, it was an old fashioned settle and a table and a chest of drawers and another table. And of course some chairs and that's all the kitchen would hold. Then of course there was the old fashioned fireplace. With the coal oven. We could read our prizes on Sundays. And we had to wash our hands before we picked them up and they had to go back exactly as we found them. We were allowed to read on Sundays. Not through the week – we hadn't to have our prizes out through the week.

I was at Miller's eighteen months and then I moved out here, Wigton way, for two and a half years. While I was there the First World War broke out.

We didn't feel much because we had our own butter and eggs and milk and everything. There wasn't the severe rationing there was this last time. We didn't feel it with not being householders or anything of that sort. We would maybe have felt it if we had been running a house. We were pinched of sugar, but as regards butter I can't remember ever being short of that – not there. And they got their meat. I can always remember when the War broke out that weekend. It broke out on the Saturday, I think, and market day was at Wigton as usual on the Tuesday. And they were loosening the farmers' horses out and leaving the carts in the middle of the street and taking them away. They were just undoing the horses' harness and taking them out and leaving the people to get home the best way with their traps. It was some government. I can't remember whether it was soldiers, some officials. They got they hardly dare go to Wigton, but they had to go to get rid of their foods. That was the 1914 War.

You see, when I was down at Westfield House I was never away from that place for two and a half years apart from my half-term holiday. And I never spoke to anybody or anything at that place. For two and a half years. I often think it's a wonder I didn't go crackers. There was just their own two selves and a daughter and a son and of course these people, they sat at one end of the kitchen and we sat at the other. And they never drew you into conversation or anything of that sort. And I wasn't allowed to speak to the hired lads. They were at you right away if you did. It was a queer carry-on when

I think about it. The lads used to maybe just say hello or something of that sort as we were passing, just like as if we were passing in the street.

They were always out in the fields and when they came in of a night there was no fire to sit by or anything of that sort. And they used to just stand in the little back kitchen place. Or else go out to the pub or somewhere. But there wasn't many pubs around Westfield House and Aikton. They had to go as far at Aikton for a pub. They would just stand in the back kitchen or else go into the stable.

I had to get washed up and peel the potatoes for the next day and I was standing in that little place as well. I had to peel a bucket full of potatoes every night. You never left potatoes and that till next day. They were peeled the night before. And if we did say anything we were whispering (and you can hear a whisper, can't you?) they would say Have you nothing else to do, Lizzie, than chatter in there? Well I didn't chatter because, to tell you the truth, I was just as shy of men as anybody else in those days. I'd never been away from home much. You can't believe it. Annette [granddaughter: sixteen] thinks I'm stretching a point when I tell her anything of that sort. She can hardly believe it. I wouldn't have stayed. I would have left them. Aye, but if you left you were chased back again. You daren't leave and go home. Oh well, you must have been doing something wrong. Away, get away back. No, they were just that way that you just daren't go home. Because it was looked on as a bit of a slur, you see, if you couldn't stick it out for six months. At term end, they used to ask you if you would stay on. I think you were too shy – you started to worry about a new place and what you would do. If you would get on okay and what they would be like. Better the devil you know.

After I got a bit older and came more out Wigton way, well, you got one or two friends. You got out more. After I left them I came to Moorhouse Hall and I was with them, Dixons, four years. I liked Mrs. Dixon. She was a grand body [the mother-in-law of Mrs. Dixon quoted in Chapter 1]. Robert Dixon and Annie Dixon, they were. She was a good sort. So I got more freedom and I met other girls.

I got a lot of field work to do there. Whatever season was on, I had to help with it. Pick potatoes and help with the harvest and such as that. Thin turnips. I've seen me loading carts when the moon was shining of a night. If it was a bad summer and they were wanting to get the harvest in, I've been many a time loading by moonlight. Worn out as well. Because you see when you come in of a night there was a lot of your work left for you and you had to start on your

48

housework as well after you got in, whereas the men were finished, once they got their horses groomed and fed. They were finished but the lasses had to carry on. Some were more particular than others, some were fastidious to beyond redemption. On the whole they were all gey particular, especially about milking things and such as that. They had to be particular about that.

At the Dixons' they had three men and they had me and they had two girls as well. And then there was Edwin, their own son, and there were three daughters. But of course they were just kiddies then when I was there. And we used to have to clean the pig hulls out and such as that. We used to have an old sow and she had a litter of pigs and I used to clean her out every day. And the barn wasn't far away from where she slept, and after I'd cleaned her out she used to go to this barn and bring what they called a bottle of straw, and it was a lot of straw tied up awfully tight with the threshing machines. A great big thing and a queer weight, and it used to go and bring a bottle of straw in to its hull and break the string and spread it all over the floor for itself. You would hardly have believed it, but I used to watch her. You got to know the animals and they knew you.

Pigs are intelligent, and they can be fierce as well. They're bad 'uns if they turn on you. There was one I was frightened of. It had just had its piglets and that's when they're most dangerous. But it wasn't this one that I used to clean out.

I would start at six o'clock – half past five and six o'clock, and Mrs. Dixon always used to wake us. And we would get up and get dressed and go right out and milk the cows. Maybe thirteen cows. Maybe somebody would help you and maybe somebody wouldn't. You might milk six and you might milk twelve and they would come in just on the thirteenth or something of that sort. And you came back and put it through the separator and you had to turn a handle the whole time. And the cream was coming out of one spout and the milk out of the other. And after you had finished doing that you went and fed all the calves with this milk after it had been separated.

Then you came in after you'd done that and you got your break-fast. And that was porridge and bread and butter. After you'd had your breakfast – not the men, I'm just talking about myself – you washed all those things up in the separator, took it all to pieces and washed it and washed all the parts in it. And you went into a big, what they call the pot house because there was always a couple of boilers in, pig boilers, one for to boil potatoes for the pigs and the other for hot water to do all the washing-up. And that boiler was kept going all day with ordinary coal fire underneath. You did all your

49

washing-up in there and all the things were scalded with this boiling water and they were set out to cool until night when you put the separator together again. And you milked again. And that was to do twice a day. And then of course after that you washed the breakfast dishes up and then started to do the house up and you were on call whenever the men decided they wanted a bit of help, maybe have to go and help to move some sheep out of a field or something of that sort or take some sheep away down into a field, help if the cows were calving or anything that was on a farm. Then they'd maybe decide to send us out into the fields and you had to go out with the men, and work in the fields, scaling manure – putting it all over the field. It was hard work as well. All sorts of jobs.

The mistress generally did the baking and the cooking but we had to have all the vegetables ready; we always did the vegetables but as regards baking she used to generally do it. And she used to make fresh scones for the ten o'clocks. That was another job I used to have to do. If I was working about the house I had ten o'clocks to take to whichever field they were working in; sometimes you had a good bit to go. Used to go in a big tin can and the food and stuff in a basket. And if they were at the bottom of the field you had to wait till they came back up the field, whatever they were doing with their horses, if they were working at the bottom of the field you had to wait until they came upon what they called hay drigs, you see. And then you just left them and they brought the dishes in at dinnertime. And that was the same at teatime as well. In between times, there was the dinner.

At Moorhouse Hall they were more friendly. They were bringing a young family up themselves. They liked a bit of fun as well. Now it didn't matter how tired you were at harvest-time or haytime, you liked a bit of fun like that. Now we got that as well because their kiddies used to like to play with us, and we used to play at all sorts of things in the field. Worn out many a time, we'd been maybe haytiming all day. It was a grand place. And Mrs. Dixon would never think of asking you to do any mending or anything of that sort. You did your own, that was all, and you could read or do anything you liked there after you'd finished your work.

I had one pound a week [this is 1918–22] and that was supposed to be a good wage. It's about twenty-five pounds for the half year and that was a very good wage for a girl. But you see when they wanted you to stay on they would ask if you would stop on. And if you said you were thinking of a change well, I'll give you so much more to stay on, and that's how it happened. You weren't allowed to spend a lot. It went home. It went home and they saved it for us. You couldn't get away then. You daren't ask for a day off. You never got a day off until your half-term was up. We got Mothering Sunday, and you got the weekend but that was only from Saturday afternoon to Sunday night. You had to be back in at Sunday night.

I went to church every Sunday night regular. That was the only place I got to. I didn't go anywhere at all until I came nearer Wigton and got to Moorhouse Hall and we got going to dances. Smashing, real old-fashioned stuff. And I tell you where we used to go to. We used to go to the Baths. They used to put a floor down on the top of the Baths. There was a lovely floor on there and there was roller-skating as well. But we used to have some grand dances. Highland Scottische, square dances, quadrilles and lancers and Canadian three-step and military two-step and all them sort. Everybody enjoyed them in those days. You put your heart and soul into them. And you know the lads went with great big boots on in those days. Just on a Saturday night. If there was a special dance you had to ask off and ask if you could be out later. You used to walk from Wigton to Moorhouse Hall after it was finished, sometimes two or three o'clock in the morning, and you were up again at five to milk. It wasn't worthwhile getting into bed for.

Sometimes I've been locked out. I daren't tell me mother I'd been locked out. I can always remember being late one night and Bob Dixon says to me the next morning, I think you'd better have your watch on your ankle, you'll maybe see it better. I can always remember him saying that. He was a rough and ready fellow but he wasn't a bad sort really, Bob. I liked him. I used to like his laugh. He didn't boss you about a lot. He told you what to do and you had to do it. He didn't play war with you unless you really slacked. He never seemed to say much to the lads either when he used to give them their orders every morning. I can always remember when he got his first car. I says, Ee, it's a wonder you can afford it. Well, he says, I'll tell thee what, Lizzie, if I wait till I can afford it I'll never get one. So he got it and paid for it as he was going on likely. It was a biggish one as well. I can remember the first car when I was a little girl. That was when we were at home in Aspatria. I don't know what age I would be, or anything of that sort, but I can always remember that car coming past our door and looking through the window. We were amazed when we saw it. I don't know who it had belonged to or anything. So that's a queer long time since.

Marriage – it's a bit difficult when you take somebody else's bairns on and we were poor. He was getting twenty-three shillings a week in 1927, and I was getting a pound a week in about 1920, so wages seem to have gone backwards. I don't know how that was. I suppose I would think myself I was better off single.

Just after we married he was out of work. Well you see he had his accident at the pit and he had got about three hundred pounds compensation or something, something of that sort. And so he put it in the bank and his idea was to pick up a business of some sort and I don't know why he wanted to pick up butching but he did, anyhow, and that's where it all went. And we hardly got any good of it. Many a time he just would give me seven and six a week to keep things going. I just couldn't make anything of it. I suppose he was trying to make the money spin out. We didn't get any good of that money. Nobody paid and he went into partnership with another fellow. Well, this fellow slouped him as well. They used to buy a cow between them and I can always remember that cow was twenty-two pounds to buy for to butch. Now that chap ordered his share, maybe eleven pounds, and we never got it yet. That was a big drop in them days for us. I can always remember we kept writing to him and once over when he wrote he said he had sent one pound last week. Well we never got it and so I wrote back and I told him we hadn't got it but I would see further about it. I would enquire at the post office. It wasn't long till there was a letter came saying that he thought his wife had put the money in and she hadn't. He was just trying it on. But we never got it. I got sick of writing. I can always remember they call him L - - - r as well. He came from Maryport. Joe L - - - r. It all went and all we could get was farm work.

It was going along Weybrig Road to Silloth. It's a farm – turned off right down – into Dundraw, they called the place. But we were about five minutes' walk from the farm so their farm was called Bank End. But we lived in Dundraw. And we had sec [such] a cottage. Terrible. It had been done up and there had been a wooden partition put up, new wood and that, I don't know what there had been there that they'd had to do this, but anyhow we couldn't even afford to paper then. And I used to scrub it to keep it clean. We couldn't afford paper or paint for it. Because when we left Flimby we had to borrow off my mother and father for to square a few debts up. I was having that to pay back as well out of that twenty-three shillings.

I think he was too trusting. He always thought, Oh yes, they'll pay sometime. But they just couldn't pay. They were on strike for twenty-six weeks. Terrible. The men folk used to just sit outside at the doorsteps and such as that and I didn't like that. It was their habit whenever they were finished. Even when they were working

Above: A view of Wigton in the late nineteenth century.
Below: The High Street, Wigton, 1859.

Across the top:
The town at the end of the nineteenth century.

Below, left to right: The town before World War One,
between the wars, and just after World War Two
(Sammy Tate's shop).

*Above, left to right: The police before World War One,
the Banks memorial in Wigton cemetery, and the Wigton Fountain,
from the original design, in the center of town.*

Across the bottom: Walter Willson's, grocers, from 1900 to 1975.

Opposite, top to bottom:
Jonathan, "The Wigton Winner",
between the shafts of the
local doctor's digby, circa 1900;
he Wigton Railway station, 1888;
and early motor cars in
the old stabling yards.

This page, top to bottom:
The Carnival comes to Wigton,
circa 1880;
Queen Victoria's Diamond
Jubilee, 1897;
and Queen Victoria's
memorial service, 1901.
The procession went up the
ligh Street to St. Mary's Church.

A view of Highmoor House,
its bell, and the outdoor staff, circa 1900.
Opposite: Elizabeth Armstrong Bragg.

Opposite: Wigton men in World War One.
Above: Willie Fell in 1976, wearing military medal with two bars.

World War One continues in France and
with more recruiting in Wigton (center and bottom).
Opposite: Richard Irving Lowther.

"Joe Bill" Lightfoot.
Opposite: Farming around Wigton during
the first quarter of the century.

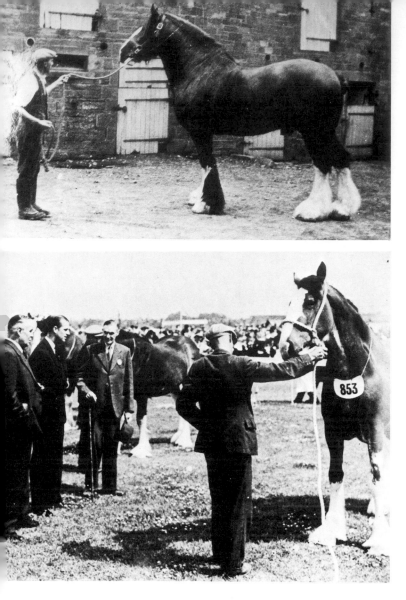

Top to bottom: A Clydesdale
from Mrs. Kerr's Red Hall stud
Mr. J. Kilpatrick (with cane),
Hawkrigg House, Wigton,
explains the points
of a Clydesdale
to the Duke of Edinburgh;
Hope's Auction Mart, 1963
(St. Mary's church is in
the bottom-left corner;
Nelson Thomlinson School
playing-fields are top right).

and they were finished they always sat outside like that, and I used to hate it. I think it was because my own father never did it. But miners have a habit of that. Just sitting on their haunches. Well he had had that accident. I don't know. And then you see his first wife, she died while he was in the infirmary. She died with cancer. You just used to wish that somebody would leave you some money. If I could just win five pounds or something of that, just get out of debt and get a fresh start. But you see when we came to Dundraw we came among all the farmers. They were all better off than we were, you know. It was a proper farming district.

Just two rooms up and one down, and there was no proper paper on the wall. It was that clay daubing and the stones would show through the wall inside the house. It wasn't levelled off with any plaster or anything. I think myself it must have been some sort of animal place – a hull as they called them. It might have been at one time, and made into a house. It could have been an outbuilding of some sort. And there was a well in that yard and I used to be always frightened for Fred falling in because the top was easy pulled off. No, I didn't like that. And then after that we went to Leegate House. It was better but I still had to work out.

That was the trouble with farm places. They always expected the wife to work out. I used to get sixpence an hour at Atkinsons' but it was mostly – you see, they sold the milk and it had to go by train. I don't know where it went to, maybe Newcastle or somewhere, so there was always this train to catch twice a day. So if ever they were going to be rushed, they used to send for me to go and help to milk and I used to get sixpence for milking either one cow or maybe up to twenty-six. I just got sixpence a milking and it didn't matter how many cows I milked, I still just got sixpence. And it was very often a lot. It was very rare I just milked one cow. And I used to have to help with the harvest.

I had to work at night when I came home. I could make the lads their trousers and such as that. I remember making a pair for John. He was very little and there wasn't any flies on, just a little hole, but Uncle John that used to live at Maryport, he worked on the railway and he had a railway uniform, green corduroy, and used to make lovely trousers, and they used to give us them to make up. I made John this pair, and I'd cut two left legs, instead of a right leg and a left leg. Well, they were no use and it was such a waste. But I pulled it all to pieces again and managed to get a pair made up, but there were joins in them. I used to do a lot of sewing in them days but of course I can't see now. Anyhow, there's no need. But if people gave you anything to cut down it was a good help.

Baked everything. Never bought any cake in them days. Bread, teacakes, scones and pastry cakes and fruit cakes. And do a big day's washing. Aye, and they were all to rub by hand or poss or dolly, whichever you used, and they were to boil in a boiler and just an old-fashioned mangle with a big wheel. I often think I don't know how ever we got through the work really. I suppose we just had to do. It was either do it or leave it.

Dad [husband] was horse man there, he was the head man when we were at Leegate House. And he mostly did the ploughing. But when it came to be harvest-time and binder work, cutting with a binder, Mr. Atkinson, the farmer, used to turn in and do part of it.

My father was still working at the pit then and he used to send me a few coals with them chaps that took skins to the tannery at Carlisle. They used to pick them off the slag-heaps on the pit-banks because we couldn't get any coal them days. There was no cars coming round with the strike, and he used to go on the pit-bank and he used to pick all the best out of the slate, same as hundreds were doing, and he got these chaps to bring them through for me. And they were a couple of nice chaps, they used to drop them off for us. It was a big lorry, D. Mark & Son, they were skin people, they gathered all the skins from the farmers and butchers and such as that, you see. It would be for to go to the tannery. And I remember once over, he had picked a good bag for us and he had got a few good ones in as well, he'd been pinching them out of the pit itself while all was quiet. And so we got this bag of coal and we were burning them one night and the bloomin' police sergeant came in and I don't know what he came in about. I think it was something about a fellow called Hope. He had been getting into bother. I don't know whether he was drunk or what, but anyway he wanted Dad to give evidence at court. But anyhow he came this particular night and he says, By, he says, you have some good coals on your fire. Where did you get that frae? Off t' slag heaps at No. 4. By, you must have been gettin' into a good seam then. We daren't say a thing because Granda would have been jailed. I'll never forget that. It's funny that that sergeant should come in that night and see them coals on the fire.

We went to Bromfield after we left Leegate House, to Mearside, and from Bromfield we went to Springclose and then from Springclose to Kirkland. Oh, I liked Bromfield and they were nice people. It was a grand community as well. There was everything in that little village. There was a church, a school, a cobbler, a telephone and post office – there was every amenity that you really needed for everyday life apart from buying vegetables or anything of that sort. But then you bought off the farmers then. It was a grand little place and he was a nice chap was the schoolmaster as well.

The house was rather damp but we had two bedrooms and sitting-room and kitchen, and a bit back kitchen. But it was damp. Stanley [the oldest stepson] left school while we were at Bromfield and he went to Stockdales. He went on farm work. He did well at Blencogo School. When John first passed his exams and that and passed for grammar school we couldn't afford to send him because they were just wearing clogs and such as that so we didn't send him. Mr. Burnett [a teacher at the grammar school] came and saw us about it and told us what we could do. He told us we could get a grant for him, for clothes. We got five pounds a year for him. Well, it helped a good bit. At least he could go to school in boots and such as that. It would have been a terrible thing to go to the grammar school in clogs. It would have been terrible, wouldn't it? As regards prestige and that. He wouldn't have gone. No. Well, I think we had thirty-five shillings a week there, this was John I'm talking about, and there was John and there was Elsie. Mary and Stanley were out working. And Elsie was starting work I think as well. There was Elsie, and Wilson, and Irwin, then. Thirty-five shillings a week. And Fred, I forgot about Fred. That was four. There always seems to have been four. As one got away. So it wasn't much in them days.

We all liked it at Bromfield. You see we were in the Co-op as well and to try and have a little bit I didn't used to lift me dividend much. But it mounted up and when I was really hard up it was there for me. And then it got that when I got a few pounds saved and I was going to get anything extra, my own father would say, Well, don't lift your money, I'll pay for it for you and you can pay me so much a week. So it left me with a little bit of capital behind us. It wasn't much but it was nice to know we had something. Because they knew that if I lifted it it wouldn't go back again. So it mounted up over the years as we grew better and everything grew better.

I think things started to get better just before that when we went to Leegate House. [c.1930] That was our first start for rather pulling together because you see Mary got work and Elsie was working then. Well, they weren't to keep and they weren't helping us in any way but they weren't to keep. That's where it was. They just clothed themselves and everything. And sometimes if they wanted anything and they hadn't any money throughout the half year, well, I used to get it for them and then they paid me at the end of the half year. There was no wages in those days. It was all cheap labour. Politics?

We weren't a bit interested in them. I didn't know one thing or another from politics. I can just remember there was an election when we were at Dundraw and Dad says to me Now vote for Lowther. That would be Lowther of Lowther Castle. And I just put my cross there and I thought after – proper Tories. Proper Tory government it was. He was rather like that. Just because his boss was a Tory we had to be. And that was the only thing I remember. I never bothered myself. After that I think we were all more or less Liberal. Labour wasn't doing very well them days.

At Bromfield we had some grand nights. Dad used to go for a pint, and he just had sixpence maybe, and as soon as he went out, Stanley, Elsie, John, Fred and me had a rocking chair just like this, an old-fashioned one though, and I used to sit in this chair and they used to sit round me and we used to sing and carry on. Just sing or have guessing games and such as that, all the time Dad was out. It was a happy time there, really, for the bairns as well as myself. And I've seen when Stan's wanted his dad to go out, him say, Have you not got sixpence for him, Mother? Then we'll have a sing. We had some good times. We had our hard times but there were happy times as well. And in this sitting-room at Bromfield, Dad used to play the melodeon and Aunt Nellie used to come and visit us sometimes and Uncle Tom, and maybe Mary would be here and bring maybe a friend with her and that sitting-room was just given up to dancing. And Dad playing the melodeon.

Well this is our twelfth house, believe it or not. This is twelve times we've moved. And when we went to Kirkland, after being at Mearside (Bromfield) and that, we weren't very well off and we lived in the farmyard. It's been bulldozed down. It isn't there at all now. It was right opposite Stampers', where Stampers lived. Well we went there you see and then they decided they wouldn't keep a head man, Hopes, so we had to look out for another place, we had to get out you see. And so Dad applied for places. A bad time then, the 30s – in the 30s, you see. Things were poor again. And he tried two or three adverts and such as that and then there was a one in Scotland at Canonbie and the chap came to see him and we asked if it was as big a house as we had at Kirkland. Not that it was a biggish house at Kirkland. We had two big bedrooms upstairs, and they had old oak beams and everything. And there was a big kitchen and there was a parlour, and there was a big long passage and there was a dairy as well. So when the chap came to interview, Dad he said to him, Is it as big a house as this that you have for us? And the chap says, Oh yes, it has a bedroom upstairs. So of course we got – Stampers were moving us, I think, in their big cattle wagon. It was an awful wet day, November. Anyhow, we got packed up and went away to Canonbie.

It was a long journey. And when we got there we couldn't get the bloomin' furniture in. There was hardly any room at all. There was a kitchen and there was no upstairs at all. It was just a loft. And there was a wall they called a hole in the wall and that's where a bed stood and it was there all day as well. Proper Scottish way of sleeping. And then there was on the other side, there was a place for another bed. And they'd had to knock a piece off the mantelpiece to get a double bed in. Well we were going to have to knock that piece off that mantelpiece to get our bed in and there was going to be two bedrooms in that kitchen. And when we looked in the oven to see what such an oven it was, there was a big hole like that in it and there was just a tray laid over it. If I'd baked in that, smoke would have belched out like anything. The oven bottom was gone, you see. So we never unloaded. Dad went up to see the chap at his house, a big fine house. He promised him all sorts of things just to get away. He said he would see he would get him another man and we said the house – we daren't take the furniture off, so we arrived back at Kirkland and we had nowhere to put our furniture, because the people who had followed us were in. And it stood in a stable for three months at Stampers and we went to Aspatria then to Granda's at North Road. To live with my father.

And so there was me and Dad and Wilson and Irwin lived with me father at North Road and John and Fred used to go down to sleep at my brother John's, at night, and come back up for their meal. It carried on like that for about three months like and then me brother owned these houses where he lived so there was a letting come up so we got a house off him. It was very small but it was better than being in with me dad because there wasn't room for us all. And he expected us to go to bed at nine o'clock as well! He used to wait till nine o'clock and Dad and me had to go walking up them stairs at nine o'clock and he was following us with a candle. Now that's true. I'll say Dad could have kicked like owt. But he had forced to keep his peace, because you see Granda and Edwin needn't have taken him in if he had a mind to say anything, 'cos you see as long as the mother and bairns are okay it doesn't matter about the man. As regards anybody being evicted. They look after the mother and the bairns but the man has to fend for himself. So Granda could have turned round and said that to Dad. He was bad-tempered, though. I used to be sort of flate on him, frightened of him, and then I got to be braver and I just retaliated. I hadn't been used with men folk being bad-tempered really. I don't know why. I think my brothers were a bit placid.

He always wanted to be his own boss. He had a good bit of say at Mearside (Bromfield – where he was head groom to prize Clydesdales). He was okay at Mearside. He liked that. When we came back from Canonbie, from Scotland, he hadn't any work or anything and we had to go on the parish at Aspatria. That was the finish though. I used to hate it. You didn't get any money. You just got a voucher and it was just for food. And I was fair shamed. Dad used to go for it and I had to go and spend it. I don't know which would have been worse. You didn't like it. It was just eighteen shillings as well. You couldn't please yourself what you went to buy. There was a list made out of things you could buy. There was no fresh butter. There was margarine and so much jam and so much sugar. They didn't half let you know you were on the parish. I suppose just because the money was being spent at ratepayers' expense.

We would be on it about three to six months. Then we got into this house belonging to me brother and Dad tried to get jobs here and there and he couldn't get anything. And then of course this park job cropped up. He saw it in the evening paper, so we went about it and, my, he didn't half go round folk at Wigton here, councillors and all them. And Canon – what did they call him – that was here at the time, he had retired then but he was still on the council – what did they call him? a deaf fellow with white hair. Never mind. He got at him and he did his best for him and got it. We were in my brother's house and he travelled for twelve months on the train till we got a house here. And then we got that house at Wiza Crescent. And we haven't looked back since. We were at Wiza Crescent and the Parish Council decided they would build a house for the park keeper to be retained by the park keeper, so we were a year or eighteen months on Western Bank. And we were there twelve months and we didn't half watch this house being built. It was smashing and do you know we've had three new houses that didn't belong to us [council houses]. Then Western Bank was a nice house. It was really nice when we first went. But over the years things deteriorate but they're fairly decent at the moment. There was three bedrooms in them houses. I loved being there. It stood on its own.

Park House was lovely. I wouldn't like to go back there now. It isn't the same. And you know, after it was built and we'd moved in, people used to see Dad in the park and Would you like to see through? He used to bring people to see through. It didn't matter what I was busy doing. But anyhow somebody had asked him one day how we liked the new house. Oh grand, he says. Go and tell the Missus to let you see through, so this knock came to the door. I don't know who it was now, but she fair laughed about it after. When she knocked at the door and I opened the door, she says, Your father says you have to let us see through the house. She thought he was me father!

They say it's very nice now, the Park. Have you been down? Our Wilson says it's lovely. I think there's two of them do it now. And you see they've staggered hours as well. But you see Dad used to just have to get anybody he could. When he first started down at the park he used to have two pounds a week and used to have to pay a lad ten shillings a week to help. He got two pounds but out of that two pounds there was ten shillings to pay to this assistant lad.

The younger two children – Margaret and Irwin – they had a lot better life than we ever had. Freedom and one thing and another. You daren't speak when we were bairns. But they would be able to argue with you and such as that. And they were better other ways. They got a bit of pocket money as we never did, all sort of things like that. And Annette, Margaret's daughter, she's having a better life again. You see when Margaret was a girl going to school, the War was on. They were just getting half educated. There was just half-day education because of the Newcastle kiddies being here, and Dame Allen school and that. And they were to teach one part of the day and then the teachers were always being called up or something. And as Margaret says, she just wished she could have gone on another year or two in a more settled atmosphere. Of course she's quite bright really and intelligent but nobody took any interest in them much because they would be thinking, well I'll be called up next. I'll be away, so why bother? But she always liked Mr. Postlethwaite. He was a good teacher. Annette's studying now for nursing. She's going in seriously for it. She goes to Carlisle one week and Highfield another for her voluntary nursing. She hasn't been going very regular lately with upsets one way and another and with the house being central heated and such as that, there's been a lot of unsettled way of living, somehow or other. They haven't been able to sit on a settee. You can't do much studying if you're not comfortable.

I wouldn't like to have lived the life that my mother lived when she was my age. She didn't live to be my age anyway. She was just sixty-five. She hadn't a great deal to do because it was a little house but she had bad health at the finish and then she went blind, so she couldn't do much. My father lived a few years longer than her – seventy-eight. Oh no, I wouldn't like my mother's life that she had.

59

Very restricted. They never went anywhere or anything. She would never have believed that Annette could lead the life she does now. I don't think they could picture it really. They would just think they would go on the same way as they had done all their lives. They would never think that things have improved much, not as regards the way people live.

Improvements have been tremendous since we came to Wigton in the 30s. Financially for one thing and socially as well. Got among a nice class of people and when we first came to Wigton next door to the Barnes', well, they were an education in themselves. They were nice people and you got you just lived like them. Well you have that feeling, well, on the whole, you can sort of meet anybody. You maybe can't talk proper English always but at least you can curtail a lot of dialect and that. When I was young you would have thought that they were better than you and you wouldn't like to have spoken to them or anything of that sort unless they spoke first. You just felt you weren't on the same level. But you see, as we grew older and grew better as regards the sort of work we did and everything – farm work's very degrading for an ordinary farm labourer – it was them days. Mind you, they're better off today, farm labourers. They have everything behind them now. And the farm labourer himself won't do things that we had to do, because we had no choice. They won't work the hours that Dad did. And you daren't speak back till your bosses them days. They can tell them off or they can please themselves, sort of.

And look at all these houses that have been built for farm labourers. They're every bit as nice as any of the council houses. There's some at Waverton, there's some at Cogo – with central heating and that. In fact, I think they're better off than them because these people with a lot of land they would have some queer taxes to pay, such as Sir Wilfred Lawson. You see, Sir Wilfred Lawson when we were bairns and Lady Lawson were people that you bowed to; when they came through the town you curtseyed. They used to come to church on Sunday mornings now and again and you stood still if you were in the street and you just bowed. That's true. Mind, that's a long time since – before the First War.

Oh yes. There were a lot of high class people in Aspatria then. At the top end of the town there was the doctors up there and there were one or two nice big houses up there where they had servants and such as that. I don't think there's any now."

Her father could neither read nor write and never left Aspatria. Her sons are architects and draughtsmen, her great-grandchildren are born in Canada and Australia as well as England. Her grandchildren have forged ahead on the back of the social and economic progress made by the working classes – scholarships, grants, apprenticeships, travel – and one of them wrote this book.

CHAPTER THREE

War (1914-1918)

In the sixteenth and seventeenth centuries the world discovered its size and spread; in the eighteenth and nineteenth centuries empires and nations old and new challenged each other for precedence in the new global state of things; and at the beginning of the twentieth century, progress was such that there was a conflict which could be described as the First World War. That might stretch a point but the two hemispheres were involved (and the four elements) and the five continents knew of the conflict although the sound and fury was substantially on the featureless fringe of the Old World. Americans, Africans, Australians, Arabs, Austrians and Albanians were involved in this vortex of violence ignited by a scene from a Ruritanian melodrama, and so were Canadians, Scots, Jews, Germans, Dutchmen, French, Indians, Russians, Welsh and many others. This is not just a resonant roll-call of nations; the mess and muddle is essential to the central notion of this chapter, which is the idea of Everyman at war. Not an original idea, not a dramatic idea, but never, surely, in the field of human conflict have so many suffered such a similar and dreadful fate – proof of technical man's new ability to centralise, bureaucratise and paralyse Mankind – and never have they spoken so little of the old virtues of war, as can be seen in the poems and songs and memories of that event. And all these interviews bear this out. Each man spoke as one representing men with none either more or less worthy of note.

The central image of that first World War is of a man – whatever race or nationality – in a slit trench, dirty and bewildered, pausing between rifle shots and waiting for the order to lift himself out of the meagre protection of the ditch and onto a muddied field strewn with mines, shells, barbed wire and dead bodies, to advance into the waiting guns of the enemy. Millions on millions obeyed the command to go over the top and in their millions they were mown down by the waiting guns. All those who spoke here – as everywhere happens with those who speak of the First World War – were above all conscious of their luck, their debt, the weight of the massive slaughtering of their friends and comrades in arms.

Many many points can be made about the convulsions revealed and brought on by that event; how it heaved the long encrusted provinciality of many Englishmen, full of scarcely credible innocence and ignorance, straight into a whirlwind of manhood, survival and the sternest tests of all; how it changed society's way of regarding heroism and even loyalty and patriotism; how women came out of the home and, fully recognised, into industry and politics; how the voices of reason were derided as treason and the braying of bullies applauded as the expression of wisdom; how war itself changed and machinery changed and perhaps the faith and works of Western man changed. These immense topics are for others. Here is a simple chronicle, told by four soldiers, all of whom counted themselves fortunate to have come through. Edwin Routledge:

"There were these posters; Lord Kitchener pointing and saying Your country wants you and he did that and many many others. Another one that comes to mind is a group of people, servicemen on a poster. He devised one where you had a Highlander and a sailor and a – there wasn't any Air Force in those days – it was part of the Royal Flying Corps but he had various servicemen all walking along together smiling and you know everything was happy and wonderful and full of glory. And the thing that struck me about that later on was that most of these men were carrying their rifle the wrong way round. They were carrying them with their butts behind them, you know over their shoulders, which was an offence in the Army when you got in. You weren't allowed to do that. You were put on a charge if you did it. And in these books that I got later on – *Salesmanship and Advertising* – the Russell Art School of Scientific Salesmanship of which Sir Charles Higham was the head, he said that the one kind of advertising that he had done and would never do again and he had nothing but remorse about it, was the posters he did for the First World War, because he said they weren't honest, and he felt that he had let his profession down, he had also let himself down by devising these posters.

It was government-sponsored. You see, what I set out to tell you first of all was that the difference between the two wars, the first one, the First World War was recruited for the first two or three years purely on people's emotions, patriotism and people's – I had a brother, the elder brother (he was a miner), well, not the elder brother but the one older than me. He joined the Army in August 1914 and him and me we talked, I was only a kid then, I was only fifteen, and he said, Well, with miners and the death rolls high in the pits, and it was in those days, it used to kill over a thousand people a year in the coal-mines at that time, and he said, Well, it's just a bit bigger risk than that. And they recruited men by the scores of thousands that they could neither clothe or equip. They weren't geared for it and men were being taken away from very good jobs that they could have been doing, coal-miners, for example, you needed coal for power, engineers that were going in that could have been used on munitions and all this, and they were taking them and putting them in the Army. They had no equipment for them at all, and a lot of them . . . they were in – they were put into uniforms, when they got uniforms; first of all they just wore their own suits with an armband on. Raincoats were bought by the million and given to them, but not uniforms, they hadn't them. And they were just hanging around in the various camps. Aldershot was crowded with them, and they were drilling with drum sticks and all kinds of things because they just hadn't the equipment and rather than helping the war effort they were hindering it, because they just weren't being used properly and they just couldn't pay them.

I don't remember a lot about the propaganda. As a matter of fact I went into the Army in May 1915 at the age of sixteen and a half. We were in Aspatria and there was a recruiting drive there and there was a man they called Beck from Whitehaven. He was in the Seaforth Highlanders and he was recruiting on Brand Row. And they said that for every recruit he got, he got an extra day's leave, and he had been at home for about six months then, persuading people to join the Army. And there was a crowd of us this afternoon or there must have been – you could detail them all by name; but some were drunk, some were over-emotional and some saw the glory of it and all this kind of thing but these lads that I was with, they were all anxious to go and I said, Well, you're just a lot of fools. I said, It's not what he's telling you. I said, They kill people where you're going and I says an old man's life in those circumstances – I don't know much about life yet, but it's not the kind of world that I want to live in. I says, Well, you get yourselves joined if you like, but I'm off. I know where Edie Stoddart is and I'm going to take Edie home. I says, You please yourselves.

She was a girl from Westnewton and I think she's still alive but she had a dislocated hip. She wore a very thick boot and she was in our house when I went in the Army and she was there when I came back. In those days Edie and others, these people, they used to go round to various people's houses, her and her sister used to come to our house and they used to make Mother a dress, make my sister a dress and this kind of thing. All for a matter of about three shillings a day in those days. They had their meals with you while they were there. And Edie was just rather older than me. We were very good friends. There was nothing out of the ordinary about it. We were just good pals. But I knew she was working, and I knew what time she finished – they used to finish about six o'clock – so I went and met Edie and went home with her and stood and talked and came back into the town. And just as I was getting back into Aspatria here's this gang all coming down the street.

Oh we've all joined up, we've all joined up, we've all joined the Army. And come on, come on, you'd better go with us. Well, I says, I think you're a lot of fools but I suppose I might as well if you're going. Well alright, I'll go with you, but I says I think we're doing wrong. I says, It's no place for us, but never mind. And one of the things which they told you which was quite wrong, well it couldn't be, that if you joined together, you remained together. Well, this couldn't happen, you see. We were all split up. I joined on 22nd May 1915, sixteen years seven months, and actually this Beck hadn't enlisted us at all. He just got us to sign our names in a pocket book like a lot of kids. Some of the men were older. There was a gang from Aspatria, a lot older. So off we went to Whitehaven on the Saturday – this was on the Wednesday night – on the Saturday we went to Whitehaven to be tested and all this kind of thing. And this was the bit that was ridiculous because they just stripped you off and guessed your weight, and they put my weight down at nine stone four pounds. If I was seven stone four it would be the maximum. And they had these attestation forms ready to fill in. And I must have been a difficult character in some ways even then because this big red-faced officer, I think it was Colonel Mason actually from Whitehaven, he says, Come on, get the thing signed. Oh no, I says, I'm reading it. Well, he says, get over there, get out of the way and read it. So I stood over in the corner and read it and when I came back to him he said, Well, are you satisfied? I says, No, not exactly. He says, Well, what's wrong? Well, I says, first of all here it says that the period of service is either three years or the duration of the war. Well, he said, what do you think it means? Well, I said, I think if the war lasts only six months and I'm still alive when the war's finished, I'm out. If it lasts more than three years and I said if I'm still alive, at the end of three years I'm out just the same. I've done my stint. Oh no no, he says, that isn't what it means at all. He says, If the war lasts six months you've still got two and a half years to do. He says, If it goes beyond three years and, as you say, if you're still alive, you're still soldiering on. But, he says, we won't argue about that. It's only a consequence. But he was right. It wasn't. He says, What's the other point? I says, Well, here it says are you willing to be vaccinated? I says, Somebody's filled in yes. He says, Aren't you? I said, No, of course I'm not. I don't want to be vaccinated. Oh, he says, we'll cross that out. Well, in the end I'd done about four years so that knocked the three years out and they vaccinated me before I went to France. So it was futile to argue with them.

Actually, what they did, they played on the emotions so it was patriotic. The Germans doing this – well, you won't know – you can't possibly remember it. But what it was all supposed to start about was a scrap of paper and that. They made a lot of this scrap of paper, that the Belgians had signed it and the Germans – I think we were supposed to sign it as well but the Germans had ignored it. But this is what they do in wartime. And then they came with the usual story of atrocities and all this kind of thing. That happens in any army. I don't care what it is, you get brutal acts, because it's a brutalising thing anyhow, isn't it? And I think lots of men lost their sense of common behaviour, like decent behaviour, through this kind of thing. I wouldn't really say that men did it deliberate. They did it in the kind of life that they were living.

There was another thing that went on like – it was Dig for Victory. You know, it was everybody that could get an allotment, all kinds of places were made into allotments so you could grow your own cabbages and your own potatoes and this kind of thing. And this was all done to beat the blockade. The Germans had some submarines, not to the extent they had in the Second War, but the submarine menace was there even in the First World War. And people called it Dig for Victory. And then the people who had been in the Army – I have a friend who's just gone down to live with his daughter somewhere in Hampshire, he was in the Dardanelles and wounded and he had dysentery and all this sort of thing, well, when he came back, instead of sending him back into the Army again, they sent him as a substitute to one of the farmlands, with one of the farmers, and quite a lot of servicemen were sent on to the land to help the farmers. This kind of thing was going on all the time but, as I say, I was away. I joined the Army in May 1915 and I didn't get back home until – I was home for a day or two just before Christmas, 1918 – but it was in April 1919 when I finally got home.

We were trained about forty miles up from Inverness. And our pay at that time was sixpence a day. One payday you'd three shillings, the other day you got four shillings. One Friday three shillings and the next Friday four shillings. That was your pay. Well, there was a man they called Pearson Peel, he was from Aspatria, he was from Harrison actually. He was a man that liked a lot of drink and he knew his way round the world. So this Thursday night him and me were sitting on a bed, like this row of blankets just outside the tent near the camping ground and he says, Now look, Edwin, you're a long way from home. I know the kind of family you've come out of. And he says, You've come into a queer life. Well, I didn't need telling that. I'd been there long enough to see that. And he began to tell me the pitfalls and the ways of the world, women and drink and all this kind of thing. Now I was sixteen and a half and he was opening a world out to me that I didn't know existed. It was completely new. And I think this is where the modern generation have it on you. They know all about this kind of thing before they leave school now. But drinking and all this kind of thing, well, I suppose even in those days I was reasonably well balanced, and I took it all and I hoped without showing too many signs of surprise. But it was, I think, the first experience of what you would call the coarser side of life. It was absolutely new to me. I wasn't completely ignorant but he was telling me things that I just didn't know.

There was a small school definitely opposed to the war but they were very very unpopular. And they mainly came from the Non-Conformists. I'm not a religious man at all, I don't accept any religion, but I think that over the years we owe quite a bit to the Non-Conformists fraternity. I don't mean the professional man at all, the ordinary lay preacher – you know the man I mean, 'cos they were the first speakers for the Labour Party as well. And there was a school of thought there as well, not a very strong one, but there was a school of thought there that thoroughly disapproved but they were very very unpopular. More than that, there was some stupid things done really. In Workington, for example, there was a family that was called Hake and they were Germans, pork butchers in Workington. Now the people in Workington smashed the shop windows and all this kind of thing because they were Germans. This is just because the emotions were being played on. If you were a German you were dirty and if you were British you were marvellous. Of course, this didn't apply but in any case – like the economics of the thing – it was stupid to start smashing property up whoever it belonged to in this country. But quite a bit of that kind of thing went on.

I went out to France in 1915, I came back late 1916 and I went out again, it must have been somewhere in 1917 that I went back, and I was taken prisoner in March 1918 and I finished as a prisoner of war in Germany, working in their mines in a paper suit. It was from March until I think it was a date in November 1918 when we actually got home, at least, when we got back from Germany.

I think heroism was at a pretty low level. I hold the view that the people don't appreciate what's going on really. I'm sure of this. There again it's emotions – I think most people who win decorations in war simply don't see, don't appreciate the hazards. They see what they want to do and they go and do it. Well, the man that gets through he's a hero and he gets a medal. But an awful lot didn't get through at all. They just simply died. They were no heroes at all. And in a long time I never heard anybody say that they wanted to keep going. There were no heroes, not really. You couldn't blame people because you were living in a dreadful life at the front."

Willie Fell:

"You just had to go wherever we were sent. The first time I was in we were at Armentières then after we finished there we moved to Ypres and we were in Sanctuary Wood at Ypres. We were in Ypres for over twelve months.

Then after that we went to Hill 60 in that time, then from there we went to M & N trenches and then from there we went to Messines Ridge and then after we finished Messines Ridge we did a long march from Belgium right up onto the Somme at Albert. We didn't go till the end of September, 1916, and we went over. We went with the first tanks ever used. That was at High Wood. It was a rough place, High Wood, and I met my brother there, Henry, at that same spot. The 1st Battalion came there. We were with the 5th Battalion, Territorials.

I was a stretcher-bearer on the Somme. I got a Military Medal there. For fetching in wounded in broad daylight. When I was fetching them in, the fellow that was helping us, he got killed, fetching them in. I got down in the trench first and they knocked him down with a bullet. We had set the stretcher down. I fetched a lot in in broad daylight, and the white flag was up. But it didn't stop them shooting. And the first night we went in [to no-man's land: to get the wounded] on the Somme we went at black dark at night. Half past twelve at night. Well, when we got back, there was nobody in the trench. Do you understand? Gerry [the German Army] had made an attack and he had killed the best part of them and taken the rest prisoners. So we marched over this ridge and we got them to dig in, and them that didn't dig in, Gerry got them all the next morning in broad daylight. He was firing at them, you see; they were laying flat on the ground and he was firing at them. First one would jump up and then the other, and as soon as they jumped up he got them. But anybody that had dug himself in, he was alright till night. Laid there till night. Of course there was a shell hole. We got into shell-holes, but there was water in them. But it didn't make any difference. We had to stop there or we would have been killed.

Then we moved from there – when we left Ypres it took us six weeks to march from Belgium to the Somme and wherever we stopped on the road was our bed. Six weeks it took us and we had a terrible lot of fellows had dysentery at the time and they were getting medicine. A lot of them died with it. This was 1916. At that particular time there were no potatoes for to make dinners. They gave us foreign chestnuts – sweet chestnuts. And we all blamed the chestnuts for the dysentery. Then we went from there, we did another long march. We marched right to St. Quentin that was – the French were holding St. Quentin, we were the only British troops who were ever at St. Quentin. Our army, the 5th Army, and General Gough was in command, and they expected them making this big attack at Ypres. Instead of waiting at Ypres he come on, General Gough, to St. Quentin, and he had a weak army. They had taken half of his army to back Ypres up. They expected him to come right through at Ypres, you see, but he come on with the weak army. Well you see, after he came with a weak army, they wanted reinforcements. They were fetching them from Ypres to the other end of the line. Well, Gerry knocked us back fifty miles. And we stopped at one place and Gerry dropped leaflets down there saying: Two million men off the Russian front going right through to Paris. Well, we dropped leaflets to him: Six thousand Yanks landed every day. Which was all bluff.

On Easter Monday morning, 1917, we went to Arras and we had about four divisions hidden in a chalk quarry – underground chalk quarry – and they fetched them out on Easter Monday morning, 1917, and we took the Hindenburg line. We went seven miles, the biggest advance that was ever made, and the cavalry was in action. I got wounded there. I was twelve months in hospital with a bullet wound. I got wounded when we were going over the top. Every officer was killed in the regiment. And as soon as we got orders to go over, I

69

hadn't gone thirty yards till I got a bullet in here, through this leg and out of the other. But it went around the bones. It didn't break any bones. I was in hospital just outside of Bournemouth. Like I made a mistake there. When we got to Southampton, if you said you belonged down south they sent you right up north. They said, Where do you belong to? I said Carlisle. So instead of sending me nearer home, they sent me further away from it.

I went straight back after it was better. I got back exactly the day before the Germans made the big push. Me and Arnold Marden went back and Arnold got took prisoner. He wasn't back half an hour until he was took prisoner – off leave from home. But he had the machine-gun and all such as that. Like he was in charge of machine-gunners. And do you know what they did with him? They cut both leaders of his legs here, in below the knee here, both of them, and he was a cripple for life. And when Gerry made this big push we carried a Wigton fellow over three miles. He lost his leg like, and if we hadn't taken him they would just have put a bayonet through him. Tottie Robinson. Me and old Tommie Hodgson of Station Hill carried him. He was alright. He lost his leg. Our lot didn't do anything like that with them, not that I know of. But I did see one time where there were some Germans down a dug-out on the Somme and we had took the front line and instead of bringing these Germans out they fired bombs down and killed them down in the deep dug-outs.

And Gerry had good dug-outs on the Somme there. It was in a sunken road just the same as a railway – a railway embankment like that, and he had dug-outs in the bottom. Well we took them good dug-outs. They were forty feet down and they were all timbered with good timber. We had poor trenches. We just had a galvanised sheeting across on top of some sticks just for to get under when it was raining, but the Germans worked like billyo. They made good dug-outs. Then we went over the top again. I was talking to Lieutenant Wills, he was my platoon lieutenant, and before we got out a shell come and it just took the top of his head off here, right off. I catched him standing. He was telling us what to do when we went over. We went through a cornfield and the corn was up that high, and he was shooting just the height of the corn and we advanced seven miles and he had planted all the ground behind with corn and wheat. Well we were going through that and he was just gun-firing over the top of it. And there were about four from Wigton got bullets at that same spot, all through the legs.

We were standing in water up to here, up to our thighs. At Sanctuary Wood, we were on a listening post. We had a lad from Dearham out here, and I was watching the men on the road at Ypres; I was watching the road and he was watching across that way. Well, we had been on maybe an hour and a half and I shouted Joe, I says, you're not asleep are you, Joe? And there was no answer back. I went from my side of the shell hole to his side, he had been hit with a bullet, killed instantly and he never coughed or anything. Joe Martin of Dearham. When the platoon sergeant comes out to us, it was Sergeant Ferguson, he was a Wigton fellow, and I said you'd better come and get the stretcher-bearer, Joe's killed. And rather funny, he had got twenty-eight days' first field punishment for not reporting scabies, like that was with not getting any clean changes.

And Henry was in hospital with scabies, my brother. But Henry got down to the base and when he got down to the base they sent him up to the 1st Battalion, Border Regiment. Well, they did nothing else but go over the top. The 1st Battalion, they volunteered for it; they were a regular regiment. He was the runner for Mr. Ewbank. And Ewbank ordered him to take the message down to the headquarters and he says, I can't go through that. They would shell him like billyo. And he spun the revolver out, Mr. Ewbank. He says, If you don't go, I'll blow your brains out. So he had to go. The Ewbanks – their father was Vicar of Boltongate (three miles off Wigton) and he had four sons and I think they were all killed except for one. We buried another of them – Walter Ewbank.

Once night we had to go and cover a wire party. They had blown a gap in the wire, barbed wire. Well, they went out to mend it and me and a lad they called Charlie Wilson of Wigton, we went out in front of them. We had to watch they didn't fire bombs at the wire party when they were working and at the finish we had to come in. There was four inches of snow on the ground and on a moonlight night, well, it's like committing suicide. Well when I come in we crept back, we got inside like, and in our own trench. Then I went to Ewbank and I says, Now if you don't keep yourself down, he was a fellow well over six foot, he was six foot seven and a half tall, they were all tall, there were four brothers of them, and you could see the moon shining on his specs ... I said to him, Now if you don't keep down ... I says, We've been out on that party. We could see your specs as plain as anything, looking back. And half an hour after he was killed instantly. They were all priests, these Ewbanks. Every one was priests. The others, they were priests but were officers in the regular battalions. Walter was in the 1st Battalion. He come from India with the 1st Battalion. He got every honour there was except the V.C.

71

Do you know what the M.M. – Military Medal – was fetched out for? D.C.M. you got a month's leave and twenty pounds. Well this was fetched out to save you – they were that sort of men, they fetched this Military Medal out. It was fetched out in 1915, and they fetched it out on purpose to save that month's leave. They hadn't plenty of men and they wanted them all. And they saved twenty pounds a year. But now in this Second War, they have twenty pounds a year pension with this medal. And we have nothing. They should have given it to everybody. They shouldn't have given one it and not the other.

[Willie Fell got the Military Medal and Two Bars.]

I was on patrol. I was recommended by another regiment. This big mansion we were in, they were firing out of the upstairs window. Well we went at black dark at night. And took them prisoners. I met this Manchester Regiment, the captain, and he recommended me for this second bar. I would have got something else if it hadn't been for the Armistice being signed. Because, well, we all got tight. Well when we were on parade the next day, there was Major Russell, he was out of the Guards and he was second in command of our battalion. He was drilling the battalion and he gave an about-turn and the officer, my officer, stumbled. You see, the officer had to come through the ranks to get in front. Well I had to follow on through but the officer stumbled and I started laughing. And he had us up for laughing on parade. That was the day after Armistice Day.

Well I wouldn't take his punishment. I asked for a court martial. Well they had to wash it out. It wasn't a crime at all. That's what did me out – I could have got a better medal if it hadn't been for that. And at that particular time, at the same place, the Prince of Wales – he come to inspect the battalion. Maybe about three days before the Armistice was signed, at a spot they called Yvoir. It's on a big river just in front of Peronne, and he was inspecting and when he come round the back he says, he asked what I did for the Military Medal. And he says, Where do you come from? I says, Wigton. And he went on to the next one. It was Sergeant Dixon. He asked him where he came from? He had the Military Medal. I come from Wigton. And he went on to the next one, and he come to John Arnison, the mineral water fellow, and he asked him where he come from? He had the Military Medal. And he went on to the next one, Dickie Robinson: four of us had the Military Medal. He says, I'll make a special visit to Wigton some day just to see what it's like!

Gerry had what you call trench mortars, and you could see them coming. He used to fire them up in the air, and you could see them coming. It was just like a petrol tin only they were round and he fired them and the explosion when they dropped, it was something terrible. They made a hole you could put this house in. And they kept toppling over like that all the time they were coming. And you could see them. We used to watch them to see where they were going to drop. One dropped once at M & N trenches, maybe about ten yards behind our dug-out and we were all outside looking to see where it was going and we all got covered with mud. It took us all day to get it out of our eyes. It was a bad trench, that. Everything had to be done at dark. Take the wounded out at dark and everything.

There was pigs all running wild and at night, when you sat looking, you could see their eyes and you couldn't tell what they were. And when they shot it it was a pig. I've seen cats shot as well. Anything that moved. In the black dark you could see their eyes glittering. The Somme was the spot for that. You found fellows on the Somme in a kneeling position, just like that with the rifle in his hand and they were all dead. Many a dozen of them dead. And every shell-hole you went in they were full of dead fellows. I know when we went in September there were dead men all over the spot. In fact, our battalion went in to relieve a Scotch battalion and there wasn't one alive, they were all dead, either dead or took prisoners. On the Somme, after 3rd September 1916, we had ninety-nine left out of six hundred.

Well, there's a fellow comes in the British Legion every Saturday night. You see, they would toss them in a shell-hole twenty or thirty at a time and toss some soil over them. All them bodies were supposed to be lifted after the war and buried afresh. He was on nothing else but graves, burying fellows, digging them up and burying them right. I've lifted dead fellows, and a fellow that was helping to lift them, well, when you lifted them wind came out of their mouth. He says this fellow's alive here. I says, If all the Germans were the same as him. I says, We've won this war. You see, when you lifted them a gush of wind came out of their mouths. We were burying them, you see.

Our colonel was shot but I daren't mention any names because it could easy come out after. He turned round and said You cowards. To shoot your own commander. He was hit in the back. It was this colonel gathered all the stragglers up to try and stop the Germans coming on and he was shot in the back. By his own men. He was shot with a sergeant-major but it didn't kill him. He lived but he was a long time in hospital with it. The next man we got in his place – he got the V.C. He gathered all the stragglers up, what there was, in – behind the lines. He gathered all the stragglers – he broke our division up that much, we couldn't find our own battalion. There was none of them – none of them could find their own battalion. They were all mixed up that much. Well, he gathered all the stragglers and Colonel Roberts got the V.C. for that attack. They never stopped after that attack because the Yanks and them got mixed up and they made their attack and went right back. We took it back in at least three days what it took him eighteen. We took fifty miles' ground back in under three days.

Them that got shell shock, they were hopeless. You had to get them away. And I'll tell you what happened with me at Arras. We were right in front of an aerodrome. Gerry had advanced on us a good bit, and this aerodrome was right behind us – our own aerodrome. We were in this dug-out and a shell came straight through the dug-out. It never touched anybody. Lance-Corporal Henry from Whitehaven was as dead as could be. It had just gone very near him. It had killed him with shock. He hadn't a scratch on him. And all of us were in the same dug-out. We were alright. It burst after it got through the door. What they call whizz bang. If I'd had it, this Ewbank I was telling you about, this officer, he wrote a letter home. He said, I've got a sorrowful job to do this morning. I had to shoot one of my own men. I've been chosen as officer in charge of a shooting party, and I shot this fellow for going absent from the line. He didn't mention the fellow's name.

We were always in the first, second or third line. Never any farther back. The only time we got farther back was when we went for a wash at Ballou. They used to march us twelve miles there and twelve miles back to get a bath. You stood two or three minutes under this tap and then you got a clean change. We went three months without a change at all. We were alive with lice. When it was warm we used take our breeches off and burn up the seams. They were full of nits and that. When we went there, they took our old stuff off us and gave us somebody else's They had just been fumigated but when you were going back, with the warm walking you were ten times worse. The nits all come alive again."

One of his brothers, Henry Fell:

"I was in the Post Office. I was a postman at Wigton Post Office. We were in the Territorials and we had to report at Water Street, Wigton, in 1914. And then we went to Caernarvon and stopped there two nights. And then before we knew where we were at, the tents went down, the bugle blew and we all had to come right back to Wigton to get rigged up for the war. So we just got back and then the next day they took us to a shoe shop. We hadn't any shoes in them days. And Mr. Johnston, the father, supplied us with shoes. So off we went to Barrow and then from Barrow to Fleetwood Barracks, back from Fleetwood Barracks to Barrow and then from Barrow to Fleetwood Barracks, back from Fleetwood Barracks to Barrow, then off to Le Havre in France in October 1914.

And then we went right up into Ypres. All Ypres was coming away, banners and all the stuff for the children, the horses, and dogs; everything they could put on a cart ... coming back out of Ypres because the shelling it was terrible. And then when we got there we went to St. Julien, and in front of St. Jean trenches. And my brother, he got wounded and died. Well anyway, we went in there and I says to him – we couldn't get any water, so I says, We'll volunteer to go for water. My brother and three of his pals said they would volunteer first. Well, one of the lads got hit with a sniper, the other two got hit with snipers and I had to go out and bring my brother back in. He was badly wounded in the stomach. And we couldn't get any water. And do you know what we had to do? We had to dig a hole in the trench and wait till the water seeped through and then we got a spoon and put it in our mess tins. We couldn't move anywhere because the Germans were too near at that time.

And after that we came out for a rest and then we went into the first gas attack. That was terrible. Do you know, we just had a little bit of a thin old-fashioned veil and cotton wool in. Well we put it over our mouths and tied it over our heads. And we used a stick like a letter T in wood with two little balls of cotton wool to see which way the wind was blowing. And if the wind was blowing this way we had to keep alert. If it was blowing that way we were alright because the gas went back on them, and it did go back. And then we came back to Ypres for a rest.

Well we got a good rest there, only for rats. Rats came out of the river. Terrible altogether. And then after that we came out for another bit of a rest, and then we went in the battle of the Somme which was awful altogether. Nobody has no idea. It was terrible. On 1st July 1916 we had to attack. It was an attack for miles – at daylight. Well do you know, they were just dropping like that, thousands all along. Germans was shooting them just as we went along. It was very early in the morning. We came from Friar Court Hill – we were resting on Friar Court Hill. It's a wooden hut. You know what a bomb would have done. It would have blown us to bits. It was a terrible battle that. And then after that battle in July we came back for a rest and then the next battle was Cambrai. That's when the tanks first came into battle. The tanks were allowed in that wood, a wood they called Fringe Wood. I nearly took a fit when I saw them. I said that's God's blessing – they're going to do all the fighting. But they had bundles of wood on top of them because if they went into a river they dropped this wood in and then they carried on over it, you see. But some got stuck. A lot got stuck. And the horses went, that's when they made their attack as well. They come back, some of them, faster than they went. Horses did like. The men were killed. It was a very bad do that. And then we never got to Cambrai that day anyway. Then we came back for another rest. We were up to the eyes. We were walking on our own mates. They were trapped in the mud in the trenches. There were that many of us. And they were alive, and we couldn't stop because there was that many going. And that's true. It was an awful battle. They were lying all over the place. It was terrible altogether. It was a real bad do. I think they were blundered myself – I do.

Passchendaele was the worst place ever I was at. It was the mud. You couldn't travel. If you got in it, you were jammed. An absolute hole. I will say – when we did get them going. What they did was we drew back, we came back, drew them out, and then we got them out. It was a very good – generals, they were good, clever, and we drew all the Germans out of their stronghold. We went back miles. I thought we were going to pull it back the same as they did the last time. This is in 1918.

We did get them going and I never knew till there was a little plane, with colours hanging down, that was coming for the finish of the war, before the Armistice was signed. And I says, What's all these? And they were hanging down, these ribbons, out of a certain place and I says, What's the carry on, and they says, The war must have finished. We didn't know because we were right out in the open. So we came across a carrot field, and we ate carrots – we boiled them and we ate them. And when we went into one café, do you know what the Germans had done? There were two of the nicest lasses you ever saw. This was a café. And because they wouldn't go back with them to Germany, with the German soldiers, they stabbed them both. And do you know they were frightened to death of us. We got them into ambulances and away. There were hundreds lying wounded, civilians as well, and we got them away. Then we came back. We were in Lille, we got back to Lille.

Now then, we had to march from Lille to Cologne after the Armistice. We had Mr. Ewbank, he was the padre, nice fellow. And he was in front, and every time we were coming to a place to rest for the night and billet, barn or anything, the band played 'John Peel'. And we knew then that when it played 'John Peel', we knew we were coming for a night's rest in this place. But anyway we marched along, the roads weren't bad, there were apple trees and pear trees and all kinds of trees.

But do you know we walked our shoe-soles off. We couldn't get our shoes repaired on that march. And there only was one shoemaker with the battalion. So our feet was worn through the soles. Then when we got into Cologne, what a change. We went into a mansion, as big as that mansion up there – Highmoor House – a lovely house. They just detailed us, see, when we got into Cologne – you eight in there, you ten in there, didn't matter whether it was a public house, café or owt – you ten in there and they daren't say no. The Germans daren't say no. Some were good with us. There was this lady where we went in. We were getting a bit dirty with lice and things and they had lovely beds. So she asked us would we take one room, eight of us, and lie on the floor 'cos she knew, she could understand English, and we were all dirty. And very kind with us she was. Then they comes round and he says, Now any of you lads want to go home that doesn't want to claim a pension? Here we are anxious to get home. Hands up, yes. Trainloads of us, hands up for to come back home. But some that was wounded they stopped behind, and they got a good pension. I wish I'd have done as well. I'd have got a pension. But I wanted to be home.

I had one leave seven days and I'll tell you what I did in London. I slept on Clapham Common, me and another fellow. I came home and then went back to London and I says we'll have a couple of days in London on our own. It doesn't matter whether we're late or absent or what. Anyway, we went to Clapham Common and then we went into the Salvation Army. They used to take soldiers for the night, free then, and a bed for you. And as we got nicely in bed, they came to see our passes. Because we were two days absent; Oh, we can't keep absentees in here. You'll have to go to Waterloo Station and get away back. Put us out of bed and we had no spot to go then. And do you know where we went? We went into a theatre in London and we got in. Now, I says till [to] the other fellow, when the thing's over sit quiet. We stopped there all night and we sat in the seat. Everybody went out, locked the doors. I says, That's grand. We'll get a good sleep tonight. And when the cleaners came in the morning, Oh, they says, what are you doing in here? Well, we says, we couldn't get out. We've

77

been here all night. They were frightened. Do you know, they fetched us tea and bread and what they could and gave us a good feed and told us to get out as quick as we could. And we were off to the station then. So we got to the station. And then they ask you what station? They had to put us in the charge of a sergeant of our regiment to take us back because we were absentees.

And I'll tell you what they done with us in France, and this is true. Anybody who had been in trenches so long they got sent back out of the firing line for a rest, for to get it off your mind. And we went back to a place they called Deauville, that's a lovely place. That's where all the toffs live. Deauville and Trouville, but we went to Deauville. A lovely camp and a lovely place. Well, we got out one night. We were allowed out. Well, as soon as we got in this place we didn't know there was a war on. You didn't know there was a war on at all. These millionaires and casinos and all these. Come on, have a drink. First one gave us a drink and after we didn't know where we were. We didn't know what we were drinking. And we says, Oh, that's grand. We're alright now. A Canadian that was. And do you know what they done? They put us in a railway wagon, and there was Belgians, French, Australians, Canadians, they were all tight and they just left you there for twenty-four hours until you sobered up. And then you went in front of your officers, the C.O. Well, we got fourteen days and do you know what they did? They tied us to a post for about two hours every night, and you couldn't scratch yourself. And the civilians going by in cars and saying, Look at them poor tommies. And that's true. For fourteen days. And you have to shave practically in the dark. We hadn't any mirrors or nothing. It was an awful carry on, that. That was just outside Trouville. It was a lovely camp, mind. And Bombardier Wells was our trainer. He came from London. He was a boxer. Gymnastics, you know – keeping us fit to go back. There was some awful punishment for English soldiers, there was. They gave you fifty-six days for next to nothing in them days and, another thing, they could have shot us for being absent. Oh yes. For those two days. But you see, with us being Territorials and not regular soldiers, we were safe: if we'd been regular soldiers they would just have shot you. There were plenty shot.

I never came across any of these atrocities, but they're very queer are Germans. I won't forget them for this last do. Gassing people. But mind, I will say they're clever. They had better roads than we have now nearly – autobahn they called them. When we got on these roads, we thought we were in heaven. They had lovely roads then, in the First War. The trains went on one side, there were trams, there was cars and what they had, and then there was a bicycle and foot-path, all on the same road. It was lovely."

Four brothers went. George Miller:

"Of course we were young, bravado, thought we were going to have a picnic, that's just where it was, and of course we had all to go in and do our bit, so to speak. Well, I had to go down to Carlisle to go through the preliminaries to be tested, and on like that, and then from Carlisle to Kendal. We were equipped with our uniforms and that at Kendal. And about six or seven of us there was, just young chaps. Then we were taken to Liverpool and shipped over to Ramsey, Isle of Man. That was our headquarters for about three months.

Well I was sent to the 5th Border Regiment. And we went from Dover, no Folkestone, and across to Boulogne. We camped at Boulogne and then went on a route march from Boulogne to a place called Etaples and we were kept there for a while and then, just for a week or two, until we got acclimatised, and then we were sent up to our respective regiments, the 5th Border, luckily it was the local regiment. I knew a lot of chaps there and I got amongst a lot of good ones and bad ones, real terrors. Our sergeant was exceptional. He was a grand fellow was our sergeant. They called him Sergeant Monkhouse. He was a good one. He was a great man, he should have been decorated that fellow. Not really strict, you know, but whatever he told you to do, you did it. No matter what it was, you did it, because you knew that he would be behind you and he would be with you, especially when we went on bombing raids and things like that. He never let you go yourself. We went in groups. Of course, at night, bombing and that, just little skirmishes, and he used to always be with you. He was a grand chap was that sergeant and the first place we went to, we went up some duck boards to a little wee place, well, it was just ruins. We went down the cellar and that was the headquarters of the Border Regiment, one of the companies, and waiting of whichever platoon you were going to be put into. So I was put into Sergeant Monkhouse's platoon and it was very very funny that. When I was down talking to the other chaps that was in this cellar, a chap come out, I just forget who he was now, and he says, Is George Miller here? I said, How do you know that I was here? Oh, he says, a chap from Aspatria told us. Well, I said, did he? He says, I'm going to show you something. You won't have to be surprised. And do you know the

79

first man I saw dead was a Wigton fellow and he had been killed by a Minnie Wafer. There wasn't a mark on him. What we called – they had these things they used to send over – they were Minnie Wafers. And the only thing you could tell . . . they used to shoot them out of the little apparatuses they had, the Germans. They used to come over all of a sudden, just with a winsy noise, and then drop right down. What a thud. And he was killed by shock. And that was the first casualty I saw and he happened to be a Wigton lad.

Well, it sort of – I says, Am I going to be like that? Of course the chap just says, Buck up now, George. I wanted to show you. Away, go on, we'll do our best. That was at night, we went up into the line, you see, and Sergeant Monkhouse he comes to us and he says, Come here; I want you. I says, What do you want me for? He says, You're just the boy I want. I says, What for? He says, You'll be my rum carrier. So that's what I got to do. I would have got paddy-whacked for doing it if I'd been caught out. You see they used to always inspect you when you went up the line, mostly to see if all your equipment was right, they wanted to see if you were carrying maybe rum that you shouldn't. Well, they used to come along when we were getting in-spected. At the back we had our bottle of water and our hard rations was in a little pack at the back, with our rifle and bayonet and so forth like. I just forget how many rounds of ammunition you went up with. Anyway we were all set and they used to come around and inspect. Are you alright, George? Yes, yes, grand. And at the back at the strap, Sergeant Monkhouse always used to push another bottle. You see, the inspection was over and we weren't caught. Well, that went on for a bit and of course it was very essential, this rum business. I didn't take much of it but it was black and strong. It didn't half make you – you know, you were going to cut all the Germans to pieces when you got this rum, and anyways I said like, Where are we going? What part of the line are we going? Passchendaele Ridge. I said, That's where they say, when you're walking, you sink into the ground. I says, Where are we at? And it was very funny. We were just going up the line and a voice shouted to me, Hello, George Miller. And I turned round and it was Tom Coulthard; they used to be in a pub in Wigton. He was killed. That was the last time I saw him and he was in a different company. He was still in the Border Regiment, but we were relieving them. One company came out and one company went in. And the only thing that we had for cover was just sometimes just a little hole with just a tin over the top. And shells were dropping all around and that was all the cover we had. And Passchendaele Ridge – it was just a mound, like that – it just went up and down like that. And that place it was a death trap if you showed your head up. And rats, they were as big as cats.

I thought it was going to be a picnic until the shells started to drop, then it put the fear on you a bit. I saw – I don't know whether I did or not, I can't remember, but it brought tears to some of the lads' eyes. Terrified. I saw two or three of them, not that I was any braver, mind, I wasn't by no means, but they were ready for running away and we used to have to buck them up. And come on, come on. Now I don't want any rum. But they used to bluff them. They used to give them a little warmed-up tea, but half of it was rum to buck them up. And they were alright. They got over their fear then. Either that or a cigarette. But you had to be very careful when you smoked a cigarette. The light. And it was surprising how far you could see a cigarette. Anyways we came out of Passchendaele Ridge. We came out on rest. And we went to a place – I just forget the name of it now – but that was the first time I ever saw a gun as big. They were as big as what the Queen Elizabeth used to use. And there was a railway, and our officer told us that we hadn't to make a noise or anything like that. We had just to come back, on this certain afternoon, this gun was going to come up. I never saw a gun as big in all my life. Naval crew. And do you know the shell that they were firing was a fifteen inch shell, circumference, and the length of it, well, I never saw it – it had to be hoisted in with a crane. Of course we were a good distance away from it, like a nice distance, we were behind it, you see, so we didn't get any shock. The shock went in the front. But this gun, what a size! It came up on this little narrow railway, a little engine brought it up, an electric engine, and the crew, there were maybe twenty sailor men with this big gun, and they fired three shots. There was an aeroplane spotting for it right away up in the sky and signalling down where the target had to fire. They were firing twenty miles away.

We used to sit down at nights and take our shirts off and all down the seams we used to have a candle. We used to go all round the seams, cracking them. Oh yes, it was bad. There were about half a dozen of us going that night on leave, so we had to be all changed and go through the steam bath and all that sort of thing. Then we got our pocket money, so many francs, I think it was a hundred francs we got to come home with, our pay that was standing on, and I thought, we're not going to get out. By gum we're not. He started to shell the little siding and, by gum, two shells dropped right onto it, like on to the side of it. Oh dear me. So we were delayed there a little bit. We had to wait till the little pusher train come right up, and we got out alright. And we got to Boulogne, across to – I think it was Dover, we landed there – then to London. And in the morning, by gum it was quick, I caught the mail train here at six o'clock and before I got up in the morning, like I'd had a little sleep, people were coming round to our house and they knew I was on leave and they were asking if their boys were alright. I says, Well when I left they were. But do you know in the paper there was the map that St. Quentin had been taken, the Germans had taken it, the Border Regiment again was absolutely massacred. A lot of our officers got killed. Now then I was on leave. I reported to go back and it took me, I should say two months, travelling all up and down. I had to go to Carlisle, to report at Carlisle. And Carlisle says, Oh well you can go back home, Miller, and we'll let you know when you can travel any further. So they let us know about two days after. I went down to London. I was in London so many days before they could let you know, then they parcelled you off from London to Folkestone. I was in Folkestone for goodness knows how long, two or three days, then across to the border and just going back and forward, back and forward, to try and find the unit – what was left.

And eventually there was these gentlemen – officers they were, they weren't really in the army but they were gentlemen that contacted you – if you were stragglers they got you together and they found out where your regiments were. And so I did eventually get up to the place. And a very funny thing. I walked into this little farm where our lot were, the 5th Border, what was left, and the first chap – he's in Wigton yet – Willie Scott, he was the first Wigton man I saw and he said, Come here, I want to see you, come here. Now on the list all the dead, and I was among them. They'd lost us, you see, quite lost us. I was there, dead. On that list. I wanted to try and get hold of that list but they wouldn't let me have it, because it was rather funny to see your name dead. Missing you see – dead. But I read it down, all the poor officers and lads that I knew, they'd all been either taken prisoner or killed. Willie Scott and the officer who was there, they started to tell us all about it. He says as soon as our train got out – we were the last train to get out of that little siding – and he says the Germans come over, and before ever they knew where they were. And that was that. Well, we waited there a little bit until they got them all collected up and we went to a big camp for stragglers.

There was one scene where we were putting up a barrage, the machine-gunners – I was a machine-gunner then – and we wondered what we were going to put this barrage up for and it was the Canadians, and they had gone mad. We didn't actually see what they'd done but I think it was some French nurses that the Germans hadn't been nice with. The Germans, when they captured them you see, the field hospital had been ravaged by the Germans and what the Canadians had seen I don't know but it wasn't nice. And they went mad. Big fellows they were. Half of them hadn't guns. Some of them had great big iron bars and they went absolutely mad. They didn't half give the Gerries something. They did that. But of course we were putting up a good barrage for them and keeping the Germans down. Of course when you saw a machine-gun firing, and it was a big machine-gun, and in each belt there were five hundred rounds in a belt went through, and could go through in about three minutes, so you may know the fire. Flame right through – and kept putting them in and putting them in, boxful and boxful we used to fire over at them.

There was another incident where the Canadians and the Australians and the Jocks, they were altogether, and by gum didn't they go. And they never took a prisoner. There were no prisoners after that week-end. They did not. Everyone we used to see, they just put him down. They were that infuriated. You came across sad things, you know, and it made you absolutely mad, you know, that such things should be done. But mind the worst time you used to have in the line was against the Prussians, the Bavarians. Now the Saxons, they were alright. They used to sometimes shout over and tell us, We're Saxons, we're Saxons. Right, we'll give you an easy time. You give us an easy time. Well we did, we got it. But when they used to shout over, Bavarians coming in and Prussians, you could look for a heavy do when they were in. And it was funny that. We used to sometimes have conversations and things like that, and I'll tell you another thing that we used to have. We used to have Woodbine Willy. He was a parson, and he used to always come in the line and always before he left he used to say a little prayer and he used to always leave you with a Woodbine, a cigarette. So we called him Woodbine Willy. He was a grand fellow that. Never had a gun or anything.

And we used to have another chap regular in a certain part of the line. I don't know whether he was a naval officer or what he was but he used to come over, but he had a signal. He always had a signal because if he hadn't he would have been shot many a time. By our fellows. I once seen him come down the line and couldn't he talk German. Sometimes dressed just as an ordinary German soldier, sometimes dressed as an officer, a German officer. Where he got the clothes from I don't know – they were pinched off the prisoners – and he used to go over and spy in amongst the line and take information and come back. He was a brave man was that but I never used to get to know who he was or what he was. We just saw him come into the line and over he went. We – maybe he didn't come back our way. He would go back another way. But I've seen that chap twice, and Woodbine Willy I saw him about half a dozen times. He always left that little Woodbine, and we hadn't to smoke it. He said, don't smoke it till you get out of the line. We had to put it into our pocket. Away he would go. He was a grand fellow, was that. And I'll tell you another thing that I used to like. The Salvation Army. They were very kind to soldiers. Everything that the Salvation Army did was free. Yes, free. If you went into their hut, behind the lines like, you went into the hut they used to always – Come on, come on. Always a great mug of tea for you. And have you wrote home lately? No, if you haven't, well, here you are – a sheet of paper and an envelope. And no stamp or anything. We never used to put a stamp on. They were just franked. And they used to put them in the box and send them home for you. They were very good that way. And they used to have their meetings and little concerts, and things like that. Yes, we used to have plenty of concerts when we were out on leave and on rest. Oh yes, and football, plenty of football. Who was it I saw once – I do believe he was an American, and at that time he was a great jumper. Well I'm not going to say, I don't think the Olympics were on at that time, but he was a great professional jumper, long jumper, and in some sports – he was the first man I ever saw jump twenty-four feet. It was an achievement in them days.

I was watching a game of football, it was England against Scotland – English boys against Scotch boys and England and Scotland. We were shouting our heads off, a convalescent camp it was. And the siren went and, oh, what's the matter – Armistice. Well, well. Now then. What's going to happen now? Things finished. And some of the boys they even said, Isn't it a pity. They were getting that used with it. So they told us to keep calm and not do anything silly or anything like that. And first thing the commander of the camp said – the canteen was at the top of the hill – what he did, he says, Oh, the canteen's not big enough for you all, and he just had ropes put down. I never saw as many barrels of beer and stuff down that hill, and you should have seen the merriment that went on in that camp. It was good. It was good to see. Drunk – they went absolutely mad.

Well anyways that got settled up and a day or two after we were all called up and he says, We're all going to send you to your depots if we possibly can find them and you'll get your orders from there. So we were sent to our depots and they saw where we were. We were 5th Border Regiment. Well, there wasn't any then. They couldn't find it. So what they did, there was six of us and, we'll send you up to this regiment. Some Lancers or something. Well they were on horses. We weren't used with horses. The colonel he went mad. He was an aristocratic fellow. He went stone mad. He says, What am I going to do with you? Can you ride horses? No, we can't ride horses, sir. Can you use a sword? No, sir. What are you out of? Well we're out of the Border, machine-gunners, naval division. I've never heard a fellow swear as much in all my life. Oh, my hair stood up on end. What he was going to do. I don't want you. I don't want you. And a great big trooper sergeant – yes sir, yes sir. He had great big spurs on his feet. Take them back to the camp, take them back to the camp; I don't want them. So we were sent back to our billet. Well what we did, we just had to sit and just bite our fingernails. We couldn't do anything else, but we got our rations. We were in billets – peasants. And what we did – we just helped this German woman to spring-clean and do everything for her. The funny thing was how they used to spring-clean. It was a marvellous way they used to spring-clean. Everything used to come out of the room, there wasn't much in like, but it was all laid with red stuff and instead of having the skirting boards on, the red stuff come up about that far. Well we were going to sweep it out. No, no, you don't do that. She could speak a little bit of English. Well, I says, what have we to do? She come with a bucket of water, it splashed up on the walls and everything and we had to dry scrub. It was marvellous how fast that stuff dried, and I often used to wonder at the front door what this little V-place was for. I got to know. That was for the water to run out, and we did that for about a fortnight.

And then we got called up to the headquarters. We were in front of this colonel – aristocratic – again. He says, You're rubbish, he says, six of you. You've been a lot of use to me, he says, by gum you have. I'm going to send you home, he says, I'm going to send you to London anyways. He says, I'm not going to have you here. And by gum that's what he did. He says, Have you any money? No, we haven't any, sir. We haven't a thing. You haven't? No. Well, how much do you generally get? Oh we generally get a hundred francs, sir. Oh, do you? Well he says, will a hundred and fifty francs each do you? It will be very helpful, sir, till we get home. And he parcelled us all off. Go and get your things. And he telt this great big sergeant, he was with us, he was our guard, we hadn't to go out of the street. If we wanted we just had to walk up to the top of the street and back again. We were prisoners really. And then he brought us down. Come on you lads. Well we hadn't much tackle. We hadn't any packs or nothing, we hadn't even our rifles. We didn't know where our rifles had gone. So he parked us into a little lorry thing and he says to the sergeant: Here, when the boat leaves, see that you get them on and don't let them off, and see that they've tickets for London. I don't want to see them again.

When we got to London we didn't know what to do. So there were officers in Euston Station and, where are you from? So we – I got word I had to go to Manchester and they didn't half bustle you about. There were thousands there. And they were saying if you have any ailments you'll not get out at all. And they keep you for months. Oh, I says, I'm going to have no ailments. I says I'm going to get out.

We went to this camp outside Manchester and we were all lined up and of course you know what it was like. Now then, you fellows, he says, here for six months or home tonight. That's what he told us. That was to say you'd better not have any complaints or else you stay here for six months – or if you haven't any complaints well you can get away home tonight. I says I'm going home tonight. So we went through the doctor and he examined us and everything and No complaints, no complaints at all. You're not wounded anywhere? Gassed? Yes. Come on then into this machine and see. Yes, you're gassed. (I'd been gassed. It troubled me for three years after.) Do you want to stay here for a pension? No I do not. I want to get home. I've had plenty of it. And I got right through that day and I was back home the same day. Discharged.

I didn't really hate the Germans, no. I just said to myself, Well you're fighting for your side and I'm fighting for mine, but I'll tell you one thing that I did see, and it brought tears to my eyes, it really did. And some of the chaps that was beside us. We were – it was practically finished. The Germans were on the run and we had an awful job to keep up with them. And in this certain sector we were coming along and there was a chap, a little wee fellow he was, a German, and he was lying moaning and crying and, poor little fellow, he had a good right to. He had – the limber that we were taking, we used to call them limbers, trucks you know, and they were pulled by horses – well, he said he was trying to get onto one and the limber had gone over his legs, both his legs; they were flat. Well he was crying and crying. I don't know whether he had any pain or not. I says, What can we do with you me lad? And he didn't care about himself. He just was crying for his wife and children. He was a man maybe say about forty, just a little fellow. And he says, You won't kill me, you won't kill me? No, I says, we're not going to kill you, oh no. And we saw a Red Cross van coming along, and we told them to come up, and they lifted this chap. Well his legs were flat. He would have to have them both off, and we lifted him up as best we could and there was an official there in the ambulance. He says, are you in pain? No, no. Well there was one of our officers came along and he asked the doctor or whatever he was, Will a drop of whisky hurt him? No, he says, I don't think so. We gave him – just lifted him up, I was behind him, and just let him lean on us like that, and he had his whisky, coughed, he had a mouthful then another mouthful. And we just lifted him up as best we could and put him into the ambulance. That's the last we saw of him."

CHAPTER FOUR
Richard Irving Lowther

One of the dangers of a book such as this is that it will turn into a display of "characters": people who project themselves amusingly or vividly, button-holers, tall-tale-tellers, round-the-clock gossips, eccentrics. England is littered with them still: to spend time in one place and to keep your eyes and ears open is to realise that Dickens could return any day and still find the flour for his recipes. And whether to cut them back or encourage them to flourish is a nice matter of taste and judgment – because, of course, under every exception there's a rule, just as the apparent grey men, when scratched, often turn out to be the real originals. Moreover, there's simple gratitude involved. In writing a book based on people speaking, it's a pleasure and a relief to come across people who speak fluently. Garrulity can be generosity, after all. On the other hand, those who speak most engagingly do not always hit the nerve or what one guesses and hopes to be the centre of the matter. So I have taken particular care here to check and screen the "natural" talkers who threaten to take over the shop.

To see Richard Irving ("Dickie") Lowther walking up the street or, pushing his bicycle, trudging through a scurry of tiny dogs along the lonnings which run out of the town and into the country, is to see a "walking miracle": as a young man he was told he would never, it was impossible that he could, walk again. What he has done since then will give a fit man pause. His action as he walks is all his own: somewhere between a swagger and a totter, he goes along at a fair old pace with his stick seeming to thrust his upper body forward and just *make* his legs take the next step. When he talks, too, it is a combination of opposites: though he received only elementary education, the tone is cultivated – and yet the local twang is there and sharp interjections come in caustic Cumbrian: only to be contradicted once again by a drawl which is partly like the mid-war upper classes whom he served in the Thirties – and partly feminine, mother-ish, you might say. Almost an actor's voice – a touch of the Music Hall.

He lives with his wife and their dogs – there are no children – in a tall old town house on Market Hill – where once the town fairs were held: now a car-park. From the window we could see over the gas works to "the lonnings" – his favourite walk. Sandy-haired, quick with his gestures, gradually relaxing and enjoying his own stories, he told of his life, which began in the last year of the First World War. For those who like headlines, Dickie, among other things, worked as a valet in two of the Richest Homes in England in the rich and aristocratic Thirties: he was a Scout Master, a goat- and bee-keeper, a champion griffon-breeder, in the Air Ministry stores for twenty years, a Catholic convert, and a man who refused to be an invalid. It will be hard to believe some of what follows – but I am sure it is true.

His father worked in the tan-yard and died when Dickie was three, "leaving my mother with six of us. She would be thirty-four then. She went out and worked. Doing housework for various people, took in washing. She had to work to bring us up."

"I never wanted for anything. A penny went a long way then. We never had any house rent to pay, because the property belonged to my grandfather. She hadn't any rent or rates to pay. I don't think she ever paid any, until later when my grandfather died. I think she started to pay then.

Wigton then was a different place entirely to what it is now. We lived down there at East End [two hundred and fifty yards away] and it was like a fair to come up to the town. You know, you were a little village of your own. There were lots of streets that I'd never been in in Wigton until I was quite well in my teens. It was really a day to come up to the street to Market Day on a Tuesday when the market was all along the street and so forth. You got a little penny sugar pig. It was marvellous.

We played rounders and denny and the chasey with the big stick. Games like that. And you see every season had the different thing. We had hoops and tops, sometimes played with the tops and whips and it was who could have the smartest top with crayon drawings on a piece of silver paper and things like that. And we never – we used to have, as well, my grandfather was a great one in the Salvation Army and we used to have Salvation Army meetings in me grandmother's for all the kids down there. And I used to be captain and we would take it in turns and have prayer meetings and all these sort of things, open air meetings. You see my grandmother just used to sit and read and we used to do all these things. It was really marvellous like. We never had much money but you never seemed as if you wanted money then.

I went to St. Mary's, Church of England. I was the first server there, and I taught in the Sunday School and I sang in the choir from, I was a boy – of seven. Father Wilson came to Wigton and I served for him. That was the first time ever I served. And E. T. Doig came after that and I served for him and then Malden came and I finished. I left the Church of England and I turned a Roman Catholic. I read the *Apologia* of John Henry Newman and, well, I read – I was always High Church of course and I came to a precipice and I thought, well, if I have to save my soul I must do like John Henry Newman. I don't know whether you've ever read his *Apologia*. He said, If I have to save my soul, I must lay on the Anglican death bed and die for ever to the church of my birth and be born again to the true church of Christ. And I've never regretted it. Of course I've made very few friends there. All my friends belong to the Church of England. Like Charlie Nurse, all these people; I've still kept friendly with them. They never rejected me because they were all very High Church. You see, I used to be a server at St. Aidan's as well in Carlisle. No, they never rejected me. Although I went to Rome I never lost the love for St. Mary's. If they have any collections or anything I always give generously to them. I think it's a personal thing really, but I couldn't be bigoted against anyone and against anyone's beliefs, whatever they are.

The Salvation Army was great fun – my grandfather went there – they were great fun because we had tambourines. My grandfather bought us tambourines and of course you never saw people coming about. There wasn't cars and all these sort of things. I remember the first buses coming down there and they were cobbled roads and we used to watch the old men breaking stones up by the tip there, you know, the gipsies coming along there. And of course that's where you learned all this Romany talk. Mort [girl], Cower [thing], Miximangen. Real Romany type, the gipsies. They used to park along the wall beside the tip. Very generous. And I learned there how to do the first hedgehog which I've done many times afterwards with the Scouts. They showed us how to cook a hedgehog. Have you ever seen them done in clay? These hedgehogs, they did them in clay, and they put them in fires, all these little fires and iron things, with the pans hanging over. They used to bury them over in the clay and then, when they took them off, all the quills came off and they're really delicious to eat. And these people just used to make pegs and all this sort of thing.

I never had any fear of them. They lived rough. The father and mother would live in the caravan and the children would sleep underneath – on some old sacks and so forth. They were very nice people and I don't think there was ever anything pinched or anything like that. I've got very good recollections of them. Sitting round – we used to sing and they used to tell us stories and so forth, round the little fire and then, of course, we were brought up very strict and as soon as my mother shouted we had to go. There was no saying, I'm waiting a minute, like they do now. You had to go there and then.

They were very swarthy-skinned and I wouldn't say, one of the big attractions was these McKenzies that used to be down there making baskets. You know about those, do you? Those McKenzies they had a big basket trade. They got to be quite wealthy really and they were in the Salvation Army with my grandfather. It was quite a big thing then, the Salvation Army in Wigton, and my, as a matter of fact, my father – they couldn't write, they were illiterate, all the lot of them – and my father used to do all the correspondence for them and my father had just been writing a letter for them when he come down home. And he dropped down dead on his way back home. The McKenzies were gipsies. He went back to the Romany style and lived down on Oulton Moss. He ended his days down there in a place that he built himself. He was a brilliant man with basket-work. And I've been with him many times and we used to go for these willows and gather the willows. Away in the country. Anywhere where it's rather marshy. Down by Oulton Moss and those places. Along by Miss Storey's there, Miss Wilson now, and that was the main place. They sold the baskets for potato gathering – you know, the farmers. They went all over the country. There were loads of them went to the station. There were four sons and him, continually working at them.

And of course there was cock-fighting and they used to keep the game-cocks. My grandfather always kept the cocks and we used to go with him to the various walks that he had with these cocks, a cock and probably two hens. Springs Wood and then away over onto Many Banks and away round there. We done this walk once a week, taking the corn round and he had another place. The cock and hens live there. That's their place and they breed there, then you get the chickens from there, they set themselves. You never gathered any eggs. Well, they're very wild and you see even if they didn't know you, they could give you a terrific leg. They've big spurs and if the spurs weren't cut off, they could go right into your leg and you could have a terrible leg. I remember once one got me down. A big black cock. I was very lucky to escape. They're a huge bird, about six to eight pounds. Course that's the big one, then there's the younger ones. There's different types. There's the stag. They tell these by their tail sickles. Did you know how you told the age of a cockerel, by the sickles in its tail? And that was part of our line. Grandfather used to sell these cocks all over the country. A lot went to Ireland.

And we always had whippets. I've always been brought up with dogs.

And there were lots of horses in the town – there was Scott's down there that had the hearses. They had the funeral hearses and they used to turn out with the top hats and the cabs. I think they had ten cabs. They looked very nice all coming out, each cab with a horse and the hearse with two. And they used to come up the town here, all in their black regalia and the horses all done up with big tassels on their heads. It was really a busy little place the East End. I think myself it was different from any other part of the town because of the little community that lived there, the Scotts and the Lowthers and the Gates. My grandfather had quite a few houses down there which belonged to him which have been demolished now.

It was very unrushed. Well I'll tell you for instance what they used to do. My grandmother, she used to have a big kale pot, and she used to have it on the fire and all the kids in the East End, when she was making broth, they all took a bowl and they all had broth there and she used to feed half of them, taking these big bowls of broth and big dumplings in. You see we never had cakes or anything like that. We just lived on poultry. My grandfather used to buy a ham once a fortnight up at Strong's, they used to have a little place opposite the market there, and they used to have the hams. And if they were sort of tainted, I don't know whether you've had tainted ham or not, it's – I like it, of course I've been brought up with it, and he used to buy a ham about threepence a pound, a good one about a tanner. He used to get one once a fortnight and that's how they lived. Used to get cow heels and tripe. We didn't know what cake was really.

I went to St. Cuthbert's, the Catholic school – because it was the nearest. Well, there was more Protestants went there than what there was Catholics. And you see you could go at three. I went when

I was three. Because my mother was out working and we went there at a very early age. The nuns would take you in. I suppose that's why I went there. Everybody round about went to the Catholic School. And of course this was all heavily populated all round here, Tenters and Market Hill, and all these children went there, and the Stampery children.

My mother was Church of England and she didn't care what other people thought. We were marched to the church at eight o'clock for Communion like soldiers and we hadn't to miss, and then to the Sunday School in the afternoon – back to Mattins at half past ten, changed again, then back to Sunday School at two o'clock and then in the choir at night and then straight home.

I think myself that there was more discipline. Mind, I like the young people of today but I think there was definitely more discipline then. And I know my mother's word was the law. If she said you were in at nine o'clock, you were in at nine o'clock. Even my sister until she was twenty-three. But you see, what was there to do in Wigton? You see, if you went anywhere in the evening well, there was nothing to do in the church – there wasn't any services through the week, just the choir practice on a Wednesday night.

We all went into one another's house and if there was anybody died or anything like that, everybody was there and they helped one another. Now, for instance, my mother she was on tap for to lay people out that died. Now my mother would come back into the house and she wouldn't go to bed. She would make a great big baking for them. You would know my mother, did you? She would bake them a great big baking, cakes and so forth and take them it. You see, this was the reckoned thing that was done then. And then when the people were buried, they had tremendous tea parties afterwards and everyone was invited to them. The kids sat second after the grown-ups had their meal. And they used to have these tremendous meals. A death was a tremendous party afterwards.

Drink was very cheap. I never saw drink in my house. My mother loathed drink. My grandfather, before he was converted to the Salvation Army, was a great boozer. That's how he went through all his money. As a matter of fact, do you know Fair View, well, that's where he was brought up at, and he went to get that house – it was going to be signed over to him as they done in those days, and he went drunk and he got it knocked off him. I think it was left to old Miss Patrickson, her mother, she was brought up; she was my grandfather's cousin, old Miss Patrickson, and she got a tremendous lot of the money. But my grandfather had quite a lot of land and so forth and property. But it was lost through booze, that, and then he got converted to the Salvation Army and he was in for I should think twenty years.

There was poverty but I could never ever remember my mother – and she must have had some very hard times – at thirty-four left with six – I could never ever remember her saying she was badly off or hard up. It was just a small house. I had two brothers stayed with me grandmother. There was only two bedrooms and a sitting-room, a small living-room and a kitchen, and a back kitchen. You see, all the boys would sleep in one room, and my sisters slept with my mother in the other room. And, well, there was three boys in one room. And then you see, with us being the youngest, as they got up they went to farm service, my brothers. There was nothing else to do.

The poor people went to the Salvation Mission in Station Road, and the Primitive Methodists or the Salvation Army. The Church of England didn't go out of its way to encourage them either. The first Sunday that I went to Communion when Wilson came to Wigton, do you know how many there were – three. This is at eight o'clock Communion. Of course he changed all this, you see. And this is when it sort of got – it would have been a real one if he had stayed. This is much later, 1936. He filled the church. That church was packed. They even sat on the window-sills and on to the steps in the gallery. He went into the pubs and hooked them out and got them into the church. There were people went into the church in clogs, old Kettler (an old boyo: bachelor: forever on the dole) and all that lot. He got them in. He married people that were living in sin, he walked round Wigton streets – he was always dressed with a little beret on, and a monkey on his shoulder – he was a wonderful man. Very High of course. You see I knew all that, the High Church. And I was his first server that he had. He saw me going to Communion regularly and he asked me to go and he give me the instructions on what to do and so forth.

Well, when I left school there was no opening in Wigton. I went to the butchers at first – Fox's. I was there for a year. I didn't like it, and I met a person who was a waiter in the Kildare Hotel and I got on with him – he'd be about my age, sixteen or seventeen, and he had gone to a school in Norfolk. And I went, that's when I left Wigton. I wrote and got into this place. To learn valeting. You didn't get any money and it was a place called the Priory, near Diss, Norfolk. And I went there and I was there for nine months. Learnt everything, to be a gentleman's gentleman. I was taught everything about clothes. Keeping clothes, brushing them, laying them out, what you would wear for different occasions, how to do a top hat with a little iron, and how to leather shoes and wax them. All that.

First I went to Ignett's, the tobacco magnate. I went to valet a Captain Ignett, but he never turned up. I was there for six months. All I did was to walk the Pomeranian. Mrs. Mary Ignett. She had six Poms and two big dogs and I used to go hacking with them. She had thirteen hunters. She proved a great friend to me.

Well, it was through those dogs that I got on with the next man. The big Airedales. I used to take them out for a walk in the afternoon. I used to go hacking in the morning with the grooms. And then we used to go off, and I met this man. Through taking these dogs – I used to meet this man every day, and I didn't know who he was. I knew he was some landed gent round about and so we used to go for a walk every afternoon; hail, rain or snow. And he had about fifteen dogs – poodles and all sorts, and so I said to him, there's one thing I would like to do before I leave here. I was leaving, you see, at the end of the six months – I was just engaged for six months, fifteen shillings a week. And I said, Before I leave here I would like to go to Cotters Brook Hall to see the   they had a tremendous lot of wild life there, pheasants and duck and all this sort of thing. They had little miniature lakes. Well, he said, if you meet me tomorrow at the gate to the hall I will take you round. So I never enquired, even then, who he was. I hadn't the foggiest idea who this man was. A charming man. He took to me – afterwards he told me – because I had red hair. He was married with one daughter; he was a widower. His daughter got married and went to South Africa. But, anyway, he met me there and he took me all round.

It was out of this world. The staircase – it was out of this world. This candelabra. It was fantastic.

He was Captain Bingham Brassey, the big racehorse man. He had a big place in Ireland. He wanted me to go to Ireland. He wanted me to go there and I wouldn't go. It seemed a long way to me then. And that's when I went to the Linlithgows.

In this time I'd met, at the Ignett's, a footman there who constantly kept correspondence with me and he went to be the under-butler at the Marquis of Linlithgow's. And he kept writing to me and he asked me if I would like to go to be the valet to the two boys: twins. So I said, yes I would, and so I wrote and I got an interview. But when I got there, there were fifteen there for interviews. All young fellows. So when I was coming out of the room, she said, We'll let you know in due course. I said, That's no use to me at all. I said, I must know now whether you've engaged me. I must know now whether I have got the job or not. So she said, Well, just wait for a few minutes. And she said, Yes, you are the person we want. I said, Thank you very much. And this under-butler took me out to lunch and I went there. I think about a fortnight afterwards.

The Linlithgows, well, they entertained royalty. I waited on old Queen Mary. This Queen Mother's mother and father. I used to do the wine to get into this thing. They used to have twenty and thirty for lunch. And there was thirty-five servants at Chester Square – 29 Chester Square. It wasn't a very big house. And I valeted the twin boys. They were eighteen. About my age. They would be going out for nights out with boys. They were full of devilment. I never once had a wrong word with them. We used to have some great times. Then the father went to India as the Viceroy.

They had fantastic wardrobes. They would have morning clothes, perhaps three suits at that, and then they would have the morning coat and they would have the ordinary coat and then they would have various lounge suits for the afternoon. It was a very busy life, because they had a clean shirt on every time. Perhaps six shirts each a day. It was nothing to change six times. You took them a cup of tea in the morning at eight o'clock. Huge bedrooms, they had, and dressing-rooms. These two boys slept in the same room, they had twin beds. And they shared the same dressing-room. Now in the dressing-room – have you ever been in one of these big gentry's dressing-rooms, big deep dressing-rooms with all the suits in? – and then you would say to them, What would you be wearing today? What's your programme for today? and they would tell you.

Well, where they would be going – perhaps an afternoon party. They would be going to lunch somewhere or they would perhaps be riding in the morning. They used to ride in Rotten Row and you had the riding-clothes to get out. You see, they would come down in the morning for their breakfast and of course they never came down in a dressing-gown or anything of that. First of all you would draw the bath for them. I think there were about six bathrooms there. Then you would draw two different baths. And then they would change – they would never come down in their riding-clothes to breakfast. They would have an ordinary morning coat on – morning clothes. They never sort of wore casual clothes like people do now. They were always dressed all the time. They would come down in the morning, they wouldn't have the tails on, they would have the ordinary morn-ing coat on and then, if they were just being in the town, they would have the morning clothes that they would go out with. And then they would go off riding. Then they would come back and change for lunch. And – perhaps they were going out to a luncheon party. You see, during the Court Season, there's all these débutantes, afternoon parties and tea parties and all this sort of thing. And they were just continually changing all the time. I had to do no washing. Prepare them for the laundry and press. He had a big pressing room. And to do the shoes for them. And the socks. Even the socks were turned outside in. Laid out on top of the shoes. They just had to put them on. Then of course the big dos in the evening – for dinner. And if it was just an ordinary dinner or it was a dinner dance, they wore the white waistcoat. You had to know all these various things. There was quite a lot to know about it. It was very hard work for very little money. I think I had about twenty-five shillings a week, and of course it was a lot of money then.

Well, they wouldn't do it today. You see then it was nothing for Lady Mary Hope, she was the lady-in-waiting to the Duchess of Kent, she used to change several times. Her lady's maids used to go with her. And there was always two detectives used to come. It was a life that buzzed with social events there. You got a lot of tickets given to you with the lady's maids to go. You see, you never mixed with the ordinary servants. You lived in the housekeeper's room. I didn't go with the housemaids and all these. There was the lady's maids. The butler, and under-butler and the valets and the housekeeper and the head cook, they fed by themselves. I think there were thirty-five servants there. I liked the London social scene. It was a way of life much removed from Wigton, of course, as you could well imagine. I loved it. I loved the people but I used to think a tremendous lot about the waste.

It was very difficult coming back. Although my mother was a marvellous cook, to come back to live here – compared with how you lived there – because the amount of food that you had there, really it was absolutely fantastic. You lived in the lap of luxury, from when you got up in the morning till you went to bed at night. You could have a drink whenever you wanted one. If you fancied a drink, there was one thing that she always said, the Marchioness, If you fancy a drink, have one.

Then I came back to go to Naworth Castle, to the Earl of Carlisle's place, and that was the most fabulous place that I was. That was *the* luxury. This is 1938. We had some marvellous banquets there. Terrific banquets. And he paid me until 1943. I went to the Air Ministry in 1940 of course and he paid me. You see, they had all the top people of the day, great entertainer the Countess of Carlisle, and we used to get Lord Swinton, Lady Claude Hamilton, one of the great beauties of the day. I don't think it was all above board a lot of it of course. Well I think they lived sort of what we would call permissive now, I think. Various gentry going there and mixing in with other wives and so forth. Oh, it's a huge place. The banqueting hall would be nearly as big as the Market Hall. Seat about a hundred and fifty. The most they ever had was seventy-five. I once had a most peculiar incident there. Sir Miles Lamson was there with his six daughters. They were great beauties, these girls. So the butler said to me, Would you come and give us a hand in the dining-room tonight? So I said, Yes. So they had the soup; it was taken round on a big silver tray, in these little bowls that you empty out, and then you put your bowl back. So the fashion of the day was these big bare backs. So I was going along with this tray, all of a sudden there was one of these dachshunds made a dart out between my legs and I fell over and the soup went right down this woman's back. The screams. She was scalded right down her back. Well, it wasn't my fault. And Lord Carlisle – he wouldn't blame me. Whatever I done was right. He was very kind to me. Of course he blamed them. They shouldn't have dogs in the place. And whether somebody had stood on its tail or something and it darted right in front of me, but I never saw such a pandemonium in my life. She had a terrible back. It was one mass of blisters, right down her back.

Every night of the week, this entertainment. Except one night and there was a servants' ball and they all came. And they waited on you.

The servants' breakfast – it would comprise, every morning there was always a big ham and eggs. You could have as many eggs as you wanted. Haddock – and of course there were various cereals and porridge and all this. Toast and marmalade. Coffee.

The war came on and so Lord Carlisle was called up to the Army and I came back to Wigton and I stayed at Wigton for a year. And then I was sent for by Lord Carlisle's men to see what work I was doing. I told them I was employed by them and they seemed to know all about I wasn't employed by them, but I was still getting the money, you see. So the Labour Exchange sent me down to the Air Ministry, the Ministry of Defence. And I was there ever after. Twenty years there. Well I was in charge of the log book section for seven years – aircraft log books. I went there into the office. I was there for a few months and then I was put in charge of ten people there on the clerical side. It was very poor money on the clerical side so I went over on the stores side after that, and a great mistake, of course, but nevertheless. I lost a lot of money by it, in later life. And then I went into the stores and I worked there.

I liked the people. I loved going. I looked forward every morning to going there. It was absolutely marvellous. The officers and everyone; everyone was one big happy family. The day was too short there. That's a queer thing to say about work, isn't it? I never longed for night there. Night came all too soon.

I got to know quite a lot of R.A.F. people there, and they were awfully nice. Everyone was the same. There was no class distinction whatsoever, until later on, till after the War, that's when the class distinction part came in. Well, it came in by – you had to use the back door if you weren't in a certain grade. You couldn't use the front door and all this. And they changed the canteen. They had different set-ups for different grades. You could have your best friend and when it came to lunchtime you couldn't have lunch with him because he was a grade higher than you or a grade lower. But even so it was still nice. I liked it.

In the war Wigton was a very gay place. They came to Wigton in their thousands to the King's Arms – they called it the Cock Loft – that was its name. And there were tables put down the centre there. And there was a band and people sang and so forth. I've seen them. It was like a football match getting out when that place got out and the pubs in Wigton got out. They came from far and near here. I didn't drink much. And coming down the streets here, in the War, on a night, of course, the pubs closed about ten o'clock . . . about quarter past ten, well, it was just like a football match getting out and coming up from the Black-a-Moor. I think that used to be the worst place. Do you want to hear what the Catholic priest said about Wigton when he came during the war? He said, I have travelled the world. Yes, I have penetrated deepest Africa but this is the wickedest little hole I've ever been in. I've met every type of sin it's possible to commit here. He was given a mission. Father Mayes they called him. He gave this mission here down at the church. He was a marvellous man really, about six foot six inches. He had travelled the world, even penetrated deepest Africa and this was the wickedest little hole he had ever been in!

I didn't go out much at all drinking because I had the Scouts and I always thought it was a bad example to show to the Scouts by going out drinking. I think I denied myself a tremendous lot. Too much really – for them. Because I lived it for seven days a week. It was very peculiar how I got interested in the Scouts. Of course I was in when I was a boy here, through the choir, when Joe Holmes was here. And I met a man down at Kirkbride called Dougal Paulin. He was a director from Newcastle, a big steel firm in Newcastle. He was a director, this man. And he happened to be the camp warden as well, in his spare time, at Newcastle, Gosforth Park. It was peculiar how I met him. It was through the black market. He used to have sweets and you see, at Newcastle, he had this allocation of sweets there for Gosforth Park which they kept on during the war. And he had all these sweets and that's how I got to know him. He used to sell them to the men there. He always had his car full of sweets, chocolates and so forth, which you couldn't get. Well, you could get them but just with coupons. And that's how I met him. And he got talking about Scouts. And I said, Oh, I used to be in the Scouts when I was a boy. I said, I'm thinking about starting a troop up in Wigton. Have you any notion of coming along and giving me a hand? And he invited me along to the first night that he started at the Parish Rooms and I was with him all the time he was here. Of course then I went to take the Wood Badge.

The Wood Badge shows that you've attained a certain standard of proficiency and allows you to pass the boys in all the various badges. You see, you got through every test right up to first-class scout. And you either pass or you fail. There's a tremendous percentage of failing. There was only twenty-three passed. I think there was ninety-six on the course that I was on. And there was twenty-three passed. And I did everything. Went on the journey and the lot, and baked. But you see, instead of going with two, I think there was five. You were in a patrol, you see. It took a fortnight. I came back to Wigton as the assistant Scout Master. I was the assistant Scout Master when I went there. Well, after three months you do the written first; it takes about two years to get it. And then you had the written to do, and then you do the practical. And it depends on the Commissioner whether he grants it to you or not. I got it. Mr. Dougal Paulin had it as well of course: he had four little notches. There was six patrols when I started. Thirty-seven boys. Because we had a troop leader.

It was called 1st Wigton. Every weekend we went to a place – our first camp was Thackwood Nook, which we took, all the badges for the camp and pioneer, and I went to Gosforth Park to pass all these badges myself and to become an instructor on passing all these badges for the Bushman's Thong. Thirty-six I had. I passed thirty-six in the Wigton Troop. But that was my continual life. I never went out for a drink during this time. This man, this Paulin, he could put enthusiasm into you, and these kids were so keen. They were absolutely great. You felt you were doing something for Wigton, really. I just lived for that.

All our work was outdoors. We were very little – we had the Nelson School gym of course but we weren't affiliated to the Nelson School: we were 1st Wigton. Everybody. And there were some very very outstanding boys. Boys that have done quite well. We won that shield down there, the Carlisle Scout Shield for six years on the running, for scouting and first aid as well. You see, I took the Medallion and six boys in the Medallion, and the first-class teaching certificate in the Order of St John. Well, you see, I didn't want them to have anything that I hadn't. You see, you can't teach children things if you haven't got a good knowledge yourself. And then I was appointed for this Duke of Edinburgh Award scheme for the bronze, silver and gold medal. For the First Aid. But the scouting days were really wonderful. The monkey bridges that we built! I had some great boys, very loyal, and during my time that I had them, I had thirty-six King's Scouts. I paraded in front of Rowallan at Keswick Jamboree twenty King's Scouts in the troop at once. There was nothing in the county that came up to it. But I don't think there was anyone else that gave their time to it. Because I just lived, breathed and slept it.

I was Scoutmaster from 1944 until 1950 and I gave it up then. Well, I had an appendicitis and George Gate took it over.

My friends are, like books, few and well chosen. I don't think I've got one person in *Wigton* that I would confide in. That I would call a real friend. I'm very friendly with – but I have to be very wary what I say to him.

I was twenty, 1938, when my illness started. Well I came downstairs this morning and I stood on the mat. It was like an electric shock went through me. And so I laid down on the settee and then my mother said I had better go back to bed. So I went back to bed and a few minutes after I wanted to get up, I felt as if I wanted to pass water. I tried to get up and I couldn't move. I was totally paralysed. I started shivering. My whole body shook going with cold and my teeth chattering. She put hot-water bottles on me in the groin here and down here. And I had no feeling whatsoever, which she didn't know, and I had a very limited knowledge of first aid and it burned me. I just had one mass of blisters from my stomach right down to my ankles. Then I couldn't pass water. This happened on a Friday. The doctor came on the Saturday. No, he didn't come until the following Tuesday. She had been several times for him to come and he never came. Dr. Dolan. And all this time I was drinking water, you see, I was feverish. And he came and he saw I was in a terrible state and he took a full chamber full of water from me – he catheterised me. I didn't know what such a word meant, but I was to know more about that in future months. And I laid there and he came each day to catheterise me until the following Friday, which would be 31st January, and he whipped me into the Infirmary.

And I was there, and my mother sat with me, for seven weeks. And I had got congestion of the lungs and I had to be tapped. And of course I was completely paralysed. From the waist downwards. Completely – bowels, bladder and everything. Then thirteen weeks after that, this abscess burst and it perforated the bladder. The complete bladder collapsed and I passed bottles and bottles of puss and I had to have a bladder wash three times a day. And then, when they got this cleared, I had to go to have this silver nitrate dropped into the bladder. There was no anaesthetic whatsoever. This is entirely different to what it is going to have a bladder inspection now. And they pass a silver catheter into you and put this silver nitrate into you. It's frightfully painful and you've got a small whisky and hot water afterwards and no one was allowed to see you for an hour. No anaesthetic.

The pain was terrific. But I was never known to shout. And I was dressed night and day. This hole in my back was dressed night and day every two hours. And of course I was all red raw from the groin right down to my ankles. And then after this burst, there was one day it was a terrific thrill. The physotherapist came and with the electricity they couldn't get the slightest movement but I had a slight movement in my right toe and I thought it was great. It was a wonderful thrill. And one night when I was laying there, totally paralysed, and the screens around me, and a face appeared round this screen. It was a man with an open razor and he said, I've come to cut your bloody throat. Well, I was totally paralysed and I couldn't move. I couldn't do anything at all and I screamed and the nurse came and they overpowered this man and got a straitjacket onto him and took him away. And then all went well. That shook me more than anything all the time I was in there, because everyone was so great. The man was a manager from the Turf Hotel at Carlisle. He was completely berserk. He went to the Garlands Asylum after that. And life went on. Of course, you hadn't any of your own food. The food was horrible that you got. Mostly cod, boiled in water and swimming in water, vile.

I was fully insured, I'd never been out of work. That was why I went into service because there was all the people loafing about in Wigton and you couldn't get a job here then. That was the reason that I went away originally.

Well, they came around. As the doctors come around, I'd made my mind up. I was definitely going to ask him. I said, I want to ask you something. I said, Do you think that I'll ever walk again? He said, No. He didn't make any hesitation. Because I'm a person that likes to be told right out. No, he said, you'll never walk again. And I said to him in return, But I will walk again. I'll not only walk but I'll ride a bicycle. He said, It's marvellous to have thoughts like that but I can't see that you ever will. But I said, I'm determined that I will. Once I get off this bed, and I will get off, and at that particular time I just could twitch my toe ... but I never gave up hope. I'd terrific faith that I'd get better.

This Miss Bachelor, a great friend of mine, a physiotherapist, and there was a terrific interest in the Infirmary in me. She was determined she could get me out of this bed, in spite of what they said. She went against them and she said, I'm going to have you out of that bed. So she got me one of these chairs that you can push round and then of course they never kept me in. I used to go all round the place, talking to people in different wards and so forth because nine months is a long time to be in a hospital. And then they decided they would get me to walk and I was sure I could walk, and I couldn't walk. It was terrible, like a baby. I'd no strength whatsoever. But I was determined I would walk and they used to practise me for a minute the first day and then two minutes. And then they got these calipers after that, and I had them for about a fortnight before I came out. And I came out with the calipers on and I had them for about – well, I come out in plaster of Paris. I had to lie in plaster of Paris at night, like a cast from the stomach down, and I had to bandage myself in this cast, and me mother used to do me feet, so that you couldn't move. You were sort of in a straitjacket. And gradually I left that off. I thought to myself it wasn't necessary. And as my mother went out I learnt myself to walk. I was determined I was going to walk without these calipers. I used to get a chair and pull myself up and try to stand and then push the chair forward, lift the mat up and go forward like that. And then I had this money coming to me and I bought myself a bicycle.

I got this bicycle, and I always remember I got this cycle and I wheeled it down here to along the lonnings there and I got on the grass and I took these calipers off. I said I'll ride that bike if it's the last thing I do. I'd a caliper on each end, and I fell off and my knees were bleeding, but I was determined I would ride it. At the finish I got on. It was great. I had to fall off. I got all the way down to East End with the thing and I fell off and my mother was horrified, but I was determined and I practised every day with that cycle.

I didn't care what anyone said. The skin was off my hands and off my knees but I was determined I would ride it. And eventually I had to go to the Infirmary. I was attending there by the way three times a week, but I used to put the calipers on to go. So I got so good on my legs that I got without this caliper. So I thought to myself – this big man was coming from Edinburgh to see me, I thought I'll go without that caliper. I got down to one caliper, you see. So anyway, I thought to myself, I'll go this day without the calipers on.

The bus used to stop at Ashley Street then in Carlisle, it stopped there and as I stepped off, I stepped on some leaves and I went right under the bus. And they had to pull me out from under the bus. But anyway I got up and I got myself down to the Infirmary. This man was there and he said, How are you? I said, I'm great. Let me have a look at you. Where's the calipers? I said, I don't wear them now. He said, What? How do you walk? I said, I don't know but I do walk and get about. He said, Walk along there. He said, I'm staggered. I couldn't tell you how you walk but you do walk. So he said, It's nothing short of a miracle that this has happened to you. He said, I can't believe now that you can walk, because I can't see how you can walk. I've never seen anybody that's had this, what you've had and can walk. You're the only person I've ever met. I was to learn about this more so when I met this professor from Newcastle. He told me exactly the same.

So afterwards, you see, I wasn't getting any money. My mother had to pay. It was eighteen pence down to Carlisle on the bus and my mother and my aunt, they were very good to me. I never could say that I wanted. But eighteen pence was a lot of money then. And I had to go three times a week down there. And of course my mother was always against charity, that you shouldn't accept anything. I suppose I could have gone and got it from the parish. I never went to anything like that. And eventually it was coming up to about six months afterwards, and I was feeling I was getting on fairly well, and I could get about. Well anyways I went back to Naworth Castle, back to work, and I found it very difficult; the stairs there, the winding staircases, but nevertheless I managed. I was determined I would manage.

I went back to valet Lord Carlisle. So then the war came, 1939, and after I'd done all his clothes up, he went into the Army and I came back home, and I was home for a year and he paid me my money all the time. And then they sent for me to the Labour Exchange and they said, What are you doing? And I'll never forget this. There was a great big fat woman sitting there. She said, Now then. You've taken a lot of tracing. Where have you been? I said, I'm afraid I've been nowhere at all. She says, But you're not working. I said, I am. I'm Lord Carlisle's valet. She said, You're nothing of the kind. You're at home. Naworth Castle's been closed down now for nine months. I said, Yes, but I've still got my retaining fee. She said, You're not working. Don't you know there's a war on? I said, Very much so. She said, Well you're getting a job. You're going to Kirkbride – she wanted me to go away to a training centre. You must go to a training centre and learn some trade. I said, Definitely not. I've no intention of going to any training centre. She said, Don't you know there's a war on? You're not doing any war effort. I said, Yes. I know quite well there's a war on but nevertheless, I said, I'm at home and my brothers are in the Army. I'm at home with my mother and I intend to stay there. So she said, Will you go to Kirkbride? I said, Yes, I'll go to Kirkbride. Well I'll go and see if there's a job suitable for me at Kirkbride. So I went down there and I had the interview, that was on the Thursday, and on the Friday I started work there. And it was a very peculiar incident that happened to me there. On the first day that I went, I was sent into this office at a place called B site, it was away across the moss, and as I got in the middle of the moss, I had a cape on, and a gust of wind came and it lifted me like a balloon and dropped me right in a big pool of water. This was my initiation baptism to Kirkbride, and I was soaked to the skin. A big yellow cycling cape. Dropped in the middle of this water. Anyway, I went there and stayed, as I have said, for twenty years.

It was very difficult at this time doing all the Scout tests but I've never let anything conquer me. You see, I think that through the Scouts it learnt me to live, it learnt me tolerance. And I found then that the greatest thing in life was to live for other people, and by aiding others, and I felt that this was my mission in life, that to help these boys, and if I could only get the knowledge – so that's why I took the Wood Badge. There was a twenty-mile hike over barren country involved. Round about Huddersfield, and crossing rivers, etc., soaked, and then build a bivouac and dry your clothes at the other end. But you see I would never let anyone do anything – I had this goal in view, that if I wanted to do this I must do it myself, because I couldn't say to a boy in later years – I had in my mind that I would do this, I would send boys – that I hadn't done it myself. The authorities said, Listen here, we don't want you to do that – the twenty-mile hike. I said, Actually that's the reason I've come here; to do the lot. It's either all or nothing. I said, If I can't do this, I've no desire to pass the badge, because I want to do everything. I said

I would like to attempt it. I said, If I can't do it then it will be alright, but I want to attempt it, to say that I've tried it. It's no good giving in unless you've tried. So they said, Well, reluctantly we'll let you go but we're not really supposed to. We cater for people like you. I said, But I don't want to be any different to any of the others. And I went and I done it. And the biggest laugh I had on that thing was – most of these people were executives and so forth, priests, a tremendous lot of both Anglican and Roman priests there and of course the people who were exempt from the war. And they were no good at cooking at all. Well I'd always had a flair for cooking, and I baked a stone of flour on a slate, an ordinary slate with water out of a tin, and made these flapjacks over a big slate on the fire and stones at each side, a little tunnel fire, and we ate jam in them. To me they were perfectly horrible but I was hungry and you would eat anything. That stands out. We didn't have tents. We had to build a bivouac with a ground sheet. And I had this Father McKenzie, he was an O.S.B. from Ampleforth Abbey, him and I built a bivouac together and slept in this bivouac. He was a great friend of mine for years after. I don't know where he is now but he come to Workington after that and I used to often go to see him. And I seemed to mate in with him.

Well, about 1946 I had a stoppage in the bladder and I couldn't pass water. I went there and I was there for six weeks under observation. I sort of got it into my head that I had cancer. I was losing weight terrifically and they found, after all many and various bladder washes, etc., they found that I hadn't and I came out again. And I was alright after that for quite a long time until I had an appendicitis. Then I was in there for Easter. It's very peculiar. I had premonitions when all these different things were going to happen. I've always had forewarning of everything that's happened to me. I've never had anything happen in my life that I haven't had a premonition of. Until this final time when I went there. I went down – this is four years ago, and I was leaking terribly. Incontinent continually, and he said to me, I'm afraid that I must have you in. We've X-rayed you and we can't see anything but we must have you in, and I think I'll do an operation on you. When can you come in? Well, I said, I'm going to London to judge the Griffon Club Show and I'll come in after that. And then it was when I went in that they found I had the tumour in the bladder, but it was non-malignant. I've had twenty-eight operations: the twenty-ninth is coming up.

I was determined I would get to the top in dogs. That was one thing I was determined that I would do, get to the top in dogs.

And I looked round and I saw these griffons. I'd never heard of them before. Very tiny. They're like an old man really. Something about them superhuman. And I formed immediately a great attachment. I said, That's my dog. I shall have one of those. So I went to George Johnston, a friend who kept dogs, and I said, I've found the dog that I want but there's none for sale. And they were very difficult then to get in the 50s. 1950 it was.

George didn't like to show himself. I think he was a very reticent man. So anyway the woman that had bred this dog of his was at the show also with a basset hound of her own. I said to him, I think we must take this woman for a drink. I said, It's only etiquette to ask her for a drink. He said, Oh you go and ask her. So off we went to ask her for a drink. So she said, Yes, she would go. I always remember we got three brandys. I brought them in seven and six – then she brought them in, and then he brought them in. And I always remember what he said to me, come on, we'll have to go, this is too dear for me. Seven and six. We got to talking and she said. Do you keep dogs? I said, Well I have two Border terriers but I'm looking for a griffon. Well, I have a griffon, she says, I've got several, but I've got one in particular that I would like a good home for. I thought I was going to get it for nothing. I said, Oh really? She said, Yes, it's a lot of kennel jealousy and they don't like it. She's a black one and my others are all red. She said, Would you like it? I said, Yes, I would. I said, What's the price? I nearly fainted. Thirty-five guineas. I thought to myself, Where am I going to get thirty-five guineas? I said I'll have it.

I worked overtime like hell. I done without everything till I got the money for this dog. Anyway, there was several things come in the way; bad hard weather, and so forth. I was longing for this dog. Eventually the day arrived when the dog came to Wigton Station. I've never seen anything like it. The box was as big as this mantelpiece here. A huge box full of straw. In the corner was this little face looking out, these great big eyes looking out and all this straw around it. And I lifted it out. She was only seven pounds weight. In this terrific box – it was for an Irish wolfhound, this box. And I brought her home and I remember she sat on here. She just sat there and she was the most aristocratic dog that I ever had. And she – I had a terrific do with her. I got her mated and I nursed her and I took her along here for a walk and a huge Alsatian jumped out and picked her up by the back of the head and shook her like a rat. I was sure she was dead, tore all her neck, and she was only two days off having pups. I had the stick and I had to batter that Alsatian off with the

107

stick. And I brought her home.

I thought she was dead. I sent for the vet. The bleb came, like when they're having pups and he said, She'll not be able to have any strain because she's nearly dead. He says, The only hope is I can save a pup for you. So he took it away and he had to do a Caesarian operation on it. And he brought it back. He said, I've brought one pup but I'm afraid it's no good, it's dead. So my wife and I worked on this pup all night. And we got it breathing and going. Massaging it and putting it in front of the fire. We both had first aid knowledge. And giving it little drops of glucose and water. And from that I reared it and from that I built up my kennel. And the mother lived but I never bred anything more from her. I just got that one bitch. It was about two and a half ounces weight, this pup, in cotton wool and I hadn't an infra red lamp then. We got one later, but then she came round and she suckled the pup herself. And reared it. But I sat up with her for over a week. I was with her night and day. When I was at work – I didn't think anything about taking a fortnight off work if anything was wrong with the dog, without pay – because they're there not because they want to be there but because I want them there. That's what a lot of people forget. They have a dog. But my dogs are number one; there's nothing comes before them, not even the wife.

Well that one wasn't a show specimen. So I bred another one from her that was a very good bitch but still it wasn't what I had in my mind that I was going to take out and cane them all, because these people lived in a phase or in a standard of life that I would never never attain. These people who bred griffons. The people are very very wealthy people, and a tremendous sort of type of people as well. I've met a lot of types of people who are very poor but these people they were the real top notchers with money. They had money to burn. And I said if it's the last thing I do I'll beat you lot at your own game. So I got this one, I bred this one, but I thought to myself she's not quite what I want. But I got on with Miss Stewart, she lived at the Hermitage Pit in Fifeshire. So she invited me to go for a holiday up there, so I went up and I saw this dog. I said, That's the dog that I want to sire my pups that I'm going to win with. So I went, it was only a puppy, eight weeks old, and I had this puppy, and I said, One day I shall use that dog. He'll be a great dog that. So later on I mated this bitch and I bred my Annabelle and I knew that I had the tops. But money was pressing. I had this house and a big mortgage on it and I was getting behind and I'd been ill and you didn't get paid then. And I said – she was nine weeks old – I said I must sell her.

I knew it was the tops. I knew this is it, this is it that I've got but I must sell her because the money was so pressing; because I was getting behind with the money and through illness and so forth and being off work. And the Air Ministry never paid big wages. So I sold her for thirty-five guineas. This is fourteen years ago and I got the cheque and three days afterwards I got a telegram to say that I must take her back. The woman who bought her had another griffon that was going mad and it was going to kill her. So there was a pre-paid telegram and I wired back. Return her immediately – will meet at Carlisle. So I went to Carlisle and she come off that train in the early morning. I went and sat on the station all night. I caught the last bus from Wigton: ten-twenty. I hadn't a car or anything and I made up my mind there and then when I got her, I said, I'll never sell you. I returned the cheque and she sent me a fiver. So anyway, I said, whatever comes I'm not selling this dog. And so anyway I got through. I still had the rabbits – I had forty orange Rex. The most gorgeous rabbit you've ever seen. They weigh about twelve pounds. I had five champions. So there was a terrific – it just shows you how things come to you. I had all money that was wanting and I had a rabbit had seven young ones and I sold them all for seven pounds each, these young rabbits. I made a fortune in rabbits. So I cleared myself up and I still had this dog and I was determined I would keep it.

I bred goats as well. I had British Salmons. Down at the Tip, where they had the allotments. Where the pigeon men were. I never had a minute to do anything. I bred bees. So anyway I had this dog and I went up to George Johnston's and I said, I'm going to take her to Edinburgh. Are you going? He said, As a matter of fact I'm not. Oh well, I said, I'm going. So I went on the train with her. Went from here the night before and the first train was five o'clock in the morning – sat on the station all night. So I took her there. I've never had a dog in a championship show before. So I looked at the books and I had her weighed up. And they were all saying, Oh, what a marvellous griffon you've got there. Where did you get it from? I said, Oh I've bred it. So I went into the ring with her, and there was eighteen in – in the puppy class. She'd never had a collar on until the day before, never had a lead on, and I won first. Then I took her into the next class and I got first. Then I got the reserve challenge certificate. And I met this Marjorie Cousins then, she's the author of the griffon book, and she said to me, That's the greatest griffon I've ever seen. She said, You'll go places with that. So when I got home I looked in the dog paper and I seen she was judging the Olympia. So I went to London but I got a lift there with Fred Sills; Sills, the dog people up at Warnell Fell. I went with them and I think I gave them three pounds for the lift down. My word, I won the novice class and the graduate class. I only put in two classes. A pound a time – two pounds. So I won four pounds. So I thought to myself, I'd had a good day today. So anyway I was sitting there. I thought to myself I'll get nothing more. And the steward came along and he said, Would you come along. Miss Cousins wants you to challenge for the ticket. It's a Kennel Club Challenge Certificate. You have to have three of these to make a dog a champion under three different judges. To be a champion it must have three challenge certificates under three different judges. You see, with these dogs if you're not entered in the open class, a judge can depend themselves whether they draw you in or not. It depends on the judge. She can say, Would you come in? If you're not entered in the open class, you can be entitled – but it's the judge's discretion.

So she invited me in. She said, Put the little dog on the table. And she said, Do you know you've got the greatest griffon there I've ever seen. She says, She's the greatest black that's ever been in this country. She says, Take her down the room. So I took her down and she said, Without hesitation I'll give it to this dog here. So I thought to myself, That's great. She says, Don't go away. I want you to challenge for the best of breed. Well, these particular two dogs had never been beaten before. I never get in a quiver about anything. To meet anyone. If it was the Queen that was coming in there I wouldn't be any different than I am to you. This doesn't bother me at all. This is how you lose points showing dogs as well. You transmit from your own brain to the dog's brain. So I thought to myself, Oh I'll never beat this dog. Twelve championship certificates, never been beaten. But, no hesitation, best of breed. I got it. So I thought to myself, now then, I've done exceptionally well today. I'm going to spend this four pounds. That was all I'd won in money. And I'd spent three pounds coming down and two pounds entry. So I was a pound down. But I said, I'm going to flute this four pounds. I'm asking everyone that has griffons here today for a drink. So I invited the lot. I had to put a pound to it but anyway it was well worth it. And I went to five shows after that. That was six. I only done six with Annabelle, six championship shows and I got six challenge certificates and six best of breed. And then I was offered at Dumfries Championship Show a thousand pounds for her to go to America.

It said in the paper 'The dog with the £1000 ears'. 'A Man turns a £1000 offer down.' My God I could have done with it as well. It was a lot of money, a thousand pounds then. 'Richard scorns £1000 bid for Annabelle.' They cut their ears off in America you know. And I said it's complete cruelty and against the law in England. And so I wouldn't have it. It was in all the national papers. But it wasn't really because of the ears – because I'd made a solemn declaration that I would never sell her when she come back on that train. You see, if I made a promise to anyone I wouldn't break it under the pain of death. I think it's final and irrevocable if you break a promise and even to the dog – she was my shadow wherever I went, this dog. She even went to work with me every day. I had a special box made for her. She sat under the desk. She was great.

I never bred from her. I was too frightened to lose her. But I should have bred from her because she was a born thief of puppies. She used to steal the other dog's puppies and nurse them herself and then I bred her brother which was to bring me the great fame. He became the second Black Smoothed Champion in the world; at that particular time he was the only one in the world. And he won ten challenge certificates and three reserve challenge certificates at thirteen straight shows, including best of breed at Crufts, which was my goal that I said, One day that I will win Crufts. Then I said, One day I shall become a championship judge. And I did. I was asked to do the Griffon Club Show and there was nine judges put forward and a hundred voting papers went in. I got ninety-seven votes out of the hundred. I drew the greatest entry that's ever been known in the world. I have reached my goal and I don't care if I never do another.

I've always found that if I couldn't afford a thing I've done without it. I can always remember going to see *Dr. Faustus*, the tragedy of Faust, at Shakespeare's Memorial Theatre at Stratford. I've been there a few times and I've seen *Antony and Cleopatra* and *Faustus*. And the seven deadly sins – pride, covetousness, lust, anger, gluttony, envy, sloth, and the greatest of these was covetousness. Now I've never been covetous and I've formed my life now and when I weigh up form and I look back on it and I think that I could go to all these places and see people that lived a life that I would never never reach, and I've never, honestly say, ever been covetous of them, and I've seen people I've had in the Scouts that have got on and done well, risen high up in the world and boys that I've taken for tests and so forth, and I've never ever been covetous of them. Like I live my own life and I'm very happy in it. I think it's a great thing to be happy in your own life."

CHAPTER FIVE

Between Two Wars

In 1918 England was victorious and exhausted. Millions of men had been lost to the British Empire and billions of pounds; distortions at home and disruptions abroad had shaken the firm comforts of the Big House. In this period between two wars, England can now be seen as a country landlocked: between the Apocalypse and Armageddon, mortally wounded but not yet struck down and forced to rise again, stagnant.

It was as if the Great War between 1914-18 had blown into the sky all the country's prejudice, complacency and injustice: for a moment a newer, more decent, more modest and more tolerant England was revealed. But that would have to wait half a century for its face to be clearly seen: what happened in 1918 was that the topsoil fell back to earth, as silt.

That is the overwhelming impression that I get from the mass of interviews. It was people of my parents' generation, those who had spent the Twenties and Thirties in adolescence and young adulthood, who form the central mass of the material before me. I would estimate that I came in contact with and interviewed over a hundred and fifty people in that age range and after all was said and read, the feeling and fact which comes through is of exhaustion, silted lives, numbness. At the end of the period, as the Thirties move towards war, there is a shift; things improve; sewerage schemes, literally, are installed all over England. It is difficult to invent a better image of improvement for that period. As the Thirties go on, housing estates are built, wages begin to rise, food production improves, the labour movement advances, a new generation emerges willing and able to recolour the map of the world and find a more suitable palette for this country – and then another war drains the land. But even so the weight of evidence, oral evidence, relating to the time between two wars supports the notion that England was in some way paralysed and trapped.

113

The shock of course had been tremendous. Our invincible navy had been decimated; our trustworthy generals had discovered no better tactics than the crudest form of trial by strength – a mass sending-in of men which had been superseded as long ago as the time of Alexander and Caesar; our politicians had fumbled and then panicked – their rhetoric increasingly grandiose as the disgust with the war grew stronger: women worked in factories; tanks and aeroplanes brought intimations of greater achievements and greater disasters; above all, although it is painful to say it, despite the indisputable tenacity and courage of English soldiers, the fact is that we needed America to bring about the kill. That was even harder to swallow then.

No king likes to be dethroned. In 1917, Russia turned its back on the world and America put its mark on the world. Yet there, in 1918, was still the British Empire; there in London was still the Mother of Parliaments; there, being hastily rebuilt, was still a global navy; there, being quickly recruited, was still a civil service and colonial administration which cared for highways and byways on the five continents; Lawrence of Arabia was a world hero, Bertrand Russell was a great philosopher, H. G. Wells and George Bernard Shaw and D. H. Lawrence were writers of world fame and stature, Rutherford was working and so were scores of other great scientists and inventors. There was no lessening in the capacity of individuals. But America had taken over. It had not yet the trappings and would never much care for the trappings of empire, but the imperial mantle had been taken from Europe, west across the Atlantic.

Yet that was neither admitted nor acted on. England still had immense responsibilities, enormous territories, and a determination to hold on. Traditions, habit and natural greed saw to that. But why? And to what? And how?

These questions are the undertones of that unhappy peace between two wars. Their muted force does much to explain the masked and trapped appearance which comes from these interviews. Like a severe pain which cannot be diagnosed, such questions take away strength.

It was as if England brooded then. The 1914–18 War had changed its world but the shock was delayed. Characters of aristocratic birth and Arabian wealth still swanned around the world in luxury liners with offensively exclusive English accents, in Evelyn Waugh novels, in Noël Coward plays and in the social sets which still made news in the gossip columns of the national dailies. No chapter telling of life in England between the Wars would be complete without some reference to them and there will be such a reference here, a woman, a spinster, who played tennis and hunted and bred dogs through strike, slump and rehabilitation. There were, moreover, still those gentle and genteel middle and lower middle-class characters who so distinguish the pages of Mr. Kipps and Mr. Chips – they went on, ostensibly in the way they had gone on before the war, lives of leisure, eccentricity and inventive tranquillity while their energy was stoked in the unseen colonies. There were still blimpish colonels and endearing vicars, still society scandals and Court gossip, still many of the big houses; and still many of the big families.

And it is here, down among the mass of ordinary people, that the burden of this chapter rests. They speak for themselves of course but, though I've been representative in the selection, there is obviously a great amount of material which cannot be included in any viable way: on the basis of that excluded material, and from what will be said, are drawn these few observations.

The most startling thing of all is how little the daily facts of life changed until the mid-Thirties. Again and again when reading of childhood, of housing, of money, of food, of expectations between 1918 and 1936, one could be forgiven for mistaking the period: it could as well be 1900 to 1914 or even the 1880s and 1890s. These stories of poverty, these hard times, surely they are Victorian, at the very latest, Edwardian? No, on they went through the reign of George V. That cannot be stressed enough. Looking back I see how my life was easier in all material ways and fuller of opportunity than the life of my father: and so I think was his than the life of his father – and on or rather back to a grim unspeakable past out of which ordinary people have dragged themselves over a century and more. Not so. Or, rather, not so neatly so. In my own case, my father's early life was not very much better off than his father's, if at all: and the early years of my great-grandfather were rather better than those of his son. Such progress as there has been has come not steadily but in leaps and pauses.

Another striking fact to me was the introversion of England. It is as if the mass of people realised, way before their leaders, that something had to be done at home before anything else could be achieved. Far from being short-sighted or contemptibly insular, I see this as the proof of that capacity not only for survival but, much more importantly, for restoration and resurgence which has for centuries been the never-failing characteristic of the English nation. And it is here, in the even sullen withdrawal of ordinary people, that a new England was being worked out. That, of course, is post-hoc and, if one bore in mind, say, George Orwell's *Road to Wigan Pier*, which described the terrible condition of life in the engine-room of industrial England in the Thirties, then it could seem just so much romantic wishful thinking. Yet I would hold to the point. It was not their wish, it was not their total preoccupation; it was blindly done, but in some way, English people were saying, "Leave us alone to lick and bind up the wounds and mourn; we are suspicious, more than that, bitterly wary of passion for Empire and ideas of gentility which bury our sons in the mud of Flanders fields; we may have won a war but we have lost a faith, a style and a confidence: the future is with us, the ordinary people, because the leaders have led us into the cannon's mouth for the last time: leave us alone."

But there would be one more and final time.

This introversion is seen most clearly in what is left unsaid or said only politely. Between the two Wars came national and international incidents and events thick and fast: in the stronghold of their struggle to heave themselves and a new shape out of the gigantic rubble they inherited, those who came after 1918 found little time or energy to participate or even to include the events in the world which mattered to them – the world of work, family, home and being the person they wanted to be.

And so question after question about that harbinger of the Second World War – the Spanish Civil War – brought such a low response that it scarcely registers on the page. There was a Spaniard who kept one of the three fish and chip shops – called, with the inevitability of common truth, Manuel – and one or two people said they had asked him "which side he was on". This war brought intellectuals from all over the world, Hemingway, Malraux, Koestler, Orwell, and socialists from all over the Empire onto the battlefield from which they sent an endless battery of reports, memoirs, poems, articles, novels, warnings, declarations – and yet the people of Wigton were not alone in appearing deaf, I would bet all I had on that. People in Arkansas and in Normandy, in Padua and Toronto, they too, mostly, were bent on trying to sort out their immediate existence in the twentieth-century trough of the Thirties. The Spanish Civil War was a significant and important event in the lives of the people of Spain and in the lives of those who went to help the cause of liberty: but for most people in England the real contact with Spain was at the Spanish fish and chip shop. This, I would contend, is neither superficial nor second-rate but an honest view of life which, while not at all condemning those who went to Spain, nor disparaging for a moment the efforts of those who fought for liberties, sees the future in terms of the immediate present, and the hope of progress in the true appreciation of what can be done on the spot.

There was almost a revolution in England after the end of the First World War: but it went away: there was almost an economic civil war to the death in the mid-Twenties, but each side spared itself that final gesture; there was almost the nervous breakdown through frustration, injustice and the craving for a place in the world in the Thirties, of the industrial working-force: Keynes, world trade, Roosevelt, and self-preservation picked through that. It was a time of the Wall Street crash and depression, jazz and frightening unemployment (today there is, thankfully, serious anxiety when the number of unemployed passes one million: in 1932 it could well have been six or even seven million), lacks all round and, still, luxuries for the few: only at the end of what must have seemed a tunnel, towards the end of the Thirties, did matters begin to improve; the middle class spread to large private housing estates, the working class to council estates; roads were mended, there was a little more money, services improved, people were coming round, a new England was emerging, there was light at the end of the tunnel: but it turned out to be the torch of the Nazi officer.

The following extracts give some idea of life between two wars. I have left out many areas of life which are more fully gone into in chapters wholly devoted to the subject – farming, for example, and factory-work, education, religion and the changing character of the professions. This, then, is largely working-class domestic interiors with occasional contrasts brought in from other neighbouring worlds.

So, in 1918, they came back from the war. And Henry Fell, who had begun life as a telegraph boy and "carried messages all over the place in the war", headed straight back home.

"And do you believe, when we came back, do you know what we had to do? Go to the Workhouse and chop sticks. And we got about nine shillings after we came back. And they said they were making a country fit to live in. Saw sleepers and chop sticks, and they didn't give us any money, and here mind, Wigton, and they gave us nine shillings and we had to have a meal, marmalade, no cigarettes. But what we used to do, we used to say, Oh, have a meal off and give us a packet of Woodbines. Instead, because we couldn't get a smoke. Now wasn't that awful after fighting for them?"

Mrs. Fell joined in. "I went back to Mains Farm. I had to be there at half past five and it was sometimes half past six or seven when I got home." "And then she would start and wash when she got home," Henry interrupted.

"And that was seven days a week, mind. Of course on Sundays I didn't work all them many hours. [Mrs. Fell took over for a while.] I used to come home for me dinner, and maybe half past ten, eleven, for my dinner, and then I used to go back at three on a Sunday. But I've seen if it's been a bad time, snow and all that, I've stayed up there and got my dinner. I got a guinea a week, for seven days a week. I worked for them when I was single, at Springclose, it's just past the cemetery, it's just like a mansion. I worked for them there, then I got married. Well they always kept two maids. It was farming, or Mr. Batty was a cattle-dealer. Well they always kept two, well they could only get one and Mr. Batty come and asked if I would go and help a bit while they got somebody. Well they never got anybody. Just me and another maid, and some of them didn't stay long. I – well you see you had to clean byres out and all that. It was hard work, but mind I liked it. I was there about twenty-five years. Before I got married I was hired by half year. I just forget what I had now, when I first went and when I left, but it wasn't a big wage. Do you know, when I first started I had three pounds for six months. I went out at five o'clock or half past with my clogs on. I was as good as an alarm clock. A lot of people used to tell me down Station Road I was as good as an alarm clock. They used to hear me clogs and I never had a bicycle, you know. I used to walk to Springclose and I walked to the Mains and there was the morning after I got married, we just had one clock then, and I don't know whether I had wound it up or not but do you know how many hours that clock had forward to go? Three hours. And it had stopped. It was a lovely morning, the cocks were crowing, and I thought it must be time for getting up. So I got up, and I used to give myself a bit of a wash and a drink of water and away I used to go because at six o'clock they would go and have their tea and a piece of teacake. I got myself away, and it was rather cold. So when I got there, there wasn't a soul about. There was a greenhouse, so I went and sat. I'm sure I sat half an hour, then the dining-room clock started to strike. I was saying to myself, They'll not be long in getting up now. Instead of striking five it struck four, and the best of it all was that morning they slept in. Twenty minutes to six and Mrs. Batty used to get up at quarter past five. The morning after I got married.

And do you know, when I first went to Springclose Mr. Batty was a cattle-dealer and he used to go to Cockermouth Auction and he used to buy dairy cattle at Cockermouth Auction and send them through to Wigton. So we used to go and wait for them and we used to sit in Wigton Signal Box and, mind, they were kind. On cold nights they used to shout, Come on, sit yourselves down. Put a big fire on for us, and some of them they used to phone to see where the cattle wagon was, to see about the cows. We were many a time in that signal box at twelve o'clock midnight, waiting of the cows from Cockermouth. And they were to take to Springclose and when it was dark one went at front and the other at the back, we had a lamp each, and we had to go across a field, and you know what strange cattle is, getting them in a byre, then they were all to feed after that before we went to bed. You didn't get any overtime then either. Mind, I liked farm work because it was interesting."

Henry Fell took up his story.

"I went back to the Air Ministry and that was the best job. I got my own back out of the Air Ministry for fighting because I had a lovely job. I was a messenger. I was a boy messenger at the Post Office, then I was a messenger in the war, then I came back and I went to the Air Ministry. I was a messenger for the Air Ministry. And then when I come retired I'm messenger here and roundabout, taking pills and running messages for old pensioners. Throughout the 20s and 30s you were just doing these odd jobs.

Jobs like pipes for Wigton sewerage and all hard jobs. We used to bike to Sebergham (eight miles away) and all over. And when we got there and if it started to rain they blew the whistle and we had to come home and we got nothing at all. And we couldn't strike. We daren't strike. The only thing we could do was to strike matches. The wife went back to work."

It was the same story from everyone. The return to "a land fit for heroes to live in" was tough.

All over the country children waited for their fathers to come back from the war. One of these was Henry Fell, nephew of the Henry Fell just quoted, son of the Willie Fell who won three military medals.

Henry Fell is a lean, tall man who speaks steadily, methodically, and with great concentration. We talked in the large house which he shared with his wife and mother-in-law. The house is in the middle of the old town, next to where the tan-yard was: a place where all the back alleys and little town "walks" used to come to as to a hub. It's quiet there now. Streets round about here have been levelled for the car-park, hundreds of people left those cramped yet cosy, insanitary but intimate cottages and terraces and moved, towards the end of the Thirties, up one of the slopes of the town to a new estate. Henry Fell is widely informed about the town – his job as a postman (like his uncle) takes him, literally, everywhere, and he has taken care to note and assess the changes, not least in his own life.

Somehow the word "typical" appears to jar the nib of my pen. Like "average" or even "ordinary" it seems to diminish as much as it describes. It is as if, aware that the reformation and rebirth of English society is not yet fully realised, the language itself is holding back, refusing to disclose the word which will identify the new Englishman. But whatever word it is, its ancestors will be men like Henry Fell, who grew up in the compound confusion of an exhausted old order, an uncertain new order and a present which was hard.

"I was born on 12th April 1915, a war baby, and I was born in Station Road, Wigton. I always remember Mother saying that she had a very hard time with having very little money because she didn't get a very big allowance, just having one child, and the people with bigger families were much better.

And I remember after the war when she said, Your Daddy's coming back, the war's over. I said, Should I go and meet him and she said, Well, we don't know what train he's coming off. And so I thought well, this is grand, he's coming back. I couldn't remember him; I knew him by a photograph that Mother had but I had never been able to see him in the flesh. Anyhow, I waited and waited near home and I saw a soldier coming in his uniform and I said, This must be my daddy. So I went towards him and I said, Daddy and he said, I'm not your daddy. But however I thought well, this soldier looks like my daddy on the photograph we've got at home, so I followed him and he went right up the lane where we lived and then I knew it was him. So he didn't recognise me and he said he wasn't me daddy but it were him all the time.

When he got back into civvie street in 1918 there wasn't any work much. He was a woodcutter by trade, a good woodcutter, but there was hardly any work and he was on and off the dole quite a lot, well really, every halfpenny counted. Sometimes we didn't have very much coal for the wintertime cold weather and Mother would say to me, Henry go down the coal-yard and get a half cwt. of coals I can manage to find a shilling. We used to have a little – we called them bogies, little soap-box with old pram wheels self-made, people used to make them bogies, barrows or whatever you like to call them, and off I would go. I would be about eight years old then and coal agent would give you the coal and it was wonderful coal compared with the coal today, it was absolutely wonderful coal. The difference today when you see the coal, today, with the coal in those days – I can't understand where the good coal goes to.

Well before that I went to school on me own. I would be just turned four, this is the earliest memories I have – when I turned four, somebody said they're going to school and I said, I'm going with you to school. Me mother didn't know anything about it so off I goes to school which was down Market Hill – the infant school. And Miss Steele was the Headmistress. She said, What do you want? I said, I've come to start school. She said, And what do they call you? I said, They call me Henry Fell. Oh yes, and you want to start school? I said, Yes I would like to start school. And she said to the other teacher, Miss Moffat, Miss Moffat, do you know this boy? Yes, I know him, he wants to start school. Well they had a bit of a confab and they decide it was alright to start school. At dinnertime I come home and me mother was nearly off her head with worry. She said, Where you been? I said, I've been to school and after I've had me dinner I'm going back. Well, she said, that's all right. What made you think about starting school? Well, I said, all the other children were going to school and I had nobody to play with and I thought I may as well be at school as playing by myself. So that was alright.

For my mother to bring us up was a real struggle. I was the eldest and eventually there was six of us altogether children; three brothers and two sisters. And to say that we were hard up is putting it mildly.

But we were never short of a bit to eat, excepting once when Father was on the dole – he was reported for working and drawing unemployment benefit. Well as a matter of fact he was cutting a gentleman's grass lawn and I think this gentleman was going to give him a shilling or a few cigarettes for doing it, but still he was working. Well it was reported to the dole, the labour exchange, and dole was stopped and it was stopped for six weeks and during that six weeks there wasn't a penny saved in the house or anything like that and Mother said to me, Go and see Mr. Moore who is our landlord, we just paid three shillings a week house rent, and tell him I'm sorry that I won't be able to give him any rent this week and probably for six weeks as me husband's had his dole stopped, has been reported working while drawing unemployment benefit. And Mr. Moore was very good; he said, Oh well you can't pay you can't pay. Tell your mother if she can't pay she can't pay and he said, I'm very sorry that he's had his dole stopped. And where we got our provisions at the shop they were very good indeed because the same thing happened there; Mother was allowed to get her groceries for six weeks' credit and the big trouble during that six weeks was would he be disallowed any benefit?

Father went before a court of referees at Carlisle and they had said he had done wrong and he would lose all his dole for six weeks and the following week there would only be one week's dole. How the devil did they pay the rent and provisions I don't know, but everything ended pretty well because the court of referees then decided that he should have his dole, that he wasn't doing a full day's work and he wasn't getting very much for it and so the next dole day he got six weeks back dole which seemed a fortune but of course the rent had to be paid and, oh, the coalman even left the coals – he said he was told I don't know whether we had to pay or not but if you leave any coals we wouldn't be able to pay you for them this week and it might be a good long while before we can pay you. But he said, It's all right, he said, you get your coal. And we didn't have very much to eat those six weeks but there was mainly plenty of bread and a lot of broth every day, cheap vegetables and a pennyworth of bones at the butcher's and in those days there was quite a lot of meat on some of the bones, they weren't like they are today when you get bones, if you get bones at the butcher's now well, there wouldn't be meat on them at all.

Well that was a crisis I can remember and of course that was only one of the several crises my mother had to go through and unfortunately her health wasn't too good and she was told when she had the fourth child, she was told she shouldn't really have any more but of course the other two came along to make the six and the great day was – I was the eldest – when I got a job. I had to get a job then at fourteen and it was really amazing in Wigton. To get a job in 1929 was amazing. There were seven boys left school with me that I can remember and I was the only one that had work to go to and I had put me name down for the Post Office four year before; when I was ten year old me mother went to the Post Office and put me name down on a list. There was a list of applicants for the job and she put it down and it just was lucky that when there was a vacancy for a telegraph boy my name was there and I was the right age – you had to be just turned fourteen. And I got the job and strange enough I could have – those that are lucky seems to get all the luck because I got chance of another job the same week and I thought, well he's – I'm lucky really because I've left school and I've got two jobs and some of these poor chaps can't get a job at all. One or two of them never worked, were never gainfully employed we should say for four or five years. One was quite nineteen before he got a job. He wanted to work but there was nothing, there was nothing round about here.

I really enjoyed school, I thought school was a wonderful thing. And I was keen to learn and was always wanting to know things and really enjoyed school. But there was no school meals. And the Infants' School, the teachers, there were three teachers, the Headmistress and two other teachers, and they were very good with corporal punishment, I can't remember any cane being used. Sometimes somebody smacked somebody's bottom but apart from that there was no cane. Of course we were only Infants but even then there were some of us pretty badly behaved at times. Leaving the Infants' School was a terrific shock because when you got at seven years of age you went up to the Elementary School and you were tossed in at the deep end there because you got introduced to the cane which was very much in evidence. It was the one thing you could see in that classroom, it was put in a place where you could see it and your eyes used to wander to it for at seven years of age you were rather scared that it might be used on oneself. But you got used to caning, we got caned often, for the slightest little fault we got the cane, particularly when we got to eleven and twelve and fairly big lads. It was the time when perhaps the teachers thought well, if we don't keep these lads toeing the line they are going to be too big for us to handle. And when we got six of the best on your hand, sometimes you got six, three on each hand, your hands would sting of a cold morning, would be stinging maybe hour and a half, maybe playtime when – you maybe get this caning about quarter past nine and at playtime you were still tingling and stinging. And lots of lads would put their hands out and when the cane was coming down they would pull their hands away, but they never got away with it because sometimes the lads would be called out to hold his hand while he got his cane. But the teachers were fairly good really, we liked them.

Mr. Scott was the Headmaster and when he – he seldom caned but when he did you knew about it, he fairly laid on. He laid on when you got caned, off him you knew you'd been caned. But there was another teacher there, he was an ex-1914–1918 War man and had been gassed or something and he was a bit of a terror, really, but a very good teacher, a teacher that was really too good for a national school. But whether it was because of his poor health, he had to take this school, or whether he had a chip on his shoulder that he was in a school which he deserved to be in a higher school really and he did sometimes take it out of us lads. I always remember him giving us a drawing lesson, well, the drawing lessons we ever had were very elementary – it was standing on a railway station looking down the lines and you're looking down the line and you see the telegraph poles; well, of course we were a pretty stupid lot of lads really because we knew that the railway lines didn't meet – they appeared to meet in the distance, looking at them – but we knew they didn't and we were asked to draw the railway lines and these telegraph poles. And there wasn't out of the twenty of us in the class, there wasn't one of us had the sense to draw them as we saw them, though it had never been properly explained to us by the teacher. He didn't explain that beforehand but we should have had the sense to realise, we were about eleven at the time, that we should draw things as we see them. But we all drew the poles the same length right down and the lines the same width along the paper which we knew that was actually the thing that we were drawing were all the same length. And he got really vexed and he really had us all out and gave us I think four canes, two on each hand. Every one of us; and he was absolutely livid with rage and we were very frightened and I always remember I always thought, well the next time I draw anything I draw it as I see it.

Elementary teaching in those days it was the three Rs; reading, writing and arithmetic was the order of the day which drawing wasn't for us lot. In fact that was probably his trouble, this chap that lost his temper, because he was trying to give us a better education than the system was allowing – drawing lessons were a thing that, well, the only time we ever got them was when he was teaching us and after the railway lines and the telegraph poles well it was thought that even he began to lose heart. Music lessons; I can only remember about a quarter of an hour a week being devoted to music lessons. There was an attempt made to teach us the scale and there was a piano played and we used to sing and I was always sorry that the music lessons wasn't much longer, trying and learn the scales, but you didn't have time to learn them because you didn't just have the time to bother about. And of course I think it was one of those subjects that, well, it doesn't matter about. We had to concentrate on the Three Rs, good handwriting, spelling and we were forever spelling – repetition spelling – spelling words *b r i g h t* all the whole class shouting out the spelling. We were fairly good spellers I think in the main, fairly good writers and when it come to very simple arithmetic, well, we were about able to count our wages and that sort of business.

The Headmaster said, Henry I think you should try and go on for the scholarship for the Nelson Thomlinson, the Grammar School – the Nelson School as it was called then, he said, I think you could pass your exam for the Nelson School. Well I thought, Well that might be alright but I wasn't really keen to go in Nelson School. It was in my mind if I could get a job when I was fourteen and earn some money it would be a big help to me mother with being the oldest of the family and I would rather have pleased my mother than please anybody. I would rather help my mother than help anyone else in the world, so I thought it over. But anyway he would persist in putting my name down to sit this exam for the Nelson School and there was about six of us sat it. And I was really bothered about it, I had a feeling I might pass and I thought if I pass I know the scholarship's free but you got to have better clothes and there's a bit of uniform to buy and there's books and schoolbag and even though I knew me mother would somehow manage to get the money someway honestly as she always did I didn't feel like imposing on her any more so I deliberately made some mistakes in my exams.

I made pretty sure I wouldn't pass and I always remember after the exam Mr. Scott, the Headmaster, said, Well I don't know, Henry, what you been thinking about it, must have been nerves he said, for I was sure you would pass, he said, you've been the brightest boy in my class – we were in his class – he used to take a class but I didn't let on, I didn't tell him that I had deliberately put some wrong answers down. And unfortunately as time got near when I was drawing to fourteen and I had to leave school I felt such a desire to go on learning more and I didn't want to leave school, I was really starting to enjoy school and I was reading in the library at Tullie House and I was getting library books, I was really getting interested in things and realising that there was more to life than just being a telegraph boy. But it was too late and I just thought I'm getting punished for not doing my best in exams now. I'm getting punished for it because here's a thing I never thought would happen to us, here I was leaving school and didn't want to leave – was really interested in trying to learn things. Wasn't it funny? It was funny, I always thought about it.

There was evening classes – it was possible for somebody with plenty of grit and determination, and you needed to have a lot of grit and determination in those days – the opportunities were there but you weren't spoonfed; I'm not suggesting they're spoonfed today but there was facilities, there was night classes and if you really wanted to get on even then, if you were prepared to work your leisure of a night and just swot and swot, well the world was at your feet. But it was very very difficult and the thing that always held me back mainly was the fact that Mother had so much to do trying to rear a family on the precarious livelihood me dad could get after the war. Sometimes he was working but it was a case of working maybe two or three months and then on the dole two or three months. He wasn't permanently on the dole like many of our neighbours – some people, some men never worked for two or three or four years, never even had a day's work. They were on – what would it be in those days, what they called the parish and it wasn't their faults there just wasn't the work – there was no work for them unless people went abroad and it was much the same abroad in some places.

The telegraph boy's job I really liked it – I got a smart uniform and a smart hat and I was a growing lad, I was about five foot nine or ten, now I am nearly six foot. I got provided with shoes, uniform and on the bicycle – the bicycle to take the telegrams. It was an easy job, sometimes I would do as far as thirty to forty miles a day delivering the telegrams and the bicycle was a pretty hefty bike, it was a very heavy bike and took a lot of pushing. But it was a good healthy open-air job and the first telegram I took out was a three-mile journey to a place called Biglands and I always remember that when I got there and gave the telegram to the farmer he said, Just a minute, and I said, What is it? and he said, Here's threepence for you. And I thought, By jove I'm on the road to fortune if I'm going to get threepence every time I take a telegram, let me have plenty of telegrams. But tips weren't as free as that, there was tips, a few tips, but you didn't get a tip with every telegram.

Ten shillings a week was the basic wage and I started work at nine o'clock in the morning and finished at five and I had half an hour for dinner and that was Monday to Saturday. On Sunday morning I worked from nine o'clock in the morning until half past ten – there was telegrams on Sunday, there's still telegrams on Sunday yet, but the Post Office was open on Sunday mornings for one and a half hours, so I could say that apart from the holidays I worked every day in the week for all the time I was a telegraph boy – that was nearly five years. And I never had one day off except when I had – what they call it – annual leave – you worked every

Bank Holiday. Christmas Day, Boxing Day, Good Friday, well, you worked them all, you worked every Bank Holiday. Didn't work *all* day, finished about dinnertime so you were really pretty well tied to that job. But I liked it and there was opportunities in the Post Office then, if you tried to better yourself you could sit exams for to pass for Counter Clerks and that was the first step. And of course there's plenty of telegraph boys from elementary schools have finished up as postmasters. And I was thinking on those lines, but I liked the outside life and I was pretty strong and, well, weatherwise it didn't matter how cold it was or how wet it was, it didn't have a great deal of effect on us and I thought, ah well it's the open-air life for me and so I never bothered any more about trying to better myself as regarding a better job.

Until I was nineteen and the time comes when a telegraph boy has got to be a postman, he can't be a telegraph boy any longer than eighteen. I was nineteen; there was a mistake made. I should of been a postman at eighteen but I were nearly nineteen when they realised I should have been a postman. Well, vacancies were very few and far between for postmen, there were no vacancies at Wigton but there was a vacancy at Carlisle, I had to go to Carlisle to be a postman. If I turned it down, well, I would have been out of a job, they didn't – you either took the job or you packed it in and that was it. So I went to Carlisle (eleven miles away) that would be in 1934, and I biked. I started work at six o'clock in the morning, well there was no public transport from Wigton to Carlisle to start work at six o'clock in the morning – the soonest you could get to Carlisle was a bus at half past six getting into Carlisle about seven which was no good. So I biked from Wigton to Carlisle, I got up about quarter past four and me mother always got up with us and I used to say, Mother you needn't get up, she said, No I'll make you some breakfast. And Mother and I used to get up just about four, she would make us some breakfast and give me bait – and off I would set on the bike to Carlisle to be there at six o'clock. Well I was always there before six. Then I had to bike back. Well, I started at six o'clock and we sorted the letters into postman's walks and then after we had finished sorting into postman's walks we used to go out to our own postman's walk and clear the boxes, prepare them and about an hour after seven o'clock we would be packing our bags and going out to deliver the letters we had got ready. And we would be back about somewhere about half past nine and ten o'clock in the morning. And then we used to have half an hour for a meal and then we went back again and did another delivery of letters and parcels. And in those days there were three deliveries of letters in the town area in Carlisle, there were three on Monday to Friday and on Saturday there were two deliveries. Now there's two deliveries Monday to Friday and one delivery on the Saturday and it's quite possible that as time goes by that there will only be one delivery Monday to Friday – but I don't think I'll be in the Post Office when that happens. I think it will come because of the telephones. People are using the telephone more now if their friends have got telephone and they have telephone, well they're not writing letters. And the people that are writing letters are mostly oldish people that haven't the use of the phone. They're dying off very quickly and if it wasn't for bills and circulars well I don't know what a postman would find to do.

Anyway, that first job in Carlisle – one week on rotation of duties, one week six o'clock to two – eight hours Monday to Saturday, you did eight hours a day Monday to Saturday – and the next week I was on split duties, starting at six in the morning and I finished at half past nine. And I started again at one o'clock and I finished at quarter to five. The split duty starting at six o'clock in the morning and finish at quarter to five at night we were booked off from half past nine until one o'clock. I used to put quite a bit of time in Tullie House [the Museum's library in Carlisle], it was just up my street. I don't think all the time I spent in Tullie House really hasn't done any good but still it was very interesting to pass the time. I did really read most of the daily papers but there was periodicals there and occasionally I had a look at some reference books for various things and I managed to go right through and look at all the exhibits. And that wasn't every day; some days I'd maybe go in the market if it were a fine day, go maybe down to Bitts Park, but I used to always be very tired on the split duty because on the split duty I was on a bike – it was a bicycle job, my round in Carlisle, and I was on a bike from say shortly from five o'clock in the morning until it was sometimes seven o'clock at night when I got back because I was fairly tired and often there was a wind blowing against us from the west. And with being on the bike on the post job I wasn't feeling terribly fresh. And I remember one night there was a terrific gale blowing and I was practically having to push the bicycle, walked with the bicycle the eleven miles because it was blowing trees down, it was impossible to ride the bike. And Mother said to me, By I don't know, I've been worried about you lad, because it's blowing some trees down that wind and your dad said it was blowing against you. I said, Well I managed to get back, I said, but I wish it had been blowing the other way."

Maggie Cook also lives in the old part of the town, in Reeds Lane, opposite the new bus station, just across a field from Henry Fell.

She's rather deaf and instantly told me that I would have to "speak up". Equally firmly she told me that she had nothing to say. She was insistent on this and stopped from time to time to assert that what she was saying could be "no good". We talked in the small living-room of her house. She had just come back from the Senior Citizens' Club which meets round at the Parish Rooms, fifty yards away. She's a compact, self-composed woman, small, black-haired, very direct. There were seven children in the family, her father was a blacksmith and came to Wigton when she was five.

"I was twenty when I married. We came here to this house, just a little room down and a room up. I can just picture it. I had a sofa and a wooden-topped table, two chairs. I had two wooden-topped tables – a lang un, and I had a little round un. We used to have oor meals off t' little roon un, and I used to have a nice red tablecloth ont' just for a bit of furniture to fill t' room un, and that would be all we had doonstairs, and a rocking chair. We've always had a rocking chair. And a prodded hearthrug. Everybody that got married got a prodded hearthrug for a wedding present somewhere or other. Upstairs beside t' bed, there's be a chamber set. Washhand stand, you know. Well, this was a big bowl and jug. They're in antique shops. They're any amount of money noo, and a little thing for your toothbrush and that and a soap dish and two chambers for under t' bed, and that was t' chamber set. At Redmaynes when anybody got married and they collected either that or a clock was two things they used to git. One or the other. And then you gradually got a little bit more and a little bit more pulled together.

I remember when we were first married, Bob and I, we had twenty-three shillings and threepence. I always remember that, because we were in Armoury Place and the rent was three and three, and a bag of coals was two shillings and the insurance was two shillings. And we had an Aladdin lamp. Well if you broke a mantle you knew about it. That was about another two shillings for a mantle. Well you had half a gallon of oil or a gallon of oil, whichever it might be. I can remember very very well sitting down with a paper and pencil and putting down what I wanted. But this was after my mother died, mind you, putting down what I wanted. And I thought, Dearie me, that came to ten shillings. My goodness, I'll have to cross off something. I'll have to do without something. For I must have something for a bit of meat or some eggs."

I walked up the town to see Mr. and Mrs. Morrison, who had also started married life in the Thirties – in a detached red-brick house on the road to the Lakes. As I went from Maggie Cook's house, comfortable as a squirrel's den, it was late morning in early summer and, from memory, and notebooks, here are a few observations on the town that morning; 1973.

There was scarcely a person around. Work and homes or cars and schools contained the great mass of the population. Except for the centre of the great towns and cities this seems generally true: life has moved off the streets, people have moved in from the weather. The roads were clean and well-maintained; the gardens were well-stocked and trim, houses despite the taxing northern climate were clearly being looked after. Exceptions to these generalisations were very few. The factory which employed almost a thousand people was silent: only the oily fumes from its long high chimney showed activity; the schools which took in almost two thousand children were preparing to let them out for school dinners, heavily subsidised by the state, carefully planned by the council's catering committee; in the centre of the town the banks and shops were busier than ever before and yet fewer people than ever before clung around them or the pavements between them: cars and town buses took them to and fro; cafés, new to this decade, took them in for a cup of tea until the transport turned up. Though Mrs. Morrison, herself gentle-mannered, graceful, having escaped, as she would tell, the physical toil which had been the life of most of the others I spoke to, remembered the mid-wars town as a quieter, gentler place, it is difficult to see how it could be quieter.

Her father, William Park, had a small boot and shoe shop: he worked in it for seventy years. His father had fashioned hand-made boots for farmers in a village nearby. Mrs. Morrison's brother – there were three children – now had the shop in his turn.

We sat in a very agreeable sitting-room; out of the window were glorious views, about to be blocked by a new private housing estate. "We've had the benefit for all these years," said Mrs. Morrison, "now it'll be somebody else's turn."

When she finished school, "I went into the shop part-time and part-time I stayed at home with Mother and sort of larked about really."

"This is one very big regret I've got, I'm afraid. I stayed at home with Mother and helped Mother. She wasn't too strong and then sometimes during the day I perhaps went to the shop and helped in the shop. But this is what life was all about then. This really is a very great regret that I had. I would love to have been a nurse but they didn't think I was strong enough. I would have been really but in those days nursing was hard work. Well it's hard today but you sort of got down and you did the really messy jobs as well and they thought that I wasn't strong enough to do this, so I didn't get away with it, but it's something that I would loved to have done really.

There was plenty to do at home though. On baking days we used to bake maybe four white loaves and four brown loaves, and ginger-breads and batches of rock buns and all these sort of things – biscuits. And it was really quite a thing. Friday morning was set aside and the table was cleared and everything was really set out. Then the milkman used to come in those days with their tins – not in bottles, and ladle this milk out. Well there was four milkmen came, it sounds a lot, doesn't it, in one day? Sort of a gill here and a gill there, and they had plenty of time to sort of stop and talk to you. Tommy Marrs used to come and he used to say, Ee, it's like Warwick Hall. Well I never knew what Warwick Hall was but apparently it's a big farm out Westnewton there. Must have done an awful lot of work or something. And then Joe Stainton used to come with his milk and he had any amount of time to stop and talk. He showed us how to grow a plant out of coal, pouring a sort of mixture of red ink over this coal and you got a fungus coming away from it. He was most interested as he came along to watch this thing progress. He'd plenty of time in those days.

People thought that we were quite lucky, I think really, which I suppose we were in those days in comparison. It seems to be getting easier all the time. But remembering as much as I can remember of my youth it seemed to be happy enough. The thing was that you seemed to have any amount of time and at the shop, somebody wanted some shoes sent out, repairs and all this sort of thing. We sometimes delivered, and we used to go out to Brookfield School with a parcel. Well then you see it was quite a long job, a walk out to Brookfield School and of course we took our time doing it. There was never any rush on. Everybody's in such a rush these days. And I mean you don't sort of send shoes out like that now. People more or less come to collect them. I suppose you would if it was requested but normally people collect their repairs and things like that now. I mean, well, if it was a case of paying for time, well, it would have been ridiculous because perhaps a pair of shoes heeled and walking all the way to Brookfield with them, if they'd been paying time, well you just couldn't have done it, could you? The shoes were about a shilling in those days. And then we used to get calendars, Christmas time, and deliver those, and we used to make great lists and go round with all these calendars to every customer. It was quite a big thing. You wouldn't dream about doing that now.

There was quite a bit of poverty at that time, yes. A lot of these poor houses that you see being pulled down. Yes, there was a bit of poverty at the time. Definitely. When we got married we just couldn't find a house and this one cropped up and we knew the people quite well that belonged to the house. It had only been up two years, so it was a good opportunity. We had to think about it because it was to buy and we didn't have the money, in those days, and so we sort of just furnished two rooms up and down and we made a list. We went out in the country for a walk one day and we sat down and made this list of all the things that we would require to set up house and then reckoned up how much money we had and then found that we had to strike all these items off the list because we couldn't afford them. There was no hire purchase then. You sort of bought a carpet and they gave you a rug over and this sort of thing. Things were cheap in comparison."

Mr. Morrison, now retired – he had worked at the factory – was sitting in as it were while we were talking. He came from West Cumberland, from one of the areas worst affected by unemployment in the 1930s: Maryport. Eighty-five percent unemployed for two years. "The depression there was heart-breaking. If anyone had any savings at all – let's say if they had fifty pounds in the bank, you had to spend that fifty pounds before you got any assistance at all. And the only assistance you got was the unemployment benefit. There was no public assistance like there is now." Hungry children with no shoes, men with no work, women with no money for families with little hope – this was Northern Industrial England.

But the fact remains that for large numbers in the lower middle class and middle class, things, as Mrs. Morrison said, "seemed to be getting a bit easier all the time".

For Miss Wilson, it was her heyday. She was the cousin of the Storey family who had taken over Highmoor House. From her own large, Georgian house in which she lives alone with her dogs and family treasures, the tower of Highmoor can be seen across the fields.

She lives on a back road a mile outside the town: breeds horses, hunts, and remembers her life between the wars with a good deal of warmth. She's a shy, rather stilted woman, "Miss Barbara" she is called by those who have known her for a long time. She smoked a lot and was most careful to correct any mistakes she made as she went along. Her brother, who used to live in that house, has gone south to be a Master of the Foxhounds. Mostly she talked about hunting, which is recorded in the later chapter on leisure. Even apart from hunting, though, life between the wars was:

"Very pleasant. We used to hunt a lot and as I said played various games, quite a lot of dances. We had a very very good time, very good life. We used to always have a cook and a housemaid. They were usually with us for a very long time. The cook used to be – the housemaids were young girls who usually got married.

We used to have a groom and a – I don't know whether we had a full-time gardener or not. The gardeners were always pretty ancient but you see it was quite a big garden. I've cut off most of the vegetable garden. I've put it out to the field. There was a tennis court at the end of the garden. We used to play quite a lot of tennis in the summer. The weather must have been better because it was just a grass court. We couldn't have played much tennis as this summer has been. I seem to remember playing a lot of tennis and all of my friends had tennis courts all over the country. We used to dash about playing tennis. I wouldn't have been so mobile when I left school. I had a hundred pounds in my account and I was absolutely thrilled because I found that a hundred pounds would buy a Morris Minor – you won't have ever seen them, but they were funny little things with two seats and they had a canvas hood you used to fold back when it was a nice day. You sort of sat up in them. That car did an awful lot for me because it made me mobile. I didn't have to borrow the family car, which I would never have got anyway. But you see with this car I could sort of go and do what I liked. This was absolutely marvellous. I was awfully thrilled with it. Of course you didn't have to do a test or anything in those days. You just drove. There was a marvellous story round here of Mr. Hope that used to be up at Kirkland. Have you ever heard of him? Well, he bought the car at a farm sale. I don't think he'd ever driven it before but he drove it home and on Tuesday there was always great excitement because there was Mr. Stamer up at Kirkland and Mr. Hope and they used to rather enjoy Wigton on Tuesdays, and it was a great thing if they got past the pond, there used to be a pond there, very often they used to go in it and had to be fished out.

But everybody was more neighbourly than they are now. Everybody knew each other very well and when you used to go out riding, people didn't have tractors, they used to be mostly working with horses then. They had plenty of time to stop and chat and it was very, very pleasant. One knew everyone very well. Much more so than you do now. Because they're in such a hurry or if they're with a tractor, well, you wouldn't expect them to stop anyway. But they used to have horses and if they were doing hedges, they used to always stop and have a little chat and ask how things were doing.

My brother used to have a pony, a hunter, and he used to do rather well. But now you see these show ponies today, they're so valuable, that they're not allowed to do anything like jumping or anything. They're merely shown and then they're put back in their horse-box. But in those days, goodness me, this pony it used to be shown, then it used to jump, then he used to play games, gymkhana things on it afterwards. I mean, you really got far more pleasure out of them. And it was a very good pony, because it used to win all sorts of championships and things, and then it used to win the jumping. It had to work, and it was a jolly good thing too.

My father used to breed cocks – gamecocks – and he used to show them locally, but the best ones went to Crystal Palace. That's where you aimed for and then he used to send them all over the country. They used to go in these wicker basket things and they were sent from Wigton Station, I remember, and all over the country. He used to judge a lot, too. He really knew all about them. He'd always been interested in game. He was very famous. One of his cocks won I think it was a medal – at Crystal Palace. He was very deaf. He'd been deafened by the guns at Passchendaele.

My mother used to breed – when we lived in Canada, my mother used to breed Scottish terriers and she showed them all over the place. She did terribly well. And once we had seventy, I remember. We used to have kennels on the side of the hill, and she sold them all over the place. A lot of film stars – who was it came once? She was very well known, and then after that they were all wanting these Scotties. Very good for business. She used to do it for a hobby.

I loved Pekes. They were very profitable at one time and then they went. And I liked pigs, they're rather super things. Awfully intelligent. Used to run them out in huts with the sow with the tether on her. I remember all the little pigs – on the top of the hill – all these little pigs used to run about loose and they used to scamper up and down the hill and they had a marvellous time. I used to feel awfully mean when they got too old for that and they had to be brought in to be sort of fattened up."

Back in the town there were lives, not as carefree, but certainly comfortable, certainly free of the day-to-day economic anxieties which pursued the majority.

John Johnston was "born and bred in Wigton. 24 King Street. Above the shop. Johnston's shoe shop." He is a lean, fit-looking man, a schoolteacher, very straightforward in his opinions and attitudes, something fiery about him. He too remembers the mid-wars period with great warmth though, being in the town, he was well aware of the other side of the coin.

"We didn't suffer particularly but I suppose some of our sort of tradesmen were better off than some, but you wouldn't call it well off. My mother always made her own bread for instance. She was a hard worker. Baked her own cakes, all this sort of thing. No money was ever wasted. Father for instance took five shillings pocket money and never any more all his life. Saved money though. He didn't drink or smoke. He played bowls and this sort of thing and so there was never any great surplus of money. For instance, my shoes, we were always well shod, being in a shoe shop, my shoes were invariably ones which got too much sun in the window. But there was a lot of poverty. Our shop was at the top of Water Street. Water Street was down the back. Well in those days Water Street was very built up and a lot of people lived up there and a lot of them were very poor. I think one family lived almost behind us, where the father was at work – Charters – about eight kids. I don't know whether there were two bedrooms upstairs and one downstairs. Very difficult. A lot of the children wore clogs. They used to come into the shop, we had a workshop behind the shop where there was a clogger, and at lunchtime they would come in to get new corkers on their clogs. And I can remember them all sitting on these four steps, four or five of them sitting with their clogs off waiting to get new corkers put on. But nobody seemed to take much harm really. They probably weren't as fit as they ought to have been, probably too many fish and chips and that sort of thing. Wigton had three fish and chip shops in those days. They can hardly support one now.

I went to school at the kindergarten – Thomlinson School. The local Infants' School was on Market Hill and it rained in and there were stories of children sitting with their umbrellas up. Father thought, Well, that wasn't good enough for us so we went – myself and my sisters went to the kindergarten, attached to the local girls' school, till we were eight – well, till I was eight anyway. Then I went to the preparatory department attached to the Grammar School till I was eleven. They called it Form 1. They were both fee-paying.

My parents had a lot of property about the town. They were fairly easy landlords, I should think. They never took anybody to court or anything like that, and there must have been a lot of people who didn't pay ... well, I know there were lots of people who didn't pay their rent – not for years, some of them. But we just didn't get it. There wasn't any money.

When I became older I suppose I mixed mainly with the boys who went to the Grammar School. Not greatly, not a lot, with the lads who didn't. I knew a lot of them, mind. I suppose this happens with a private education. A paying education at the time, more so than it would now. We played rugby and they played football. The school holidays were different too. We got longer than they did. I think in those days the Elementary Schools used to get about a month or something like that in the summer, and we got two months. These sort of differences. We weren't particularly popular. I never had any problems, sort of falling out, or fights or anything like that. I always got on well with them. But again partly I was probably better off. That made a difference too. My father, as well as having a shop – to some extent landlords in the town – and they had quite a lot of shops, houses, and a lot of people lived in the houses – and this may have made a difference too, because I was a landlord's son. The property was all over the middle of the town ... what's now the bus station, used to be Tickells Lane, it was a slummy property. Quite a lot on Market Hill, some in Water Street, Half Moon Lane, some down Meeting House Lane – various places in the town. They used to come to the shop and pay. They usually paid in the shop. Rents were very little. I can think of one, for instance. A chap called Staff, old Staff. He lived behind Reeds Lane and he had one room, upstairs, and he paid one shilling a week, and the time that I remember it the rates on the place were sixpence and the Income Tax, I suppose, was round about tuppence halfpenny. I remember being disgusted because my mother wouldn't put a new roof on. It would be very old. My grandfather bought most of it, you see. And it just passed on. Until eventually it got knocked down.

We used to do a lot of cycling – a few friends. We used to go off – for three years we camped at Ullswater for instance, and there would be about twelve of us each time. And we used to bike there. John Park and I built a two-seater canoe covered with canvas and we fixed it up on a trailer behind the bike and pulled it behind the bike to Ullswater then got in it and paddled across – hair-raising. But there were very few people camping up there then. We camped at Silver Bay. You couldn't camp there now. We had a great time. You could hire a boat for twenty-five shillings for a week. A big one. The biggest they had, we used to hire for a week. We took most of our grub with us. We used to raid the larder, sort of thing, before we went for tins and of course we bought potatoes and all that sort of stuff when we were there. It didn't cost very much. I can remember doing one year on thirty shillings for a fortnight and bringing presents back. There were three tents that we had available. Three people had tents. We used to get some – a couple of times we borrowed them from Aspatria Scouts, a bell tent, then we used to bike a lot at weekends. All lads. We didn't think anything of biking to Keswick (twenty-four miles). This was just the start of the ride sort of thing. I've biked from here down to Great Gable; biked to Seathwaite (thirty miles), left the bikes, climbed Great Gable, biked home. I've been to Pillar too. I remember once biking to Buttermere and leaving the bikes at Buttermere and climbing over the top of Haystacks, round Ennerdale and up to Pillar, walking and then back again, and then biking back home. We must have been fit."

One of the families in Water Street referred to by John Johnston was the Charters family. I went to interview Mary Charters, now Mary Reeves, and it was here that I felt at the heart of the fact and the myth of working class life in this period.

Water Street, now largely demolished, once boasted a hundred and two houses in about a hundred yards. Back alleys, courtyards, slits between cottages gave it a feeling of a warren and indeed part of it, the most heavily populated part, was nicknamed the Rabbit Warren. Up to six houses could share an outside lavatory. Coal heating, tiny rooms, a great deal of unemployment and large families – Water Street had the reputation of being the poorest and the toughest street in town. All areas, all towns, all cities have this sort of place – whether it's the West Side of New York, the East End of London, the back streets of Naples, the poor and the overcrowded in the world's urban conurbations everywhere then would point to the central, always somehow legendary example of the harshness and bitterness of it all: that, in Wigton, was Water Street.

Yet, of course, it is never so simple. No one I spoke to who had lived in Water Street wanted to condemn it out of hand. And indeed it was difficult to take people away from memories of good neighbourliness and childhood games and get the barest details of life there. Very few conditions are lived through without a multiple response: in one sentence Mary Reeves would both condemn and celebrate.

We spoke in the house of her sister Jessie, in Station Road opposite the police station. Jessie's boy, Wayne, who needs special schooling, was there and the sisters made a very loving fuss of him throughout the interview. Jessie's daughter also popped in and out: as in many other houses, the tape-recorder was the signal for a family gathering.

Mary is a smallish woman, slim, a smoker, intensely willing to help, speaking with some passion.

"Well the house I was brought up in was one up and one down and a kitchen. My mother had nothing in it but beds upstairs, a bed settee in the living-room for my father and her, so that the children weren't where she was. That is the type of house we were brought up in. The lads were locked out on a Saturday while we were bathed in one of these old-fashioned – what you used to wash clothes in. We were put to bed, the lads were brought in and they were bathed. That's when we were children. There was four boys and two girls, until Jessie was born. I mean we were grown up when Jessie was born, but there was the four lads and Jean and I.

Most of the houses were the same then, in Water Street. We were all the same, no hot water, nothing, yet my mother's house was spotless. We had a cold water tap and there was these old-fashioned gas things when they first came out. They used to boil the water in that, or they would put a bucket on a gas-ring and boil it in that, and just keeping this bucket on to fill this tub up – that's how we were kept clean.

In bad weather we just used to all sit round the fire. Mam used to sing. We would tell stories, and we had a great time when we were kids. My mother could sing all day and she would sit up all night on her sewing-machine. We wouldn't know it then, just to make us a few extra coppers to get us a few little luxuries. This was when we were kiddies, and she would make all these clothes for kiddies in Wigton for Easter, sit up all night to finish ours off for Easter Sunday morning, and old Mrs. Thornton at the garage, she used to wait for us going up the street because she knew we would be beautiful.

We were really well off as regards the rest of the kiddies in Wigton 'cos Mam was a dressmaker. We were lucky, but mind she had to work hard, and when you think, she used to make a pair of pants for ninepence and provide the material. That's true. We never went hungry, never, because, as I say, it was good old-fashioned tatie pots, and on washing days she used to send us to Sarah Jane Thurlow's with a big jug for tuppenny broth. She lived in Water Street and she used to supply all Water Street with broth. And you used to go with this jug and you used to get it filled for tuppence and then go to the market to Phyllis Hogg and get your jug filled with milk for a penny. And that was our dinner on a Tuesday when they were washing and that. They hadn't time to cook. They had to wash in their kitchens with the old-fashioned dolly tubs and poss sticks, and we used to go down the lonnings – this is true, you know where the lonnings is, hook them on to the barbed wire and sit and wait till they dried. We used to take our turns. Mam would say, Git away down and watch the clothes at the lonnings and then Jean'll go for an hour. And that's true, and if you weren't there the cows ate the shirts. That's perfectly true because they once ate me father's.

We had a good mother. We were lucky. There were some of them that my mother, as poor as she was, used to send a meal to. And like my mother had all us kiddies, but there was some of them would have gone hungry many a time if she hadn't sent them, and that was in Water Street. She was never harassed. Do you know what she used to do – she had us all small, she used to come down to St. Cuthbert's School for us, she used to take us out of our school dress, put us into a clean frock to walk us up the street to the park. When we got to the park, she used to take our clean dresses off, put our school dresses back on, to play at the park, and then dress us again before she brought us back up. Now how could anybody be harassed these days? Every Sunday afternoon every one of us were packed off to Old Carlisle with plate cakes and everything. I had a very very happy childhood. I never knew what it was to go hungry, I was always well clothed, so I couldn't say otherwise.

I went to St. Cuthbert's, the Catholic school. Dad was a Protestant, it was Mam that was the Catholic. Now my dad liked a drink but he never touched a drink on a Sunday. He made the dinner while Mam took us all to Mass. He never interfered. I respected his religion just the same as I respected my mother's, but we never had – and it was never drummed into us, you have to go, you have to go. I sometimes think the reason we did go to church so much was because we were frightened of a Monday morning – hands up who wasn't at Mass. I think that's the reason that we didn't want to miss Mass. People say that when you go to that Catholic school religion's drummed into you. We had about half an hour a day. It was Catechism. That was all we ever had. We had morning prayers the same as any other school does. Religion was not drummed into us. People get that impression because it's nuns down there. I mean, to us it was just a normal school. Now there was once a scare when we were at school that all the Protestants had to leave. Half of them went and turned Catholic because they were terrified they were going to have to go to the National School. Marjorie Wilson, Jean Pearson, they turned Roman Catholics, although the nuns told them that it was just a rumour. Oh, we want to be Catholics, then they can't chase us. So religion can't have played that big a part.

I think there was too much singing and poetry and things like that. Course, every time any visitors come to the school, I had to stand up and recite Mark Antony's Oration on the Body of Caesar, and I'll never forget one day saying it. And it was Tom Woodgate and Donald Norris, and they kept saying, Lend me your lugs [ears; Cumbrian dialect] lend me your lugs. I stood up with my hands clasped. Friends, Romans, Countrymen, lend me your lugs. They got six of the best over that off poor old Mother Catherine. She's dead and gone. There was too much of that sort of thing I felt. I'll tell you what there was, a lot of favouritism. That was the big thing down at St. Cuthbert's. Too many favourites. You get strangers come into the town, and they would think, oh they spoke different to us and they were something different to us, but they hadn't been brought up as well as what we had been brought up. But they were everything.

We used to go to the Salvation Army youth club. Hands up who was at the Salvation Army and we were like this, terrified. Yet we loved to go. Because you see to us there's only one God and as a child, even although you're a Roman Catholic, you don't think, well there's a Protestant God, there's a Catholic God, there's a Salvation Army God. It was Latin in our church. Half of us didn't understand it. We went to church, we stood up when everybody else did, we knelt down when everybody else did, but when you're a child you don't take these things in. It's only when you get older that you really understand Mass because I certainly didn't as a child, because it was Latin. Everything was Latin. As I say, you stood up when everybody else did.

We wouldn't have dared do anything wrong because we would

have had to go and confess it. Now with this permissive society, if they had to go and confess all these things they do, well that kept us on the straight and narrow. Because you would be terrified to go in the confession box and tell the priest what you had done. I've asked questions. I can always remember asking Mother Patricia – they used to tell us this story about Adam and Eve and Cain and Abel and it still baffles me, when Cain slew Abel he went into a far off land and took upon himself a wife. I said, But where did he get the wife from? They were the only four people on this earth. But they still can't give me an answer. It's only two weeks since I asked Mother Patricia about this. Oh, be off with you Mary, be off with you, and that's what I got. All these years after. Well you would have thought she would have tried to give us some answer? I wasn't trying to baffle her. This is the sort of thing we had to put up with.

I kept my religion up right until I got married. And when we went to the priest about getting married, he says, I'll marry you but not at the altar. You'll be married in the vestry. He said, You had no right to fall in love with a Protestant boy. Oh, I says, Father, I says, I met my fiancé at a dance. I says, You don't think when you meet them you say Are you a Catholic? If you're not I can't go with you. And he refused to marry us at the altar. So we went to St. Mary's (Church of England). He refused to marry me at the altar. I says, You don't think for one minute that I am going to stand in that vestry and be married and my mother and my family sitting in church. I says, When a girl was married three months before me, pregnant, married at the altar but because her fiancé promised to turn a Catholic, you said they could be married at the altar. I says, No, if you won't marry me I know somebody that will marry me, and we went and we were married at St. Mary's. But I couldn't settle. I went and was re-married. The worst thing I ever did, because you see I had to divorce that first husband of mine. Well if I hadn't have divorced him I could have married my present husband in church. So I had to be married at the Registry Office, so according to the church I'm living in sin. So I don't go to church now because it just upsets me when I can't go to the Sacrament. Here was me, an innocent party, had to divorce my husband for cruelty and one thing and another, but because I had to divorce him, he would have killed me, the surgeon at Carlisle said, I can't take the Sacrament.

It's two years ago since Mam died. Nobody knows how I've felt when at Requiem Mass I saw my brothers and sisters going to Communion and I couldn't go, and I was her eldest daughter. I couldn't go because of some stupid rule, and I was innocent, but this is the Church, you see, and that's another thing that's putting everybody off the Church ... this birth control. It's stupid. I mean, look at my mother, nine children. I used to say, what did you feel like, Mam, when you knew you were having another, when we got older. As soon as I knew there was one there, she said, I was happy. I had nine, and I wish I'd had another nine, and I wish they'd all been lasses, she used to say, and she was never harassed. And with a man that never worked, because he was so badly wounded. He was wounded at the Battle of Zeebrugge in *H.M.S. Vindictive*. He wore a caliper on his back. He had two holes in his back that you could put your fist in, a caliper on his leg and a brace on his back, he wore. He had a full disability pension. Twenty-five shillings a week and I mean I suppose we were more fortunate, I said, than others. But there was a man with a brain. I mean, my dad was a clever man. But he was so severely handicapped. He took an office job at Kirkbride but they said it was too much for him. He was wounded on St. George's Day at the Battle of Zeebrugge, and I still have the certificate that the King of Belgium at that time gave them all.

When we were kids there was this slot machine outside Thomlinsons and we put this penny in and got these three dog cigarettes. They called them three dogs, and two matches. We'd be no bigger than that. And we would go down to the station and smoke them and then we would go under a tap in Vinegar Hill and gargle. Please God, don't let Mammy know we've been smoking. This is the sort of thing we did when we were kids. And we used to swim in that dirty old beck round Tenters and that one round the Baths. But the handiest place was on your way to the Baths. That beck. It was like a sluice, and we used to get in the deep end. I've seen a bag with rats in. I mean that was the only thing. We never saw any slime or anything. We got many a hammering for it. Mam giving us money for the Baths, which was about a penny then, and rather than spend this money on the Baths we would swim in the becks.

We were Water Street gang and we used to collect the stones for the lads when they were fighting. They used to throw stones. Just them little pebbles mind. But we used to collect the stones for the lads. They used to arrange the fights. They used to say, should we have a fight tonight? Do you want a fight tonight? Okay then. No provocation or anything. We would go down the lonnings, the Market Hill lot would go down their way and the Water Street lot would go down their way and that's where – we used to collect them the stones and sort of meet half-way. We used to throw stones until one of the sides gave in.

Dad liked to take us for walks and he would point out anything of interest he thought you should know, he would tell you. And if there's anything you want to know, ask me, he would say. And it was the same with any problem. Don't go and ask questions in the school-yard about – we didn't know what he was talking about then, come and ask us and we'll try and tell you to the best of our ability. Like me mam was the same. I suppose we were fortunate that way that we had parents that we could ask. And I used to say to Jean, I haven't a clue what Dad's on about. If you go wrong we'll never frown on you. What does he mean? We didn't know what he was talking about. We didn't know what he meant, that if we should have a baby or anything he wouldn't put us out. He would always have a home for us. We didn't know that this is what he was meaning till we were older. It was something that wasn't talked about. But as I say even we didn't know what Dad meant. But I suppose it was his way of letting us know that if we should go wrong he would be there ... Well you didn't know anything until your periods actually happened. You heard snippets from other girls. Then I went to my mother, Oh it just means you're growing up. That's all you got. Never a lecture, never. My mother never lectured us, because friends of ours would say, Oh we can come in your house and your mam will say, Go on and have a good time. I'd had a lecture off my mam, Div't be gaan with lads and all this. We never experienced that. My mother used to say, I trust you, therefore you won't betray my trust. And then when you did find out you thought to yourself, Oh does my mam and dad do that? Which it should have been nice, you thought it was terrible. It's awful when you discover actually how a child is got. Oh, fancy my mam and dad doing that, which is a perfectly natural thing. Now there's Debbie and Donna, Jessie's kiddies, I don't know exactly if they know what happens, but they know exactly all about babies, and where they grow and everything. If they come and ask me a question, I answer them honestly. Because I believe in it myself.

But for manners Dad was very strict. We weren't allowed to speak at the table, we had to say grace before we had a meal, and we had to say, Please Mammy may I leave the table? Very strict, and one thing my father was very strict on, he never abused me, he never lifted his hand, Have you washed your hands? Always. That was something unheard of in our childhood days, but we always had to wash our hands. Now people they didn't bother in them days. But discipline was very strict. We were never allowed to speak back. We were never allowed to argue with one another, birthdays we had to send each other a card, and always kiss goodnight and God bless, and we still do to this day. Our boys, Gordon, Robert, Ernest and them, they'll come in that British Legion Club, before they go out they'll walk over and kiss the three of us goodnight. Always."

In one respect Wigton is fortunate because there has been Redmayne's, the Cumberland Tailor, in the town all the century. There are shops in most of the towns in Cumberland; the speciality, not surprisingly, is Cumbrian tweed, farmers' hard-wearing clothes, and hunting gear; the factory is in Wigton; and the workers are today, chiefly, women, as they have been since the First World War.

Edna Stamper, the same generation as my own mother and as Mary Reeves, worked there. I went to talk to her in her house in what remains of Church Street – a few houses from one side of a street which used to run like a dog's hind leg through the middle of the old town, higgledy-piggledy full of courtyards and dark alleyways, mere slits in walls which led to pub yards or back onto the High Street, warehouses, auction pens, the graveyard; for children an adventure playground: now a very fine car-park. It's thoroughly appropriate that Edna Stamper should end up here because she is unashamedly sentimental about the town, its past, her childhood, her friends, its life – all from the point of view of an ordinary young girl who has always above all loved fun, "a bit of frisk", enjoying herself.

She is among the most entertaining people I've met. In the street where she hobbles with difficulty now because of her bad legs, or, at night, in one of the pubs where she holds forth, winkles out gossip or gives up some of her treasure of gags, limericks, reminiscences, jokes or rhymes – she's good company, the best.

Illness has drawn her face rather tightly: it is anyway the face of someone seemingly born to encourage others to laugh along with her. Droll. Her hair is sandy and fine, her eyes deep socketed and, despite the laughter and the jokes, seeming to be observing as much as amused. Her accent is broad; like town celebrities the world over, she would find it hard to travel because people would not understand.

I've unravelled some of the dialect spellings here to make it readable. But the sense, the darting style and the spirit above all, belong to her. She began by recollecting her employer "the *old* Mr. Redmayne".

"Sarah Routledge, she worked in Redmayne's till she was sixty-five. She got her pension there you know. And every year Mr. William Redmayne used to fetch her one of these cream cakes with 'Sarah' written on it and she used to gather pennies for what she called Black Babbies every Friday, 'cos he was a missionary, you know, Mr. William Redmayne. He was always on the go, he was always going abroad, he was very interested in the natives over in Africa, he used to fetch these lantern slides back; and he used to give us these slides down the bottom in old lonning there, where the Theatre Club is now. Used to be the Salvation Mission.

I've had many a bit of frisk in theer! Aye, I always remember going in theer to have a supper. Aye, it was candlelit and it was pie and peas. You were gaan round with a candle lit trying to find peas. Used to be threepence to get in. Them days'll nivver come back though. And then we used to have games like 'keep a bobbin like a dainty little robin'. You used to sing

Keep a bobbin, keep a bobbin,
Keep a bobbin bobbin all the time,
Keep a bobbin bobbin like a dainty little robin
Keep a bobbin bobbin all the time.

Then you see when you stopped at somebody they had to get to the front and the other went to the back. Till we were all in a great round ring. So we used to have some fun. I missed the old Salvation Mission when it finished in there, because after that it finished altogether.

My grandmother worked in Redmayne's, all her life till she was sixty-five. And my mother. She worked there. My daughter worked there and I did. We all worked there. It was easier as it got to like me daughter's stage. But when I was there I started five shillings a week and me mother used to give me sixpence but mind you you could buy a lot for sixpence in them days. You got a tuppenny packet of Woodbines, fish and chips, you got them for threepence, then you just went for haporths of sweets and they never weighed them. You used to get great big handfuls in bags. I would like them days to come back.

And Highmoor Mansion was on the go then. It was beautiful.

When I left school I went to be a hairdresser for a week where the old post office used to be. Well, on top of there there was this woman, they called her Mary King, and she had set up this hairdressing business. So I got a start with her. I was there a week then me mother found out there was no wages, you had to pay *her*, so she took me away and put me in Redmayne's. See, in them days they couldn't afford to let you do that. So she took us away and I always regretted it because I would have loved to have been a hairdresser. But you got no money for six months. And you had to pay so much to do it as well. So it was no good to me mother that. But I only got five shillings when I went in Redmayne's, when I first started, and when I left at twenty I had twenty-eight and six. I was just due for a rise. I think it was thirty shillings the next rise.

They were all in Redmayne's round about me. May Middleton and them all. So through that I went with them and I was quite happy to go with them. It was hard work but I never bothered. I used to go in and I used to get into a queer state. I used to get mired [confused] now and again. They put me on the press. I was always in amongst like Mount Everest. They used to fire [throw] them at me here and fire them at me theer – a great big heap. You couldn't see me for trousers to press. And there was these heaps of trousers for the Garlands [then the local hospital for the mentally ill]. They used to make them all for them. And then there was heaps of flannels, sportswear, then there was the suits continually coming in; everything kept coming in, and there was only me doing it. At the press. Well, it was impossible. It's not like that today you know. They've three or four on the same job now. And they put me where they could nivver find me – 'cos I was buried. I always remember our boss, Moseley, he used to call me Dean Swift. And do you know I used to answer till [to] it till I found out what it was. Do you know? Dean Swift? It was a horse that was last in a race.

We used to have some laughs in there. I always remember just below us there was pipes underneath. Well, with the continual steam coming through it used to rot the wood and I was pressing away this day and I used to get the job of shutting the windows – well, you had to push them up, so I'm here pushing them up and, I don't know what I did but it went with a bang and the glass fell down into the bottom into the yard. Well, I was in such a state 'cos I knew what Moseley was like with me. Well I went home in such a state 'cos the buzzer blew just then. So me mother says, Well, you'll have to go back. It's no good worrying yourself about that. She says, you'll definitely have to go back. So I went in, and I was in such a state and I was here pressing away, flate [frightened] of him coming down, you know. Do you know how he shouts – he shouts Dean Swift. Well, I come down in such a rush, this thing underneath, it gave way and I fell down into the engine-room. I disappeared altogether. He says One minute she's there, next minute she gone. I tell you, I used to have some fun in there. I would give myself a bit of a jerk, but I landed easy. Then there was another time when I was down below I got in the lift and got stuck and they couldn't get me out of the lift. I was stuck in the lift.

And these things used to come in, you know; these clothes. Vicar's clothes and all sorts. We used to have sec [such] a laugh. I used to say, see where he is? [Moseley.] He's down in bottom end there. Quick . . . I used to put them on. He's here . . . and I couldn't get them off. He catched me two or three times, wid them half on and half off. Mind, old Moseley was strict with me. He was nivver off me back. He was always on top on us. But I was that type, I was that thick I nivver noticed. Often when we used to go till the toilet, I used to go to the toilet for a puff, and there used to be a crack in t' wall. So I'm here sitting in the toilet and I used to shout, Who's that? It's Mary. Look through the crack and see if he's theer. Yes. Oh, I can't go out yet then. Who's that? It's Jinny. Look through t' crack and see if he's still theer. Aye. Well you know, many a time I was theer half an hour. I daren't come out. And he used to say, I will put your bed in there. I will. I'll put your bed in it. And Sarah Annie Galloway, she used to make you laugh. Well, she was very religious. She wouldn't tell a lie. So he used to come down and say, Where is she now? Nobody would say. They wouldn't split on me. So he used to always go to Sarah Annie and Sarah Annie couldn't tell a lie. She used to say, Toilet, Mr. Moseley. Is she in there again? Go and fetch her out.

And sure as shot if anything come down with a red ticket on that was urgent I burnt it. Sure as shot. Owt urgent. I did summat wrong wid it."

I talked to Joseph Johnston, the baker, beside his oven, built eighty-five years ago with twelve cartloads of sand on top of it to keep the heat in, still cooking hams, baking bread and cakes and teacakes as it did in his father's time and his grandfather's. And the same recipes are used. For teacakes "Just flour, lard and salt. No compounds or fat. And yeast."

We talked about food and the price of food between the wars.

"In those days, of course, my father was a game-dealer as well. Maybe on a Tuesday, when he was busy in the shop, he would say, Go and skin rabbits maybe what he sold over the counter. Of course they had to bring them up here and do them on this. About ninepence each them days. That was a big price for a rabbit. We used to get maybe a penny for the skin off Charlie Murray the barber. He used to buy rabbit-skins, lead, pewter, he had a warehouse. I think it would be maybe where that hairdresser's shop is extended on to him now, and he used to hang them up for the full season, rabbit-skins, hare-skins, and dry them till the spring. All these old poachers such as John Hogg and these fellows travelled the country, well they would maybe get a rabbit-skin off a farmer's wife and that was a meal to them when they come back to Wigton. Well they used to go to Charlie Murray's with the skin. Well he would maybe give them a penny if it wasn't a torn one, maybe a penny halfpenny because of sympathy, and Charlie used to send them to London I believe when he got a consignment.

My father also took farm sales on then and that was on account of so many farm sales – was that farmers were going bankrupt. The farm itself wasn't being sold, they were more or less tenant farmers, but going bust, and he had these sales on. Well the Auction Company used to ask him to go and make the teas for them in the barn, and maybe if it was not as big a sale as he anticipated or a wet day, there was food left. Well in those days Water Street was a big housing estate as you would call it today, and word used to come round, Johnston's have stuff left from the sale, and they used to send their kids for a pennorth or whatever was going and they used to fetch a bag and he used to fill them up for a penny or two pennies or whatever. They were that hard up. That was the pattern every Tuesday night. There was families used to come after the Auction for bits off the tables, pennyworth or twopennyworth or whatever was going. What was left from the farmers, bread and butter, or whatever was cut up. They used to come and send their kids. It was really a hard life. There was an old fellow used to come, I don't know whether you've heard of him, Tin Whistle Billie. Well, he was a bit simple maybe, but he wasn't that simple with money, and he used to – I've been out all day Missus, I've only threepence or whatever it was, for trying his tin whistle at farmhouse doors, and he used to come at night. Maybe buy a candle and half a pound of sugar. Maybe spent tuppence or something like that, and taking it over a week, he could live for about ninepence with our shop.

The price of food. Well, when this oven was – I can remember, used to go down to the gas-works for coke. It was Wigton Gas Company in them days and they used to send a horse and cart full up with side-boards on, maybe three-tier side-boards, full of coke for twelve shillings. Well now it's about one pound twenty for a cwt.

And a cart that size would maybe hold fifteen to sixteen cwts., and that's the difference. Hams as well in them days. They used to come from Kirkbride, ham. Maybe weight a forty-pound weight ham. Well today that ham would be sixty pence a pound instead of five-pence. But business was good because you see we were a penny for a teacake then, and threepence for a white loaf, like a two and a half pound loaf. Well people lived on plain food then, bread and teacakes. There wasn't so much cake wanted, people hadn't the money, and I find even today when money gets tighter you sell more teacakes. It's a better meal for them and cheaper, a teacake with a bit jam in even today than buying meat and things, and it fills them up better. So whenever times are bad, we more or less prosper. And as times get good, they go off this way of eating and living. Even now, I don't know whether it's just this district, but money's tighter and they seem to be drifting back that way.

On Market Days we put on a Meat Tea: it was a plate of ham, or ham and tongue or beef, mixed up, or anyway you wanted it, and bread and teacakes buttered and cake, and you could eat as much as you wanted for one and six. Or if you want to call it a plain tea, it was a shilling and that was the same. And that's how it is today. But really it's just thirty-five pence today for a meat tea. Well, the customers I should say are the same customers or customers' sons as what were then. Farmers come in, used to come here when I was a boy. Maybe seventy or seventy-five. And some say, it's eighty years since I was in here. An old chap from Caldbeck. Old Mr. James. Well I should think he'll have come for eighty years.

Market Day was a big day. Tuesday morning, you start counting eggs. Farmers' wives used to bring their baskets of eggs in and my father, with being a game-dealer, of course bought these eggs and butter for baking with, and all the eggs were to count off the farmers' wives, from their baskets into our baskets, and then the butter was the same of course and put onto slates in those days. Big blue slates to keep cool. There wasn't fridges and things. Well, there wasn't electricity then in Wigton. And then game used to come in. Well it was all to handle and take away from the shop to the warehouse. And then the rabbits would be to skin, people wanting rabbits, hares, maybe partridge or a pheasant to pluck which was very rare because they were too expensive for local people. And then as the day went on there was rabbits and things to take to the station. Then we had to go to about three different markets. Workington was a big rabbit town, Leeds and Bradford, and the game, it went to London. And it had to be in London by four o'clock in the morning to catch the market there, and of course that was my day. But the town was more or less full of horses and traps, cars, farmers' wives doing their shopping, selling, getting whatever they wanted. It was more or less like Woolworth's is on a Saturday, Wigton would be. People stirring around, pushing to buy things.

We used to start in the tea rooms maybe ten o'clock in the morning, the customers would be coming, whereas now you're lucky if you get them at half past eleven. And then it carried on until maybe seven o'clock at night on a Tuesday. Well they used to sell sheep, I've been in auction at half past eight at night, when they were selling sheep for five shillings each. They breed these things different now. They don't have them all ready at the same time which they used to glut the market, and that was it. You see in them days we had to put eggs down with waterglass when it was a glut in the spring – Eastertime, for the winter to bake with. Ninepence a dozen in those days. And you used to put them in these big bowls and pour water-glass over them. It's like a lime, and that kept the eggs all winter. Well you see nowadays we haven't got all these jobs. Same with butter – it was put down in these pats of salted and it was scarce in winter. And like work's easier today and yet it's harder. It's changed in so many ways. For example, I should say I worked more hours than my father worked because he had less auctions to cater for and he didn't make as much variety of stuff for to sell in his shop. And he had a much easier life than what I have. You see with the costs of labour I can't employ people like he used to do for a start. You see, he used to have a woman come, and I think she got four and six for a day. Well that day was eight in the morning till maybe eight at night and that was four and six. Well, it's just not on today."

The theme of these years is, overwhelmingly, first finding work and then keeping it. But the possibilities of confounding expectation must not be overlooked. Mary Reeves, for example, whose father had a disability pension and six children all at school at the same time, managed, in the ravine of the grim and hungry Thirties, to go to tap-dancing lessons.

"I went to Rita Irving's. She was from Carlisle. It was a shilling a week. In the Parish Rooms. And she would only be about seventeen herself when she took us as girls. And I'd be about seven year old. And she used to come every Friday night and we used to live for these dancing classes. As I say, Mother would make that shilling for me wherever she got it. She'd sit down on that machine. Oh and it was sec a lot of money. And I always remember saying, oh these tap-dancing classes are starting. And Ginger Rogers and Fred Astaire were on when you went to the pictures on a Saturday afternoon and oh they were marvellous, and I wanted to be able to dance. Ay, if you want to gan lass you'll ga. And then she would put on these shows and you had to provide your own costume. And it would be packed, and Mother would get this material and make frocks and that. Rita Irving used to say, You would think you were the one with the money, Lizzie. 'Cos if I said put two yards in Mary's you would double it. Things was great. I know we're better off these days. Now I went to tap-dancing classes from I was about seven years old and I, this was after I'd left school because she had stopped coming to Wigton then – we used to have to go to Carlisle – so Mam says, I don't mind you going, I'll pay your bus fare, I'll buy your materials and I'll pay for your classes but, she says, no sneaking off to the pictures in Carlisle.

Well, there was going to be a pantomime. It was *Babes in the Wood* at Her Majesty's Theatre. Mother had got all the materials for my costume, everything. But I went to the pictures with Betty Barton and she wouldn't let me go. Well by that time I was about sixteen. Well I'd lost interest really, because I'd started going to ballroom dancing and that was the finish of me tap dancing. And do you know I still have a pair of me tap shoes till this day? You started off with black patent-leather ankle-belts, and then you got red tap shoes. I remember one Christmas, I would only be about nine, praying to God, Please God let Father Christmas bring me some red tap shoes. And lo and behold Christmas morning here was me red tap shoes. I went to bed in them that night. And me mother let me."

In September 1931 Mary Charters started work at Redmayne's, the clothing factory, for eleven and fourpence halfpenny a week, five days a week, eight to five thirty with an hour off for lunch. "Machinist. Eyes down and away with it." "Very fortunate to get a job in the town." "Making men's clothes. Jodhpurs and things. Gentleman farmers' stuff."

As the Thirties went on, things improved for the working classes; not enough and not fast enough, it might well be said, but there were improvements and one of the ways this showed was in the way people pulled themselves up through work.

Norman is Henry Fell's younger brother. Henry, who followed his uncle at the start of this chapter, is tall, Norman stocky, Henry deliberate, Norman more expressive; Henry private, Norman a man who has taken up union work, council work and all manner of causes. But both have clear memories of the mid-wars period, both remember the one room up and one down in New Street which housed them when their father returned with three Military Medals and went off again to make money felling trees or on the dole. Like Henry, Norman was expected to pass the scholarship which, when he was eleven, would have taken him to the Grammar School and, so the expectation and the tradition went, away from manual labour, away from casual labour, away altogether from the world of work which was the world their parents and relatives lived in. Like his brother he failed the examination – indeed, even because of his brother; and then began the long haul to a job in which he could respect himself and use his skills and talents, the road to some sort of reward, satisfaction and dignity.

"We were sitting for the exam and I went in the morning, and there was a teacher Mabel Briggs. She was a wonderful teacher and I were in her class. And she said, prior to starting the exams, she said, Now you must concentrate because I think you've a good chance of going to the Grammar School. So we had the first part of the exams in the morning and oh I tried hard, and I felt I was doing exceptionally well. Until I went home, dinnertime. And my elder brother said, Under no circumstances must you pass for a scholarship because, he says, if you do, we'll never be able to clothe you to go to that school. And when I went back in the afternoon I just didn't try . . . And that is the position. When Mabel Briggs, the school mistress, said, What have you been doing this afternoon? When the exam results were known she said that she knew there was something wrong, and the wrong part about it were that I didn't try at all, because I knew the fact was that I wouldn't be able to go – I couldn't dress to go to that school.

I regretted very much that I didn't get the scholarship, because I always felt that I were of a standard that would – I could – at least have benefited by a further education – when I was nearly fourteen, George Scott he came, he said, Got a job to go to, Norman? I said, No. There was a vacancy that occurred at the solicitors at Wigton, Rigg & Strong's, and Mr. Arthur Moffatt worked there, and he approached Mr. Scott, the headmaster, to see if he had a good lad who were fit to go into the solicitors' office. Now I had not attained the age of fourteen; I were about three months off the age limit at the time, and you can only leave school at certain periods, and it was even so then. And George Scott said, Well, Norman Fell's going to be leaving school soon, in fact, he says, if we can get him off school, he's the man for you. Those were the very words that George Scott said, and Arthur Moffatt said, Well, if we can get him off, released, then we'll give Norman a start. But I couldn't get released from school, to take this job, and John Larkin, who was three months older than I, was fortunate enough to be able to leave the school, and he got the job. Well, after that, George Scott kept saying to me, Now then, you're not to go to any type of a job. You'll wait until I find you a job. Now the next job he tried to find for me were in Redmayne's. And he were unsuccessful owing to the difficulty at the time of finding work (this is 1934). And he said, Well, you're not leaving school. And I stayed on at school for a few months. But there was no jobs available, and I got fed up doing nothing, so I went round the town myself, and I was fortunate enough to go to Aird's. The plumbers. I don't know whether it was fortunate or unfortunate really, but this is the way it went. I went to Aird's and asked them if they wanted an apprentice plumber. And they said, Come in. And we talked away, and they said, Yes, they said, we could do with a good lad. And I left school against the headmaster's advice because I wanted to earn some money to help my mother at home financially. Well, my first pay at Aird's was five shillings a week. Now out of that five shillings a week I used to get sixpence pocket money. And that to me was a lot of money, in them days. And five shillings was a lot to my mother. So I automatically couldn't do much with sixpence. You couldn't get in the pictures at the time unless you had eightpence. So I used to save it up until I bought a blow-lamp which cost eleven and six. It was a Swedish blow-lamp – I can always remember the name – in fact I've got it – I treasure it, I've still got it – and then I used to get little bits of scraps of solder, and I used to pray for a hard winter so that I could start mending burst pipes. Now this is – if I never move off this seat – I used to mend burst pipes and they would say, How much now, man? And I would say Two shillings. Well, two shillings was four weeks' pocket money, and I've seen us mend maybe as many as twenty or thirty burst pipes in a winter – sometimes more – sometimes fifty. And I worked away for three years at Aird's, at five shillings a week.

I'll give you an instance of one job – we had a police house to do at Caldbeck (seven miles away: in the hills), the plumbing. And Mr.

Aird says, Have you got a bike? I said, No, I've no bike. He says, Well, you'll have to have a bike. I said Why? He says, Well, we've got a job at Caldbeck and, he says, you'll have to get there. And I said, Well, what can I do about a bike? He said, Well, he says, you can hire one at Harry Moore's garage. And I used to hire a bike, and it cost me a penny a day to hire a bike, so that I could bike to Caldbeck to do – to help to do the plumbing on the police house. At Caldbeck. Now that is one example of where my pocket money went. Sixpence – six days, sixpence. To hire a bike to get to work. My mother still got four and a tanner, and I gave Harry Moore my tanner pocket money. Well, the burst pipes, that was what kept me going. I used to pray for a hard winter.

Six days a week, we started at eight o'clock in the morning to five o'clock at night. Now we were supposed to be on the job at eight o'clock. And we would finish at five, and it was a good run back from Caldbeck, back on a bike. And a hard push there. And then Jimmy Aird who I worked with, as a son of the family, he had a motor-bike. And a sidecar; he came along and he said, We'll use the motor bike and sidecar in the end. So that eased the problem. But at the start of the job we had to bike. We had to bike to Caldbeck, we'd bike to any job that was round about two to three miles here or anywhere. There was no talk of transport – you had to find your own, you had to get there.

Now I had five bob a week, and I was frustrated because we were only doing repairs, and the only new house we ever worked on was the police house at Caldbeck, and Brackenlands estate was on at the time, and I was ambitious – I wanted to be a plumber; if I was going to be a plumber, I wanted to be a good plumber. I wanted to know what new house-plumbing were going to be like, and everything; and I wasn't getting anywhere. And I said to Aird's, if there's any chance of us, I said, Brackenlands houses, I said, Mr. Reay's doing them, I said. How are we going to get any plumbing work – like, real plumbing work? And he says, Oh, he says, we just get the jobs when they come. Well, they got the gas-main, I helped with laying the new gas-main from I think about the church here, right up to Brackenlands. To Brackenlands and Brindlefield estate. I worked on that gas main, with Vince Edmondson, and that were a bit of good pipe-work – we were starting to do pipe-work. Well then, I'd had five bob a week for three years; we had to put stamps on at that time, and I think the stamps cost one and ten – I became of an age when I had to put one and tenpence worth of stamps on, a week. And that meant that five bob was going to be knocked to pieces.

So I went in and asked for a rise. And Mr. Aird, old Johnny, the old Aird, I don't know what his first name were – he says, A rise? He says, Who do you think you are? he says. When I was an apprentice, he says, *I* used to have to *pay*. We used to have to pay to serve our time, he says, you ought to think yourself highly honoured that you work here and getting paid, he says, to be a plumber. You should have been paying us. Well, I said, I'll have to have something more, I said. There's going to be one and ten for stamps and, I said, I'm only getting five shilling a week. And he gave us a two-shilling rise. Now that was the time when I had to start putting stamps on, now then, that were when I were sixteen, I think. I think it were sixteen. So I'd five and tuppence a week and my stamps of course. Well, we put up with it for a bit longer and then after the third year I again asked for a rise, my mother couldn't manage; things were getting desperate with helping Henry at Carlisle in the Post Office and that. And I had to again ask for a rise and he says, Oh no. I couldn't give you a rise. You should be paying us. That's all we could get out of them, You should be paying us. (Mid-1930s.)

And one of the workmen, rather than have me leave, was going to be willing to give me a two-shilling rise out of his own pocket. That was Jimmy Aird, offered to give me two shillings; I couldn't agree with it at all. And Mr. Reay was building the houses at Brackenlands – he was doing the plumbing. And I went up one dinner time to see Mr. Reay and I explained that I was an apprentice plumber. I'd worked for Aird's for three years, but I wasn't getting anywhere at all as regards new house-plumbing, and I wanted to advance myself in the new ways of plumbing. Copper pipe had just come out at that time, and everybody called Willy Reay a jerry plumber, because he was using copper pipe. Now then, I mentioned to Mr. Reay about a start, any chance, and he said, Aye, when can tha start? I said, I can start on Monday. So I went back to Aird's and I told them that I'd be finishing, and I'd give them a notice that I was leaving, a week on Monday. I think I arranged with Reay that it would be on the notice from Aird's – I said, I'm leaving, and I didn't tell them where I were going to, but I said, I'm leaving; because I couldn't afford to stay, at the wage. I said, If you'll give us extra money I'll willingly stay – because I liked Jimmy Aird – he was a good man to work with, and Vince Edmondson – they were two good craftsmen and I enjoyed working with them. And I had a little bit of feeling that perhaps this copper *was* jerry plumbing. And I felt, now then, I don't want to be a jerry plumber.

Anyway, as I couldn't get a rise, so I went to see Mr. Reay, and

I started work with him, I think – I could find the date – for Mr. Reay. And I worked away, copper pipe, and learnt to use copper pipe, and we started doing private houses on West Road; John Black's bungalow was the first one, and Bob Pattison's – there was Bob Pattison built four houses. They were for the – I'll try and think of the tenants – there were Tom Bell, Lenny Bell, George Rumney, Josh Ferguson – them were the four tenants. Now Reay were doing the plumbing there, as well, so that was where I started getting into copper pipe plumbing – on private houses.

Well the first week I received my pay off Mr. Reay; it was in a packet – I felt the packet and I could feel two coins – two half-crowns I took them for – and felt, Oh, this is grand, same money anyways and I'm quite happy. Stamps was on and I took my pay packet home and I said, Here, Mother, there's my pay off Mr. Reay. And I gave her the pay packet, and she opened it; she said, There's – oh, she said, Mr. Reay's made a mistake! I said, What do you mean he's made a mistake? She says, There's one pound, and a ten-shilling note and five shillings – thirty-five shillings – he must have given you the wrong packet. So I went back to Mr. Reay and told him, My mother thinks you've made a mistake with my pay, as I was only getting five and two at Aird's. And he said, Well, Norman, that's your wage. You get thirty-five shillings a week. Did you take that packet home unopened? I said, Yes, I did. I said, and I gave it to my mother. He said, Well, that's a good lad, he said, here. And he gave us two half-crowns and says, That's for theself, and don't give that to tha mother. And he says, Tha'll never take hurt as long as tha gives tha mother money like that, he said, you'll never go wrong if you look after your mother. And every time after that if I got a rise off Mr. Reay I always got the five shillings on top, for myself. That was the difference of what jerry plumbing and the old-fashioned plumbers that I worked for in the first place.

Well, thirty-five shillings a week, well, we were moving to the stage, well, we're getting somewhere now. My mother could look people in the eyes. We started – you know our house – we bought a three-piece suite and started to get a bit of four by three carpet. And – things that we'd never seen before – into the house. And my wage – I had a better wage than my brother Henry had, who was working on the Post Office in Carlisle, and I was still just an apprentice plumber. Well, I worked on and on with Mr. Reay, and the times were hard – very hard. And it got to the stage where Mr. Reay was thinking of paying people off. He even mentioned to me that he was going to pay his own brother off and keep me on. And I turned round to him and I said, Mr. Reay, I said, I would rather do anything than you do that. I said, After all, Jack's your brother. I said, I feel that I've reached the stage now when I feel I should go to a bigger firm to complete my knowledge of plumbing before I finished my apprenticeship – because it were a broken apprenticeship in any case.

And I applied for a job at David Thompson's at Carlisle, and I was successful enough in getting a job. And I told Mr. Reay I was leaving. And I was starting with Thompson's of Carlisle. Well, I went to Thompson's of Carlisle, and I got the Union rate there, I think it was one shilling and five pence an hour, and I were really a qualified plumber. I started as a qualified plumber at one and five an hour and I went to work on Hadrian's Camp because at the time there was a threat of war and Hadrian's Camp was just started to be built. And I started to work there – I went to see the foreman plumber there, a Mr. Walker, and he started me on the job, and we started working on the spiders. They called them spiders – these were the buildings on Hadrian's Camp. Now then, at about that time, or somewhere near that time, we moved from round Hospital Cottages to Western Bank, which was a council house. It was one of these houses that were built for the soldiers returning from the 1914–1918 War, of which my dad was one, but in them days those who came back, they couldn't afford the rent, so they were rented to – Dr. Gordon's wife, the tenant previous to us, her husband died – well, in fact I think you know what happened to him, don't you? Well, I think he committed suicide. And his wife went to live in a council house. Anyway I wouldn't like to say I'm sure of that. But I think that is the point. Anyways, to get down to brass tacks, we went to live in this house; it was a three-bedroomed house, living-room, kitchen, back kitchen, and everything was lovely. Henry was working, I were working, and my brother Jack – my brother Jack had started as a telegram boy in Wigton for the Post Office, so he was working too. And my dad was working, that was four. Money was coming in, and we did feel well – we are getting somewhere. And I felt that it would have been better if the money had been there when we were young, instead of having it all at the wrong end."

A small point: ninety-five percent of those I spoke to instantly mentioned the same place when I asked them where they had gone on holidays: Silloth, a seaside town twelve miles off, with lovely greens

157

and a good beach on the Solway Firth. A day trip to Silloth, it was the universal treat.

At the end of the Thirties, Water Street moved south of the town to Brindlefield. To land once owned by the owners of Highmoor House then, at the end of the Thirties, falling on hard times, the deer park down for grazing, the mansion knocked into flats, the bells removed. Mary Charters was eleven or twelve at the time of the move.

"We thought we were well off, because we had gone into this house with three bedrooms and a bathroom. And all we did was answer the front door. We thought it was great. If somebody knocked at the door we thought it was smashing. And do you know, the funny thing, before these houses were completed we used to go and play in them. There was Jean Coates and I, and I used to say, this is our house and this is yours. And lo and behold we got No. 12 and they got No. 13. We thought it was a palace.

All Water Street lot were together. There was Sarah Jane Wilson, well Sarah Jane had about No. 11. This house she got was built specially for her, 'cos it had five bedrooms and there was two above Mam's house, it was supposed to be that when they grew up and were married, Mam was supposed to get these bedrooms but she never got them because Sarah Jane's family never left. But it was all one happy family. The lot moved. Queenie Fisher, Queenie Studholme, Sarah Jane Wilson, Annette O'Hare, Asbridges. Alice Chicken and all them lot. They all moved. It was nearly all the same clique together. Maggie Carson, who used to have the sweet shop down Vinegar Hill. They all moved up together, and Sarah Jane would come in, Has t' a penny for t' gas, Lizzie? I'll see if there's yen on t' sideboard. And she would just lift it. And away wid it. Everybody helped one another then.

But there wasn't the atmosphere that there was in Water Street. We thought it was great, because at that age we thought it was smashing having a bathroom, but there wasn't the family unity and that that there was in Water Street. Everything seemed to drop off – as far as I was concerned. Of course, we hadn't the haunts to go to. Church Street. The middle of the town. We missed Water Street terribly."

As often, memories of hardship and memories of happiness are hard to disentangle. But the move up the hill marked the beginning of the end for the old Victorian and pre-Victorian clay daubings and little snuggled huddled cottages in courtyards, back alleys and narrow streets in the heart of the town. It was almost like the beginning of a migration, this journey to the edge of the old community, and the journey would be taken up again after yet another war.

CHAPTER SIX
Joe Bill Lightfoot

Familiarity, especially in a book such as this which intends to be of use to students and scholars as well as being of general interest, is rather distasteful but "Joe Bill" it has to be: he would be called nothing else and yet the easy-going implication of the name is not by any means true. Joe Bill Lightfoot has had a difficult, strenuous, at times even a bitter life and he talks about it urgently.

Yet here is part of the trouble for those of us who do books like this: if only they could be issued as L.P.s or in cassette form (though no one, at the moment, could begin to afford to do it so), because it is the sound of the voice which is so important, the emphases, the intonation, all the possibilities of complexity which are proscribed to the writer here because to describe the voice would have to lead to a description of the character, background and thoughts of the man: to do that would be to lay claim to knowledge which no one could have unless he did a full-length study. Even then, fiction would be better.

So one states a few, the barest, facts. Mr. Lightfoot is proud of the fact that, though a pensioner, he carries not an ounce of spare fat. He is a regular though not a particularly heavy drinker. He walks a little like a cowboy, one of those old-timers in a John Ford Western. Though he speaks vividly, the words, when typed, have a slightly unfamiliar look in their arrangement. And yet to include only those whose sentences ran emolliently through the typewriter would be to deny much of what exists in this country. Hazlitt observed that the finest educated minds could be toppled by men of no formal education in a battle of pub wits. While not describing Mr. Lightfoot as a wit, I would say that the tenacity with which he makes his point is representative of many of those who have to live on by words alone. He speaks a fairly broad Cumbrian.

We talked in the front room of his council house, which was built after the Second World War at the western end of the town. Photographs of the family, all about. Two children, both doing very well; grandchildren; good furniture: spotless. The gardens, front and back, were like show-pieces.

Mr. Lightfoot had thought that I was "only joking" when I asked to interview him and was surprised and puzzled that I actually turned up. His wife, who looks as young in her way as he does in his, brought us some tea, he sat on the very edge of a deep armchair, as close as possible to where I was sitting, and, without any hesitation, began.

"I was born in 1908 at a little place called Bolton Low Houses (two miles from Wigton) and was brought up in a very poor family and there was five of us, three boys and two girls. So it went on, we got older and older and we had nothing to eat hardly, and I think everybody was alike, old Ginger Blackburn, all the Parkers, all the Tolsons and that, and so my mother had to go out to all these confinements, she was what they call a midwife. So I think everyone like in this generation, like you know the younger generation I'm talking about, in Bolton, I think they were all brought into the world by my mother. She had no training whatever, but it was always Bella, I'll have to send for Bella. Bella was there with the white apron on. And there was the Carruthers, and an awful big family of Temples, all the big family of Jimmy Ward's, all the Blackburns, all the lot. Well all of them were brought into the world by my mother.

And then my father, of course he was a big gardener and he was a big friend of Johnny Wren's, a fruiterer, where Henry Sharp is now. Well he used to do gardening and between them they used to show and I don't think they were ever bet or beat with beetroot, potatoes, everything you mentioned they showed up at Blennerhasset, Aspatria, Cockermouth, Wigton, Thursby, every place. At all the agricultural shows, at all the flower shows; flowers and vegetables.

So like the first place he judged was Cockermouth and then he got on up to a place called Ecclesfield. He was judging every week. So it was all through that – he never drank, he never smoked, I never heard him swear, he never gambled, but his own downfalling, of course he was a good father, but the only downfalling, and I blame for our poverty, only why we couldn't get nothing to eat, was just through him showing. But of course again it was his hobby, but the money, if you reckon up, all the eighteen shillings a week, I've seen my mother crying many a time. You just couldn't live on eighteen shillings a week. So of course again he was maybe taking five or seven shillings of that for to get up to a show. Of course the trains were cheap up to Aspatria and Baggrow and then there was his money for entry. Well as I say that was maybe six or seven shillings. But you couldn't live. That's why we got nowt to eat. So the only thing we had to do was to go down to Bolton beck, grapple a few trout and I've even eaten cock liggies. I don't know whether you know what a cock liggie is. Well I've eaten them. And while we were out fishing, that was down in Kerrs bottom at Bolton at the bridge, there was what we called yow yarlings, a sort of flower with a white scabby flower. Well we had the big fork and stick for sticking trout as well. We used to dig into the ground and howk these yow yarlings up and they were as big as your nail. Only a bulb at the end. Well we used to take the peeling off them and I'll tell you what they were like to eat. They were just like a ground nut. The taste I mean. We'd eat away at them and that's all we got, half past eight, nine o'clock in the morning till the beck and maybe not come back till about eight o'clock at night, and that's what we lived on. We fed ourselves. On yow yarlings, maybe cleaned the fish, and pinch a little bit of butter or a bit of lard or whatever there was.

Old Joe Mallinson used to be in the shop at the time. Old Joseph Mallinson. A little bit of lard or get a bit of rind of your ham or his bacon, put it in a paper, then get an old tin lid. If we caught any fish, get some tin to make a little fire, put the bacon scraps or whatever there was into your old tin lid, then put the fish in, and that's what we got.

I went down the pit when I was fourteen. I left school on the Friday night; I went down the pit on the Monday with my father in the cage. Scared to death. But I wasn't so bad when I got down because it was all arched, all electric light. I thought it was lovely. Beautiful. But then when I got into the low, maybe four and a half feet high, had me back down, had my old lamp on, an old cord round my neck, and short pants on, no shirt – what they call a dickie, that's a vest, and all black dark and that. Well I went to work with my father. Hadn't been down – I was pushing a tub, I had my old lamp on here, pushing away, lost me light. I was all in darkness. In them days, there was no electric light, it was one of those old-fashioned lamps, and I'll tell you where you'll see them, of course like you used to see them, all hanging up in the Black-a-Moor Pub. I don't know what the light was made of. But of course like if it went out, and then there was batteries down the pit, so you put a steel on here and you put your lamp and you just rubbed it and then you got your light again. But I was never as frightened in all my life.

I was what they call a trailer. And so a trailer, of course it's a bloke that pushes tubs, up the coal-face, of course they fill them and then when that tub's full, it runs on wheels, and then I take it maybe a hundred and fifty yards up to a big siding and then I bring an empty back, and that's the way it goes.

Always hungry. I got very embarrassed sometimes, but it happened all the way through the line. A person or a child, of course I'll take the child, what I mean to say, up to he was fifteen, up till he was sixteen even, he didn't know what a pair of shoes was. All clogs. Off Willie Park. I think they cost seven and sixpence. Well I never had a new suit – when I was a boy, up till I started at the pit at fourteen years of age. The only thing I got, the only thing I had, a jersey and what they call, a sort of one of those hard collars with a stud in. I don't know whether you've seen them studs, have you. And of course you can twist the end bit anywhere for to get in the hole. Well of course they were called celluloid collars and of course you could wash them. And the only pants I had was a pair cut down, either from my father's or from a pair she had got given off somebody, and a handkerchief. You just didn't know what handkerchiefs were. Bit of old shirt tail to put in your pocket. And if you sort of lost that well it was this – finger and thumb. Well at about fifteen and a half I got my first long pants. At Redmayne's. First long pants of blue serge and a pair of tawny red shoes. Well like you know how I felt. Shirt and a collar.

The place we lived in up New Street. Well of course in them days they were all sort of bungalow-type. Two rooms. There was my father and mother's room, and then the one room for all the five of us kids. Only one bed in the room and the rest on shakky downs. Just a mattress. Only a mattress just put on the ground. Of course that was for the three boys. And that acted as a bed. As far as lavatory was concerned, all dry at the bottom of the garden with a bucket in. Who used to get that job, a filthy thing? Me. Joe Muggins. And the only place you could empty that, like we had a garden maybe the length of this, maybe twenty-five yards, and the only place you could empty that bucket was to dig a hole, empty it in, and then put the bucket back again. Then we had the ash pit. Of course you would know about the ash pit. In Wigton when they come round with the cart, go round the ash pits and put the ashes in. It was a sort of hole. It protects the lavatory. So Dave Armstrong used to empty that with his horse and cart, but that's the only thing we had. And bluebottles and midges, I never saw anything like it in all my life. I've seen Water Street there, you couldn't move. It was hose-piped every Tuesday. Fetching the cattle in and doing their jobs all over the street, all the sheep and that, all coming down Water Street. Filthy. Never saw anything like it.

And as I say it was rough. As as far as meat was concerned, I know meat was cheap, but you just couldn't buy it. So therefore what we used to have, either dry bread and jam or butter and bread. If you got butter on your bread, you didn't get any jam. If you got jam on your bread, you didn't get any butter. If you fried, and very rare, a little bit of bacon or something, then when the fat was cold you put that on your bread. But Woodbines were twopence a packet. Sugar a penny halfpenny a pound. Twenty-four eggs for a shilling. Old Billy Tut used to come up to Bolton – Fresh herring, fresh herring, at the top of his voice. And they were all in barrels. Lovely herrings. Maybe twenty-four for a shilling. Well it was cheap. But meat, we never saw it. Vegetables: garden full. We never saw them. He wasn't growing for the house. He was growing for the show. Even his celery, it used to go to the show but it never come back. Same with his beetroot, it went to the show, it never come back. And it all went to the show but it never came back again. And that's why we were hungry. He sold it or gave it away. If you're taking maybe four lots of potatoes and you're taking maybe three or four lots of beetroot, in a small garden – I've seen my mother after my father went to bed at night, and then she would sneak out and take us some potatoes up. Maybe at eleven o'clock at night. But you couldn't blame her, because she was hungry as well. Everybody was hungry. My mother cried over the washing-tub and she was following the washing-tubs six days a week. Two and six a day. Up at morning. I'se crying, me mother's crying, all the others are crying, there wasn't a fire, there wasn't a bit of tea, there wasn't a bit of sugar, no nothing.

General Strike. Just used to get up. We had no soap. Just a bit of a wash. Of course they used to go off to school. They had nothing to eat. Here's these little boys taking their bait bags, but for the love of God what they had in them I don't know. I've gone into a field many a time for my breakfast, a raw turnip. I've stole potatoes out of a heap. I've dug in. I've put the fire on. Never washed them. Just put them in the fire – potatoes with their jackets on. I've seen me sit maybe two or three hours. It's what we lived on. They don't know they're born today.

In about 1926 I would be about eighteen. Eighteen. I got a job at Billy Harrison's up on the farm. I had nine pounds for the half year. But before that I worked down Allhallows Pit. I also worked up at Bolton New Houses School where there was a drift. I also worked for Tom Dand which was down the gill, but of course I wouldn't say that was a job. 1926. Yes. No soup kitchens like in Wigton. They sent it up in anything they could get hold of. Old baths, zinc baths, and they only got their ration, a basinful. Just the same at night-time. If it was winter, if it was cold, you just didn't sit up. But it's marvellous. I've taken no hurt through it all. Like I'm sixty-four in December and although through poverty and everything, I feel well, and I've always been a hard worker, that's what I say for a long life now, never mind sitting at home. Plenty of work, a little smoke and a good pint of beer at threepence. Everybody the same. Reuben Graham, like Jack Dalston – he drove the van with bread – of course, them days, Mary Jane Cowen and Mary Ann Blackburn. But they were just the same. Instead of wearing shoes, like these shoes with a clasp on, old frock and a pinny. And their hair in plaits or hanging down their back, and skirts down till here. But you see – today, there's no comparison. What, that was nivver sec a thing. There was nivver sec a thing as a tin. But for to eat out on. If there'd been tins in them days, with your meals in, then you could have lived. Because they would have been cheap, but today – no, give me today. I wouldn't like to go back.

The first schooling that I had, and as I would say with Dougie Parker and Kitty Blackburn. I was in Miss Bell's class first. Very nice person. I respected her. I can meet her on the street now and stop and talk. Lovely person. And she used to bike all the way from Wigton, rain, snow, or owt. There wasn't any snow-ploughs. And then as I got older I went into another class, old Sarah Grindley, up at Boot Farm. Then she used to teach down at Wigton. Well, I gets into that class and a flaming trick I did, I should have been strangled. There was dry lavatories. Of course there were three at the bottom of the yard. So every dinner time, after they'd had their dinners, it used to grieve me and aw, good dinners teachers had, aye, we used to watch them. After they'd had their dinner, straight till the lavatory. Well it was just a playground – no books or owt – but just a flag in the back. And a field in the back. So this day I gits a bunch of nettles and me and John Arrer we jumped over the top of the wall and we just waited. Just let's old Sarah get nicely at it. Tickled her with the nettles. What a hiding we got. Nivver no more. Pulled the stone flat out and tickled her bum with the nettles. Yes.

I'll tell you the school master at the time, Jimmy Johnston. Now his son, Norman, he had the boats – your dad will know – but old Jimmy Johnston, you talk about learning owt, I nivver learnt nothing. Well there would be maybe thirty or forty in his class. He would start a subject but he didn't stick to that subject. He got on talking about his younger days and what he did. Well it pleased us. And as far as what he was going to talk about, he never learnt us owt. And that was every day.

So this day, we were talking sums, but if he got bad-tempered, he used to come with all this bloody common slang. But as I was saying Douglas Parker, like we were doing sums on the board, so he puts them down. Like he asked us what it was. And Dougie Parker, he was a dull but, well, I was the same myself. So up goes his hand, he says, Right, come on then. So he went up to the board. So he just says, Douglas Parker, your nose grows darker and darker. Put it in the bower wow, stick it in the middy. And the cane, didn't he use it? That's what's wrong today, Melvyn. It's exactly what's wrong today. They say, Divnt use the stick. I say it isn't used often enough. We daren't talk back till him. We daren't talk about sex. We sort of couldn't mix with girls. Very bad-tempered, very bad-tempered. Discipline – my father, if he said – well, I've got a son and daughter – if he said, be in at half past seven, you had to be in. Now I was the same with my two. That's why I've never had no trouble. They're both doing well. I've never had any trouble. But I never hit them.

By my father – what! We had to go of a night down the field to gather the sitcks in for the fire. In them days, it was put them in the oven for to dry. Well I'd maybe forget, but if we forget, even if we were in bed, it was a simple thing for him just to go down the field in the dyke and get a few sticks. But no, out of bed. I got a halfpenny a week. I got a halfpenny every Saturday. He used to bring his eighteen shillings in this bait tin. On a Saturday, a halfpenny. Now I could get that halfpenny. I could go into a shop at Bolton, old Mallinson's, in them days all boiled sweets, in these big bottles. Of course I think they're the same today – I could go on the booze for halfpence man. Old Johnny Raine, I could get halfpence of ice cream as what I'm getting for my shilling today. But as I say I was roughly brought up, not by my mother mind, no, no. My mother was the opposite. She would say, I'll tell your father when he comes home from the pit, but she never did. If we did owt wrong, I'll tell your father when he comes from the pit. But she never did. Because she knew what he would have done. But as I say he was a good father, but as I said, before all his garden stuff, all his showing – that's why we got eighteen shillings, and you take six shilling from that . . . Of course like it's bad to believe. Like we know stuff was cheap. You could get a brat of stuff for ten shillings. A pinny-full I should say. But you called them brats in them days. Like an old coarse apron.

I liked it working at the Allhallows Pit. Eighteen shillings a week and so, like the first job I had was driving on the shaft level. Like an old pony called Charlie. Like an old Cock Robinson, he was what they call like an onsetter and so it means that you've got a big wire goes right from the bottom of the shaft right up to the top, it has a bell on it at the top. Now he's got a bar at the bottom. If he wants them tubs to go up in the cage, one, two, and then when the cage comes down you've got the big sump. Of course there's two cages, like double decker. Like you have four men in a cage. You see when it comes down with the men in, like they've got these things called keps, like they come out for to hold the tub for to get the men out or else it would go right down into the sump among the water, and so therefore he lets the bottom ones out first and then he just fills that in again. And then the cage goes right down into the sump among the water, it's full of water, then all the other men gets off. Like you've got all the men out, and then all the tubs come from down the dib, of maybe two miles in, but down to 6 South it would be about three miles. Of course that was bottom of the dib. Well all these tubs used to come up on a rope, it was driven by a great big engine on the pit top. They come out of the shaft and then like you took that rope off and they went right down to the bottom into these sidings and then of course they were put into cages, a couple at a time, and that went on up and down, like your full uns going up and empties coming down. So I used to put me empties on and I used to take them a hundred and fifty yards up by, and of course these chocks – that's a piece of wood with an iron, and then when your wheels went over it, it stopped it from running back. And then of course they used to go down the dib and that's the way it carried on. I didn't leave the pit. It closed down. At that time, which I say it should never have closed down. I'll tell who the manager was then – Elder, and he lived up the Boltongate road, up there, and then of course the other manager was Mears. But why it closed down I don't know. But we were right down in Crookdale, coal for evermore.

And I went on to farm work. You started at about quarter to six in the morning and then it would be half past six at night, six o'clock, it could be seven, especially haytime, it would be eleven. You would work the overtime, and you would get nowt. And then if thou asked for a weekend off it was like asking for gold. Of a morning now, up, one and a half hours' work done, all the byres to muck, all the milking to do by hand, thou never got washed, no. Come on man, come on, damn. Then thou come back for thee breakfast. Great bowl, although there was plenty of new milk, a great bowl separated milk and a bit of cheese, two slices of bread. Oot. Like you were eating the last bit when you were gaan out. Then thou come in for t'dinner. Same.

Potatoes and a bit of meat, but of course this was old Fenwick of Lesson Hall. Like I'd finished me meat, and Mrs. says to me, she says, a bit more meat, Joe. I says, Yes please. WHAT? he says. I says, No thanks. I only had three places. And then I went to George Twentyman's. In them days all the byres all paving stones. Like they're all concrete today. Like they're all mucked out with a muck scaler and that, but I went, all barrow. And all paving stones. So I was theer maybe four weeks and it didn't matter how I cleaned that byre of a morning, he used to come in half asleep, maybe half an hour after, and he would come in, like he was an awful bad waker, he would come in. Ee man, thou's nivver cleaned this bloody byre right. So it went on and on and I never said nowt back. But this morning I took particular care, I swept it and there was no muck lying about that I could see, there wasn't a bit of muck lying about. So I'se sitting milking and I'd about three parts of a bucket of milk and he comes in. He hadn't gitten into the byre anyway, and he started again, Ee, you can't ... and I just got up off me copy, and I just planked the flaming bucket of milk ower his head. Now, I says, I'se off. He says, Thou's not. I'se off. So we gaas to have break-fast and the Mrs. comes till us, she says, Oh divnt gaa, Joe. Take ne notice of him. Cor blimey, me I stopped four years. Couldn't do nowt rang [wrong]. But why did he complain all the time?

But what used to dishearten me was I'm talking about these bad old times. Well mind it's understandable. But God love him, I agree with him. Do you know something – I've seen them, Melvyn, this is the truth, mind, they maybe had three or four stirks, about that big – calves, but I call them stirks – I've seen them have to sell a stirk a week before the half year was up just for me to give me eight shillings. I've churned and I've seen them all making butter with these flappers, then market. No machine. I've seen me churn for three-quarters of an hour then up on the top of the churn, how you knew it was ready – there was a little glass and as soon as that glass was clear, and then the butter was right and then there was a plug in the bottom, and like you pulled that plug out and that's where you got your milk from. God damn, they were worse off than even me. Talking about today, well you know the price of land, look what John Barnes made off one place. He pays eleven thousand pounds for it, and gets forty-five thousand for it. Forty-five thousand pounds. But he would have about seven farms altogether. Well, aye. There's John Kerr at Redhall there. See what he paid for his place. I shouldn't say paid, he never worked in his life. Poor old fellow, he's dead. I never saw him with his jacket off but yet he got all this money left.

And now he's gone and there's somebody enjoying it. That's what I want to do. Nothing. But what's the use? But look at my point of view. As I say, we come into this world, what with? And that's the way people should go. You can't do without it but I say if you come in with nothing why the hell should you leave anybody anything? Go out with nowt. That's my idea. Like I'se a funny fellow.

And then I went on the dole. I was on the dole for seven years, on means test at Carlisle. All the old farmers round the big table, Have you been seeking work? Old Fargie Feddon was on from Greenhill, Have you been seeking work? I says, Thee give me a job and I'll come. Now, only for saying that I was knocked off the dole. Well, I was getting my seventeen shillings off the dole. Well, why go and work for a farmer for ten pounds for the half year. No. I was at Bolton Low Houses. On the dole.

That's where we were living, up at Bolton Low Houses, when we got married in 1933. On the Friday, I was married on the Wednesday, I went to draw my dole on the Friday and I was very much surprised when I got twenty-five shillings. Twenty-five shillings for two of us. And I was married at Mawbray Church and comes home, no honeymoon, and we come home to this house at Bolton. Well, Willie Lightfoot, like we were the best of pals and that, they had the garage, well I went to bed first anyway. Well, I couldn't get into bed because it was all sawn through and through like with thread. Then when I looks underneath the bloody bed, here's a great set pot, you know what they boil clothes in, one of them. So like for just for to show no ill feeling or owt about that, like her father says, Now here's a rabbit for your dinner tomorrow. I can always mind [remember] that. Of course, there were plenty of rabbits down there. They gave us this rabbit. So next day she had prepared for dinner. This was the first dinner. So I always mind we had potatoes and cabbage, a bit of dry bread and a cup of tea. Now she puts mine on me plate and puts her own on. So I gets half-way through it – I'se playing away and I sees these two lile black things. What the hell's these, Evelyn? Two partles – well, that was the first kick off. She hadn't cut the heart and the eyes out!

I got married and I think I would be off work eighteen months to two years, then I got a job. With Kettler and them, old Harry Graham at Kirkbride, always bothered with gout after he'd been on the booze. So we had to go on this pipe track, at Abbeytown, up to Mawbray, and up to Allonby, so I got a start, me and Kettler. It was to bike, mind, all the way there. Ten mile. Eleven pence an hour. And the first day – stiff, hands all segs, even bleeding, but I wouldn't give in.

I stuck it. I stuck it. If there was one job there was a hundred for it. That's why they had to make this means test as a gag. If they were to own up with it, they all knew there was no work but they had to have this bloody means test. Anyway I was laying these pipes at Abbeytown. I'd been there three days and so Kettler and this Graham, like they were supposed to be bottoming out, like shovelling a trench out, like it had all been dug out but they were trenching up for to put the pipes in. Like it had an awful lang shank and all they had to do was go along and throw it out. So this day Harry Graham was off. I learnt through Kettler. So of course I was sent with him for to bottom out. Now, he says, when Granger walks that way, he says, thee ga with him. Kettler was just standing, doing nowt – what, old Kettler. He never had nowt of a Friday to lift. He'd sub all the way through, and same with Harry Graham. Always had gout. I divnt know what he meant by gout – always had gout. They can speak of Kettler – he was a lad, they can speak as they have a mind but he definitely beat the Maker's. He would have lived where thou and me would have sunk. Not through intelligence, mind, but of course the sneaky way he went around it. Well Kettler used to be a mancher. Like he's in with Tomboy and Nimble. Well of course they lived at Fletchertown. Well what they used to do like in them days they had what they called a hearthrug. So they used to make a raffle a week and then, of a Saturday night, the fun of the fair they had – Tomboy and Nimble and Kettler. But never no bugger ever won this raffle. Never. Used the same mat. They only had one mat but nobody won it. Of course they would start it up at the Highland Laddie, up where Bell's cut meat up at. Well they used to start there, all tickets. The whole hearthrug wasn't wrapped up, just underneath the arm, took it out, all the colours of the rainbow, beautiful. Then they would come down to the Crown and Mitre into there, into the Crown, into the Kildare, across to the Half Moon, Lion and Lamb, and that went all the way round the pubs. As drunk as jinny owlets. And then when they got bloody tired they would throw the mat to Kettler and it was put out of the way. And that went on for weeks.

They used to have these carnivals. So it was this carnival, like Tomboy and Nimble, they used to follow all the carnivals and so like they got a brand new tub from the pit, like it had never been down the pit, with four wheels on. And it wasn't just filled up with coals, there would be a board across – like a few coals put on the top. And this old horse Charley drawing it. And then the next year he had old Tomboy as a bear. Like he had him dressed up as a bear. And a great chain around him. So like after the carnival was finished, plain as a pikestaff, up where the fountain is now, here's old Tomboy with his great lang chain. It was a plough chain, that's what it was. He gets the plough chain, he fastens it around that lamp post at this side, at this end, he locks it, but you see they would be half drunk before they went in the carnival. So he looks at Nimble, he says, Where the hell's thou going? He says, I'se gaan for a drink. He says, What about me? Oh, he says, bears can't drink. No, all ever Kettler lived for was tricks and money. I could give you a daily routine. Up about ten o'clock, up to the top of Union Street, then he would crawl along to where Jimmy Blair had his shop at, and then into the King's Arms. But in them days it was just a small place, a bar and fire. That's all Kettler wanted was the fire. Because I would say he never saw a fire. Then he used to go over till Bell's, pound of tripe, and he would go and get his pint and fire and tripe. And that was his dinner. Then it come till five o'clock and he was there again. What he could hook, or what he could make on the horses, or what he could sponge, it was his life. But mind I got a big shock when he died. I didn't know there was anything wrong with him. But there's Tomboy the same day, they were in all one clique.

When the War came, I was a foreman for Costain's at Silloth, putting them hangars up. Putting all the hangars up, putting all the concrete roads in, everything. Reserved occupation. Then the job finished. Well it just wasn't complete but just on its last legs. So the boss come, he says, will you go to Liverpool? Aye, I will. So I takes about thirty or forty men from here with me and we went down. I was sent out to a job at Bootle, a cheese factory. Flies – I've never seen nothing like it. All the pubs you went into, flies, more flies. Terrible. And we played there for about two years. All through it. I saw Bobby Temple and all them, they were all there. All in uniform, and I'll tell you these bombs and that was coming down. Of course like, as far as we were concerned, like, we might as well have been in the War. I tried to be in. I was only in a month. I was no good. He says, What are you waiting for? I said, Me grade. He says, You have no grade. See. So like I come out of theer and started on the buses and I was only at work five weeks and I had this big stomach operation. Of course, they knew that. I didn't. An ulcer. So I had three parts of it taken away – the stomach. But getting back to Liverpool, like I was talking about them bombs and that coming down. Well, Sammy Murdoch, he's the boss of the State Management Scheme now, he's what they call like – like he's the boss of the builders. So I'd been there three weeks before he came so he was sent there and he come into the same digs. I warned him. I said, As soon as them sirens go, out of bed, underneath. So this night the sirens went, I out and under the bed. He would have a peep through the window. He put his head through the window and this great land-mine come down. His hair – it did that and that. It went white overnight, only through that.

I came back from Liverpool and I went to drive for Nestles Milk. I would bring the wagon home at night, get my own milk, eggs, and of course anything I could pick up. That was the only time I was well off, as far as eating was concerned, because farmers gave me taties, they gave me eggs, and I could have as much milk. All this milk that was sent back, it wasn't up to standard, because maybe you'd putten water in or summat of that. So I used to bring it back, but I had a great bait tin like that, and a spoon. Make me own butter and sell it. I was well off. Then they come for me on the buses. Well, in them days if you wanted to change your job, well you had to go and see this officer. It was a law that was passed. Like you just couldn't change your job. I could get off, but they got me off. My first wage was two pounds fifteen. I said, Mr. Spear, this is no good for me. Get my cards out. So he says, Now listen. He says, Give it a chance. I would give it a chance. He was on that phone to Whitehaven, so like they come through to see me. Oh, give it a chance. Now they put me hours in I never worked. Why should they do that? Only for to keep me. Like probably two pounds, fifteen – it went up to over five pounds. I didn't work them hours. It's how they kept me. And I stopped for twenty-eight years. Because they couldn't get men.

In them days we had no uniform. We just wore our clothes and then what nettled me, after the War finished like, you got your uniforms, and then they put a big notice up – you've got to work in your uniform, not in your own clothes. Because they could then get plenty of men. Now the biggest wage I lifted there, up till I left, was nineteen pounds. Now lady conductors, in the black-out, I was sorry for them, double-decker and single-decker buses, all blacked out. The only thing they had to work on was a flashlight. It was pinned on here – their chests. The only thing I had to drive with, I could only see ten yards – they used to ask me, how did I manage? Oh, I could see. I was telling lies. All guesswork. These masks – the mask they fitted on the lamp to keep the light out from the aeroplanes, and how I managed I don't know. You ask your dad about conditions. And then when the lights come on again and I took them masks off, I thought I was living in heaven. I thought I was living in another world altogether. I run over a horse, I run over a cow. I couldn't see nowt.

Then I started me own business. I kept me job. I says to the boy,

172

he was going to the Nelson School, I says to him, What would you like to be? Well, I've always given him plenty of time, just the same as I told the fact of life at an early age, just for me to keep him right. And so like I asked him I said, Would you like to be a green-grocer. He said, I would so. And so I said Okay. So I rigs an old stall up and I puts it on the Fountain there [a square in the town centre]. So I had to go up to school to get him off. I just forget his name who was there now. So he says, Yes, certainly Mr. Lightfoot. So I gets him off and gets him onto that. And now then, I was doing well. He was on that stall from nine o'clock in the morning till half past five or six o'clock at night. I was doing well. But of course that shop that Miss Turner come in. Well, we were an eyesore to her, she says – that great big stall I had on there, it was blocking the side of her shop and she was losing money. As I should say not with the locals but with the strangers, because they couldn't see the shop. So she comes around to me. She says, will you have this other shop next to hers? I says, yes. A pound a week. I took it. Just nicely gets a start.

I goes to Carlisle and buys a van. So we goes down to Proudfoot, the fruiterers, I goes down to Dockers, I goes down to Messiter. He let you have your sugar and all sec as that. I says, Give me a good credit. Yes. And the thing they liked about me was I was honest. I says, it's for the boy now, so I says, that means I'll have to be guarantor for him. Okay. So I gets a month's credit, never looked behind me. And I gets his banking account, like you pay in and take out. I did me own books, bank to cash and cash to bank and all sec as this. My accountant was Kyle of Carlisle. He used to be up the steps where Sammy Tate had his shop. So I bought this van. It cost me four hundred and fifty pounds. Of course, that was when stuff was very dear. I paid it through the bank – I never paid for it straight out. Well, we played about until this conscription come about.

Well he wouldn't have the Army – Cyril (my son). He wouldn't have anything but the Navy. Well, I says, listen, lad. It's just a matter of time like, you'll have to go so you might as well go and join up now, which he did. But for to help me out, Billy Walker – he's just died and he was Inspector of the buses – he gave me a hand out in the shop. Matt gave me a hand out in the shop but before that I had a couple of girls in the shop, very honest. A Wigton girl and a girl from Westfield here. And so like I gets this certain bus conductor – mentioning no names – he said he would travel the van three days a week. Well, I had Waverton and round by Great Orton and Aikton, all them on a Friday which would fetch me maybe two hundred pounds and odd in. Of course that was

173

when the boy was driving, mind you. So I played away a bit. And this round was dropping and dropping and I was wondering why. And it just came out as easy as . . . although I was weighing that bloke's stuff up, I couldn't fathom it. And Thompson, the manager of Walter Willson's, he came to me. He says, does Mrs. So-and-so get her stuff off you? You see, she was spending five and eight pounds a week with me. He says, Now the only stuff she's getting off me is butter. Well, I didn't sell butter. So in the meantime I had seen my van coming down from Brindlefield. I had also seen my van coming out from this way, he had been at his sister's, supplying her as well. And so when I asked him about this, I says, Why have you been up to Brindle? Oh, he says, to get washed for the pictures. So I took it for granted. A fortnight after Billy Dodd comes. He says, You're losing money. He'd bought a television in six months. *I* couldn't afford one. So I'll tell you, after the boy went to the Navy, well I got that bloomin' fed up, I had that much to do and that much to think about, and I says, now then. If I've got to be twisted, I've been well twisted. And I had hundreds out owing to me. People pass me in the street now, How do you do? I went to my bank manager, Saul. Of course like he was a magistrate. I went till him. He says, Joe you can do nothing, until you catch him. He says, Have you caught him? I said, No, my accounts do. But I never did catch him. I couldn't prove nothing. Now how it happened to be, but I had no hard feelings against these girls, neither one nor the other. One says, I'm not taking owt. I says I know you're not. And the other girl says, I'm not taking anything. And then the penny dropped. She says, Oh, you've been putting tins of Plumrose meat on. You – I hadn't put it on. I says, He put it on. Well, that Plumrose meat in them days, very dear. And he'd putten jam and all sec as that, unknown, I hadn't put it on the van. But they should have told me. But that's what he was doing . . . It's been a hard life but I've finished up alright. I don't want anything. I've got a clean home, I've got everything I want.

What I'm talking about now is this, I've always said it, science will beat man. In them days education, like what we've been on about, they says to me, Did you get educated? No. In them days they never went to school. They couldn't force you to go to school, that's why they were so daft that I had to use a gripe [fork] to scale muck with. I had to use me hands to milk with. All this modern stuff today, even women, even women are modern. Even men are living longer. You take your milk today, it isn't the same milk because it's interfered with. You take your bread today, it isn't the same, because it's been interfered with. Then they ask me why are people living – in our old days if a person died at fifty-nine or sixty, poor old fellow, but you

174

say poor old fellow now at eighty. I mean to say, no, I wouldn't say, it isn't much better. I'm talking about the poor, mind. I'm not talking about the high-ups. I'm talking about the working man. But that's what's wrong with the country today. It's all these high-ups. In them bad old days, as far as I was concerned, as far as your dad was concerned, nothing, they didn't want to know you. As far as class distinction. What's happening in the world today is this. And I love it. The working man is of the same structure as the big man. He's got his motor car, he's got his television, which in them days I couldn't compete. But as I say like, the living conditions, yes, we're in a different world altogether than what you were back in the 12s, 15s, 14s, when the horses were coming through. Even in the First World War when the horses were coming through Bolton with their cannons and spurs and belts. Everything's changed.

I'm sixty-four now but so help me God I'm pleased I'm going out. I wouldn't like to be here thirty years after this. I'm glad I'm going out. And as far as God's my maker, although my father was a preacher there wasn't one took after him, but I've got my way of life as well. And what I say is this. In church, in all sort of religions, all these religions, unbelievable – I've never seen it nor you've never seen it. Now I'm not saying, I don't want you to think for a moment that I don't believe in God, I don't want you thinking I'm an atheist, because I'm not. But this is what I think. All this is just a case of politics. The same. I vote Labour because my father and mother were Labour. That's been brought down all through the years. Now then, as far as my father was concerned, I used to often ask, I've never seen God, I've never seen Christ. No, he says, if you saw them, then you would believe. And then we got onto destruction. But I say this, of course I say I'm not atheist, but I often stop to think – I often lie abed awake and I think about it. If there is a God, then why does he allow all this? If you can tell me another way, of course He's Almighty God, but as I say if it is Almighty God, why shouldn't he put his hand out or stop this or stop that? No, it's queer. Like for instance the Mormons, again, it isn't only because they believe in it, he's a sort of sun worshipper. Well, why worship the sun? I've gone through it all, I've gone through all the Bible, and now they're trying to change it. And then when it comes to now they're trying to play this rock and roll stuff in a church. And I think that's a last resort. Admittedly I don't go to church, but the only pleasure that I get of a Sunday night, it doesn't matter who's here, who comes, I'll be sitting there listening to the minister and that sermon. I love it. And that's what keeps me going all the week. You needn't go to church to be good."

CHAPTER SEVEN
Farms and Farming

In England for centuries there has been a "drift from the land": to the cities, to the colonies, to new, independent countries. The deserted village and the dying village were as much part of our past landscape as the thatched cottage and the village blacksmith's shop. As the first of the highly industrialised nations, England drew men from the fields and into the factories, offering higher wages, hours which at least had a beginning and an end, and, often, infinitely superior housing.

There are three chief ways in which farming has changed in this century. The units have become bigger – a bland way of saying that many small farms have gone under, even moderate-sized farms have had to hold on fast, larger holdings are much more profitable. There has been, especially since the end of the Second World War, a vast increase in mechanisation: horses have gone, tractors have come in, the milk stool has been succeeded by the milking-machine, the pitchfork by the combine harvester, the countryman, to a certain extent, by the mechanic. Finally, with the mechanisation, the heavy protection and subsidies which farms have received since the Second War and the sharp rise in land values, the life of the average farmworker has changed amazingly. At the beginning of the twentieth century it would be true to say that many farm workers would have recognised their condition, detail by detail, in the novels of Thomas Hardy, novels set in the 1840s and 1850s: by the third quarter of the twentieth century, the labourers' world, though harder than most and less well-paid than most and subject to a greater number of variables than most, is altogether lighter: lighter on the body and lighter on the demands it makes on the hours of a day. This chapter in one way outlines the changes in farming this century.

Wigton sits in the middle of the Solway Plain, a rich farming district, with plenty of warm rain from the last reach of the Gulf Stream and deep soil suitable for most crops. The town is almost at the natural centre of this plain which partly accounts for its success in previous centuries as a market town and even today, despite the motor-car and lorry which can take buyers and sellers to Carlisle or up to Hawick in Scotland, over to Hexham in Northumberland, or down into Yorkshire and Lancashire, even now it is extremely busy, week in week out throughout the year, and boasts the largest horse-sale in the North of England.

One of the largest farms is owned by Mrs. Kerr who lives at Redhall, a most substantial farmhouse set a few hundred yards back from the road, a mile from the town to the south. Mrs. Kerr is now a widow.

The house was exceptionally tastefully furnished with chests and Sheraton chairs and other antiques they had bought over the years. The farmyard was almost uncannily neat and tidy: as if no cloven hoof had passed that way for months. Mrs. Kerr herself is a very handsome, lively woman, more like the headmistress of a good girls' school than a farmer's wife: she went away to school as a girl, to Sedbergh, a girls' boarding school. It was "rather spartan but I enjoyed every minute of it. I really did."

Her father was a mining engineer, manager of the Whitehaven Colliery (forty miles from Wigton) for "a number of years". They lived four or five miles outside the mining town; in the country. This was in the Twenties.

Her father was killed in the pits in 1928. He had been down the mine supervising the restoration work after an explosion in which thirteen miners had been killed: a second explosion put an end to his life. That was in February. In November, she married John Kerr and came to Redhall.

When she came to the farm in 1928, they owned (as distinct from renting) one hundred and fifty acres, arable and mixed farming and, most famously, a stud of Clydesdales. These were the great farm-horses of this time; a massive, even heroic breed which did heavy work in war and peace. John Kerr, her husband, orphaned as a boy of two, was brought up at Redhall by his spinster aunt and bachelor uncle: the uncle started the stud: John took it over when the old man was crippled. He was then seventeen.

They bred themselves on the farm, but more importantly they had grooms who took the Clydesdale stallions all over the country, from farm to farm, servicing the mares. When Mrs. Kerr arrived there were about fifteen stallions.

"We travelled these horses to different districts and they were hired out. Some were hired out to various districts and then we also had, oh, maybe half a dozen that travelled the area of Cumberland you see, from Carlisle down as far as Millom and some of them were away the whole season. But always at weekends we had maybe four or five used to come home for the weekends, stand at home over the weekend. And there was one man to one horse. When I first came here all the ploughing was done with horses, you see. There would be about four pairs of horses kept regularly for the work here. And then, of course, when the tractors became available, we went on to tractors and, of course, it did away with the work horses. But when I first came here the men used to go out every morning with a pair of horses. Three of them would go out doing various things on the land. Then the horses were gradually beginning to go out and horses weren't needed for the land. The tractors were there, all the horses were needed for were a few for showing and export. We used to export quite a number. Canada and the States for these teams of horses, you see, and for these big brewery places, you see. We exported . . .

When I first came here, my husband did do a bit on the land, not very much. But over the years, I mean, business took him away so much that he just supervised, he didn't do anything, because any business that he had, he concentrated on that. But he supervised the men and planned the work, but he didn't actually do any manual work because he was away a considerable lot, you see.

When I came here there was hot and cold water in the bathroom and everything like that; it wasn't bad. I've never lived anywhere that hadn't a bathroom. Oh yes, there was a bathroom and hot and cold water and everything like that. And then after the coal range we got a solid fuel cooker in the kitchen and then, oh it must be twenty years since we renovated this house, and made it what it is today. And then we eventually made our own electricity, but we'd to make our own for quite a long time. We had storage cells. I had two maids. You see, John had had a housekeeper and a maid before I came . . . Well, they had had housekeepers for a good number of years, you see, after the old aunt died, and they had had a house-keeper and a maid when I came. There was a housekeeper who would have liked to have stayed but I said to John, No, I'm starting off with a clean slate. I'm not having any – I'm going to be the house-keeper here. I'm not having anybody that's been here. It wouldn't have been policy. So I had two maids. They lived in. I had two maids for a good number of years and then, you know, when they got bad together I just had one. And this person whom you met in the kitchen this morning, she was with me in her younger days and she has now been with me for over twelve years. I used to help with the cooking. One of the maids and I did the cooking, because, as I say, we had men to feed. Then you see we built two cottages here. Well, one man lived in Longthwaite Farm and we built two cottages up here at Redhall and the men went into them in 1939, the year the Second World War broke out.

The farm workers were exempt from service. I don't really think that it affected us very very much. We still had the staff that could carry on with it. Of course, during the war there was a ploughing order that you had to obey; depending on the size of your farms, you were told what you had to plough to grow extra grain and extra potatoes and all this sort of thing. It didn't affect our way of life very much. No, I don't think so.

John started doing the Young Farmers' Movement here in Wigton after the war. They wanted one started and he was approached and he got them started and was Club Leader for a while until some of the older end grew up, you know, the like of Billy Mars, Jimmy Kirkpatrick and these ones. And then John, you know, he obviously kept an interest in it but he gave that up because he had other commitments and let them carry on, but he was interested. But I mean I never took any active part in any sort of parochial or things in Wigton. Of course, we are not actually in Wigton Parish; we are in Waverton, you see. But I never entered much into anything like that. Though I belonged to the Inner Wheel Club at Wigton. John was in Rotary, of course. Yes, it is the ladies' side of the Rotary. Your husband has to be a Rotarian before you can join the Inner Wheel and I was a founder member of Inner Wheel.

We do all kinds of charitable work, organising different things. We used to visit at the hospital, visit at High Field and we used to raise money for sending Christmas parcels to the aged and the deserving and help for the blind and cancer research. I'm not in it now. After John died I stayed in for a little while after and then I resigned because I felt that I'd, you know, I'd taken part in it and I didn't feel like joining up. You see, Rotary and Inner Wheel do join socially and we help each other and, of course, on any social functions I didn't feel I wanted to go without a partner. And so I thought it over quite a lot and so I resigned five or six months ago. I used to join John in different things. We used to go away a lot together. He went on business but we could combine the business with pleasure and we always used to go to the Highland Show every year. And he judged the Highland Show about nine times – the Clydesdales – and I always used to go with him for that and we used to meet some friends socially. But I mean, round the Wigton area he was a magistrate for a good number of years.

Now, since his death, I'm just carrying on the way that I knew he was going to carry on. I was always interested and, well, let us put it this way – John expected me to be interested and it was a joint effort and he expected me to be interested and to know what was going on. He was away a lot, you see, and it was expected of me to get out and about and see that things were kept moving and, therefore, I had a real interest in what went on. And, fortunately, it's as well I did do that because I knew what he was meaning to do and we discussed everything – everything was discussed – in every aspect. And I'm having to begin to put my thinking cap on now and begin to do things, but anything that I can't manage now on my own, well, James and George Kerr, they give me a hand, you see. They are the executors, they are John's cousins. One's on Green Rigg and the other is on Newby West and they are very good at giving a hand with all these various forms and what not if I can't manage them."

Two other farms were added and over five hundred acres were leased for grazing. Mrs. Kerr has three daughters and one of them has bought a farm and some of the land from her.

Mrs. Dixon, who, in the chapter on the Big House, described her childhood in the town where her father worked at the railway station, eventually married a farmer and remembers the day she first met him.

"I met him when I was coming for butter when I was fifteen. The road was flooded. We often talk about this. And I was following him because I thought if he was working here, he would know the way past the water. And just in the bottom it used to flood. It was an old lane. It had been the road to the farm, and it was flooded level, and he jumped and he looked back and he said, You'll have to jump, and I said, I daren't. He said, Well, throw me the butter basket and jump and I'll catch you, which he did. Then he went on and left me. And I often say, My goodness, what was I thinking of at fifteen? So off he went, and I followed him there, and I came back the other way – along Oulton Road. They told me to do that. And that was getting dark early, about seven, so it must have been about spring – and that was during the war years. Well, just after the war finished. He was at the Nelson School. We started courting right after that. Then of course a few years when you float away from one another, still aware of one another, I suppose, and we sort of met up again when I was twenty. Married when I was twenty-five."

Edwin Dixon was the only son of a farmer who farmed two or three miles from Wigton. It is the farm where Mrs. Dixon now lives out her retirement as a widow: her son farms it. When they married, though, Mrs. Dixon and Edwin Dixon first tenanted an eighty-six-acre farm – mixed – nearer the coast. They had one boy to help them and, said Mrs. Dixon, "I worked jolly hard. I helped in the fields."

"Thinning turnips, mowing hay, thrashing day when I had to go on the top thing, and I used to bake everything myself. We had the hard days. Still had the hard way of living. Then I had the two children. Used to put Vera in the pram and Alan would creep up the stitches with me, thinning the turnips. But on the whole they were very satisfying days. Used to churn butter. Still got the old churn there. Once a week, bring it to Wigton in the pony and trap to sell, and eggs. You had to live on your butter and egg money. That was your housekeeping. Christmas poultry, turkeys, always busy.

And then we bought a little car and we got to going off, although it was a nice pony. I often think it was lovely having a pony and digby. I mean, you were something with that. Go off on a lovely drive round the quiet lanes.

I was always up at half past six. Edwin got up about six and brought the cattle in and then I had to get up to cool the milk. We'd gone a bit modern and got a milk-cooler, and I had to pump the water up out of a tank inside the cooler to cool the milk. And I had to go to the byre and carry the milk in buckets and put it through the strainer on the top. That was when we went on the milk, but before that we used to separate the milk as we brought it in. Well, it used to be rather hard and Edwin used to get a bit discouraged and he used to say he wanted something easier than farming. I suppose he'd be like most lads. He'd be getting sick of being under his father. We were just farming altogether, and he used to say on about it and what he would do, so I said to him, Well you can stop grumbling. I'm sick to death of you grumbling. There's a pub to let in Wigton. Just send yourself off and apply for it. I can just see him yet. He gasped. Anyway, he did, and we got it, much to his surprise. No bother. We were just in three years. We'd just gone in when the war broke out. So of course he had to farm as well in wartime. He was farming although we were in there. I think that was the hardest part of my life. It was hard work.

We came back to this farm, Edwin's dad's, in 1942 and there were thirty-two horses on this farm. There was two hundred and fifty arable and then there's reclaimed woodland and there's the tarn. Edwin bought a tractor. His dad was a horse-man. He bred horses. He had stallions. A couple of stallions or something. And that was one of his jobs. They used to take them round for service at the farms. Well they kept their own bulls here which the neighbours used. Course the pattern was altering then. The first year we were here we had a very bad harvest. 1942. We were bringing corn in at Christmas. No labour, no staff, and Edwin bought an old wagon from Walter Willson's and it had Daisy White on it. We always called it Daisy. So we were leading corn without Daisy, because I was learning to drive. Before we came here I drove, we had a little car. We used this old lorry and got everything in with one boy. And of course Edwin worked very hard and then he started with sugar diabetes. He had been ill. Then the children had to work hard. Vera was nine and Alan was coming twelve by then, and they worked hard as well. Alan wanted to leave school, so his Dad got him away. But he left school and he had to farm on and we all had to work as a team. Went onto the milk. We got a milking machine – bought it at one of the dairy shows. Edinburgh or somewhere like that. But we didn't do any new building. Alan, my son, will have gone in more for that. Alan's gone in more improving by building. Alan has four hundred gallons of milk per day. He has his own bulk tank. You see, Edwin was a mixed farmer. He liked sheep. We always had lambing and then he had this breeding of these Herefords. We had cropping as well. There were turnips to thin and corn to stook. Then they got, this is when Alan was growing into a young man, they got a combine harvester. We had our own thrasher and that sort of thing. And the thrashing day, well we call them thrashing day but it was threshing really, when they're threshing the corn, and that was the hardest day. Maybe sixteen of our neighbours would come and help us on that day and you went in turn to help them. Your annual crop, you thrashed it and put it on the grainery. This is the 40s and 50s.

Edwin's father only lived eight months after we came back. He was a sugar diabetic as well. So we really had a hard time. I took in visitors. They came for the fishing. For a period we gave up the milk – well, it was this abortion thing – I don't know what they call it, the place wasn't right for it, they'd had a bad time – so we went out of milk for five years and that was the period when it was hard. Went on to long-term policy which was feeding. And I tried by taking visitors, summer guests for the fishing and the farm and looked after them well, and I liked doing that. And I'd work hard for all the things I needed in the home.

The stackyards are no more now. There's a great big shed on it. Feeding place where they come and go, come into the milking parlour and go back. Everything's altered. Alan's more advanced. We paved the way to that. Alan's gone more in for the milk which he likes and he doesn't keep any sheep at all. He's all milk and feeding and cows. He grows barley now. We used to grow mixed. Mixed peas, oats, barley – hops and peas and barley, and mixed it. Then of course we grew for our own cattle. There's a tarn down there we have, full of pike, huge pike – we were just talking about them last night. There's plenty of people wants to come and fish but at the moment we've let it to a few policemen. When Edwin was ill and couldn't look after himself, he let this cousin have it. His feet were bad with sugar. He had operations on his feet. His toes taken off and that sort of thing. He was an ill man but he looked very well, and he still kept his hobby. Nearly killed himself but he loved his shooting. And we reared pheasants. He was always keen. We've always reared them. Then we had pens. There's still the remains of some of the pens there. The week Edwin died there were six came up into the shed where he had been working on. I thought, Well, bless him, I'm sure he's a pheasant now. I always feel as if he's wandering on in his spirit. I've a happy feeling although I'm still a bit sick about things. I still feel that he's here, because he used to go out, his poor feet, take his dogs with him and his big sticks that he has and he would go and wander where he could. He had little places made where he could get over with his bad feet, used to go struggling off into the wood. It's all reclaimed now, right across there.

You were asking about the things that have struck me most – we had a series of farm fires in this district. I can't tell you the year, but anybody will tell you that remembers. And we were on Christmas Eve. They came up this shed and set fire to all the stuff there and there were some calving cows, one with twin calves, and they had all to be let out. It was an awful Christmas and I think from then Edwin was never a well man. Went into Wigton and we were the last fire. They were all round – some fire-raisers, but they never found them. Dreadful. He was never well after. For six months Edwin and I were never in bed before 3 o'clock. We sat up every night, went to bed at three and Alan got up. Watching everything, because all the time they were searching and firing round about. The police made their headquarters up here. We had an awful Christmas. All that middle part was burned out, and there was one cow, it had the hide burned right off its back. And Alan had to let them out, and this man we had living in the cottage then, and let them all out. Alan thought they couldn't let them out. The fire was so bad. They just opened the doors and the cattle were raving mad. And Alan said they just had to find their own way out. If they didn't, that was all they could do 'cos they couldn't go in any more. It was that hot and smoked. I remember what a Christmas we had. Everything tasted of fire. Well, we couldn't eat. We put a goose in the oven and forgot to turn the oven on. So I think that was one of the real nasty things that happened to us in farming."

Mrs. Dixon's life, in terms of her work and her achievement, is rather like that met with in gentle romantic novels. Nothing gentle, she would rightly say, about the beginning of it – thinning turnips in the open fields with two small children about your feet and a raw wind blowing: but from stern beginnings, through inheritance, to a definite comfort, the farm still in the hands of a Dixon, like many of the farms about Wigton, still in the family, and humming like a well managed plant.

More numerous were the labourers who started with nothing and finished with very little more and only if they were lucky. Bob Stephens was one of these – now white-haired, retired in a small rented cottage, still prepared to hedge and ditch and job around the place, a slow-speaking careful man whose memory is clear and without bitterness. He was born in 1904, and he went to the great hirings, where hundreds and men and women went each half-year to stand around and wait for a farmer to make them an offer.

"When I got hired at this place in Cockermouth (twelve miles from Wigton) at the hirings, it was when Wall Street dropped overnight (1929) – I had twenty-four pounds for the half-year up till then. I came into Cockermouth and I could only got twelve pounds. That's what they had dropped by and they never got no better for a lot of years. It was a lot of years before it ever got to be more money, then through time it got to be twenty-three shillings a week, that was the basic rate. That was when things were beginning to pick up again. But a lot of farmers had had a bad do and they were hard put to it, they hadn't much money, their stock wasn't making much and probably a lot of them had only started from scratch.

You came to a hiring and you got hired and you had to work for six months, you see, it was six months' contract. If you come into the hiring and a man fancied you, you know, he would ask you if you were for hire and he would ask you where you came from, what they called you or such as that. How old are you, have you ever been on a farm before? If you had not been on a farm before then that fetched your wage down, you see. You could practically do nothing, as they put it, you had to learn, and that was how you gradually worked your way up. If you were good at your job, you picked it up, and if he wanted you to stay on another six months he probably gave you a pound more, and if you wasn't satisfied with that pound more, well, you could go into the hirings and see if you could get another pound more. But you wouldn't get much more than a pound. It was barter; you were bartering your labour for a pound or two and your keep. Sometimes your keep wasn't a great lot, you know. It all depended on who you were with. People who was good feeders, fed you. People that wasn't good feeders, didn't feed you. They fed you on practically nothing you know, bread and cheese, porridge, a bit of jam. Maybe a dinner every day but that was what you got – you got your five meals a day, your breakfast, your ten o'clocks, your dinner, your tea and your supper. You got your supper as near six or after six as could be and there was nothing more till breakfast-time the next morning. You were probably two hours to work next morning before you got your breakfast. Sometimes rather longer if there was a bigger farm and there was somebody off ill and there was more work to do. Some farms was good, very good. Some was bad. Some didn't care. They didn't care whether they fed you or not, you see. The best places was where people fed you the best.

I was a long time before I got married. Some men wanted to get married when they were young but still had to continue in farm work because they couldn't get other jobs. And they were hard put to it in them days because they'd still got to live, especially when they were married with a family. It was all right when you were single, you had no troubles. Generally, when you got married you had to apply for a married man's place, probably you didn't get in the hiring when you were married – you watched the papers and see where anybody wanted a hired man that was married, and then there was always a cottage provided, you see. There was very few that was hired in the hirings that was married like.

The mothers came to see lasses, young lasses off, gave them advice before they went. But the lads they didn't bother about – young lads or men. They used to say ta ta at the house and get the bus to the station and that was that. And you never see them for maybe about three months and then you come home and had a weekend at home and then went back again. It was only six months, you see. Then you came back after six months to the Fair and start all over again. I think it was quite alright. You know, you were getting away from home and getting some work to do. And it was lovely going up there, and I spent eighteen months with that old man – he was a bit obnoxious at times. I can always remember me and him fell out one day and he said, I'll pay thee off. I said, Alright. So he went into the house and got me money, there was no cards then – he got me money and he started to talk to us and he said, I tell thee what, he said, we've just had a row now. Give us money back and thee can stop. So I stopped and I was with him another twelve months after that. It was alright like. I got hired at different times after that and I come to Cockermouth, went away down Wigton. You got some good spots and you got some bad spots; you had to what you call 'fry the fat with the lean' in them days.

Well at a lot of spots it was bread and cheese four times a day nearly and a dinner at dinnertime – maybe not much meat in. But of course a lot of farmers in them days were hard up – they were hard put to it you know – there was some of them had a job to carry on. *They* were skint. I was at one place once for six months over and I never got an egg – all the time I was there I never once got an egg. But it isn't that way today, I don't think. Farming is changed now. Better to their servants and a lot of their servants stop better with them. But of course you know, when I was young we wanted to work with horses. Every young man wanted to work with horses 'cos if you were a ploughman, well, then you were supposed to be a good chap.

You got your own back on farmers sometimes. You maybe didn't get your own back on farmer you lived with, you maybe got it back on his neighbour. I can remember one – we used to get these long tubes of cardboard that almanacs come in. They were round and about that long. We used to blare down them just like a cow call. And there was one spot we went to, and he was abed, and we got up on loft and we blared down blarer, as we called it, and he got up and come down and he looked in byre and he walked round and he says, Well, you're alright; there's nowt wrong with you. We could hear him as plain as that. So he went back again. So we blared again and he came down again and had another look. And he says, Funny that, I can't make it out. He was talking to hissel. So he went back and after a little bit we give him another or two and a bit harder next time. And down he rushed and come in byre with a walking-stick and he gave those cows a hiding and he says, Ye buggers, I'll larn you if you won't let me get to sleep. Well, we had handkerchiefs and caps and all sorts at our mouths to stop us from laughing because, if he had heard us, he would have hit us with the walking-stick.

A farmer said to a farm labourer once, He was a clever man who invented daylight, and farm labourer said, Aye, he was a cleverer man who invented darkness.

There was hunting, which we followed on foot, and pubs. There was a lot of people at a hunt and a lot of drink and a lot of talk and a lot of singing. And I reckon many a time you darcdn't strike a match for you'd explode it. It was that way sometimes because there were some awful characters used to come it. There were, when they got among the drink you know. Oh, it was lively, very lively. Once there was a stewpot – tatie we call it – in the middle of the table and there was a good few of them come in. There was Henry Stevens and there was John Willy Kay and Alf Turnbull and a few others, and Tyce. And Tyce said, Hunters? He said, You're not bloody hunters until you sup blood out of this. And he took his knife out and slit fox's throat and put it in tatie pot and said, Now, lads, get into it, and they did. They didn't bother because they were that hungry. And they eat it up. He was a gay lad was Tyce."

There was a prevalent view, all but impossible to support statistically, that in the Thirties and Forties there began another drift from the land: that of farmers' daughters who, for the first time in considerable numbers, decided against looking for husbands exclusively among the farming fraternity.

Margaret Ellis was one such. Brought up on a substantial farm near Wigton, having "a fabulous time" on the farm as a girl, nevertheless "I always said I'd never marry a farmer and I didn't." She came to live in Wigton and the shock was great.

"You were sort of brought up to a farming life and you accepted it. It was a life – you hadn't known anything else but farming and I think this was it. You thoroughly enjoyed it while you were there and yet, when I left home, I thought, well I'll never get used to town life. I thought this is dreadful. As soon as you stepped out of the door you saw all these people. I thought this is terrible, I'd never seen this before in my life – all these people. And you used to think if you went out and did anything they were sort of watching. And I thought it would take me years to get used to it, but I accepted it very quickly. You sort of felt, I couldn't imagine this, and everybody sort of coming and saying, Good morning, and I just couldn't believe it. And of course you lived on a farm and you just didn't see anyone whatever you were doing. You sort of were on your own. The family were around you but yet you just didn't have any strangers around. And it was such a change. I'll never forget going out with the first rug to shake it and there was everybody from the other houses, because there's about eight little houses all round where we lived in this little yard place, and I thought, gosh, has everybody come out at the same time? I thought I'd better wait until nobody's there. This is how I felt at first. I thought, what a change. It was terrific. I worried about it a little bit. I used to think, well, I'm bound to get used to it and I did very quickly really. It didn't take so long because I like people, even though I was not used to mixing with people an awful lot, I still liked people. And I used to think it was rather nice. And I suppose really they were trying to be very kind and to make me welcome there, but I still went out to the farm each day. Every afternoon. I couldn't get there quick enough.

We were not allowed to go out until we were seventeen, then of course we must go two of us together because my sister was slightly older than I am, and we used to always go together. We were allowed the car about twice a week but that was all. And you were only allowed to sort of go to the big balls, Farmers' Ball, Hunt Ball, things like that. We were not allowed to go to just an ordinary dance, an ordinary village dance. Father was rather strict on that. Then I think about a couple of years after that, when we started to go, he thought, well it was alright. He thought we were old enough to go out and we used to go to the local dances then. But up until then, no; it had only to be the big balls. It was just after the war and I think people were still very frightened. I think most parents were, about you going out. They just didn't like you going far away, and I think this is it. If you had a party you had them at home. And you entertained a lot at home, you often had friends. Christmas time, birthdays, anything like that. A friendly get-together and it would be all over by midnight. Just quite a friendly party, neighbouring farmers and friends, girls that you'd gone to school with and such as that – you didn't somehow be very friendly with the boys at that particular time. You lived a very quiet life. So it was quite nice. We enjoyed it."

But families still held on to farms and in the Wigton area, as all over England, there is a caucus of families – not gentry much less aristocracy, but solid farming families which have been there for a number of generations. One of these is the Dixons. Mrs. Dixon married into that family, one of her brothers-in-law is at Thursby – a village half-way between Carlisle and Wigton – John Dixon. He rhymed off a few of his relations round about.

"There's Moorhouse Hall where Father was brought up on, there's Lessonhall where my cousin lived, John Dixon. Well my brothers are all farming. I have a brother just across the road from me, my youngest brother. My second brother, he farms at Newlands, Hesket New Market; Gordon farms at Lathes, has a partnership in the White Heather; John Wright, a nephew, he farms adjoining Gordon. And Dixons of Bank End, they're relations – half-cousins or something like that. All in the Wigton area."

His father rented the farm and then bought it, two hundred acres, for four hundred pounds in 1922. On these two hundred acres he employed a first horse-man, a second horse-man and a cow-man. And of course there were four sons growing up to help. In 1926, though, to keep going, he started a milk-round in Carlisle – six miles away – which meant his getting up at quarter to four. In 1930 another milk-round was started in the village of Thursby itself. John Dixon went to the village school and stayed there until he was fourteen: "As soon as it was one o'clock when I was fourteen, I was away from it. You thought about nothing else but farm. You were brought up to it, and you thought about nothing else but work." His life was very like the life of labourers.

John Dixon's brother-in-law, Joseph Benson, is the auctioneer at Hope's Auction Company and it was in the small offices beside the empty auction that I spoke to him about the changes in farming and marketing since he joined the company at the end of the Thirties. The auction is in the heart of the town, a substantial spread of pens, offices, parking bays, a new pub and restaurant serving it (The Stocksman) with its own fields round about it. When it's not full of beasts it's a playground paradise for boys fast enough to evade the caretaker's clutches. Usually though, at night and on days when there is no trade, it has a peaceful, harmonious feeling about it, ancient and settled despite the tubular steel which long ago replaced the wooden pens.

Joseph Benson, a fresh-faced, handsome man in his early fifties, who still hunts and lives just outside the town, was brought up in the town where he went first to the National School and then to Brookfield, the Quaker private school on the town's western border. We began by talking about the auction circa 1940.

"There would be a terrible lot to do with horses. The horse-sale time, that was always at the end of October. I think this would be recognised as one of the largest sales of horses in the country. You could have a catalogue entry of anything from a thousand to fifteen hundred horses. Mostly Clydesdales in those days. If they were taking foals, yearlings and two-yearlings, you would have anything up to a thousand Clydesdales. People used to come from, well, you might say Land's End to John O'Groats – horses being sold as far as Southampton, Portsmouth. People from Aberdeen. I think there would be tremendous horses bred in Cumberland and there was always a lot of good studs; Hawkrigg, Tarraby, there's a lot of stallions kept in Cumberland. I wouldn't like to hazard a guess as to how many stallions would be kept in Cumberland in those days. They used to send them from Cumberland all over the country to do the season's travelling. But I think if anybody was looking for good Clydesdales in those days they would come to Cumberland to seek them. There would be Clydesdale horses exported out of Cumberland for years and years back.

They classed it as a large sale until tractors came in, which was about 1944–45. They would start to get small numbers, and it came down to a two-day sale, I'm not sure when that was, then it came to a one-day sale. It is now back up to a very big sale, it's a one-day sale, and it's a very big sale at the present moment. But if you get about twenty or thirty Clydesdales, all told, you do well. It's mainly ponies; fell ponies, hunters, just anything at all now, any breed. There's not as many farmers and dealing men as such come now. You would get a dealing man coming and buying twenty or thirty Clydesdale horses and you used to put them into railway companies and Co-operatives and various things. You don't get that sort of person about now. You get quite a few dealing men that deal in ponies and so forth but mostly individual buyers now.

During the war, you had to plough a certain amount; they specified a certain acreage which you had to plough. Well, the horse just couldn't get through it. They had to get tractors. Contractors then started to creep into it. Chaps that could afford to buy two and three tractors and ploughs and so forth and went round ploughing for other people. Of course, there wasn't as much labour either, when the war was on. But I went into the Forces in 1943. But even then, in the war, a big percentage of the farmers used to drive into the town by pony and traps. You could stable a horse in the Crown and Mitre yard, you could stable them in the Half Moon yard, there was stabling in the King's Arms yard, there was stabling at the Blue Bell – the stables would be full on a Tuesday with people driving into the town. There was quite a good stabling; mostly in yards behind pubs really. But there was a lot of stabling done in Wigton in those days. I wouldn't know where you could go now to stable one.

During the war the selling of fat stock was done away with and they introduced a grading system for our own fat stock and they weren't sold by auction. You entered them and they were graded and they were sent – the Ministry of Food used to send you a list. You used to send your entries into them – how much stock you were expecting on the following Tuesday – and they would send you an allocation back, and you had to send twenty cattle and about a hundred sheep to Sunderland or something like that, twenty cattle and three hundred sheep to Manchester. And they were graded and loaded at the station or went by motor vehicle to the slaughterhouses direct. And this was called control and decontrolling didn't come in till about 1954, I think, when they were put back into the market to be sold. The butchers didn't used to buy the stuff in those days alive. They got it all from the slaughterhouse. It was fair; I think it worked out. But the butcher didn't choose his meat. He had to take what was there, whereas now he can buy what he wants. The government was always a very good customer. A lot of the stock that was fed in those days you couldn't sell them nowadays because what they wanted in those days, the farmer wanted plenty of weight because it was so much a pound they got. And the more weight he had for his sheep the more he got for them. So he could feed them until they were about hundred-pound weight. He could feed his cattle until they were thirteen or fourteen cwt and as fat as he could make them. Whereas people now don't want fat. So it wouldn't be very popular nowadays. Not the type of stock that was being sold then. The trend has changed and they want a lighter animal, a lighter pig, and a lighter beast, and they don't want any surplus fat.

The dairy herds have increased tremendously. You would never have thought of a man with a hundred cows in those days. Thirty to forty cows was quite a large herd. And there's any amount of people now working a hundred cows in this area. There was no silage in those days. It was all hay whereas now a lot of the cows are never tied up. They're in what they call loose housing – cubicles and they haven't a chain round their neck. The byres have been done away with. It's all done for easier handling really, because there isn't the labour force on the farms that there used to be. I should think ninety percent of people will make their own silage. They use more manure now and they keep two and three times more stock on the farms than they used to do, with the use of manure. And with this loose housing and so forth they can get more cattle inside. Everyone has more stock. It's a great stock county is Cumberland. Wigton's a great stock area. I should think that it would be one of the best stock areas in the country.

In 1940 it was mainly shorthorns. There's very very few herds of shorthorn cattle left. I think the Ayrshire cow crept in first, they seemed to think it gave more milk, and then the Friesian and then they found out that the Friesian cow produced a very good bullock as well as a heifer and the Friesian-shorthorn cross was a very good cross and I think everyone started to use a Friesian bull. And I should think ninety percent in the county will be black and white (Friesian). And now the Charolais has crept in. He's very very popular indeed. It's a very popular beast. Very popular with the butcher. I think this has come to stay, marked as a dairy beast mainly. It's a commercial animal.

Farmers' sons are being better educated. I mean, a lot of the farmers who were farming in 1940 would probably leave school when they were twelve or thirteen, all they did was hard work. Now there's a lot of paperwork attached to farming, book-keeping, a big lot of paperwork, and they have to have a better education. It's a very skilled profession now is farming.

This company's been in existence since 1890. It was good fore-sight of the company, really, when it was all made steel (the pens). It doesn't need any repair hardly and there's no fire risk to it. And to have it all under one roof you kept all your customers together, and you needed less staff really because you had to keep moving from one ring to another in the old days whereas it's all central now. You see, on a Tuesday we sell the pigs at half past ten, then we start the cattle at eleven o'clock when the pigs are finished, we start the cows at sort of twelve to quarter past and then we start the fat sheep at one o'clock when the fat cattle are finished, then we start the store sheep at about three o'clock to half past three when the fat sheep are finished. So we don't have two rings going at the same time. In 1938–40 the first prize dairy cow used to generally make about twenty-eight to thirty-two pounds, something like that. Now it will make nearer two hundred pounds. Fat cattle would be making thirty to thirty-five pounds each, now they're making anything from a hundred and fifty to two hundred pounds. Fat sheep would be making two or three pounds, now making eleven, twelve, thirteen, fourteen pounds.

We have a book there that goes back to 1920 for all properties being sold by this company. The price of farms have altered. Here's a very good farm which sold in 1930. It is a well known farm and it was a hundred and sixty acres. It made six thousand, two hundred and fifty pounds. It could make seventy thousand today probably. Rents, they used to be one or two pounds an acre. Rents on farms now are ten pounds an acre. Some more than that I should imagine. Ten pounds would be quite common to rent a farm. A lot of people have bought their own farms. The Auction Company owns a lot of land. We farm ourselves about three, four hundred acres. We've lost an awful lot to building – Greenacres. That stretch all belonged to the Auction Company. Brindlefield was the Auction Company, the school playing-field was the Auction Company, the houses on Station Hill that's just built was the Auction Company land.

The farming community is much better off now. They live a better life. It's a hard life, but they live a much better life than they used to. Young farmers today have a much better life than their parents had. They work hard for it but they have a much higher standard of living. Once upon a time when a man went to look at a farm, either to buy it or rent it, he wouldn't take his wife to look through the house because the house didn't matter. But now the house counts a great deal. It didn't matter what kind of a house it was in those days, as long as it had the land. I won't say the land comes second now, but the house is more important. But all farmers have got a much higher standard of living. They deserve a good standard of living really. Most of them still get up at six or six-thirty in the morning and they're really never finished. You can finish milking at six o'clock at night and you might have a cow calving or two cows calving or some sheep lambing or something. Or you might have a field that's got to be sown. They have no regular hours, farmers, but they're in that position they can take a day off. They come to market on a Tuesday, they can go to the Highland Show, they can go to the Royal Show, but it's a hard life. They do work hard."

Llewellyn Evans was born in 1939. One of twelve children, he was brought up on an eighty-acre farm near Wigton and loves the work. Marriage, though, and the larger wage-packet took him from the land to the factory, where he works in some frustration, missing farm work. Of the five brothers, three have continued in farm work, two are at the factory.

Llewellyn owns a bungalow where he, his wife and two boys live, on the southern edge of the town, looking over to the fells. He would like a much bigger garden and in all ways is constantly full of the memory and the idea of farming.

"There was more pride in it than there is today. It's too commercial for my liking today. It's forced, forced today. Once upon a time they grew things with taste but I think today you know they sell this fertiliser to boost this, that and the other and everything seems to be pushed. When you see cows eating grass today they'll eat the hedges that's never touched the fertiliser parts, they'll eat all round the hedge backs, everything rather than eat this that's had the fertiliser on it. It's really force work that they're eating this. So you know, it just shows that the taste's gone really. A lot of them today, if they can't do a job they just sit on it – they don't want to know about it, that's my opinion. If you sent a chap with a spade to build a hedge up today, he would say he'd want a tractor and bulldozer to hew it out. And put a wire fence up today rather than, you know, make a tidy job of putting a hedge up and one thing and another. No farming today. There isn't farming today; it's just industry. It isn't farming.

Money. That's the only thing, money. I didn't realise, you know, when we bought this house what it'd entail. I was working on farm work, you know, to make ends meet. Like it was just hopeless really on farm work 'cos you'd your travelling and you're – you hadn't a chance to make anything else 'cos you were working from dark in winter till dark at night, you know, and Saturday and Sunday work. You used to always have to work either every other or maybe, if you were on a good farm, maybe once a month; nearly every other week end. You never had any time to spend with your family. I think this is the biggest drawback. When kiddies are small and that. I never seen them really, when I was on farm work, living in. When I went into factory I practically seen more on them than enough.

There's only one thing I'd have liked, you know, and that would have been me own farm. Other than that, to work for somebody, it was ridiculous."

Miss Wilson, Miss Barbara, too, has seen a great number of changes. None more disturbing to her than what is happening just a hundred yards along the road where she finds she has a new neighbour.

"He's been a farm manager in Tanganyika and he's set up the most fantastic – well, I don't know what it is. He must have spent two or three hundred thousand pounds at this Kirkland place, this farm here at Kirkland. He's got quite a lot of acreage on the Wiggonby aerodrome. He's got a farm called Black Brow at Wiggonby, he got both Spittal and the Mains, he's bought the whole lot. And all he does is grow barley for his bulls. Scores, hundreds of bulls he has, inside, in those sheds, and all his fields grow barley for them.

You know it's just ruining the country, it's going to ruin the countryside, this, because I was always led to believe you couldn't have grain off land more than two or three years running. Well, this is going on for years and years and years. And the fields are all abounding in twitch and all these things. Well, apparently there must be some way of killing it and carrying on, but you see there's all those farms that have disappeared. It's rather sad, isn't it, you see, those whole families that have gone. And he has the latest thing in everything that ever comes out. And he didn't like me much as I've got all this grass and I think he'd like my land on this side of the road. He said, If I had my way there wouldn't be a green field in England."

CHAPTER EIGHT
Kenneth Wallace

Kenneth Wallace lives in a spacious old house which he rents from Miss Wilson. It's on the opposite side of the road from the man who grows barley to force-feed bulls.

Kenneth Wallace is a striking-looking man, broad featured, black wavy hair, well built, amused with the world. When I spoke to him he seemed to hold nothing back. His daughter, whom he was teaching to drive, was in the house, his wife was shopping in the town, his son was about to go to Northern Ireland with the British Army.

Perhaps Kenneth Wallace's mix of life-styles is one that could only be discovered in the countryside. His regular work is in Wigton at the factory but, once through with that, he is to be found around Miss Wilson's house, helping with the horses – that's been his passion since childhood, riding, breeding, hunting and caring for horses.

This, of course, is virtually impossible inside a large town, but apart from the intrinsic value of what Kenneth Wallace has to say, I believe him to be representative of something far too little credited but prevalent and, I would guess, fairly widespread. Unexpectedness. Superficially, Kenneth Wallace's life could, on any official document or in any sociological survey or in any historical account, be made to appear typical of millions of people who came from large families, went through a war, were tossed about by the world and finally settled into a large factory to raise two children. But underneath that, as so often happens, is so much that is usually neglected: aspirations, bad and good luck, ambitions held and sometimes almost realised and, above all, a life which, when examined at length, defies classification. Though others may not hunt on their days free from the factory bench, there are many, and an increasing number of work-people all over the Western world whose leisure pursuits take them way out of the expected circuits of their daytime jobs. Kenneth Wallace stands for those who manage, somehow, with little to support them, to fashion the life they want on top of the life they have to have.

He was born in Wigton, in Station Road, in 1921.

"A very nice happy family of five, plus two parents of course – seven. And a very small house which the town was littered with in those days. Well, actually I think we were lucky because we had an attic, we had two up and two down – but it was three storeys and then the attic on top. We were luckier than most actually, and other than Bill, my eldest brother, we were all born there and more or less reared there. Mother died there and we all grew up in Station Road. So really it was always our home base from the family origin, if you know what I mean – from the start of the family, other than Bill, he was the odd one out, but he was still born in Wigton. Well, we all just departed from there as we grew older and left school, we all went to the same school – the National – and we all left at an early age of fourteen, except Betty, she went on to Grammar School. And of course she had to leave when Mother died and that sort of curtailed her career. Well, she never got off the ground sort of business because she was actually going to be a teacher. She had all the qualifications and what have you, but it never got off the ground, as I say, so that finished Betty.

Dad was a foreman joiner – a foreman carpenter, shall we say. He was never – I can never remember him being out of work which was another great asset in the town because there was a great labour force but no work to do.

I always thought Station Road was a grand place to live. The point was there wasn't that many houses where you could get mixed up with – I mean, you take Station Road and New Street, we all played together but we didn't go far away from it to the other parts of the town. You can put it, in a way, it was rather a couple of select streets in the town, as far as we were concerned. We used to meet everybody at school which everyone does but once school was over we had our little select gang and we didn't bother anybody. And this is another thing, I think, where the barefoot area, you know, in the summertime, nip around in bare feet . . . well, we had the little river, the Bob beck as we called it, to play in and one thing and another. And there again it was our own little area. We were never tied up with gangs at the South End or Market Hill or anything like this and we never got into any serious trouble. I mean, we used to rob orchards and things like this which was the way of life in those days. We used to go to the pictures once a week. We used to make our own enjoyment because there was more then. Everything was seasonal and you used to find that it cost you nothing to get a hoop or a whip and a top. The girls had hoppy beds and skipping and one thing and another and it was all on a no cost basis because it was the only way you could work it. Yet we wanted for nothing to do. We were always well occupied. Never in the house.

As a working family I always thought we were very comfortable. We hadn't any money because nobody had any money but Father was working and we got round. It worked round from week to week. But there was this element and they used to come to school really badly put on, and they'd had no breakfast and they used to rely on the milk supply at half past ten. And if we took a piece of homemade gingerbread or shortbread or something like that, they would ask you for half of it. And this was the way you started to feel – why can't you bring something? Mammy has nothing. There's nothing in the house. And of course these were genuine people; that the man was on the dole always. There was no work for him. And there were masses and masses of families like this, but we didn't feel in any way superior to them because they would come and play with us and we would go and play with them. You could go in anyone's house, you could go the town circuit, and you used to go with threes or fours and people's doors were always open. You could walk in and get your apple or orange at Easter. And of course there's no money again, but the apples and oranges were there. And then they used to come to your house and do the same thing. And of course in the afternoon you were off rolling eggs and eating as many as you could, making yourself ill nine times out of ten, because there was no tomorrow. Nothing would wait for tomorrow. You thought if you didn't hide them somebody would nick them by tomorrow, so the best thing was to eat them. And of course by nightfall you could neither speak, laugh, cry or anything else because you were choked up with eggs and oranges. But I always found Easter was a nice time of year because of this.

Christmas was rather more poverty-stricken than Easter because – another lad and I, we used to go to Harry Moore's showroom and stand on the door and we did it for years and years. And we would stand on a Saturday from nine in the morning to the Saturday night or, as I should put it, Christmas Eve, until midnight. And we would rush home for a bit of bread and jam and back again, and stand on the door. And he would wait till I went and I would wait till he went. And there again we got no money at all, no money for doing this. Open and close it. Letting people in and out and showing them round and what have you. We got no money at all but we thought, now we'll be well in at the end of the day, and we used to be. Mr. Moore used to give us a big game each. Well, actually, he didn't give us anything. When we'd locked up and everybody had gone, this was getting on for midnight, he would say, Now just take what you want. A game each or a good toy or something like that, or a little train set which of course they were just built for people's pockets in those days, two and six, two bob. And we used to get the choice of anything and I was always rather superior at home on Christmas Day because I had a big game which everybody wanted to play with or this train set or a dirty great knife or something. Something we couldn't afford in daily life. And I think I've sort of done that way all my life because everything I've got I've worked for. I've worked, not so much for financial gain, but just to keep something rolling and keep you above pie, if you know what I mean. It just keeps you out of the deep – you don't owe anybody anything and you live rather comfortable, but one has to work for these things, you see. That's the way I find it. And I've thought Wigton is a grand little place for things like this. There's so much here.

I started as a groom – I started as a boy in the stables at fourteen. With Mr. Ivinson across the road. He was a dealer. He had hundreds but there was no fixed number because they were coming and going every day. Twice a week we were perhaps taking twenty or thirty off the train from Ireland. He used to nip over to Ireland twice a week. We were never off the roads, bringing them in, selling them, taking them away again. Even while I was still at school. He would come with the car and pip the horn at four o'clock and get out of school and he had a little bull-nosed Morris. I'll never forget it, with a dick seat at the back. It had a little dick in it and it used to fall down. Come on, Kenneth, get in. Jump in the back. Now you hadn't a clue where you were going or what time you would be back. My parents knew where I was. They would just assume that I was away with him. Actually I could have been kidnapped, hijacked or anything you liked and there would have been nobody any the wiser. But they didn't bother. They would bother if it got late evening. Where is he? He hasn't been in for his tea or he hasn't been in for his supper. Old Ivinson would never tell you where you were going. Jump in the car, or I would be at the Showfields, playing cricket or football, and just a pair of shorts on, perhaps no shirt, and a pair of plimsolls. Come on, jump in this car. And off he would go. You might end up at Cockermouth or something like this and there's me sitting in the dickie seat at the back. And he would see this man, maybe a farmer or maybe another dealer, buy this animal. Go on then, take it home (sixteen miles away). And you had to get on it or lead it, whichever, if it was unbroken you had to lead it, or if it was a broken horse, one day it might be a Shetland and the next day it's an eighteen-hands Clydesdale, and you just got on the best way you could. And this went on for years. A marvellous life. Marvellous.

It taught me one thing. It definitely taught me one thing that – even today you can take me to a place, I don't care where it is, but I'll bet I can go there again.

Well I don't suppose any lad in this country had a more easier undertaking than I had in leaving home. And it wasn't for anything that was done at home at all. It was just that my life was horses. I started with John Wilson, just as a pro tem job. And well I must have started on about the Saturday, and he farmed at Old Carlisle. They had about twenty cattle, milk cows, they used to milk them by hand and they used to nip down into Wigton with an old van and I was delivery boy. But on the following Wednesday there was a lady used to come to Ivinson's to buy ponies and I happened to be in on the Wednesday night and she knew me very well because she had come for years. She said, Hello Kenneth. What are you doing? Oh, I said, I'm doing the milk-round. Oh, you've left school, have you? Oh yes, I've left school. I left about a fortnight ago. Hmmm. And where are you going to work? I says, Nowhere yet. She says, Have you nothing in mind at all? She says, I know where there's a good place. It's just through Lancaster. Well, Lancaster to me was the end of the earth. I'd never been any further than Silloth (twelve miles away). I thought where the devil's Lancaster? I didn't know where Lancaster was. However, the amusing part of it is that she went home that night – she lived at Seascale – and I carried on with my milk until the following Sunday morning, and I was nipping about the town with a basket of bottles and a pocketful of cash and old Bill Appleton – I happened to be in Water Street – he comes running up. Kenneth, here. I says, What's the matter, Bill? He says, Miss Burnett's come. You've got to go. You've got to go now with her. I says, Right. So I ran into Teresa Calvert's. I says, Teresa, give John Wilson this milk and this money – I threw the money on the table – I'm off. Tell him I'm finished. Well, the period of my milk job I got paid nothing because I wasn't there when it finished. I ran down Water Street as fast as I could.

This was my first job with horses. I ran down to Ivinson's yard and she says, Now, Kenneth, I've got a marvellous job for you but you must come with me now. I says, That's alright. So I ran in home. I got myself changed into what was my best suit and nothing else. I ran out. I said to my mother, I'm off. She says, Where are you going? I says, I'm going to Lancaster to a job. Of course, there was tears. And Ivinson brought Miss Burnett over to tell her exactly what was going on. I was blunt to the head and nothing would stop us. And so within the half hour we were off. This was on the Sunday morning. I landed at Seascale with her and had lunch with her and she put me on the train on the Sunday afternoon to – with a little piece of tartan ribbon in me jacket lapel. Now, she says, Kenneth, you must get off at Lancaster Station and, she says, there will be a gentleman there to meet you. Well, I was maybe rather more fortunate than most. I could almost read. And there was a lot in them days could neither read or write. I could read anyway, and of course we journeys on and journeys on and I thought what a long way, what a long way – and I was only going to Lancaster. Just a bit of a kid. What a long way we're going. And should I have come or should I have not. I'm leaving home, I'm leaving everything. However, we duly gets to Lancaster, a massive big station. I'm looking round. Lost to the wide world. And this chap comes and taps me on the shoulder. Are you Kenny Wallace? I says, Yes. He says, You're the man I'm looking for. He says, Come on. And we walked out of the station into the smartest car I ever set eyes on, in those days. It was a Daimler and I'll never forget the colour of it, a real racing green. Oh, I thought, this is going to be some place. He was a little thickset chap. Very nice but very bossy and prim in his way. And we got in the car and nips out of Lancaster, along this big main road. Oh, I thought, this is grand. I'm watching points here and there and then we're out of Lancaster about six miles. And he shot off to the right and up this road about two miles and comes into this drive. A massive big red house, stables on this side. I thought, what a cracking place! This will be a real job. And of course I couldn't wait. Jumped out of the car, right into the stables. This groom was there. Hello, what do they call you? Oh, Kenneth Wallace, they call me. Where do you come from? From Wigton. I says, I've come to work here. Oh, he says, have you? He says, You're the boy, are you? Alright. And showed me all the ponies and horses. And of course I'd nothing to get changed into so I just mucked in in my best suit for the day. And Mother sent the rest of the things on during the week and that was the first set off.

And during that season, that summer season, the Royal Show was at Newcastle. I rode there. The Royal was at Blackpool. I rode there. I rode in the ring. Actually showed. This chap had two children and they were at boarding-school, you see, and these were rather early shows and they weren't home. The Royal was at Blackpool, the Great Yorkshire was at Sheffield, and the Royal Lancashire was at Blackburn. They were four of the biggest shows in the country. And I was in the top two all the way through. We had some marvellous stock. And I haven't any photographs left. I was thrilled to pieces. But he took me back into Lancaster the next day and bought me a pair of breeches. Ivinson bought me a pair out of Redmayne's once. They cost ten shillings. And this fellow rigged me up properly and I felt like a king. I did. I felt like a lord. The Prince of Wales was at the Royal that year at Newcastle, him that's just died. And it was a totally new experience horse-wise for me, other than company-wise or seeing everything, because I hadn't been out of Wigton – tremendous experience travelling. I was all over the country that six months of the summer, all over England – British Isles, other than Ireland. I mean, a horse-box in those days was something – well, you would class it as a Rolls today. I'm talking 1934 and to have a private horse-box in those days, and everything laid on, it was super. Actually, when you were at shows, people would hardly speak to you because they thought you were Lord Muck. I was pleased some of them didn't, because I couldn't have answered them. I didn't know what they were talking about half the time. And this is the way life went on.

Hindley was a director to Blackpool Football Club in his latter years. He's dead now, of course. Albert H. Hindley. And when I found out about him, it's rather remarkable. His wife was a very eccentric woman and he had been in his early life, I think he was a porter on a railway station. He wasn't society-bred or anything like that, and I think he'd been a porter and then a chauffeur or something like this. She wasn't a woman nine out of ten would have tied to. She was a little nattery woman, very eccentric, and finicky and all this, that and the other. And he was a real down-to-earth fellow but he didn't throw his weight around as he could have done. And I was very happy there. And when his children came home he had a boy the same age as me and a daughter two years older, and there was a young chap lived down the road who used to go to school with Peter, his son, and he used to come up and ride and it was free gratis. When they went out, I went out. Wherever they went I went. And it was a sort of life I'd never been used to. I was amazed at everything. The way they lived. I mean, the food in itself was fabulous. I mean, fresh salmon and big hams hanging here and there and, well, I was living like a king in my own right. I was. Absolutely living like a king and I never realised just how, well, you couldn't call us peasants, but how low in status we were in Wigton until I'd been away and come back.

Now I'd been away, about four months, and we were that busy I never got home, I never got back home at all. Until one Sunday morning, he says, Come on, Kenneth. We'll have a run through the Lakes and I'll take you back home for an hour. And he actually brought us back. We came through the Lakes, Cockermouth, and down into Wigton. In this big Daimler. And it stood in that yard entrance yonder and I think half of Wigton was there having a look at it, because it was some car. Whose is this? Oh, it's Kenneth's boss. And then it got around. And even himself, he came in our little kitchen and he sat down. He had a marvellous dinner with my mother and father and he says, This is marvellous. He says, You know this is my way of life, and that's when I first got the gist like that he wasn't what he sort of pretended to be, that he was of working class. You could tell actually by the way he talked and that, he wasn't society. But I thought he'd been rather more than what he was. And he really enjoyed his dinner. We had a bit of roast beef and Yorkshire pudding and new potatoes, and the way she did it, it was out of this world, the way she cooked – and a bit of apple cake afterwards.

Everybody in Wigton seemed very rough then. Crude, real crude. And of course you couldn't put everybody on that scale, the way I was mixing and living then I mean, I was still working class but I've never found it as rough anywhere else since we'll put it that way – as it was in Wigton then. This is where the slang element comes in. And I found – I was sitting in the house with Mr. Hindley and our John ran in, and Mam says, Look who's here? Oh, it's him, how do? Are you alright, John? Yis, I'se alreet. And he whipped round and went out again, you see. And that was the first words that got me ... where I was always, Yes sir, no sir. But John says Yis. I says, that's awful, to myself. I didn't mention it. And it was just that one word – yis. Ee, I says, that sounds awful. And then of course my father started talking and then there was one or two more of them in, and I was just sitting listening. I was rather dumbstruck. I daren't open my mouth in case I let myself down, or made an ass of myself the other way – the way I'd been talking which didn't apply at home. It was very embarrassing, because Mam would ask us, Are you alright, lad? And this that and the other. Yes Mam, I'm fine. I'm grand. And Mr. Hindley, Oh yes, he's a grand little fellow – I wasn't so little like. He's a grand little fellow. Now we're looking after him, Mrs. Wallace. Don't you worry. Mother would say to Mr. Hindley, He's alright as long as there's horses there. When he writes home, in his letters – which are few and far between – about one every two months or something like that – he'll say, now I hope you're alright because I'm fine and my horses are marvellous. And that was the letter. Love Kenneth, you see. And I started with three shillings and sixpence a week and I used to send two and six home, but I used to wait till I had a ten-shilling note to pop in the letter, so I would write once a month.

I was there one full show season. I would be there about nine months, I should think. And then Peter came home. Actually it was his wife, she wasn't very well, and he got shot of quite a few of the ponies. Because they were outgrown, you see, with the children, and he just kept one or two and he kept the groom on and he said, Now I'm sorry, Kenneth, boy, he says, the showing season's over, which is our great thing, and he says, There's no work around here of any consequence. So we'll just keep one or two to ride about and I haven't any work for you. Oh, I says, that's quite alright, Mr. Hindley. I'll soon get another job. He says, You will, lad. You'll soon get another job. And, he says, I'll give you a reference. So he duly gave me a reference, ran me into Lancaster, and I was back where I started. We were on the station but, in the interim like, I'd travelled a few miles and knew where I was going. So I landed at Wigton Station with me cases. And walked up home. And the following week I was in the factory.

1935 I would come into it first. Yes, it had been going about three years. Of course, Dad was foreman joiner, you see, and in those days it was more or less open house, the factory, for everybody in Wigton that wanted to work. There was a lot that didn't and still doesn't. But I went in there – a very uneasy time, because I wouldn't settle, or I couldn't settle. I didn't like this indoor life and smelly and one thing and another. So I was on the lookabout, you see. Always on the lookabout. I was at the factory and a dealer came to Ivinson's yard and he lived at Odham Castle, that's near Ecclefechan, Lockerbie, Dumfriesshire. And another chap I knew, of course. He says, Where are you working, Kenneth? I says, Down at the factory. He says, You don't want anything there, do you? I says, No. He says, Well I'll give you ten shillings a week if you come to me. I says, Righto. And you see, all my jobs starting and finishing, they were instant. Instant dismissal, one way and another. So I went into the house and my father was in, probably getting shaved, ready to go out at night. He went up to the pub every night for a pot. Can I finish at the weekend, Dad? Yes, where are you going? I've got a job near Lockerbie. Oh, alright. So I took this job.

Dad knew that horses were our Bill's [elder brother] life and mine. All he tried to do when we came home was give us a licking, sort of business. He used to keep us happy with a bit of cash, but he knew fine we wouldn't settle in there. You see, Bill was in there and was studying in the Tech. College in 1933 to be an engineer. And he just dropped it like a hot coal and wouldn't go any further. And he just went onto horses and that was it. He never stopped. He's had a marvellous life with them. Professional huntsman for fourteen years. He started at Brayton with Sir Wilfred Lawson. He's had a marvellous life out of it.

I took this job but it was totally different from the one I'd been doing. This is where one gets experience. This was a big hunting livery yard that liveried for the gentry of Dumfriesshire. Now this is where the cash was in those days. Lord this, Lady this, Sir this, Captain this, and they were all titled people that used to come about. All rode in scarlet. Marvellous turnout, you know. But it made it terribly hard work for us because all the bits and everything about them were steel and they'd got to be burnished every day with silver sand and then the burnisher; the stirrup irons and the big double bridles and what have you and – but when you saw the result of your work it was a very pleasing sight to see a gentleman of about six foot three or four with a scarlet coat on and top hat and mahogany-topped boots sitting on a big grey horse that you'd just done. And there was only two of us there. We had about fifteen or twenty horses. We used to get up at about half past four or five o'clock and we'd dip in the cold-water bucket and get cracking. He used to feed and I used to muck out, which was my job, and then we used to take three each for exercise down the roads – of course they were all drives then. There was no traffic. You could take three – ride the middle one or ride the outside one, whichever was easiest. We used to ride the middle one and take one each side you see. And nip out for about an hour, just walk, on a nice cold frosty brick morning, and come back. Get in about half past seven and by that time you could have eaten the horse you were sitting on. And nip up for breakfast. There again I was getting what the townies weren't. I was getting my eggs and bacon every morning while they were living on crusts. And I knew they were living on crusts, bread and jam, bread and dripping; what have you. And I was getting my porridge and egg and bacon, back down again and a wash, and back down, at it till midnight. But whatever ailed one in those days, you hadn't so much as a headache – but cuts, bruises, abrasions, it was all done stable-wise – veterinary-wise. You used the horse medicines on yourself. Zinc and lanolin, sulphur and lard, iodines, balsams and all this. You didn't look for a doctor. You never had time to look for a doctor. If you got a wound or anything you would just get some horse iodine and pour it on then bounce about for the next half hour, but it did the trick. You got a sore bottom – you just used to clamp zinc and lanolin on and away you used to go. And you'd get kicked. I've been kicked all over the place, put off, thrown off, trampled to death nearly, and you always come back for more. You just take it as the danger living today, as these, as anybody does; National Hunt jockeys, racing drivers, motor-car drivers, what have you. They just take it as a way of life and we used to do the same.

She was a race mare this. We were training her for a point-to-point and I used to do her and she had a skin like silk but really really fine. Very very fine. She couldn't stand a brush on her. Lots of horses couldn't. And you have to do them all with cloths and soft hay wisps and one thing and another, and I used to get on marvellously with her. This morning, well, we'd been out exercising, we'd come in and of course you have your braces off and you're just in your shirt or your vest. You have to get mucked in for an hour and a half. And the sweats – even hard fit the sweat's belting out of you when you're doing these race horses. It's no easy game at all to do them properly. I had to groom them properly and massage them. You do their muscles and one thing and another. And she must have been feeling out of sorts this morning because I was just about her loins and she just walked away from us and she gave us both back feet. Just whipped in smartly. She kicked us in the stomach, she knocked us into the corner of the box. I split my head down the back and sort of rolled over and she came back at us again. Her ears back, teeth, and one thing and another. So I swatted away with me hand and gave a big shout and they came running, you see. What the hell's going on in here? Oh, I says. I got my wind back. I says, I don't know. I don't know what took her but she really went to town on me this morning. And of course the boss says, What's the matter? Oh, I says, it's me head. And I had masses of black curly hair. I couldn't see through it. When they clipped the horses they used to give you a bit of a trim up – you hadn't time to go to the barber's. I don't know what it was like then. But I always wore a cap and I could stick it up under me cap. But he says, It's like dressing a bloody great Angus bullock, this, and he's pulling me hair apart to see where me head's split. And he just got this horse iodine and tipped it in. Well I was going berserk. And of course I'd forgot all about me stomach then, when he started pouring iodine in this. But I wasn't injured in any way. She just got me on the soft part and they're that quick, it's more or less instant. They're not like a great Clydesdale that just clags you and holds you down. It's just instant, like this, and it's away. You just sort of feel a bit flinched for a moment, then it leaves you. That was just one episode. There again there was no fear. I wasn't frightened. I was more concerned of what had made her do this, you see. That's my concern. Because I'd done her for months and I knew she was ticklish and all this. She used to climb the wall when you were doing her and the teeth were going and the feet were going, but never with any intention to kick you. I mean, when you're doing horses, feet are going all the time, back and front, but they never purposely kick you. But this morning she turned really vicious. And whether there was something bitter – I wouldn't know. I don't know to this day. But after I got straightened out I finished my job and she was alright.

As long as there was horses there I had no ambition whatsoever, and that's rather funny that. I hadn't any ambition at all. I was happy. I was doing a job for little money and, as I say, sixteen, seventeen, eighteen hours a day didn't deter me one little bit. There was more than me, of course, but it's a dedication with horses. It's a dedicated life and you've got to think, eat, sleep and drink horses. You're always with them. You've got to be aware of their every worry, their every care, and if you're not dedicated – I mean, I don't know what it's like in other walks of life or other animal life at all – I've no idea – but if you're not dedicated to horse life you might as well never start. You might as well never start in them at all if it's going to be for a twelve months and you say you get sick, hope it out, well, you'd best stay out. But they're a thing you've got to live with, know them and once you know them, I mean, the biggest thing about a horse is – I mean, if a strange horse came into that yard tomorrow the first thing I would do, and lots of people know this, I would read his mind. You can. I can't tell you how but you can. You must get to know what he's thinking and more often not on the ground but on his back. You get on a strange horse and I can tell you within five minutes or even less what that horse is thinking; with the movement of his ears, his tail, his head or his actual action. I could tell you if he's going to put me down. I could tell you if he's going to run away. And these are the things that grow on you and you find through handling so many different horses. It's a premonition – there's a great premonition and anticipation in horse life. I mean you've just got to be just that jump ahead. It's like having a car, you've got to be quarter of a mile ahead of your car, and it's the same with a horse.

207

You've just got to be that few strides ahead of him and beat him to the punch all the time you see. But a horse-man can read a horse's mind just clockwork like that.

By the time the war started I'd been back to the factory twice. I was in a racing stable, I was in this big livery yard, I was in this show yard, then I went to this riding school in Leeds. They had about forty horses, and these are totally different walks of a horse life, and I was gaining experience in every angle, and I was going through it in my own way. And I was doing this – and I'll say that I had no ambition, but I, really at the bottom of me I had an ambition to know horses from start to finish. In every way – or in every walk of horse life, this is what I wanted to know. And you can only do it by changing jobs. I had a reference from every job and I didn't have a job that I couldn't go back to.

It would be in 1938, Mam died. I was at Leeds when she died, and I went back and the boss' son, he was the same age as me, and we had these forty horses. It was a big riding school and I've seen us have about a hundred and seventy of them on a Sunday from Leeds. We were going morning till night and of course you had to go with them. I would take about ten or fifteen. Somebody else would take about five or six. And this is the way it used to go. And there was two gentlemen came one day from York, I think they were from York or somewhere near York. It was just about the scares were on. They were starting to mobilise these peacetime – what was peacetime armies, and one thing and another. These two gentlemen came, and they asked Billy Stevenson and I, would we like to join the Yorkshire Hussars. And as fully fledged horse-men, which we were then, we would walk into sergeant stripes right away and then become instructors or some such thing. And I was all for it. I says, This is grand. It will be another change. I was all for it. So I wrote home that night. I wrote to Father – Mother had died that same year. Would you please give me permission to join the Yorkshire Hussars as an auxiliary to start with? So that meant Saturdays and Sundays or any evening we had free, we could nip over. In fact they were going to pick us up. And I was on pins waiting for this letter coming back. And on the top was a big NO. It wasn't even on the bottom, it was on the top. No, you are not going to join the Yorkshire Hussars. You will come home. So Billy didn't want to go. Well, he didn't want to go really. There was him and his father and they had a big concern. He says, I can't go so it's maybe just as well your dad said no. He said I would have been uneasy. I would have wanted to go if you had. We were grand pals and great mates. And so that went phut and I came home about a month afterwards. And I'd risen to the mighty sum of ten shillings a week then and my keep. And Kirkbride aerodrome was well through in the form of building. The main site was up and A and B site were up and Dad says to us, Now you want to go down to Kirkbride and get yourselves a job. It's big money. Oh, I says, that's alright. So I went to the dole office at first to see Jimmy Tennant, and I'd never been on the dole in me life. I didn't know how to go about anything, and I walked into the office as if I was walking into jail. I was terrified that he would probably either chase me out or put us down New Street in jail for doing something. Because I hadn't experienced anything like this at all. And well, what do you want? Jimmy Tennant. Knowing him later, he was a grand little chap, once you got to know him. I says, I've just finished the job. I would like a card to go to Kirkbride aerodrome. There you are then. So I got this green card and off I went on me bike to Kirkbride aerodrome (six miles away).

I got a start down there, with some steel erectors, and I never asked about money. I never asked how much an hour or how much a day or how much a week. It never entered my head. And this is how lax one can be. I don't know how it is, but I just wanted to get into something. However, I started and the first week I think I got a tenner. It was seven to ten pounds anyway but we were working till eight o'clock at night from seven thirty in the morning. It was summertime and it was really grand. I was enjoying it. I couldn't understand this seven to ten pounds. Well, I was a millionaire overnight. So the following week there was a terrible wet day and Willie Moffat and me we nipped off to Carlisle because we couldn't stand it any longer – our pockets bulging with this cash. I bought two suits, three pairs of shoes, a pair of boots, and umpteen pairs of socks and shirts and I come back loaded. I just couldn't help myself, I thought, this is marvellous. This is a grand way to make money. And I went on there, I was there months. Then I broke these two fingers about – matter of six weeks before my age group came up for enlistment. And old Dr. Dolan – I went down for a medical, of course. Billy Johnston and me out of the little toy shop. We went together, we were the same age. And I went down and old Dr. Dolan, he says, Come in lads. I brought you into the world, I needn't examine you. But, he says, you're stripped off anyways. Then he says, You needn't go any further, young Wallace. We'll send for you later. Well, I was going to the rehab. about three mornings a week to get my fingers straightened out and I was deferred for twelve months. And then of course, like all the rest of them, I was anxious to get away. And in that twelve months, or getting on for nine or ten months, I volunteered and they wouldn't take me, so as I say I was deferred for twelve months and I went under the next age group.

I was twenty-one actually but I was more when I went in. I was twenty-two. And I went in the Air Force, courses here and there. I went in as a fitter armourer eventually, attached to the Dambusters latterly. They were the last squadron I was with. I had a grand time down there. And then I went to – I did my term, five to six years. Never out of the country, of course, much to my disappointment, because I wanted to travel. And, you see, when you went on the station with half these boys with tears in their eyes and their mothers seeing them off, well, that never happened to me because I never wanted it. I'd been away all my working life and it didn't bother me, just jumping on the train and going. It was just another job, sort of thing. I enjoyed it, just because it was different and the community I got on well with.

When I came out of the Forces, I went up to this butching in Scotland. In Galloway. He asked us to go and work for him. I said I'd never done any butching before. But of course, it's as it is now, everything was killed for them to come into the shop, and I got the job. I was always handy with a knife. Even if it was just cutting a bit of chicken up. I went round on the van with him for about a fortnight or three weeks, just for variance. He says, Right, you take the van. And I did that for two years and I used to come down home pretty regular, about once a month or something like that. And of course Irene and I had been going together long before the war, the usual falling out and back in again – I never went with her while I was in the Forces at all. I just went freelance. I hadn't any ties at all. And we met up again, I think it was one Friday night in the Market Hall. There was a dance on and I was down for the weekend, half sloshed as usual, and we met up again. And it just seemed to take over from there, where we'd left off sort of business, and I wasn't long up there. I says, We'll get married and I'll come back home. And I jumped into Charlie Hetherington's sawmill and Irene was working at Robson's at Carlisle. She was making more money than me and I was at the sawmill about twelve months, I think. And I went back into the factory in 1949. And I've left once and been back since 1949. I'm in the coating department. I've been in there this latter, with a seven-month break; since 1949 I've been in the coating department. Other than that I was all over the place before; stores, joiner's shop, but this has been more realistic, shall we put it? Shift job, on shift work – I was never on shifts before.

I went back to the factory in 1949 and I was married and I stuck it until 1953 and I was sick to death of it. Really sick, right up to the neck. And there was a job come vacant. Well, they chased me to death – at the farmers' hunt kennels at Welton, they chased me to death to take it. And George Fairbairn, it was his first season as master, and they came down to Wigton and back again, and they came down, and I was at Skelton Show and he tapped me there. I was at Penrith Show, he tapped me there. And I was ready to hold of the bit because I was sick to death down there and I was losing – actually he gave me, he says, Now if you're coming – I couldn't leave home, you see, I couldn't leave Oulton. I couldn't take Irene away from her mother through being an invalid. So I says, I've got to have means of travel, if I do come. He says, I'll buy you a motor-bike. Well, she wasn't for it, at all, but I was that sick. And old Ivinson had died. I used to go to John Dixon's at Low Houses and I threw cautions to the wind and I says, Right. So I just rang Fairbairn up and I says, I'll take that job, Mr. Fairbairn. He says, When can you start? I says, I'll start at the weekend. I'll work a week's notice. He says, That's fine. And that was the 53–4 season.

I was the stud groom there. I was in sole charge there. There was nobody else. And I really enjoyed it. What a change from factory and shifts. I really enjoyed it. And I was out seven months exactly and Fairbairn took the Tynedale Hunt, he left there, so of course they changed staff. So I thought now there's nowt with me staying here, because I was losing about three or four pound a week now travelling, and I was getting back on the same state I was as a boy; getting up early, get us up about four or five o'clock, and there again with horses long days. It didn't matter when I finished. Many a time, eight o'clock at night when I was coming back. And I thought, dash, no – I'll have to settle down. So I packed in on the Saturday and started on the Sunday afternoon at the factory, at two to ten shift. And that was my sixth time in there and that was in March 1954. It was the weekend after the point-to-point. I saw the point-to-point through at Rosebank and I think it was on the Saturday that day. And I finished on the Saturday night and started at two to ten on the Sunday. I just nipped up to Western Bank to see Mr. Routledge. Of course, Father had laid the ground prior to that, but I just used to start in on my own job at two o'clock tomorrow. And I just got the bait bag and away in at two o'clock on the Sunday. And that was it, and that was in 1954 and I've never left since. And I think in that time, it's only about two months ago, my back went and I lost two days, and that's all I've lost through illness since 1954.

I've never missed a shift, through illness. I've missed through other things but never through being off through illness, actually one shift.

I'm not in the least union-minded. I'm not biased against the Union. It's a great thing. It's a great thing for the individual worker, to safeguard him against bad management or bad employment in any way. But I'm not one for this hysteria business. Go with the masses like sheep. I mean, one has to have principle and one has to try to be an individual as well. And you don't get it, you don't get it in industry. I mean, even this small industry down there – there's that much backbiting and two-facedness that you just can't live with it. I mean – how can I put it? there's chaps down there if you went to them tomorrow and says, Right, you're working for a shilling an hour less they would never turn a hair. They would say, That's alright. And then against the fighters and the rebels that want more, it isn't even a vicious circle. It's just bite against bite, if you know what I mean. And you've just got to sort of compromise between the two – which we have a lot of them down there. And there's a terrible differential between them of the town or the the town men from Aspatria, or even Carlisle, that are union-minded and want more and are fighting to get more. But they've no backing because these others, ex-farm mostly, they can come out of there and go and do a stint on the farm and get a bob or two. They're not interested in big money at all. There'll never be a strike down there, and, I quote, never. There'll never be a strike down there because there's too many independent workers. And they're independent in their own right inasmuch as if they got paid off tomorrow they would jump in a job the same day. They would just nip back to the land. And this is what makes a man independent. He's not fighting for his bread and butter. But the town men can't do this. They can't do this. When they're paid off from there, that's them finished. They've got to go round building sites or other industries to get another job. But these country lads don't bother. They can start work tomorrow on a farm on a good basic rate, as it is now, and it's giving them a total independence from the town man altogether. And this is why the Union isn't strong down there. It's strong in membership. Everybody's in but yet you couldn't get the factory out. You couldn't get them out as a whole. And I think this has applied for the last ten to fifteen years anyways. You couldn't drag them out at all. It's quite impossible to get them to come out.

So as life goes on, as one door shuts another one opens. Old Mr. and Mrs. Cox that were in here, the family had left them and it was too big. They'd been here twenty years and it became vacant

World War Two:
An Air Force group, 1943
(author's father is at extreme right, second row down),
and the victory parade, 1945, in the High Street.

Harry Watson's Rugby Union round-up

ASPATRIA gained their 16th win of the season, beating COCKERMOUTH, the cup-holders 14-3, by playing the more progressive and forceful football. Their performance was worthy of

ball line. Both sides also missed penalty chances.

Keswick took the lead in the second half with a penalty goal by David Hume and he also converted one of the tries that were added by

WIGTON II travelled to beat BRITISH STEELS in the Shield League 28-3. They were faster and had more penetration and the Steels got their three points from a penalty goal.

trouncing at WHARFEDAL 46-0. They were on the defensive for most of the game an Wharfedale ran in 11 trie and one was converted.

VICKERS played th better football to be

KING MORE OF OUR HAY

ugh the hay crop of England and
n an average year is worth £85—
llion at current prices, we could
ore of it, and it is now of vital

Opposite: Harry Watson.

*Above: Watson, president of the Wigton Rotary Club,
presents a heart machine to Dr. Tom Dolan (left)
and Drs. Guy Jones and Norman Gray, in 1971.*

This page, top to bottom:
Nelson Grammar School, early 1930s;
first pupils at St. Ursula's School, 1946;
the National School, now unoccupied;
and St. Cuthbert's R.C. School.

Opposite: Kenneth Wallace.

Opposite: David Pearson.

*This page, top to bottom: Wigton R.U.F.C., 1907–8,
winners of the Cumberland Shield; Wigton R.U.F.C., 1965,
Cumberland Cup winners (David Pearson standing fourth from left);
and Wigton Harriers A.F.C., 1910–11.*

Top to bottom: Wigton Cricket team, circa 1900; Wigton swimming team (who beat the Swedish Olympic team in 1928); and the hunt, circa 1930.

Opposite: George Johnston.

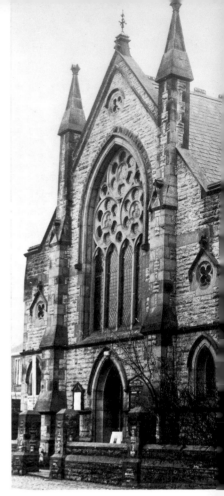

*Across the top: St. Mary's Church (C.E.),
the Methodist Church, the Congregational Church,
and a nineteenth-century water colour
of the Wigton Vicarage.*

*Below: Wigton church choir, 1904;
Wigton church choir, 1947 (the author is second
from left, front row);
and the Church Missionary Society campaigning.*

Opposite: A stand at the British Industries Fair, 1936,
and two views of the Sidac factory.

Above: Joseph Graham.

Opposite, clockwise from top left: Penrice's, coronation year 1953;
Redmayne's the tailors; and the end of the Wigton City Council, 1974—
Edwin Routledge (left) becomes chairman of the Allerdale District Council.
Wigton 1976—the car-park, inside Saunderson's in King Street,
and a view of King Street.

The Carnival revived, 1975.
Four generations: Elizabeth (Armstrong) Bragg, Stanley Bragg,
Melvyn Bragg, and Marie-Elsa Bragg.

and I just happened to say, in passing one day, I think Barbara and I were riding past here – I says, It's a grand big house and that. She says, Yes, isn't it? All the front was all trees. You couldn't see it. And everything was crowded over. Just little small lawns. And the talk went on. I said, I would like to live there. She says, Well, the way the horse population's going, I think you'd better. We were breeding them. Went into ponies. She says, as soon as they get out you can come in. They went out on the Saturday, I moved in on the Sunday, post haste. Brought Mother with us and we've been here ever since. And there again, horses have never done me any harm all my lifetime. I wouldn't have been living like this without a horse. I would have been living in a council house on the estate. Possibly in Wigton, maybe not.

I still go hunting myself. But it's all changed up here. Etiquette's dropped off. I mean, they come out in jeans and not hats and head-scarfs and anything. Let them come, we're pleased to see them. I don't mean it in that manner. The hunting etiquette has gone, the manners gone in the hunting field. I mean, in the early Thirties we daren't look round if you were standing there with the colonel's horse or something like that at the meet, you daren't look round. You had to have boots polished, leggings polished, bowler hat, the lot. Now you can go in your wellingtons and jeans and a cap on and anorak on, and that's you. There's been a tremendous change in the horse population in my time. I mean, the horse population then *was* a horse population. You got the lights, you got the heavies, you got the small, you got the tall, you got everything. But now they're more or less on a uniform scale. The heavies have gone; there's no heavy horses. No Clydesdales or Shires or anything like that. You've lost all the heavies altogether. They're few and far between, as much as you like to see them. There's a few farms keep one or two, but that's all. There was stables all over Wigton at one time. You could count ten stables.

And this is where the dealer used to get his horses from. Old Ivinson used to do nothing but stand on the street all day Tuesday morning watching them come in. And if a fresh one came in at all, he was right at them. And of course the price then was twenty-five to thirty and he would buy it. He would bring it down and give the man some old scrag to take away with him. You can borrow that one to get him home and use about the land. He would look after it well, it cost him nothing, and he give him twenty-five or thirty pounds for his horse. We would get the clipping machine at it, put a saddle on it and see what it was like to ride. Next thing he knew, there was a dealer there the next day come to buy it. Probably sell it for forty pounds. Now in those days ten pounds was a lot of money. Even today if you're turning over something like ten a day you're doing well – he maybe not made ten, may three to five, something like that. But this quick return, and even then it was big money. And this is the way they went on. But the thing was, with horse-dealing and horse-dealers, unless – I always found – unless you went on a specific standard, I don't think they ever made much money. You see, take a dealer like Ivinson, as I've said earlier on, one day he'd buy a Shetland, next day he'd buy a Clydesdale. Now, if I'd have been dealing round here, or if I was dealing round here now, I would go for the top-class stuff. I would specialise, and it would take a while to get your name through – sales, you would have to show at sales and take horses to sales. These big sales – Doncaster, Kelso, Leicester. But once you had sold a good animal or two, your phone would never stop ringing. I've an order now for as many three-year olds as I can find, and I'm talking big money. Five hundred a piece. Money no object. But they're just not there.

It's all changed. In the Thirties the hunt staff at the hunt ball, their local hunt ball, used to stand in livery at the door, not taking tickets or anything, just standing there. For ornament. With their scarlet coats on and white breeches and boots. They were the huntsman, the first and second whip, the second horse-man – our Bill's done it many a time. I've never done it, mind. I've never been in hunt service as a whip or anything like that. They used to go to the hunt balls and stand at the door, and they're on duty. For what reason, other than ornamental, I had no idea. But what used to happen, the hunting farmer – the hunting gent – he used to get them tanked up. And by night, half-way through the night, they were to carry home. It was, in itself, a way of giving them an evening out, but all restrictions were barred. They couldn't move off the spot. This is the way etiquette was in those days. I'm not for this at all, I'm not for it. I'm not for it in any sense of the word because you're always a servant. You're dedicated to your job but you're still a servant.

There's plenty of professional huntsmen made their way and made big money. They've bought farms and one thing and another. They've been very good at their job and they're recognised gentry in the country now in some counties. There's old Barker of the Pytchley – he's a big land-owner but he was just a professional huntsman. And it's the way of life that one can't understand and one can't tell unless one's been associated with it. You see, the huntsman in himself, it costs him practically nothing to live at all; nothing. And I mean nothing because his daily work, they bring casualties from the farms to feed the hounds and he'll nip down to this farm with the Land Rover and trailer for a cast cow or a dead horse or even a sheep. And while he's there he'll probably get a double whisky or two double whiskys off the farmer and a bag of potatoes. Now he'll go to another farm, he maybe gets a ham thrown in the back, and all hunt balls in his region, him and his wife and the whip and his wife get complimentary tickets. And the huntsman got that way that God-fearing men, they got that way that when they went in the pub everybody had to buy them a drink. And they were real little lords in their own community. And this is the way the huntsman was. And this is the way the huntsman lived. You can't ask him for a drink; he's a huntsman of the Pytchley or the Warren Chase. The same element applies here to complimentary tickets and if a farmer saw Bobby Hudson walk in the Kildare, he'd jump up and buy him a drink. But that's not putting Bobby on any pedestal. I mean, if you – in olden times – Frank Smith of Dumfries, he was a marvellous huntsman, one of the best old horn-blowers that was ever known. If he walked in a pub, you would see them stretching. They would be five inches taller. They would nearly stand to attention, in the local pub.

There's only one regret . . . that I would like to have had not a lot of money but enough finance to get my way through this horse life. I've no other regrets. I don't want a lot of money. I would just have liked to have not had to go into industry to make a living. I would like to have made my own way the same as you feel that you're sort of freelance, you're your own boss up to a point, and you can make your own way. I would like to have done that. That's all. But of course it would just have been in my own line, the line I know. But I meet people, you get around, and it's a very full life when you weigh it up. It's a very full life because it isn't seasonal; you're going twelve months of the year. If you're not doing one thing you're doing another. You make an awful lot of friends. You make enemies, too, when you're dealing, but if you've any tact you can get over that. Which businessman hasn't an enemy? I don't know the original – I came back to horses again, the original horse people are gruff, they're rough, but they're grand folk, if you know what I mean. They're far from being greedy and narrow-minded and all this, that and the other. Because I think it's the whole mixture of mixing with people all their lives and meeting different people. I mean, one day you meet the tramp, the next day you meet the lord. And it gives you a great insight into life.

I mean, take Irene there, for instance. She never met people – since we got on these latter years – that she would have met if I hadn't have married her. I mean, I'm not being upstartling or anything like that but I can walk in the Kildare and John Brockbank [a big farmer and horseman] will be sitting. Hello Ken, come and have a drink. I'll go and plant down beside him, but I wouldn't go in if I couldn't afford to go in. This is another thing. I'm not living above my means by going in there, because we don't go out that often anyway. But when you take your wife out for a drink, why not take her to where there's a nice chair to sit in, rather than stand at a cheap bar? The drinks are the same price. Half of them are frightened to go in. They can't talk to anybody when they go in. They're sitting in a corner like mice. Now this is all wrong. They've never been anywhere. And three parts of Wigton are like this, Wigton lads. If it hadn't been for the war, they would never have left the town.

And that's what our Barry quoted. He got himself a job at Carlisle and then he come down into the factory. He says, I'm not stopping there. He says, I'm going to travel. He quoted to me one weekend, I think it had been an August weekend, or an Easter weekend or a Whit weekend, some of the lads coming in on Tuesday morning from their weekend holiday. Ee, what a weekend we've had. Where've you been? We've been in the British Legion. Sitting drinking. Saturday afternoon, Saturday night, Sunday lunch-time, Sunday night – and they come back in there in great glee. He says, That's not for me. I says, Right lad. I says, It isn't. I says, You get yourself away. I says, I won't hold you back. I says, There's only one thing – the night before he went we were up at the Sun, and I was real tight. And I put my hand on his head. I says, There's only one thing I want you to do, Barry. He says, What's that, Dad? I says, You can go where you like, do what you like, at any time you like. I says, We've done all we can. I says, Never bring any trouble to your mother. I says, Other than that, you're free. And he's done just that. He's best of squad, best young cadet, and he's taking the Army life as he meant to take it.

He went in for three years, to do three years justice. He hasn't gone in to loaf, to lie about. He's doing his utmost. He's been to Hong Kong. He's been all over the place. And he brought a lad up with him, maybe six months through the basic, and he brought a lad up with him that had been in eight years. And I got this lad to one side one night. We'd been out for a drink. I said, Mick, what's he like in the Army, I says – he just throws things about here. He says, Don't you believe it. He says, Bloody hellish, of a morning, when he's going out. Everything has to be just so, polish here, polish there. He says, It's murder.

You daren't speak to him. Now, it's funny this. And yet he comes home and his shirt's here, and his trousers there. He knows his mother's there to gallop after him. But it's in the bringing up. It's there when it's wanted."

CHAPTER NINE
The Factory

The western side of the town is dominated by the factory. The chimney has always been tall, taller than the church tower, taller than the mansion tower, taller by far than any town building – most of which are two-storeyed: it had to be tall to take the harmful and poisonous chemical fumes into the sky. But when a west wind blows, not such a rare event in England, the fumes drift over the town and visitors wrinkle their nostrils: most townspeople say that the smell means work. As it does, today, for almost a thousand employees. The factory feeds the town.

Of those so far quoted in this book, Kenneth Wallace, Norman Fell, Llewellyn Evans, Edwin Routledge, Johnny Morrison, Billy Lowther and his father, all worked at the factory and this is before we have reached the chapter devoted to it.

At present there is a boom. The "old factory", set off at the beginning of the Thirties on the site of extinguished industrial ventures, makes cellophane paper, clear, transparent paper which is used for all sorts of packaging; around cigarette packets, for example. That grew slowly in the Thirties, Forties and Fifties: in the Sixties it was taken over by Sidac, an international and multi-national corporation which built a new factory cheek to cheek beside the old factory, and still, into the Seventies, the expansion goes on. More and more skilled workers are being brought into the plant: twentieth-century affluence has come to Wigton largely through these paper-works: environmentalists will find significant satisfaction in the fact that affluence and effluence go hand in glove: the river Wiza, once famous for its trout, now runs with chemicals, and the fumes cannot possibly have a beneficial effect on health.

On the other hand, a recent survey proved that people in Wigton are longer lived than anywhere else in the country (and it is by no means a spa town or retirement centre!), and no one with a spark of common sense or a survivalist's instinct would hesitate for a second: first the tools for civilisation – of course tools are sometimes dirty – and then, later, the polish. Few things are more sickening today than the sight of those who have, and those who have long had, bemoaning the sweat and grime which accompanies the have-nots on their understandable drive to climb towards civilised comfort; few things – except the coincidental anti-materialist philosophy, invariably, in my experience, held onto by those whose basic needs and indeed whose creature comforts, are well provided for. Inside most communes is usually one capitalist whose money (from where? the usual hidden sources of labour) carries the can and several well educated professional or embryo-professional people whose base expectations have long been satisfied.

All this to say, simply, that I'm glad of the boom: I'm glad that people I know can move out of two-roomed damp gardenless slums into three-bedroomed council houses with bathrooms and lawns; I'm glad there is more money about for sweets and treats and holidays and clothes; I'm glad that the sons are six inches taller than their fathers and that *their* sons show signs even of overtopping them; I'm glad there are insurance benefits and union rates and better working conditions and more of the happy things of life for more people, people who, on the whole, are not materialistic, not greedy, not the pawns of industry which snobbish journalists and despairing academics in their life-lined jobs describe, not mean, not grasping, not falling away from nobility because they are reaching towards a respectable style of living. The factory represents the work and will of people wanting to better themselves, without hurting others, and there is everything to be said for that.

It also represents a considerable amount of tenacity, local ingenuity and, of course, hard work. No one waved a magic wand in Wigton. What's there had to be found. Johnny Morrison was one of the men there at the very start. It was 1932. There were four employees.

"The joiner, myself (a fitter), an electrician and a labourer. Of course there were the executives, such as the manager and the chief engineer, and then Mr. Lever, he was more like a storeman. But for employees there was just the four of us. We gradually spread our wings but very very slowly, because money was very scarce at that particular time. Just had enough capital to erect the machine, the first machine. The factory in the first place was built for artificial silk by British Netherlands Artificial Silk Company, they had a factory here and I think another one at Dumfries or somewhere on the Scotch side, and they got all the equipment in and they went broke. Well, they found out that this artificial silk process was the similar process as transparent film which they're now making. Sort of cellophane paper. Instead of spinning the thread for artificial silk you make it in a sheet, or as you say, well, we call it rayophane, it isn't cellophane, and a lot of the equipment in the first stages, it came in for paper manufacture. Only they had to build a special machine for running the sheet – the silk frames were scrapped, and they just started from there.

Unions were in their infancy then. I don't think they could have got us a higher wage. They hadn't the money to pay it. And you see the reason why we got this first machine, it was built by a firm at Preston called Thomas Dryden and Sons and I think they built it with the expectations of getting another order, which was like a long-term loan if you follow what I mean, which proved very beneficial to them and they built the second one. What we had to do in the first place, we would dismantle a lot of these spinning frames. We were in the viscose section, overhauling the various machines which had been standing idle for so long. And then you would gradually employ another man, probably another fitter, and then another, and then there would be another electrician come. But I think we had just about four for quite a number of years.

We started our own apprentice scheme just before the war. Now the majority of the fitters down there they're all their own products, if you follow what I mean. They've all served their apprenticeship – well, the majority have served their apprenticeship there. There are a few outsiders. Manpower's gradually been cut back and machines are working themselves, more or less, it's just a push button, and the working conditions are much better. They're more safety-conscious, too. When we first started, we didn't realise what caustic soda was. I've seen my finger nails practically eaten off with the damned stuff and we didn't know what we were playing with. We weren't told. But we soon found out. Now there's instructions to tell people – they're educated into these hazards. At that particular time, factory inspectors didn't come round as often as they do now. There wasn't the same interest taken with general factories as there are now. You see now a factory inspector will pop in at a factory any time. Well, we never used to see one when we first set away. When I served my apprenticeship, we didn't know what a factory inspector was. We didn't think there were such-like men.

There's so many advantages now to what there were then, when

I was an apprentice. Take for instance the fitter himself. I mean, he had to provide all his own tools. Now they're provided for them. Their clothing, it's provided; there's protective clothing if you're going into a department which requires protective clothing, that's provided for them. It wasn't then. You just had to go in as you were, and if your clothes got burnt with acid or whatever you were working with, well, you had to make good yourself. As time went on there was allowances made for that. And the wages structure is much better now. We got four and ninepence a week. They get about fourteen pounds. Also the times. We used to start at seven thirty and finish at five thirty; now they start at seven-thirty and finish at four-thirty. And on a five-day week. We used to be on a six-day week. Seven-thirty to twelve-thirty on a Saturday. I was out all night many a time. When we just had the one machine, we were called out maybe at eleven o'clock at night, and be there till six or seven the next morning, because you just have the one machine, and you had to repair it. In the early years there was very much a feeling that you'd got to keep the factory going, because there was nothing else. That was the feeling. You had to keep it going. That was the big success in the factory. I mean, they make a much better quality paper here than they do at the parent company at St. Helens. I think that's the whole secret. It's still bred into a lot of them here now. They must get the best.

You see the apprentices now they spend so much in the factory. I think they spend about six months, and I think they go to the Tech. at Carlisle for two years, then they come back to the factory. But during the holiday periods at the Technical College or whichever school they're at, some go to Workington, during the holiday periods they come back and work in the factory. And everything's provided. All their expenses are paid, all their books are found. When I served my apprenticeship, I had to go to the Technical College at Working-ton. And we used to have to go after work to evening classes. Well, these children go to day classes, if you follow what I mean. And we had to provide all our own books. The only concession we got was working on the railway we used to get passes to Workington. But there was no time allowed off from work at all.

I don't think they're as good a craftsman as they were in our days. See, an apprentice, when we served our apprenticeship, we used to go right through everything. We would start off with a fitter at the first, and then you were put on a machine, you were maybe put on a lathe, then you were put on a trimming machine, and possibly milling machines were just coming in then. You were put on a milling machine, and then you would go back with the fitter, and stay with him. Whereas now, an apprentice fitter in the present day, the only thing he does, he does fitting. Any machine men, well, they're trained for the machine, such as a boy going on a lathe, he finishes up as a turner. A boy going on a milling machine, he finishes up as a miller. The trade's been split up. You see, we were fitters, turners, we could braze, we used to go with the tinsmith and learn that, and we used to go with the boilermaker. And that's why the marine engineers, from Maryport and Carlisle they were, were so good when they went to sea because they had had experience with the boilers.

When you take – for instance, you start work at sixteen and you get four and seven a week, you wondered how your parents – dirty overalls to provide – and it's a rough job, engineering. And when we were apprentices, we used to lark about quite a bit and quite a bit of clothing went for a burton. Fitters at Maryport, they were like students at college. When I served me apprenticeship, I should think there would be about fifty of us. And during the fair-time, they used to get the fair coming to Maryport similar to what came to Wigton, but during the fair, well we just used to take ourselves the afternoon off. Used to go up the street in the boiler suits, and the steel rules in the pocket, big men, and possibly pushing each other, and walk round the butcher's shop and out again and go to the fair and take the fair by storm. Not pay for a damned thing. And they just used to stand and look at you. They knew it was innocent fun, just the same as you get your rags at college. But, as you say, the present-day apprentices, I don't think there's the same – well, you see, we had to work because you knew you couldn't get anything else. Well now, there is opportunities to a certain extent. They're getting hard to fill at the moment, but you'd always that behind you. If you've a job, keep hold of it. It was up to you to work as hard as you could and make the best of it."

Mr. Morrison's brief outline gives some notion of the development. Now the factory spreads along the river, threatening to take over the town's park which was once happily marooned in green fields.

The old and new factories are easily distinguished. The old like many an archetypal industrial pile in England, looking at once ramshackle and elaborately organised; cooling towers and long sheds, loading bays beside the railway lines and old flaking green paint. The new factory seems to gleam of concrete and aluminium. There's a clank in the old and a hum in the new; the old looks like a struggle, the new appears effortless. And, it seems (from observation, this, and conversation – not statistically proved) that the old is manned by more of the old originals; by those men who were taken on in the Thirties and Forties and the touch-and-go Fifties. Physically smaller men, none of the "strangers" who work in the new plant and buy their own houses on the edge of the town; council houses not mortgage, bike or walk to work not motor, still with the knowledge of the difficulty of finding and keeping work and the necessity of holding down work however unpleasant.

Most people, when asked if they liked the work, said exactly the same thing, word for word "You've got to". It was a fairly cheerful fatalism. When asked what they would do if they won the football pools most of them said they would stop work "for a start".

On the other hand there's undoubtedly boredom, resentment, frustration and pain of all sorts in that factory as in any comparable place. One man I spoke to expressed some of this most directly. What follows is his story.

I have decided not to name him. This is the sole anonymous contribution in the book. The reason is, quite simply, that although he was keen to tell me, he would, I judge, be embarrassed and even harmed by having his name to this in print.

This man comes from a large and very very poor working-class family. Food and clothes were a real problem. He began work in the factory in the Thirties. His work has been generally reckoned and recognised to be outstanding. He has always worked in the factory.

"I believe in God, I divn't mix with many people; I'se honest, I don't tell lies, I hate lies; I'd rather have a smack on the jaw than tell a lie. Maybe sometimes you were in that predicament where you've got to maybe tell a lie to prevent something serious but I wouldn't tell a lie deliberately, say till anybody like I've done this and I've got that and I've been there. There are some people that do that, isn't there? There are people like – if I find out that people are genuine with me, I'm genuine with them. Like on a number of occasions I've given money away to all sorts of people, just to try and help them and see that somebody does care about them.

I've seen me, when I was a boy – instead of doing the garden that I was supposed to do, I've seen me cut across those fields to the show-fields. And I've seen twenty and thirty grown men running up and down the field after a ball, each side, running after a lile ball. And somebody would come over for a game, oh you can't play, you've got clogs on. And the other fellows would maybe have a clog or a shoe on, maybe a soft shoe, a left-footed one, and they would carry on like that. Like people today, I know by our lads like, I've seen rugby balls, two or three in, two footballs. Them fellows couldn't get a ball them days. They had to go and beg and pray and ask people. Willie Wallace, old Gally Wallace, they used to ask him if he could lend them a ball. Get on their knees and they were excited to death because they were going to get a game of football. Excited. They would maybe rush home and get a cup of tea or whatever there was to eat, these men, likely same as I was when I was a boy, and rush and go down to the showfields, and pick sides. Terrible, thirty or forty good craftsmen, running about that field and there wasn't employment for them.

I started down at the factory at about a pound a week. I enjoyed it then. It's a bloody rat race down there now, absolutely. It used to be enjoyable going in. Mind you, I wouldn't like you to take my word for it. It's a pure rat race. About twelve months ago there was seven hundred pounds' worth of stuff pinched out of there, couplings that belonged to the machinery. Now the five fellows that were involved with it, they got one of them about three or four months after, but there was five of them involved. Now out of them five, there's two of them got promoted. And one of them, a real snake. Now we used to have to put our waste into a trailer, but consequently if they were having a bad do, some of the lads they maybe do it for a few days, just lackadaisical, that's all, this fellow that was on the tractor, he was playing hell about bales not being in, so therefore us lads that were in charge of the job got a lobbicking. But I found out what he wanted the baling for, because his other compatriots was putting the stuff over there and they were taking it out and selling it between them. And them's the type of fellows they're employing down there now. And George Stephenson (the manager, who came up from the factory floor) turned round and employed them. Mind you, he's a fair lad is George Stephenson. I'll tell you something else as well. If you come up now, mind you, they're very reluctant to deal with you, these young fellows, because they think you're wanting the bloody job off them. In fact, we should have had the job off *them*. They shouldn't have been allowed to be in there, in my opinion. I agree with the top men, but not young ones where they come and dictate to you down there. They ask you about the job, then in two or three months they come and tell you what to do. That type of fellow. Some of them will do anything to get their own ends.

I should have had a dozen gold watches for the ideas I put up, and they're all in use down there. Saving them thousands. Them old machines – us lads brought them up to date. But you see they say this, Oh well, you're on the staff now, you're expected to see these things. But how does it come these fellows that's getting hundreds and thousands of pounds a year extra, they don't see them? You see what I mean, how does it come they can't see them if it's good enough for me to see? Not that I want anybody's job because I haven't got the qualifications to do it, but the practical side, the fellows that's with all the B.Sc.s down there, some of them can't see wood for trees simply because they're maybe not interested. And I'm going to tell you something. It's knocking interest out of everybody down there. I've seen me fully eight hours down there. That's one thing I do. When I go to work, I go to work, and when I get out of that gatehouse it's finished with me. As long as the mill's going right like, I wouldn't want to wish it any harm. But I'm going to tell you, they want a bloody good shake up from top to bottom. There was a thing just happened a few weeks since. They run out of pulp. They couldn't filter it fast enough. And there was nine empty tanks one night and we shut a machine down. When I goes back after the weekend, everything had been shut down. Somebody would have to answer for that. But if it had been any of us, it would have been instant dismissal. For a thing like that, but one will cover the other up. Now I don't believe in whips or anything like that. I don't believe in a thing like that. But I believe in justice.

Wages have improved, yes. Wages are good for what you do. But it's a boring job. You get paid for boredomism down there. It's a boring job. But my job like, it isn't so boring because you're always at it. There's always something going wrong and you're always learning. But I can't understand a good lad like George Stephenson putting up with them fellows he has running about him. I'm going to tell you, there's one trying to cut the other's throat. Like I divn't want to cut anybody's throat. Like everybody do a fair share of work, but these young uns today. Like bosses – they would ride ower any of them, some of them, to get their own ends."

The rest of this chapter on the Factory is devoted to the work and politics of three men who have played a central rôle in the making of the factory: Edwin Routledge, now retired, in his seventies; Norman Fell, at the time of the interview on the sick-list with high blood pressure and unable to regain a job at the factory, in his fifties; and Billy Lowther, thirty-five, perhaps the outstanding success story of the place.

In talking about the work, particularly of the older two men, I am also going to include their political lives, chiefly because, in both cases, work and politics are so intermingled.

Wigton is at the edge of the Penrith and Border Constituency – which is largely agricultural and solidly Conservative – one of the safest seats in England: a slight shift in the boundary, however, could make it part of a West Cumbrian constituency – largely industrial, formerly coal-mining and solidly Labour – again among the safest seats in the country. To all intents, then, it is at an English political cross-roads or at least junction because that third power in the land, once a giant, now more of a ghost, the Liberal Party, was formerly extremely strong in the town, attracting, as it always did, much working-class support as well as keeping the faith of the inheritors of the Whig Grandees.

As I said in the opening chapter, there was little response when I spoke of politics, little general response. However from about five individuals there was a clear commitment: two of these men are represented here.

I spoke to Edwin Routledge in his council house where he lives, a widower now, alone. His two sons are a few miles out of the town, each in his own private house. The estate on which Mr. Routledge lives owes its existence to his foresight and determination in persuading the Council to buy far more land than they intended to buy for council housing after the War. He is adept at persuading others, especially on the numerous local councils and committees on which for the last score of years he had generally served as chairman. Now a third of the town lives on this estate – its counterpart can be seen the length and breadth of the land. Broad, pleasant houses generally three-bedroomed, semi-detached, large gardens, safe for children, shopless, publess, a fair hike from the centre of the town, for many families the first experience of comfortable living they have enjoyed.

Edwin Routledge is short, stocky, very sober, very sharp off the mark, a self-made politician in the old mould, a man who could be the Mayor of a city, the leader of a national union or a Member of Parliament. His memory is clear and full. He is impressive.

Before letting Mr. Routledge speak for himself, it must be said that no one in Wigton arouses so much passion. Although time and

226

again he comes near the top of the voting for the Parish Council, there is no one else who causes so much antagonism. This is partly the flak which is aimed at any self-made success in a local community (he's also a J.P.). Partly because the whole area, whatever the national government, has been to a great extent socialised during his time (I almost wrote "rule") and people resent his power over them; chiefly, though, because, having been a Union man, indeed one of the founder Union men at the factory, he (to quote from the previous anonymous contributor) is thought to have "left the lads in the lurch". He took a management job and "started to dictate. He had been running with the dogs and now he changed to the fox, ruined both really." This charge he still feels keenly and refutes.

He was born into a large mining family; after working in the pits he went into the Army as described in Chapter 3 and after that ended up in the South Yorkshire Collieries looking for work. The collieries closed down, he came back home, to his village eight miles from Wigton, aged thirty-one, and heard that there was to be a silk factory built in Wigton.

"I went in as an engineer's labourer to put in the plant. It was a change, but it was by no means as hazardous or as dangerous as I had been used to and from that point of view it was quite congenial. You worked in fresh air; you worked in clean and decent surroundings, and I thoroughly enjoyed it. But unfortunately it closed down in March 1930 because, as I say, of the economic depression.

The depression really looked to be all over the place. Then the silk factory proper started. There was savage competition for any jobs that were going, because of the high unemployment even in a place like Wigton, which was basically at that time an agricultural community. But there'd been a jam works that worked during the war and for a short time after it – a very haphazard career. The jam factory, as a matter of fact, it made jam for the troops in the First World War – some of the people had a go at it, and then it changed to making sweets. But in the end it closed down, and it stood empty for years – and we got this artificial silk factory. It didn't last. The silk factory folded up. And then there was, from 1930 – from March 1930 until, well, in my case, August 1933, practically no work at all. You got odd jobs here and there, but the unemployment in Wigton at that time was colossal, really, for a small town. The Labour Exchange was in Union Street, and I've seen them standing four deep – about half the length of Union Street – waiting to sign on;

this was terrific for a small agricultural town.

Some of the things we did would be better not mentioned, because, you see, I always believed that – from 1931, you know, I had a wife and two children and the dole was twenty-seven shillings and three-pence a week. Well, I'd no scruples about this at all, that if I could make an odd shilling anywhere, well, I made it. And I took the view that – I must be honest – but at the same time I'd a duty towards a family. And in those days shillings counted. And, as I say, I could turn my hand to quite a lot of jobs. I used to do bits of things for the farmers, mend the harness for the horses. I used to mend the field gates. I learned to milk cows – I used to hand-milk on occasions as far as sixteen and up to twenty cows in a morning before breakfast-time, which was a colossal change from being a miner. I learned to load hay. I learned to load corn, and I could do almost anything on a farm except plough. And the farmer used to give me two horses to go and plough, and I couldn't get out of the habit of using it like a barrow, and wanted to push it. And the farmer used to say, You don't need to push it, Edwin – you've got two horses to pull it for you. But I never mastered the art of ploughing. So, that was one of the things that I couldn't do. I've loaded corn for him with old kid gloves on because there was so many thistles in their corn that I couldn't afford to have my hands pricked – and he used to laugh; he thought it was a huge joke. Well, to me it was simply being common sense to keep your hands protected. And I did quite a bit in this line for years. I learned to sole shoes for the family. I learned to sole clogs, and put clog irons on, and I don't mind telling you, I used to do it for other people if there was a shilling in it. I had all day, and I hated doing nothing.

I was living at Oulton at this time [two miles out – a village]. We lived in Oulton for the first four and a half years. And I used to go over the fields and collect brambles and sell them, and whatever they say about Dicky Thornton – he's dead now – whatever they say about Dicky, I used to take my brambles and my mushrooms, whatever they were, and sell them to him. And he used to be very generous. He used always to pay me for the weight of the basket as well. And when you think about it, I was selling brambles for anything from about twopence halfpenny a pound to him, and the weight of the basket was about four pounds, maybe it had only about ten pounds of brambles in it, you see. And he was always very good to me that way. There's a reason to this – I had a brother-in-law, aye, a brother-in-law who was very helpful to him – he was a good motor mechanic, and used to do all kinds of things, and this was one of his ways of repaying, you see.

There used to be a man, he was superintendent of the bus station, a man called Willis Pierce, he also was an ex-miner – rather a different type of person to me because he used to go to chapel and the likes and this was never a strong point of mine – I was never a chapel-goer, but we used to discuss the problems of education mainly about the place, you see. We used to agree at that time and it was perfectly true that the educational standards in Cumberland were low by national standards, and we always used to come to the same conclusion about Wigton – that Wigton was low even by Cumberland standards. This was perfectly true. One of the reasons for it, you see, there was so much slum property in Wigton, dating right back to middle 1800s, eighteenth century, and whatever anybody says, environment is a lot to do with how people turn out – what kind of outlook you give them. And there were some real cases of real poverty in Wigton. And of course there were enterprising young men, too, that – they used to do all kinds of things when they were signing on – they used to go and chase cattle for Hope's Auction Company and make money that way. Wigton was in a pretty poor way, I would say.

The Quakers did a good job. The Quakers from the Friends School (at Brookfield), they got a Society going to provide cheap gardening tools, cheap seeds and all this kind of thing. I got a jolly good gardening fork off them at one time for two shillings, which even in those days would have cost you at least six. And they bought cheap seed potatoes, cheap seeds of all kinds, and let the unemployed have it. Then there was a place, just beside the public conveniences, beside the bus station – there used to be a fire station there, and the library was there at one time. At one time they ran some night classes there, you know. The coach-builder, he used to take some classes, woodworking classes, all kinds of things went on. People did that, but it's pretty difficult to get a man to go into that kind of thing when he's so impoverished he's got nothing to spare at all; it's so terribly depressing to a man not to have a job and not to be working at all, you see. And these classes went on – I didn't go to any of that kind. I used to go to classes on (and this is maybe where I got my boost for local government) I used to go to W.E.A. classes on what we called 'Social Problems' – but we did hospitals, trade unions, Co-operative movement, and I took political economy at one time. The only time I ever saw inside a university was I went to Durham for a week on political economy just before the – I was working then, of course – but went to Durham and we had this seminar – there was only five of us then in the group I was in. I was the only one from Wigton and we ran this course. And it was just when everybody thought that Russia would be signing an agreement with us, you know, and I took the opposite line. And a lad called David Newman, he was a Jew but he was a nice lad, he took these classes, and he said to me, What are you going to give as your paper? I said, Oh, I'll give one on our relationship with Russia. Oh, he said, we'll wait until Friday then, and then, he said, you'll have an agreement to include in it. I said, Do you think so? He said, Well, of course, he said, don't you? I said, I most certainly don't. I said, There'll be no agreement. Oh, he said, you run a bit wide of the mark. But I wasn't – the agreement was never signed.

One thing was rather remarkable – you might think this is rather funny in a way, but I think it was perfectly logical – times were so bad, you see, that a pound note was a pound note and really, you had money if you had a pound note. And I always kept a pound note in reserve – even if the wife didn't know about it. But my attitude was this, you see – I'd her and I had two young children, and they got no insurance benefit at all, in those days – only the man was insured, if he had any insurance at all – like National Insurance. And I thought, well, I've got a responsibility to them, and that there may be some time when they needed a doctor, and you had to pay for it, and I thought, well, so far as a pound will go, I'll keep that as an insurance, you see.

You asked why I started in politics, or when I started. Well, as I say, there was no Labour Party, so in those days (when I was a boy) you were either Liberal or Tory. Now miners were Liberals, because they were the lesser of the two evils, you see. And of the hundred houses in Harriston [a mining village where he lived] at that time – a hundred and two or a hundred and three, somewhere about that – about half a dozen were Tories, of which my father was one. And I led a dog's life. And if you want any cruelty perpetrated, and you get kids amongst kids, they're the people, as you probably know. Well, I went through hell for about twelve months, you know, on this 1906 Election. And I thought, When I'm old enough, I'll get to know what politics are all about. And the consequence was that I turned out to be a pretty informed socialist. And I had the pleasure of seeing my father vote Labour before he died – as far back as 1918 he voted Labour. And, strictly against all the rules, when we went to vote, he showed me his ballot paper.

I passed the scholarship for the Grammar School, for a 'free' place, but we couldn't afford the fares and the clothes. I was a Trade Union secretary at the age of twenty-two. And I always knew what I believed in and was always prepared to argue about it. But I could never see any opportunity of getting away from it. I could never see any opportunity of making a career out of it. It all came at once – in 1946. I was heading straight for a pretty good career at that time; I could have got a candidature fairly easily, through the Municipal Workers' Union, but I got the offer of this job as personnel manager at the factory and – that was the way I went. Oh, I knew for a long time I could get – if I had a mind to apply myself – I could get either a political berth or a Trade Union berth. I could have done either, really, if I'd had a mind. But the wife used always to say, Well I don't want you away from home, Edwin. I want you at home. And for that reason I never really pushed it. And actually when the opportunity came she said, Well, everybody's told you you should be doing something better. And I ran the local Ministry of Information during the Second War from Wigton. There used to be an old parson, you probably knew him, the Reverend Cantlow. Well, I met Cantlow first when we were doing things for kids coming from the east coast, you know, the evacuees. And then I ran the Ministry of Information and he was one of the committee. And he used to say one or two things, but one he always used to say, Look, Routledge, you're wasting your time. You ought to be doing something different. I was just working on the clock at the factory at the time. I was paid by the hour, you see. And he used often to say, Well, forgive the expression, Routledge, but for an uneducated man, he said, you're wonderful. He said, You're wasting your time. You know. And this always stuck with me, you see, and when I was offered the job of personnel manager down there – I took a week before I told the wife and daughter – the only people interested really – what had happened, and they both said the same. Well, what does Mr. Cantlow keep telling you? You see? But I didn't look at it that way.

The factory as we know it started as British Newrap. I just went in as a labourer. I had to have a job of some kind and I was prepared to go in at the bottom of the ladder and prove what I could do when I got inside, you see. I earned elevenpence an hour. Elevenpence an hour and one week in three, when you went on shifts, you worked sixty-six hours; gross pay three pounds and sixpence, take-home pay two pounds, eighteen shillings and tenpence. For sixty-six hours. I worked Christmas Day, Good Friday, Easter Monday, the lot. At elevenpence an hour. The conditions were reasonable; you couldn't complain about the employers at all. The wages were low but they were much in line with what was being paid in the area. At that time you used to have area wage rates. Carlisle would have its own wage rates, West Cumberland have another rate, but they were all between elevenpence and one and a penny. Oh, you couldn't complain. I remember once David Read who was headmaster of the Friends School at one time – Quaker School; he was a nice chap, and he stopped me on the street one day and he says, Well, what about the new company? And I said, Well, quite candidly, Mr. Read, if you can't work for British Newrap, you can't work for anybody. It's a completely new experience for me to go to a firm where you just have to get on with your job and nobody bothers you. I've been used to working in the coal-mines. Now, I said, the ordinary coal-miner, he had to work without supervision, because, if you were twenty yards away you couldn't see him anyhow. He had to have a great degree of responsibility because any mistakes, any foolish things he did, they might rebound on somebody else. And the stake was your life all the time; gas, roof-falls and the likes. And this bred a tremendous sense of responsibility in the miner. And even when I was personnel manager down there, when times were so bad, they'd say, if you were a miner he'd give you a job. But that wasn't because he was a pit man at all; it was because you knew that the pit man – you could send him to do a job and you didn't need to worry. He would do it and he generally had enough intelligence, he had to use his intelligence to make sure that he survived. And he used to do the work for you the same as what he did – that was his inborn habit, you see.

I was one of the first members of the Union, but I didn't start it. I took a share in it. And it was rather a – the man that did start it, at least one of the men that got credit for starting it, he didn't know the first principles about being a good Union man. But it started one Friday, there was only about a dozen of us were members, and the boss, old Mr. Lonsdale, he got to know there was a Union in the place. So he, he got one or two in and said, Look, all the Union men in here, get out of the Union by eleven o'clock or get out of here. That was his ultimatum. Well, his chief engineer, Wolstenholme, he knew a certain man, and he says to him, Are you one of those Union men, Johnny? He said, Oh yes, I'm one of the thirty-six. Oh, he says, there are thirty-six of you, are there? He went and told the old man and the thing was stuck like that. Actually there was only about ten, you see, but it got started from that point. But it was never a very aggressive Union. It was the Municipal and General.

On one occasion the Municipal Union man, the organiser, old Charlie Edmunds, he came to discuss wages with the management and nobody had the courage to go with him. And in the end Edmunds named three that he knew were in the Union and they were going in with him and they were frightened. And Wolstenholme, the chief engineer, he comes to me and he says, The boss wants you in the meeting with the Union man. Oh, I said, I've got nothing to do with it. I said, I'm a member of the Union but I don't hold any office in it at all. Oh well, he says, never mind, he said. The old man thinks you should be in. Now this is how your reputation follows you, you see, because I thought that nobody really knew what my politics were or anything else, but everybody knew. So I went in and we discussed it and we discussed the wage increase and that sort of thing. And the old man said to me, Well, what do you think about it? Oh well, I gave him what I considers a good argument and we got our increases that day. But, you see, I'd been dragged in without any authority at all. But people were just frightened because they used to tell you, if you're not satisfied, there's a man waiting at the gate for your job. We were terrified to be out of work; this was the reason for it. The reason was quite obvious.

Mr. Lonsdale was the managing director – he lived at Wigton Hall – but him and his brother had an air-conditioning business in Bolton. But he came up here as managing director. And there was a man they called Sam Jackson who was a man with a spinal curvature, he'd been a British Consul in about Oslo or somewhere. Campbell that lives on Station Hill, you know, he didn't come in originally as a director – he came to put money in the thing. Well, he soon found himself on the Board of Directors, you see. Now there were no local men amongst them really, not one local man.

I became branch secretary in the Union. And what the branch secretary did; first of all, he got his members' money in. And I had a method there. I used to go round the mill with little squares of cardboard. When a man gave me his contribution money, I used to put his clock number down, and how much he gave me. And if you made a complaint or a suggestion or anything that made an enquiry, I used to turn the card over and write his enquiry or whatever it was on the back. I used to go round the mill and I used to take, oh, quite a bit of money at sevenpence a time in those days. Well, when I got home at night, I used to enter all the contributions in the contribution book, check up on who was lagging, falling behind. And then I used to take all the complaints or criticisms or suggestions or whatever they were off the back of the cards, list them in the book and then, as I dealt with them, I used to strike them off and date it when they'd been dealt with, and what the outcome was, you see.

You got half a crown in the pound of the contributions you collected. It wasn't a full-time job. I used to interview the managers about various conditions. I was in a unique position this way that nobody, nobody at all, resented me as a Trade Union official. And the relationship was so good with the boss at that time that we used to go in – you weren't supposed to go in by yourself, you were supposed to take another Union member with you – but I used to frequently go in by myself because you could do so much better. Now this wasn't being a Judas or anything else. This was just a question that you could meet the manager on much better terms, because you could discuss things more freely, and he gave you credit for having a bit of intelligence. And the relationship between him and me got to be so good that in the end he'd say, Alright, then, you draft the notice and I'll sign it. Absolute hundred percent confidence in me, you see. Then he offered me the job of personnel manager. This was what happened in the end, you see. So far as that was concerned, it was just at the end of the war, and the shift men on shifts, they worked twenty-one days and had a day off every three weeks, two weeks in three, and a Wednesday they worked sixteen hours; eight hours, eight off, eight on again, you see. Which meant that you used to start your cycle of shifts six o'clock on the Thursday morning, and by the time it got round to ten o'clock on the Tuesday night you'd done your twenty-one shifts, so every third Wednesday was clear. Now you can understand that this was a bit of a grind, you know – the men wanted a shorter working week. And I helped to negotiate it, to get it down to forty-eight hours, six shifts.

Well, we discussed it quite a bit, and as I say we got it agreed to nationally. And then it went on for weeks and nothing was being done to try to apply it. So I said to the old man, as we used to refer to him – the managing director – I said, Look, Mr. Lonsdale, if you don't do something about this forty-eight-hour business you're going to have trouble on your hands. I've helped you all I can, I said, the men are getting restive. They've got a forty-eight-hour week – working week – and they want it implemented. And the old man, he's an awful man for swearing, he says, Well, to tell you the truth, Ted, he says, I've got no bugger that can organise it. Oh, I said, if that's your trouble, I'll organise it for you. He says, Can you? Well, I said, I'd be all kinds of a fool to offer to do it if I couldn't, now wouldn't I? I said, There are one or two things about it. First of all, I'd have to have an office that I could work from – you can't work from a greaser's bench out there. Oh, he says, take the boardroom, he says; you can work from the boardroom. Well, I said, now you realise, don't you, that for every six men you employ now on shift it'll take another one. It'll take seven men to do what six are doing now. Somebody has got to engage a learner. Oh, he says, you do it. Oh no, I says. I'm Trade Union secretary, and I can't do anything like that. And, I says, the men you've got now, I says, it's going to make all kinds of changes. So, I said, somebody's got to interview your departmental managers to see where to place these men and where to fit the new ones in. Well, he says, you do it. Well, I says, I'll interview your managers but it looks a bit comic, doesn't it? I said. You've got a whole batch of managers, all kinds of clever people, I says, and you've got to rely on me to show them what management's all about. So anyway, I went in the boardroom and started on this job. This is 1946. And they were absolutely fascinated at seeing somebody able – sitting at a desk – to move men around. I worked out a seven-week cycle to get man A back to man A's job; it took seven weeks; and I put every man's shift down, for every day of the seven weeks. They were absolutely fascinated by it, you know; they couldn't understand how it was so easy. And it was easy if you knew the principle that you had to work on; and I'd done it for about a week when Mumdio, the technical director, he says, Look, he says, you know this job backwards, he says, I think we'll give you the job. And I laughed and I says, Well, I says, I'll think about it – never thinking there was anything in it at all. But when I came out of the office he was waiting for me, and he says, Look, he says, I meant what I said. Oh well, I said, if you mean it, I've got to give it serious thought, haven't I? He says, serious thought? I'm offering to take you from an hourly paid clock-man to put you on monthly staff. I said, I know you are. And, I said, my name's going to be mud with half of the men in the mill, and the women because, I said, I've done all things for all men in here, things that you knew nothing at all about. I said, A man who's doubted the loyalty of his wife – he's come to me and talked about it. I said, If a woman thought her husband wasn't tipping all his pay packet up, so she's come and talked about it. I said, They'll come and talk about problems that I'm embarrassed about. Many have come with their Income Tax. I said, I've done all kinds of things for your men because I think the person that can should do for the people that can't. Now, I said, half of these people are going to say as soon as ever you got the offer of a decent job for himself, we go down the river. And that, believe me, I said, it takes some thinking about. So I might as well tell you this; within this next month or six weeks I'll be offered a candidature for a seat in Parliament, I said. I'd have the seat to fight, I says, and the offer's coming along. So, I says, that's the way I stand about it. And that was where it stemmed from, you see, that the old man, he met me next day, he said, We've given you Muckley's job, Ted. I said, I know, you said you would, but, I said, I haven't said I'd take it. And it took me a week before I told my wife and daughter as to what it was all about.

Quite frankly, what made me decide to take it was that, as I told you earlier on, my wife had had this trouble. We'd known all the bitterness of short time, unemployment and the likes and this was a chance of putting some more money into her hand. And if it hadn't been for that consideration I wouldn't have touched it with a barge pole. I'm not going to tell you what the salary was like but when – at the end of the week, you see, the old man sent for me and he said, Well, have you made your mind up about it? And I said, Tell me what the salary is and I'll tell you. Well, he mentioned the salary and I said, Forget it and I said, I wouldn't touch it, I said. One way and another, I said, I can make more than that, I said. I know I've got a low wage in the mill, much lower than what you're offering, but, I said, I get quite a bit out of the Union one way and another. So he added another fifty pounds, bearing in mind fifty-pound increase was a lot of money in those days. Well in the end I said, Well, let's strike a bargain here. I said, I'll take it for that figure – for six months. At the end of six months, if either you say I'm not doing a decent job or I say I've had enough, well, I'll go back in the mill and we'll forget all about it. You can find somebody else. But, I said, if at the end of six months you say you want me to stay, and I say I'm willing to stay, I want another fifty a year. Well, he says, you drive a hard bargain but, alright! Well, I said, I'm not particularly worried whether you drive a bargain or not. I said, I can quite easily get a boiler-suit on again tomorrow morning and go back in the mill, I said. It will be no punishment at all. Alright, he said. And every year up to the year I retired I got an increase without ever asking for it. And when I retired, they gave me a pension thirty-one-eightieths of my salary, for which I'd never paid a brass farthing.

And I was chairman of the national group that negotiated wages. I must have been the lowest paid man of the lot, but we used to meet the directors or general managers of the other companies. The leaders of the Trade Union had its meeting in London. We used to meet in Spring Gardens, Manchester first then we used to meet in London. And I was the chairman. And when they wound it up, this when I was leaving, they bought me that watch as a present. And the chairman of the company, Mr. Pountney, he sent for me the last day and he says, Look, Routledge, I've always admired the way you went about your job. I was going to give you a half-hunter gold watch as a personal present from me to you – nothing to do with the company – just as recognition of what you've done. I've admired you always because you never left anybody in any doubt. You always lived for what you believed in. But he said, Never mind, get yourself something durable and send me the bill and I'll send you a cheque for it. And you can go to one hundred pounds. And I bought myself a mahogany bureau bookcase – ninety-three pounds fifteen: sent him the bill and he sent me a cheque. Pountney – he never lived in Wigton. Used to stay at Wigton Hall. He used to come up for a day or two; he was a very active man. He was all over the place. But I remember old man Lonsdale had a stroke and Pountney and Mumdio remained joint managing directors but Pountney was also chairman of the company. And he used to tell me, he says, I don't need to ask anybody, Routledge, what I do here. He says, Virtually I'm in charge. At the first meeting he held, very soon after he took over, he called a meeting of all his departmental managers and said, Look, gentlemen, if we don't do something about it, we'll all be looking for a job. He says, we're putting thirty thousand pounds of film on the floor every year. He says, We're putting all our raw materials, our labour, our overheads and everything in. Instead of selling it, he says, it's going on the floor as waste. Because they couldn't get the sheet through the mill, you see. And from that point on, he started to take an active interest in everything that went on. Nothing was too small, nothing too big for him to handle, and it was no good going to him with fairy tales. If you went in, and I did – well it was nature to me – if you asked a straight question, you got a straight answer. And he did some marvellous things in my opinion. If he hadn't taken over when he did, inside a couple or three years, it would have been a dead duck. This is 1949–52. There were seven hundred men there then.

But for myself, my own life, when I took this personnel job it was just as I forecast, you see. I had a pretty difficult time, you know, for a good bit. Nobody would believe – not very many would believe – that you could change your occupation and still retain the same beliefs. Now I was a socialist when I started – I'm still a socialist. But there are a lot of things the Socialist Party do that I wouldn't like to be associated with. I don't mean that they're mean or anything, but they're just not the kind of socialist things that I would do, you see. But I could see this coming because, as I say, men and women would come to you with all kinds of problems and if you didn't know the answer you were honest enough and said, I don't know but I'll try and find out for you. And I used to go to no end of trouble to keep the men and women satisfied.

There were two people, two people in particular, that used to put people up to all kinds of things to come and complain about. That they weren't getting their justice all the time, or holiday pay, or protective clothing, and this kind of thing. And I knew, according to the line of argument that they used, who had put them up to it, you know. And because you wouldn't give way, because you wouldn't let them have their own way, they built resentment.

The whole thing was this, you see, that they thought you'd sold a pass. They thought that because I'd been a Union official and I'd done all kinds of things that had nothing at all to do with the Union for them – but as soon as ever I had the chance of getting on the bosses' side, all that I was interested in was being a boss. It was the farthest thing from my head. You know, the only thing I wanted to do, as I say, it offered quite a bit more money, which I didn't want for myself, but I thought I knew that my wife was entitled to a better standard of living and more money in her purse if I could provide it. And the sole reason I took it on was just that. But nobody would believe you.

You learn to fight back. There's a man in the town, I'm dying to tell him sometime that I've always lived in a man's world, you know. He keeps needling me at times, you know, and he's led a protected life. He's never worked among anybody but boys, girls, kids, you know. He's never seen an angry man in his life, you know. And I'm dying to tell him someday like, the difference between a man's world and a boy's world. He'll get it one of these days.

I had a real rough time like as personnel manager for a bit because some of these men resented it. And then I got a feeling, well, some of the bosses, you know, were in a strong position. They tried to make life intolerable, too, but largely, I think, it was probably my own fault. I was never any good at soft soap and this kind of thing; if I didn't believe anything, I just said so.

I don't think that my attitude changed a great deal when I was on either side. I think that basically what I did when I was Trade Union secretary; I applied the same principles exactly when I was on the other side. I took this line, you see, that when I was Trade Union secretary, if the members were wrong in my opinion, or if their logic was wrong, or if their history was wrong, what they were building up to, I told them; if I thought they were making unreasonable demands, I told them. And the same thing was when I went to the management side. If the management were being in my opinion unreasonably greedy, you know, like, not forthcoming enough, I used to tell them. If the men were making demands which I thought were unreasonable, I told them. And, believe me, it's the only way to carry out negotiations. Be true to yourself. Be true to yourself, and be fair-minded, and if you do that, well, the man on the shop floor learns to respect you. He learns to accept that what you do, you do in all sincerity. You lost some friends. And some of the people that wanted to be friendly were rather cautious because of the attitude of other people. When we moved into this house down here, one lad who was just a chargehand now, he came and gave me a bit of a hand to put the furniture right, and do bits of things, and do bits of odd jobs you've got to do in a new house. And he took no end of criticism from some of the men; because he'd come to help me.

I think that after about two years I had some regrets that I didn't try for Parliament. I thought, you see, when I went in for the job that I understood the pitfalls, I understood what was going to happen. But I think if I'd fully appreciated the amount of bitterness it was going to cause, among people that you'd always termed as friends – inside the mill, I mean, not friends you meet outside, but friends in the mill, friends that you'd talked to, friends that you'd shared things with – I think if I'd realised just the amount of bitterness, I'd have been frightened to start on it. It was never what you could call an easy life; there were certain people on management side, you see, that rather resented your having come from the ranks. And, believe me, like, some of them you'd nothing but scorn for their mental ability – their capacity, you know. But they couldn't, they just couldn't understand somebody coming off the clock, hourly paid, right into top management. Because nobody could argue with me. And one of the bitterest critics – he used to do all kinds of things which were not just wrong but unfair, you see. But he couldn't prove me wrong, you see. And I think that was the strength in my side, you see. I knew Trade Union law, I knew the Factory Acts, I knew factory law, I knew where I stood. I knew what I could do, and what I couldn't do. And I wasn't prepared to infringe, you see. But when you came to the crunch, as they call it nowadays, whatever you'd done, you could prove it, and nobody would ever attempt to interfere. And the only person that really wanted to know what you were doing was the chairman. And he used to say, Look, Routledge, you've got your problems; I've got mine. If I want to know, I'll ask. So in that sense, you see, you were on a standing with a director, as regards what you were doing. Nobody could, nobody would dare to challenge it because of the arguments you could produce for what you were doing. And when the unions put in for a rise, generally at national level, I used to send a memo to the chairman, Mr. Pountney, and a copy to the others, saying that the engineers, the electricians or municipal workers had an application in for a wages increase, and all they did, they used just to come back, you'd just send it back and say, Alright, tell me what it's going to cost. And before ever you met the unions, at all, you had to sit down and see what the application was, see how far you were prepared to go; and see where the point of agreement would be. And then work it out, how much it was going to cost.

Wigton's never been what you could call positively-minded on politics. They had a record of Liberalism, but it was based more on friendliness than on political beliefs, you know. This was one of my handicaps, when I came to Wigton. When I came to Wigton to work in the factory first, like everybody else I wanted to keep my job, I didn't want to be out of work again. Often I didn't draw my *Daily Herald* until I was on my way home at night. If I did buy it, I used to fold it up and shove it in my pocket and never take it out while I was in the mill. And for this reason, you see, I didn't want to be involved. But one day, it must have been about 1936, 1935 – something like that – Willy Wigsten used to be a chemist in the place, called me in. I don't know what it was about now. He says, Look, Ted, you're a bloody socialist, what do you think about this? I said, Well, how would you know? He said, Know? He said, It's shouted from the house-tops, man, he said, the dogs are barking it. And I thought I was suppressing it, you see. That job to me, like, it's been an experience – a long experience, thirty-one years and about three months. That you look back with a great degree of satisfaction, you know.

What dumbfounded me when I first went into the – in to see Lonsdale as the manager about various things, he had a girl, he picked her up off the packhouse floor, you know, where packing tables, and they said she was clever, like, and she was actually acting as chief cashier. And honestly, I gasped when I saw – you got to bear in mind, you see, this was my first introduction to the management side of the thing; I'd always seen it from outside and been a bit puzzled at times, but you couldn't form any opinions really. But I got inside and saw what happened. Now this girl, she was clever up to a point, you know, but nothing in the – nothing like being a company cashier, or anything like that. And she used to talk to him and blind him with science about making the packing-cases about a shilling a piece cheaper than what they'd been made, but what on earth did it matter, you know? It was film that they wanted the costing on, but that didn't matter. Well, later on they started a – I went in one day, and you'd two girls in, two girls out of packing tables, and – they were after a rise, you know. They wanted twopence an hour more, but he wouldn't give them any, and they sent for me. And I said, Well no, you can't really because it's not part of the national agreement. We deal with this at national level, you can't start doing it locally. Well, he said, never mind, girls, he said. I tell you, there'll be a bonus in your packet on Friday. Oh well, the girls got up and went out. Thank you very much, Mr. Lonsdale, that'll do. So when they went out, he said, There you are, Ted, he says, that's got rid of them. I says, Yes, got rid of them for today, but, I said, you say there's going to be a bonus in their packet next week. And again he said, I b—— well tell you there's got to be. Alright, I says, I'm not arguing, Mr. Lonsdale, I says. Tell me, I says, how are you going to do it? He says, I say it's got to be done. Well, I said, yes, you say it's got to be done, but, I says, Jack Sharp starts making wages up on Monday, I says. This is Friday afternoon; Jack Sharp starts making wages up on Monday, I said. I don't know; I've got to tell him, I says. You don't seem to know, I says, how on earth can you give them a bonus next Friday? He went through the roof, you know, but when he came round, Look, I said, if you want to put a bonus into operation, Mr. Lonsdale, you must study production, the capacity of the people, what they're doing and all this kind of thing. I says, It'll take you six months to get down to any basic figures to start to put a bonus in. So it's useless to talk about it now. Oh well, he says, I didn't think about – go and tell them, will you? I says, Yes, me go and tell them, I says. You know my name's mud – they'll blame me for everything. No, I says, this is your fault but they won't blame you, they'll blame me. And this is what they did.

Now look, I said, I don't want anything to do with it really, but, I says, you're the experts, I says, but here at the present time we've got forty-two people – girls – packing food. I says, I can show you on the scheme that they put out that you could reduce these forty-two women to twenty-eight. And the twenty-eight women would be costing you more than the forty-two are now. Now, I said, believe me, I said, the only justification for the bonus is when you save money. Not spend more. I says, In theory, if you reduce the number from forty-two to twenty-eight, I said, that's reducing it by fourteen. Seven of those people's wages should go as bonus, and the other seven should stay in the company's pocket. You're not saving money,

I says, get it done on time, and material, because you get a better job done, I says. You run all the risks of the day once you put people on measured earnings because they'll find out all the short cuts to make more. And in the end I thought, well, anybody can be a destructive critic, so I sat down one day and I worked this scheme out. I took it and I showed them – I saw the old man, and they wanted to know how it worked, you know. And I demonstrated that the thing would work. Fine. But the mistake I made is I got all the bonus schemes in the place to do after that."

Norman Fell, quoted in Chapter 5 on Between Two Wars, is one of those people who has crossed swords with Edwin Routledge: in the factory, on the Council and in public debate. Yet in their stocky independence, their determination to be educated and to know about things, and their devotion to the needs of others as well as their pleasure in the organisation of others, they are similar. Unlike Edwin Routledge, who came to Wigton when he was thirty-one, Norman Fell was born and brought up in the centre of the old town. He was eloquent about this. His brother Henry has stated that family background which in Norman's mind is even more vivid: "it was humiliating to be going to school with clogs on, darned socks, breeches, my backsides patched on the breeches ... I used to feel embarrassed." Of his mother he says, "I always do blame the poverty of the early days for my mother's premature death. She died when she were forty-nine. I think she starved herself to feed us when we were young. That has always been in my mind." His relief was in street games and country gains – mushrooming, a penny a pound. "I can remember three of us setting off for mushrooms and we went into a field one day and it was white with mushrooms; white. Everybody wondered where we'd got them, myself and my brother Henry and our Jack." He worked first as a telegraph boy, then as a plumber, then he went into the Army.

"When we got out of the Army, which was something everybody was eagerly looking forward to after six and a half years, we were just waiting to be demobbed. Well, all I wanted to see, was to come back to Wigton and see the Fountain. I wanted to get back home. Now when I got back to Wigton, I'd quite a number of affairs with girlfriends, but I'd never considered marriage or anything of that, you see. And I went to work at Broughton Moor on the dump up there.

That was where I met my wife. My wife was a West Cumberland lass. And I met the wife, and I got myself married, and the problem then were – I were also working – first I worked in Barrow Shipyard. I went to Barrow, and my wife – we were courting then, you see, my wife said, Well, if you're going to Barrow, it's just like being away in the Army, i.e., you're not going to be at home. I went to Barrow Shipyard – they wanted to know if I was in the Union, you see. So I had to produce a Union card before I could even get an interview. I produced the Union card, and I were interviewed, and I did start work at Barrow. I went in lodgings – and Barrow, there was trouble again – they always wanted too much strikes. The strike menace was always there because of the low wages. There was still – I feel – I think at the time the wage was about three pounds fifteen a week. Well, money was the main object in life – you had to have money to live. And I felt that we should fight – start and fight for better wages, you see. And I were at the age of twenty-seven, I think, then. I felt that it was time that I took a more active part in things. Anyways, I got myself married, I came along to Wigton – we got married at Maryport, and we lived in at Wigton, for a while, for a week or two. Not very long. Things didn't go on so happy there. And I had to start looking for a house. And I went to see one or two councillors regarding housing problems. And I went to see a certain councillor – it was Willie Dixon, I can tell you who it was – Redmayne's manager – and I said, Excuse me, Mr. Dixon, could you spare a few minutes of your time, I said. I'm wanting to know if you could help us regarding housing accommodation, I said. I'm married, and I'd like to know if you could, if I could have a few words with you, and then perhaps you can help us. And the very words that Mr. Dixon said were, I'm sorry, he said. We've plenty of our own people to look after without strangers, he says. We've enough people of our own without strangers, he says. Goodnight. I said, I may be a stranger to you, but, I said, I'm not a stranger to Wigton. I said, I'm a stranger to you because I've been away fighting for this little town for six and a half years, I said. I think it's time I stood for the local Council, so that we could really give people a chance, at least, of discussing the problem – their housing problems, with the local councillors. And from that day I started actively as a Trade Unionist. I started work at the rayophane factory, we formed a works consultative committee, we formed the factory benevolent society. This is 1946.

I started as a pipe fitter at the factory. I went to see Mr. Wolstenholme, and he said, Where do you work? And I said, I'm working in

Barrow Shipyard. He says, When can you start? I said, I can start any time you say. A week on Monday? he said, and I said, Yes, very good. So I left Barrow and I went down there, and Mr. Wolstenholme started us. And, well, being a Trade Unionist, we automatically started a benevolent society which I were a founder member of. Gibbons, myself, Andy Gibbons, myself and a few more – the founder members. We then started wanting more pay; we asked for increase in pay, because some of the apprentices were being paid threepence an hour below the rate. A lot of discussions ensued, and it took us nearly eighteen months to get the pay put right, but we were right – I were right in the end. I were the shop steward, and I proved right; they had been underpaid, and they were given a lump sum payment each, plus the extra pay. Mr. Routledge was personnel manager then, and I told Mr. Routledge, I said, They're bound to get it, I said, it's theirs by right, I said. Nationally, it's understood they should be getting this money and, I said, you're trying to hold them back unlawfully. I was supposed to be wrong all the time, but in the end there was a lump sum payment made, back-dated.

And I were then an active shop steward, you see. We used to have our Union meetings and just at that time the Labour Party – I were a member of the Labour Party – I can't just remember which year it were I joined the Labour Party now, but it could be found out – I joined the Labour Party and we decided to have more industry in the area, too. We asked Lord Adams to come through to Wigton, but Lord Adams would never come; he'd never meet us, he never ever came to Wigton to meet us, as a Trade Union or as – what d'you used to call it? – the – the Wigton Trades Council. The Wigton Trades Council asked Lord Adams, and everything was always fired back at us that there weren't enough workers available for the factory. We can absorb all the available labour, he said, at one meeting – Mr. Dixon (Redmayne's) and Mr. Routledge (the factory) said at the time they could absorb all the available labour, and that stopped any chance of any industry coming. Now then, the Labour Party decided to contest the Council elections. Now then, Mr. Routledge had been elected as a Labour councillor and he'd gone Independent, you see. And Mrs. Fox was still a member of the Labour Party and she was a Labour councillor. And we decided we'd have a go at the – we were still waiting for housing, of course, and we thought we'd have a go and try and get one or two men on – local men, Labour men.

It was a five-pound bet plus Mr. Dixon's answer to me that made me stand for Council, really. And we stood, and I was successful on the Parish Council. But I didn't get on the Rural. So that knocked us back again anyways. I still didn't get a house – I got an old condemned house. I got to the stage where I had to take one of Mary Ann Moore's houses in Proctors Row – a room up and a room down. And I said, Here we are; going back a full cycle after the war, to what I was born in, and back in it – a room up and a room down. And a wife and young kiddie expected, you see. And our Margaret were born in that house in Proctors Row. And I waited until – we were very active in Trade Unionism and everything now on the go at the factory all the time – and the next election we stood again. Now at the next election I was elected on to the Rural Council, and the Parish Council. But, prior to that, we had a public meeting, and I stood up on the platform and I said, Now I feel we want somebody on this Council that's going to look after the interests of the working-class people. And, I said, that's the reason why I'm standing. And I said, And if I don't serve you in the manner that I feel is required, I hope you'll throw me out, the next time, I said. But give us a chance. We've been and fought a war, and we fought for this little town and, I said, all we want now is decent houses to live in. I said, We want to get rid of all the slums in Wigton, I said, because I can remember the old slum property and, I said, I would like to think that if I were elected as a councillor we could start and get rid of slums and have decent housing. And I was successful. I was a successful Labour candidate. Now I stress that point. Labour.

I went on to that Council and housing was my main topic and it always has been ever since. I judged every housing case, I've never refused an interview to any person from Wigton, Silloth, Aspatria or wherever they may be – if they had a housing problem I discussed it with them, and I've done my utmost to help them if it was at all possible. I've never been parochial on any of these events, and I used to discuss it with Labour members from elsewhere. They had what was called a Labour Group. But we had a Labour Party in Wigton. We had a Party that had formed and had bought its own public address equipment – speaking equipment – we had three to four hundred pounds of funds, and then we got an agent who came along, part-time agent, Bill Cowan, and he came to show us how to run things, you see. Well, I think we were running things better on our own. But Mr. Cowan came along and they started a draw – a hundred-pound draw, selling tickets, to build the funds up. But in the end we started losing our funds – we lost our speaker, we lost everything, and the Labour Party just went squash. And I had to leave my job at the factory.

Now then, the reason why I had to leave my job at the factory were, on being elected to the Wigton Rural District Council, I were approached and congratulated by the managing director on my success, and told that I would see Mr. Routledge and he would tell me which committees I should go on. Now I resented that very much indeed. In fact I told him that under no circumstances would I discuss *any* committees with Mr. Routledge. I stood for Wigton, and the public of Wigton were the people I were going to represent, no one else. Six weeks later they came along and they offered me a staff job. Four pounds a week extra, throw your overalls away – you'll have all the staff benefits, everything – and this is Mr. Mumdio, the managing director. Throw them away, he said, because we're going to give you this position – you're on the staff, and you'll be in charge of this end. Now then, there was Mr. Mumdio, Mr. Routledge and myself were the only three people that knew about this so far; amazingly I thought a bit about this, I thought, This is very attractive. But I said, What are you going to do with Mr. Riding, the man that's in charge now? Oh, he said, we're going to sack him. I said, Well, thank you very much, but my principles wouldn't allow me to take the job – principle and sentiment, I said, I couldn't. Thank you very much, Mr. Mumdio, I couldn't accept your offer. I did say something else, but I don't think I'd like it published, not while he's alive, anyway, because it was appertaining to somebody else. But I wouldn't even say it, because, you never know. But I were put on the spot.

I went round to see Riding; he was a Communist, you see. Now I was always Labour and he was very very red hot Communist. He used to preach it. He used to tell me about how Edwin Routledge used to read the *Daily Worker* behind the machines and one thing and another. Well – I don't think he read the *Daily Worker* behind the machines; Riding read the *Worker,* Routledge read the *Daily Herald.* But anyways, getting away from that, I said, Can I trust you, George? I said, Can I trust you with something, I said, I don't want you to go running to the main office or anything. I said, I want you to listen to me and bear with us, I said. Yes, he said, I'll do nothing. I said, Well, they've offered me your job today. And he says, You what? And I said, They've offered me your job. I said, Mr. Routledge and Mr. Mumdio, Mr. M. and Mr. Routledge, because he was just a go-between, they've offered me your job. I said, Now don't go running round that office, I said. I'm telling you because, I said, they'll know that I've opened my mouth. Well, I was amazed because he turned round and he says, I don't f—ing well believe it. You understand my point. And I walked away and back on to my job, and he went straight to Mumdio and asked them was it correct. And then there was witnesses there – they told me that he says no. Said I was lying. I got a letter from Routledge saying that I would report to a certain department 'or else'. Now then, I was in rather a peculiar position – I wanted to know what the 'or else' was, you see. He says, Or else we'll pay you off – you understand. Well, I was flabbergasted. I was absolutely flabbergasted. You couldn't expect much else because I'd broken a confidence, you understand, by telling Riding. And Riding never spoke to me for eighteen years, after that. And I was rather perturbed, but anyway, when I were in Routledge's office, and he explained the 'or else', he said, Or else you're finished. I said, Thank you very much, and then I applied for two jobs. I was successful in both applications so I went back in to see Routledge and said, Excuse me, I said, Could you clear the room? There were a girl in the room. I said, I'd like a word with you in private. Oh no, he said, you can't just come barging into my office. I said, I've come in here to do something today that you would never do. I turned round again and said politely, Leave us alone, to the girl, and I said, Would you mind going out? And she went out. I said I'm tendering my notice, today, I said to Routledge, because the last time I were in this office you caught me with both hands in my pockets. I said, I was flabbergasted when you said the 'or else' meant I was going to be sacked, I said. Well I'm here today with both hands in my pockets, I said, I've got a job in each pocket, and I'm tendering a week's notice, and that's summat that you'd never do. I said, And you've got all the men in this factory, I said, there's at least seventy-five percent of them – you've got them in your hands like that, I said, because they can't do what I can do because I have a trade – I can move. But, I said, these men are tied, and they're being tied just because you can play about with them; you can ——!

And I had a right heart-to-heart talk, and I said, You are the man responsible for me leaving this mill. And he tried to make excuses; well, like, this is personal, it – but it's true, he knows it's true, too. Anyways, I went to work with Laings, and I still kept up my activities on the Council. But prior to that, while I worked at the factory, and I worked there for quite a while, I used to have to ask permission from my employer, which everybody does, to attend Council meetings. Now then, I was in the unfortunate position of being told that I weren't able to attend the Council meeting because if I was missing from the factory I'd be holding up production. But Mr. Routledge, the personnel manager, could go to all the meetings because – he was personnel manager. I said, Well, to make things easier, I said, you go to all your meetings, Mr. Routledge. Oh but, he said, I come back at night and make my time up. I said, Well, wouldn't it be alright if I went to my meetings, and then came back at night and make my time up? I said, Then, I said, we could stagger working. I said, I wouldn't have to claim anything off the Council and I could do my full-time Council work. But they wouldn't accept that. So I reckoned, and I always have reckoned – I've been a part-time councillor – not a full-time councillor; because there's no room for full-time working-men councillors. And that is what's been behind all my problems – the problems have been all my life – that you cannot be a full-time councillor and be a worker. Because no employer – every employer I've had yet, they say, Either the Council, or your job.

But there was a man did a lot of work for unions. That were George Riding. George Riding was a – even though he was a bit of a Communist, he knew what he was talking about. And I had to soft-pedal with him a bit. And then, you see, they offered me his job. And if I'd took it I'd have been – all Wigton would have said Norman Fell took George Riding's job off him. But I will say this, I could never say for a minute that George Riding – he had his facts right, but he had the *Daily Worker* and, mind, the *Daily Worker*'d give you a lot of trouble. Winston Churchill always used to get the *Daily Worker*. He bought three papers; the *Times*, the *Express* and the *Daily Worker*. That was Winston Churchill. Now then, I can remember chargehands, chargehands, all Union men, promoted to keep them quiet. To me, I felt there was a price – there's a price on everybody; and the price they offered me – well, my principles wouldn't allow me – I said there's no price. Mr. Mumdio turned round, and he said, You'll never get anywhere in the world, Fell, if you rely on principles, he said. I said, Well, thank you very much, Mr. Mumdio, but I'll still stick by them. I said, I don't care, I said, money's second to me. I said, My principles won't allow me under any circumstances to accept a bribe."

At the time I was interviewing in the town, Norman Fell was trying to get a job back at the factory. Although the new factory was expanding and although he worked on the installation of the plant itself for the new factory (as a skilled plumber) no job could be found for him. In his opinion this was because of his record in the Union and because of the fight he had, while on the Council, to do something to ameliorate the harmful effects of the fumes coming out of the factory chimney. This was eventually done, but at some cost.

What hurt him most, in my opinion (though he would never admit this and perhaps I'm wrong here), was that men he had worked with and boys he had trained, now in positions of authority, reached out no helping hand.

He lives on the same council estate as Edwin Routledge: Greenacres.

Across the fields and up the hill, Billy Lowther lives in a house he and his brother built. They've also built a house for their mother. He and his brother have bought some fields behind these houses and his brother is steadily raising an attractive private estate, two or three-roomed bungalows now selling for about fourteen thousand pounds.

Billy Lowther's father worked at the factory. There's a strong tradition – as there is in most factories – of men "getting their sons a start". I was at school with him and to everyone's surprise he failed to pass for the grammar school. He went to the secondary modern school. His further education, though, is very much part of the story of the factory: he was the first Wigton apprentice to "make good" and his career reads like a text-book triumph.

Typically, I spoke to him in his office, early on a Saturday morning. He was to go to a ten o'clock meeting to work out what was to be done to meet a crisis brought on by the power workers' strike. It was more than worrying because once the machines shut down it takes days to start them up again. His office is in the new factory.

He is rather short, very direct, a generous smile, slightly balding, slipping a little uneasily into and out of the Wigton accent which he likes but clearly considers rather inappropriate for his position as site manager. He was made a J.P. some years ago. He's been at the factory twenty years: He's now thirty-six.

"When I was about nine years old there was a fellow across the way who used to repair – he had a lathe in his workshop a fellow who had always wanted to have served his apprenticeship as an engineer. Who would have liked to have worked as an engineer but couldn't get a job, when he left school, doing that. So he had taken another job, and as soon as he'd got himself sufficient cash gathered together, he got a wee shed in his back garden, and got all sorts of tools and equipment, and started doing wee engineering jobs for the farming community – milking-machines, repairing them, and this type of thing, at weekends, repairing people's wirelesses, and this sort of thing. Now they then moved to a new bungalow opposite where we lived. And I remember going across and being fascinated by the fact that he had a lathe, I'd never seen one before, and he used to build model engines. And they were completely to scale; he used to buy castings and this type of thing. Now I was fascinated by all of this, and my father used to say from a very early age, I have been a labourer – I want you to be a tradesman. And he used to say this to both my brother and myself. And this was absolutely sort of pressed upon us by the fact that my father sincerely felt that by making sure that we became tradesmen, he was doing us a good turn, that we were going to do better than he'd done. And I remember going with this very same fellow; these people didn't have a family and they used to look on me almost as their son to some extent, and I used to go across and help him in this workshop, and get all oily and what have you. I used to come back to my mother and say, Why can't I have a boiler-suit like him? And I remember going up to the secondary modern school when it first opened, looking round there, and here was metal workshops there which was more elaborate even than what this fellow had. And this aspect quite attracted me, so for a start off I wasn't all that bothered which school I went to; it seemed to me that if one wanted to be a tradesman, then this was the school to go to.

I never realised how ill-informed working people are about the educational system. And because I worked as a fitter, an apprentice fitter, along with a lot of the people who are now working for myself, for that matter, I get them coming to me to ask me for advice. Now I say, Why don't you go along to school? And these men are extremely interested in their affairs, but you know I was again brought up not to swear. And when I started work everybody used to be f——g this and f——g that, and, digressing for a minute, that if they couldn't swear to describe themselves, they were lost. Now if they went along, for example, even a church service, and they heard the vicar, certainly his vocabulary to him was nothing extraordinary; it was perfectly understandable, and he would use the words that he did automatically. But these blokes used very simple language, and unless they swore, many of them couldn't speak, and this still applies today. Now most of these men are extremely interested in their children, and because people don't turn out, and – I've had this out with Ivan Stowe (head-master of the comprehensive) – because they don't belong to the parent-teacher associations, it doesn't mean that they're not interested, which he seems to automatically think must be the case; it's the fact that when he starts speaking to them, they feel slightly inferior for a start. They have difficulty in explaining – in asking the right sort of question.

I don't know how many people come to me and saying, My

boy's at the grammar school. I would like him to be a fitter or an engineer. And I say, Well, how many O-levels does he have? And they tell me, Oh, he's taking eight. And I say, Well, have you never thought of some other job? And they say, Well, what do you mean? Well, would he fancy being an architect? They think that's a cut above them. You might think it stupid of people thinking that, nevertheless people do. But it's understandable. And the thing is that – so – these people used to talk about their wee boys or girls coming home, and how they had homework, and how they would maybe sit and answer questions and this sort of thing. And my father was working all the time. He worked long hours. During the war he worked twelve hours and was in the Home Guard on top of that. My father was the sort of fellow who always had a part-time job. To get more money for the house, he used to go and work on farms during the summer; harvesting, during haytime, and this sort of thing. He was always hunting out work, and he didn't really spend a lot of time with us in comparison to what I saw these fellows spending with their child. I hadn't realised that he hadn't spent the time. I can never think of equivalent periods in my life of when my father came back and sat down and started asking me questions about what I'd been doing at school. And this type of thing. He was the type again who never went to school to find out how we were getting on. But was extremely interested nevertheless in how we were doing. The reason why he didn't go was that, in his way of describing it, they used far too big words, and he couldn't understand them.

I get inundated with filling in tax forms, with filling in bits of questionnaires and forms and this type of thing for people in this factory who I've worked with. And they come and they always sort of start and say, I know I can come here and I don't have to sort of put up with all that fancy sort of patter. And in that way I get down what they want – or try to. But you know, there was one fellow recently applied for planning permission to build a garage on the side of his house. He went to the Council offices; he got a multi-purpose form, and he filled the thing in, in his own way, put his name at the bottom and sent it in, you see. Summers, who was the local surveyor, wrote back and asked him what he wanted to do. And he came to me and said, I wonder if you could help me. He said, I've filled these forms in; there's more red tape than enough nowadays. I've filled these forms in, he said, and he sent them back; he says they're not right. So, he says, will you look at them? he says. So I looked at it. It was a multi-purpose form. He'd put his name at the top, and he looked at these headings which were sort of vague because it was multi-purpose, and he thought nothing applied, so he crossed everything out and signed his name on the bottom. But here was Summers writing asking him what the hell he wanted to do. I tried to explain this situation to him – Summers, in fact, was being quite reasonable. And he says, Oh, it's all beyond me. You look after it; I know you will. And I says, Righto, and I said, For God's sake, don't tell anybody, because I'll be plagued to death by other people. I tell everybody that comes to me not to tell anybody.

By the time I came to leave school I'd got it into my head that if I hadn't become a tradesman I'd have been a complete failure. My father to some extent unwittingly had brain-washed us to that extent. Now I always fancied, again because of this fellow over the road, being he used to play about with motor cars as well, and I'd always fancied being a motor mechanic. And I applied for a job as an apprentice motor mechanic at a garage and was not accepted. And my father told me about them having people called fitters down at the factory and would I fancy being a fitter. Well, I hadn't a clue what fitters did but he told me they wore boiler-suits, and that was at least half-way there; they got oil on their hands and that was three-quarters of the way; and they used spanners, and that was seven-eighths. And so I didn't take all that much persuading, to perhaps try and become a fitter. So I came down here and was – my father approached Edwin Routledge – Edwin Routledge being the personnel manager at the time – and Johnny Morrison who was in charge of the fitting shop, to ask if there was any chance of a job for his boy. This again is a slight difference from what we have nowadays. At that time, if anybody had worked in the plant a long time, it was very much a sort of, My boy's coming up to leave school – Johnny or Edwin or Mr. Mumdio was the director – Will there be any chance of a job for him in the factory? And more often than not they would say, Send him down. And they would try and fit him in. So I came down and they told me at that time that Johnny Morrison – I was sent for, my father approached them, and they said, Right, send him down. And Edwin Routledge said, I'll send him a letter when he must come.

So I got a letter, and Johnny Morrison said to me, You want to be an apprentice fitter? and I said, Yes. And he said, Why? And I said, Well, I've always been – I've always liked playing with motor-cars and this type of thing, and tried to explain what I used to do across the road. And he said, Ah well, fair enough, and he said, I'm only allowed to take so many apprentices to the number of tradesmen that I have. So at the moment I've got my full quota, but in six months' time Ian Thwaites will be coming out of his apprenticeship which will again make a vacancy. But if you have a mind to come in the meantime, as a sort of tea-boy cum sweeper-up, in the stores, the general stores – (in which we kept all the engineering spares and parts and also brown paper used for wrapping the film and anything whatsoever to do with processing, any spares and stocks and what-have-you were kept in the stores) – move into there for six months and, if you do a half decent job in there, then you can come into the shop and serve your time. So I took this job in the stores and, sure enough, I was the tea-boy and sweeper-up. And I tried to use that time, mind you, on Johnny Morrison's advice to get to know all the names of the various bits of engineering equipment that we had in the stores. And I found it extremely useful because when I came across back into the shop we used to strip a pump down, for example, and I knew which was the rotor and the stator; and I knew the names of all the various bits and was surprised to find, sometimes, that the tradesmen didn't know its proper name. They used to say, That rubber thing. Or try and describe it – from the shape; but I knew its name through having been in the stores.

So I went then to serve my time as an apprentice fitter. I had no G.C.E.s. I was told that you have to go down to Carlisle Technical College on day-release. And so I went down to Carlisle Technical College on my own and was told, Well, have you any G.C.E.s? No. Have you passed any examinations? No, just the end-of-year examinations at school. And he says, Well, in that case, you'll have to take a preliminary – what are you doing? Serving my time as an apprentice fitter. I see. Well, you'll have to take a thing called 'City and Guilds' – ever heard of it? But before you can do that you'll have to take a preliminary technical year in order that we can assess you. So I took this year – I took this preliminary technical course, and then I did – probably a bit of luck – the examination went my way. I worked hard, mind you, and got extremely good results, sort of ninety to ninety-five bracket and, looking back, an extremely simple paper, mind you. The sort of thing like 'describe a Leclanche cell' or this sort of thing. Anyway, very simple. I went the following year; this again is a difference between when I served my time and now. We have a training officer now, the personnel manager knows about all the courses which are available. Edwin might have liked to think that he did, but he didn't. He hadn't a clue; not surprising, it was just coming on. It was something new. It was a good thing for the company to send its apprentices to the Tech. They'd possibly been approached by them to see if they would. We liked to look on our-selves, like we did then, as a forward-looking organisation, and they would agree, but they hadn't a clue what the courses were. And they certainly did nothing to tell us what they were. And all we did was arrive at the Tech, explain that we were apprentice fitters, and what have you got for us, so to speak. And rely on them to put us on the right course.

I remember having passed this preliminary year and going down to sign on again. The term ended in June and it was more or less closed for the summer and you started again in September. I was going one day per week, by the way, on that preliminary year. I was given day release. That was pretty good for that time; the bulk of the industries in this area insisted on their apprentices going at night. Now I went down with another apprentice fitter and I said, Well, what do you do now? And he said, Well, we've got to sign on for a thing they call the City and Guilds. And so I got my form and prospectus and I filled this City and Guilds thing in. And there was a couple of lecturers standing about, checking forms and making sure that you'd filled them in correctly ... prior to your going and paying your fee and becoming signed on, as it were. And I saw this fellow; I hadn't a clue who he was, and was going to walk up to him with my form. And there was a fellow shot in front of me and handed his form, and I sort of moved back as he shot in front of me and looked back to see if there was anybody else. And I saw one of the fellows who took me in the preliminary year. So I went to him. And he said, I see you've signed yourself on for a City and Guilds. And I said, Yes. And he said, Don't do that. Sign yourself on for an Ordinary National Certificate. And I said, What's that? And he said, It's a much better qualification, he said, and I can tell you that you'll get it, no bother at all. He said, It'll be better than a City and Guilds. You sign on for that. Well I was worried. I was frightened to do wrong; you see. What would *they* think? It's putting it a bit strongly, a servant/master attitude; I'd been brought up with, you know, but certainly the bulk of people I worked with at that time in the factory were very careful about their attitude to management. We were tapering off from the hiring and firing period, but nevertheless this was very much in their minds. And they're much more outspoken now; there's no comparison. People would feel a grudge and we would discuss it in the cabin, but it would never get further than that. It would just be between ourselves. And when I say ourselves, I was sort of on the outside, but as a little apprentice sitting in the cabin I used to listen to these fellows' grudges – grumbles about management. And when I hear some of these people nowadays talking about management, they don't understand – they can't understand what picture the working fellow has of what's happening.

I can see a lot of things that our fellows do, because I try to get myself back to those days, and they're not all that much different. And I can see which way they're going to move sometimes, from those days. And here was me being told to sign on for an O.N.C., Ordinary National Certificate; I hadn't a clue what it was. It was different from the City and Guilds. And I thought if I come back and tell them I've signed on for something different to every other apprentice, I might get the sack. And so I said, No. I can't sign on for that because everybody else in our firm signs on for this. And he said, Look, I'm not going to let you. And then he said, Are you mechanical or electrical? It might sound unbelievable now but I thought that he was on about mechanics – motor mechanics – and I said, I'm not mechanical or electrical, I'm a fitter. And he said, I'm not meaning motor mechanics, he says; anything like that is mechanical. I said, Oh, I see. He says, It's a general sort of course, for mechanical engineers. Well, I argued with him, and he said, Look, if you don't fill the form in, I'll fill it in for you. You're wasting yourself. You go in for O.N.C. If the company complain, tell them to ring me. So I filled the thing in for an O.N.C. And came back. And I remember, frightened like, going into Ted Routledge's office, and he said, What have you signed yourself on for? And I said, Ordinary National Certificate. And he said, What was that, Ordinary National – and he finally said, What is it? It's something different. We've never had a student done it before. Why? I was being a little unkind; maybe Ted wouldn't want to let an apprentice tell him that they had such a thing at the Tech.

And so I signed on for this course, went down to the Tech, and I remember the first lesson. I sat in the class – I was there about a quarter to nine – two or three lads got in – and I realised that they'd all been to grammar school, they'd all done algebra; they'd done a number of things which you could tell from the gist of their conversation. Now the first class was maths, and I remember the maths fellow coming in and saying, Good morning, Welcome to this class. I think I'd better fill you in, he says, with what you'll be doing sort of over the next three years. As part of all this he told us how there was only about – I think it was thirty percent – who had passed the examination at the end, and actually get an Ordinary National Certificate. And he told me how, if we went on to get a Higher National Certificate, then possibly only two percent of the people who started off with it – there's be a lot of people get it, of course; there's a lot of people start, but there's be only two percent of the people now sitting here would pass. I was thinking, Hell, you know, I'm obviously in the ninety percent of failures for the O.N.C. and the H.N.C.

He started off and he said, Now the first thing we do is logarithms, but, he said, we never touch it because everybody's done them. Then just by chance he turned round and said, There isn't anybody who hasn't done them? I put my hand up. I'd never heard of them. And I can remember there was a hoot round the class, and I went as red as a beetroot. And then he said, Oh, fair enough, we'll do them. They're in the syllabus. Well, he effectively ended up teaching me, you see. And of course he used to say, And what is the logarithm of a so and so, and of course, if you're all fresh to a subject to some extent you're all on the same level and if people's struggling, then fair enough, and even if they are struggling you sometimes never know about it because they're lost in the group. But since he was teaching myself directly, everybody who'd done it before felt it frightfully simple. He was asking me, What's the logarithm of so and so, and of course I was taking a bit of time, because I'd never seen a log book before. And one fellow got up at the back of the class – he's a good friend of mine nowadays – but he stood up and he objected to the fact that I was in the class. He said, I say, we're being held back, he said, by this student. It's obvious that his education is such that he should not be here. And I don't like the fact that the rest of the class is being held back. And he said (this was one of the older fellows, by the way – he was about twenty-two or three) he was in his own private business. So he was giving himself a day off. And this accusation, it sort of stuck; it slighly embarrassed the lecturer. And he sort of said, Well, it's in the syllabus; we've got plenty of time to cover the course, so we're going to stick with it.

So when I came home that night I thought very seriously; and must have been on an edge between, maybe it *was* too much; maybe I was trying to do something I shouldn't be. And I should get on to the City and Guilds thing. But it was more a fact that that bloke had said that this student should not be here, because I said, I'll stick it out. And I'll prove to that bloke that not only can I do the class but I'll get higher marks than he does. And this meant that I had virtually to spend four nights a week and sometimes weekends going through logs, doing all sorts of programmes, using logs on my own. After a long day at the factory. We started at half seven till five and sometimes I was working with a man who believed that because he'd had a hard apprenticeship that it was part of the necessary training. And I used to be thinking – algebra – what's 'a' multiplied by 'a'.

I'd never thought about it in my life. How the hell can you multiply 'a' by 'a'?

And at the time my job at the factory was largely manual. We used to fetch and carry for a start, inasmuch as if any tradesman wanted anything from the stores, we had to run and get it. If there was any holes to be knocked in the ground or the walls with chisels to hang up whatever we happened to be doing – maybe brackets or something on the wall – we had to drill the wall to get the wall mountings. Then the apprentice was always given the job of hammering these. I can remember my hands being covered in water blisters, doing this. But that's not to say that in comparison to my father I'd have thought I'd had a relatively easy time. I was merely unfortunate that I was with a man who thought because he'd had a hard apprenticeship that all apprentices should have it hard. I thought on the whole it wasn't too bad. We had to work hard, mind you. I've seen myself – the second year, you see, at the Tech – at the end of that first year – I've always been lucky, I think, in exams. To some extent they've gone my way, although I have worked hard. I'm not *naturally* bright – I have to put the work in; and I got distinctions in every subject. So that pepped me up a bit. And I went and signed on for S.2. There wasn't sufficient companies prepared to let students, let their apprentices off, and so they couldn't run a day class. So we were on four nights a week. And under those conditions I finished here at five o'clock, ran home, got washed because I was covered in oil and grease, and used to eat a sandwich coming down the road (half a mile), catch the twenty to six bus into Carlisle. The class started at half past six. I walked to the Tech (half a mile). More often than not it was was necessary for me – because of the lack of education between sort of eleven and sixteen – the class finished at nine, the bus went at ten past nine – and if you wanted to stop – you were allowed to stop back five or ten minutes after the class to ask any questions – but I very often had to stop back, and it meant I missed that bus. And the next bus was ten o'clock. So I was getting into here, I was getting home at half ten. Back to work at half seven. But in comparison to my father's days, it wasn't all that bad. I liked doing it, you know. The blokes in the shop, we used to have some hellish good laughs.

Anyway, I was going four nights a week. I'd got my Ordinary National Certificate, and I was called into the office by the principal. He said, We will give you a technical state scholarship on your results. To go to university. And the college would put my name forward. And I said, Well, I'll have to think about it. And I came back, and I thought, Will I have to break my apprenticeship? And I'm not going to be a tradesman? And I mentioned it to my father, and he said, I always wanted you to be a tradesman. Do anything you like after that but get your trade. And I took their advice and went back and said I wouldn't bother. I'd go on and try and get my Higher National. So he said, Fair enough. He tried to persuade me, by the way, but I wouldn't have it.

And so I went on to get my Higher National. Now at that time, when I was an apprentice, there was absolutely no automatic equipment whatsoever. It was all very straightforward and simple. But I noticed, in the two or three years of my time in the fitting shop, that slowly but surely we were getting more complicated equipment in. And we got a German machine which was full of electronic equipment. Looking back, very simple – we still have it – but we thought it was fantastically complicated. They put two electricians on the job, working alongside a German electrician, a fellow from the company. And he was going to explain to them how it worked so that they could repair it. These fellows were so frightened of it that they went – they both went ill. They went off ill. I suspected there was nothing wrong with them but they thought they would have to carry the onus of having to repair it when it went wrong, and they couldn't understand what the hell he was on about. This was the end of the 1950s. And everybody said they had German measles. We had a lot of difficulty in getting anybody who would be prepared to even take on the onus of trying to repair it. The onus and responsibility of trying to repair that equipment. We had periods of where we had to send for a man from Germany to come and repair this piece of equipment. And it would take him ten minutes, and he had to fly across from Germany to do it. And this was the first piece of electronics and everybody said, half said, We want nowt to do with that. And the other half said, Thank goodness. We've got to get to know about this sort of thing. If we don't we're kidding ourselves. And we'll start to drift backwards because there'll be other people prepared to look at this equipment. So I thought, by gum, I should really get to know about that. If I'm going to be an engineer that's worth his salt, I'm going to have to understand this sort of equipment. So I go down to the Tech and I started my first year on my Higher National Mechanical on a day-release system. One day and one night – I signed on for an O.N.C. in Electrical, which covered a bit of electronics – four nights. So that gave me two classes one day and five nights. Which meant that I virtually had to spend the whole of my weekend doing homework and this type of thing.

I have a lot of sympathy with apprentices nowadays who, in fact, don't tackle it the hard way. More sympathy than what some people have who took it easy themselves. I wouldn't advocate what I did for everybody. If you wish to do it this way, well, fair enough, but I don't really think – it was hard work in a sense because I was having to spend longish hours, but I quite enjoyed what I was doing. I didn't sort of look on it as a bind really, apart from there being June and July, when examinations were coming up, and it was glorious weather. Sometimes – I can remember my latest examination was on 23rd June and the first two weeks of June were absolutely glorious, and I was going in at nights, swotting. And some nights I'd actually thrown water on my eyes to stop going to sleep. But I thought that, because I knew I had some homework to do – well, this was of my own making, if you get what I mean. There was other apprentices in the shop who were certainly going to classes and doing their City and Guilds and no doubt, in their own way, working reasonably hard. But this business of going in for this electrical thing was purely my own initiative. Nobody suggested to me that I should do it.

I can remember being moved into the drawing office because of my examination results, and sitting behind these three fellows. And I can remember one of them having a bit of an argument with the other fellow and he turned round and said, Don't be so bloody supercilious. And I said, What the hell does that mean? you see. And I got myself a dictionary and every time they used a word that I hadn't a clue what it meant, I used to pull the old dictionary out and see what it meant, to try and improve my vocabulary. Now I wasn't conscious of having a poor vocabulary until I got into the drawing office. I'd been able to speak perfectly well down in the fitting shop and explain myself as I thought reasonably well. And I wasn't conscious of the fact that I couldn't really describe myself – and had a very poor vocabulary. It was only when I was placed with these other people that I thought, Hell, I've never heard of that; I've never heard of this. The lads used to say, Oh well, you'll soon pick it up, you see, and give me a few words of encouragement. So I moved from this business of where I realised I had a poor vocabulary and I should be doing something about this, maybe, so I can speak a bit better than what I did when I was down there. I can get my point of view across better, I think.

I also had the – in terms of living better – I would say when I was in the shop I saved a bomb, you know. I was on apprentice's wages and because I spent so much time in classes and hadn't virtually any social life at all, I saved about a thousand pounds between sixteen and twenty-one. And I was most proud when I was twenty-one when I got it to four figures. But I never felt short of cash because I just never spent it. And anything I wanted, I got; it was mainly clothes. I didn't have a lot of things, but you know if my jacket was getting a bit tattered then I got a new jacket. I then was moved in the drawing office. I got my car whilst I was in there, and I started to ease off. And I've since become a member of the Round Table where I go out for a drink. And nowadays I don't have to think all that much about my money. It's not that I'm extremely well off, but I mean I can sort of go out for a night and spend five pounds and not come out wondering how we're going to live for the rest of the week. At the time when I wasn't earning a lot, I wasn't spending very much. I wouldn't say that I have a tremendous lot of expenses now. Just, as I say, if I go to the Round Table and go out for the night; five pounds seems to go nowhere sometimes, but maybe you start to eat quite a lot better.

I can tell you also, the first time I ever went away for the company; I went to have a look at some equipment they were considering buying. And the director of the company – there was about thirty thousand pounds worth of equipment; I was most proud that I'd been picked to go and have a look at this company to see if we should, in fact, place an order with them – and I met one of their sales engineers who took me along to the engineering director. Rather a posh sort of fellow, and he said, I'll take you out for lunch. Will you accompany me for lunch, Mr. Lowther? And I remember us going into this restaurant and he said, Would you like – I got this menu which I could understand perhaps a tenth of it. And he said, Would you like me to recommend something? And so I said, Yes I would. And he said, Well, I'll tell you what. He said, I recommend lobster, it's absolutely beautiful. He said, It's their main dish here and it's marvellous. So I said, I'll have lobster. I was expecting him maybe to have lobster as well, you see, because I'd never had lobster in my life before. Anyway, this crab-looking thing arrives on a plate and they poured some brandy over it and it went up in flames. And then he put some sauce over it and one thing and another and finally I got this thing on that plate and I thought, My God, how do I eat this? You see? And there were four knives and special forks for me and I wondered, why the devil he was bringing me these? And then, much to my dismay, he wasn't having any – this other fella – so I couldn't see how he sort of tackled it. And he was talking to me in a very high-faluting kind of way. And if I look back to them moments, I put myself back to the days of the – you know, I can equate these to now, when some of our fitters, some of our process operators, they have the same sort of feeling you know; most embarrassed. Anyway, I looked round the room to see what everyone else was eating. The back of it, unfortunately, was covered in sauce and it took me time to realise that it was cracked, you see. But it had some trimming round the thing and I sort of started on the trimmings in the hope that maybe somebody would come in and they would order lobster! And I remember saying, Well, the first thing I'll do, I'll get its legs off – I'll have to get its legs off. And I started to cut its leg, and the bloody thing was so hard I'd no sooner got started and the blooming thing jumped from one end of the table to the other. Thank God it didn't land on his plate. And then eventually I must have had enough courage to sort of say, I haven't a clue how to eat this damned thing; will you show me how? And I was never so embarrassed – I look back on it now and laugh, but I was never so embarrassed. And he must have thought that they'd sent a complete idiot. I thought two things; one from my personal point of view and secondly from the company's, you know; Hell, who's this fellow they've sent? But I knew about the equipment.

I don't look on myself as one of 'them', having been one of 'us', sort of thing. But nevertheless I think that to some extent that must be true, inasmuch as from time to time I found it necessary to rouse people for having done that or t'other. But what I've tried to do is be fair. And I have had indications in various ways of where people you see, fitters don't work for me really, we have a fellow in charge of the fitters. There's a fellow in charge of the electric people, there's a fellow in charge of the electronics people, there's a fellow in charge of the instrument people. And these fellows I had working for myself, and occasionally there's an argument brews up between the men and the fellow they were working for. And it does please me quite a bit whenever I tell people this; it does please me quite a bit on two or three occasions I've had to come along and they say, Whatever you decide, we'll go along with it. Because, even if it's against us, we think it will be fair. Now I deliberately tried; if we've been doing something which was unpleasant, to explain why we were doing it. And how it might well be in their best interests. Profit in this country has become a dirty word, and I've tried to explain to our people we're in a new plant and we're making no profit at this time. We're in the black as it happens; we're doing a lot better than anybody ever thought we would do; we're expected to make a loss three years; we're in the black already. We've got a long grind ahead of us, and I keep saying to these fellows, I cannot guarantee that when we're making a lot of profit that your wages are going to go up as well. But what we can all say is that there's bound to be a better chance of getting a good wage out of a company that makes a good profit than what there is out of a company that's making no profit. So their chances are bound to be greater. And in my opinion they will get better wages and conditions if I've owt to do with it. Certainly. I'll make sure they do. In other words, I see a need to explain what's happening because there's a lot of things that happen – I look through the old records and I can look back to days when I was sitting on t'other side of fence, and I never realised that management were doing anything of the kind.

When I look back and see minutes of meetings of what they were discussing at the same time as you're calling them – sitting with these fellows in the cabin – we were being talked about and discussed in all kinds of ways. I never realised and neither did they half the things that were being done; they didn't know the reasons. I think that most people are extremely fair providing they're satisfied that the reasons are fair and square. You know, if you're above board. If they think they're being taken for a ride, then they suspect it, and it's extremely difficult to get this across. But it's a long hard grind, this sort of thing. It's a bit like, you know, somebody in an area that builds up a lot of respect – he goes out one night and he gets drunk or something, and he rapes somebody. Fifty or sixty years of respectability is lost in one night. It's possible. You've got to be awfully careful what you're doing because maybe one thing which they think is unfair is sufficient to undo the goodwill that you've tried to build up over the years. But I think it's better to go back – I've gone back to our blokes and said, I reckon I was wrong, at that particular time. And I should have said so-and-so, but it was just my judgment. And at the time I was speaking I thought that I was right. You see, there's always a body of men – and we have a body of men – who, regardless of what you did, you would never be able to satisfy them. In the shop floor day – the shit-stirrers. But they've got to have shit to stir. Well, the point is that at least eighty, I would say ninety percent in this plant want a fair deal. But if that other ten percent can point out to them that – to the ninety – that they're not getting a fair deal, that they're being taken for a ride – can point to all sorts of examples of the 'us' and 'them', then they get a lot of sympathy out of this body of people, and before you know where you are they're all going with them. It's perfectly understandable. But I look back and see what was being discussed and organised by management for the benefit of the men, and I was one of them. And I never realised it. They probably thought, the management, that the only reason why we didn't realise it was that we must be a bunch of ignoramuses. You know, surely to goodness, they'll realise it. I've had case upon case where I've turned round and said, We'd better explain this, and I've had thrown back, Everybody knows about it. That's what I said: Is it me that's wrong? I may be out of touch. And I'd go round to a few blokes who I know and I'd worked alongside with and I said, Do you know about so-and-so, Jack? No, I know nowt about that. And it's not the case at all. It's like the old telescope, you know, looking at it from the other end. People become so engrossed in their jobs that they think everybody knows about it as well. It's a bit like a well-read man thinking that people are bound to know certain things, though they're not bound to know them. And you need to keep reminding yourself."

CHAPTER TEN
War (1939-1945)

In portraying the First World War I stuck to men, all of them in the Army, all of them with experience in the trenches on the front. That was the dominating fact about that war, I thought, and the interviews bore this out. Space did not permit me to give the women's point of view, for example, although there was plenty to choose from. Nor was there the space to talk about the town, about the various quirks and resettlements of fortune brought about by the war, the conscientious objectors, such as Mr. Tate, the Methodist, who went eventually as a stretcher-bearer or the boy who joined at fourteen and went through to the end, returning, after three and a half years' service, in the week of the birthday which made him officially eligible for the Army.

In this war I'm going to jump all over the place, giving some weight to the life in the town, some to unusual situations – like that of a prisoner of war – without neglecting of course the shank of the matter, the war itself.

Some things have come through already in the words of Kenneth Wallace, Richard Lowther, Joseph Benson and Joe Bill Lightfoot – and there's been evidence that both farmyard and factory did well out of the war, the former even better than the latter. In later chapters on Education and Religion, for example, this second war will be seen more clearly as a watershed in the century. But it must have a section of its own.

I was born a month after it started. My father and his brothers went through it just as their father and his brothers had done in 1914–1918. We moved in with my grandmother, a large house in a council yard, a council house but big enough to house us and sometimes other families too. There is too much that I remember: my own testament would, I think, take away from whatever value I have as a reporter. But there are one or two obvious points which should be made. (If, throughout this book, I seem to stress the obvious, it is because I believe it to be the most important and the most forgotten aspect of the lives we live: just as no one "saw" the postman in the story by G. K. Chesterton, because he was so naturally and obviously there every day, yet the postman did it: the obvious is often at the heart of the matter.)

There was deprivation. Even in my own working-class household there was a story of better times gone by. Outside the sweet shops gaudy machines rusted against the walls. These, we were told, had once held cigarettes and goodies which could be got at by putting in a penny or two and twisting a knob like you did at the fair. Somehow these empty machines stood for a feeling of affluence which did not reach the streets again until the mid or late fifties when new machines took their place. For councils and businesses and individuals had begun to knit a society together towards the end of the Thirties and there were prospects.

The Darkness, too, I remember, the policemen coming round to check the blinds. Queues outside the shops; cars, few, small and black; tanks in the streets and single lines of soldiers marching along the gutters; damaged aeroplanes at Kirkbride where Richard Lowther worked and Joe Bill Lightfoot and Kenneth Wallace and my father worked for a time. The six o'clock and, as I grew older, the nine o'clock news on the radio. Hate games with Hitler and the Nazis as the unimaginable monsters. Terror stories of Japanese tortures. Funerals. Visiting friends of my parents where son or husband had been killed. Letters from my father. My mother took on cleaning jobs about the town, taking me with her on the back of her bicycle. We managed. Like the majority of married servicemen, my father sent back all his pay.

Where, then, to begin in what proved to be an international holocaust starting in the fine old European tradition of frontier extensions and ending across the globe in Hiroshima and Nagasaki with the mind-blowing, world threatening atomic bombs?

May Reeves, née Charters, during the war, was a young woman enjoying herself:

"You thought it was great; these Yanks came to Wigton and you thought I bet they can jitterbug because they're Yanks. It was fantastic. For teenagers, it was heaven. We just didn't realise there was a war on. All we were doing was having a good time. I had brothers away fighting; naturally I worried about them, but we were having such a good time that you didn't realise that they were away actually fighting in the war. We were too busy enjoying ourselves all round the place.

Dances all round. Of course, there was Anthorn later on, where the sailors were. But we had Kirkbride (Air Force), we had Wiggonby, Wiggonby was Air Force, and 14 M.U. was Air Force, Abbeytown was soldiers, and of course Wigton there was soldiers. We thought it was great. I often say to the young ones now they don't know what a good time is, compared to what we did when we were teenagers. I would go to a dance every night if there was one. We would walk to Oulton, and walk back from Aspatria. We just didn't care. If we got there we didn't care how we got back. Anthorn was free. Most of these camps the dancing was free. There was always a band. In Wigton it was more hillbilly, but you were get out to these aerodromes and that and to us it was Glenn Miller and Tommy Dorsey and all these things, 'cos they played that type of music, and it was great. I can always remember Victory Night everybody celebrating, and me sitting listening to A.F.N. all night. We loved music. Frank Sinatra and Bing and all these. The best dances I would say would be Kirkbride and out-of-town dances. They would start about eight o'clock. You didn't bother about drinking then. You didn't drink. If you did it was a shandy. But they would start at eight, and if it was during the week, finish about one, sometimes two, but Saturdays of course it had to be finished about eleven-thirty. It was the slow fox trot and tango and quickstep and, as I say, jitterbugging and all this sort of thing. Out at Waverton and Caldbeck they did the Dashing White Sergeant – not in Wigton. They would have a Palais Glide or a Canadian three-step, but to us that was hillbilly. We were town girls, we felt. We felt we were town girls because we used to see them coming, these farm girls, hired, and it was a joke. Are you for hire? They were yokels compared to us. You thought so at that time. They would never wear make-up, and where we would have four-inch high-heeled shoes, they would have these brogues and things like that. And we went to Hunt Balls and we would have a long dress and that, but we wouldn't enjoy it the same as we would these hops. I mean, we went because it was a dance, and if you liked dancing in those days, you went because it was a dance. But it wasn't like the hops.

They were strict about your age then going into pubs. And at that time you looked your age. I mean, you can see a girl now of fifteen, she'll look eighteen or nineteen. I mean, when we left school we had ankle socks. I always remember, I was allowed to wear rouge but never lipstick, and sneaking off to a dance with lipstick in my pocket and putting it on when we got to the dance – till you were

266

about sixteen, then you could put the lot on. When I was seventeen I was going to marry an American! I went into the N.A.A.F.I. I wanted adventure. I went into the N.A.A.F.I. and I went to Salisbury Plain. I said, I'm not sticking in Cumberland. I'm going to join Southern Command. So Ruth Calvert and I joined the N.A.A.F.I. and this was during the war. And we went down to Salisbury and I was engaged to this American soldier and I was to be married. And I thought, Oh, it's only because he's a Yank and I got this beautiful ring, and I was frightened to go to America. And do you know we wrote to each other till twelve years ago when he was killed, and he never married that American. Now that was paradise. When we landed at Salisbury the town was full of Yanks. We thought it was great. Although the war was on, we didn't think about the war. Too busy enjoying ourselves. So in that respect we were just like the teenagers of today as regards dancing and boys and music.

Wigton was blacked out, but it never lacked life. On a Saturday night and Sunday night it was the rowdiest place in Britain. It was, although it was black-out. It never lacked life. It was good. There was no fights. It was all good."

Equally honest about this life in the town was Raymond Huntingdon who now works for the Council. He was nine when war broke out. He gives a child's eye view.

"Apart from the black-out, apart from there being members of the family not at home, in this instance our Sidney, Malcolm and Archie weren't at home, and apart from the fact that you couldn't buy sweets, I don't think it made one haporth of difference to me. In this area, it's well known that we were very fortunate that eggs and butter and ham and this sort of thing were always available. Everybody was on the black market. You weren't thought of as a black marketeer. People weren't making prodigious profits, etc, out of going round selling this and that and the other, but you always got more than the town dweller. So far as we were concerned evacuees brought it home that there was a war and there were some others that were unfortunate and were not at home. They had to come over here because we were deemed to be a quiet area. If you went up on your bikes and you went down to Kirkbride or Silloth you saw that there were aeroplanes. But to me – your family weren't at home. You knew members of your family weren't at home. You heard of somebody's father or sister or an elder brother being killed. I think it brought it home a little more to you then. The only way that war came to us really was in Pathé News at Joe Cusack's Picture House. That was war to us or what was on the wireless. During that period you didn't get oranges, bananas. I remember as a boy our Malcolm coming home, of course he was in the Merchant Navy, and he brought three bananas. And I ate a banana sitting on the church wall and threw the banana skin down to watch people's faces and look for comments seeing a banana skin lying on the front of the church. Nobody had seen a banana. There was kids who didn't know what a banana was.

I remember going to school with lads like Jimmie Bulman, Billie Moffat, and myself, and digging trenches down the far side of the dyke there, 'twixt the allotments and the school playing-field because the Germans were coming to machine-gun us. Where we got this from I don't know, whether this was all in our own minds. You know what kids are like. The school asked us to do it – I don't know whether it would be a directive at all, but yes – there was a line of trenches dug the whole way up the far side dyke there for us to go out into in the event of German planes coming here to machine-gun the school. This was what my interpretation of it was."

I suppose that another in the series of obvious generalisations is that while the beginning of the First World War had something of the nature of a crusade about it, the Second World War, as far as most Englishmen were concerned, was a bad job that had to be got through. And people were much less ready to sacrifice themselves, much more determined to carry the standards and the lessons and the gains of peacetime life into the war. Compare Willie Fell's implicit assumptions in the First World War with his son Norman's in the Second.

"And then in 1939 war broke out. When I went in the Army, you know, I was always supposed to be a Communist, because I always thought we were entitled to our rights. Though I were never a Communist. I never ever were a Communist – it was just I expressed myself really. I used to demand the officer to come and have a look at the meal and ask him personally, Do you call that a man's dinner? I did this at Clacton where there was a thousand men, and we were in training, and the food – well, it wasn't fit for pigs. And I asked for the orderly officer and I demanded that – I asked him personally if he thought that was a man's dinner. And he agreed with us that it wasn't, and they were near to rioting in the mess-room at the time. And we were all told that we would get a good dinner. And the food improved a bit. But I was always labelled then, even in the Army – I was always supposed to be a trouble-maker. I weren't a trouble-maker. We were only asking for what we thought were right. If you have to fight for your country, you should have been fed, and we were in the Army for two bob a day; make no bones about it, it wasn't a lot of money, two bob a day. And I weren't at Clacton long because about nineteen days later I finished up in France.

We were in France in December of 1940 and I remember 17th January we were billeted in – we were under canvas in snow – it was one of the worst winters that I've ever known. We used to meet the French people, and the French people used to say, Well, English soldiers good time, French soldiers Maginot, you know. We used to get all this palaver from Parlez-vous français touch, you know. And we couldn't speak a lot of French – I couldn't – but I seemed to pick it up fairly quickly – the fundamental parts. We used to do guard duty without bullets, rifle between two and guards without bullets. And we had no live ammunition at all. I never seen live ammunition until we'd evacuated from France. We were given five rounds and had to aim at a petrol tin, and we never had any training whatsoever on that sort of thing.

And we came out – I didn't actually come out of Dunkirk – I came out of Boulogne. But we had retreated all the way back from Belgium, from the Belgian frontier where we were reinforcing gunning positions, until we came to Boulogne. And being in the Royal Engineers we had to unload wounded and put them on to a hospital ship. We loaded eleven hundred people onto this hospital ship, just outside the dock area – it was a Red Cross ship – and I don't think it got more than a mile out when it was bombed and it went down. So we'd worked all day – and I think the majority of the wounded would be lost. But that Red Cross ship was sunk outside Boulogne and we witnessed it; we eye-witnessed the Germans bombing it, you see. And the next day I can remember was the tank brigades coming in; the armoured columns. We unloaded two hundred and odd tanks at Boulogne. And these tanks were going to show Gerry what we had to put into the war, you see.

And I can always remember vividly all the young soldiers saying, Where's the mademoiselles? Where's the brothels? you know. And I said, You needn't worry about the mademoiselles, or anything like that, I said. Your worry is five kilometres up the road. I said, The

Germans. They're five kilometres up the road. And twenty-four hours later the same men were coming back with no tanks, no nothing. And we were saying, Where's your tanks? And they said, We've been absolutely annihilated. And it meant that we had to leave Boulogne. Sorry, we didn't leave Boulogne. I didn't come away from Boulogne. I'd got a gun there. We moved on to a bank at the top, it used to be – I can't think of the name of this place – it's a camp. It used to be an old camp and it's two miles outside of Boulogne. And it was in the evening and we were laid out, given fifty rounds of ammunition I think we got in the end – and our officers led us out. We were supposed to be 'no retreat and no white flag', that was the order. And we laid, and we could see from the position we were in – we could see the whole town of Boulogne in the valley – in the bottom. And we witnessed the tanks, the German tanks, coming into Boulogne, going into the square, and into various parts of the town, and I felt, well, this is it – we've had it. The end of the war. The barrage balloons, the German fighter planes and every one of them went up in flames; I guess it wasn't a non-inflammable gas at the time, and they shot all the barrage balloons down.

We were in this position and we were told we had to move – well, we jumped into these – we had lorries at the time – we jumped into our lorries. And then they started strafing us, the Germans' planes started strafing everything on the road. And there was that much carnage on the road, I've never seen so many people dead in all my life, and never will again, I don't think. And we got to a certain part where the Germans were strafing and we said, Well, out lads, and we ran out. And it was dusk – it was nearly dark. And I remember – and I'll always remember it – I ran, and there was a strand – one strand of barbed wire – and I think I was the first to it. I shouted, Stop, lads, there's barbed wire here. And we dropped down. And when we settled I could see the foam on the waves off the cliffs. We were on the edge of the cliffs. And there was one strand of barbed wire which would have meant that we would have absolutely committed suicide; we would have run right over the cliff edge. And I'll always remember that.

But that is one of my first experiences which I have had – I've had about nine lives. I think that was one of my first lives. And there was about forty of us and we were – if it hadn't been for one strand of barbed wire – we were panicked. As far as I was concerned, we had no opposition to the Germans in the war, they just strafed at ease. We had to then march by foot till we got to Calais. And we were put in the third line of defence of Calais. We still had our own rifles and that, and we were given orders not to fire unless we heard movement, you see. Well, we did and we fired. We were told, Keep your eyes open, keep your mouth shut, be quiet, and listen. And if there's anything else coming up there – up any of these streets – they're Germans. Next morning there was no more noise in the street. We had a quiet night after that. And next morning we went and we found two or three women and a few children lying dead, not Germans, and I felt that that was the first time that I'd had an encounter with death. Actually I couldn't say that I shot anybody, but I fired a rifle in anger, something that I'd never wanted to do. Instead of being Germans they were innocent civilians trying to get back to their premises for the night. And I shall never forget, that was impressed on my mind, you see, and I felt what is all these wars about?

Anyway, to cut a long story short we managed to get away, I think it was from Calais. I got away from Calais. We had a hectic journey, but really we were bombed when we were in the water, and I finished up on a destroyer and we did eventually get home. Well, when I got home when I got to Dover, I got a train to London and then went right up to Carlisle and then I came home. To see Mother and Father and the family. And I told them, As far as we're concerned, the war's over. And people called me defeatist at that time because I said this: If Gerry comes on here, we've lost this war. And I still – like in my own mind, I still think that if he had have come over, we'd have lost the war, but that's immaterial like and I doubt if it's much good for any book.

Then Russia entered the war, and I was no longer classed as a Communist. I were a great fellow because the Russians were in and, oh, Russians were that, that and the other. Russians were our allies then, and there seemed to be a different atmosphere, and more respect. If you complained, you'd have better treatment in the Army. And I was quite happy. Quite happy in the Forces after the Russians came into the war because we felt we had a chance. But they wanted the specialists, and the specialists' job were – it was for the Pluto pipelines, which was the fuel lines which were going to be needed when the invasions came along. And they wanted thousands of plumbers and fitters.

And we started work, we had a network of pipework all over the south of England, including tanks and storage tanks, pumping station at Lydd, and along the coast at Lydd – we used to hide pumps in bungalows, camouflaged, and in the holiday bungalows and chalets. We were on the pipelines all over the south. We were only on certain portions – nobody knew the full impact of the whole network because this was one of the best-kept secrets of the war, as everybody knows, this Pluto. But we worked for about eighteen months on these oil installations. But that was an experience where my plumbing came in useful – I were doing a useful service. Now about the same time we were practising on another effort which was called Fido, which was a fog dispersal unit. And we worked on Fido, and we didn't know what this effort were. We were putting the pipework round the tanks and the petrol lines and a ring of pipes right round an aerodrome. And then they tried it out and we were all eager to see what this Fido really was going to be. And the first Fido installation was at Felixstowe, and the bombers were coming back – Wellington bombers were landing at Felixstowe. And if they were crippled and there was fog well, they were sent to Felixstowe. And the first crippled bomber to come back was coming back with his undercarriage – it wouldn't come down. And his wheels wouldn't come down. And they sent it up to Felixstowe and when they put the installation on there was a ring of flame – an absolute ring of flame round the aerodrome. And the plane landed – and landed successfully with no undercarriage. Due to the fact that Fido had proved itself. And we know now that was the first proof of the Fido scheme which was used later after D-Day in France and various other places."

A feature of the town in the war was the number of evacuees, predominantly schoolchildren, shifted from the more heavily industrialised areas, away from the bombing. Raymond Huntingdon describes them.

"We had two types of evacuees. We had the Dame Allen school which came, which were the grammar-school people, and they of course were the upper crust. We had the other evacuees that came with the short hair-cut. I can remember them. Little wee tags on them, like shifting cattle about. The vast majority were Geordies (from the north-east: Newcastle and adjoining towns: shipyards). And they lodged with people in the town. I remember one lad, Michael somebody or other, stayed with Mrs. Aggie Parker Moore up Longthwaite Road here. I remember Jimmy Ellwood's wife had some. There were the Dame Allen people ... others that stayed in the town. There was a little lad called Booth that stayed on. I think there'll be a number of people who came as evacuees, whether or not their parents were killed, whether they hadn't much of a good home life, but a small number, a very very small percentage would stay on over here with the people that they were evacuated to stay with. But a very small number. I don't remember any evacuee here, that if I met today I would know. They were alone to themselves, sort of thing. They were townies as against us country lads, basically rural area. I can't remember any evacuees ever playing in our immediate circle in, we'll say, eight or ten lads. I never remember them at all playing."

The Miss Bells had evacuees. I lived next door but one to the Miss Bells for years. When I was a child they had already retired from school-teaching and moved into a house which used to be the old grammar school. Yet, so charged is the expectation of space, that when I went to talk to them, it did not seem a particularly big house nor they particularly old. Both of them have died recently and like Mrs. Carrick's death, their going was remarked in the town as the end of the old ways. You could see why. They were brought up in genteel comfort – not affluent, not ambitious – they went to the local school and played in the lanes and fields with everyone else, yet their father's little business gave them a cushion against a world which was hard on you. They would get treats that others did not get, more food or more varied food, clothes, just an extra dress, a little pocket money, the occasional trip to a city in the Midlands – not much, not wealth, nothing to detach them from the lives of their contemporaries who left school at fourteen to work in the jam factory, but enough to palm their way.

Out of this had come a great deal of sweetness. They were quaint in their last years as they came, Victorian ladies, up the lorried streets to do their shopping, but not comical: they knew too much. People were glad to be recognised by them – old pupils, old friends. They carried an atmosphere of peaceful ways about them just as markedly as some people "give off" a feeling of violence: in all towns or cities or communities the world over, I think there are those like the Miss Bells who have come to bloom in a past period and retain both bloom and period until their last days: "old timers" in the mid-west, old men in black berets and ancient overalls in Provençal villages, old ladies in black throughout the Catholic Mediterranean, ancient sages with almost transparent skin in villages far from Toyko. They are the true reminders of what we were, and what they always appear to have is serenity.

For all this, and for all that I'd known them all my life and been clucked over as they'd clucked over my mother and hundreds of

273

others, the interview with them went badly. Quite simply they did not believe they had anything of interest to say and kept going out to make cups of tea, show me the garden, the bedrooms where "the scholars" used to sleep, the view, offer me a glass of sherry which I drank to their great satisfaction (and mine), every mouthful appreciated by all three of us. Naturally, when the war had come, they had volunteered to take in both soldiers and evacuees.

"We used to have soldiers staying: and others would come to supper. We used to be rationed with food and all that sort of thing. And we had no lights. We had evacuees of course. And two nice girls; they still write to us. They came in 1939 and stayed until they were able to leave. And the Headmistress was down the very day they went to see if we would take some more. But Dr. Goldsborough said, No. We had done our bit. And Arthur (our brother) was at Kirkbride and they commandeered his car and of course we had to get up early to get him out. So Dr. Goldsborough says, You've done your bit, so don't take any more. Send them to me, he says, if she comes again.

We were paid seven and six a week for each of them. We got that from the government, and then we used to give them pocket money every week. Arthur used to give them money and we used to give them money. We were out of pocket, I can tell you. I used to have to give them something to take to school for their morning break. No wonder they always keep in touch with us; we were good with them. Because we were sorry for them being away from home, and they were both only children. And they were very good pals. But they weren't homesick. And we used to take them about as much as we could while they were here, and we used to leave them in the house and let them have their friends in when we went anywhere."

A marked contrast – though this is not one hundred percent true – between the wars is how much more readily and how much more vividly most people remember and are prepared to talk about the First than the Second. This again is not an original observation but there appears to have been in that First War a traumatic element which, though by no means absent in the Second War, did not affect the whole body of men as it appears to have done in 1914–1918. If, out of all the carnage of 1939–45, one can take the most terrible salient feature, one would point to the Jewish Question: this, I think, and here I am aware of treading where everyone should be fearful, this was experienced by most of those I spoke to only towards the end and even after the war. I remember as a child "knowing" about it and, unless I romanticise, I believe that I remember real terror and dread at the thought of gas chambers: machine-guns were frightening but they could be imitated in childish games, as could Spitfires and even Big Bertha. But the image of the gas chambers and the facts of the extermination camps imprinted themselves later, slowly, on my consciousness and on the minds of all of those I spoke to. This does not imply, I think, any callousness or lack of sensitivity; it was just that the fighting itself and the struggle against the Germans took up all the energy. Here is Joseph Benson who had a long and at times extremely dangerous war: yet, having talked at length and in great detail about the cost of calves and cows and horses and farms in his time as auctioneer had only this to say, in total, despite my trying to get more, about the Second World War.

"I was in Germany, France and I saw quite a bit of fighting. Then I finished up, I spent the last two years as a drill instructor at the Guards depot. It was a good life. Very strict, it broke my heart at first, but it was a good regiment.

[Did you feel angry against the Germans?]

Not really. You were there to do a job, and you felt that angry you didn't want to get shot if you could help it. You'd rather shoot them than let them shoot you. But no, not really angry.

[And the Jews, for example?]

We didn't hear much about that at all. I think that everybody was just fighting to win the war and get it over as soon as possible. I think that this was what was in people's minds."

Perhaps this is to over-emphasise the point. But whereas there was the overpowering image of the trenches in the First World War, there seems to me to be no such central fusion in the Second World War for Englishmen (apart from Dunkirk). Stalingrad was a symbol for Russian and German: the A-bomb provided an exclamation mark for the world: for the Yugoslavs it was a war of liberation, for the Poles a war of survival, for the Danes a war of resistance, for the French, exhaustion. Most of those I spoke to, those who saw action, were modest, matter of fact, very prosaic. Even Glenn Ritson, the solicitor, a tall, ex-public-schoolboy rugger captain, whose short service career had the glamour of a war-film:

"622 Squadron at Mildenhall in Suffolk was a new squadron formed from an older squadron, the older squadron provided the backbone and then new recruits were sort of added to it. And so you got a mixture of old crews who'd been at it for quite a long time and new people coming in.

I wanted to be a pilot and I applied for that but it turned out that I was colour blind to quite a big extent and also I lacked some accommodation, I think, in one eye so we had to choose something else. And I chose a bomb-aimer because a bomb-aimer acted as second pilot. I thought I would get some flying in that way, though not very much. But I only flew – it was a total of three missions. It's a bit hazy now. We did the trip over Heligoland, I think it was, and then we did another bombing trip – I just can't remember where it was now. And then we did the first Berlin raid, the first big thousand-bomb raid on Berlin. And it was in that raid that we were shot down. It was 23rd September 1943, I think. We all went on different routes, of course, to Berlin and it was mapped out. And we actually got to Berlin and we actually let our bombs go, and it was just turning back over the target that we were hit by a German fighter. He came along behind and settled down behind the tail, and then he opened fire, then just drew his nose up and I saw the lines of tracers coming out in front, then just lift up and go right through us. And, luckily, I wasn't hit actually, but the pilot was and he shouted to us to bale out. The whole thing was on fire and I was really very lucky to get out because I was in the front, locked in.

And you're supposed to be let out by the navigator when you're getting out. He unbolts the door. And he had been shot as well and, so I learnt, he couldn't open the door. So I remember putting my feet up on the sort of – part of the turret in front below the guns, and then just pushing back as hard as I could. And I burst the door and flew out backwards, right down into the bombing hatch below. And managed to get the trap door open myself and went out, and I was only just in time because I pulled the ripcord straightaway and no sooner had the parachute opened and sort of steadied me, with a jerk, when my feet hit the ground. We must have been extremely low indeed. There were three of us got out, out of the seven. I didn't meet the other two afterwards – it was a night raid – but we finally came together. The Germans picked us up and we all went to the same camp.

Landed right in the countryside. It was beautiful rolling country near a village called Göttingen which is near a castle, and I sprained my ankle badly. So I followed the drill about trying to bury the parachute. And you can imagine trying to bury a parachute, with your bare hands, in hard ground. Very hard ground, near the edge of the wood. But we managed to bury it with the help of the wireless operator who was also the upper gunner. He landed quite close to me and he helped me to crawl into the wood. We managed to get these wretched parachutes buried somehow or other, and we were found almost immediately within an hour or so by the equivalent to our Home Guard. They were mostly farmers. They immediately sent for the Gestapo who arrived later on. There was not the slightest hope of escape because it was actually dawn when we landed and we could see these people working in the fields all round at a distance, and I had this badly sprained ankle. It was like a football, and the idea of trying to run away and get away was out of the question. So the mid upper gunner with me – he was hurt as well, not badly, but he was hurt – and there was no question of us being able to get away at all. We were surrounded by people. And these landwomen obviously sent word to the Gestapo and they came bowling out in a huge, open touring car, like an old Bentley, with grey leather coats and all the rest of it. They tried to get out of us more than the permitted information – which is, what is your rank, name and number. They tried to find out which squadron we were on and how many planes and all that sort of thing, and we steadfastly refused to answer, and luckily they didn't attempt to torture us or anything like that. There was no heroics involved at all. It was just that they saw we were determined not to say anything like that and they didn't bother any further. They then took us back to the village and eventually we were transported to Frankfurt which was an interrogation centre where people were taken when they were first taken prisoners, and were put in solitary confinement there, and questioned again there.

The mid upper gunman and I, of course, were separated from the moment they captured us. I never saw him again until after the war. You see, he was a flight sergeant and I was a pilot officer and of course they separated us from camp point of view in any event for that reason, and I didn't see him till afterwards. They interrogated us quite carefully; both the normal Air Force, the Luftwaffe people, and also they sent in the bogus Red Cross people. A man comes in, a dear old man with white hair, saying he's there to help you and he's going to help you get parcels through and your parents notified, just let him know just what your squadron is and he'll help. And this sort of thing. And as soon as he saw that we twigged he left us alone right away. I wouldn't answer – we'd been warned about him, of course; he was part of the drill. The Luftwaffe put very straight questions to you and they accepted your answers. I mean, they were very courteous and sort of saluted and all the rest of it and all this sort of thing, but they used to produce magazines like *Flight* and *Aeroplane*. We used to see them at school in those days. They used to have breakdowns of Spitfires showing all the construction, and they produced these. When they found we weren't prepared to give any information anyway, they just sent us back to our solitary confinement blocks. And then we had the bogus Red Cross man around, and that was really all that happened to me, personally. They kept us in solitary confinement. I was there, I think, for about a month.

Strangely enough, it wasn't very trying because I've always been used to being able to amuse myself and I've never needed a lot of other people to enjoy myself. And it didn't really bother me. I was perfectly alright by myself. The only thing that did annoy me was the place was absolutely crawling with cockroaches and I loathe cockroaches. It was the only thing that really put me off. And lack of air. They kept the window shut all the time. I used to lie on the bed and congratulate myself on still being alive. I was thankful about that. And then, after about a month, they moved us right across by cattle truck right down to Eastern Silesia, to Breslau. And I went in an Oflag there which was one of the most famous of the prisoner-of-war camps. It's the one that had the wooden horse escape in it and that happened before I arrived there; but we had the big escape afterwards, which was the tunnel. I don't know whether you heard about it. But they shot about forty of the prisoners on the excuse that they'd resisted arrest, which of course they hadn't. This was to try and stop escape. It was a dreadful thing to do. They just rounded them up in bunches and shot them. After they'd escaped, when they were captured, they just bundled them up and shot them, and made various excuses afterwards which we knew were quite incorrect. Of course, nobody would be stupid enough to try and resist capture. That wasn't the point. The point was to annoy the Germans all the time. Keep them busy rather than do anything heroic. The films about escapes are very good actually. They're extremely accurate. They do show how life went on there and I really couldn't find any fault with any of them at all. *The Wooden Horse* – all of those. They're all good and very well done indeed – and it's just how life was.

Quite honestly camp life wasn't too bad, as far as I was concerned. I was never tortured or anything like that. We had some worrying times, particularly after the escape. They brought in machine-guns and we obviously thought they were going to mow the lot of us down. But apart from the worries like that I never had any ill treatment at all. I was very lucky. Some people did, of course. Not in our camp but we heard stories filter through of ill treatment in other camps. Our camp was solely for Air Force but we had a mixture of nationalities. There were Canadians, South Africans, and a lot of Polish. We had a Wing Commander Day in charge of our camp, and he's mentioned in these films as well. Another Squadron Leader called Roger Bushel, he was in charge of all the escape efforts. He was a wonderful character. He had everything worked out. Everybody was given a job at the camp who volunteered. You didn't have to if you didn't want to. They wouldn't make you join the escape group unless you wanted to. But if you volunteered to do it then they allocated a job to you. You either dug in the tunnel or you helped to make uniforms or supports or you kept watch for Germans coming into the camp and things like that. And everybody had a job.

The Germans couldn't make officers work but they did make the non-commissioned people work. They went out on working parties. We couldn't, so we never went out of the camp. The men went out and sort of did forestry work and things like that. And I think they enjoyed it. Actually, I would have loved to have been able to go out and do some work rather than just pace about all day. They saw something different. And they could sometimes speak to the local Germans living around in the village nearby. That was all a change. It's rather funny to explain about the Germans. We'd been drilled into us that if we were taken prisoner it was our duty to escape if we could and give the Germans as much trouble as possible. And everybody was briefed on this and everybody carried that out. I don't think there was much anti-German feeling in the sense that we loathed the Germans. It was rather doing the job that we had to do.

I think a lot of people in the camp quite liked the Germans as people. The guards we had, most of them, were ordinary Luftwaffe policemen, nothing to do with the Gestapo, and they were just quite ordinary people and quite pleasant, just doing a job. A lot of them were old men. And we got on very well with them. One old guard, he had a birthday, we learnt, so out of our Red Cross parcels we baked a cake and when he came in to inspect the rooms to see that nobody was doing anything like building a tunnel, we produced this cake for him and sang 'Happy Birthday'. And it reduced him to tears. I mean, that's one side of it. The other side of it was that we did everything we could to annoy them. We had certain contacts, officers who were picked out to speak to the ferrets; these were the people – there were about four of them – who came into the camp regularly every day to look for tunnels and escape things. And they had long, pointed iron rods which they used to put into the sand to see if they could find tunnels and things. And those officers who were appointed used to speak to them and used to try and get as much information from them as they could, and try and bribe them and generally cause as much trouble as possible. Some of the Germans we saw were the people who were making sure that we weren't trying to escape, and these were the unpleasant ones. They had an unpleasant job to do and they were picked for their hardness to do this job. But I think all prisoners realise that the people who are our real enemies were the Gestapo and these ferrets, as we called them, were under the direct orders of the Gestapo. The ordinary guards were just ordinary German servicemen and they were perfectly alright. They were doing a job and loathing it, most of them. They were always terrified of doing anything wrong in case they were sent to the Eastern front, against the Russians.

We were allowed to write so many letters, one letter a month or something; and I got some letters through from home. All the letters were censored, of course, so you couldn't put very much in them. It was nice to get news of home, of course, and to know what was going on there. I joined the escape team and I was appointed to the security side of it, which was really keeping tabs on the Germans and organising watches so that we could notify the people who were working when the ferrets came in, so that they got all this complicated stuff out of the way before the huts were searched. And that was the side I was on, in that. We used to have an organiser of a group of us and he used to tell us exactly what to do and we had shifts and things like this and so forth. And we just used to hide in various vantage points, and then when the German came through the gates into the compound, we would sort of give a signal to somebody else in another hut. And this went all down the line until it finally got to the hut in question where the work was being done. And of course they immediately covered everything up. Hid everything away.

There was a very big long tunnel and it really was a wonderful effort altogether. And everybody who had worked for the security group, the escape group, was allowed to have a ticket to draw who should go out. They thought they'd get about two hundred out and they said, We'll dish out tickets and the first two hundred will actually make an attempt to go out. And if they get out, anybody can follow, if they want to. And my ticket, I think, was about 204 and I was bitterly disappointed that I hadn't got one of the two hundred. Though afterwards, when I heard what had happened, I was really rather thankful that I hadn't got out because I would probably have been one of those that was shot. It hadn't leaked but, strangely enough, there was a raid by our bombers that night and whenever there was an air raid by our bombers, the siren went on the camp. As soon as the siren went, there was a special guard came out with dogs, Alsatian dogs, and they kept walking round and round the perimeter of the camp. This was as well as the guards up in the boxes at each corner of the compound. And as luck would have it, the tunnel had just broken and half the people had got out when this air raid started. And the siren went and of course round came the man, the guard with the dogs, and as soon as the dog got near the entrance of the tunnel, which was just across the path, of course the dogs found it immediately. And people actually pouring out of the hole of the tunnel at the time. And that was the end of that. Immediately the alarm was given and there were Gerries flying everywhere.

After that there was talk of digging another tunnel at the other side and from memory – I'm a bit hazy about this – I think it got started. But it never got any length or anything. It never got outside the compound. And then of course the next thing that happened was that the Russians advanced and the Russian front moved right up towards us and right up to the camp and we were evacuated. They marched us out and they put us into cattle-trucks and we were moved right up, right across the south of Germany, and up to a camp at Bremen which had been occupied by some Navy people. And we were in that camp there for only a short time when Monty advanced right up to Bremen. And we were moved out of Bremen and we were marched all the way across the top, right up to Lübeck. It's quite a long way, that, and it took us about ten days. There was a blizzard blowing the whole time and we slept out every night. And we got to Lübeck and went into some barracks there that had been used by the Germans. We stayed there until Monty came up to Lübeck and literally liberated us. It was the last place to be freed, actually – Lübeck. It's at the bottom of Denmark."

There was a large German prisoner-of-war camp near Wigton, and Mr. Lightfoot is pleased to remember a man called Muhler, "stiff-built, strong fellow, a blondie, grand worker" who was "his". He was dropped at the gate at seven-thirty each morning – "he brought his own food in a tin but I never made any difference. He used to eat inside with us." He made toys for the children and, so stories go, the German prisoners, some of them (because the place is small), spent evenings singing in harmony in the local pub with no thought of escape. No one tried to escape, people said. Muhler's swept-back hair style was much imitated by the lads who had lately moved from Water Street up to the new estate on Brindlefield.

Andrew Savage, whose health kept him out of the war, had a direct but idiosyncratic response to the question: What was Wigton like in the war?

"Oh, it was – it wasn't bad like. It was quiet, there was a good few troops an' that here and we had plenty of entertainment in pubs an' that. I met a Communist or two. A big chap, he used to get in Hare and Hounds. Oh, he'd be a chap of seven foot. An' he was that big they couldn't git a uniform for him. He always paid wid silver and he was in ivery night, drinking and playing darts an' that. He was interesting. An' there was a little young soldier used to git in – well, they were badly paid, you know. Well, we used to give him a beer and get him to mark dartboard [keep the score]. Well, we used to bring him a glass of beer in if we iver won, but soon as the captain come in, about half-past nine, he had to go. This captain used to play darts, see. Well, soon as he come in this boy had to go. So I got at Freddy [the landlord] first. I said, Freddy, why's he going out theer for a bugger like that, I said. If he wants to be among lads, tell him to git in t' room with Lawrence an' them in theer. (They used to go in other side.) So anyway I said to this boy, Now, when he comes in tonight thee sit still. So anyway he hands in and I said to this boy, Just sit theer a minute. And I said to the captain, There's a little boy here, a grand lad, I said. He hasn't much wages and we give him a glass of beer or two and buy him a few cigarettes to mark that dartboard. But, I said, as soon as you come in he's got to go. And, I said, this is a working men's room, this. Oh well, he said, I like a game of darts, and, he said, I've haven't told the boy to go. Oh well, I said, that's better, but the boy might be a little uncomfortable. But anyway he gives the body behind the bar a pound note and says, Bring these drinks in. She fetched drinks in and he told her to keep change. Poor lile mite [poor little lad: the young soldier] he pinched a lamp off a bike soon after. He committed suicide over it, poor lile bugger. Aye, a bonny bit kid he was an' all."

Some people, as the war went on, used it to satisfy a secondary purpose. Frank Moffat, for example, a solicitor, had always wanted to go into the Navy and been forbidden by his father. His call-up, at the end of the war, gave him the opportunity. There were so many support, supply and supplementary jobs in the Second War even then, while the Normandy landings were being planned and the Chindits were dropping into the Burmese jungle, men could look on it, to a certain extent, as a chance to re-order their careers. An odd fact but true to report is that many people calmly considered what they themselves could get out of it in a way in which, I would guess but could scarcely prove, had not happened before. Men in all ages went and still go to war for adventure and loot: pressed men are forced to go; trained soldiers are trained to go; armies in defence of their country or an idea go to fight for that cause.

A number of people I spoke to, however, quite definitely saw the Second War – as it ground on and became what has been called a Total War, involving so much industry and all the population – as their chance to, one hesitates for fear of implying cynicism which there was not, express release, in some way complete themselves. Frank Moffat, for example, spoke of the Navy as his "university". This, I think, is bound up with the mentality which must obtain when an entire country is at war. For then the translations from civilian to service life are so numerous that there inevitably appears, to those whose life has been in a groove, a richness of choice which a force majeure insists they make. Possibly a medieval knight would go off to the wars for a couple of months for no more pressing reason than to relieve the tedium of life in the family castle but the characteristic of the Second World War is that, perhaps for the first, perhaps for the last time, a very great number of men (extending from my own findings) used the war for their own ends. This is to select a minor part from the major: there was universal conscription in England and when your papers came through you had to go. Perhaps to make the point at this length is to labour it; but I think not. It is, for me, part of the really deadly character of large-scale war that so many can be so necessarily involved without even the saving compensation of feeling the urgency of the conflict. War, in short, can, to some degree, become just another stage in life.

To conclude, I thought it would be interesting to follow Henry Fell through this war as we followed his father and his uncle through the First War. Norman, Henry's brother, was at Dunkirk, and then came back to England. Henry, talking most deliberately, as he did, with scarcely a pause for questions, looking at the carpet a few feet in front of him to keep his concentration and remember things as clearly as he possibly could, went much further afield.

"I was at Carlisle until just after the war broke out and I wanted to be in the Air Force so I went round to the recruiting place at Carlisle and went into the recruiting office. And the sergeant said, Well, what do you want? I said, Well, to join the Air Force to get into the war. Well, he said, what do you want to be? Well, I said, I would like to get flying. Well, he said, you've got a hope, chum, he said, you've got a hope. There's thousands wanting to fly now. He said, We've got a lot of fliers but we've got no planes to put them in as yet. Do you want to be a driver? Oh, I said, I can't drive a motor. We'll soon teach you to drive. Oh, I said, no – I didn't think of going into the Royal Air Force to drive a motor. Well, he said, that's the position, and he didn't seem – there was no urgency about it at that time. They weren't dying for my services and I could see that. I said, Well, and come away. There's one thing, I thought, they can do without me easily enough. I found that out so I thought, what should I do? I didn't fancy joining the infantry really. I was a fit fellow and I thought, well (still am a fit fellow) and I felt an A1 man. I thought, really that's where I should be, where they really have to be fit, but I thought I would see me mother first and see what she says. I said, I think I'll join the Army, mother. Well, what about your job? Oh well, I said, job's all right. They'll let me go, they soon get a postman. And she said, Well don't rush into it. She said, You know how your dad was in the other war and when he come back there was no work or anything. And I said, Well it was nobody's fault that really, was it? Well, she said, no it wasn't – it was the aftermath of the war but, she said, think about it – don't rush into it. This war seems to me – it doesn't seem to be a real war, she said, it isn't like the last war – they're just playing about, she said. So she said, You'd be more good in the Post Office than you would be playing about in France as far as I can see. So I said, I'd like to see some places and that and see things and, I said, it will be one of the few opportunities I'll get for free travel as I can't afford to travel. You got the fares to pay and they pay all your fares and everything; there's nothing to worry about, there's free travel – and the only travel I can do is free because I've nothing to pay for. But anyways I thought, well think it over. And eventually she said, Anyhow, you're at the age when they'll send for you when they want you; you'll soon be called up. Oh well, I said, I'd rather be a volunteer than a conscript. Well, she said, it doesn't matter – volunteer or conscript, when they send for you that's when they need you. If you volunteer you're just going to go and mess about some place in France or somewhere just wasting time. So I was called up 8th August 1940 to the Royal Army Service

Corps and I was very pleased to go because it was murder in civvy street on our job. I was on station duty at the time and we were working in black-outs at the station and there was a lot of more mail and people going and short of staff and working a lot of overtime. I was pleased to get away because I thought, well the Army can't be any worse than this. And it wasn't and with being a fit fellow, I said, I wish I'd got in here a bit earlier because, I said, this is just suiting me. And we were physically training and drill and the food was quite good and I felt very fit and well, ready for anything. But we never got any Army Service Corps duties; we got put into an infantry battalion – we were still Royal Army Service Corps but they made us into an infantry battalion and we had to stand by for invasion. And we had to sleep at nights with all our equipment on and our boots on.

It was in Nottingham in the remains of Sherwood Forest, and when we weren't on picket we were on hard training. And it really was murder, that particular period, and sometimes never got our boots off for maybe three days. And your feet – mine was killing us. And so this night, I always remember this night I'd been forced to take my boots off, even though we weren't supposed to take them off, we were to be ready, for instance, if any paratroops dropped we had to be ready to get there before – on top of them before they could do anything – that was the idea, you hadn't time to put your boots on. And they come round with a little blacked-out torch and of course there was Fell with his stocking feet and Sergeant took me name and I got fourteen days C.B. (Confined to Barracks). That wasn't any real hardship; it wasn't any hardship because we weren't getting very far anyway. But if that officer had had my feet! Well, I was nearly – if I hadn't have took them off that night and eased me feet for the two or three hours that I managed, I think I would of had to have gone in hospital with them. I put me boots on but I didn't fasten them up. I said, Well he won't come back again but I won't fasten me boots up. But I didn't take them off, I left them loose, and next morning me feet felt a good bit better. And so I wasn't on any drills because I was onto this Defaulters Parade and they found me a job in the cookhouse so – mountains of dishes and all that – but it wasn't punishment because if I'd been on drill I would have been on me poor feet and that would have been worse still.

The money was very poor – I got ten shilling a week and a married man got seven shillings a week on top of that. Well, his wife got an allowance. What a married man got hisself was seven shillings, a private, and a single man – private – you'd get two shillings a day, that's fourteen shilling a week, seven days a week. You got the pay on Sundays, they paid you every day in the Army, seven days a week – fourteen shilling a week. But they never gave you any more than ten bob; the other was posted all to your credits because, well, you were obviously going to survive the war and you would need some money when you came out. But that four shilling would have been handy every – if you gets our fourteen shilling, but we never got it – we got ten shilling a week and the rest was going to your credits. But every now and then, well very often, there was Barrack Room Charges – damages. We were living in tents; I suppose tents are barracks when it comes to brass tacks – any damaged tents or anything like that, well, we had to pay. And often there was two shilling off your pay, instead of getting ten bob you maybe get eight. Say, what's this? 'Barrack Room Damages.' And some of the married men were getting five shilling a week. Now, if they smoked, that would just do – there were no cigarettes issued in Britain. If we went abroad we got cigarette issue but not in Britain. Those lads that like a cigarette, well, that's just what it was, cigarette money. There was no – if they went out and some of them went out, had a couple of pints of beer, two or three pints of beer on Saturday they were broke. And nothing to look forward to until next Friday payday. There was quite a bit of trying to borrow and there's no doubt that some did sell Army blankets occasionally. There's some of them sold their kit and that – they got caught – most of them got caught. It was a big mistake, I think, to pay people that poorly – it did tend to encourage those that were that way inclined to steal, flog stuff and that. And I've no doubt about it, there's plenty would send plenty of fellows on the wrong road for the rest of their lives. I didn't approve of that business but I was lucky I was a single fellow and ten shilling a week – well, I liked a fag but I managed quite nicely.

So we set off to go – we didn't know where we were going but we got embarkation leave. And when we come back we were kitted out for abroad – tropical kit. And we got on the train – troop train – and didn't know where we would be going but we had an idea, well, we knew we were going to a sea port but we thought it might be Liverpool. After a journey from the south of England, this train seemed to be going all ways, it was in Staffordshire it was in – but eventually it was in Wales and in Staffordshire, but eventually we got to Liverpool. And we got off the train and marched right down to the docks and embarked on the ships in Liverpool Harbour. And it took quite a long time to load the ship up. In fact they'd been loading them the day before. We were some of the last troops to come on it and I think there might have been five, six, seven thousand on that boat.

It was very overcrowded and I thought, well, I watched the last troops come on, very soon we'll be sailing. We had these hammocks to sleep in, well, most fellows never seen a hammock in their lives and there was a bit of fun trying to get into them. And most fellows settled for lying on the deck. So I thought, well tomorrow morning we'll surely be sailing, I said, because there were four or five ships and some were drawn off the quayside and we could see there was troops on them. There's enough for a convoy and I thought well it's a good target for German bombers. And one of the dockers said – one of the dock men come on the ship for some job, to put some water in or something like that, he said, I wished to hell these ships of yours would get away, he said. If Gerry gets to know that you're lying here, he said, he'll be dropping bombs and they'll maybe not all drop on you, they drop on us as well. But anyways we were there three days. I thought there's a possible chance that they might change their minds and let us off but eventually the tugs come and took us off. That would be 1942 – May 1942 – and of course with lifeboat drill and one thing and another they couldn't do a lot with us on board. The infantry fellows – they trained the infantry on board; well, they took all the space on the ship. Consequently us chaps we didn't get bothered with any drill or exercises. It would have been a change if we could have done but the most important men were the infantry and they were keeping rehearsing their drills, and we used to watch them on the machine-guns and various things that do with their drill. It was a bit of a bore for us. Of course there's a wonderful game called Housey Housey which is called Bingo now, and if anyone had told me that Bingo would ever be a national pastime well, I would never have believed it. But we played Housey Housey to pass the time away and, with one thing and another, we went across the Equator and had a bit of a 'do' – they let us know we were crossing the Equator. I suppose you can go anywhere from the Equator, you can maybe turn round and go back. But we didn't know where we were going and – our ship broke. I remember getting up one morning and I always liked to look round and see all the convoys, see if they were all there, I would just count them – the submarine warfare was at its height and they were pretty tempting targets for the Germans, these convoys. But I gets up this morning and I said, They've all been sunk. There were only us – we were all by ourselves on the ship. Oh, I said, by jove, they must have sunk them last night. I thought, well our ship's going very slow, and it was and it was only just going along. So I saw one of the crew fellows and I said, What's wrong? And he said, Oh, we're having engine trouble. I said, Well they've gone and left us. Aye, he said, they've left us but, he said, by the time they mend the engines they'll probably catch up with them. You could hear a lot of banging going on down in the innards of the ship and eventually they got the engines going again and I think it was twenty-four hours before we caught up with the rest of the convoy and went into Freetown.

It was torrential rain and then the sun shining and the steam was rising off the ship and we weren't terribly clean – water was a big problem on the ship. We were overcrowded on the ship – I mean to say, it couldn't be really helped, ships were being sunk and troops had to be got abroad and they packed in as many as they could. And the water supplies weren't terribly adequate. We were rationed for water. If you didn't get your water between a certain – it was on for about an hour at night, and if you were queuing up to fill your canteen and if your – sometimes you were behind the queue and when you got there water was knocked off. Sometimes it was knocked off in less than an hour because they said it had been on an hour and maybe been on only half an hour and you didn't have any water. It didn't matter so much until you got into the equatorial waters and it was pretty warm and we weren't feeling so very fit. We didn't get a chance to go ashore. So we were very pleased when we started to come out of Freetown and of course we were guessing where we were going – we could only be going to Burma.

Well, it was Singapore then; well, Singapore hadn't fell then – Singapore was still British and we thought we might be going to Singapore against the Japanese. But my idea was, I think we'll be going to North Africa, Egypt, but I wasn't sure and wasn't really caring. Anyhow we eventually come to Capetown and we had a lovely sight of the Table Mountain with the tablecloth on – the cloud – we saw that quite a while before we saw Capetown's port. And we all – nearly all the convoy got into Capetown. It looked a pleasant place from the ship but we wondered if we were going to get any shore leave with being aboard ship for about nearly six weeks then, well, over six weeks. And we thought, well surely they'll let us have a bit exercise on the land. And it was a welcome announcement that, except those troops that were required to do duties on the ship, at one o'clock there would be shore leave. Well we let out a great cheer for shore leave – we didn't have any money; we were going ashore but very few of us had any money to buy anything. They never gave us any pay, but I wasn't bothered about that because I thought just to get onto terra firma. So I always remember when I walked down the gangplank and set foot on the quayside how solid it seemed – I couldn't get over it – with great army boots on. And I said to my pal, I said, Eh, I said, dear me – solid country is South Africa, isn't it? Well, it feels solid. He said, Well I suppose we've acquired sea legs and now we'll have to acquire land legs. And it's a terrible long way from the docks at Capetown to the dock gates.

Well really, the hospitality was amazing. Of course they were dishing out cigarettes and this lady gave us I think about two hundred cigarettes each. It wasn't just a brand that we were used to but we were very grateful because, as I said, we hadn't a sausage.

Well we went up into Egypt, into North Africa and we come back and went into Palestine and then into Syria. In the Royal Army Service Corps we weren't on the offensive but we were well in it because, in fact, I think we were really worse off than the infantry because we were having to cart stuff up to them to fight with. One of our jobs was to get the stuff off ships when they have been stored and take it out into the desert, because they kept looting these places. It was no good putting anything in the warehouse because lots of stuff was getting laid in the docks because you hadn't time to put it under cover. And then there wasn't any place to put it in and it was a good dry climate. There's places in the Sahara where I don't suppose it ever rains – I don't think it's ever rained in a thousand years. That seems a long time but I'm sure there's never been any rain for around a thousand years. We used to just dump this stuff out in the desert somewhere and put camouflage things over it and I'll bet there's some of those dumped there now. Maybe two thousand years from now somebody excavating will wonder what they have come across. But we were moved back from there to Syria. There was a bit of a do in Syria, in Palestine and then that was settled up.

I saw quite a good bit of action. It didn't really worry me. I never thought I was ever going to be killed or anything like that. I don't think anybody does. I think you always think it is going to be some-body else. It's just as well, isn't it? Most of the time we weren't more or less on the line. It was a bit monotonous. You weren't in action from start to finish. The first night we were in Egypt we were in tents and somebody had a wireless – I don't know how they had a wireless. And they put the wireless on and a voice – good English – said: Well, we know you have arrived, you chaps that come in that convoy. We know you have arrived and it took many big ships to bring you here, he said, but by the time we've finished with you there won't be enough of you left to fill a rowing-boat. And that was propaganda. I liked it. Well, I thought, I can see the funny side and I thought, well, that fellow has got a good sense of humour. And of course there is one or two, very few fellows believing it – one or two of our lot that looked very serious about it – they went very serious when they heard that. Of course most of us knew it was just a lot of kidology. We used to get a lot of that sort of business. Another thing was Alibaba Muirhead and his forty thousand thieves have arrived in the land of the Pharaohs. Well, that was General Allen – the Australian general – and the forty thousand thieves were two divisions of Australians had arrived in the land of the Pharaohs. And this radio fellow – he spoke perfect English, I am sure he was an Englishman – and he had an English type humour. Well, I thought that bit reference to Australia was pretty good. Alibaba Muirhead and his forty thousand thieves arrived in the land of the Pharaohs! Quite honestly, I wouldn't have missed him!

The things you see on a battlefield shortly after it has blown over, it's amazing. You will see money blowing about, pound notes. Those high explosives when they go off – terrible things, this high explosive. It absolutely blows fellows to bits and that. Everybody has photographs of his wife and children and that sort of business, letters from all that they have kept. Well, everything would be scattered all over the spot; letters, fellows' letters from their wives, money and pound notes floating around in any bit breeze there was. Some had English money. I don't know what they were gonna do with it. I never had any English money. You couldn't spend English money out there, but some fellows likely come abroad with English money. It's strange to see among the battlefields. It isn't really as horrible as you think. It is just strange to see – the things you see lying about the dead bodies. I noticed the bodies but I noticed the personal effects. You see, quite a lot of fellows, you think they were asleep. Like they are not all mangled up. Thou knows there's something wrong. It is surprising how many corpses you would see that you think were asleep. Whether it was with the pressure or what, I don't know. It just sort of – I don't know what it was, but something. Well, high explosive or something causes pressure somewhere and kills them. And I have seen the tanks burn and the fellows couldn't get out and, well, that was terrible – to hear them squealing. The heat and they couldn't get out. You could just hear them being burned to death. The men were on fire."

CHAPTER ELEVEN
Harry Watson

Harry Watson's name is labelled on Wigton weekly in the *Cumberland News*. Though his reports now go to the nationals, Sundays and dailies, he keeps close watch on Wigton and has reported on it for most of his working life. He was born in the town and, though his father was a joiner and his uncle had a partnership with a local newsagent (his uncle ran the printing side), there was no question of him being kept on at school.

"I left school at fourteen. I was in the shop for the first year and then I started serving my time in the printing trade and I went right through the printing trade. This was on the *Wigton Advertiser*: 1931 onwards. It was a weekly four-sheet paper. And from there I went into the printing trade and I served my time as a printer. Have you never seen the old machinery and boxes with the alphabet in? Well you – if I can just remember it – you used to work in sections. The big boxes for the As and the Cs and the more used letters, you see – A, B, C, D; E was a very big one, F, G – two slots you know, it was like case set out in different squares for your alphabet, for your letters, and it was all hand-set. We used to set the four-page *Advertiser* complete every week, about six of us.

And, as well as doing that, you were doing jobbing printing: funeral things, dance bills and catalogues, show catalogues and stallion cards as they used to call them, you know, for John Kerr's Clydesdales, the Entries. And in my spare time I was taught to be a journalist by Robert Scott Wilson, he was R. S. Wilson. He was the reporter; he ran the *Advertiser*. My uncle was downstairs; Robert Scott Wilson looked after the upstairs. He wrote the *Advertiser*. He was a very good journalist. He was a marvellous shorthand writer. He was a Wigton man, just the same as my uncle. Now the way he trained me – he sent me out to do something and he only ever told me what was wrong with it. If it was right, he never said a word.

And he would send me to Caldbeck Sports on a Saturday and I'd be up there by nine o'clock and I'd get back at nine o'clock at night and he'd maybe give me ninepence extra. He used to pay me extra for little things like that on a Saturday. Apart from that, I got six shillings a week. We used to sell about fifteen hundred copies a week. It would be an economical proposition these days. Caldbeck Sports would be a biggish report, yeah. And I used to sit there till the wrestling finished about nine or ten o'clock at night. Course, then he used to mince it for other papers, of course, just as I do now, you see – we put so much away. I used to do the rugby reports and the football reports as well. Chapels, sales, I used to do everything. That was while I was training to be a printer as well. I used to still open the shop with my uncle in the morning at seven o'clock, I would be home for my breakfast usual time, as when I went to school, and back in the printing shop at nine or nine fifteen.

R. S. Wilson died when I was about nineteen, so I carried on the paper writing the lot. And I gained most of my experience then because when he died I took over most of the freelance side as well. And I covered my first murder story when I was nineteen. The John Demon murder; he murdered the farmer Percival at Aikhead. 1936. He murdered him for a few coppers. He worked for him. He was a farm worker, this boy, and he'd been – I think he'd got mixed up with a girl at the time and, not that there was anything wrong with it, he was just going with this girl and he wanted more money or something. And he asked the farmer for more money. He needed more wages. So he laid in wait for him one night and he attacked him. He hit him with a pick in the head; it was one of these short-handled sort of picks like a brick-layer would use. And then his son came on the scene and he attacked him as well, and he was at death's door. Now that Percival was Isobelle Thompson's uncle, Mrs. Hill – they were farmers. The son laid at death's door for a month or two before he started to recover. I covered that murder story. There was a hunt for him and they found, Luke Mouncey found him hiding amongst some hay on the farm – hadn't gone any distance at all. He never got away anywhere and he gained nothing by it at all. I think it had just been temper. He was hanged that boy.

I did this for the daily papers and I got an awful lot of experience from that which I would maybe have taken years to get. The *Daily Mail* would come on and say to me, Now if you have any doubts, you know, ring us up and we'll advise you, and all this business.

I did get an awful lot of experience from that. And then I took over the paper. I did it until I was twenty when I went into the war. Then the *Advertiser* stopped.

In those years the news was the Annual Tea and the Annual Bazaar at the Congregational Church – that was one of my jobs always – the Primitive Methodist Tea in New Street, that was another one – there was the sports and they used to have talks at the Mission in Station Road. I did a piece on Tommy, the blind man; he was speaking one night. He was a man from Silloth. A remarkable man – he used to travel all over the country and he could nip on and off the buses and he knew where he was, wherever he was then. I covered that one week. He talked about just his experiencs as a blind man; I still have it actually. I did one on the Canadian, Mr. Reay, the ex-Mountie, how he got his man. And I used to go to all those, and there used to be quite a bit of that sort of thing. As I say, there was the sport at weekends. I did the police court every two weeks – at the police court, in those days. Riding a bike without lights, and drunk in charge of a bike, such as that. In fact, I'd one of those after the war. And there was a lot of farm stuff and committing a nuisance and all this business.

And I covered sales of farms and all this, and the auction reports were always covered every week, and still are. This is the funny part about it. I went for the auction reports as a boy on Tuesday nights or Wednesday morning and the special sales on a Thursday, and I still collect reports and I still send them to the *Yorkshire Post*, the *Glasgow Herald*, the *Scotsman*, *Newcastle Journal* and the *Preston* paper. I still send them every week. I've been sending the auction reports for about forty years. Sometimes there is the horse-sales; there are three reports in the winter; three reports every week – and these papers still take them all. Wigton Market is one of the foremost markets in the north. Cockermouth's poor, I'm told, and West Cumberland – poor markets. Wigton has the far bigger, has bigger sales than Carlisle weekly. They also have the edge on Carlisle for the horse-sales. These are the biggest in the north of England and it has been really a thriving market town. The town's full at the moment on Market Day, it comes and goes, but it's a different pattern now. I mean, people stood with their baskets along the forms, selling their butter and their eggs.

You remember the fairs when you were young, the fairs were up and down the streets; the streets were full. Stalls all the way up the streets and up High Street. And the pattern used to be, in those days, all the farm lads and lasses used to come into the town on a Saturday night and a Sunday night. And they used to walk from Market hill to the church and back again. And the town was literally full; there was hundreds of people on the street Saturday night and Sunday nights; just walking and walking. They used to all meet.

The difference is total because Saturday nights and Sunday nights now Wigton is deserted. That is the biggest change I think. And I often think about that because the town was full; it was sort of exciting, you know. People were in their best. You see, there was nothing else to do. I never remember fights or anything like that. Nobody was; there was no fighting. Even the police courts – there was not much, never any fighting on the charge, you know. And I used to do the country rounds, round by Oulton and Gamblesby and Biglands and – I think I was a little dreamer, you see – I was always thinking about these things. And it was always going through my head about what I was going to do or intending to do. It was all – I didn't want to do anything else but what I did do. I did have chance to become a tailor, of course; my grandfather had a tailor's shop in Station Road. But I fancied journalism.

We didn't do much campaigning journalism, except there was a very strong member of the Good Templars Lodge running in Wigton at that time – in the Thirties. The Good Templars, campaigning against drink. That was the only campaign and they used to have a man here every year, for a week, talking to people and trying to stop them drinking so much. There was quite a bit of drinking in those days and my uncle used to lead the field in the temperance business. Very much down on drink, because the poorer people suffered when the husbands took a lot of drink because there wasn't money for anything else. I think that's really why they campaigned against drink. There was that, mind you.

More people drink now. Well, nearly everybody drinks nowadays. Most people take a drink; a glass of sherry or something. I'm not a drinker really – I stop at two sherries when I go out because, if I'm driving – well – but I stop at two anyway. I'm not – I don't like drink a great deal. I think I still have a little bit of a guilty complex – well, whenever I have a sherry and I hear something about my uncle, the man who really put me on my feet and started me off in life – was the bread and butter of my career really – my uncle Richard, the best man that ever walked – and he had these religious convictions all the way. He was an out-and-out tee-totaller and had no time for, well, I don't say that – he was an out-and-out tee-totaller. I don't say he'd no time for drinkers but he was always trying to gather the flock, sort of thing. And stop other people drinking. And he was the kindest man. If he thought a woman was a bit hard up through her husband drinking, he would be the first to give them money and he would never want to know anything about it.

But people weren't severe. It was a nine-day wonder, of course, when anybody got pregnant. But I don't think they really bothered. They were understanding, I think. I think people are pretty tolerant about that sort of thing and they were in those days. I think a lot of people, you know, as I say, a lot of folks 'had to get married' then, more I think than do now. I think it's the general temperament of the people. They are sorry for people more than sort of call them and ostracise them. That's the feelings I have on it. And, of course, that reflects my own feelings because, as I say, that's how I feel. I remember cases used to come to court and, you know, for illegitimate children and things like that. When I look back, I knew lots of people had them and nobody seemed to bother much about it.

There's been a levelling out, a little bit of levelling out. In my days, of course, the police ball was the event of the year. Five bob, supper and dance, that was – as soon as you were old enough you went to the police ball and you were 'in' sort of thing, you know. There again, nobody thought themselves much better than anybody else, I don't think, even then. Although there was a bit more middle class, when I think about it – the people who monopolised the tennis courts and such like. I think they would think themselves a bit more middle class. The opportunities were there for anybody that wanted to, I mean, I used to play tennis and I used to mix with everybody. I didn't – the boys who played on the football team didn't have much – well, none of us had much, we all had a struggle to find a tanner to go to Carlisle to play football on a Saturday. I mean, John Park of the shoe shop – he was one of the team – well, maybe he wouldn't have as much difficulty as I had. Kippy Tennant, Kippy's father was the dole – Labour Exchange chief.

I went in the R.A.F. Clerical duties which entitled me right away, without trade test, to have extra pay. Well, I'd just had trade test and I passed this well, granted I was in. I got an extra one and three-pence a day – well, that was quite something. The average people were only getting two bob and then I changed my trade after I'd been in it a couple of years. I think I was promoted to corporal and I went into – I wasn't very happy with the job, it was a bit hum-drum – well, I went into Code and Ciphers after that. And I was, after the course I was promoted to sergeant. Actually I went to India and that was it. I didn't have any more promotion.

We were attached to the Indian Army actually. I was never

actually in Burma; I was on the verge of Burma, sort of thing. I was based at Dumdum; Dumdum Airport which is the place for Calcutta, for landing in Calcutta. When I was posted. The things about the R.A.F., you always went on your own if you were posted, not like the Army, in a block. Wherever I was posted I went on the boat at Liverpool and I didn't know a soul when I went on that boat. But when I went to India I made a few friends and I took ill and I was in hospital a couple of weeks. So when I had got out, everybody had gone and I was posted on to Bengal. H.Q., Bengal – to the place there. Started afresh there, not knowing a soul, sort of thing, and after three months' refresher course, the postings came out and again I was posted to a place on my own. And I said to the postings officer, I said, Oh, for crying out loud, I said, this is deadly. I said, I no sooner get to know people, get into a football team and get organised with everybody than I was posted on my own. Well, he said, taking a look at the posting list, he said, you've got the plum posting; just you be quiet and sit tight. And I went to Dumdum Airport and stayed a couple of years. I was sending messages all over the country, operational messages and this, that and the other. From Area H.Q., Bengal. And then I went to Dumdum. That was an operations room, you see. We did everything there; we'd transport, American aircraft, American bombers, the lot. And we'd be passing signals, messages, concerning our own planes, people travelling and where to pick up people and droppings, where they were dropping stuff. All in code.

We used to change them every day. We had a type code which was done on an elec typewriter; there was different drums and drum settings and everything. I enjoyed most of it. The thing I did enjoy most in that job was breaking down the corruptions, you know; breaking down the signals that wouldn't start. I used to specialise a bit on that sort of thing. You get, well, all your codes have an indicator either at the end or the beginning or something and, well, you just get corrupt indicators, you get two, three or four wrong figures or something – through bad wireless op stuff – and the messages won't start. Well then, if you can't send messages you've got to send back for a checker for that message, and it takes time. And if it's immediate or most immediate or urgent, well, I used to always go in after the other watch and the first thing I used to do was to try to start the messages that didn't start. Nine times out of ten I could. Our codes were always intercepted. We knew this. But I don't think they could break them.

When I came back it was a case of looking for a job. Because while, as I say, I went away the paper closed down and my uncle, of course, died just before I left and the business was sold. I didn't have a job to come back to. I went looking. I got back on the Wednesday and went looking for a job on the Thursday. Well, jobs were difficult, you see. I mean, 1946 there just wasn't many jobs. And I went to the *Cumberland News* and they'd just started a man who was a district reporter in Wigton. I saw Bob Forsyth there, who was editor at the time, and he said, Well, why didn't you write to me and tell me you were coming back? I'd been a freelance for the *Cumberland News* before I went away, I did all their stuff before I went away. And he said, I'd have kept the job open for you. But it didn't work out that way. I went in to see if they'd started this man and he said, There might be a vacancy across the road in the *Carlisle Journal,* he said, and if you get fixed up there, the first job that's going on the *News,* I'll see you get it. So I went to the *Journal* and it was Friday. I was in the *Carlisle Journal* offices and I got back home on the Wednesday and the editor of the *Journal* said, Well, as a matter of fact there is a job – when can you start? I said, I'll start tomorrow if you like, so I'd thirteen weeks' leave, I started on the Monday, so I picked up thirteen weeks' R.A.F. pay. Which was very fortunate, and also I picked up thirteen weeks' wages as I started work right away. But that's just how jobs were. It was a case if I didn't get in there where was I going? I'd have to leave the town or go elsewhere.

I went to Carlisle and worked from Carlisle: city works, city council, city stuff and everything. And in about six months to the day I'd a telephone message from Bob Forsyth telling me that there was a job, if I wanted, as district reporter at Wigton. And he said, What you make as a freelance is your own business. So I took it. It was ten bob a week more. I'd five pounds when I started on the *Journal* after the War. That's what we started at – five pounds. And when I went to the *Cumberland News* it was five pounds ten, so it was an extra ten bob. I was lucky, of course, with working at home and everything, it cut the travelling. And there again, working on a district I was allowed expenses and things for travelling.

I'd got married during the war. I got a week's leave and decided to get married in the November just after, would it be, about a year – let me see, I went in in January. I went in January and I was deferred service in May and decided to get married in November. And her mother said – Ruby was nineteen, I think it was her mother said, Anyway, will we leave it for six months or something. So we put it off and got married in April. I don't know why, but mothers are like that, I suppose. Anyway, our John [his son] when he was getting married and going to Canada, his wife's mother said, Will you wait until she's twenty-one or something? So John waited six months. He said, Well, I thought I'd better please her – I was taking her daughter to Canada. We got married in April. It was difficult getting a house at that time, getting something. I only had about ninety-eight pounds gratuity after six and a half years' service – well, it bought a second-hand three-piece; you couldn't get the stuff, you know. You got dockets for everything in those days, for curtains and furniture. And it was only an odd occasion when, well, what I got didn't cover a three-piece at all – I could have got a brand new three-piece for forty pounds, but because I couldn't get the coupons to get one with I'd to buy a second-hand one. And it cost me thirty-five. It was a bit tight, you know.

Reporting politics was different then. I used to go to Rafferty's [the Communist's] speeches at one time. The first one I ever took I thought wonderful – you know the stuff that he dishes out. But it never appeared in print. He used to travel around speaking at Wigton and all over the place. It was real good stuff, it was real down-to-earth truth about the way people had been treated and such like; the way they were pushed back, miners chiefly and such like. It was pretty grim in those days. But of course it was the news-papers – it was the Cumberland newspaper that wouldn't print it. I couldn't do much about it; I was just a freelance, you see. I couldn't do anything about it. But I thought it was a bit bad and that it should have appeared.

But there again the *Cumberland News* was a Conservative paper at the time and it had very strong leanings that way. I knew I needn't waste my time going to a Labour meeting because they wouldn't put it in anyway. It was wrong. That went on for a few years after I joined the staff of the *Cumberland News*. I think they finally realised they were in a Socialist town [Carlisle voted Socialist] and the Socialists bought the newspapers and then they stopped being so bigoted. And they changed their name from Carlisle Conservative Newspaper to Cumberland Newspapers. It was actually a Carlisle Conservative news-paper when I went to it.

They give a fair share to everything now. I can send in a Labour meeting now and they'll put it in. They do give a very fair report and I've never had to be told how to write my copy or anything like that. Yet you always have to give a good report of a Conservative do; and they do flog the Conservative candidate.

Otherwise the news is pretty much the same, I should think. There's just been the same type of thing – there's been a couple of murders locally and things like that. At one time when – you remember Borne – was he here when you were a boy? – he was Borne, the Superintendent. He was a terror and he smartened the town up. He was the man, if he used to see a couple of fellas lounging against a wall, he would walk up behind them, you know, he would stand there till they got up and he would walk behind them. A real policeman, he was. And he was very hard on the criminals and he was as good as any law advocate in prosecuting. There was a period in the mid-Fifties there when 'the lads' were in their heyday. They would go and pinch potatoes out of the farmer's field and wheel them past the police station, inviting the policeman to say, Where the devil did you get those? It was just stupidity really. There's been a few real crimes in the area but always petty stuff – but they did go to jail. They've been in jail once or twice. Because I know we in the Rotary Club used to help them when they came out trying to get them a job – maybe a pair of gum boots to start with. Somebody would maybe come and say, One of these lads has got a job but he's got nothing to wear much. And maybe we would rig them out. They have mellowed, you see, these lads – they don't now. There is one cheeky 'laddo' left – aye – he's still cheeky and hard-faced. But the others have mellowed. They break in the Rugby Club and they'll be half tight – they won't get anything but they'll leave a cap and there'll be a policeman sitting on the step with it when they get here. But I don't think they send them to jail now, no. It's always been petty stuff – there's never been any hard crimes. And you always know who's done it.

There used to be a bit; a lot of fights from Saturday dances, so they stopped the dances and there hasn't been any since. It's the White Heather and the Lido now – there's one on Saturday, a schemozzle at Silloth where the chap was stabbed with a broken bottle or something – his chest cut up a bit. But I thought it was a stabbing the first I heard about it. And then half his stomach was hanging out was the second version. And the one I got from Henry Graham was he'd been cut on the chest with a broken bottle – and that was the true version, of course. There's a lot of it at the White Heather now. Mary Addis' boy was beaten up. He was coming from Moota one night and somebody offered to give him a lift, stopped the car and beat him and another boy up. He was taken to Hensingham Infirmary.

It has become fashionable at the moment that men have fancy women on a more public level. It's always gone on but they're a bit more open about it now.

The Council has been a pretty good council in Wigton. They've done quite a lot of work. They haven't done so much in the house-building; they've done a fair bit but I think they could have done better. They've completed some water schemes, they did the town sewerage, you know, three years ago – now that was a good job. They've sewerage to Caldbeck and water at Caldbeck and they didn't have that a couple of years ago, you know. They've done a fair job, but nothing special. They've succeeded most in cleaning up the town; they have cleaned the town up, they have improved the town, the car-park. The new car-park they are putting in behind all the shops, I think that's a very good thing. They are going to extend it, you know, right up the whole block; right up to the church. It's all going to be done. That's one of the biggest things they've done and, of course, people have been shifted. There's nobody living in, I shouldn't say, poor property – there might be the odd cottage or something but I don't think so – not that I know of anyway.

The private developments have really gone ahead. More so in these last few years. You see, when they started to build along this road, it's all interesting because the first four houses that they built they sold two and they couldn't sell the others. Because I wanted to buy some land off Crozier and he said, No, it belongs to Wills – the whole length of it. He said he couldn't sell me any. The next thing I knew was that somebody rang up and said, Harry, there's some sites going up along your road. Wills can't sell the houses and he's going to stop building. So in the meantime, Jack Robson and a lad from the Council bought sites and then Wills took two more and then he took another two and then I got this one and then a chap from Carlisle got beyond me. But we wouldn't have got in here at all if Wills had seen this boom coming. They were priced at two thousand seven hundred pounds these bungalows at the bottom, and the one with the Roman roof was two thousand, seven hundred and ninety, and these couldn't sell – they couldn't sell at all. 'Cos it was a lot of money. People were starting from scratch. Well, this was it, I mean – I built this place but I built this out of purely what I had in the first place – with my freelance work. I mean, I couldn't have done it out of my wages coming in. I do a fair bit of news for the *Telegraph*. I do a column on Thursday and every Friday for overseas and a column on a Monday and on West rugby down to Barrow-in-Furness: and I do work for the Sunday *Sun*. And I do them probably a full programme every Saturday. I cover quite a few matches for them. I do Carlisle, I do Wigton and for that day I ring up and get one of the lads who had been playing. Or speak to the men who have been watching, and in a lot of places the man has to be ready for me. You see, they are quite keen to have their reports in. And the fact they get in the *Daily Telegraph* and things like that, you know, well – and they do play ball with me. A lot of them ring me and I tell them what time to ring me and then we don't cross up on the phone or summat. And then I do so many matches every Saturday for the B.B.C.; I mean, just match scores, just results. I do about five or six for them every week, and maybe a dozen for Border Television. But the B.B.C. want theirs by six o'clock – I mean, ten minutes to six.

I do upset people, being a reporter. And of course they upset me sometimes. I'm a bit of a quiet nature really. If I do upset anybody or if I have a row with anybody, it isn't of my choosing because it upsets me more than it upsets them. I get myself a bit worked up about it. Now Edwin Routledge, of course, he's had more publicity than any man in this county. He rings me about all sorts of things – I mean about business. If he was at a Council meeting and I couldn't get there, I'd get him and say, Did you have anything interesting today? and I know he'll give me a good report. But I upset him because, just like I'd upset anybody else, nobody tells me to keep anything out of the paper – that, to me, is like a red rag to a bull. When I was at the Council meeting when there was a reference to the chairman's allowance being put up from a hundred to six hundred pounds I thought it a bit funny and wondered what it was all about, you see. Mrs. Bailey called out and said, Can you tell me, Mr. Chairman, why is your allowance being increased to six hundred pounds? Well, he said, I was hoping you wouldn't mention this, he said. I hope you won't put it in the paper. He said this to me, you see, and he said, The Council is coming to an end and we all do a lot of work for the town and such like and I thought that we might have a dinner. And that was why he was raising the allowance, to pay for the dinner for the councillors. Well, Mrs. Bailey said, I don't agree with this, and she said, we all give up our time but so do a lot of other people. And of course Bob Sayers got up and said, I agree with this – I think it's scandalous, he said, spending rate-payers' money on dinners – why should we have our dinner?

Well, of course, the financial officer was sitting beside me and he said, You're not going to print this, are you, Harry? and I told him I would please myself what I did. And I began writing it down, you see. So I spread it over about four columns in the paper. Well, I met John Wills in the town yesterday. He said, Well, I hear you put that in the paper: it was just for the committee, wasn't it? Oh no, John, I said. It wasn't for the committee: it was they told me not to put it in. He said, Aye, I heard about it. Aye, I said, and so did a few other people there. And, I said, I'm not having people in this town turning round and saying Harry Watson was for it. But it was wrong. I said, You're a rate-payer, and me. I pay three times the rates everyone else pays, I said. Let's all have a dinner."

Like all fine local reporters, "everybody knows him" and the man they know is always neatly dressed, quiet, sharp-eyed and good-tempered. Nevertheless his obstinacy and militancy now in being prepared to take on people with whom he has to live his life indicates a much more bracing attitude, more liberal and more spirited. From being the camera on the town he has gradually also become a watchdog. This swing on the part of the provincial reporter is behind the national trend but then national reporters do not live next door to their subjects and their readers, they do not have the constraint of knowing people very well, constraints which can be stifling.

His reports on Wigton will soon span half a century. They would make an absorbing record.

CHAPTER TWELVE
Education

The subject of education again leads us into those myths of England's past which debilitate the present. There is an uneasy notion, particularly among those in positions of power and authority – those, that is, over the age of fifty to fifty-five who were educated between the Wars, generally privately, by men who had themselves been educated before the First War, even more exclusively – that "standards" (never defined) are falling, that the wider net has brought in a lesser haul, that the opening of the gates had led to a lowering of the tone. It is *that* which bugs them, in my opinion. The *tone*, not the facts. Facts prove the opposite; yet just as the rich ran from the Riviera with imprecations when those a little poorer arrived, just as the ski slopes lose their value when other classes come up them – so the snobbery which in its dying years has clamped a last grip about England's throat, preferring to see it sink than swim away in a new direction, calls down and causes gloom about education now.

Those in authority in this country have, over the last two hundred years – in the busiest period of Empire – gone to fee-paying schools or slogged their way to universities by scholarship and patronage to discover themselves among fellows whose connections were closely bound by the interlocking nature of the private schools: and so the outsiders had to conform simply to survive. And from there the corps went into professions, politics, the civil service, big business – as directors or major shareholders – and so on. That was the system and for what it was intended it worked extremely well. On all sides it can be defended and even, by its admirers, praised: even the exclusivity which galled local observers for generation after generation, even the strict sense of hierarchy and the snobberies and hypocrisies which held that together, can be justified in terms of the colossal tasks to be done by a tiny island suddenly at the heart of the biggest empire the world had ever known and in the front of the race to industrialisation: the educational élitism gave the country cohesion, apologists would say, and it would be difficult to argue against them.

But like an old snake-skin which will not be shaken off, the system persists though the situation has changed out of all recognition. It is said that the Spain of Philip II began its long decline from superpower to stupor by excessive attention to the endless possibilities which can be drawn out of an elaborate administrative system. Too many forms led to ossification. We have that possibility too, but more dangerous for England, I think, is the clinging to the dead forms of snobbery. We all love a Lord. We all love pageantry. We like our Gilbert and Sullivan policemen, and Beefeaters and judges in their fancy dress and the army dress uniforms which cost a fortune and the military bands which cost more than our orchestras. It would be disastrous, though, if we continued to regard them as the finest flowers of our society, as the indices of our lives, just as Ascot, Henley and the Boat Race must be seen as enjoyable events, not as the apex of our society.

And if this seems far from education, then consider the simple fact that to most people in this country, an image of success is the vision of a family, in the full and expensive regalia of top hat, tails, new hats for the ladies, new dresses, hampers full of rich food and champagne, meeting others of that ilk on a race course in the middle of the country in the middle of a working week. And those people are perpetuating a notion of life which came about through the riches of empire. Nothing intrinsically wrong with such a survival – nor in any of its countless parallels all over the land, except that it presupposes an England which is not dead and need not die but must step aside if there is to be a future. For it presupposes privilege, not only in wealth but also in education, and it declares that the attainment of privilege is a worthy aim for society.

Not so. Not until the Age of Leisure is fully on us. For the privilege was always on a mortgage – and the repayments were made by cheap labour in Africa and Asia, comprehensive investments world-wide, a time when England was the world's oyster and all the grit of others brought us pearls. That has not entirely gone, but it is far enough away to make the meeting of like souls at Royal Ascot not enjoyable (which it clearly is) but frivolous (which it need not be). Frivolous not because I am a puritan, nor am I envious: frivolous because we cannot forever talk in abstract terms about "class" and "systems" – we must have examples to follow – and as an aim in life, the life of a nation as energetic and fertile as ours, Royal Ascot is now inadequate.

Unless, that is, we want to become a toy-town of the Western world, an animated museum, a pack of complacent caricatures, forever strolling in and out of our glorious past down the hill of a gutless future. That may be the case. Certainly the first point to be made about education over the past seventy-five years is that while it has changed enormously, it has also stayed the same. Private schools (called "public" schools, reminder of the times when they were available to all) persist and multiply, feed the older universities, staff the civil service, man the professions and so on into the establishment. This is not the place to argue the case for or against them – it is, in the end, very dangerous in a free society to tell people what to do with the money you leave them after all necessary taxes, and if they choose to spend it on private education it is hard to find an abstract argument of whatever force which does not smack of authoritarianism. What can be said, however, is that the continuity in that area of our educational life has obscured the achievements of the majority and it is that majority which forms the bulk of this chapter.

For if we are to have a future world rôle then can it come from a system – such as the private system – whose ethos, tone, methods and manners are so fixed in one particular past – the imperial amphitheatre? Just as the public schools grew up in the nineteenth century to meet the demands being made by colonies and the growth of internal legislation, so the expansion and democratisation of education lately embarked on could lead to ways of meeting the new demands of a post-imperial world which at present threatens to leave us marooned in all our glory. If there is to be that release of energy which alone takes countries and people forward, then it must be to the mass that we look – for through taxes, unions and votes, the mass now has the power. And on the hopeful side for England, there has been a recognition that just such a basic reorganisation and investment in the majority could unlock the energy. Of course it is frustrated by a private system which takes away much talent and interest and concern; and by competing doctrines of secondary education; and by the still worrying inertia of a country which, even in the last quarter of the twentieth century, manages to transfer so few genuinely working-class children to university (but as was seen with Billy Lowther in the factory, universities are not the only way).

Yet when such theories and assertions are done, simple observations remain as soundest evidence of the life we have. A day in the schoolroom for someone in 1900 was a very different thing from a day at school for a child today. Not only are the children generally better fed, better dressed, given more encouragement at home and less cruelty at school, they are taught, generally, in brighter buildings with more aids, more and more varied books, more variety in the curriculum, proper games periods and so on. There is so large a reservoir of world-weariness and apprehension about education at the moment that to state and to reiterate obvious advances is to be accused of almost irresponsible optimism. But the overwhelming fact over the last three generations in Wigton is that more people have been better educated as the century has gone on. This is a story of success.

Before 1914 the common picture is either dark or idyllic. Many of those I spoke to referred to their schooldays as "terrible", "didn't like it one bit' – surprising, really, when it is remembered that those interviewees were at least seventy, and at seventy childhood traditionally appears like a rose garden. But there was a clear majority feeling – particularly among the men – that school had been drudgery, a waste of time on all sides, something they looked back on with scant concern. These were people, I would guess, whose life at school had been accompanied by complaints at home that they ought to be out earning a living, ought not to be a burden on the family, ought to work. In those days, and in the working classes lingering strongly through until today, the feeling was that school was for children and the drive was to be a man. After the comparative simplicities of ordinary arithmetic, spelling, writing and reading, there was little which could be taught that could be held or seen to have wider application to a world of work and marriage, and besides this the discipline, especially for the boys, was especially harsh. For them, there was little joy in it. Joe Bill Lightfoot touches on that side of the matter.

His teacher was one of the Miss Bells who represents the sunny, simple, Beatrix Potter side of Edwardian schooling. Joe Bill was proud of the fact that she remembered him, despite the "trouble" he thought he had given her, and it was a point of this pride to speak to her for a few moments whenever he saw her on the street. So did other older pupils.

In fact, Miss Bell's progress up the High Street on one of her morning shopping expeditions would be a smaller version of a walk-about by the Queen Mother. She dressed, in style, like the Queen Mother and her complexion too had that gentle Northern freshness. Her sister, also Miss Bell, dressed in complementary pastel shades. They lived together in this large house which used to be the old grammar school just a few steps from the yards where their father built coaches and then their brother Arthur "took up the motors". Gentility was their chief and antique characteristic. The world of Jane Austen, of perturbation over the minutiae of domestic arrangements, of pre-occupation with this small world was not far off: but nor was a stouter side. The world of *Lark Rise to Candleford*, country life as it had to be lived, including Miss Bell's bicycle journey every morning to her school, in the foothills of the fells, three miles away, "rain, hail or snow", "never missed a day". The two Miss Bells spoke as one, sentences completed for each other, gentleness and quietness absorbing the questions with subduing disclaimers that they could not be interesting enough for anyone to want to know about. Yet Miss Bell was for many people the perfect schoolteacher. She had the infants from five years to seven. By seven, all of them could read, although "I never used the cane". "I had a method, I couldn't tell you the name of the method but it was my own. The inspectors used to copy it. Oh yes, I could teach reading." She taught in the villages around Wigton throughout her life and retired in 1950. I spoke to her just before she died, in 1973, and even then there were flowers and cards from old pupils. "I taught everything except needlework." Her sister died a few months later.

Joseph Barnes went to school in Micklethwaite two or three miles from Wigton: Miss Bell went there as a relief teacher at one stage. Joseph Barnes, who is now retired after a lifetime as a painter and decorator, was the son of an agricultural worker and his schooldays come out of a late Victorian picture book.

"I went to school at Rosewain and that was quite an adventure really in those days. Of course there was no buses and there's a public footpath from Micklethwaite right out to just beside Rosewain School and that was our route. Now if it was an extra heavy rain the Wampool used to flood and so of course it was clogs and stockings in those days. Off they came and you waded through the water. We didn't get cold. I think nowadays the average youngster would get pneumonia. Peg out. And that carried on until I was twelve, and the school got overcrowded. It's only a small school. You may know the building. And so there was – well, it'll be the Education Authority, they decided that the elder boys had to leave – and that was Grahams of Spittal and Fenwicks of Bridge House and Bells the butchers – Anthony, the late Anthony Bell. Well, Fenwick and I went to Wiggonby. That was further still. And there again we were on the public road all the time, but there again there was a flood. We had to wade through that. But, as I say, I honestly think myself that it hardened me up for after life because I've had a wonderful bill of health.

It was very old-fashioned teaching we got, though. Like what I mean to say, when I was looking at some school-books a year or two ago at Wiggonby, I was there taking the contract for the outside painting of the school, and so during me lunch hour I had a look through some of the school-books – well, they were different altogether from what we had. Of course they seem to be learning them all the phonetic side of spelling and that sort of thing and – but somehow or other we sort of got through it. Now I believe they've started them off printing, then after they've taught them to print, then they teach them to write. Where we were taught to write from the beginning. And, when you come to think about it, it was bound to be harder really than the present way because like printing, they're printing exactly what they see in the book where when we were writing it, of course, it was a different design altogether.

We had to learn a lot by heart. Like Wordsworth poems for instance, and Tennyson's 'The Brook' and that. And of course there was sort of a standard set of songs that you used to sing, of course, 'Rule Britannia' and that sort of thing. The songs were like 'Men of Harlech' and 'The Minstrel Boy' and, now then, I'll remember them all after you've gone. And of course, as I say, there was always fresh poems to be learned, and by the way, at that time, one of the strong points was the religious education and that seems to be more or less in a lot of schools nearly a thing of the past. In fact there was a special exam by the Diocesan Education Society each year and the different schools vied. Oh, there was a shield. And the school went for top scoring; well, they got that. Incidentally, Wiggonby got it more often than any other school. He was a great master that, there's no getting away from it.

We played football, but of course we hadn't a proper football. We just kicked about as best we could."

Willie Johnston's father was a grocer and butcher. The first school he went to was the Infants'. "A Most Terrible Place," he said. "Conditions – Terrible. Sanitation – Nil. Very bad. It was damp and cold and a terrible spot." His father paid for him to go to the Nelson School. At that time, Mr. Humphries was the headmaster. He was a Doctor of Divinity and, according to Willie Johnston, "he had a very funny way of educating. He would line you up and ask questions. If you didn't know the answer you went to the bottom of the class. Sometimes a perfect dunce would end up top. And these were the positions you took home with you." Willie Johnston's own stay there was brief.

"I wouldn't say I enjoyed it tremendously. No, I didn't. I was a nervous type of a child. I had no confidence in myself. That was my trouble, as a youth. I grew out of it later but, oh my God, I hadn't the confidence to think I could do well and I'll tell you, those days when I went to the Nelson School, my father used to pay so much a term – and I'll never forget the reason why I left. I got a report one day and it had on the bottom of it – 'Has the ability but will not try'. Immediately go down and give your notice, Father said. You're going back no more. That was the finish. I never went back again. That put paid to my schooling at the Nelson School."

Even the son of a tradesman could be given such rough and ready treatment. The great majority went through the statutory period, learning more about obedience than the world of information. "Discipline was tough." "You *had* to sit still." "If you didn't do what they said . . ." They were rather impressed by the strict schools they had passed through.

And it would be a mistake to assume that the changes were steady. The same teachers stayed at the Infants' School, Miss Bell, Miss Steele, Miss Moffat, Miss Ivinson and the awesome headmaster, Mr. Scott, from near the beginning of the century until my own infant schooldays in the Forties. Nor had their methods changed. We were drilled like little chocolate soldiers and we chanted out our multiplication tables as ritualistically as the Chinese sing the songs of Mao. (Arithmetic was to the Imperial Englishman what Maoism is to the Chinese.) We said our morning prayers in unison and in unison said "Thank you, Miss Ivinson" and "Good afternoon, Miss Ivinson" and before a legal move could be made we stuck up our hands in what now would be seen as a gesture of revolutionary solidarity. "Please, Miss, can I go to the lavatory?" Naughtiness, though, especially from boys, and most especially from likable boys, was also, in some way, "written into the constitution". But all teachers at that Infants' School could quell even us, the post-Second World War generation, with a single rap of the cane on the desk. A cane, incidentally, which was in active use throughout my own schooldays until the mid Fifties. The great changes came at the end of the Fifties – the changes inside the schools and in the buildings themselves. Previously changes for the better had been largely as a result of the amelioration of conditions outside.

Mr. Postlethwaite's father was an engine man in the mines in West Cumberland. He became an insurance collector, taking his son on the wide country rounds into the hill and lakeland which butts the industrial coastline. He came to Wigton to teach in the early Thirties and many of those in this book were taught by him, as I was. He served under the legendary Mr. Scott and saw the system change from Victorian hardness – bare wooden benches and slates, chalk, cold fingers, chanting, concrete playgrounds, no lighting, few books, poverty – to Elizabethan opulence – glass-faced white concrete schools in acres of green fields, gymnasia, books galore, teaching aids, occupational guides, the comprehensive idea. His own story is that of many clever and determined boys anywhere since there ever was a ladder for an ambitious working-class child to climb. His teaching experience bridges that great mid-century change which took England from the squalor and certainty of insanitary red-brick to the ease and uncertainty of glass.

He's retired now and I saw him when he was fishing – his private passion. We talked then about a trip he'd been on to New York to visit one of his daughters. The most vivid part of his description was the telling of how he had raced "home" from the airport on his return. "Couldn't get back quick enough." A few days later we talked in his house, a detached house near the middle of the town.

"I won a scholarship to Whitehaven Grammar School. Two of us passed. We were the only two from the school who passed the scholarship in my particular year, and we were the only two as far as I know who passed for quite a number of years. In the whole of Egremont. In those days I think there were as few as twenty scholarships to Whitehaven Secondary School for the entire area, and that includes Egremont, Cleator Moor, Frizington, Parton, Distington. The books were free, the travel to the school was free. And that's what we got. Clothing, uniform and so on were provided by parents. Quite a few bright boys simply couldn't afford it.

The first thing which struck me at the Grammar School was the fact that the teachers wore gowns. And everything was just this little more genteel. Teachers didn't belt you over the earhole or across the backside if you did anything wrong; you were told off but told off in a much more genteel manner. The fact of going to the secondary school made you into an embryo little gentleman. Not the same as St. Bees Public School which is again, if you like to used the word class, in a higher class again. Gentlemen's sons, of course. Whitehaven Grammar School was for the bright boys of the area.

The syllabus was the old-fashioned grammar-school syllabus. Latin,

French ... the usual stuff; languages, maths, history, geography and so on. Just the usual grammar-school syllabus. Very little attempt made to make the subject interesting at all. Certainly no slides or films or projections or even models. You were taught from a book. The teacher talked to you and told you what page to turn to in the book, he wrote something on the blackboard and that was all the teaching. The only time we ever did anything practical – we did a little woodwork but not much. It wasn't much thought of in those days because it was a waste of time. You had to get through examinations and woodwork didn't put you through examinations. Apart from that, the only time we handled anything or did anything with hands as distinct from our brains was when we did chemistry or physics. That was quite a change, going into a place where there were benches with glassware. A tremendous change from the local elementary school. There was no original work. There was nothing about your own thoughts going into anything. You simply turned back what had been told to you.

The only outside activity that I can remember in my days at the Whitehaven Secondary School were two fellows; one was the Latin master and one the P.E., I think. They took us for Scouts and that's about the only outside activity we took part in, and they weren't very keen. They were supposed to give us an hour on Tuesday nights or whatever and usually they would come in about half an hour after we were supposed to start. They used to teach us the Morse code and various knots and this was it. We never went camping, for example. We wore Scouts' uniforms. There's much more concern these days with giving the youngsters activities. You've still got the academic side of things, of course – you must have it – but an awful lot of work has been done recently, encouraging the less able children academically to use their energies in some way or other, even if it's only football. I mean, in those days that I'm talking about when I went to school, we had a school football team but they only played maybe two matches with little villages or towns nearby to which they could walk. They had to walk to the football matches. They weren't taken on buses or anything like that.

At school you did precisely what you were told, no more, no less. If you went to school in those days, there wasn't a sound or the headmaster wanted to know why. I went to a school in Egremont and the headmaster used to sit in the room and there were two classes in this room and if there was a whisper from a boy in any of those classes, he was standing up looking, frowning ferociously, to see who had whispered. You daren't talk. It was a really hard discipline. You either behaved yourself or else – children were to be seen and not heard.

311

The old idea; when you're a child, you do not speak to your elders until you're spoken to.

This is probably the basic attitude – that you were, did what you were told by the person who was superior to you. There was no question of respect and liking for anybody and doing what they wish you to do because (a) they knew better than you and (b) you respected their viewpoint. It was fear all the time.

I've seen some children get some horribly sadistic hidings. They would be getting four strokes as a general thing. They'd be lashed round the classroom if they'd been rather worse than usual. If they had to be given a really good thrashing, and I mean a thrashing, I don't mean just a couple of whacks across the backside with a cane, they were taken into what we called the porch in those days – the cloakroom, and given a real thrashing in there. And, incidentally, parents used to come to school in those days, occasionally to complain but very frequently just as often to tell the headmaster that if their boy wasn't behaving himself, would he give him a real good hiding. I've seen this happen quite a number of times. The parents depended upon the school master to keep the boys in line. I've seen mothers come to school – give our so and so a hiding if he's been misbehaving. And for what we would consider very minor things in these days; answering back to their mother, he won't do what he's told, simply because he's said, I won't go down the street for a message, I'm going to play with so and so. It's unbelievable in this day and age.

Don't get me wrong. I can't ever remember most boys actively hating a school master. In fact, in some peculiar way we had a great respect for them. In fact we almost liked some of them. Very few indeed though. I can only remember one of my school masters whom I actively liked. In fact, a friend of mine and I bought him a present. He emigrated to South Africa. We bought him a pipe or something, but we liked him. The school master was not quite a gentleman but a semi-gentleman. We respected him. He wore a collar and tie, which is something you very seldom saw in ordinary life. People went about – shirts without collars and the studs stuck in, the stud was always stuck in.

There was very little sport in school, only football as far as I can remember. In fact when I was at school there wasn't even a games period. And the boys who were in the school football team simply showed ability in the school yard at playtimes. There must have been some school master who was interested in football and gathered them together and got a football team going. And nobody ever dreamt of staying on at school after fourteen.

I must admit that I stayed on at school for no specific reason. Possibly because there weren't many jobs going and I might as well be at school doing something which might earn me a better job in the future. But there was no real specific reason. Had a job come up, I'd have probably been a grocer's assistant or something. I had interviews – talking about being a grocer's assistant, I had an interview for a job, I always remember, when I was about fifteen or so in Egremont Co-operative Society as a clerk or something. Fortunately, as it turned out, I didn't get it, otherwise I'd have been stuck there all my life. So I stayed at school. Almost by accident became, somehow or other, what they called in those days a student teacher. Did a year's training, went into the local school – incidentally back to the school where I'd been taught as a boy which was extremely difficult 'cos everybody in the place knew me, and I was just a kid of seventeen or so.

I must have been about seventeen when we took what was then called the Higher School Certificate and, having got through that, then I really had to start looking round because I couldn't go on at school for ever. I came into school teaching by pure accident because there was a Further Education dance at Egremont and I there met the fellow who was then Director of Education, G. B. Brown. And he said to me, well, I don't know how I got talking to him in point of fact, he said, Apply for a college, young man. So I applied for a college, got in at the college and here I am.

This student-teacher business was to fill in the year between getting into college and going there. I went back to my old school and, my God, it was hell on earth. You can imagine going back, not much older than some of the kids I was attempting to teach. They knew me, they knew my family and we'd always lived in Egremont. I knew them, they'd always been used to calling me Bob and here I was trying to be a respected school master amongst it all. It was almost impossible. But, my goodness, it broke me into teaching, shall I say. I've never suffered quite so much since. In fact it was a very heart-breaking period for me, that, and for everybody else who did the same thing. A lot of people did the same thing. But my parents were frightfully proud I was going to college. Because – and I suppose, again without being big-headed, I'm saying a lot of things which sound big-headed but it's perfectly true – the town was proud of me. I was a boy from Egremont who'd made good, because there wasn't employment in the town. What did everybody do? They either hung about the streets or managed to get a job at the mines, and a boy who'd made his way as I had, well, I had something to be proud of.

But I must admit, they talk about teaching being a vocation – the teachers of my age and era were almost forced into teaching if they wanted something a little bit better than manual work. We had to do something of this nature.

It was Dudley Training College I went to and that was one of the most enjoyable experiences of my life because I left a type of education where you did what you were told, even up to the time that I finished grammar school you did precisely what you were told, when you were told and how you were told. Going to college is a completely different atmosphere. There's an atmosphere that you're a young man now, we rely upon you to do your work without being pushed. We rely upon you to put forth ideas and to talk about what you intend to do. Discuss your own ideas and to argue with other people, a different type of education completely. Practically no formal teaching; an awful lot of discussions, an awful lot of argument, an awful lot of mistakes but the end-result proved its worth, I think, in that when you finished you could think for yourself, at least you could talk for yourself. The basic course was for what they then called the elementary school; that was the basic training. There were slight variations of aspects of the type of teaching you were going into in these schools; for example, I did maths – I could handle the maths side.

When I came to Wigton I was supposed to be able to go into a classroom and teach every subject that that school taught, including music. And my music is completely nil. And I have taken music lessons and the kids probably knew more, some of them knew a darned sight more about music than I do to this day. At college I found people more or less like myself but from all different parts of the country. And, whatever you say about Wigton being typical of the country, every bit of the country has its own particular outlook and its own particular views upon life and about how things ought to be done. And when you get to a training college you meet all sorts of people with ideas which are at complete variance with your own. And you learn to assimilate some of their ideas, reject what you really don't believe in but accept some of them. Again you got an atmosphere there in that possibly some of them were like myself, who weren't awfully sure about teaching, but you got people who were talking about teaching, talking about handling kids, talking about new ideas. And gradually you found the whole place becoming one sort of unit of thought directed towards educating the young. Even though in the first place when you first went you were still a bit unsure as to whether it was really what you wanted to do, you lived in an atmosphere of educational outlook and possible educational progress.

I came to Wigton on 6th February 1933, on a temporary basis. I was twenty-three. And I went to the National School, the Elementary School. When I came to Wigton I found that the people here were completely different to the people I'd been used to living among even at Seaton, which is or was basically a mining area, but more so Egremont where everybody was, in my youth, very serious about life. They lived a tough life, some of them didn't know where their next job was coming from, some of them didn't work for years. I got the impression here that nobody cared about anything. Oh, tomorrow's another day. But down west in the mining area you were thinking about today, the immediate problems. Wigton, oh, if things go wrong today, they'll be right tomorrow. Different outlook altogether. They had a saying in those days, 'Owt'll deu.' I'd been brought up all my life to be quite serious about things, and I found people here – and I've come to believe that they're quite right. There's nothing very serious in life really. We all die, I suppose. We all come to the same end. So why not have a bit more fun while you can. Do the job to the best of your ability. But when I started it was this attitude of Owt'll deu, well, to me, it wouldn't. I wanted to see things done properly. I don't want to name names but I've found kids in the school when I first came here, oh, if they couldn't get something right it didn't matter. Let's get it finished with and let's get out of school. And this attitude was rather foreign to me, coming from a hard-minded community. I was just as foreign to them in my outlook as they were to me. They conquered me. I didn't conquer them. And I'm happy to have been conquered, incidentally.

One of the first things George Scott, the headmaster, said when he got to know me, he says, Robert, do you know that this school was condemned in 1910? He said, I remember an Inspector coming through that door – I was in the classroom at the top of the stone steps leading out of what used to be the girls' yard – he put his umbrella to the ceiling and he touched it and he said, This ceiling is far too low. The school would be condemned 1910 and I arrived in 1933, so it took quite a few years after that to – well, it's only a couple of years since they've been out of it, isn't it? Built in 1810. You were scrambling about there in 1950 yourself.

Well, my temporary business became permanent, so to speak. Actually the point was that I think a lot of life, it depends on how you get on with people. All life does, doesn't it? Well, I got on very well with George Scott. I was almost like a second son to him, but I'd a great regard for old George Scott. I didn't agree with many of

315

the things he said, I used to think he talked the most awful rot some-times, and he probably thought I talked the most awful rot – but we got on very well together. He used to believe in the old-fashioned type of education and I wasn't too sure that this was the right thing to do. This wasn't the right way to handle children. But it was a differ-ence of era. Difference of time rather than difference of personality.

The thing I remember most about that classroom up there was I was teaching a lesson, shortly after I'd arrived actually. It was a rather hot summer's day and I had the door open – there was a big, heavy door at the top of those stairs you may remember. And I was teaching this class, with my back to the door naturally, and quite suddenly every girl in the class screamed at the top of her voice and jumped onto the seat. And it's a most peculiar thing to say but I can quite distinctly remember saying to myself, I may not be a brilliant teacher but I'm surely not as bad as that. And what had happened was a great big rat had run up the steps. Behind my chair there was a hole in the floor. Then one day we had a scratching in those metal cylinder things there used to be at the back of the classroom. I never knew what those were for – ventilation or something. So I got sick of this and eventually I said, Well I'll find out what this is. And I pulled this ventilator thing away from the wall and there was a starling there and it stunk to high heaven. It had been there about three days, fluttering, trying to get out.

Physically it was a horrible old place. There's no need to be senti-mental about it. I got to quite love it in the end but it was a horrible place. I don't know whether you – you're not supposed to know this – that boys' yard at the back, there's a little gutter flows down behind the wall. There's some sort of party door or something goes through it. When there was a lot of rain, this little gutter used to flood underneath the door and the entire playground was flooded. Even-tually they built sort of staging round the side of the school so that the boys could reach the lavatory, otherwise they couldn't. But before that was built, boys who came to school in wellingtons were at a premium because they carried the other boys across to the lavatory, across this flooded yard. And some of the walls used to bulge out-wards; there are sort of metal ties across some of those walls to keep them into place. And if there'd been a fire, say, in the ground floor that place was an absolute death trap. I mean, you went out of the upstairs room down those steps. Some of them were wooden steps and some were stone steps. There must have been a hundred children up there, or thereabouts, and had there been a serious fire down below they would never have got out – an absolute death trap.

Walter Purdham used to be on the ground floor, and Abe Ray used to occasionally take music lessons in this big room that I used to be in at the top of the sairs. Abe Ray was taking a music lesson one day, he was the only one who could play the piano apart from George Scott, and Walter was in the room below – and one day Walter looked up and he saw this foot dangling through the ceiling. The flooring was rotten. Abe's foot had come right through the ceiling. He was up to his knee, his foot dangling through the ceiling of the room below. Oh dear, oh dear – education.

For a teacher the point was in those days there were no such things as free periods. You went into school at ten to nine or whenever you were supposed to be in, you signed in incidentally – the teachers signed in, clocked in saying what time they'd arrived, and clocked out at night say what time they'd left – and from the moment you entered the room or the youngsters came in from the playground, you taught and taught and taught. You didn't have time off for marking or anything like this. Any marking you did you took the books home with you. Any preparation of lessons, which a young teacher must do, no teacher can teach without preparing lessons, you had to do at home. The result was your job was – well, it started at nine o'clock in the morning and finished sometimes nine o'clock at night. It was a twelve-hour day. But it was quite remarkable what some of the children produced actually, and I always found that when I started teaching I taught in very much, not quite, but very much the same way as I had been taught – three Rs and so on. But eventually one started introducing more interesting things and it was amazing how – what a set of good work the kids turned out. It sounds simple, making table mats, hexagonal table mats and painting them and varnishing them, on top of an ordinary wood desk such as they used to be in the old days no benches or anything – quite remarkable what they produced. I mean, it sounds simple, it may sound rather silly.

Discipline was still severe, of course. But I always used to impress upon them if I punished them I punished them because I believed they'd done something they shouldn't have done. I never punished a child because I was in a bad temper, for example, as I've seen teachers do. I've had boys, I've punished boys at this new school if they were getting off the track and they've accepted the punishment. Get over a desk and get four across the backside. But I've always made it perfectly plain to them exactly what they'd done and that I'd previously warned them that I think this punishment was completely deserved. And I've always found kids will accept punishment if you make it clear to them that they have done something that they ought not to have done, having been previously warned or given a chance before. Kids are wonderful things but they will not accept injustice. And, I mean, everybody makes mistakes and I think I've always realised very shortly afterwards when I've made a mistake, in that sense.

Then, in 1944, this secondary modern system started. I always thought it was one of the most wonderful advances in education the country had seen. The Wigton one was the first in Cumberland, and the big thing about it was that even though you reached the statutory leaving age you were encouraged to stay on and do something else if you showed any aptitude for any particular subject. A thing that had never been known before because – you remember the old school – the big point was there just wasn't room for youngsters to stay on. What did you do with them if they did stay on? You either had to attend to them individually, which you couldn't do, teaching class all day long, or you just let them potter about. But as soon as the secondary modern school business started – it was a wonderful advance to my mind. We got girls staying on there. There's a girl in this town who is now a nurse, she's married, I don't know whether she does nursing now, but she was one of the nurses in the town. That girl was a C-stream girl in the secondary modern school. Now a C-stream girl isn't very bright, let's be honest about it, academically; that girl stayed on at school, worked so hard and was encouraged to work hard, and eventually got three or four O-levels and became a district nurse. This was a thing completely unheard of in the past. Boys staying on to do a course in woodwork or a course in metalwork, children being encouraged to stay on to take this shorthand-typing course. Absolutely unheard of until the secondary modern school started. As I say, again basically because there just wasn't room for them in the old-type school. It was the facilities which improved so dramatically.

It's almost impossible to describe the change. Not only in the building, in the tremendous area, playing area, they had, but the change in the complete outlook upon education. We still did the basic things, of course, but so many things facing us, there was such a variety and such a richness of opportunity in many respects, it took us some years to grasp them. It was a tremendous change. I mean, even from a physical point of view – the fact that there were separate rooms for woodwork, metalwork, two rooms for housecraft. Then of course it was also, as you were saying, the time when there were new ideas coming into education. You didn't knock the tables into a boy or girl; you encouraged them rather than made them and children responded. One of the things that I noticed up there was immediately the children appeared to be far brighter in class. Coming out of an old gloomy building into a brand-new white concrete outside and beautiful pastel shades in the classroom, the children seemed to respond much better to what you were trying to get into them.

And we had a gym, it was a wonderful thing. We'd never seen a gym before of course. As far as education in our section of the field was concerned, we didn't know what a gym was. Labs, typewriters, then of course we probably sickened ourselves to some extent in over-utilisation of the facilities. We'd all sorts of clubs and societies and teams that were never dreamt of before. We ran ourselves into the ground, sort of thing. We did too much. It was a very hard time for the teachers, very hard indeed. We were encouraged to take children on Continental holidays, we were encouraged to take them out into the countryside, we were encouraged to take them camping and all this sort of thing. And it became very arduous. And there was much more sport. Walter Purdham and I started a little competition in this area. That was the origination, I think I can safely say, in the sports activities in this area. We started off by having a competition between the local schools for some little cup I got people to subscribe money for. And from then we grew and eventually we got a sports team that went to the County Sports. All the children in Wigton had run in their local little school races but they'd never got out of the town at all. And it was a great thing for them the first time we took them, I think, down to Whitehaven to run against the rest of the county. We only took about fifteen to twenty youngsters but what an experience for them! They'd never seen anything like it before. And the little beggars ran their hardest. One of them was Agnes Riding, and Isobel Pearson who used to live on Station Hill. They were extremely good runners and I almost wept when they didn't win the race. Because the little beggars tried so hard.

And people were gradually getting better off in the Fifties. This is an important factor, you know. In the first place, even in 1949 after the war, when people were sort of settling back to their jobs, it wasn't everybody who could afford to keep their kids at school. The farming community, for example, they wanted their lads out of school to help on the farm. But it grew and eventually it grew to such an extent that we were having difficulty in keeping the numbers down; we were getting too many staying on. And occasionally they'd go on to technical college. Talking about Billy Lowther, he's a case in point. And there were several like him, quite a number like him who, say, took a course, what we call the light engineering course, sort of bridging course between

319

school and work, doing things that they would likely do, say, in the factory down there. Now it didn't end there, of course. At the end of each school year when the children leave there's a youth employment officer comes along. And we used to be very keen on impressing upon them that their education wasn't finished. They would go to a job, say, in the rayophane factory down there and then think of going to technical college. Basically, it all came down to use of apparatus. It was the provision of new apparatus that we'd never seen in schools before. Talkie projectors, television and this sort of thing, slides. Many more books, and much more money was made available at that time for books and equipment and this sort of thing. And there was more contact with local firms.

Every year or maybe twice a year, when the youngsters were due to leave, we got the factory people and Redmayne's and Carlisle firms, youth employment officer, to come in, set up their stalls in what is now the canteen up there, with their literature on, people representing various factories or jobs sitting at the desks. We invited the parents and the children to come along – those who were leaving or those who were maybe not leaving for a year to talk to these people, to get to know what went on in various jobs. We also took children out to factories and showed them what factory work was like, what they could expect when they left school. Again Wigton factory, Redmayne's, various firms in Carlisle, print works at Cummersdale, Carr's, all these local firms where it was possible some of them might obtain jobs. We even had a scheme once, some years back, about ten years back now, we actually allowed boys to go out if they, say, wanted to be motor mechanics or something of this nature, we'd contact, say, George Huntington and ask if he would have this boy for a day. He maybe didn't do much. He maybe just carried a spanner or two but he saw the sort of work they were doing. Even how dirty they got and that if he wanted to be a motor mechanic, this was the sort of thing he had to do. We tried to bridge the gap between school and work. This was completely new. We tried to foster parents' interest by having a parent-teacher association, by, as I say, having parents come up when their child was about to leave school, by inviting them to come up when we thought their child was sufficiently bright to benefit from some of these extra courses we were able to give them. In fact, invite them up and say, we want to talk about your boy or your girl.

It was the 1944 Education Act, basically, which changed the whole picture. By making more money available, by making better facilities, by making better buildings, surroundings, and by drawing in all these employers and saying, We've got these children; they're good at this or they're good at that. Then drawing in the parents and saying, Your child's good at this or good at that ... And then the next change, at the end of the Sixties, was to comprehensive education.

The teaching profession was very much divided about comprehensive education, and I'm afraid a lot of the teachers in schools took sides. And I think it's true to say that most of them did not want comprehensive education. I must admit that I'm one of them because I feared very much – I've built up maybe a picture of the secondary modern school which sounds bright – it was bright. We felt that we were doing a damned good job for the community, even if not in the educational field, which we thought we were, in the field of transition from school to work. We thought we'd done an excellent job there and we'd done it with what were termed and are still termed disabled children. And the fear amongst teachers was the fact that when comprehensive education was largely brought about in this country, that these less able children would not get quite the same care that they had in the past.

The idea, of course, behind comprehensive education is that every child should have the same chance and that the brightness of bearing or outlook of the brighter children would rub off on the less able children. And that's a very doubtful supposition, to my mind. Again, my attitude – we mentioned before that attitudes probably suffer from your practical experience, and I felt that all the work that we'd done up there in the past might be swallowed in a bigger community. Now don't ask me to pass judgment, it would be unfair if I did. I'm biased and I must admit it. But I still think that the secondary modern system was an excellent system and I doubt very much whether the present system will be quite as effective in the fields we've been talking about.

Let's put it this way: if you are headmaster of a big school like this comprehensive, what does the community judge you upon? It judges you upon the list of passes in O-levels and A-levels that you see in the local newspapers. They judge you upon that. So what's a headmaster going to do? He's going to say, I'm going to get plenty of A-levels and O-levels in my school. The other stuff is less visible. It's less immediately of news value. And so it may possibly take rather a back seat. Or let's put it another way. I very seldom found that the children themselves were disappointed by failing the eleven-plus but I often found the parents were disappointed. And I rather feel it was the parents who were rather more disappointed than children. Nowadays people are much more conscious of the advantages of education and naturally parents are saying, Well, if my child's going to get the best education possible for him, he's going to be in a grammar school. And if he doesn't pass the eleven-plus then he's not going to go to the grammar school.

But the old system again was excellent in the sense that the eleven-plus was certainly not the be all and end all of a child's chances of getting to a grammar school. Every first year we had up there, that is the first year out of the primary school into our school, we looked at them very carefully and we maybe found eight or ten children who we thought might do better in a grammar school, who were sufficiently bright to do well in a grammar school. Now we contacted the local grammar school and pointed this out and what happened was that these eight or ten children were tested, given another test. In the second year we did much the same thing. I even badgered the Director of Education and Mr. Stowe here two or three years ago about a girl who was showing tremendous promise in music. And I wrote to the Director and he said, Well, if you get Mr Stowe to agree, we'll transfer this girl down to the grammar school – and this girl was in her third year. Three years after she had failed the eleven-plus. And eventually I got her into the grammar school and she did quite well. We were always watching them and looking at them, always re-assessing, always trying to say, Well, if they're academically inclined, let's have them in the grammar school.

So I'm cynical and I say that this is the type of education they had in the days of Henry VIII when you dumped every child into one school and said, Right, let's teach them the Latin or whatever. And you can't treat children like that. You can treat paper in the factory like that but you can't treat children like that. You've got a thousand or more individuals in there. They're all individuals in their own right. You've got to give them – you haven't got to give them their head freely but you've got to look at them and assess them and weigh them up and say what they're best for and try to do the best for them. And I've always been a firm believer in the fact that a school should be a certain size – I always say five hundred but some put it much less. Now you said the kids liked me. Do you know, probably one reason why they liked me was because I liked to think I knew them all. When I was acting headmaster at the secondary modern school for about eighteen months, if I saw a child I didn't know in the school and couldn't name, I used to think to myself, I'm slipping. Now in a school of a thousand, you don't even know the staff. It's – to me it's one of the prime essentials of school mastering is that you know your children. From the lowest standpoint, if there's any trouble you can always pinpoint the little beggar that caused the trouble. But from a broader outlook, that you try to do what you can for them according to their abilities.

My personal opinion is that in the not too distant future they'll start splitting comprehensive schools up into – well, they'll have to rebuild their entire schools into a sort of campus where the kids who are sort of academically inclined will carry out one course of instruction, another set with carry out, say, technical-type instruction for factory work and another type will do agriculture and this sort of thing. And you'll have another type who are almost educationally subnormal that you've got to handle in different ways again. But if you mix them all together and try to teach them and you say, there's no streaming and you've got educationally subnormal in with kids with I.Q.s of about a hundred and forty, if there are any such children, who do you teach? Do you aim at the highest academic level? What's a little fellow who can scarcely read going to do? If you aim at him, where's the other lad going to get his academic attainment from? I still think that children should be separated into groups. The only trouble is the dividing line and you've got to have a flexible dividing line, and my ideas aren't revolutionary – they're what a lot of people think and they're built up over forty years of experience.

The attitude in my young days was you got a job and you worked. And you worked if you could in your own area because you lived among your own folk. Parochialism, I suppose. And I hope that I've been bold enough and liberal enough to allow my children to have their head. See that they did their homework, shall I say – see that they took full advantage of the educational opportunities. I never had a television. I said I'm not having a television in this house until my children are away from school. I don't know whether it was selfish or whether it wasn't. I didn't make an issue of it. I just didn't have one. And then I never interfered with my children in any shape or form. If they wanted to go to America or South Africa or whatever they went. They made their own minds up and I'm delighted about this, that they weren't tied to our apron-strings. They did just what they thought they would do. Even my youngest daughter, who is still in England, she went to work as a hotel receptionist, and she wandered about north Lancashire and various hotels. But if she wanted to do that, fair enough."

Charlie Allardyce would regard himself as typical: he started at the National School, at eleven, about the time Bob Postlethwaite came to Wigton, and left when he was fourteen.

"I think school for me, it was hard work. I never used to try and play truant or anything like that. I always went to school. But I felt that when I was just about ready for leaving school, this is the time that I was getting the idea of things, the idea of learning. I would have liked to have gone on from there.

Looking back on it now I think the teachers were pretty fair. They were strict. Of course, we had our dislikes. We liked one teacher better than another. But no, they must have got something through to us. Subjects – we all had our favourite subjects, of course. If we did wrong we were brought out and given the cane, and this was pretty regular. Two or three times a week you would have six of the best. I gather this doesn't happen now. There's no canes now at all at school. Lines, we didn't get lines or we didn't get kept in. Kept in at playtime instead, if we'd done something wrong – Right, you don't go out; you stay in. But we didn't get lines as such. We got punished there and then for what we had done and that was forgot. That was it. I think possibly if I'd been given homework to do I might have got on better, especially, as I say, towards the end of school when I really thought that I could start to learn something then. Mr. Postlethwaite was my teacher. I respected him. I really did like him; he was a good teacher. He was very fair. He used to dish the punishment out, of course, but I thought a lot of him. At that time he was really clever, because he knew a little bit of everything. He was a grand storyteller and I think maybe I couldn't understand how one man could be so bright and intelligent that he could go from sums on to history, on to geography and then he could do his gardening, woodworking, playtime or games period. He used to go out and referee the football matches. He would do everything for me. I'd no other teacher while I was in that form. Every year, of course, we used to get a step up and you got different teacher. Started from the kindergarten stage – the real infant stage, nearly always women, Miss Ivinson, Miss Moffat, Miss Steele.

We used to go by Standards then – One, Two, Three up to Standard Seven. Now Standard Six and Standard Seven, you were getting on to the thirteen- or fourteen-year-olds then. These were taken by Mr. Scott, who was the headmaster. He was Standard Seven. And then later on Mr. Postlethwaite, he took Standard Seven. And it was then that I really started enjoying school – when I had to leave. When we got to about fourteen we were allowed to call them by their Christian names. It was a great boost, this. It was 'Bob' Postlethwaite and – not in class, but while we were in a games period, playing football – you were able to call him Bob and he would call you Charlie.

It wasn't Allardyce do this, Allardyce do that. It was, Charlie, will you go and do this or will you go and do that? Yes, Bob, aye. And this was great fun for us. We felt really big. But we wouldn't do this with the women."

Before Bob Postlethwaite was beginning his teaching career in Wigton, Mr. Stowe was at the local Grammar School. He was born in Scotland, son of a Methodist minister in Renfrewshire, and he came to live in Aspatria, eight miles from Wigton, when he was eleven. He won a scholarship to Wigton Grammar School in 1927, from there he won a scholarship to Oxford, and after the war he returned to the school as headmaster and stayed on to manage the transition to comprehensive education. Bob Postlethwaite taught at the sort of school which takes in seventy or eighty percent of all children: Mr. Stowe's longest experience before 1953 had been at a grammar school which took in about twenty percent of those who passed an examination when they were eleven, soon known as the eleven-plus. Now that this has almost completely gone, there are comprehensive schools which take in everyone, except the small percentage which still goes to paying schools as in the days when it was thought, understandably, that to control such a vast empire we needed a large, coherent, well-drilled élite. Mr. Stowe, then, was part of and returned to teach what became known as the Meritocracy: the brain-spine of Britain, those who would not become directors (that was still in the family or on the old boy network) but departmental heads or even managers; those who would, generally, populate provincial universities, go back to teach in grammar schools, fill out the lower ranks of the professions, the civil service, local government; at best, edge into the elastic but exclusive compounds of the well-off or well-born, at worst "sink" back into the proletariat. He came to Wigton as headmaster in 1953.

"I think retrospectively that it was extremely useful to know the people and to know the area. And to be able to speak Cumbrian when you needed to. Because I think this was a short cut. It would have taken me – to learn Cumbrian, as it were, at that stage would have been quite a job.

I must be very careful because I don't think I can be absolutely frank about what the school was like in 1953. It had obviously changed very markedly since my day in the 1930s because it was a mixed school whereas it had been a single-sexed school. [The Girls' and Boys'

Grammar Schools amalgamated in 1951–2.] I, of course, didn't quite inherit the antagonism between Nelson and Thomlinson but remembered it from a boy. I knew that this had existed on both staffs and that there had been a good deal of antagonism to the idea of joining together. But fortunately, when I came, a lot of people had left or just before that a lot of people had left, whether it was post hoc or propter or not I wouldn't know, but most opposed to the idea in general had left. And again I must be very careful because I don't want to be unfair to the gentleman whom I succeeded. He couldn't have, in the one year when this had been taking place – this unwilling amalgamation – he couldn't really have moulded them into anything like a unit. So I came to something which was a difficult job from that point of view. For a start, I haven't got a fetish about uniform but I am very attached to it because I think uniform is an outward and visible sign of modern spiritual holiness, if you like, and it was an extremely scruffy lot that I came to, among whom you were yourself. And you may remember that we immediately sort of sought out uniform which would incorporate certain parts of the two uniforms and tried to get this going. And this is one unifying and smartening influence. And bit by bit, of course, the staff changed too and eventually you begin to build up at least a tradition of efficiency."

This is putting it mildly. What happened, so it seemed to us who were at the school, it seemed to people in the town, was that a rocket got underneath the school when Mr Stowe arrived and the school changed in an enormous number of ways and in a very short time. It never occurred to us, for example, that we would have so many young boys playing Rugby for England or some people capable of taking Oxford exams and so on.

"I put an enormous amount of work in; in fact, at the end of the first year I think I nearly had a nervous breakdown. I was very nervy for a couple of months at that point, but I got over that. I taught far more than was really sensible but again I liked teaching and again though, I must set the example; if I wanted any sort of standard I must be prepared to do it myself.

I wanted a grammar school with academic standards within its limits. People who were not afraid of working hard. Where they would have reasonable ambition for a start. Where, and again education had obviously moved on a good deal since the Nelson School

326

itself, where they really do widen their mind, take other interests, where they wouldn't all think of going to Newcastle or Durham, the neighbouring universities, where they wouldn't all want to go to the nearest college of education, training colleges and also come home at weekend. Because I'd moved around a lot since then with the war and with my own life and so I wanted Wigton School really to open out in the people we sent out. And I wanted them to be, I think it isn't presumptuous to say, socially aware. I don't mean party politics at all. But I'd done so much in connection with the press and with information, world events, current affairs and so on that I was very interested in this. And I wanted the school to be aware of modern problems, if you like."

In the 1960s, by the Act of a Labour Government, the school, like hundreds of others, became comprehensive.

"Well it is aimed, its aim, obviously a cliché but it is still its aim, is social and, if you like, intellectual justice. It avoids the division into sheep and goats at eleven, although I never thought that in Cumberland this was as grave a thing as generally the country made out, because they operated Late Entrance as they called it. In other words, after one year in the non-selective school you could be selected for the grammar school and this was done. Theoretically you could be also relegated in the opposite direction and this I did with only, I should think, about three people at the time when this was operative. And this was far more difficult and I thought inadvisable. But now, because they all come to one school, you get, basically, social justice, equality, you have also, theoretically, and I think in practice, got intellectual equality of opportunity because they are all in the school. And we make it part of our philosophy, as it is part of any proper comprehensive school's philosophy, that they must be able to be fitted in as they move up the school at a point which suits their intellectual ability. Now there is vast argument in general in this country – which gets tied up with politics, too – as to whether there ought to be any selection inside the comprehensive school. And in this I'm unreservedly retrogressive, if you like; conservative, if you don't attach the political label to it – it is just utterly nonsensical. People are of different mental ability and they cannot all take G.C.E. Therefore, at some point, you have to start streaming inside the school by one method or another. I think it is wrong to start streaming fiercely and obviously immediately

327

they come here. And we do not do this, other than in a fairly innocuous and disguised, slightly disguised manner for the first two years. And there is only the beginning of selection by ability by the course that they choose to follow in the third year, when you start your second language. If they want to start a second language, they have got to drop something else. You don't put them on a second language if they've shown themselves to be no good at languages anyway, you see. Then in the fourth year, when they start selecting the course that they want to follow through for another two years to external examinations, they then select themselves, by their choice, into G.C.E., C.S.E. or basically non-examination – who would follow this record of personal achievement and other things that I was talking about.

You see, Melvyn, good always needs to be qualified, doesn't it? As I used to say to you in the Sixth-Form R.E. Is it as good academically for the academically bright? I'm not quite sure. We were, and this is, talking about *this* school. I can't generalise about comprehensives in general because circumstances differ. We were lucky in that we were an established grammar school with roughly five hundred and fifty people who amalgamated with – took over is the unkind word – a similar sized, slightly smaller secondary modern school.

The buildings are not as bad as they might have been. We took over all our grammar staff and all our grammar traditions of work. We lost in our catchment area a certain part, but not a devastating part – and therefore everything was favourable for being able to maintain at very nearly the same level the academic attainment. No, the only reasons why it would fall a bit, and I think it has probably fallen slightly but certainly not dramatically, would be first of all the trauma of the joining up. Both for staff and for pupils, not only for our staff but for the people who joined us. The disciplinary question among the pupils was acute for the first year because those who came to us were determined to show they were as good in some ways as a grammar lad and lass. And the way in which they were as good or better was in being naughty. This is just being cynical but you see what I mean – there was almost no incentive to them to assert themselves in the way that came easiest to them. Now when you get a problem of discipline which is fairly acute and has to be fought all the time, then your energies are dissipated and the energies that you were able to concentrate on the academic side have to be spread out into discipline. Furthermore, you get staff coming together who are not used to teaching the sort of children that they find now in certain parts of the school.

You are faced with the dilemma as Head or as the management team – do you therefore, in fact, continue running two schools within one or do you try mixing? I'm talking now about staff, and we decided that it would be wrong not to try mixing wherever it made any sort of sense. You can't put someone on teaching Sixth-Formers who has never taught any and who has never got the academic background. There were quite a few graduates from secondary schools and people who were at least capable of teaching to O-level. Therefore we purposely mixed and we purposely made our own, asked or got the consent of our own heads of departments to teach the less able. But neither of these groups, you see, was immediately suited to do it and they had to learn. So this is a fair dissipation of what had been a concentrated energy. And I thought myself at the time that it is inevitable for the first three, four years, maybe five, I don't know – you will not have the same smoothly working mechanism that we think we had in the grammar school. I'm still of this opinion. I think we moved out of the disciplinary quagmire after a year, year and a half, which doesn't mean to say we have no trouble now, but I am quite sure we are not preoccupied with it to any extent.

The big change in attitude has been that the gospel of work has become the gospel of enjoyment. I think it is hedonism that is the most marked change and you see this ties up with so many things. It ties up with the academic unwillingness of the Sixth Formers to do other than smile sadly at the thought of three hours' solid work per night which I did, as I was telling you, and which you would do. And this is again unfair to them as some of them still do. But I am talking now generally about their attitude. I think those who didn't do it in your time and mine were possibly rather more guilty, felt rather more guilty about not doing it than they do now. I think they first of all are determined they are going to have their pleasure, if it means going to a dance on Wednesday then they go to the dance on Wednesday and they'll fit in their homework some other time if they have got to do it, you see. And I don't think this happened when you were their age, not to the same extent.

Sexually I think there is an enormous change, but this is reflecting the change in society. I don't know half of the things I'm sure that go on. Not in school. We have a Fifth Form Health Week or so called where this is brought out explicitly but much more in general. I think I am far more outspoken with the Sixth Form than I was with you and I thoroughly enjoy arguing with them about sex before marriage, for example. But I am never quite sure whether they are being honest with me. I wonder if there is a certain amount of holding back and what I learn about them afterwards makes me wonder, as I say, and how far sexual freedom has permeated the Sixth Form. But in school they play the game."

Though he could stay on until sixty-five Mr. Stowe has chosen to retire at sixty.

"I intend to learn something more about music. I like choral music, as you know, very much. I don't know much about classical music and I've saved that up for my retirement. I'm very interested in the law and I'm extremely happy to be a Justice because this is something that you can devote more time to and you can go on with as a hobby, as doing your job in a local magistrates' court. I want to do some more language, believe it or not. I want to do something which one day perhaps you might help me with. I want to do some translation. I think to be done properly you can't, I think, do it properly just in the odd times that a school master has. This is a secondhand writer, as it were. I am not original; I couldn't write like you but I know that I could translate well.

Almost in preparation for retirement we moved six miles out of the town to Anthorn, by the sea. We rode out, liked the look of the houses and I rang up the same night and asked if we could have a sort of option on them, and we haven't regretted it in the two years. In fact, we like it very much. It's a lovely place. It's a nice little community which is still forming and I'm chairman still of their community association which I enjoy, because it is trying to weld things together and I've almost spent my life since 1953 trying to weld things together. And it is good to get away from the children. I've found this, for me, was one of the wearing things about going comprehensive, believe it or not. I used to know all the Grammar School children, not by name – I think I knew them all pretty well by sight and I used to speak to them in the streets and they would greet me fairly cheerfully. Then when we went comprehensive I found it immeasurably depressing to be looked on not as the boss which was, I think, fairly amicable as a term of reference but as 'Stowe' with an unpleasant S. We're out of school now, 'nowt to do wi' him'. What's he talking to us for? You see. Of course, endeavouring not to be seen, not exactly shouting abuse but you could feel, and I think this is not just me, I think this is their attitude to teaching, discouraging."

There remains that small percentage (about 7%) whose education was privately funded. It still persists. Curiously, the sisters at the convent, whose order is dedicated to help the poor (which they do), run a fee-paying school, St. Ursula's. And there's the Friends' School, a Quaker boarding school on the edge of the town. Others leave the town altogether; Glenn Ritson, the solicitor, went to St. Bees, a public school on the coast of West Cumberland.

"I liked the position of it and also the sense of responsibility that they gave you there. A lot of it was left to you to do yourself and you accounted for what you'd done later, which I think was a great help. It brought your character out and made you do things which probably you would never have thought of doing if you'd still been at home. Things such as looking after your own clothes and making your own bed. And also it left you to work on your own and I always feel I managed to do a lot more work there than I would have done if I'd still been at school at home, because there would have been all the interests at home after school. And friends and so on and so I think that was a great help that way. I did much more work than I would otherwise have done. I'm sure I was very lazy in those days.

Later I was put on the Old Boys' special committee for helping to raise money and things like that for the school. I enjoyed that. I used to go twice a year to meetings and so on. I haven't been so much recently. The Old Boys were very good indeed. They produced a tremendous amount of money to do all the things that were necessary – extending, rebuilding a lot of old-fashioned buildings and things of that nature, building new blocks – a new science block and woodworking and metalworking shops. And also they built a new school hall – that was the biggest project. Before they'd used some large classrooms as a hall, which was not very satisfactory.

When I went I felt I had a Cumbrian accent compared to most of the boys there but this may have simply been through being worried about it, with first going. But I did have that feeling and I think that most boys did unless they came from a background where they had no accent at all. But I think they were a very mixed lot indeed. I was lucky. I found that I could get on with most people and I had a lot of friends there. In fact most of my friends really are connected with St. Bees because I was away from home so much. Very often sons of professional people already there simply coming back and joining their fathers or their own family firm or something like that.

I loved playing rugger and I was captain of the First Fifteen in the last year. I loved that. I lived for it, as most people did. I think it was more a sporting school at that time than it is now. The emphasis has changed recently. It's much more academically minded now than it was. And I was very fond of gymnastics as well. I used to spend most of my time in the gym. But I joined in everything at the school and thoroughly enjoyed it."

It should be said, to emphasise the complications which exist, that Glenn Ritson is arguably one of the most approachable, well liked people in the town. Not at all detached by the process which, in its larger application, divides our society still.

Now the comprehensive experiment has become a reality for about ninety percent of the children and this has coincided with a vast increase in the facilities available to teachers. The schoolrooms themselves – even in the older buildings – are infinitely livelier places; tables set out as in a restaurant rather than desks lined up as in a medieval schoolroom, the work of children on the walls not just reproductions of Italian paintings of Christ, more books, more aids, more fun. Helen Connolly was eight when I spoke to her about a day at school. She had been going to the Junior School for two years and that day she had written a story ("two and a half sides") about an old house being demolished. "I just described what it sounds like when it's old and then when the bulldozer came and the sound it made when it was sort of killing it." What was most impressive, though, was the number of other activities she pursues at school and through school. Not only swimming and general games, but special gymnastics – after school – "Hand springs, cartwheels, rolls and back flips" – the choir, the orchestra (two instruments, both learnt at school), projects – one on owls ("twenty-four pages"), another on ponds, trips to museums, the wild-life park, Edinburgh, Newcastle – all, though, it seemed to me, in much the same gentle and amused frame of mind as Miss Bell at her private school seventy-five years earlier. The boundaries, however, are dramatically wider and the scope much vaster than Miss Bell could have dreamt of, or wanted, or thought proper.

At last English children are being taught, in the majority, to reach out as far as they can, not to be crabbed or confined by the past or by class or cash: and to some extent the children are the masters now.

CHAPTER THIRTEEN
"Letter"

This is one of the many letters I received from local people when assembling this book. It represents not only a thwarted life working itself out, but that number of English people who could be dismissed as eccentric if you failed to understand their strength.

"Saga" of a Poor Wigtonian, by Tom Jackson

"Thomas James Jackson, born September 15th, 1914, Tickell's Lane, Wigton. Father: Thomas Jackson, railway signalman; West Cumbrian Irish origin. Mother: Elizabeth Jackson (née Craghill), disowned for marrying beneath her. Her Uncle Edward founded the Keswick confectionery firm of Craghill. Her cousins included Canon Robert Walker of Causewayhead and Ethel Davidson, the Carlisle milliner. Her brother Jerry owned the Maple Leaf Dairy and Fruit Farms, El Monte, Los Angeles. Her brother Walter made his pile in Australia. Her elder sister, Mrs. Fearon, owned two farms in the Bolton Low Houses district. Her parents were small farmers who owned property all over Great Broughton. The 'marrying beneath her' bit will be readily understood.

My reminiscences may sound BITTER, but bear with me. Dad had only one leg, yet trudged to and from his Rosewain signal box, aided only by his crutch and stick, in all weathers. (Seven miles a day!) The L.M.S. took over from the M. & C.R. and closed several signal boxes, including Rosewain. Dad, my Uncle Johnny and 'Old Splasher' (John Mart) were given stone-breaking jobs, but mechanical crushers put paid to that. Came a miserable time for Wigton, the Twenties and Thirties, the sad indignity of paupers' coffins, the soup kitchen at the Market Hall, the distribution of used clothing and footwear by the local police to children of the poor, Mr. Batty's gift of milk to the needy, the teeming 'Bastille' [Bastyle' in the vernacular, otherwise the workhouse], appalling slums and crumbling property that earned Wigton's landlords a bad name throughout the district.

1926. Dad and other recipients of 'Parish Relief' chopping sticks at t' Bastyle, under 'Simon Legree' (Workhouse Willie Mattinson). The bundled sticks were sold at Johnny Holdsworth's barber shop in Old Lane. Same year saw May Pringle and me win TOP AWARDS for best essays on British Empire. (Prince of Wales Bronze Medals. Poverty forced me to 'flog' mine.)

1927. Won Certificate of Merit for reporting a lecture. Honourable mention for a report on film of Victor Hugo's 'Les Misérables', starring Gabriel Gabric.

1929. Left school. Delivered papers, Friday and Saturday, 1/3d. a day (walking to Waverton, Parkgate and back), Sundays, 1/- (plus a thick ear if slow on the job!). Visit from Uncle Jerry from U.S.A. (His daughter Margaret, my cousin, a prig and a snob who referred to us as 'those paupers'.) Uncle offered me a job with him, but Dad dangerously ill, so no go.

1930. Bad mistake! For a few bob a week extra, began billposting and window washing, with E. Grant. Bad boss. I played banjo in band to earn a little more.

1931. Owing to being bullied and flustered at work, fell from a height at Dalston and was disfigured for life. No compensation. Off work for months.

1935. Fed up with low pay and bad conditions. Aspatria pal doing well in Bushey. Tipped me off about vacancy in lab. at Ellam's factory. Biked there in two days and nights. Didn't know job was only temporary through regular man's illness. Job ended. Only vacancy available was in abattoir. Being of the Jhain faith, I refused. Biked home in same time, but harder going. Old boss offered me more money to resume work.

1938. Discharged from Territorials with blind eye caused by my accident. Boss committed suicide. Girlfriend's father accused me of being involved and ordered me out. Married West Newton girl in October after working temporarily on farm.

1939. War. Rejected on account of blind eye after volunteering for Tank Corps. Tried for war work, but Manpower Board tied me down to window-washing (my pet hate!).

1940. Moved from haunted house at Langriff to one-room accommodation at rear of old Queen's Hotel. Bad place. Moved to paternal grandfather's ancient cottage at the Moot Hall, Ireby. Happy period, but got banned for life from driving a car through accident whilst learning. (Knocked bridge parapet down. Got bill for £87!)

1942. Moved to council house of ill omen at Wigton. One tenant ejected for sub-letting. Another couple parted there after constant disagreements. My wife and I had constant rows over the bad company she encouraged.

1958. After 16 years of bad debt, I could no longer continue. (I still have £'s owing me in Wigton!) Cost of living rising daily, yet people refused to pay any more until Bobby Hampson put his foot down. I took up stores work at Kirkbride aerodrome, but during my absences wife was unfaithful. I left home and lived at my Aunt Jane's cottage. Twice won top award for my unit for smartest and best kept stores and equipment section. Contract for cinema posters (own designs). Contract to play thrice weekly at Crown & Mitre, Wigton, where I first met my REAL soul mate. Band bookings at Winter Gardens, Morecambe; Royal Oak, Keswick; Queen's Hotel, Silloth, and all over Cumberland, Westmorland and South of Scotland. Won vocalist contest at Canonbie.

1961. Moved from flat at Waverton to council house near Long Meg Mine, where I worked as storekeeper, sign-writer, accountant, explosives-checker, caretaker, stoker, stretcher-bearer, security man and loader – all rolled into one! Splendid neighbours.

1963. Accident. Furnace blowback put me into hospital. Favourite nurse was Margaret McLellan, late of Market Hill, Wigton. Very kind and most efficient.

1964. Healthier job at Low Plains Quarry. In charge of conveyors, site-clearance, sign-writing and alterations. Grand boss and workmates. Boss got me a Queen Anne cottage nearer the work. Three happy, prosperous years. Visited Scotland on vacation.

1967. Quarry petered out. Only job going was on security at Penrith By-pass camp. 3/8d. an hour (McAlpine's.) Assistant got 3/7d. an hour. We had to do 95 hours a week to make a living! Exorcised caravan ghost by Romany method. Poem on Penrith traffic conditions accepted by 'Penrith Observer'. Posters for Regent Cinema, Penrith.

1968. Working as painter and sign-writer for Hetherington and Son. Officials from Ministry called thrice to invite me to apply for post at the Shap Abbey: as curator. Application successful. Passed as civil servant, custodian and sub-accountant. More articles, plus drawings, for 'Observer'. First T.V. appearance. 'Cumbria' editor called. Articles accepted. Editors of 'Observer' and 'Eden Valley Church News' came later. Articles accepted. Strong letters from publishers about 'Eric the Saxon' being DANGEROUS subject, liable to upset aristocracy. Major Diggle of Cape Town wrote in praise of my 'Cumbria' articles. His father, Bishop Diggle, had confirmed my Mother. Major requested my 'Cumbrian Ghosts' for scrutiny, then accepted mss. for publication. Peter Travis and I worked on his second books of 'spooks'.

1969. Invitation to meet Frau Elisabeth Strauss at Ivanhoe Hotel, London, for Annual Dinner of Strauss Society. Wife and I only members in all Cumbria. Article accepted as an ultra-special for 'Tritsch-Tratsch', the Society's mag. Attorney-at-Law Edwin C. Jeffries, San Diego, visited Shap Abbey. Offered to market my 'stuff' in the U.S.A. (Unfortunately, Americans didn't like the TERSE British style dictated by my editor.) Two batches of mss. (AND publishers) disappeared in U.S.A. No acknowledgement from Holland for mss. of 'Eric the Saxon' (per Major Diggle).

1970. Wrote massive work on Cumbrian and Westmorland folklore. Considered too big, too expensive to produce. Stockwell of Ilfracombe accepted it, but required a bond of £741. Janay interested, but required subsidy of £180. They want first chance of 'Castle Dracula', having praised the prologue. Won only prize to come north in 'World Works' essay contest. Various periodicals now publishing my work. Second and third T.V. interviews.

1971. Gifts from overseas visitors include new Strauss book, souvenirs from Vienna, cards from Louisiana and American books. Now Honorary Brother of the Order. Visit to Herts. and London. Hammer Films working on one of my scripts. More letters and signed photos.

1972. Twice offered my old job back with quarrying firm, now back in production, but am in tied house. Not keen to sacrifice civil service pension and a month's vacation each year, either. Autographed photos and letters from Peter Cushing, Ken Dodd and Ken Goodwin. Publisher John Blackie and his Edinburgh University Madrigal Singers expected at my place IF weather improves. Representative of Robert Hale (publishers) called, but considered my work TOO TERSE, and blamed my old editor for spoiling my style. I'll never regain it now. Wish I'd stuck to my guns and done it my way. Praise for my paintings: 3 'Draculas' (Wigton, Penrith and Norfolk clients), 'Royal Scot ascending Shap' (Tebay Railwaymen's Club), 'Flying Scotsman' (Shap client), 'Shap Church' (Canadian client), 'Johann Strauss' (three of these for myself). Composed words and music of 'Lakeland Rhapsody' and another piece for Keswick Mountain Singers. (Praised by Press.) Two visits from Tyne-Tees T.V. people. Using my published work for documentary on our 'Transylvanian' legends. Lots of good material to hand but can't get rid of the impression that the editor and his assistants will oppose any attempt at extending my style to a full, descriptive one. Being accused of being a long-winded,

old Dickens sticks like mud! If I write as the editor insists, I'M TOO
TERSE; if I write more descriptively, I'm a b—— old windbag!
What the devil DO they want? My local pal strongly advises a good
co-author who has no psychological qualms about a well-meaning but
stubborn editor wielding his verbal 'big stick'. I feel that the Old
Boy is so obsessed with brief reports and the saving of valuable
newspaper space that he considers longer styles wrong. What would
Dickens and Shakespeare have had to say about such an attitude?
Brevity is all very well, but in literature it conveys little or nothing in
the readers' imagination.

Director of Tourist Board taking his time over writing foreword
to my 'Guide to the Cumbrian Transylvania', methinks! Invitation to
appear on same bill as N. Mortemore, the poet who contributed
verses to my work. We are doing a charity concert at Renwick. Mr.
Mortemore reading his own poetry. I'm doing Negro plantation
melodies on traditional banjo and Strauss waltzes on Viennese accor-
dion, plus Chopin, etc. on guitar. Highbrow audience. (GOOD!)
Must remember to avoid anti-Norman conversation. The name
Mortemore is another form of Mortimer. Both stem from the town
of Mortemore, Normandy. Seymour is another Norman 'monniker' –
and he's writing my foreword! The Craghills of Crag Hill, Westmorland, knocked hell out of the Normans during the 30 Years' War
of the Lakes. Ma was a Craghill! (Better 'keep mum' about Mum!)

Dear old Vicar pushed lawn mower in my back garden. Makes
himself at home at my place. Enoch wrote today, also Sir Gerald
Ley. (Fellow railway 'fans'.)

Border Television followed my 'Observer' contributions with keen
interest and featured me in three interviews in connection with those
items (ghosts, dialect and vampires). Now Tyne-Tees T.V. have
enlisted my help in a subject featuring the 'Transylvanian' legends
of East Fellside and Edenvale.

Soon, other magazines welcomed my work after some successful
articles had been published by 'Cumbria' and 'Eden Valley Church
News'. John N. Charters, author of 'Brampton Railway' for Oakwood
Press, wrote to me for help with his second book, but shied off when
I invited him to be my co-author in a work called 'Railway Reminiscences'. I worked with the Rev. Peter Travis on his second book of
northern ghost stories. My 'Eric the Saxon' met with widespread
opposition because it cited the Normans as eleventh century 'Nazis'.
My pen-friend, Major Diggle, had accepted my 'Cumbrian Ghosts'
for South African publication. He negotiated with Northern League
of Amsterdam for publication of 'Eric the Saxon'. The Major's

ancestors are included in the story. They smashed the Normans at the Battle of Chat Moss, while Eric and Earl Boethar of Eskdale beat the Norman scum at the Battles of Grasmere and Rannerdale. This is all genuine history which our Lords and Masters FEAR, hence the ban. The exposing of 'Quislings' of 1066 was another factor. Did you know that traitor Saxons like Smith and Walther (later Fitz Walter), actually fought on the Norman side at Senlac? Or that the worst traitor of all was Edward, the so-called Confessor? Revelations like that earned me a number of very nasty letters.

Malcolm A. Seymour, Director of the English Lakes Counties Tourist Board, is writing the foreword to my 'Guide to the Cumbrian Transylvania'. Poet N. Mortemore has contributed two Helm Wind pieces. Various friends have sent appropriate photos.

Having had my old flair for descriptive writing 'purged' from me, I shall have to seek a co-author for my next projects – 'Eric the Saxon' (revised), 'Castle Dracula' (the only GENUINE sequel to Stoker's classic, based on real historical fact), 'Lair of the Vampire' (Cumbria's 'Transylvanian' legends in one story) and 'Railway Reminiscences'. If interested, Melvyn, or if you know of anyone who would care to tackle the descriptive side, I'd be glad to forward rough story drafts. Christopher Lee has praised them and has been trying to interest film concerns in them.

All the VERY BEST, Melvyn, and good luck with your work, lad. 'Willkommen zu mein Translyvania!' Cheerio for now!

Your sincere admirer,

(signed) Tom Jackson."

Still in the town is Peter Stubbs, now entering his sixties, who has struggled with a lifetime of illness and a passionate, almost medieval devotion to Philosophy. He left school at fourteen and, self-taught, has contributed to *Mind* and reviewed Commentaries on Aristotle for the *Times Literary Supplement*. He lives alone, a bachelor, as is Dr. Loveday who forced through a massive thesis on the preposition "à" in French. Both these men, like Tom Jackson and others, are in different ways a testament to the drive for cultural achievement so often thought to exist only in the context of a cultured community. Each of them worked alone and made a mark.

338

CHAPTER FOURTEEN
The Establishment

It is a fascinating question – where power and authority lie today. Who rules and who serves, who controls and who is dependent. Parliament, the Unions and Big Business would be the obvious and acceptable answers – but how far does Parliament merely codify and legislate for situations and circumstances which have already arisen in the country? Where is the head of Big Business? – in the factory in Wigton employing almost a thousand men, run from Wigton? from London? from Holland? from America? And the Unions, though they have force – is it much more than a set of good brakes? What can they institute and sustain? It is when you try to see what happens to a group of people in a single community and reflect on what outside forces control their lives (an individual is too limited in such a survey as this) that the accepted divisions of authority become misty.

Children out of the home are in the hands of the teachers; the system though is determined by the politicians; the politicians are persuaded by the thinkers; the thinkers are influenced by their own experiences at school. And when the boy goes to the factory, he joins a union and a firm – one can make him redundant, the other call him out on strike, both can improve his wages; the firm can determine his type of work – within its limits: his own ability is a big factor here – and the unions can determine the conditions of work. The work depends on the large group of companies, which could depend on an international bank: who knows when, to save a paper percentage, company accountants might not call for a close-down of the Wigton factory? Even more fundamental, the product could be superseded or rejected: the transparent cellophane paper could go the way of the old brown paperbag which, even in my childhood, stood in high hundreds on the counters of all the shops.

And this is only the beginning. The law ensures he will not do certain things and perforce do other things – from paying rates for street-lights which don't interest him or playing-fields he never uses or roads he will not motor on, to subsidising people, activities, and occupations for which he may have no sympathy. An Englishman's life today is hung, drawn and quartered compared with the liberties of the fortunate few in the past: compared with the majority in the rest of the world, of course, he is a prince.

The enquiry over where power lies can only be referred to here in passing: what can be said is that – having seen something of the way in which the authority in work was organised and reserving a special chapter for religion (Chapter 18) – we can look at the way the town allows its daily life to be run. In trouble or in turning outside self and family to find the first contact points with the "County" which now takes and gives so much, people would go to the school or the church for particular answers; but for a general worry, it seems to me that people would go to the council offices, to their doctor, or to a solicitor. These three parties – the Law, Medicine and the State – represent most of the direct connections most people have with the country at large and it seemed that the lives of the men – all men – involved in those occupations would, together, allow readers to draw conclusions as to the nature of those who are put in authority over us – often by their own efforts, sometimes by the efforts of others, occasionally because of those traditions which are at once a threat and a strength to our continued way of life.

Frank Moffat is a solicitor. He lives on the north-west hill of the town, in a fine detached house, quiet road, large garden, grown-up family; he is a lean man, wary but direct. We drank a little while the interview went on and the afternoon turned to evening on Station Hill.

"I was born in this part of the world on Station Hill in 1927 about a hundred yards away from here and, apart from a few years in Park Square towards the end of the war, I have never lived anywhere else but this part of the world. Whenever I move, I simply move not far enough to justify getting a removal van. I simply hunk the stuff along myself. My last move actually was from across the road. We did a swap. One of those amicable arrangements whereby I paid a certain amount of money. It was a make-weight and we spent one May day transporting furniture backwards and forwards. It was an amusing sight actually because some of the furniture, with our various volunteer helpers, was brought backwards and forwards and we eventually finished up over there with one particular bed which had a frame for another bed which was over here, and we hammered the thing together and wondered why the devil it didn't fit so well.

My father wasn't qualified. I think he started off in about 1913 as a solicitor's clerk, at three shillings a week, and he was in the same business when he died. And of course I followed on from that. In his day it was Rigg and Strong. Now it is known as Beaty and Company. The premises are the same, the clients remain the same, and the family connection's carried on, it's simply a change of name.

In those days the office would be John Strong, the proprietor of the firm, and old Billy Easton – he was a long standing clerk, he'd been there from 1880 something – and there would be old Joe Lancaster who was the father of our recently retired managing clerk, Arnold Lancaster. My father would be there as junior clerk and I think they probably had one other, possibly two other junior clerks – five, possibly six, there would be at the time. They would be handling only a fraction of the business we have today. They just couldn't have coped in those days with their methods and systems with anything like the volume of business that we have.

In these days we have photostat copiers, we have fully trained competent shorthand-typists and secretaries; and of course we have long since ceased to produce legal documents in handwriting. They just couldn't have attempted to cope with anything like what we have to do, apart from the fact that the complexity of modern life is such that there are so many problems cropping up from everybody's point of view and the immediate reaction of many people, when they have even the slightest problem in this town, is immediately to say, Right, I'll just nip along and see Frank Moffat. I'll go and see Brian Hunt, or something like this. And they simply plant it on to us and expect you to sort it out. Some of the problems are the type of thing which if they sat quietly at home and spent ten minutes of their own time and applied their mind to reading an explanatory leaflet or something like that, they could very easily do themselves. Things like filling in a very simple income tax return. They just don't bother to do it now. They plant it on to somebody else's desk.

I'd left school at fifteen and a half, gone straight into the firm, decided that I would do law and, early in 1943, I was articled to the present partner. And I had in fact by sheer hard work and getting off to an early start, passed my intermediate law exams before I joined up. I took these in late 44 and got them so that when I came out of the Services in 1948 I was half way qualified.

The system that we adopted there, by consent from my employer so to speak, was that I would learn for half a day the routine of office work and the practical side of things and the other half day I could lock myself in a spare room, in those days we had space because staff were missing – I locked myself away in a spare room and studied. With assistance from these correspondence courses, from what I think was called the Metropolitan College of Law. It was quite a good one actually. This was interspersed with weekly visits to King's College, Newcastle, which was an obligatory thing. It didn't get a degree but it had to be done. The Law Society said that one had to put in one year's attendance on a part-time basis at an approved Law School. I used to travel through to Newcastle every Thursday morning and come back late on Thursday night. I learnt nothing there but I had to do it. Looking back, I sometimes think I missed out by not going to university and taking a law degree but in those days law degrees were rather frowned upon by the legal fraternity. In those days anybody who applied for a job with the letters LL.B. after his name was immediately suspect by the average acting solicitor as being somebody who probably had a fairly good technical knowledge of law but damn all common sense or experience with which to apply that technical knowledge. Nowadays things are different. One normally expects that the newly qualified solicitor will have a degree; in fact, this is what my son is doing at the moment.

The first wages I ever received were when I qualified at about the age of twenty-three. When I joined the Forces and found I was getting two and ninepence a day to start with, I couldn't understand why other people who joined up with me were complaining bitterly at what they got at the end of the week. They got about twenty-two and six or something like that. When I got twenty-two and six I thought, this is tremendous. I can do things with this because I'd literally up to then been living on handouts from father who, towards the end of my pre-joining up time in the firm, was giving me what I thought was a handsome sum of ten shillings a week. With that ten shillings I could take my girlfriend to Joe Cusack's Picturehouse, on the back row, two nights per week and I could manage on ten shillings a week. I could buy the odd packet of Woodbines. I didn't drink at all. You didn't have the opportunity of going off somewhere, not travel of any kind. You made your own pleasures in the town. I was quite happy. Incidentally, when I did start work my ideas of a thousand pounds a year as a qualified man were rudely shattered because I was offered and had to accept the princely sum of three hundred pounds per annum, gross, which represented five pounds, twelve shilling and sixpence per week, I think.

Obviously, in starting off with the firm and starting off as a qualified man in the capacity as an assistant solicitor on a salary, one had one's sights on getting into a partnership. So this I went into about 1955 I think on a junior basis and, of course, at various intervals since then the partnership turns a glimmer of eyes to the point where in fact at the moment I am, I suppose, senior partner.

The *type* of business hasn't changed in the legal fraternity for heaven alone knows how many years, probably a hundred years, in a little town. It hasn't changed in a big town either really. Certainly my experience is confined to Wigton, a small town, and the general run of the legal practices in an area like this is a mixture. You've got to be a jack of all trades and probably master of none. But it boils down to basically three types of work in general terms. One, and this is bread and butter, is conveyancing. This is the sale and purchase of property. Farms, houses, building sites; you name it, that's conveyancing. Second, and this is a type of business which never dies out, probate work. This is dealing with deceased people's estates and winding them up, in accordance with the will and in accordance with the intestacy provisions. And the last general sort of category, shall we say, miscellaneous, this is litigation. This is where you get disputes either civil or in the criminal courts; court cases, court work. On the fringes of all these there are various other things like drawing up wills, you don't put these into any specific categories but they've got to be done, and in a small town like Wigton where you are not running a big enough practice to specialise, you've got to act not only as a lawyer but you've to apply a hell of a lot of common sense in dealing with people's personal problems. Some of the problems that I am or have been asked about really haven't much to do with law at all. You tend to become personally identified with your clients because, being a small firm, you get to know them on a personal basis. And they tend to come into you with ostensibly a small legal problem and they start talking to you about all sorts of blessed things and you're expected to listen and to give them advice on family and goodness knows what. Strictly speaking outside the terms of pure law. You're expected to do it and if you don't do it they'll probably go off somewhere else and somebody else will do it.

In a part of the world like this, families tend to be pretty loyal. You get grandfather and father and son dealing with the same firm traditionally. It doesn't always happen but more often than not it does. If they have a legal problem at all it's automatically passed down the family, Alright, go and see our family solicitors. That's Beaty's of Wigton or Rigg and Strong as it used to be. And quite a lot of

343

our business is from that type of clientèle.

You could say that people who deal with us are middle class on the whole but it depends where one draws the line between what is working class and what is middle class. I don't like either of these expressions. I find now that I am getting more and more clients of an age and in the type of job requiring legal assistance on various things which would never have happened in the past. I find the man who works, shall we say, on the shop floor, for want of a better word, at British Sidac coming in to me at the age of twenty-six or twenty-seven and saying, Look, I want to buy a house on Highmoor Park Estate. It's going to cost me five thousand, three hundred and ninety-five. I can put down six hundred pounds. I want a mortgage for the rest. I've got a wife and two small kids aged four and three, and this sort of deal is quite on the cards now. Twenty years ago it would have been a sheer impossibility. It's changed for the better. It's the changing society and changing standards of life that have made this so.

It's had its effect, of course, on the price of houses as well, as you probably gather, but certainly the people who could never have contemplated buying a cottage can now quite blithely entertain buying a house. In fact, some of them come in to me in their early twenties, wanting to borrow money and succeeding in borrowing money from building societies where their monthly mortgage payments absolutely appal me. Considerably higher than I am paying on this place, or what I could reasonably expect to afford to pay. Course there was another point here. Very often you find that the wives are working as well. Possibly as a school teacher or a girl going back as a secretary to some firm, and two incomes coming into one house. The volume of work that we are doing now will be at least five times what we were doing twenty years ago. Mainly in conveyancing. We go through the same procedures but we go through it a jolly sight faster. We've got to. And we have more efficient staffs now. Of course, with photostat copying, that really is a boon. We can produce various documents which are required in conveyancing work simply by feeding paper into a machine and letting it come out the other end. Whereas in the old days to do a job on this machine which takes five minutes would have taken a typist, a skilled clerk with a lot of experience and quite good at the typewriter, maybe two days to produce. Because we don't have two days in this time to do this; we just can't do it. The extra benefit we get, of course, is that the photostat copy is exactly as the original and shouldn't need any checking.

Generally speaking more assets are being left. This again is a sign

344

of the times. People now have the opportunity of acquiring and accumulating assets and because this is so more and more, I think, are making wills. I think I make, personally not the firm, but I personally will make in an average year something like a hundred and thirty to a hundred and fifty wills. I should imagine that if my father made more than fifty in a year, it would be a pretty hectic year from that point of view. But nowadays all sorts of people make them. Particularly, in many instances, people who are contemplating a holiday abroad. They're flying out from Manchester Airport on a Saturday morning so they land in to me at three o'clock on the Friday afternoon confidently expecting that I'm going to drop everything to give them my undivided attention and provide them with these wills, just in case anything happens to the aircraft. More money is being left. People have more assets but there's a tremendous difference. I deal with estates which basically extend from, literally, ninety-five to one hundred pound assets up to the sort of fifty-five, sixty thousand pound mark. These obviously are farming people with considerable expanses of land and well stocked and all this sort of thing. I don't think I ever dealt with an estate above sixty-five thousand pounds, although no doubt these are on the cards some time in the fairly near future. But you can't say there's any average on this. It depends entirely upon the late client. The majority of estates I deal with are below the estate duty limits, which used to be twelve thousand five hundred. It's now fifteen thousand. Most of what I deal with are below that.

Miscellaneous work's changed probably just as much as anything else in terms of pure volume because of the complexities of modern life. The people of Westminster first of all churn out, they decide in principle that a new law is required to cover a certain set of circumstances in a certain sphere of life. So this is laid down in principle and I think it's then handed to the Crown Office who have lawyers there responsible for drafting these laws. Then eventually they become law and so much of it is churned out with insufficient forethought and with a lot of laxity on the part, I feel, of the Crown Office staff. And the result is when it gets to the general public as an existing Act which is law, nobody understands it. Quite frequently even the lawyers do not understand it. And life gets more and more complex and people have more and more reason for coming in and asking about their personal affairs and how they are affected. Things like the capital gains tax which arose in 1965 had never been heard of before in this country. It's with us to stay. This is one thing which creates extra work. Another thing that cropped up a few years ago

345

was the Land Commission Act, which was the most ill-conceived piece of legislation. It's died a death since. It might be resurrected, I do not know, but even the Lord Chief Justice admitted he couldn't understand it. This created a lot of complications. All sorts of things. You get consulted about matrimonial problems. I am frequently consulted about appearances in court. You get the disputes between two adjoining owners as to who owns the branches of a tree which overhangs somebody else's fence. All sorts of things. Some are absolutely trivial – to me – but obviously not trivial to the people who are consulting me. To them that happens to be their most important problem at the time. To me, simply one of another hundred and fifty at the time which I can ill afford to give time to, but you've got to do it.

In the last year that my late father was the Justice's Clerk for this town, 1957, in that year the total number of cases dealt with at all times through the Wigton Magistrates' Court was two hundred and ninety-six, and for the last few years I have been handling seventeen to eighteen hundred every year. Now in those days we sat at half past nine on a Wednesday morning in my office to deal with juvenile business. We would get through that and be down at the court premises proper in New Street at ten o'clock to deal with the proper adult regular court. When all the criminal business had been finished we then carried on within enclosed doors with the matrimonial disputes and more often than not we could be out of that court by about twelve thirty or quarter to one. Now I have separate days for juvenile courts. I sat this morning, for instance, I sit on average something between eighteen and twenty-four Mondays during the year. I sit twenty-six times at the regular court which frequently lasts until seven or so at night. And sometimes we have so much business we have to hold a lot of it over until the next morning. And I hold twelve domestic courts every year on the second Thursday every month and sometimes these can go on well into the afternoon. That's apart from any special people like criminals who are suddenly arrested and have to be dealt with on the spot. So that domestic problems have obviously increased. I am spending more and more time on domestic problems every month that goes past. Domestic problems, incidentally, will include from my technical point of view affiliation proceedings. I suppose this is a sign of changing times.

In the old days it was somewhat unusual and certainly a very great disgrace for any girl to have to go to court and try to obtain seven and six a week from the putative father of a child. Nowadays they come through quite frequently and nobody seems to bother much.

346

And the vast majority of the domestic cases, the pure matrimonial cases, are from relatively young people. People who have been married as short as eighteen months. It's very rarely we get one from a couple who have been married any length of time. Not divorce. We can't deal with divorce. We can make orders against a husband, in fact, technically we could do it against the wife, but it's usually the wife making application against her husband. And her basis of complaint must fall into one or other of several categories; for instance, neglect to maintain, adultery, desertion, cruelty, those are the four basic ones. And as a result of this, the magistrates, if they find the case proved, can order the husband to pay so much a week for the wife and so much per week for the children, etcetera, etcetera.

I think there are three reasons for this increase in the number of cases. The first is the increase in motor traffic, and the second is the fact that life is simply much more complicated and the third, which grieves me considerably, is that in these days the police authorities bring to court matters which they would never have brought in the past. They seem intent upon filling their books and showing the vast amount of crime that there is in the county, not crime in the strict sense but little offences. For instance, this morning I had to spend a considerable amount of time dealing with a case of a fourteen-year-old boy who was accused of riding his bicycle without due care and attention. And he had done nothing more or less than I had done times without number in the past, and you have no doubt done as well. And we had the same sort of thing at the juvenile court three weeks ago. You can't just throw them out because technically the law has been broken. I pass comments quite forcibly at times to the police authorities, to Inspector Graham. He says, well, he is controlled by his head people at Carlisle and there's nothing he can do about it. If they send a file back with "prosecute" on the front of it, he's got to bring the case. The net result is that we spend literally hours in court, both adult and in juvenile court, dealing with matters which quite frankly in many cases I think should never have been brought to court at all. But motoring I think is the big thing in the increase in business. Bumps and accidents. And driving without L-plates, driving without supervision, the breathalyser is now in of course. If cars had never existed I think I could get through my court in an average day in two hours.

Another thing of course which has caused an increase is the changing standards. There's an awful lot of rowdyism, fighting, assaults and this sort of thing now which didn't happen in the past, but it does now. Now it seems to be a question of not fighting things

347

out with fists. It's a question of putting the boot in, as they say, butting somebody in the teeth, kicking them when they're down, all this sort of thing. And this frequently causes injuries which give rise to a rather more serious type of charge when it gets to court.

At one time I was a firm believer in corporal punishment, but I'm not now. I don't know when I changed, I don't know why I changed. It's probably I'm more mature, I'm older, probably a rather more reasonable man than I used to be, but I do not agree with the police thumping somebody. My point about too many cases being brought is not that these should have been dealt with by the police administering a good thumping, in the first instance; it's simply that they're bringing a type of case very often which really, on its merits, doesn't justify being brought. The trivial sort of things, really trivial. But I shouldn't advocate that the police should have the power to thump anybody. I think it probably goes on occasionally. In the category of violence I would include the type of offence which we call breach of the peace; this is like a gang of youths coming out of the Market Hall after a Friday night dance and really kicking up a rumpus in the town and cursing and swearing and probably having a few blows exchanged with one another, a sort of general rumpus. For want of anything better, the police usually prosecute them for breach of the peace; they have upset the neighbourhood. This sort of thing happens very frequently and, including that in the category of violence, I think there's more of it going on.

But as I said in my third reason for the increase of volume of business that I have to deal with is the fact that the police are bringing more cases than they used to. They probably have more policemen available; they're a younger type of policeman who are probably very keen to get on. They like to bring the occasional case just to show that they do exist and are doing their job. And the two things work together and I think the general effect of the two factors is that it is responsible for this in all kinds of criminal activities, or illegal activities. Theft's a thing that goes on quite frequently. There's been a big increase over the years in what you would call burglaries, technically breaking and entering. I mean, there are legal distinctions of burglary and so on; but entering somebody's premises and stealing something, there's been a lot of increase in that sort of thing over the years. Offences against the person are on the increase, which include assaults. And I suppose, in a sense, will include breach of the peace because this is disturbing the general populace of the town. There are offences against property which involve theft, obtaining property by false pretences, breaking and entering, putting your fist or a brick through windows, wilful damage sort of thing.

But the vast majority of offences are committed with motoring, which covers a multitude of different things. You'd be surprised how little you can do in a car and technically remain clear of the law. Then you get the fringes like failing to pay your National Insurance contributions which, I suppose in a sense, isn't exactly fraud but it is depriving the Revenue of the income which the Revenue is entitled to. And you get not having television licences. Here again this is an offence against property in a sense that the Revenue is being deprived – all sorts of things. My average court list will be in terms of numbers, let's say, eighty cases. Of those eighty cases, again, very much a rough average, I can reckon that sixty-three, sixty-four of them have something to do with motoring.

Another great recent change has been in the value of money. With farms it was quite possible, a matter of ten or twelve years ago, for a man to pay seven thousand, seven thousand five hundred or eight thousand for a farm which would still be sufficiently big to be a workable unit, to be able to provide him and his immediate family – that's wife and possibly a couple of young kids – with a living. It wouldn't have been big enough to provide a living for two grown-up kids working in partnership with father, but certainly provide a reasonably good living. And this could be purchased for seven or eight thousand pounds. Fifty, sixty, seventy acres. I don't mean necessarily immediately surrounding Wigton. I'm thinking particularly of the type of farm that has sold on the low side, the Biglands, Gamblesby, Aikton area, Cardurnock, Anthorn and that part of the world. It's never been a particularly popular part of the world from the farming point of view, although the farms are good. But it's never been particularly popular as regards price. In fact, in those days if we got a job which was a purchase or a sale at ten thousand pounds or upwards we thought we had got a plum job. Incidentally, the scale legal fees on a transaction of ten thousand pounds are exactly one hundred guineas. It's the only scale charge I can remember, off the cuff, without looking at my charts. But this was reckoned to be a plum job. Nowadays it's quite common, we're actually buying at the moment a block of land for a client in Leicestershire at sixty-eight thousand pounds – this is to add to his existing farm. We're doing another two jobs at forty thousand pounds. And these are for farms which are under the hundred-acre mark.

I think quite frankly that if I had not been so involved with my father with the firm of which I am now, in fact, the principal, I would have felt I could have done something better with my life than to have stayed in Wigton. But I had my roots here from the home point of view and, as it turned out, from the business point of view. I could see possibilities in it. There was a future for me in Wigton. A future which probably one in a hundred in Wigton had ready laid on for them. Had it not been for that I think I would have uprooted from Wigton. And I like the place. But I would have tried my luck somewhere else.

My son's reading law. He's just finishing his first year at Liverpool. He's going for the law degree which is the equivalent of the Intermediate Law Society's Examination. He's then got to do another two years, finishing up at the Law Society school in London. I fully expect, and this is his intention at the moment, he will come in with me. And of course, in the fullness of time, he will take over. But I have another son David, my younger son, and I think he is inclined this way. So therefore for a start I have two sons and I am and have been for some time acquiring a business. I haven't been handed anything on a plate incidentally. I'm buying this business and I've worked jolly hard to get where I am, but at least I have something I can hand over to a family, the next generation. And I have a daughter. And it's quite on the cards that she, too, might want to qualify in law in which case the three of them together really could run a highly efficient practice in Wigton. There is a tremendous amount of scope.

The volume of work that we're getting through is probably five times as much as we were getting through fifteen or sixteen years ago. There's certainly scope. The other thing is that now there are only two legal firms in the town. When I started work there was Harry Twentyman, Ritson's, there was our place, Hetherington, Duddings; there were five firms. And years before that there was old Bobby Lawson in Park Square, a fellow called Gibson, there was a fellow called Crooks – there must have been seven or eight firms of solicitors or individual solicitors practising on their own. Now there are only two. And it's not just the town we're covering. My rivals up the street and I cover an extensive country area. Our stamping ground is literally, say, from the coast at Allonby, right round by the fells, Uldale, Ireby, Ruthwaite and sort of thing and out Dalston way and right round the coast at Aikton, Cardurnock, Kirkbride, Anthorn, Silloth, Aspatria; all this is included. That's apart from the fairly frequent jobs in Carlisle and not just a few jobs much further afield. I've been recently buying houses at Barrow-in-Furness, I've sold property in Cornwall, dealing with property in Leicester, basically because of the family connections. Several generations of a family dealing with the same firm of solicitors and they uproot themselves from Cumberland and buy a much bigger farm in the Midlands but they still retain the connection. All their legal work is done at arm's length two hundred miles away, but they still do it if the loyalty is still there.

Of course the personal contact is the thing that creates goodwill. When I say personal contact I don't mean being able to see them every day because you don't. But the long-standing personal contact that has built up, the fact that they have confidence in you and you know them personally makes a difference. Occasionally you lose the odd one who goes away and after twenty years he's gone. He's always dealt with you in the meantime but twenty years after, he's gone. He's found that there is another solicitor in his local town, much more convenient to be able to pop into his office rather than to write a letter to us or to telephone. And he disengages and goes elsewhere. This is inevitable. But it cuts both ways. We get incoming clients who come into these parts and change over from some firm in London, to us."

Glenn Ritson, whose father and grandfather were solicitors in Wigton, tells the same tale. One third the number of firms doing ten times as much business for a much much wider spread of people while the difference in income and style of living between himself and the majority has narrowed considerably: and been welcomed, genuinely I believe, by both Frank Moffat and Glenn Ritson. The biggest change, Glenn Ritson pointed out, in the working life of a solicitor was the change of pace. "In my father's day everything was very leisurely. It was nothing to take a whole day doing a conveyance or part of a conveyance and you travelled probably by a coach in the very old days and sometimes by trap. And he's often told me that he used to spend probably a whole day going over to see a client with a document to sign, taking it over in the trap and getting it signed and bringing it back. And these days we just haven't time for that sort of business."

The undisputed Kings of the Growth Industries in twentieth-century England have been in the Public Sector – the money, energy and manpower which drove the machines and mills of the nineteenth century turned to the internal structures of a cruelly inequitable country and produced school systems, road systems, hospitals and old people's homes, sewage systems, water systems, council houses, street lighting, social benefits, library systems, swimming pools, parks, playing-fields – relatively inadequate, perhaps; over-wasteful with resources for the size and strength of our economy, perhaps; open to criticism on all sides – but compared with the amenities available to the ordinary person seventy-five years ago, the world we live in now is palatial. For the majority, life is better than their parents would have dared dream, and the weight of this has been borne by the state at a national and local level.

In the new council offices – which caused such an outcry when they were built a few years ago, because of the cost, and yet, within a few years, were too small for their original purpose – I spoke first to Colin Graham. Born in 1913 in Aspatria, eight miles from Wigton, another to gain a "free place" at the Nelson School, from which he considers himself to be most fortunate to have gained a job as an assistant for Aspatria Urban District Council when he was sixteen. Aspatria was then a mining town: unemployment was very high. The council he worked for had been set up by the Local Government Act of 1884. Wigton, too, was an Urban District Council and these councils operated with local men, largely independently, and economically. There were three people who did the administration for the Aspatria Urban District Council. Colin Graham began in the bad year of 1929, with fifteen shillings a week working nine to five, weekdays, nine to one, Saturdays.

"The Council was, in effect, a small entity on its own and it had its own insurance clerks and houses; about eighty houses. They were the highway authority, street lighting and they had a park, well, you know the Aspatria Park – they looked after that. And allotments, library, fire brigade – those were our areas. Nothing to do with schools, for example. Then the Local Government Act of 1929 placed a duty on the County Council, that is the Cumberland County Council, to review the boundaries of all the districts and parishes in the country, this is, including the boroughs and the urban and rural parishes. They started on this probably after 1929, certainly by 1930, and they came forward with a scheme of amalgamations. I don't know for certain but I should think it was mostly the widest reaching review in this country and reduced the number of Local Authorities drastically. Well, we'll take Wigton. There was Wigton Urban and Rural, Holme Oultram, Aspatria were all amalgamated into one. Longtown Rural, Brampton Rural and Carlisle Rural were amalgamated to form the present Border Rural Council. And, of course, they did the same down in West Cumberland. The only two to survive, small parishes, were Keswick and Cockermouth, and the reason for that was that they were looked upon as the holiday resorts with special circumstances and they felt that they ought to remain independent.

I got a job in the Finance Department as first assistant to the, what was then known as the Chief Financial Officer, and that was Mr. Sanderson who was the Clerk to Aspatria Urban. There had been three of us at Aspatria. Now there was – well, there was Stan Easton – do you know him, Mr. Easton – his widow lives with John Johnston. And Frank Easton and Alan Easton. Mr. Easton was the Clerk, Willy Carrick was the assistant clerk, first assistant clerk and George Coulthard who isn't here – he died a couple of years ago – and John Johnston who was in my department where I worked. That was four; myself, Sanderson, myself, my wife, who is now my wife – I met her in the office, she was, she worked for the Wigton Urban in those days, she was transferred. And there was another one, there was four and four makes eight. Three collectors; eleven, and three Public Health Inspectors, that's fourteen. A Medical Officer, who was part-time of course, fifteen. About fifteen or sixteen in the council offices in George Street. At first we had an awful job to bring all the accounts of the four Authorities into one – that was our job in the Finance Department.

I think it functioned very well and between 1934 and war breaking out it was amazing the number of small schemes and housing schemes that we got off the ground. We started quite a lot of villages, about ten or a dozen that had never had sewerage. That was one of the main advantages of the amalgamation – the rural areas benefited far more than the former Urbans because the former Urbans had always had this and the villages hadn't. And we started providing, in the first place, sewerage schemes. We did quite a lot; Fletchertown, Abbeytown, Newton Arlosh, all around. They were all started and finished before 1939, so I think really the Wigton R.D.C. did a good job between 1934, when it was formed, and 1939 when all capital schemes were stopped because of the war. Water and sewerage. They didn't build houses until 1939 and that was the Brindlefield Estate.

In 1936, the Housing Acts of 1936 came out then and it placed a duty on all Authorities to get cracking with all slum clearance. The District Council then, Wigton Rural, appointed Mr. Blackburn – you know Mrs. Blackburn – as a Public Health Inspector with special duties of dealing with slum clearance. And it was his job to go round and make himself known and survey all the houses and make representations to the Council about which houses he thought should be replaced. Well, he concentrated on Wigton and condemned quite a lot of houses. But, of course, you've got to provide replacements and that was how Brindlefield was started. Water Street, all the little alleyways down there, you'll know them better than I – all had to go.

I spent the war in submarines – and went all over the world and came back in 1946, early 1946 I think, about February or March. And then Mr. Easton, who was Clerk of Wigton Rural, retired on health grounds, or was going to retire. It was advertised so I applied and I was fortunate enough to get it. In 1948; I came here in July 1948. It was pretty well as I'd left it except I was on housing because the demand for houses in those days was tremendous and they were building houses all over the district, in every little village or town. There were houses everywhere, and water supplies came more into the picture. We wanted to extend our water scheme. All capital schemes were stopped just before the war and we started again our water scheme, the old Aspatria and Silloth Joint Water Scheme, into all different parts of the area. Laid mains over to Thursby and, once the water was there, then of course you could start to develop a sewerage scheme. Unless you have a good water supply you can't have modern drainage schemes. But housing, oh housing; my time was taken up on contracts for housing and water schemes.

We had eighty houses at Aspatria, twenty-six at Silloth, that's a hundred and six; we had about a hundred and seventy-eight and ninety at Brindle, two hundred and seventy. We now have about two thousand; since 1948. I think the greatest concentration is in Wigton, with more in proportion to other places. We have about four hundred down on the Western Bank, there's Brindlefield, the Highmoor, Kirkland Avenue, Fell View; all these have been built since the war. We used the services of the North-Eastern Housing Association to build our houses. Well, this is something new. In 1936, I think it would be, the Government decided that for the benefit of those in what was known as Distressed Areas that they would give a special subsidy to housing associations who built houses on behalf of the local authorities, and the North-Eastern Housing Association was set up with headquarters at Newcastle, and they opened a branch at Maryport and offered their services to local authorities in Cumberland. The Wigton Rural decided that they would employ the Association to build their houses, the object being that they would get this additional grant. There were subsidies to local authorities from the Government for building houses, but in Distressed Areas there was this extra subsidy so the Council decided to use the N.E.H.A., and the houses in Brindlefield were built by them. After the war, and this is controversial, they decided to carry on with the Association

354

and have done ever since. There have been various attempts to drop them but they have never succeeded and the Council have always built their houses through the N.E.H.A. So they have provided the houses, we provide the finance; we borrow it, of course, from the Government and pass it to them. Any subsidies that come from the Government we pass over to the Association. We select the tenants and the Association collects the rents and keeps the properties in good repair, and that's, very briefly, it.

The houses are the Association's. They buy the land, they engage the architects and the contractors. We've got to approve the siting and the types of houses and the plans and so on, but they build the houses and they belong to them. I think the N.E.H.A. have done a very good job.

We have now about thirty; twenty-nine and one part-time staff now compared with, say, 1945 when I said about sixteen, about fifteen or sixteen. In the old days I told you about the sewerage scheme, well, at that time we didn't have an Engineer and a Surveyor's Department, we had three people who were known as Surveyors, Public Health Inspectors or Sanitary Inspectors in those days. And our Surveyor was Mr. Spencer. Do you remember him? Mr. Blackburn and Mr. Miller who was at Silloth – and they were known as Public Health Inspectors and Surveyors. And in about 1954, because of the volume of work on sewerage and like matters, the Council decided that they would have a Surveyors' Department, and relieve the Public Health Inspectors of their surveying duties.

So we set up a new department in 1954. That department has undertaken quite a lot of sewerage schemes and similar jobs on their own in the Parks before the Parks were set up. We used to employ consultative engineers and architects and so on in private practice to do our schemes. The smaller schemes are now being done by our own staff. A few of the bigger schemes are still put out to consultants. That is one of the reasons why staff has increased. There are eight in the Surveyor's Department that we didn't have before. The Parks Department has ten, the Treasurer's have nine where they used to be four, but a lot of additional work used to be put onto the Finance Department, and that is why they have had to expand. It's just a case that we have, in fact, undertaken more of the functions that were available to us in the past.

Street lighting has expanded tremendously. I think when I first came in 1948, there was street lighting in Aspatria, Silloth and Wigton and I think in Abbeytown, and that would be about all. Well, they started on street lighting and we were determined that every

355

little village would have a few street lights and we have now got street lighting in all the hamlets and villages and in recent years have been bringing that up to a better standard. These are things, the powers were there but they weren't being used. And we have, over the past twenty-five years, been expanding, putting into effect the duties that weren't being done before.

I am, in effect, the Chief Executive Officer and I think we have an efficient system insofar as it keeps in touch with what is going on. There's very rigid delegation, the Council to the office, and they prefer to keep an eye on things themselves. It means more work for us, of course, and I think from that point of view it is better for the councillors; they know what is going on and they see everything in the Minutes. And they can bring things forward, they can question matters, challenge them if they like – which they do occasionally. And I think it is to the benefit of councillors and the public themselves, but there is a drawback in the delays which do occur. This is where the public don't really appreciate that because we only meet once a month, and these things have got to go through the procedure, it means that anyone who wants an early reply has got to wait until it has been approved by the Council. But, by and large, I think it is working pretty well. Now then, I know we are coming to Allerdale [with the new change to an even larger area authority which took place in 1974] but when we move into Allerdale I have six Authorities like ours all amalgamated into one. It will be impossible to carry on like we do; they will have to delegate to their Officers. They would have to decide the policy then and then say to the Officers, you get on with the detail.

I am not in favour of the huge Authorities; I think they are rather impersonal. But they can be efficient. I think that applies in commerce as well. Some of the bigger companies are very efficient but impersonal, and this is what I'm afraid of. At the moment people can come into this office with a complaint, they can come and ask to see me and it has always been my policy that if anyone comes to me I'll see them. And if they have a complaint we'll deal with it. They can come in enquiring about plans, about houses, about roads, buying houses, all kinds of things. I should think there are very, very few people in this town that haven't had to come into the Council office for some reason or other; to make an enquiry or complaint – and we can deal with it right away, they can see the person who is in charge. In the future, they won't have that facility. And there is no guarantee that they will see the person they want to see. They'll probably see someone who will try to help them but, as I say, I have tried here, at any rate, that if any person wants to come and see me, I'll see them. That's always been my policy."

Colin Graham lives in the town but doesn't, as he says, "mix much", preferring, with his wife whom he met at work, to "make his own entertainment". That has always largely been to do with natural history, bird-watching, rambles, gardening.

Something of the quality of being a councillor comes out in Norman Fell who went onto the Council after the Second World War in order to devote himself to housing and has been an outstanding councillor. One of his main problems, though, has been to find the time to attend Council meetings which are held on weekdays (i.e. working days) through the day, usually in the afternoons. He tends to compare his disadvantageous position not with the easier situation of local business or professional men but with Edwin Routledge's ability to take paid time off work at the factory in which Norman Fell himself worked for some time. He is against the system of amateurs, barely paid "part-time" councillors which comes directly from the days when those in authority were those who had the necessary money to buy the leisure to take the time required. In that sense, the Much Lauded Amateurism was a high-minded barricade against working men.

"I've always been against this - against the old system; the old system of councils. I've always been for this proportional representation I feel that it's going to be the best type of government, and I've always been for it. Now then, to get down to council work. I would say we'd have to have another good afternoon, you and me, because I'll tell you now council work, to me, if your face doesn't fit, it's a waste of time. And who can be a full-time councillor and a working man at the same time? The officials of the Council are getting forty and fifty pounds a week, and the councillors who are there to represent the public could at one time only claim a pound for four hours, and two pounds for a full day. I've seen when I were earning five pounds a day; I went to a Council meeting and I could only claim two pounds for the day. And yet your officers are sitting and meeting – you understand my point? And your officers sitting there with forty to fifty pounds a week; and they'll sit right through the meeting. Full-time councillors are out as far as I'm concerned; you can't be a full-time councillor unless you represented either a firm or a political

357

party or you're a man with plenty of money.

Then I worked for Rolls-Royce for seven years. I had a good wage and a good job, and I were quite happy because they did allow me to have a day off any time I wanted to go to my Council meetings. And I could go there and speak my mind and nobody ever complained. But it meant taking a full day off when only half a day would have sufficed, you see, because I couldn't travel. I couldn't get up there. Because once I went in the morning I had to stay there all day – or else. So I had to take a full day off, for two hours in the afternoon a meeting. Well, it were a shame to take a full day off. I didn't think that it was right and I was rather tied. And the only way I worked it, I went on the Health Committee in the morning and the Housing Committee in the afternoons. I had two committees, and I made a full day. And that's the only time I could devote to council work, being still a part-time councillor, you see, owing to circumstances. Now then, you see, if you're not in your committee, it's no good going to the full Council meeting and raising the matter unless you're on the committee, and if you haven't attended your committee meeting ... I reckon a councillor, a full-time councillor, should be able to attend all his committee meetings and he shouldn't speak, if he's missed a committee meeting, who is he to raise it in the full Council? And if I had my way – I've asked for meetings in the evening so that we could attend then, with John Donnelly and myself – we've tried to get meetings in the evening so that I could attend. But we were beat by the Council. If you want to have all the time you need to be a councillor, you do what these fellows have done at the factory. Like this present fella, he joined the Labour Party, he took the trade union shop steward over, and he's now personnel manager. You understand my point? Now then, he were a member of the executive committee of the Labour Party for Cumberland, he went on to all these committees, then got on the inside of the trade union, and then when the job came along, that was the price. This happened time and time again.

So, is there a true socialist? What is socialism? What is the meaning of the word socialism? There isn't a true socialist – I think every one of them has a price. And the true socialists are the poor, and they'll always be poor. That's my attitude. Because – principles; what's principles today? You see, I don't bear anybody a grudge; I've no grudge against Edwin Routledge or any of them – understand? I only feel I'm afraid I've missed a lot, but I've no grudge whatsoever.

I'll tell you about two fights – one I lost, one I won. First – the Parish Council. Now then – the one that I lost. Well, I was always

358

behind the local lads and their pigeon lofts and allotments; in fact, I fought tooth and nail, and I thought I'd clinched it, in committee. They had the allotments beside the Tip – they'd been there for years, generations, years. Well, it used to be a bone of contention, and we had inspections; some of the allotments were a pleasure to look at and others were a disgrace. But the point were that it were somewhere for the lads to go to, and it was somewhere for them to occupy their spare time. Some of them kept dogs which – they owned dogs and things like that which really they shouldn't have been keeping on the allotments at all. That was one of the reasons why I think we were beaten in the end. They were using them for garage space and things like that, but the innocent had to suffer for the other people, you understand my point? Now then, the issue were the closing of the allotments altogether. Doing away with the pigeons; pigeon lofts. Now the Pigeon Club had been in Wigton as long as I can ever remember, and they'd always been on the Tip. Now I wanted – I wanted the Pigeon Club men to be given a portion of the land for a nominal figure – five pounds. Get them to fence it off and say, That's yours. Keep it tidy and that's your Wigton Pigeon Club land. And it's up to you to form a committee and look after it. And the allotments – well, I tried to get the allotment-holders to form an association, you see. But you couldn't get any interest – that's the trouble with Wigton – there's lack of interest. Now then, the allotment men; they wouldn't fight. The pigeon men weakened, and there was only a few that really tried. They started moving their lofts, you see. And in the end I got to the state where in committee we agree we could give them a portion of land. At the full Council meeting which I was unable to attend – now that was where I was beaten. By the chairman's casting vote. Edwin Routledge was chairman. And that was, to me, pigeons – it's a working man's hobby. And they've lost it. It could have been the break-up of the Club. I'd have been happy if all the Pigeon Club, if they'd a bit of their own land and they'd run their own Wigton Flying Club, you know, with the lofts and everything on their own piece of ground.

Now then the fight I won – on the Urban District this – there were a time when we were on about the chimney at the factory. Now then, I were on the Health Committee for years, and I used to – I always used to ask if the smell from the chimney, the chemicals coming out was detrimental to the health of the public of Wigton, in view of the fact that if you had any coins – and I save coins – they tarnish; go blue. Silver goes blue, and the atmosphere – I know through working in the mill that you had to drink milk and one thing

359

and another if you were in certain areas. And I used always to ask at the Council meetings – at the Health Committee, and I were a member of the Health Committee – is the pollution of the air due to the factory at Wigton detrimental to the health of the public? And I was always given the answer, Definitely not. Now then, I couldn't be satisfied with that because I always felt that there was that many people – that many sudden deaths – deaths at fifty, forty-eight, between forties and fifties, and this is just my own feeling about it, you understand? I feel, Isn't it funny that these fellows go like that? And in my own mind it's possible that it could be natural causes and then again it could be – their lives could be shortened through working among chemicals such as they have down there.

So I did raise it at a meeting that an atmospheric test be taken in Wigton. And, after a few times, it was done. And the atmospheric test proved that at certain times the pollution of the air was detrimental to the public of Wigton. Now then, it was mentioned then that something would have to be done about it. Well, I said, this was in committee and, as you know, I feel that if this committee had been public – if this committee had been public and the Press would have been there, they would have heard the discussions in general, you understand my point? And there'd have been publicity given, and the town would have known that it was detrimental to their health. Well then, the scheme – they got on about a scheme for getting rid of the pollution and their scheme were going to cost, oh I think it was a hundred and twenty thousand pounds. And the factory said they couldn't afford it. We were given to understand on a number of occasions that this scheme would be in hand but they couldn't afford it at the time. Well, it went to a meeting, and I got on about the air pollution. And I said, Can't afford it? I said, Well the profits last year were a million and three-quarters. I said, Surely if a firm can't afford a hundred and twenty thousand pounds out of a million and three-quarters there's something wrong. Now then in my own mind I think that after that, the chimney was erected. For I harped on and harped on at Health Committee meetings, and my old friend Barwise used to also help. And I maintain that factory could have put the chimney up long before that, but the profits were more for the directors' pockets than for the public of Wigton. In my mind; you understand my point? I felt that the profits of the directors were coming first and the health of the public second.

Now then, my own doctor, my own doctor was Dr. Goldsborough, stated to me – he said, If you want to shorten your life, stay where you are, when I was working at the factory. I said, How do you mean, doctor? He said, If you want to knock ten years off your life, stay at the factory. And he says, That's my advice. And this when I first went to see the doctor, the first time I ever went to see him in my life. I had a problem. And he started naming the men that had died prematurely. He says, If you stay there, he says, you'll knock ten years off your life."

The stock English Establishment figure in every community is the doctor. Society, so runs the truism, now accords doctors the reverence once reserved for priests, as well as the respect and consideration always given leaders. Despite the movements against many of the modern tools of medicine – particularly drugs; despite the increasing scepticism about the real value of men with a body of knowledge so often fundamentally simple or suspect; and despite the general tendency to be critical of those who seem to claim authority in any field whatsoever; the doctor stays at what is still, for most people, the centre of a world changing but not unrecognisable.

Dr. Dolan was born in the town. His father was a famous local figure, particularly for the fact – reported everywhere – that he would treat the poor for nothing (this was in the days when all medicine had to be paid for). Dr. Dolan – "Young Dr. Tom" as he was called, though in his sixties when we spoke – met me at his house, a pleasant, detached house on the West Road built a few years after the Second War, backing onto fields: he was playing croquet when I arrived.

"When you qualify, you don't go straight into general practice, you expect to do two years anyway in hospital service in various departments under the guidance of the various consultants. And then, when you've done that, you have a better idea of what you're going to do if left on your own.

So I went down to Weston-super-Mare which was a nice little hospital of about ninety beds and there were only two of us. And instead of sort of being detailed to, say, medical wards for the whole time, you got the whole lot to do. You've medical, surgical, maternity wards, your skin wards, X-ray, ear, nose and throat and everything to do, which was a great advantage because it was all set in one hospital. You simply went round the lot. You were very hard-worked and I am very sympathetic to young hospital doctors who get put on. But you do, you get a tremendous lot of hard work to do. I mean, you can start operating at nine o'clock in the morning and you can be still at it at six o'clock at night, with just cups of coffee in between time because you don't have time for anything else if your list is big enough.

And then I came back to Wigton to help my father. The first year I did just about a mile radius on a push-bicycle. Then I bought a car and I extended my limits. I don't think the illnesses have changed an awful lot. They were mostly 'flu, colds and things like that – usually chest cold, sore throats, earache, rheumatism, asthmatics, stomach troubles. I would say chest and stomach troubles; they are the two prevalent ones – all along. Cancers are on the increase for the simple reason, I think, in the past they were put down to – certainly in your chest anyway, it was galloping pneumonia or galloping consumption or something like that.

The biggest change was the National Health Service scheme which came in in 1948. I think it's a very good thing ... for the majority of people. But there are a few who spoil it like everything else. I mean, say you get a pneumonia which needs a lot of visits, well then I, like Father, we would just charge them a lump sum for three weeks' treatment. Or maybe a pound for three weeks or, if they were badly off, nothing. But people couldn't afford to pay that then, five shillings a time for every day for about ten days, so I think in that respect that the number of visits a doctor has to pay now he hasn't got to weigh up, you know, am I going too often? Can I afford it? Which was the idea before – that's better.

Whereas now you get all these things, or you're entitled to all these things and I think that's good because a doctor can now go and visit them as often as he likes if they're really bad. They can also get all sorts of various appliances, for your arms, for your legs, for your back, for your shoulder – and all sorts of things which you couldn't get before. Since the National Health Scheme in 1948. The benefits you can accrue from it are tremendous, both physically and therapeutically, so I think the National Health Scheme is extremely good. I don't know how it affects the town doctors say, like, in the cities but for the country doctors like Father, who never used to send a bill out, he also benefited. Other practices would be the same as ours. They wouldn't charge. It would benefit us because we get paid a set sum for each patient we have per year, so we know what we're going to get. So financially it benefited us in that respect.

But the people it benefited most. We noticed straight away, in 1948, that the number of attendances at the surgery jumped, I would say, about thirty percent. So it increased your work that much whereas before, if they got a cold, they would get a packet of aspirins and

362

maybe take two twice a day or two or three times a day and be happy with themselves and never bother you. Or if they had a bad knock on the knee or something they would just put a bandage on and maybe a bit of iodine and take some more aspirins and hobble on with it, but now they come up. But I think it's quite a good thing. I wouldn't be against it.

The health of the people has improved tremendously; that's been marked, and the main things are that you don't see diphtheria now, you see much less tuberculosis. There was a tremendous lot. I don't know the statistics but I think more or less all over England, certainly in Cumberland, there hasn't been one diphtheria case for, I would say, ten years. In the past there was so much tuberculosis you couldn't get a bed in a tuberculosis hospital before. But now you can get one with no bother at all. This mass X-ray unit has picked out the early cases and mostly they get better in three months, and so it goes on. Diphtheria's been stamped out by the injections that you get for your children. You get a triple shot for diphtheria, whooping cough, tetanus and poliomyelitis. And of course they get these school meals now. They used to get milk, they don't get that now, but they get their school meals. And of course before, on account of the wage the family got, they were lucky if they got a midday meal. They ate bread and dripping for breakfast and maybe when they got home for lunch it would be chips and bread and butter. And when they got home for tea it might be an egg and something else, whereas now they get a properly balanced meal at least once a day. Of course they're earning a lot more now than they used to do and so they are generally much better fed all round. They're better built all round, definitely. The ailments that have become more common, I think, are stomach complaints for the simple reason – the high pressure of work and the rush – the coughs with smoking, but you can't stop those things. If they have an ordinary day job and they get their meals at regular times, all well and good. Now those who work on shifts, say three eight-hour shifts, they have their meals shifted every week. That doesn't agree with digestive upsets – it sort of tends to upset them. I mean, most people now on the day shifts, the day work, say at one o'clock when they come out for their meal they invariably get chips. A lot of that fried fat and stuff is no good either.

I got three months on psychology. You get a lot of depression and anxiety on account of shift-work, low wages, inability to keep up payments and also you get that mainly through family squabbles or through family tiffs, as you might say. Or through incompatibilities of husband and wife or a very overbearing supervisor or shop steward or something like that. Or if you've got to do some work that you don't like to do but you had to do it simply because you have to get a wage. All these add up and you get quite a lot of what you might call psycho-neuroses coming up to see you, and they take an awful lot of time to get better. You can't get them better by medicine alone. You've got to spend about half an hour talking to them, maybe once a week or once a fortnight anyway. And even then you can't get through to them all the time. They improve for a little bit and then something happens and off they go again.

I would say that's on the increase alright. I don't know that it's because people are spending more or want to keep up with the Jones's when they can't – they get into difficulties or they're spending more than they should on bingo and betting and cigarettes and drink. You see, if you were to take cigarettes and drink, the money they spent on that out of a man's wages, he'd be well off. I mean, I would say the average man spends at least a fiver on cigarettes and drink in a week. The family is bound to suffer as a result of that. We find it very hard to get the time to deal with such depressed cases. You see, we have now an appointment system and I find that if I have to deal with, I don't know how Dr. Jones and Dr. Gray work theirs, but I find if I have any like that I try and see them in an evening when I finish surgery. Then I can give them half an hour or more. Or on my weekend when I'm on duty – Friday, Saturday, Sunday, Monday, Tuesday I can see them in the evening and give them a time. But you can't possibly do it in an ordinary surgery consultation, unless you have, say, one set session for such like people – then you can do it. But the ordinary G.P. hasn't got time for that in his ordinary day's work. It has to be done outside your normal hours, say after half past six or seven o'clock.

Another change is the increased number of drugs there are nowadays. You pick out what you want and you discard the rest. You just gloss over them, so to speak, and you start using them and by degrees you find they're either an improvement on the old thing or they're not as good. In that case you either continue using them and drop the old ones or, if you find the new ones are no better and probably pricier, you drop those ones and continue using the old ones, till something comes along that will better it. But you can't possibly remember them all. That's why this little booklet we get is so useful.

As regards the laboratory work, well, that is a lot easier because there's a set pattern for these things and unless there's some sudden break through on something on a disease like rheumatism or something like that – to find the cause of it or the cure for it – there's more or less a set pattern. You get your blood estimations, your urine, your sputum, your tissue – if you cut a bit off you send it to the laboratory and things like that and they do it for you. You say I think this might be a cancer and you send a bit of the stuff, cut a bit of the stuff off, they'll tell you yes or no. Of course, that's up to them. But if we send a blood for an estimation or a blood count or something, all we want to know is what the blood count is, what the haemoglobin is, and we simply send a specimen off and they send us the answer back. All these things have not what you call varied anywhere near as much as the drugs. They'll still be stable for a few years, maybe five or ten years. So the laboratory side of our work is more or less stable.

But there are new concepts abroad all the time. For example, the treatment of osteomyelitis of a bone, which is an abscess formation of bone. Before they used to simply strip your bone down and gutter it out, put some antiseptic in and wrap it up in plaster of Paris and leave it till it stunk like hell and they opened it out in about four or five weeks and it's granulating up. Whereas now what they do, they'll probably cut that little bit out and they'll put a bone graft in from somewhere else. These people that have all these bad backs and things; they cut a bit of the spine, they cut a bit of your bone off from here and they stick it in and it keeps your back straight. A lot of ear operations and heart operations have come on. You can get different operations on your ears which you couldn't get then. You can get valves put in your heart now which you couldn't get then. You can get heart surgery now which they wouldn't even dream of then. You can get blood vessels replaced in your body which you couldn't get then. The amount of advance in surgery is tremendous. More so than in medicine.

And so the older people now are better than the older people in my father's day. A tremendous lot better. But housing and so on has helped the general health. There was one family in Water Street when I started – they had two bedrooms, one up and one down. There were eleven in the family and so they slept in the two rooms. Now when that family went to Brindlefield they got a house with six bedrooms in when they moved up there. Course, since that family now have been married they've taken two bedrooms off and there's only four left in the house; they've put them on the house next door. And say down Water Street and Tickell's Lane, for instance, Tickell's Lane – there were four houses up there with thatched roofs or tin shacks on the top. Well, they were very damp, no damp course. They were very damp and they were very draughty. Down Water Street there were about two lanes on the left-hand side which – one had four houses in and the other had two. They were just about the same. The houses up Court Square, they were a little better, but they were still damp. The walls were damp. You had to keep the fire on to keep it dry. And you put your paper on your wall, and maybe after three or four months it would start to dampen off. And when they moved to new houses there was a tremendous improvement. Of course, there are about two families, I think, that haven't improved. Well of course when their children grow up, they will improve. But otherwise everybody's improved.

And food has improved, both in variety – there's more variety of food now. It used to be then bread and dripping and butter in the early stages, maybe chips and egg for dinner or chips and sausage or sausage and mash or bangers as they call them; for tea, maybe bread and butter or a scone and cakes. Whereas now most people get either cereals for breakfast, milk, or they get an egg and bacon and for their midday meal, if they're school children, they get a square meal. For the grown-up people, well, they do get a decent meal in the midday, then they get a dinner at night, as they call it.

On the whole I think we've reached a pretty high level now in health. I don't think it'll improve an awful lot. They're now living, I would say, about another ten years longer than they used to live last century, and I don't think that we can do an awful lot more as regards the health of people now. If people take notice of what the social services and the medical practitioners and the hospitals tell them."

When Dr. Dolan died, about a year after that interview, the funeral was large, the crowd mixed in class and age. It is a fairly safe bet that his death would be remarked on in almost every house in the town – he was always top of the poll for the Parish Council.

CHAPTER FIFTEEN
David Pearson

As the biographies or the "portraits" approached the present, it became much harder to ask the questions because the people concerned were often my exact contemporaries and I knew "all about them", i.e., knew the answers to all the opening questions, and they were very awkward both about what they thought I ought to know and what I needed to discover. Some interviews did not work because of this too close and yet constrained relationship.

David Pearson was born two years before me. He lives a couple of miles outside town on the road to the Solway Firth, on a hill looking over to Wigton and beyond to the Lakes, south, while to the north he can see into Scotland. He is married with a family and teaches physical education at the Comprehensive – he is, in fact, head of that large department. He's also been very active in the Rugby Club which, directly involving fifty or sixty men each week and indirectly pulling in two to three hundred – apart from the general interest stored up in the town, has become one of the chief focal points for the leisure and interest of the town. It could be said that a "sports culture" has grown up around it – a club, quizzes, dances, fashionable visiting parties or trips – different from the old obsessions with football and swimming, though perhaps only in being more affluent.

It seemed to me that David Pearson represented a number of aspects of the predictable, and the unpredictable, which go into the making of many Englishmen today. He was educated publicly, and then privately, having failed his eleven-plus, and his father, a joiner, wanting to give him a chance; in the Army it did not occur to him to become an officer, in private life he still sees and spends evenings with the friends of his childhood who, as he says, work on "the dust carts" and so on – not jobs which traditionally you would expect to be held by men playing darts with the head of a department; and

367

if this sounds old-fashioned, snobbish and out-dated, then I am pleased it sounds so because it seems to me that with David Pearson's generation we are approaching the time when the old restrictive barriers might break down as they must if England is to escape from the suffocating spell of the past.

"My father was a joiner, and then after that he was in business from the time he was seventeen years old. And after that he developed into the timber trade, as a timber merchant. As far as we know, the family's been in Wigton for about three hundred years. They arrived up here from Liverpool and they had a joiners' business and their wives used to work in the weavers' cottages opposite for Banks of Highmoor. They did do a lot of work for Banks of Highmoor. I can remember they did all the joiner work on the Skinburness Hotel. It was what they used to do. They'll walk out there on Sunday evenings, work for six days in the week, sleep in tents out on the Skinburness Marsh there, do all the joiner work, and then come back Saturday afternoons or Sunday evenings and walk to Skinburness and back.

Once I'd made this point of going into teaching, the headmaster said, Look, get an early call up into the Army so that you come out and don't waste a year. I was called up into the Army in September and you see, in two years' time, in order to catch the college term, I actually asked and was granted a six weeks' leave of absence from the Army, cutting my National Service down from the two years to twenty-three months. I got out early to catch the college term. I applied to a couple of colleges while I was in the Army and I wasn't accepted at one – Leeds – I wasn't interviewed, and I was accepted at Sheffield when I was in the Army, for a general course on teaching – two-year course. I did my basic training at Portsmouth for my National Service. The Army I think definitely opens you out. It makes you think. I seriously believe that if everybody put a stint in in the Army the country would be in a far better state that what it is now. I hate to think, these fellows that were causing trouble up at Stirling University, sort of giving the V sign to the Queen and that, I'm sure had they been stood on a square for three or four hours in complete silence, and standing rigid to attention waiting for a G.O.C. to come round and inspect you – and when he comes in a Land Rover half a mile away from you – and goes fast past you, you feel as if you're there for something anyhow. At least you're respectful to somebody.

Anyway – sport – this certain battalion, which was at Didcot near

Oxford, they wanted some Rugby players into their battalion. I mean, there's a lot of this goes on in the Army. And I eventually found myself fiddled, drilled into this 14th Battalion R.A.O.C. to play Rugby. And I think I must be the only person in the British Isles that's played Rugby in Army cup ties for two sides, because this battalion they knocked us out. I think it was in the third round, the 14th Battalion knocked our training battalion out, and then I played for them two or three games later, when I'd been posted to them, in the next round. So I thought that was a bit of a fiddle but that's the way it goes. I think my own game matured in the Army. Played in some good games, and we played for some teams as well. I fortunately got into the first team which was sort of made up of more or less officers and maybe four or five of us who were sort of upper ranks, but the captain was A. N. Other rank, he was captain of Scotland actually. That was Sergeant Bruce. And we got on quite well. Not that I wanted to be an officer, I didn't. I wasn't interested. All I was interested in was getting two years quickly over with and getting out. Anyway eventually I went up to college and I was accepted at this college and I started there in September 1957.

College was a two years' holiday. My grant to go to college was – well, I worked it a bit. My father was in business and the first year he got an accountant to make the form out, and I think I only got something like a pound a week but everything found, which wasn't too bad. I wasn't bothered about the first year because I'd saved up two or three hundred pounds in the Army, out of my four pounds a week. I'd kept it back. I think I spent about eighty pounds in the first term at college, bought a suit or two and a few pairs of shoes. I enjoyed that. Just walking down the street and I'll have that and that. No, I enjoyed college. I think the grant in the second year was round about ninety pounds for the year. We had all our travelling paid for, and all our accommodation, plus meals. You had to go into more detail on your advanced level subjects than your sort of B subjects, and just a general teaching course. I found it good and interesting. Lectures in the first year lasted through till about four thirty and there was no evening lectures. We had our activities after that. And the second year was even better. Whereas you probably had just two afternoon lectures and the rest of the afternoons were free, which we found was good from our point of view because we could get so much more sport in. This was part of the course as well – I did physical education, P.E.

When I came out of college I applied to Cumberland and I was interviewed for Cumberland. And at the interview I said, Where are you sending me or what job am I going to get? And they said, We can't tell you. I said, Well, I'm not going to accept it. I'll get a job down in London. They said, Oh, oh. And I was interested in a job in London actually because with being down in Wales – at Cardiff for my third year at college – the attraction was you could go back and play Rugby for Welsh clubs, and they would always stand your train fare plus any expenses and this sort of thing. And so the money would have been better down there. So eventually they turned up and said, Look, if we offer you Netherhall School at Maryport, would you accept it? I said, Certainly, because the school had just been recently built and it had very good facilities. And that's what happened. I eventually finished up at Netherhall. It was a boys' secondary school, four hundred boys at the time. Real tough boys as well, real good blokes, real genuine lads. Anything you would do for them – I more or less started off getting the odd fixture at Rugby and this sort of thing, and even the scruffiest of lads used to turn up on that bus. And after we had played and got back to Maryport they used to say, Thank you very much, Mr. Pearson. And that used to make me think that you were doing something for them. And lads that were not in school on Friday – they knew that they were playing on Saturday morning – you had to have a quiet word with one or two of them – make sure he's there. Oh, he'll be there. He's just off today. But he was on the bus on Saturday morning. They were skipping school but they were on that bus on Saturday morning. I would say the children were tougher down there than in Wigton. This is West Cumberland. The mining area. I wouldn't say they were any worse off financially, because their parents would probably be making more money than what people in Wigton were. But you still got the children turning up – I saw black holed gym shoes, in the middle of winter, down at Maryport; this was happening in 1960. It's maybe happening now, I don't know, and looking half fed and a bit scruffy and generally sort of a run-down mining area.

I came back to Wigton in about 1964. I felt it like chalk to cheese, moving from Maryport to Wigton, because they were rough and tough out there whereas Wigton kids were meek and mild. You could find a fight going on in the playground nearly every day at Netherhall. They used to play Rugby with gym shoes on the yard, really hard cases. Play flat out on the concrete yard and really tackle. No Rugby touch. On the yards at Netherhall in front of the school there. Tough. I learnt how to discipline them. Well you used to show them the old army technique. You jump on everything. If anybody sort of picked up a pencil, put that pencil down. You really had to get a grip on them. And keep them that way. Right up till, say, four o'clock. At first. I can remember sort of dragging a lad down the stairs, two or three flights of stairs, to the headmaster's office because he had said something to me. I just got hold of him and dragged him down the stairs by his collar. He was probably in his second year then. I never had any more trouble from him or that class for the next two years. I don't know if they would accept it now; if the teaching profession would accept it. Although the parents come to me and says, Well you know what to do with him if he bothers you. Smack his lug (ear), and this sort of thing. But there's the odd occasion when it does spring back. Not that I'm heavy-handed. I haven't collared a lad for, probably eight years. You always sort of issue threats and this sort of thing but you never seem as if you get round to carrying them out.

It's not just a matter of teaching P.E. There's the time-consuming job of going with teams, you know, going with teams to matches, accepting teams in to play school matches. I probably have something on every night, except Mondays. I keep that free. Usually finish about five or six o'clock. I mean, on Thursday night it was ten o'clock, so you can put as many as a twelve hour stint in, no bother. There's no extra money attached to it but you do it because you feel you want to. My wife doesn't agree with it, mind. We do games training, skill training rather than brute strength; gymnastics, swimming. We don't get long enough on it. I mean, we're down to one period of P.E., one period of swimming and two of games, that's in the first and second year. Once they've reached the second year they've dropped their one period of swimming and they only have one period of P.E. Now that's cut down from forty minutes to thirty-five minutes a week. Well, if you work out how sort of long it takes to get down to the changing-rooms to get changed and in fact, after your lessons, you demand a shower or you want a shower if you've been sweating a little bit, how long are you getting in a week? You're probably getting about fifteen minutes' P.E. which is not long enough. Where an academic school is concerned, let's be fair, it's more important that they're doing school work. They can do the P.E. at lunchtimes or after school with us.

My own Rugby's been with Wigton and I think probably 1962 we started developing. We won our first Sevens, I think it was in 1960 or 61. I'd been skipper of the side down at college and when I moved down to Cardiff I felt as if I was a sort of third stringer because they were so good and so advanced down in Cardiff. They were really sort of educated on the Rugby side. And they were just sort of building up at that time, but the side we eventually formed from that year, there was seven full internationals from that year, and the following year. And our skipper was Clive Rowlands who is now national coach to the Welsh Rugby. And you felt – I didn't know at that time and I don't think these fellows knew either, they were just young fellows just come out from their National Service and sort of moved into this college, and fortunately everybody moved in at the same time and we had a real cracking side. I mean, the first time we sort of appeared out on the Ebbw Vale ground, you got twenty thousand people watching you. Well, this is sort of a bit nightmarish moving down from Barton Laws in Wigton and down into a team like that, and you're sort of saying, What's the rumbling upstairs? There's a few of them watching, some Welsh fellow would say, and when you get out there you find you're up against Arthur Smith who was captain of Ebbw Vale in that year – a fully grown international. And I toured with them. We played every week. But what they used to do, we used to play on Wednesdays for the parish side and then on the Saturday the lads would play for their own town teams, like Tredegar, Llanelli, Ebbw Vale, these teams, and Glamorgan Wanderers, and so there was no matches on a Saturday afternoon, just the odd one. It used to be interesting to play on Saturdays. When we got our team together on a Saturday, we used to go up the valleys and play. I can remember playing against a team called Gleneith, who was a feeding club to Newport, their best players were automatically transferred into Newport first team. And we arrived on this little ground and there was nobody watching when we walked out and suddenly about three or four hundred people appeared out of this little doorway. So I said, Where have they come from? And he says, Oh, they've just come out of the bar. So these three or four hundred watched the game, really interested in the game. And I think we lost by a couple of points. We had a good game. And I can remember we were getting changed in the changing-room and I was sitting, Rowlands was sitting there and he said – this fellow came round with these tickets, like Joe Cusack's Picturehouse tickets, a long stream of them – and Rowlands says, Well, I'll have eight or nine please. So the fellow gave him these tickets. So I says, What are these for? He says, Oh get yourself seven or eight. So I said, I'll have eight please. So he gave me these eight tickets. So he went round all the players and they quoted how many they wanted. So eventually I plucked up courage and said, What the hell are these for? Oh well, you take them up to the bar. So we got changed and that and we went up to this bar and what the idea was, that you gave a ticket in and you got a free pint. So you had your beer paid for the night. You got eight or nine free pints. That was a good system. And for Tredegar and them you were always allowed two pairs of boots a season. You were given five pounds and they said, Look, if you want to pay any more for your boots – well, we all used to buy them from Foster's of Bolton. They were these sort of kangaroo hide boots and you paid anything you wanted. Say six or seven pounds a pair. Well, it was worth quite a bit of money and you could claim ten pounds on that for expenses, and this is the way it worked.

I came back to Barton Laws in Wigton in 1960. Nobody had been much interested really in Rugby at that time. No crowds and no bar in the Club. Quite a few people said, Well, if you have a bar you'll ruin your Rugby club. And then in 1960 fortunately a nucleus of players arrived back in Wigton, lads like Keith Warwick, Mike Stoddart was back for some time, John Hope, sort of a group of young players. And this blended together with the older players. I think that's when it started, the snowballing off of Wigton Rugby Club was away back in 1960. And then we went on from strength to strength, if you know what I mean.

I got on to Wilf Akers who was then running the F.E. in Wigton and was a Further Education tutor. There was only one class going, I think, some Women's Institute or something like that. So I asked him if it was possible to use the school gym at the middle school, that is the old secondary-school gym. And we did sort of train under Barton Laws street lights; the big lamps used to come across there and we used to train there during the winter. And I felt that it would be better if we got somewhere where we could train. I was just sort of a member of the committee. No, I think Blob or somebody was club secretary. He was for a year or two. And eventually we pinned them down to having this gym and we encouraged players to come and train and I can remember on one occasion fifty-four people training. On one winter's night I counted them up – in a very small gym. And I thought, well, this place has got something to offer. Fifty-four fellows training in a small gym and I think that's when it started. We won our own Sevens in 1960 and we've won trophies every year since.

In 1960 we started negotiations for a new pitch. I'm not saying that I pushed it a lot but we did try the local Parish Council for a piece of land behind where Len Saunderson lives. To buy a plot of land to build a club-house and to introduce the bar, you see. I mean, you could see the possibilities of a bar and finance, which was turned down, by the Parish Council. As soon as they said you would not get access we just dropped the whole idea. We toyed with the idea of building a pavilion on the other side of the river, on the other side of the Wiza, that's in Hope's Auction field. We also toyed with the idea of going behind – opposite where Harry Phillips lives. That fell through. Then the next site I was trying for was down near the Rayophane, that's behind Greenacres, between Greenacres [the largest New Estate] and the railway line. There's a large field there. Now that probably would have been ideal; what we wanted, because I still feel that had we been closer to Greenacres, that's where the money is. For every night drinks, so convenient. And it would have been better bar-taking and better bar profit all round. But still, we couldn't manage that. The next one I tried was Highmoor Park. This was about 1965–66. Unfortunately John Studholme's father had just sold out to Border Engineers so I think that same Saturday I saw Dougie Johnston, who is managing director of Border Engineers, and had a chat with him. And he said, I'm very sorry but it's building land really and I'm sort of committed to build these a hundred and sixty houses or something. And he said, I would like to help you in any way I can. Please come back if I can be of any help. So then I approached Harriet Mattinson who was the other side from John Studholme and I think that's probably where it would have rested had not I been talking to Mr. Bland on Lowmoor Road one day. I just mentioned to him that he had two good fields and he said, Yes, I'm sick of cutting the hedges. He says, How much would you offer me for them? So I just said, Well, I'll give you four thousand pounds, or said, I will certainly try and raise four thousand for you. This was for seventeen and three-quarter acres. I should have bought it myself. But anyhow I appeared at this meeting away back in 1966 or 1967 and it was at the A.G.M. down at Barton Laws (which was Council land), the last A.G.M. we had in the Rugby hut down there, and I put it to them. At that time I think I mentioned that we were fifteen years behind any other Rugby club in the area and this idea would certainly advance us fifteen years ahead of any other club in the area. And I said, This fellow wants four thousand pounds for his fields. And we could set up like a community centre or a sports centre. That was the idea. And we got a very small sub-committee together, then straight after that A.G.M. we visited Albert Bland and he agreed that he would sell us the land. By the time we got the funds together and raised our fund-raising functions it took us about a year, you see. With the price of land going up, he was asking over five thousand pounds. So we did a survey on the fields and clinched it. So then, in order to build what we wanted we had to get plans. Anyhow, we got the money through and the architect was paid and everybody was paid. It was done as cheap as possible, let's put it that way. We invited tenders in from various firms and eventually Thomas Armstrong's of Cockermouth was accepted. There was a bit of a problem getting the money through. We had to go to Newcastle to a board meeting over there. I tried about eight or nine breweries to sponsor us and eventually there was only this one who would sponsor the idea. Newcastle Federation who I sort of understood from West Cumberland. I knew one club down there. I'd had their beer. So there was four of us landed over there one Saturday in Newcastle and we eventually talked them into letting us have twenty thousand pounds – well, access to twenty thousand to which the chairman replied, Certainly. And if you want any more, please come back – because they thought the idea was tremendous. The committee members were trembling at the knees, being responsible for all this money. I can remember Betty Ellwood having a word with me about her father (Jimmy); he was worried sick about this sort of money involved. Jimmy was really concerned. He was a guarantor, one of them, but he said, If I die I don't want this wrapped round my family's necks. They were a bit concerned about it. And Ben Wilson as well. But I think they're quite happy now.

The original intention was to invite as many sports clubs as possible up there – I think I sent out letters to the Throstle Nest Bowling Club, asking them if they would like to join us, or asking them to come along to the meeting to discuss this situation. Wigton Tennis Club, Cricket Club, the Squash Club were obviously interested and the Wigton Football Club. Now the reaction was, the Tennis Club were interested, the Cricket Club were interested, the Squash Club were and the Rugby Club. The Soccer Club, their reaction was as soon as you get off Barton Laws we can get our pitch a lot better. So they didn't join us. They wanted to stay down there and use our old facilities. The Bowling Club, they said they would like to join the Park Bowling Club – which seems quite a pity.

We owe fourteen thousand pounds now, that's all. That's all we owe on the land and the buildings. I think it's been an asset to the town. I think the problem is – well, we've struck down the Market Hall dances in the town. This is a pity; there's not many dances in the Market Hall. And now that we've established ourselves as a reasonable club we are attracting the better type of players into the town team. This is what happens. As soon as anybody sort of moves into the area and they are sort of keen and interested in Rugby they say, Well, where can I go and play? And they say, Well, Wigton's the best Rugby club round here. Get down there. And this is probably what's happened to five or six of our first team players. They're graduates moving into the area, to Carlisle and here and down as far as Whitehaven, and they get to know that's a decent club, a decent sort of set-up and they move in. And they just ask if they can join us and then they play for their places like everybody else. They'll travel forty miles. One chap of ours, he's a centre, he works at Sellafield – Dave Dewhurst – but he just lives at Gilcrux. But he could quite as easily have played for Cockermouth or Aspatria or Workington or Whitehaven. But he was more or less attracted to Wigton.

We can run three teams easily. During the holidays when the students are at home, you can quite easily get four out. We won the Cumberland Cup for the third time in succession last season and we won the sort of second team championship which is whereas you've played a league throughout the season, when the top teams play off and then you have a semi-final and a final – the second team won that for the second time in three years, and they were runners-up last year. They won the Blaydon Knock-out which is a Sunday competition openly played and where you play with fifteen men from a pool of, say, twenty and you play ten minutes each way. They won that last year, I think for the second time in succession. And then we were victorious again in our Sevens and runners-up at Workington Sevens. I think we won the Dumfries Sevens this year. It's difficult to keep track. Nowadays they have access to training any night. They can go up to the Rugby field and train themselves any time of the week at any time, or they can go to a class on a Monday night where they can sort of do the heavy stuff, like weight training, two-hour session there down at Carlisle Tech. College. We have access, or we had access, to a gym last year on a Tuesday night where they can turn up and do their training themselves, not with an instructor on a Tuesday but with a P.T. instructor on a Monday. He works out schedules for them and training programmes, weight programme, that's the heavy stuff on a Monday. That's John Wood at Carlisle Tech. The main training is on a Thursday whereas general fitness training is reasonably light, ready for the Saturday's game. And they're coaching for about an hour there – you know, a two-hour session. But we are trying to get some training lights on this next season to do a little bit more outside. We improve our fixture list every year. We try to get better teams every year, sort of to execute the poorer teams, I think that's the word, or draw them down to second team standard.

I got married in 1960 and my father and I worked out the plans for this small bungalow which is next door and unfortunately he died.

We'd just made the lintels for the windows and the doors and he had a heart attack and he died on the street. And I was left with this problem of bashing on. My brother was a joiner so we were alright there. So we made a start and eventually we built this bungalow next door. At that time I was looking round for a house in Wigton, when I knew I was going to get married, and I couldn't find anything sort of suitable. I hadn't any money and no access to any either, and I couldn't find one. And I tried for planning permission at Waverton and that fell through. Fortunately this farmer had another field up here and there was only this house next door to us and one further down the hill that was standing up here. And Sheila and I came up here one day and we had a look at it and we thought, well, what a marvellous spot to build. So I got this planning through on it and I built it. And the farmer came along to see me and he said, Would you like to buy the rest of this land further down the road? Well, I said, I certainly would like to buy it but I haven't got a penny, please go and sell it. So he asked John Wills if he would come up and John built two houses there and then I thought – we had our David then – and I thought, well, if ever we need a larger house . . . I did a six-week stint on the motorway as a labourer up at Penrith to try and get some money together to buy this piece. And I bought this plot about seven or eight years ago. I enjoyed working on the motorway. I work every summer. I've worked on demolition, I've been a pipe-layer, I've been on dams and these sort of things.

I like to mix with different blokes. They thought I was a jailbird when I was on the motorway at Penrith. We had a student coming round – he must have been doing a thesis or something on motorway labourers and there was this chap from Keswick and I working together, Geordie, they called him. He was a rough and ready fellow, a big strapping bloke, and we used to work together. And this student came round and we pretended that he was a Hungarian and couldn't speak any English. This poor student, he didn't know what to do with us. He just left us. We kidded him on that we had just come out of jail. It was quite interesting. We mixed with quite a few Scotch fellows. And I remember at that time there was a murderer up in Glasgow on the loose and we got talking about guns and revolvers and these sort of things. And one of them just sort of casually said, Well, if you give me two quid I'll fit you up with whatever you want. And I thought to myself, if I'm mixing with these sort of blokes, I'm not sure what I'm going to do here. One bloke spotted that I was a teacher. I used to take the *Daily Telegraph* to work which was stupid really, I suppose. I didn't want anybody to know what I did for a living. I just said – I had my cards and everything from the County Council – I used to walk in the Education Office and say, Look, can you fit me up with a set of cards? And they would fit me up with a set of cards and I used to just go to them at Penrith and the first time I arrived there, on the first job I tried, I didn't have any cards. So this is where they got a bit suspicious. They said, You must have cards. I said, Oh, my wife's picking them up at the dole office. Alright, you can start working. This lasted for about three or four weeks. I said, I haven't got any cards. And I kept taking this *Daily Telegraph* to work. And this student – he was a Penrith lad. Eventually we used to talk together and he used to mix with them and he said – this was the day before I was leaving – he says, That paper, can I do the crossword? He said, Why do you bring this paper anyhow? I said, I just like reading this. And he says, You're not a labourer. So I told him then. I said, I'm leaving tonight. Come down with us and have a drink. So I asked the foreman to come down as well. And often the foreman asked me to go back and work for him, on different jobs.

It was hard graft. We used to leave here at quarter past six in the morning, go by car to Carlisle, pick the mini-bus up at Carlisle and out to Penrith, down to Ullswater dam, work on the dam down there till eight o'clock at night, set off back again to Carlisle and back to Wigton. I found I was getting home round about ten o'clock. And then trying to get a pint in. And then going to bed at half past ten – and the same for six weeks. But I was looking for money, you see. I just felt as if I didn't want them to know I was a teacher. I would rather I was just an ordinary guy. Somehow I don't know if teachers are any different – I don't think they are.

And when I built the house I'm in now I did all the labour work to the bricklayer. I just employed one bricklayer on this house. I tell you what – I photographed a house down in Staffordshire and I tried to get it through the local planning, more or less just the same, and they wouldn't accept it. And eventually I finished up with this sort of design, from the outside – I knew what the inside layout was I wanted anyhow. And I got this draughtsman friend of mine to sort of draw up the plans and this is what we eventually finished up with. I started this 18th July 1971 and I finished it 1st May 1972. I've been in a year now. I finished it in ten months, to live in. I mean, the lawns have only been down since November. This is it. I tried to put the best of materials into this one and I think this is big enough for what we want, although I pay too much rates on it. I say that, but I think I can afford them. I hope so anyhow. I have three or four

378

bedrooms upstairs and they can accommodate us quite well as a family house. We've a playroom, dining-room, living-room here, laundry and kitchen and a toilet and drying-room.

I love it around here.

I think if somebody came and said, Here's another fifty pounds a week, I would think twice about moving, for even that much sort of money. Now I'm sort of head of the P.E. department. I have four full-time staff. I guide them along as best I can, and I have about nine part-timers working. I've found that I've just about finished on the Rugby side now, on the playing field anyhow. I think I'm a bit too old for it now. So I'm hoping to push along with this Civic Trust a bit. I think that's a damned good thing. I think basically because seven or eight years ago I was working, sort of sub-contracting, for the demolition man, Fye, who was knocking down Church Street. And I worked for him for six weeks, sort of sub-contracting; buying roofs and flogging the slates off and this sort of thing. And I felt it was a bit of a shame. I mean, there were some lovely buildings up there and there was some lovely stonework. Some marvellous carving in the stonework. And I think this was a start of it. And then I had a sort of an interest in buildings. I think it's taste, and I don't think you can give anybody taste either. You can't breed taste into people. I think you've either got taste or you haven't. I mean, quite a lot of these architects at present, I think they're way out. They have their own ideas but you still can't introduce taste to them."

CHAPTER SIXTEEN
Time Out

The biggest change in the place of leisure is that it has become widely
and generally recognised, as the century has gone on, as something
not only available but desirable, and not only desirable but useful. It
is the useful which would have stubbed the belief of the majority
twenty-five years ago. A man could have his hobby, just, after the
day's work, the allotment and the jobbing about the house but to
consider that an alternative to work – play, pleasure – was Useful to
a life would have been thought lunatic. This is the revolution – that
leisure brings fulfilment. The majority of people in this country have,
over the past three generations, approached the area of demands once
cordoned off for the exclusive use of the well-born and wealthy: what
has happened is not so much change as spread.

Previously though the poor could have hobbies, it was the better
off who had pastimes and the well-off who had "other interests", while
the wealthy cultivated their minds and bodies: today more and more
people see ways of aspiring, sometimes comically, sometimes successfully, but the way is open, to the condition of the wealthy. Once only
the very rich – like Mr. Banks who owned Highmoor House – could
afford to travel abroad; now schoolchildren from the junior school
swarm over the Continent in coach-loads: once, seventy-five years
ago, working men would fish for food; now, like their richer pre-
decessors, they confess to fishing for "relaxation" – another word
which would have been thought wicked in the world of work before
the First World War.

Once only the wives of the very wealthy took it on themselves to
dare to enjoy company outside the domestic compound: now working
wives such as Mary Reeves enjoy and organise a range of leisure
activities at the British Legion. Horses are now for fun, not the
plough. And superimposed on these obvious expansions are the impact
of the motor-bike and the motor-car (one only in Wigton in 1900 –

approximately one thousand five hundred now), and the wireless, television, the gramophone, libraries, night classes, clubs, sports, back gardens. A curious fact is that though drinking is said to be on the increase, the number of pubs in Wigton, with a more or less static population, has dropped from about thirty-nine to thirteen (if we include the two big clubs). And around the town the houses of the rich – such as Greenhill, a mile away on the south side, built by Duddings, the solicitor, with an upstairs landing the exact length of the nave of St. Mary's church – have been turned into hotels and motels catering especially for weddings and functions from the town. The churches themselves have fewer attendants today than at any time in the century. By your works, the Bible says, ye shall know them. Increasingly this century in this country people wish to know themselves and be known by their play – by the time they take out of time taken for earning.

Homing pigeons and coal-miners are a combination which is irresistible to symbol-seekers – the men under the crust of the earth, digging black minerals while their grey-white birds fly scores, hundreds of miles often across the sea, coming back to the little lofts in the villages above the pits. Wigton, too, has had a Homing Society since the beginning of the century. Jeff Bell joined it in 1917.

We talked at his loft down in Birdcage Walk. Other lofts were round about. The birds wheeled and swooped in formation above us, like squadrons of tiny aeroplanes under remote control. The full breasted chuckle-cooing and the scuffle of movement came from inside the loft – a large shed with a porch and entrances for the birds. Other pigeon men joined us as we talked. It was a summer evening – not hot but warm enough to sit out. In 1917, Jeff Bell joined the Boys' Club.

"There were not a lot of members, maybe about fifteen, I should think. Of course, in them days I just can't remember how many, you know, but I know there was a lot of lads such as myself and Tom (my brother). We used to fly in what was called the South End Club and they had a lot of adult members – Pattison lads and a lad called Storey. There were Hill's boys, you know joiners, and there was Blair's lads, West Street. All round that area everybody had a small loft, not a lot of pigeons but small lofts and we used to race from about a hundred and fifty mile. A shilling a bird. But the big club, well, Willy Wallace would tell you more about that because he was a real goer, he's been an old member and of course he's eighty now. But I can mind Ellwoods and Bob Gate and Willy Wallace and Sinton lads

381

and Fishers. Fishers used to play on here as a matter of fact and Bowmans and Mathison Johnston. I can mention quite a few which have always been interested in pigeons, you see.

We lived in 17 West Street then, past the Drill Hall, and we had a garden and we used to put the pigeons top of the garden. We made a loft. And it's bred in the loft a pigeon with the homing instinct. They reckon they were first started in Greece but I don't know and nobody knows how they do it because Wigton birds, well, four of them are about four hundred and fifty nine mile this week, but they don't know how they get back. They have a very good memory, a pigeon, a very good one. But of course, mind, they've to be trained stage to stage you see. But that's how, you see, when they are young birds, when they start flying round a bit, you hod the wing a bit, you know, you start and train them about a week before they start racing. And you go maybe just a mile. You get them used to the basket first, you put them in overnight; the panniers. And you put them in overnight for maybe two or three times till they get used to the basket and then the first toss you give them is about, the first flight, is about a mile. Then they go in stages a wee bit further on and a wee bit further on. Till the first race point about sixty mile, that's the first race point, but between home and the first race point you can give them, we'll say, a dozen tosses, you see. Four mile, seven mile, ten mile and fourteen to fifteen mile and up like that, you see, till you get to maybe twelve mile off the first race. Then they get used to it. They've got to be trained. Food's nothing to do with it but you give them good corn, you know. Some people say corn makes no difference but it does. You've got to give them good food, you know. Especially when they're babies in the nest. You've got to give the old uns good food. This is what I believe in. Some people believe differently. I believe plenty of food when they're in squabs and squeakers you know, and when they're growing they need good food. You've got to watch them. And clean, you've got to keep them clean and that, you know.

You do lose, it all depends on the weather. The weather is a big factor in pigeon flying. If you get good days you get them all back, but you get a bad'n and you'll start to lose them. Well they've all metal rings on, each bird that's in the N.H.U. [National Homing Union] has a metal ring and that metal ring is in a book, comprised of all the metal rings sold that year. It goes to Cheltenham now, it used to be Gloucester, to the N.H.U. headquarters and then they know exactly who belongs to those rings, you see. Each member gets, we'll say, I'll buy thirty, well they are nearly all in consecutive numbers, you know, but if I lost a pigeon, we'll say, and it went into a fellow's loft in London and he reported it to the Secretary, N.H.U., in Cheltenham, he would know exactly who that pigeon belonged to, you see, and he lets you know. Now in the old days you had to send for it, you sent so much, we'll say ten shilling to bring it back again. But nowadays you needn't claim but, if you don't claim within a month the fellow that got that pigeon can claim it. That's how they do. But every pigeon that races has got a metal ring on.

When they go away racing, on the other leg they put a little rubber ring on which has a number and that number is taken down on the sheet. You put all your ring numbers down, you see, your colour, your sex and all their numbers down and that rubber that's on that pigeon is put against it. Now when it comes home and it's in good time and you want to clock it in, you've got a timing clock. There's different kinds of timing clock, well, mine's a Box Clock and you turn a handle. Now that handle when you turn it it prints on a roll of paper the exact time that that pigeon's in. You take the little rubber off the leg, put it in the thimble, I'll show you a thimble, you put the little rubber ring in the thimble like this, shut it, put it in the slot and turn the handle. That's the exact time that that bird has flown in. And at six o'clock, this is Wigton Homing Society mind you, we go and the Master Time, what they call the Master Time, well, that's the main clock you're set off it and you're checked off it. You set them at eight o'clock tonight, all the pigeons are set off at eight o'clock at night with the Master Timer. Now when the bird comes in it's timed in and at six o'clock that night after they're timed in you, he shouts, Get set, and he turns and you turn your clock and it prints again the exact time. And if it's lost or gained, you see, 'cos sometimes the clock'll lose or gain but there's variations, but the Secretary and the Clock Committee they're working to the exact time, the exact velocity. And that's how you know who's won, you know.

This cross-Channel racing from France, they are what are called Federation Races. We race against Carlisle and Brampton and Penrith, and Longtown, and different towns, you see. In the East Cumberland Federation, round about Carlisle, you see. We fly against them. But that's just in the Federation Races which is specified, such as all the Channel racing, you see. You fly against them. If your velocity's better than them, of course, you're alright.

They have been sold for a thousand pounds. It all depends, you see. The people that buys them they just buy them for breeding purposes and sell the youngsters off them, you see. Mind, I wouldn't

383

like to give a thousand for one. But a good one would, they have made a thousand pounds.

I come here of a morning, every morning, and I let my old ones out and I clean the young birds and the old ones out. I don't let my young birds out, not till night. Every night. Aye. Every night. During racing seasons but closed season, when they're not racing, well I come down at night and maybe let them all mix; they just run about in the full loft. But now they're mated, you see, the old birds are mated, the young birds are separated from these ones, they're mated and you raise them to eggs or youngsters, whichever you think's the best for them. But the youngsters, some mates them up but I don't think you should.

You could put in three hours a day easily. Aye. That's when you're racing. More than that. It's a hobby itself. The prize money, well, we've a good little club and the prize money is pretty good, it's twenty-one pounds a race. But that consists of a pound a point, you see. If you win you get six pounds, if you're second you get five, fourth, three – four, three, two and one pound you see. Of course you have pools as well and you pool your pigeons; they are up to two and sixpenny pools, penny pool and sixpenny pool. This is in just the local races. But when water races, Channel racing, long distance, well, you can go up to a one pound pool. And of course you can fly in specialist clubs as well, such as the Social Club, the Cumberland Social Club, and of course the Federation and the Cumberland Combine, and the Vaux Usher. But this year we didn't fly in the Vaux Usher on account of the disease in Carlisle. They wouldn't let us fly. But they do say they are gonna let us have a race further on for our section. We'd a race last week from Leamington – it was two hundred and eighty-seven miles – and they took about five and half hours. There was a velocity of about sixteen hundred and fifty yards a minute, well, that's fifty-five miles an hour. I've seen them do more than that. I have won races over eighteen hundred yards a minute but, of course, that's a tail wind, you see, that's an easy wind. If you get a head wind, well, it could be from six hundred yards, you know. It all depends on the wind and the weather. We've had our share of the prizes. But of course, as I say, it was a lot of years we just flew in the Lads' and we started racing before the Second War in the big Club. And then, of course, when the war come on, Tom and I we both went, you see, and that sort of keeps us back a bit. The Club has twenty lofts now.

The Club costs you three pounds a year membership but the Sweep's the main thing – each member has to sell so many – and they do, they sell very well. That keeps the club going. There's different committees for different things, you know. Clock Committees and, you see, they'll be setting clocks now, you see. Aye, they'll be setting clocks now. There'll be twenty clocks.

It's an expensive hobby; the food is very expensive. I mean, if you want to feed them on decent feed it's at least five pounds a bag. Five pounds a hundredweight. Well, it all depends on how many pigeons but I keep maybe about twenty-four young uns and twenty-four old uns, shall we say, well, that won't last more than five week. Five week. You don't toss it at them, you know, you keep them slim, you know. But it's five pounds a bag. As I say, it's rather expensive but it's a hobby and that's it. If you like them. Old Bob Gate, you know, is an old Wigton fancier. He used to say, Pigeon flying's a disease, and I'm sure it is an' all. Because once you keep pigeons and you're interested you'll always keep them, you know. It's the poor man's racehorse."

All over England, now as in 1900, within at most an hour's drive from the centre of the largest cities, the Hunt goes on. The unspeakable, according to Oscar Wilde, in pursuit of the uneatable – but he was too harsh. Foxes are vermin: ask any farmer with feathers and bones for chickens after a foxy midnight raid. Riding horses over rough countryside is exhilarating. Hunting dogs are an exciting invention, too recent to be cast into the tomb of relics. These three elements together have provided exhilaration and relatively harmless occupation for generations of English men, women and children – and it is to be hoped the Hunt will go on.

Yet, insofar as it represents the sport of the upper classes, it has gathered opprobrium. People in top hats and velvet jackets riding over fields recently ploughed by men in tattered trousers held up by string: all that fever over a pest when the attention paid to real or rather human pestilence was so negligible by comparison. Again and again it is important to go into England's past from the viewpoint of the present – not to catalogue fault and unearth guilt, but to show how far we have come and from what, and how far we must go to emerge from the grip which once was our hand of strength and is now the death clasp of a dying time. To that dying time belonged not the Hunt but what the Hunt stood for: it stood for those who could afford well bred, well groomed, well fed, well dressed, well equipped horses when most of those around them were hard put to afford well dressed, well fed, well equipped children; it stood for those who had days to spend at play when all about were those whose days were drained in work: it stood for privilege and was a token of power.

Barbara Wilson, "Miss Barbara", comes from a family which hunted as "naturally" as other families went hungry: nothing "natural" about either condition but it must be emphasised that seventy-five years ago both were considered by society as a whole – excluding the Radicals, the Socialists and the better Liberals – as perfectly "natural". Horses have always been in the family and hunting has been her sport around and about Wigton for a considerable portion of this century. She enjoys it and takes great care to pursue it thoroughly in all particulars. Now a lone survivor of the age of Jorrocks and the Squirearchy, she is to the countryside, on her immaculately groomed horse in her impeccable dress, a reminder from times past like the Venetian tower which tops Highmoor House where her cousins used to live.

Her father implanted the love of animals, especially horses.

"Father was deafened by the guns at Passchendaele. He went to Canada but had to come back here. He was unable to conduct business. He was always very keen on horses and game birds and things and he used to amuse himself with that. And he rented some fields down the road and he used to operate from that. We had this little field behind the house. Old English game was his favourite. He was very famous. And he hunted. And he used to bring on young horses and that sort of thing. And he was a very good judge of a horse. He used to show a lot of horses. Anything connected with horses he was very interested in. I always had a horse about me, and dogs; he was very keen on dogs, too. He used to have his pointers. He used to shoot a bit.

I started hunting in the school holidays. In those days it was the Cumberland, which was hunted by Sir Wilfred Lawson.

There are fewer packs now. You see, since the motorways have come, such a lot of land has been taken over by the motorways and such a lot of the country has been divided that now in the south, it hasn't happened up here yet, that a lot of the packs have had to amalgamate: so there are fewer now. People were much better dressed before this last war. They were properly dressed then. Now very few people are. Quite a lot of scarlet coats and things about then. There are odd ones now, but not very many.

Now I hunt about three or four days a fortnight. I've only one horse now. So it's what it can do. But it can do more than they could pre-war days because they used to have to hack to the meet, and she gets carted in the horse-box to all the meets, so I think she's able to do a bit more work that way. But anyway I couldn't hack to the meets now because the roads are so slippery and so fast. It's quite amazing to think that one used to be able to ride quite happily in Wigton, get the paper and all that sort of thing, or ride through Wigton to and from a meet. I mean, if you went into Wigton now you'd have had it with all the traffic and the roads so slippery. It's quite amazing.

I don't think any of the people round Wigton were sort of particularly keen on hunting or anything like that. I never knew very many people around Wigton. I never have done. I don't think very many people would have liked that sort of life really, that I would have much in common with. Of course there's always Miss Parkin. She's absolutely fabulous. Rode side-saddle on old Sampson. When Sampson died the last time she rode him she was over eighty and he was about thirty something. They were the most fabulous ages between them. And there was a wonderful old man who lived at Abbeytown, somewhere near Abbeytown, and he and the horse were a hundred and twenty-five between them, but I never saw them. For Miss Parkin it was her complete life, hunting. She wasn't interested really in anything else. She was frightfully knowledgeable, of course, having hunted all her life; she knew the short cuts through everywhere, how to get from A to B and which fences were wired and which you could jump. She was a marvellous person. She was awfully good to the young when they went out. She looked after them and was very kind – after you got over the initial fright of the sight of her. She was rather formidable. My people had known her all their lives. She and my aunt were friends. I always knew her. I found her a bit terrifying when I was young but afterwards I found she was very very nice. She was very human.

I don't hunt with the Farmers now. Ever since my brother took the Cumberland over, he took the Cumberland over in 1956 when he came out of the Army, and I've always hunted with the Cumberland since then because I haven't enough horses to hunt with both. And we've had some very good runs on that side of the country. John Brockbank's got the hounds now. When my brother went down to Dorset in 1966, John Brockbank took the hounds over and they're at Westward now. We hunt the west side. So I think the west country sort of people roughly, Wigton, Caldbeck, then we would go over to Castle Inn, to Bridekirk and sort of skirt along to Gilcrux and down to the sea. But we don't hunt near the sea very much except occasionally we have foot meets down there. That's roughly the area. Then down to Wigton, Wigton down to Kirkbride on that side and then gradually we moved over to the sea, but we didn't hunt below Wigton very much because it isn't ridable.

It's very good on the fells. We had some very good days on the fells. We meet a lot up round High Ireby and round that way. I think it's a super bit of the country. Binsey Fell is a horrid place to ride over but on a fine day it's lovely. It usually isn't fine. Been on there in driving rain and snow and fog when you were terrified of letting the person beside you out of sight because you wondered what would happen. Quite sort of scaring sometimes, because, you see, the fog just comes down like that. It's quite amazing. But you know, then it's jolly good out the Cockermouth side by Milston Moor and out that – Isel and round there, it's very good. It's more unspoilt than this side of the country. You seem to get round it better. We've made the country pretty good to get round. We've put up an awful lot of hunting wickets every year and it makes it possible for Bobby Hudson, who is now hunting the hounds, to get round quite well. It isn't much fun if every time you come to a wicket you find it wired up and you've to get off and unwire it and almost do a major repair when you put it back again. But there aren't very many people hunt with the Cumberland now. We're just a small crowd but we all enjoy it very much.

There's Mrs. Fisher, she lives at Crags near Cockermouth, but she's in London most of the time. She's up occasionally during the hunting season. And there's quite a lot of farmers but the backbone of the Cumberland hunt are the Watson family. They're absolutely marvellous. They're from Cunningarth. They give us the most wonderful opening meet every year and Mr. Watson carts the hounds about and the hunt horses to all the distant meets and his lorry brings them back again. I think it's absolutely fabulous the amount he does for the hunt. And of course his daughter comes out hunting quite a lot and his man with some of their horses and they're the absolute backbone of the hunt. We're most terribly lucky to have such supporters.

The committee are mostly farmers, nearly all farmers; there are a few exceptions, of course, but they're mostly farmers that live all over the country we hunt in. And they're awfully good. I can't think how in all these years they've managed to keep it going but we always seem to. It's absolutely wonderful. Now we've got a sheep fund that is helping rather well. We buy so many ewes every year – but don't buy them every year but we have so many ewes which are constantly being replaced, and then so many farmers take them, the ewes, and run them with their own flocks, and then when the lambs are sold in the auction, the money that the lambs made, the price, is put into a hunter cap and then we get what the lambs have made. It's absolutely marvellous. It's put us on our feet really. It was jolly good these people taking these sheep and running them, isn't it? All they get out of it is their wool. Some people take up to about ten ewes each.

Pre-war you could more or less jump any fence and you were quite safe but now you've got to look if there is any wire about and that's been the biggest curse for hunting. It was coming on before the last war but since farming has got more intensified as it is now there's barbed wire everywhere and of course these attested cattle, that put an awful lot of barbed wire up. Oh yes, you don't go cross-country like you used to. You've to go from wicket to wicket really. There are some places where you can jump quite a lot but very little now compared to what we used to do."

Of course, people make a mockery of theories when you are close up to them; which is why most revolutionaries need the seclusion of a library – testing their ideas in the mumble-jumble of everyday life would be very distracting – and "Miss Barbara" is generally liked: I'm not aware that her owning a large house and going out to hunt is resented nowadays. I'd guess most people would think it a pretty tough option, caring for all those rooms and riding a horse on the fells on wet days. It is as if – not that the world has passed her by – but the sting has been withdrawn by time and change. Power is no longer on the hunting field: and new wealth turns to skiing and motor-boats and deep-sea fishing as well as hunting.

Something which has grown in popularity has been Rugby. This is nationwide. It seems to me significant that when the new Rugby club came to be built it was not inside the town but on the edge of it, beyond the school and a road of private houses, and the place itself is a mini country club. And, as we saw with David Pearson, the Rugby club has become the focus of a great many men's private energies.

In any community of this size in England, since the Twenties, there have been an increasing number of organisations and societies. Craft societies, sporting societies, institutes, choirs, circles, committees, for men, women and children. And one of them was the Anglican Young People's Association – the A.Y.P.A. This was started by a vicar of the Church of England and should, to be correct, come in Chapter 18 on religion, but it was always more social than sacred. Clubs are clubs and when I was looking for places to go, I joined the Methodist Youth Club – for the table tennis, the Roman Catholic Club for the socials, the Salvation Army for the "evenings of joy", besides being in the A.Y.P.A. and the Church of England choir.

The A.Y.P.A. was a very gentle affair. It met about six or six thirty and was over by seven thirty or eight p.m., once a week in the Parish Rooms with the hard-backed chairs, the holy prints and the piano in the corner. Agnes Sinton and her husband Fred did a great deal for it when I was younger; Agnes, who was training to be a confectioner when she first joined, briefly described its fairly gentle progress.

"I was in the Church youth club – the A.Y.P.A. – and we used to have our dances and things like that. We used to go to the Drill Hall on a Friday night and sometimes we used to go to the County at Carlisle with a friend from work on a Saturday night. But I think the A.Y.P.A. took up most of my time from when I joined. I wasn't regular at church. I went to Sunday School but my father, he was a Communist – it wasn't that he stopped us, but I think you pick up what your parents do, and I didn't go to church. I remember going quite a bit when my grandmother used to take me, my mother's mother, Mrs. Peacock. She used to take me. They were – they had always been big church people. My grandfather was a sidesman, and I think my grandmother thought it was terrible that these two little girls never were taken to church, and I think she made my mother send us to Sunday School. That was all; if my grandmother took me to church.

At that time the A.Y.P.A. really was thriving. We used to meet on a Friday night. One week we would have a speaker, someone to give us a talk, and then the next week it would be either dancing or quizzes or a game, something like that. And we used to go to Carlisle A.Y.P.A. once a year for their birthday party, and Maryport, and then they used to come to us. And we used to put a concert or a play on every year in the Parish Rooms. We used to have a trip on a Bank Holiday, round the Lakes, or Morecambe, and we used to end up in a pub somewhere for the night. Yes, it was very good."

Her husband, Fred Sinton, has transferred his energies into the Rugby club, where he is one of the twenty who keep it going.

In a sense, the leisure of each contributor so far in this chapter has been predictable, from the working man with his pigeons to the school teacher running the clubs they once enjoyed themselves, and the lady of means out hunting. John Dixon is a farmer, one of the Dixon clan which crops up all about Wigton, brothers and cousins farming and connected with farming; but at the outset, when his father tenanted a small farm, John Dixon could be seen driving a cart, delivering milk around the village every morning. He went to the village school, left when he was fourteen – "at one o'clock on the day" – and has never lost his local touch, drinking locally and so on: at a time both building up the farm enormously, hunting and owning a string of racehorses. Just before I went to talk with him, the Queen Mother's favourite jockey had been round his stables (eight horses).

He began by hunting while playing truant from school and joining in on the milk pony. He hunted with the Cumberland Farmers, the pack which is next to Miss Wilson's hunt.

"All the country's wired up now, with attested cattle and all this. You could have some great days when I was young. You could go over the country and jump hedge for hedge in those days where you can't now. It's mostly road work now. Trotting up and down the roads. It isn't the same today. I never go now. I just maybe go to the house meet, put an appearance in. Still interested. It's very well, financially, our hunt. We make a lot of money every year. We have this big barbecue every year. We had eighteen hundred people there this last year. At Howrigg. We had it two years here. Two very successful years. It's been on about nine years. It's a big concern. It's taking a lot of organising, but it still goes well.

There would be fifty to sixty riders when I started, when Crofton Hall was on the go. There used to be the fox earths in Crofton Hall. Fox earths – they had them made and the foxes used to go in them and they used to put the flag over the end and then they knew where they were for when they had the meeting at Crofton. And all horses used to line up around these fox earths, and they used to put the terriers in and off the fox went up the park. And the sports set off. There was a big following then – Miss Parkin used to go – they were good days; real good days.

We got the milking over in the morning, the stock fed, and then it was after tea job. You were usually back maybe four or half past and stuck into your work again, and you didn't mind if you worked all night as long as you'd had your day's hunting. Well it's only on a holiday they might get forty to fifty today. Like on the Bank Holiday in January and Christmas holidays, but a lot of cars today follow them; they'll follow in their cars today mostly. There's no sons coming into the job at all. They're more interested in tractors and fast cars today. With my own boy, John, well, he rides the racehorses, exercise and the gallops, but he wouldn't go out hunting. He's never been to a hunt. We turned to racehorses after the war – one or two good point-to-points, and we started to breed.

I've quite a few now that we've bred. I used to just go along and buy cheap and bring him home and hunt him a bit and then maybe go point-to-point and then race him after that. It's quite interesting. If you'd come today, we've had an interesting man here today. A man who rides all horses for the Queen Mother and trainer. He just left an hour I should think before you came. He was up here on holiday and so he's been all round our horses today. The Queen Mother has fourteen horses, he said.

That one in that photo – I bought him at Wigton Auction at the horse-sales for about forty-nine pounds. Well, that day he won. He knocked the last hurdle out but nevertheless he went on and won. He won two hurdle races and two flat races I think. Them's the kind I used to like to ride, the cheap ones, and make them. He was in the milk cart before I got him. And there's this one here, this is Victory Man – again, he just beat a short head on the neck in the Topham Chase at Liverpool. Just come in between there. That's my daughter leading Joyful's Daughter. She won at Carlisle. We're breeding from her now. This is another one, half share with this lady – she came from Ulverston. She won quite a few races for us. These two won the first race and the last race after the war in the point-to-point at Rosebank. And this is a horse of Robert Tinniswood's, Oil Chimes, we trained him for him.

It just had to be the spare time for the horses though. Exercise was done at night in the spring of the year when the point-to-point was coming round. I had to just do it then. This is me at Rosebank on a one called Singing Rover. I finished second that day, but it hit this jump here and came on its knees, but I managed to stick on and finished second that day. It had bad legs so that the only way we could make it ready for a race, we used to take it down to Skinburness and swim it in the sea. We won at Carlisle. As soon as we went onto the beach it used to go straight into the sea. It was a smashing swimmer. And this horse, he won us a few – he was a real good horse this, but he broke his leg. This is my first winner; it was trained up at Clifton Hill. This is young Harry Glaister. He was killed off one of those horses. He won that day – a horse called Irish Gift. He won at Cartmel that day. You can see Joe Benson walking in behind there. I think I sent Joseph with them that day. We were at Hexham. A grand boy was Harry – he was just like one of the family. We broke our hearts that day. This was the day he was killed – he was winning easily and he was coming into the last, maybe, a young horse, and he just took the wing instead of the hurdle. You were a good friend of his and all, weren't you? I remember that. He would have made the tops. And you knew him, he had asthma, and he was at our place about three months and he lost it altogether. He was just like one of the family. This was one, we bred this one here, it was my mother's horse, they called him J.M.D., they called Father John Matthews Dixon so we named it after his initials. And he's winner at Ayr this day. This one, Brief Sparkle, he won – a friend of ours, he was a butcher in Lockerbie, Jackie Fawcett, he won quite a lot of races.

I do it just for my own pleasure; I don't bet. I just enjoy the job, that's all. I think I've maybe gone rather more onto the racing side because of the changes. I should think I would still have hunted on if the country had been right. But there's no pleasure running up and down roads with horses."

The hunting instinct is still powerful and it would appear most powerful of all in those who really know about and care about the animals they so cheerfully set out to kill.

Mr. Lightfoot is a farmer whose farm has been captured by the town. When he was a boy, there was a mile, largely of open fields, between himself and the church. Gradually by Council and by private buyer, the fields have been taken and I spoke to him in the week in which he had sold the last fields and the farm itself to the developer who was planning a new private estate. Like John Dixon, Bill Lightfoot went to a village school, cycling up to Bolton with Miss Bell. Like John Dixon, he had hurried through his farm work in the early morning to snatch a day's hunting. He was more one of the lads, I'd say, than John Dixon and revelled in the traditional country slaughter-sports. Shooting was the first sport he mentioned after hunting.

"We used to get partridge. There were hundreds of partridge then; you never see one now; like, there *is* partridge but you never see many. They've done away with all the weeds they used to feed on with this weed-killer, such as red shank, and all the weeds that used to grow, they spray them all now. There isn't any seeds for them to feed on. And we shot pheasants, rabbits, there were dozens of rabbits; and I used to keep terriers.

Do you remember Mott Wiggins? Every Sunday him and me used to go after foxes and badgers. Roundabouts. Just let the terriers in at them. And dig them out. And game-cock fights. We used to go to a lot of them. Used to have them up at Islekirk, at Redhall. I can remember going up to Islekirk with me father and Billy Barnes of Street and Willie Hope that lives at Thursby now, and Robert. And they called in the Sun coming back; there was a bit of a row struck up over these cocks; and Willie Hope says I'll fight you for twenty pound any time – till Billy Barnes of Street. So the fellow that clipped them out, they called him Jack Lowman, so they went in that stable there and they clipped two out, and there was an old body called Mrs. Watson in the Sun there, and they just pushed all the chairs and they had a fight in the kitchen. Forty-four or five years ago. I liked a cock fight.

There's a fair bit goes on still. I'll tell you who has a full set of spurs, he had two or three pairs, and boxing gloves as well – you know, the one with the rubbers on when they used to be practising so that they couldn't kill one another – Joe [illegal]. There's still a lot of wild duck. But on Sundays Mott and me went for badgers. Caldbeck way. I've seen us go that way but we used to go where the earths was, Crookdale and Aikbank, that old railway bank at Aikbank, come through by Blaithwaite, used to go there. An old pipe there at Aikbank, once got four badgers out of it. Fletcher Gale was with us that day. Terriers would bait them. Then we would club them. If you got a terrier that was keen it came off worst. Awful big claws on them. A good baiting terrier, the badger used to follow it out. Went to Speedgill one night, Mott and me, and there was a badger in a hole there, and it was sitting on a flag, on like a slab, and him and me let the bank away, and we watched them performing. We could see them fighting. It was on a bank like that. We just bashed away with spades and let the lot down. I would like to have had a camera. The terrier was playing it round the corner where it was sitting. Every time the terrier put its nose round – what a film you could have got. It was the only one that ever I saw actually inside the earth. I took the terrier away in the finish and shot it. Thirty-nine pounds' weight. We just buried them. Never bothered."

Fishing is the most expected country sport although there are thousands of fishermen in English towns and cities. Where I live most of the year, near the middle of London, there's a heath which has its ponds stocked by the local council and little boys sit in patient rows as they do in the country. There were so many fishermen to

394

choose from that in the end I decided to stick to someone already in the book, Mr. Postlethwaite.

"Fishing, some of the happiest days of my very young life in my younger days were spent in a little village called Calder Bridge. We roamed the woods, we chased rabbits, we looked for hens' nests, we went fishing. My grandfathers, both of them, my father, my uncles all fished, and I couldn't avoid fishing. My first fishing-rod was a little fir tree which my brother cut down for me after much pestering from me. My first fishing-line was a piece of what they used to call sugar string, very fine white string. And my first trout was caught in Calder Bridge, standing on a rock, a little boy of about ten years of age. But don't get me talking about fishing or I'll be here all day.

The most peaceful sound in the world is the sound of a running stream. Worries just leave you. That's why I used to fish. I've seen me come back from school in a furious temper, could have fallen out with anybody in sight, put the rod in the car and gone fishing and forgotten all about school and about naughty children and all about irate headmasters and all about rows – wonderful. Well, I've fished in the Waver and the Wampool. I think I even fished in the Wiza once or twice. Very tiny streams of course. Like everything else, once you've achieved something in life you want something a bit better or a bit bigger. In fishing you catch a one-pound trout, you want to catch a two-pound trout. You catch a lot of sea trout, you want to catch a salmon. I'm afraid I've caught them all now. My fishing started in this area in the Waver, the Wampool and the Wiza, some wonderful trout-fishing, and then these days I've moved further afield. I catch bigger and better fish so I go fishing up to Canonbie now. There is sea trout and salmon, but it's a wonderful mind easer is fishing.

Nothing ever happens in this world unless somebody does something. Things don't just happen and even fishing you've got to make things happen in the sense that if you want fishing at Coal Mire, which was a derelict pond due to them excavating gravel for Kirkbride aerodrome, which filled up with water – Dr. Jones had the idea of putting trout in. So we worked on it and we put trout in. And then we go and catch them. Take them out again. Some people might think we're fools, I suppose. The fishing has changed in the sense that man changes fishing. And the big changes in the local rivers is this cleaning them out. You see, these rivers have flowed for goodness knows how many hundreds or thousands of years and once man interferes with them he ruins them. Do you know that they cleaned out the River Waver from Waverton downwards and the first thing that happened was the great flood came and it wiped out banks down towards Waverbridge which it's utterly incredible to see. And it's simply the result of man's interference, thinking that he could make the rivers flow where he wanted them and the river will not flow where man wants it to, it will flow where it wants to flow. And you must leave vegetation on banks of rivers. The Waver was a series of corners and holes and hiding places and roots under the bank and there used to be trout down there and the trout aren't half as big now as what they used to be from what I can gather. Lots more people fish these days, too. There's more money about, there's more leisure time. It used to be almost a gentleman's pastime at one time but it isn't any more. Everybody fishes – well, everybody can afford to fish nowadays."

For most people, though, the great revolution in pleasure has come through the bicycle, the motor-bike and the motor-car. Charlie Allardyce, who works down at the factory, would regard himself as fairly typical. His mother would walk or go by bus: he biked or went by car.

"Well I suppose we all thought we were going to get a new bike for Christmas every Christmas, but this didn't happen. I know the first bike that I had, I bought it off Roland Richardson, cost me five shillings, an old red racer with low slung handlebars. No brakes, of course. It hadn't any mudguards on. So – I was left school, or just about leaving, I would be about fourteen when I got this red racer, and of course I wasn't allowed out on it until I got brakes fixed up and one thing and another. So just down at the bottom of Union Street there was a chap called Salkeld Irving, he used to fix bikes, so I took it along to Salkeld with bits from other bikes and one thing and another – nothing new was put on, of course, it was just a make-up job – we managed to get an efficient brake – so I was allowed out with the bike. And then gradually I bought myself a couple of mudguards off somebody and fixed those on myself – couldn't afford to put it into a repair shop and have it done up or anything like that. So that's how I got my first bike, and I kept that bike for years and years and years. Most of the other lads had bikes. Nearly all tried to get racers, three speeds of course was the thing. If you had a bike with a three-speed on, oh, you were the tops. You could fly past anybody else because you were changing gear. We used to do a fair bit of cycling, get down as far as Silloth, up to Keswick, two or three of us, just on a Sunday. It was the only way you could get – we hadn't the money to go on buses in them days. So I suppose the bike was the only way of getting about."

It also led him to an interest in hound trailing – a peculiarly local sport. Specially bred hounds, rather like fox-hounds, run, following an aniseed trail over a ten-mile course, often in the hills. There's betting on it, but not very high: the interest and excitement is in the owning, training and racing of the dogs. With my father, Charlie Allardyce had a lot to do with building up the Wigton Club in the Fifties.

"After I came out of the Army, and I think I had about seventy to eighty pounds gratuities – Army gratuities to come out with – and that's what I bought my first car with. A real old banger it was. 1936 model. And I managed to keep it on the road, and then of course, wages got a little bit better after the war and with saving a little bit and doing a lot of repairs to the car yourself, then I managed to keep changing. It always cost money when you changed. I never changed the other way where I made money out of a vehicle. I always had to add money too. It just went on from there till you managed to get a new one. Anyway I bought myself the car, the old banger, after the war because it was about seventy pounds gratuity I had and all the lads I think who were let loose after coming from the war, we used to collect in the pubs. I think the favourite pub was the Lion and the Lamb and I suppose it was with going to the pub that I got on with the hound-trailing lads. And I didn't keep any hounds myself – not at that time anyway but I got interested in it. I was in big demand, of course, because I had a motor-car. Anybody was that had a motor-car at that time. I never thought about girls or anything like that so any pocket money I had to spend – I didn't go dancing very much or sweethearting – I used to spend my money on the car. So I got into the hound trailing. And oh I was interested for a number of years in trailing.

Your father was in the Black-a-Moor then of course. It more or less became the centre. Your dad was interested in hound trailing and with him having the facilities of a room where we could meet, I think gradually the lads from other pubs that were hound trailers used to

397

come down to the Black-a-Moor and it was then decided that we would form a club. Because there were chaps with hounds that had no means of getting them to these trails. I remember Robinson lads, they had quite a good success with their hounds. They used to run about in an old motor-bike and side-car and, of course, they bred puppies, they bred hounds, and their friends would get them and this is just how it snowballed. So two or three of us got together – your dad, myself, and we decided to form this club. And we used to run buses from Wigton till as far as Moresby and Egremont, Shap, Penrith, two or three times a week and on Saturday afternoons, evenings and Saturday afternoons. And we got up to somewhere about a hundred and fifty, two hundred membership. It used to be two and sixpence, the trip on the bus wherever we went, and we had a thriving little club. I was the Treasurer, your dad was the Secretary, we had a committee and we did things right. We banked all the money and we paid by cheque and it was all done on the up and up. We promoted trails ourselves. I think this was a big boost for Wigton – for trailing like. This is – in this little bit of this Wigton and Aspatria area – as this was known for hound trailing. It took a little bit of money to put a trail on – you had the insurance, advertising, you had the trail mixture to pay for, the trailers – the chaps who laid the trails, they had to be paid so much, and it took I think about forty pounds in those days to make a trail. Of course you had the prize money as well. This was a big slice, about fifteen or sixteen pounds prize money. Anyway, we made money out of this and we had a thriving little club. And Wigton was well known for hound trailing at that time. We had some decent dogs in the town and they were winning. Of course, people follow a winning hound and for quite a number of years we really enjoyed our hound trailing. There would be thirty to forty dogs in the town.

Your father and I had one actually. Yes. It must have had a wooden leg. It wasn't much good. We never had any success with it. Neither of us had the facilities for keeping this hound so we had a chap who used to look after it for us. I used to chip in to buy the food for it and we used to take it to trails. I don't know whether it ever got round a trail, never mind won. However, that didn't last long. But we were still interested. I don't know really how it died off. I think as people got better off and the years went by, people decided that they would have their own motor-cars and gradually the buses got thinner and thinner, there wasn't as many travelling on the buses, and it just folded up at the finish. But it's still going strong, this hound trailing, though not as strong as what it was in those days.

Well, as I say, the first car I ever bought from a farmer from Abbeytown. This was in 1947. It was a Flying Standard, ten h.p., black and blue, and it used to shine like a shell. In those days they used to put a really good coat of paint on. It was really good. And when it was polished it was really good, it used to shine. It was an old rattling old thing, but however it used to get us from A to B. I just picked it up how to repair it, etcetera. I used to get these *Practical Motorists* and things like this and instant tips. I couldn't afford to put it in a garage for servicing. I had to do all this myself. But I did garage it, yes. I put it down in Mason's Garage. I think it cost me about two and six a week. I hadn't a separate garage – it was in with all the rest. I remember if you used to come in late of a night time, about ten o'clock at night, you maybe had to shift about half a dozen cars to get your own in. It was as bad as that. Not that there were many cars, but it was just the way that people opened the doors, put their car in, shut the doors, didn't think anybody else was coming in after them. Anyway, any maintenance that had to be done, I had to do myself. It was nearly always going wrong, but luckily it never let us down when we were going to trails. But it did used to give us a bit of trouble. I think this is where I learned to maintain the car myself. I used to take the cylinder head out and put new piston rings in, decarbonise it, set the points up and the plugs up, renew the brakes – linings, things like that. It just had to be done by myself because I couldn't afford to put it into the garage to have it done.

Anyways, how I got shot of that one, we were going to a trail at Crosby, just out west, just beyond Aspatria there, and your dad was with me actually, and we thought we would have a drink at the Stag's Head before we went down to the trails. And we saw this big black Standard. It was a twenty h.p. car standing outside. So we went in. I knew the chap that was inside, that owned the car. How's it running, you know? Oh, not so bad. He says, It's a bit too big for me. I'm thinking of getting rid of it. I could do with something smaller. Of course the first thing I asked – How many miles do it do to the gallon? My own was doing about thirty-five, thirty-six and Oh, he says, it will do twenty-five. I said, Never. Yes, he said, it will. Anyway, we had a straight swop. There and then. He says, Well, I could do with something less – I says, I could do with something bigger. I could get more people in to take them to hound trails. So log books were swopped the next day and the next time I saw him at the trail meeting I said I'll bring my log book, you bring yours. Just a straight swop. No money changed hands at all. So I kept that one for a little while. It was a grand old beast. You know, hound trailing, we used to go to the half-way line and see what hounds were in front at that stage. And with this great big 20 h.p. Standard I had, we used to be right way to the half-way line and see what was in front, dash back, put a few shillings on what we thought was still going to be in front when it crossed the tape, nine times out of ten of course we were wrong, the thing maybe had broke a leg or something, I don't know. But it was useful for taking people to trail. And I think about this time the buses were tapering off – the club was tapering off. At that time people were starting to buy cars of their own. And I used to take a few of the lads that couldn't get anywhere with the hounds, I used to take them around in the car. I think this is when I really got interested in hound trailing. Wanting to own a dog of my own. Anyway, to go back to motor-cars, I would keep that for a while. Gradually I would save a few pounds up and I got a better car, and then I got a better still, then I got a better still.

I haven't had a terrible lot as cars go, in that time. Maybe about ten. Since 1947. I remember the first one that I bought new was in 1960. It was the very first time that I was able to buy a brand new car. It was a Vauxhall Victor. And it cost me eight hundred and twenty pounds to put it brand new on the road. Well, I had worked up to the point that the car that I had traded in to buy this new one brought me in somewhere about four hundred and fifty pounds, and I'd saved a little bit of money, so I bought this new car. I kept that one for six years and I sold it for two hundred pounds. So I lost a hundred per year on that car. Well, I weighed myself up and I thought now I've kept this car for six years and I've lost six hundred pounds, and I've finished up with a car that's only worth two hundred. So I thought to myself if I can, in the future, I'll change my cars more frequently and I'll perhaps not lose as much. So this is what I've done ever since. I've ran a car for eighteen months to two years, and changed – bought a new one again, and perhaps I've had something like a hundred and fifty to two hundred to pay every time I've changed. It's still costing me somewhere in the region of a hundred pounds per year but at least I've got a new car all the time. I found that it didn't cost me as much for repairs, I wasn't needing new batteries and new tyres and things like this. So that's just the motor-car.

Now I've a Ford Cortina. Well the buying price of one of those now is twelve hundred. I used to be a Vauxhall man after I had the first two Standard models, then I bought a Vauxhall Viva. Then I had a Vauxhall Wyvern, and I had a Vauxhall Cresta, and then I bought, in 1960, the Vauxhall Victor new. After I sold that I bought another Vauxhall Cresta and then I changed. I went on to a Renault – French make. I kept that for about eighteen months and then I bought a Standard Triumph, then an MG 1100 and now I have the Ford Cortina. This is the first Ford I've had.

I think perhaps why I've kept on with motor-cars and why I bought one so soon was at that time I had no intention of getting married. I thought I'd stick with my mother. And I suppose the other lads that I went to school with, they got themselves married and had a family. They couldn't afford a car. Until now; most of them have bought cars now. But at that time, just after the war, they came out of the Army and they got themselves girlfriends and they got themselves married and started to raise a family, well, they couldn't afford to buy motor-cars. I stayed single, so this is why I was able to buy the motor-cars. But just thinking now, I think most of the lads that I went to school with have cars now."

The most striking thing about this chapter so far has been to see how far the leisure world was and to some extent is a man's world. There is still the very very strong tradition of women staying at home in the evenings, certainly until their families are grown up: before then, the world of Mary Reeves still runs strong – dances, dances and dances with pubs beforehand the new element.

Susan Allen, though, born after the Second World War, could well be seen as typical of a new generation. When I spoke to her she was just finishing at a London college. I had seen her at a pub near where I live in Cumberland, playing the guitar with a large group and singing folk-songs – something which has gone on for some years in England, but in Cumberland and in Susan Allen's generation it is new and on a larger scale than you would anticipate. Her interest in folk began with listening to Joan Baez records: her interest in music was cultivated at the local school. There was the new twentieth-century development of a school orchestra – now there is even a junior school orchestra.

"I was in the school orchestra. I used to play recorder 'cos we hadn't really much woodwind. So I used to play recorder for it. And also the County Youth Orchestra, which used to meet once a month at Derwent School at Cockermouth. Our school, well, we had a clarinet player and a cello then, and our school seemed to supply all the percussion section for the tymps. It was great. I don't know how that worked out, but we always did.

There were various musical things going on which I was also in. Choir, orchestra, recorder group; there was even a folk group started at one time, but it didn't last. Joan Baez, Dylan, that sort. Julie Felix was on the go at that time. But gradually throughout the Sixth Form I became more interested in traditional music rather than the contemporary. And I did get a record-player in the end and I did start buying records. Not American folk. Traditional British folk, English folk. Much more since I went to college because Cecil Sharp House is on the doorstep, the headquarters of the E.F.D.S.S. – English Folk Dance and Song Society – and I go there pretty often. I use the Library. We search for songs and things and go out to ceilidhs and things, go round the London clubs singing . . . the traditional English ones, particularly rural I think. And through that came interest in aspects of English rural life now – dance. At the moment they're having clog dancing lessons at Cecil Sharp House, but he insists on doing the Lancashire tradition and not the Cumberland and Westmorland because it's most people. And he doesn't know anyone in Cumberland who does do the Cumberland and Westmorland tradition. And I've got some dancing clogs made by Joe Strong of Caldbeck and he didn't know anybody, so we're stuck doing Lancashire at the moment. See what happens, anyway.

Most of the songs I get, the best ones are the ones I hear first – I get a much better idea of them than if I just get them straight out of books. And so the ones I have are those I hear around folk-clubs in the first place. When I do go to Cecil Sharp House, I went down and I say, Any books on Cumberland folk songs? Oh, they say, they have massive files on things like Somerset. Come to Cumberland there's about three thousand cards in. There was one book, *Songs and Ballads of Cumberland and the Lake Country,* in fact I found that in a secondhand bookshop in Keswick this last summer – so I got hold of that. But it's mostly written by the local bards. Cumbrians seemed to have tended to do this with the actual folk-songs, the traditional ones, already handed down ones, have got obliterated beneath the ones poets like Robert Anderson have written. And then the Music Hall came and you've got all the Music Hall ones and the other ones tend to have been forgotten, because this area is more cut off perhaps than other areas.

I was at Boltongate Pub at New Year, we went to Boltongate with this girl who plays the fiddle. And we were sitting there talking, and I mentioned some old songs and was trying to sort of see if anybody knew them. And an old bloke turned round – Thou's fishing, aren't thou? But I didn't get very far with that. They like a good foot-stomping chorus song in preference to – traditional songs. Like the Carlisle Club is all Tom Paxton or the Irish ones which always take over any club for chorusing. The best nights we have are up at Ireby, the Sun. It's not an official folk club. It's just more or less a singsong. There's a lot of old people come from Keswick. A bloke called Tom Thompson, I think he comes from Curthwaite, and he had formed a few local folk clubs apparently but he knows quite a lot of the old hunting songs. We get singing some of the old hunting songs. Joe Bowman and all this. And he's taken some traditional tunes, mostly Irish, and puts his own words to them. Cumberland protest songs, one of them, and the other one is 'Working on the county'. It's about a roadman – on the roads. And there's also another song about some-body that used to live up at Sandale. I don't know if you've heard a song called 'Bloody Orkney' which the troops in the last war wrote when they were in Orkney, because there was absolutely nothing and they transcribed that sort of to Sandale because they used to live up at Sandale. And a song called 'Bloody Sandale'. I've got them upstairs, the words, with some gaps but I can fill some of the gaps in, 'cos they sang them again last week. Ireby actually is the only pub I do go up to, because of the singsong. Or if somebody calls for me through the week who has a car, 'cos I haven't, then I will try and persuade them to go up there because I know the regulars. I know the landlord and landlady and the people who come in. But the only other time – sometimes I meet my friend Sandra Fairweather, say once every holiday to have all the crack, to get all the crack and see what's been going on during the term – and we'll go down to the Blackie which happens to be handy for her. And then Thursday nights I go out to Carlisle Folk Club which is in a pub, but apart from that, not so much."

Her mother's generation would go to the cinema at least once, more likely twice in a week, Susan never goes. Her mother's generation would never dream of a day when they could "slip down to the Blackie for a drink" and in her grandmother's day the only women who did that were "gypsies". Susan's friends and contemporaries have cars and in a way she has gone full circle because she now sees the benefits of the place despite being away from it and wants to work nearby. This is a straw in the wind but the great movement, which grew even more powerful this century, that to get on you had to get out seems to be slowing down. This idea of a full life now includes

403

the amenities and local pleasures which Cumberland holds.

For Susan Allen, Cumberland is an unexplored landscape of folk-songs; for Miss Wilson it's well kept wickets and good hunting country; and for Jeff Bell it's pigeons and pigeon men. Others follow their own paths: to Joseph Johnston, Wigton is alive with men who breed budgerigars while for David Pearson (*another* David Pearson) it is marked out by its darts players; and so on. There is more leisure, more time for leisure, and an other-planetary observer might find it difficult to distinguish the leisure from the work, so devoted are people to it.

But still, for most, Time Out is holidays. At the beginning of the century, for Joseph Barnes, painter and decorator, holidays were one-day trips once a year to Silloth, twelve miles away, by wagonette, praying for a fine day. Silloth was the fabled land for thousands of Wigton people up until the 1950s. "Going to Silloth" for Joseph Barnes was going to the fashionable resort, being extravagant, showing your mettle. Silloth was independence as well as luxury. That lasted through childhood and adolescence into manhood. In the Thirties, he began to go to Blackpool for a week – being a bachelor helped, he could afford it, but a great number went then. Blackpool was the seaside, holiday crowds and glamour.

"The reason why I went to Blackpool was that Blackpool always like – this is going back a few years – it always had a big array of stage stars and I like a stage show. Now then, a lot of these people wouldn't leave the London stage to go into the provinces but they went to Blackpool. Of course, the money would be good and that sort of thing. And so there was always plenty to do at Blackpool even if it was a wet week. And so that's why I went there. But as the time went on, of course, I was getting older and Blackpool was getting busier. Wages were just gradually increasing and people were having more holiday and I was beginning to feel that, well, you could hardly walk along the prom without being jostled to death. And then people – the travel firms – were starting talking about tours. So I travelled all over Britain on tours – this is after about 1949, mainly with the Ribble. They put on very good tours. They were just a week's holidays. They arranged everything, and you had your own private coach.

And then folks said, Why don't you go abroad? And I said, I'm going to be patriotic; I'm going to see Britain first. And I've been in, well, I should think there have been some places that have been bypassed, but I've been in the majority of towns in Britain. Then where I was working, the people were talking about going to Switzerland . . . so I thought . . . Joseph, we'll try it.

Then it was coach tours like when I started; like going abroad, and then more recently I got onto the cruises and these Mediterranean cruises, like they really are good. And now I'm off with Trojan Tours – 'In the Wake of Ulysses', it's called, and everywhere *he* went, we're following on."

Into the Greek myth on a trip which, in his youth, would have been dismissed as a dream or a fantasy. "Trojan Tours" – a long way from Silloth.

CHAPTER SEVENTEEN
George Johnston

Leisure has always been in the past the reward of power, wealth and intelligence. Nowadays for those sections of society which can afford it, it has become suspect: even play must have the colouring of work if it is not to be condemned as an over-privileged squandering of assets. And the old age pensioners, the senior citizens, sometimes complain that they have been condemned by society to a life of leisure which they call mere uselessness. For the virtue of work is still extremely widely accepted when other virtues are held only in a token manner. And so there is the paradox. More people have more leisure than ever before; and yet the idea of leisure and the élitism which sustained and defined it has gone. The fox-hunters, the jet set, the metropolitan gambling set, the provincial social-literary gentry, the host of upper-class custodians of our past imprisoned in their great houses by genetics and traditions, the herd of clubmen or the gossip column fodder, the Sloane Rangers – these cliques and claques linger on but in exile from the feeling and chief energy of contemporary life. Only pop stars, sports stars and those who win the football pools enter the general imagination and are accepted in it as people entitled to leisure – and those people are, usually, of working-class background or they claim working-class background and so have the justification of long deprivation to account for their spree of worklessness; but even there, the times steal up on them and you open the daily paper to read that they are opening shops or clubs or whatever; working.

Yet, as was evident in the previous chapter, which was just the tip of the town, the roll-call of hobbies and pastimes, addictions and private passions could have spread up and down the streets until the pages dripped names and preoccupations, became an encyclopaedia of play: footballers, cricketers, bowlers, fishermen, bird-fanciers, dog-fanciers, tropical-fish-fanciers, hikers, cyclists, motor-cyclists, swimmers, nature-lovers, singers, actors; there's a theatre club, there are choirs, there is a new library now – readers, television enthusiasts, gardeners, model-engine-builders, drinkers, card-players, domino-players, musicians – there are several little bands, woodwork enthusiasts, Scouts, Sea Scouts, committee-men, flower-arranging women, photographers, scholars, crossword-addicts, darts fanatics – there are billiard rooms, young farmers' clubs, church clubs, the Civic Trust, and those who like to sit or stand and watch, and though the development of suburbs and the motor-car between them have swept people off the streets after the shops close, there is yet in this as in every English community a densely interwoven thatch of voluntary activities giving great personal pleasure and sometimes social benefits, an unseen seething, a life often lived in greater awareness than work-life or even family life – but yet it is not the Leisure which moated the existence of the privileged classes for so long. For, above all, it does not see itself as a reward for riches or birth – although it often is, in some measure, just such a reward – nor is this leisure an expression of the ease to be enjoyed by those who have succeeded in certain ways (most commonly in the way of outwitting their fellow-men, and getting a living at their expense) and climbed to the top of the masses – though that persists a little here and there – nor is this leisure the sole possession and mark of one class which imposes on itself a certain style and certain duties – better, many would say, if it were – no, the most important distinguishing characteristic of the New Leisure is that it sees itself as work. However enjoyable, useless or far-fetched the activity, however playful even, the leisure is the shadow of the work and marches in step with it: somehow it has to earn its keep – to be felt to be therapeutic, profit-making, or fulfilling. Work is becoming lighter; hobbies more exacting; work less manual, less exhausting, less preoccupying for many – or not preoccupying in a satisfying way; leisure fills out the need for stretching oneself, for endeavour, for testing character – and in this way it begins to assume the characteristics once belonging only to work.

Flosh House stands near the middle of the town. Only fifty years ago it was on the edge of the town. A fine double-fronted nineteenth-century house, large by contemporary standards, local sandstone (the old schools and churches and older houses are all in this soft dark brown stone), in its own grounds, part bought by compulsory council purchase for old people's bungalows. George Johnston, son of George Johnston, son of George Johnston, and father of George Johnston, lives there with his wife Cynthia and their one son. Through the day he runs and works in the large boot and shoe shop which he inherited:

his mother, who lives in a flat above the shop, also works there, so does his wife. Local farmers will have used Johnston's for generations, for hob-nailed thick stiff skin-tearing leather working boots and carpet slippers for the evenings.

George Johnston was born a few years before the Second World War. He tells his own story but to link it to the previous chapter and to the introductory paragraphs at the head of this chapter, a couple of points need to be made.

We spoke in one of the back rooms, a room characterised by numerous and excellent prints of game-birds; the house is full of accumulations, collections of things, easy to characterise as a fortress of middle-class values. Yet George Johnston went to a local school, he is friendly with – not patronisingly but in fact – people of very different levels of income and wealth. His own life, the taste for wines, the love of France, the interest in books, is kept apart and neither isolates nor insulates him from the people in the town who give him his livelihood and with whom he lives in intimate knowledge of past and present gossip and local news.

More importantly, from outside we heard the dogs. He is the leading authority, probably in the world, on basset hounds. He used to show them, now he concentrates on breeding them, advising others and writing about them. The time and attention he gives to what began as an occupation for leisure hours is comparable with the attention given to the shop. The leisure activity has also its profit-making side. In many ways it could be said to demand more intelligence, certainly more patience, more skills more regularly employed than the "real" work in the shop. It is voluntary, self-impelled, independent of worldly need: and yet it matches the work so closely now that it could be called more than the shadow of the work, has become the necessary counterpart, a place for the virtues of work to be exercised freely.

George Johnston is lean, black-haired, weathered, and scrupulous in his talk.

"I was born in 1937 and brought up here in this house. It was built by a family called Pattinson and I don't know the exact date when it was bought. My great-grandfather bought it, exactly when, I can't tell you, but since that time he lived here and then he was followed by his family which included my grandfather. He would have maids. That was before my time but certainly he did have maids. I think he would have a gardener because there is quite an extensive garden.

Gardens and ornamental greenhouses, conservatories, so he possibly had a staff of three or four at that time because there was quite a large family of them. And at that time, well, houses of this size had staff anyway. The first school I went to was the Wigton Infants' School which is just further up the road. I would start there in about 1942 when Mr. Scott was the headmaster and Miss Cameron and Miss Moffat, Miss Steel and Mrs. Lancaster, they were all teachers there then. I would go there until what, five, six years after that and then I moved on to the National School which is immediately next door to this house. Went there until I was eleven, sat the eleven-plus but didn't pass, and then went from there to St. Ursula's School which had just been opened by the Sisters of Mercy Convent. From eleven, I went down after G.C.E. exams, by which time I would be about sixteen; left school and went into the shop for two years.

By this time my father had gone into the shop. He hadn't taken over, my grandfather was still alive. But he was a very old man and it was obvious that somebody was going to have to take over from him because at that time he would be seventy-five or seventy-six. Still active in the shop but, as I say, it was just a matter of time until he had to come out and retire, so my father left the factory and went into the shop. As a child we didn't move far from Wigton at all. My friends came from the immediate neighbourhood. Boys and girls all of the same age and, as I said before, having a large garden with trees and a fairly interesting sort of garden, we were able to play away and not get under anybody's feet. And so all the school holidays we were always in the garden, all the time. Eight, nine or ten of us, all the time.

I was interested in dogs and I think it was a good excuse for him to expand, you could say, his hobby by encouraging me. He had a perfect excuse then for indulging in extra dogs and things. But I was interested so he had to have these things. We'd have another dog show to go to or something like that. There was always something. Always. Bantams and mice, apart from my father giving me them, my grandfather did, too, although he wasn't a breeder as such. He always liked animals about the place and I think was quite happy to see both my father and me showing an interest in these things.

I had been on holiday with my school to Italy and Belgium and Switzerland which I enjoyed and I certainly enjoyed travel. But certainly National Service was the first time away for an extended length of time. We had to register and then a short time after that you got your call-up papers and mine asked me to report to Portsmouth which I thought was a hell of a liberty when there was

Carlisle Castle and the Border Regiment and things like that. So I had to go all the way down to Portsmouth with another boy from Aspatria into the Royal Army Ordnance Corps. We did our basic training at Portsmouth. Looking back on it it was a shattering experience because it was the first time away and certainly the first time in close contact with boys from a different environment to mine – city boys, Glasgow, Liverpool, Manchester, Birmingham which – these boys, of course, formed the majority of National Servicemen. What bothered me most was certainly the lack of privacy, and certainly the city boys were much more mature than I was anyway. I can't speak for the boy from Aspatria but certainly we found ourselves extremely introverted and very very quiet. And didn't do much mixing at all because I don't think we were able to, because we just weren't up in playing cards and gambling and things like that that these other lads had been brought up with. We were just out on a limb, the two of us. They were already drinking, they'd had experience of sex, by their talk anyway, and on and on like that.

On the first night out the majority of these lads made a bee line for the nearest pubs because they had obviously been missing this, that's all there was to it. We went out once, John Yeast was his name from Aspatria, and I don't think we went out again. I think we were absolutely scared to go out into Portsmouth which is quite a large city, plus the fact you couldn't have gone any further south – and for two boys from the extreme north, there again it was a shattering experience. Hundreds of miles from home. Oh, it's a strange thing, Melvyn – a strange thing. And I think after three or four weeks we were given a twenty-four-hour pass. It seemed ridiculous to come back to Cumberland in that twenty-four hours but both of us did (four hundred miles). Couldn't get back fast enough. Everybody was amazed when we asked for train passes and things; they didn't believe we could do it. I think it just meant about eight or nine hours at home but we done it. I think both of us went back quite happy after that; we realised there wasn't any alternative, you just had to get stuck in and make the best of it. Shortly after that another arrival at Portsmouth was David Pearson and two or three other Cumberland boys arrived. So there was, in the latter weeks of Portsmouth, some people you could have contact with.

Looking back on it though I wouldn't have missed it for the world. Definitely not; I wouldn't. Because we were so sheltered. I was anyway. I can't speak for David Pearson and the others. Although certainly much later, even when I was stationed in Germany, arrivals there who were Cumbrian boys had had exactly the same experiences as we had, this lost – this feeling of being lost. But certainly very educative, yes. I wouldn't have missed it for the world. It developed a feeling that there is a vastly different way of life going on to what you lead, to what we had led, and that this way of life that we saw was the most common. We were sheltered, too sheltered at that time. And yet at the same time the background we'd had, closer family ties and smaller communities, gave me anyway some strength to be independent and not be easily led by these faster-talking and faster-thinking lads from the cities who just wanted to gamble and booze and dash after women and things like that. I think it gave you, although as I say we were slightly lost in that environment, we still had some confidence in ourselves to stand up to it.

I'd been training as a clerk so I went into offices in the unit in Germany which includes spares to all the N.A.T.O. Forces. The only other serving man in the office was a corporal; he was a very nice man called John Simms. He wasn't a soldier in any sense of the word, he was an ordinary man, a decent honest man to be with and we got on very well. His hobby was going out and trying out various types of German food and wine and things like that. He wasn't a high liver by any means but when he was in Germany, he thought, alright I'm going to, as far as I can, live as the Germans did. On his pay at that time he could afford to but I couldn't – but he used to bail me out several times. And we used to go into these country cafés and restaurants and have ourselves good meals. We tried various German meals, wines and beers and we used to have trips off to other German towns and cities that appealed to us. As it happens, he had a hell of a do in Germany because he came from Portsmouth which was the twin town for Duisburg where we were stationed and he got out to all these official functions and big city dinners, burgomasters' dinners, and he was always being presented with beautiful books. And being a book-man I thought, well, why the hell can't I get on this racket? He was a decent chap but he never invited me to any official dinners, anyway – be that as it may. I took over from him. I got promoted to corporal when he left and I took over from him. Weeknights and in winter there wasn't an awful lot to do and, as I say, we were a small unit on the outskirts of a very large industrial town. And there wasn't an awful lot to do, if you didn't drink or go out with women, well, there wasn't an awful lot to do. And, as I say, Simms was always given beautiful books which we couldn't read because they were in German, of course. But they were beautifully illustrated and bound and he would come back home with a fairly sizeable collection of beautiful books – and the bookshops in Duisburg were fantastic.

Wonderful displays of books which we were always browsing through. And the library wasn't that bad but nothing exceptional, but still we read magazines and anything we could get our hands on really.

I had no intention of staying in, though, however pleasant it was. No, never. Never. This was a foregone conclusion with everybody on the camp, officers included. No never. They only asked me once. No. As I recall, I seemed to come back without any fixed ideas other than taking up life as I'd left it, which meant going back into the shop and continue on from there.

I'd been on leave once. I'd always known Cynthia because she was a customer in the shop but I'd never had any romantic thoughts about her. Come on leave once and went to a dance in the Crown and Mitre at Carlisle and she happened to be there. Gave her a dance or two and plucked up enough courage to ask to take her home and, by my surprise, she accepted. It was a bit awkward because I'd a friend with me on leave and who was staying with me, so I'd to dump him here on the way up to Reathwaite (three or four miles away, in the fells) and let him play third man in the back of the car or something. I just forget what happened now. Anyway, that's how it started and when I went to Germany we started to write to each other and got more and more serious and got together again when I came out of the Army. We sort of went steady from there. I had just been out of the Army a year, I think it was a year, when my father died. We'd got engaged and had arranged to be married in the August. However, my father died so we cancelled the wedding for two or three weeks and eventually got married in September 1958. I was twenty-two. Everything was worked out then. There wasn't any alternative. I mean as I said, I'd been in the shop and enjoyed it and with my father dying so suddenly I think all we wanted to do was to get back in action again with the simple reason of making a living. Anyway, apart from me there was my mother to think about. She had to – obviously she was fairly young still, and I had to think about her future which was tied up in the shop. Cynthia knew Wigton obviously and in the beginning, of course, there were problems – an adjustment for her as well as for my mother and for me, too. I think it all worked out fairly well. And, as I say, with having a large garden Cynthia was very keen on gardening so this suited her, she was able to lead a fairly outdoor life which she had been used to. And with having dogs and other sort of forms of livestock she was able to look after them, too. So this would help to cushion her coming from the farm down to the town. Definitely I think this did help her. Though I'd always liked country life and things like that, it certainly would never enter into me to be a farmer, and I didn't have much in common with Cynthia's parents – which is a polite way of saying that I don't think they approved of their daughter marrying anybody else other than a farmer. But we got on alright and that was that. Her brother was older than Cynthia and he was still unmarried at the time and we became very good friends and he often used to visit us and we'd have various trips off and that. And, as I say, when he got married we were the best of friends. Very frequent visitors. So in one sense, apart from finding a good wife, I found a good friend at the same time. But her parents and I never saw eye to eye completely, which is natural enough. I mean, everybody has to have their own ideas and, as I say, they were rather disappointed at the time that Cynthia didn't marry a farmer.

Our son's life, he's eleven, is already very different from mine at his age. George is more outward-looking. He doesn't stay about the house or garden as much as I did. I think a child today who has been brought up on a diet of television and mass media, and the glorification of sport, if he is that way inclined at all, well, the opportunities for indulging in these sports are there and this is what George does. He takes full advantage of the sports facilities in the schools that surround him and always has done. He very seldom plays in the garden as such and he makes more use of the playing-fields than I ever did. He is in all the teams he can get on, whatever they are for; Rugby, cricket, football. If he can get on a team George is happy and content. He is more of an extrovert than I was. He is certainly more of an extrovert than my father was. I think television has had a lot to do with some changes in character of children today. They have seen more of the world and their own country through television than we ever did and the system of education which George has been through, younger teachers than we had, very young teachers – and also, in his second school, the open play system of teaching which is encouraging them to look further than their own immediate vicinity. He has to look out books in school, he has had to look out projects and things and I think this carries through into his private life at home. He looks more outside the home than I ever did. Touch wood, he isn't a child who has needed any discipline; he hasn't been any bother. He's been fully occupied with his hobbies and his sports, therefore he hasn't got into any mischief apart from normal boys' things when he has to be disciplined. No, I don't think he's had any easier life than I've had or what my father had. As I say, my father and I were both interested in animals, dogs especially, and we were sort of occupied in our childhood by that.

There are changes in the business as well as the family. At the shop – the biggest difference would be the widening of customers. When I went in almost every customer didn't go anywhere else. Now all that has broken down, although you still have regular customers as every shop must have. You certainly deal with a wider section of the community than before, definitely. When I went in in 1953, the basic system of trading at that time was on credit and the bulk of your customers were farmers, they dealt on six months' credit. They bought goods and settled up every six months at Martinmas and again at Whit. This still continues but certainly on a much lesser degree in that it doesn't form as much of your income as it did before. This is all broken down as those original farmers' sons and daughters have grown up. And fashion has started to move fast. With every fashion change there is a change of footwear and we have moved through the winkle-picker stages and brothel-creeper stages to blue-suede-shoe stages and stiletto heels; you name it, we've had it. Clogs have done. In 1953 when I first went in we used to do a large trade in clogs; that is now completely finished. The young ones wouldn't wear them. The clogs have finished and it wasn't so long after that that the heavy farm boots more or less disappeared. Those with the big nails in the bottom and with a very turned-up toe. Very thick cow-hide uppers all completely finished because the young farmer wouldn't wear them. Too heavy, certainly too heavy and too uncomfortable. Because their diminishing coincides with the coming of the first moulded sole footwear, and also with a bigger variety of rubber boots which are light in weight, easier to slip on and cheaper. And it just was the death knell for heavy farm boots. And apart from the trade diminishing in the shop, well, quite a lot of manufacturers went out of business. Even if you could have sold them, Cumberland was one of the last places in England to continue selling them. But gradually it died out because you couldn't get supplies anywhere and the young farmers today want lighter and lighter footwear all the time.

The person who would buy only one pair of shoes a year still buys only one pair a year but these are older people, people whose minds are set in a bygone era. Times have changed, Melvyn, and as you've said there is more and more money about and this is reflected. Every shop in Wigton should be taking more money and certainly the young people have a much bigger buying power than we had. Money isn't any objective, if the article is of use to that person he will buy it. It doesn't matter whether it is every week or every other day, he still buys it, a particular shoe or whatever it is. In general, footwear is less durable than it used to be in that a shoe isn't expected to last as long as it did at one time. So you have got a higher turnover in that respect anyway. Today you have got more fashion changes, instead of every year or two when a fashion developed, now a fashion can develop at the drop of a hat. It just needs a new pop star on television or somebody to arrive from America and you have got a new fashion overnight. This has to be catered for by the clothing trade and automatically by the shoe trade. This again encourages buying and the young people have got the money to buy with. But apart from the young people, the younger married people and the middle-aged people also buy more shoes nowadays because nowadays, in my opinion anyway, there are very very few old people. Whereas at one time a person once he got to fifty or fifty-five was considered old and, therefore, wasn't in the running for very bright colours or anything fashionable, that's a thing of the past now. A person is just as old as he or she feels and you've seen very smart people whose age you just can't tell. They could be seventy or even eighty, fashionably dressed and very well dressed. These people still buy. But the person who you or I would consider smart today is more casually dressed than what an older person would consider smart. The older person's idea of smartness to you and I would be too formal, far too formal and over-dressed. Everything would have to match. The lady with the matching handbag, gloves, shoe and hat were dressed, over-dressed, Melvyn – more of a casual, to you and I a much smarter look, certainly more informal. All these rigid dressings for weddings and funerals, it's all gone by the board. Nobody does it today.

More trade done now than it used to be means more buying, more selling and more paperwork, and Mother does the paperwork; invoices and book-keeping, that sort of thing. And it is certainly much more work for her. Especially now since V.A.T. – that means a lot more paperwork. But we manage it quite well, working amongst ourselves, we can arrange our holidays without getting any staff in at all which we think is a big benefit. I can see to the dogs. That began with Father. He had dogs all his life, since he was a boy, various sorts of dogs, and I think he would begin breeding in a serious way when he was in his early twenties, would be sort of the early 1930s. Various breeds he had and varying degrees of success. And then when I began to show an interest in them he had Dandie Dinmont terriers at that time. An ancient Border breed and you as an author should know that Sir Walter Scott was a breeder of them. They actually take the name from a character in *Guy Mannering*. Anyway, we had that breed at that time and we had quite a lot of success with them. They were very bad characters in that you could never trust them with children.

We showed them all over. By this time we had a car. My father never drove, although he set off to learn, but he never passed any tests. However, my mother did so she drove and then when I was old enough I began learning and passed my test so we used to go to shows in this car; Birmingham and Leicester, Edinburgh, Glasgow, and we used to go to the London shows by train. We showed fairly extensively then, yes. This would start when I was about eleven or twelve.

We did quite well. They were very difficult to breed and, as I say, had very difficult natures so we, neither of us were very happy with them. And he saw some basset hounds at a show in London and I believe he had one or two in 1939, but because of the outbreak of the war he had never done anything as regards breeding or showing them. I think they went back to the person he had bought them from. So we decided then we would take up with basset hounds again. So we bought a nucleus of stock, this was 1950-ish, 1951, and we kept basset hounds since then. Father died in 1958, so I just continued breeding them, as I say, right up until now. We bought one bitch originally and bred from her and kept some of her progeny, and then we bought another bitch and extended from there. The most we ever had was possibly twelve to fifteen. They have very large litters – averaging eight or nine a litter so obviously you had to sell them, you couldn't possibly keep them all. We didn't want to keep them all anyway because we just wanted to keep what we could manage ourselves and look after them ourselves. So we used to have this ten or a dozen which was quite easy for two people. And when my father died I'd to cut it down to less than that. And now I average about six to eight. It's just plenty. I breed about two litters a year and sell most of the puppies.

You could equate dog shows with the football league; first, second and third divisions. Your lowest division being local shows and then your second division being what is termed as Open Shows, which are open to dogs who have won major awards at other shows. These are held in most parts of the country. But the top league, the Championship Shows, of which there are about thirty or forty held, all breed championships are held in Britain every year – these are held from Edinburgh down to Bournemouth and Torquay. These are dogs of all breeds and open to dogs of any type. The winning dogs in each breed qualify for a Kennel Club Challenge Certificate. If your dog is fortunate enough to win three of those with three different judges it becomes a challenger which means it is at the peak of its career. If the dog is a titled champion, that's as far as it can go. To get a dog made up to a champion means, in the main, fairly extensive showing and fairly extensive travelling. It can be a very expensive hobby. So my father and I used to go to most of the shows which had classes for basset hounds, which, in the early days, was possibly just seven because they weren't very popular then. And we were among the founder members of the Basset Hound Club and so we have really been in that breed since its very beginning and pioneered it through to what it is today, one of the most popular hound breeds. So we did travel about quite a lot.

We'd had them a long time and I was always interested in what had gone before them in the history of them and their past and things like that, and old breeders and their stories and the history of the breed in France. I was always interested in that and used to collect all sorts of items, cuttings and pictures and prints on them, and built up quite a large collection on that theme. And it was always at the back of my mind that some day I would like to write a book on them. And then quite out of the blue the invitation came from Hutchinsons asking me to do a book on them to fit into a series of dog books which they were going to publish. So I accepted and set to work and wrote the book for them which was published in 1968. And automatically one thing leads to another, it depends how far you want to take it. And it just so happened that at a particular time in the late 1950s we were in need of some new blood in the kennels, so we decided to import from France. And that is really the theme which opened the door to connections with French breeders and with France. The hounds we had, they were very much inbred. There wasn't a wide range to choose from, the breed had virtually died out during the war so there was need of new blood anyway. The only source of it was from America or from France. Well America, as far as we are concerned, from the point of view of expense was out of the question anyway. France being much nearer and more accessible, we decided on the French hound and eventually located one and bought him and brought him across in 1959. So that, of course, opened the door for connections with French breeders.

The basset is a hunting dog and, therefore, to enable it to hunt it has to be constructed properly. To be constructed properly it has to be balanced, and that's the thing you look for first of all, balance of the dog. Once you've got that, well, you can start and look for specialised points. It's the easiest thing in the world for a man to look at a dog and tell whether it's balanced or not. You must have seen an athlete, a top-class athlete, an Olympic champ, always beautifully balanced when he is moving. If you compare him with the men who come last – when he's finished they are coming in last – beautifully balanced to the end. He's run with economy and style, hasn't he? The others are last because they haven't had the balance, and without balance they can't have style. Their legs have wobbled, their shoulders are down and they are pumping their lungs. It's as simple as that, and the same with a dog. A dog should always be beautifully balanced when it's standing or moving, and you can't put a foot wrong. After the balance, the basset is the French word for dwarf or low set. So you are looking for a dwarf hound, a very very low hound and a very long hound; that's your meaning of the word basset. Then you have got that typical head which, to the layman, resembles a bloodhound, lots and lots of loose skin, wrinkled and long ears, very sad and sorrowful expression. Hound colours, three colours: black, white and tan, lemon and white, yellow and white; typical French traditional hound colours. And then, to further your description of the word basset, your dwarf has deformed limbs, a dwarf – your basset hound's in the front leg is the same, yes, deformed limbs in that they are twisted and turned like a Queen Anne chair leg. This is to support the big deep chest which comes right down between them like a cantilever principle. But the ordinary dog man who is used to straight-legged dogs, well, these are deformed limbs. But for a purpose, to support a very heavy body, for it weighs at maturity sixty to sixty-five pounds. A very big hound.

The first bassets appeared in a litter of normal-sized hounds in France in about the fifteenth or sixteenth century when these deformed puppies with these deformed limbs I've just mentioned were produced to normal-sized hounds. And it is thought that at that time the person who bred them kept them out of curiosity and then possibly bred them again together and perpetuated a type of animal. And bred from there. And the first mention of them is in 1545. I think in a French hunting-manual the word 'basset' appears for the first time. And it became quite popular in France as a hunting-dog. In their heyday in France they were used for hunting with sportsmen with guns, and the early guns, as you know, took quite a long time to load and set and then aim. So they needed a dog which didn't chase the game on too fast; any hound which chased the game too fast automatically put it out of the range of these men who were busy loading big blunderbuss types of guns. So the little hound which didn't unduly harass its quarry, chased it on at a sedate pace was perfect for these sportsmen. And then in France, as you know, this dense undergrowth – it was able to penetrate that where a larger hound wouldn't face it. The basset could worm and wriggle its way along it.

The most money you can win at a dog show is your two pounds

for the first prize, which is basically regarded as – most people who show dogs – as petrol money, that's all there is to it. And you have to be fortunate to win the first prize. Some other special prizes, special cups and shields and things automatically carry a lot of honour and so they are contested for; you know, breeders' cups, progeny cups and things like that. We've won some. Yes. Best prize I think we've ever won is for having dogs made up into champions, which is an honour in itself anyway. About eight or nine champions, something like that. Possibly the greatest honour came when one of our dogs became the first British export ever to qualify for an American Field Trial Champions title. The first hound that's ever gone from Europe, in fact, that's won a title like that. This was just last 1971 or 72 when that happened. It was bred here and exported to a place in West Virginia. The Americans are very keen on these field trials and, as I say, it was the first time a hound has ever gone across from Europe which has qualified in America. You see, it has been considered an American province and no intrusion at all so, as I say, I think that would be the greatest thing because not only does it prove that your dogs can look good but certainly proves that what you are producing is still capable of performing the functions it was bred for.

The puppies take a lot of looking after. It's a full-time job which it would be impossible without Cynthia. Because she – I think it's a woman's job to rear puppies. Puppies are like babies and it's a woman's job to rear babies. Little bits of extra individual attention – and they have more time than a man would give them. I think this pays off with puppies. And, as I say, without Cynthia it just wouldn't be possible. Very very difficult to rear and your losses, even with careful attention, can be considerable. In recent years it has paid, yes, and paid handsomely. I'm including the book in this which has been a big success and which has paid handsomely. And certainly the puppies we've exported in recent years, we've had good trade for them. If you take the whole period of the time we've bred them, your expense and your income and balanced that, it possibly would either break even or you would go on the debit side. But in recent years it has paid handsomely. George isn't interested in them as I was at his age, no. He likes dogs and likes going to occasional shows but he isn't, he certainly isn't as fanatical as I was on them. But he still likes the little perks of a trip to France some time and Denmark. We sent some dogs to France to a man who is a prominent breeder in France and, with getting to know him and the other French breeders, well, they are good friends that is all there is to it. So you are visiting friends apart from visiting France or anything else.

In Wigton we have no social life; virtually none. Virtually none because all our interests are interests which have taken us outside Wigton, the dogs and things like that. And I do quite a lot of reading. And when I was writing the book well, as you know, that takes an awful lot of time. So that kept me busy for one year anyway. And then I was asked to write another on French breeds which involved a lot of translations and things but I've been very lazy about that; I haven't got much done on it. And evening classes, we did. Cynthia went to cookery and keep fit and I went two or three seasons to French. Other than that, apart from odd and very very occasional visits for a drink somewhere, we haven't any social life in Wigton no, none at all. And certainly I'm not a member of any Round Table, Rotary, Freemasons, nothing like that. I'm not a joiner, Melvyn. I've not a lot of time really. As I say, dogs – and then everything I enjoy doing is either in the house or in my own garden. I haven't that type of outside interests. There are lots of other dog-breeders in Wigton whom I'm very friendly with, but I never mix with them socially, and I don't suppose they've a lot of time either. Oh, it isn't an empty place, I certainly find everything I want in Wigton, but I need to look outside our own environment for activities.

Wigton has changed. And the biggest change is that the caucus of families at the middle of the town has gone completely. You can't keep generations rigid and rigid communities any more. Wigton can't be Wigton. Wigton can't be Wigton in Cumberland and it can't be Cumberland in England. England isn't any more anyway, it is in Europe now, and this is where Wigton has to look to. It has to look outside its own parish and this has happened. It had to happen. The education available to people, those who have taken advantage of that education in the main haven't been able to find jobs in Wigton. So they have had to go out of Wigton, so this is your most intelligent group of people going out of the town in every generation. Education has filtered down, everybody is better educated today. There are no dunces in classes any more, he is equipped to do something. The boy who was in the corner and ignored when we were at school, it isn't happening any more. The old rigid ties have gone and needed to go and I think Wigton is healthier for it. The old persons are still in the town, as I've said before, but those old families are not tied to the town. They are able to get out and see life as it is outside, but they choose to live in Wigton still despite that. It must say something for Wigton. And getting back to what you said before, well, they wouldn't stay in Wigton if they didn't enjoy it. Therefore, Wigton to them must still be a cosy town. It is to me. But you can't live in Wigton any more, Melvyn. I mean that in the sense that you must go outside Wigton and anyway it would be more or less physically impossible literally to live in Wigton. At one time you could have found that people had never been out of Wigton, never been outside it, and going to Carlisle was a big event. Now I doubt if you could find one person. There's a good thing. You stay in and you isolate, if you isolate you stagnate.

And I think one of the big changes socially has been, is that on the whole the farming community has changed its place in the social structure. When I left school, when I was at school there were, of course, a few rich farmers and there always will be, but they were people who had estates really – most farmers, with eighty to a hundred and twenty acres, were working very hard just to make it. And they were called 'dirty old farmers', in a sense they never had much money and childhood and so forth; they never had anything, and they kept complaining. But that has changed round rather radically. They are the rich men of society now, as it were, the Wigton society. Around the town are these farms which by town standards and by the standards of most people in this town, I would say almost everywhere in this town – half a dozen exceptions – are extremely wealthy places. There are good places worth a hundred thousand and that's been the major thing. The other thing, I would think, would be the opportunities which British Sidac, which was British Rayophane, has given to local men to work themselves up in managerial positions in there. When my father was there I doubt if there was a local man who was in a managerial position, even in a minor managerial position – I don't think you would have found a local man. Now I think the policy is to seek out local men that are capable of doing these jobs and they've found them. I think this has been another theme in that you've got men in that factory, because it's a big concern, it's a massive concern, and yet at Wigton level anyway it has been run basically by Wigton and district people which I think is a good thing. Coming back to what I said before, I think the major development has been breaking down these aged ties, not just Wigton ties but family ties. But Wigton men have come back from the last world war anyway in Wigton with wives from the south of England and other parts of Britain. And other boys have gone away and come back with wives from other parts of Britain. I think this has had a big effect in Wigton in that these wives are in Wigton, their husbands are Wigton boys and are confined to Wigton in thought or in sense anyway.

On the other hand, there has to be continuity. I would certainly like to think that one day George would live in this house. It's been a good house to me, it was a good house to other generations of Johnstons. It's a house which has always been lived in. It isn't just a good house, it's been a lived-in house and it has always been a happy house. And I would like to think that George can live in it and be happy in it. But, as I said earlier, he is more outward-looking. I'm quite content in Wigton as I'm content in this house, the shop, and I potter about in the garden. I've the hounds and the goat and things like that. He has this tendency to be more outward-looking than I am, and as I say that would put the odds at sixty-forty against rather than fifty-fifty that he would stay on here."

CHAPTER EIGHTEEN
Religion

There is a royal flush of religion in the town as everywhere in the U.K. There are Quakers, Primitive Methodists, Congregationalists, Wesleyans, the Salvation Army, the Salvation Mission, a local evangelical sect, the Church of England, Plymouth Brethren and Roman Catholics. At one end of the town is a school founded by the Society of Friends; at the other, a convent founded by the Sisters of Mercy. Again and again in this book, people have talked of their religion: Mrs. Carrick, with whom the book started, was the first.

Generalisations apply here as everywhere else. The practice of religion has declined. Churches are markedly emptier. Observances are fewer and less well attended than twenty-five, fifty or seventy-five years ago. The graph has bumped along throughout the century, but the mass possession of cars, television sets and that extra capital which promotes mobility provided the final charge for the surge away from churches, organised religion, established religiosity and the observance of the Sabbath.

Yet, perhaps as the clearest memorial we have of the force of an old civilisation, religion lies about the town still, still practised, still held to, discussed still, a minority, a diminishing minority, but not finished yet. The churches may be, are, growing emptier, but the youth clubs, social clubs, and allied satellites of religion which sustain the idea of the Bible in some diluted form still persist.

But the Victorian Religion is largely gone. Though Northern Sundays are quiet and restrained in the town, that is largely because scores of people are down at Kirkbride aerodrome watching the "Hell-Drivers" or in the Lake District climbing every mountain, or playing sport, motoring, fishing, working in the factory, gardening. Vicars are still respected, perhaps even more than they were although there is less awe: but now we can see how exposed and rather pathetic their place in the world is. Boys, especially boys, some of them, still find the confusion of adolescence compounded by a confusion of religious mysticism: fewer nowadays than twenty years ago, I would suspect but have no proof. The suffering Christ has paled beside the suffering on the screen seen daily from Asia, Africa, South America, hospitals, crashes, wars, droughts, famines, floods; the pale Galilean, as Peter Stubbs said, seems merely to have thrown his life away. And the Sermon on the Mount, too, though it may indeed be part of the underpinning of a humanitarian attitude to life, is less quoted or used as a standard now by politicians in their speeches or welfare workers at their tasks – talk is of a more practical, less passive kind. The Kingdom of Heaven is no longer for most anywhere in space: even those who hold to it are forced into deeper conundrums of puzzlement and seek the eternal life promised for so long, in trans-migration of souls, the words of an Indian guru, or some impenetrable bio-chemical spiritualism. Yet the large questions still remain, as old and as big as the hills. Who made us? Why are we kind? Why do we love? Why do we hate? These questions are ultimately religious questions and man will never cease to ask them even if he institu-tionalises the answers or even if he erects a society which claims that it does not need the answers or the questions: though such a society *might* be the society of the future and it *might* be all the better for putting down religion. The balance-sheet of religion is not proved to be favourable to Light: the forces of darkness, many would argue, have done as well out of Christ as the counsels of Light. The fanatic-ism engendered has been more influential than the tolerance.

And yet – the good people I know and the good people one reads and hears of have so often been Christians. Fact one. Fact two: the possibilities for peace, or the possibilities of non-wars – for kindly interchanges within a creed which has also been midwife to immense cultural artefacts and music and wisdom – are at the very least an impressive tribute and, for many, clinching reason for continuing faith in this age of inconsistent beliefs. Example and tradition are the two pillars.

In the town the churches and church-buildings – halls, houses, vestries, convents, the church yards and church fields, the alms houses and cemeteries – stand as monuments somehow beached and yet not absurd. Perhaps there will come a day when only superstitious old women use them taking in new-born babies to touch a font or kiss a cross. Now, though, the shell holds, just, transparently thin, but once or twice a week, two or three gather together in His name.

For this chapter I have chosen three people who present a range, I think. Sammy Tate, now in his eighties, a lifelong Methodist;

Mother Philomena, in her middle years, the Mother Superior to the Sisters of Mercy and headmistress of St. Ursula's, the private school; and Noel Sharp, who began in a factory, went into a Catholic Order, left it and is now married – he is in his thirties. All are religious: each has found in it other things besides mere obedience to the doctrines.

Sammy Tate was born in 1891 in Fletchertown, a mining village five or six miles from Wigton. He was an active Methodist from childhood and he still is. He sings solos around the local missions. He runs the Senior Citizens' Club; he tells his own story.

"I'm the second off the eldest of nine. I had a sister older than me. She's dead. We lived at Fletchertown until I joined up in 1915, and then I joined up under St. John's Ambulance and went down to Whalley in Lancashire to the Queen Mary's Military Hospital and I was there all the time. Joined the Band. And that's where I met my wife, of course, down there. And then after the war days I came back and joined my uncles in the drapery business at Fletchertown – Tate Bros. And then after that I was with them when this business came up for sale in Wigton and we just bought it.

When I was a boy, before the First World War, there was something on every night of the week. Monday was generally what we call the Band of Hope. That was a temperance thing. Of course, you had the special singing books. Songs against Drink. All that kind of thing. 'Joe Perkins was a white man'. This is one of the things we used to sing '. . . boasted he was free, but a bigger slave o'er land or wave, no man e'er could be.' And, of course, with being a village it didn't matter whether you belonged to the Methodist Church or not, you could go to the Band of Hope. Tuesday night I think was what they called the Class meeting. Well, they used to meet there and somebody would maybe give an address and if anybody had had an experience during the week, it might be some blessing or it might be some bereavement, but they felt they should let other people know what had happened in their lives. That was the idea. It was a testimony really. We, as youngsters, when it came to our turn, we would probably read a verse out of the hymn-book or something like that. Something that might apply to something we wanted to say. They gave everybody the chance. Wednesday I think was choir practice. We had the harmonium – well, I shouldn't say it was a harmonium, it's the same instrument that's in the chapel yet today. And it was a lovely tone organ.

It was a mixed choir. You got the four parts, you see. I started alto

425

when I was just about seven or eight. There were seven of us. Seven altos. And my uncle was the choirmaster. He lived at Fletchertown then. He worked at the colliery as well. And of a Sunday night, he would do this with us – we were singing too hard. Keep us down. And we could sing then, you know. Then of course I went from there right to baritone. I've been at it ever since. Thursday night was the Wesley Guild. Well, as I say, there were four different sections then and there was a secretary for each section. There was one secretary over the lot. There was one secretary for each section, you see, and that secretary was responsible for the arrangements of that evening. It might be a social, there was devotional, there was literary – I don't know what the other one was. But there were four; which made the month up.

Somebody used to come and give you a talk – it might be some literary subject. Or devotional. Well, somebody would maybe come and give a talk of a devotional character. They would very often give their address and then ask if anybody had any questions to ask, they would be very pleased to explain. And then, of course, the social evening, it was generally more of a social evening, where you had games and such as that. No dancing. Dancing was never allowed on Methodist premises. No dancing, gambling, or anything of that nature. No Theatrical Entertainment either. Methodism was pretty strict then. Of course, you weren't allowed to be a drinker or anything in those days. A lot of them don't bother today. But it was alright, because you were brought up strict, you never thought anything about it because it was strict, you see. Methodism was strict in those days.

Friday night, well, later on after I got a bit bigger, I think it was Friday night was the band practice. I played the E flat. It's one of the big instruments. It's next to the double B. And with being in the band at home, and then when I went to join the Forces, and they asked if anybody could play a brass instrument, we had to step forward. Of course, once you were in the band you were okay.

Saturday night you got ready for Sunday. On Sunday there were two Sunday schools and two services. You started your Sunday School at half past ten and you finished about half past eleven. You started again at half past one and finished about quarter past two. You went right into the service at half past two, probably out about half past three, you had your tea, and sometimes you used to go round the village singing, in my earlier days. They would sing for the Sunday night and then go in for the service at half past six, followed by a prayer meeting. It was a full life in those days.

Methodism was born in singing because Charles Wesley and John

Wesley – Wesleyan Methodism was founded on John Wesley – and they wrote a lot of the hymns, and Methodism was what we call 'born in song'. It could be strong stuff as well though. One night they had a chap, Osborne, he was an auctioneer at Silloth, and he said something. And there was a lot of us young chaps in. And some of them – well, something he said, they started to giggle a little bit. And he picks up the Bible and he bangs it down on the desk. Aye he says, you'll laugh yourselves into hell but you can't laugh yourselves out! We've seen some wonderful things really. Every now and again they used to have these missions, probably a fortnight mission. And they would get a proper missioner to come and conduct services every night of the week. He used to have these services and he used to get a lot of converts to Methodism that way. People would come in and they could speak pretty powerful in those days. And people took more notice then than what they do today, because they just sort of laugh it off today. But not in those days. You would say it was more of the style of what the Salvation Army is today. In Methodism then.

Today? Well, it's like most places today, like most churches, it's – there's one or two running the place you might say today. I mean, there's my cousin's daughter, well, she's secretary for this, secretary for that, secretary for Sunday school, organist, and she has ever so many jobs in the church. That's the fault today. You can't spread it over so many. I think they just have one weeknight meeting in a week now, and I think it's what they call the Fellowship meeting. I think that's all they have now. There's no choir practice or anything like that now. Well, I think the Sunday School is still in the morning, and the afternoon meeting and evening meeting. They aren't as hard pushed as we were. I've seen my old uncle, he was the superintendent of the Sunday School, start at half past ten, and when it came to half past ten he would have his watch out on his hand, and if you went in – You're late, Sam. He was very strict on punctuality. I'm afraid I've followed him because when I was superintendent at Sunday School, as soon as ever it came half past one, if I had a pianist I didn't care if there was nobody else in, it would come half past one, I would start. I never like to be late.

Today we still have a strong Sunday School. I think there's about a hundred [scholars] but the trouble is today when they get to school-leaving age they leave you. In our days we had a young people's class, we called it. And it was for those who had left school and wanted to stay on. That's where you were able to get your Sunday-School teachers from. But the primary, which is the youngest of the lot, the beginners and primary, they're the strongest part of the Sunday

427

School. When you get up to further on you lose them. At the church itself, if you get twenty to thirty at a service you're doing very well. When I was choirmaster before and after the war we used to have twenty in the choir, I've seen of a Sunday night, have to put special chairs in for them.

But still Methodism keeps a very high standard even yet today. I mean, if you're a Methodist you're looked up on. If they know you are a Methodist they look up on you. You should have a certain standard, you see. I think if you're a Christian it depends a good deal on how you live your life. If you're a Christian you ought to set an example to other people. This is my way of life, and when people see you going, well, they'll say, If Sam Tate said it, it's right. I mean from the standard of your life, that's what I mean. Of course, I mean that's been said more than once of myself without any bragging about it. If Sam Tate said it, you can depend on it's right. But no, I think the standard of any Christian in any Christian church, his standard ought to be that people can look up to him at any time."

When I first knew Mother Philomena, over twenty years ago, she had just started a social club at St. Ursula's, the private school run by the Sisters of Mercy. She is very clever, merry-eyed, Irish and now the Mother Superior.

We spoke in her parlour in the Convent of St. Cuthbert's; cool, the nunnery, built of brown sandstone like other important Victorian places in the town – church, school, nunnery and the old orphanage and the house for the priest, all set out neatly on the north side of the town. It is not in her nature or in her profession, calling rather, to talk about herself and I appreciated the effort made to help when it was clearly not easy for her to be talking of herself and of her own work. She sees herself very much as one of an Order, one among many in the Church.

"I come from Ireland, from the south. Wexford. There were six in the family. Three boys and three girls. I came fourth. We come from farming people. My mother's side does. But my father's side were mostly trade. My father was a tradesman actually. Actually just had a craft, a very good joiner, shall we say – and his father before him. Growing up I often thought of being a nurse. I should say I wanted to be a nurse mostly, to work for other people. And now and again, perhaps, the thought of being a nun cropped up in my mind but

I didn't seem to become set until I was about seventeen.

Then I met up with the Mother Superior at the Convent here at Wigton. She was over travelling around in Ireland and she thought I might become a nun and the seeds seemed to be sown from that. So I came to Wigton in 1935 and the training started here. You see, the Sisters of Mercy, the Mother House is in Dublin. Each branch of the Sisters of Mercy – they are all independent. So this house here in Wigton, the Convent, is an independent convent of the Sisters of Mercy. And we are all independent, though we have branch houses. We have two here in Wigton. Egremont and Maryport. But that is the unit of the Wigton Sisters of Mercy. They came here in 1857. In 1857 five sisters came from Bermondsey and settled down here. It's very interesting. Two of the Sisters had been out in the Crimean War and later on went to London to receive their medals from Queen Victoria.

In 1935 it appeared a very small place and I thought the Convent was very small as well. And the Sisters very homely. I had expected something different actually. Coming to England from Ireland, we thought everything in England was so big and magnificent and I was quite taken by surprise. Wigton is smaller than Wexford. The training has changed but the set-up is the same. When you come to the Convent you are called the postulant and you stay in that, shall we say, set-up for six months or it can go on to a year. In that time you get to know about the Convent, the people you live with; you get a feel for whether you want to stay and be a nun. After six months you are asked, Do you wish to continue? Then you ask for the habit – to be allowed to wear the habit of the Sisters. And that was called the Reception. So you received the habit after six months, which I did after six months, and then you continue. You are dressed up now in the habit of the Sisters of Mercy but you wore a white veil for two years and of those two years you spent one in what we called the Spiritual Year. You gave most of your time to reading spiritual books and studying the constitutions of the Sisters of Mercy and you took part in manual work at the Convent and very little visitation because during the Spiritual Year you were supposed to just live kind of a spiritual life. Not go out much, not study, except the spiritual side – scripture, history of the Church, that kind of study. That was for one year. (The Spiritual year could either be the first or the second year of the two years.) And at the end of the two years you asked to be Received. You asked to take your vows.

We called it the First Profession, which meant that you then took the vows of poverty, chastity and obedience. And for the Sisters of

Mercy the care of the poor, sick and ignorant for three years. So that was all part of the set-up. It was three years and two, that was five, five and a half years you were in the Novitiate. And during that time you could leave and go back out into the world if you wanted to. But usually, if you took the vows, you stayed on for the three years. And at the end of three years you asked to be received to perpetual vows. And that is for life. Then after that, of course, you left the Novitiate and came and lived with the Community.

In those days you didn't *decide* what to do, you were told you were to study, you were to become a teacher, or you were to do other work. And I felt I would like to teach. I loved being with children and so eventually I started to study because when I left Ireland what I had wasn't very much use over here in England. So we have to study and get our G.C.E. over here, so that we could be ready to go to college and get trained. Eventually I went to Sedgeley Park College, Manchester. It is run by the F.C.J. Sisters – the Faithful Companions of Jesus. There were a number of sister students and we lived together. We had our own room for meals and we all went to all the lectures with the other students at the college and took part in whatever they were doing. And the social side, well, mostly we looked on. But today that is all changed. The sisters just fit in in the colleges today and all mixed up. They haven't got a room. Not usually now. They just fit in with the other students. I was very happy at college. I loved every moment of it. Both sides – the social and the academic side.

Actually I didn't go to college in the beginning – I had to wait because other work turned up. I was asked to take over being in charge of the children in the orphanage. We had about fifty children – that was in 1943–44. We used to make and sell altar breads and that helped to subsidise the keeping of the children in the orphanage.

They usually came from broken homes or where there was a bereavement – the mother had died – rescue societies, came from them. But it was mostly parish priests who sent them along, arranged for them to come here. We had them from about three years of age. We had two dormitories and then they had a playroom and a dining-room. It was rather congested really. That was the chief reason why we gave up in the end; we just couldn't cope.

We still do youth work. We have a youth club for the boys and the girls are also part of it. We started off with two youth clubs in 1954, one for the girls and one for the boys. And both went very well for quite a long time but gradually the girls' club died out. The girls went down in numbers and eventually it was given up. But the boys continued to do quite well and it's still very active to this day. I took over the boys' club. I started off the boys' club with a few boys from my class in St. Cuthbert's, the senior class. We have most facilities that you find in any club, except a gym, but we use the gym up at the school one night in the week. The boys are able to come in four nights of the week. We have all sort of activities which includes football and we have teams in the C.W.A. – that is the Christian Welfare Association – and we have football teams in the City Youth – Carlisle and City – Youth League. We have table tennis and we've been in the Carlisle and District League team in playing at home and away every other week. And in the club itself we have billiards and table tennis and darts, chess, draughts; all the small games. We have a T.V. room and a reading room. And when we have mixed – boys and girls – we sometimes have dances with groups coming to play. There isn't a girls' club but the girls come along to the boys' club at the weekend. They come in every Sunday night, or Saturday night if we have a dance on a Saturday night. And if we have anything on in the middle of the week, like a film show, they're welcome.

I should say the Catholic community doesn't seem to have changed much really. When I came to Wigton, I seem to remember it was about five hundred Catholics in the town. It's still round about the same number now. The attendances at the church are quite good. Well over – I'm not quite sure really but we can get quite a full church for the morning Mass and usually over a hundred come to the evening Mass. Up to three hundred for both Masses together. We have a number of Catholics in the town who are indifferent to living up to their religion but we also have quite a good number coming to church. The Sisters go to Mass every day. The last thing we would want would be not go to Mass each day of the week. And we go to Mass every Sunday and most of us go to the second Mass. So we usually go to all the services that are on in the church during the week and on Sunday.

The choir is in the church in the morning – we have a mixed choir – and in the evening we have a male choir, and the male choir is still going very strong. Since the days of Canon McNarney when we had broadcasts on the Home Service we have kept up a very good choir. The present parish priest is Father Michael Scandlon. He's a native of Kerry and he lives in the Presbytery. He hasn't got a housekeeper at the moment so he comes down to the Convent for his meals and a Sister looks after him. Goes down to the house and tidies it up once or twice in the week. He's the priest who looks after Wigton and the Catholic parishioners in the town and he also says

431

Mass for the Sisters. When he says Mass in the church – and one day in the week he will say Mass in our chapel where we keep the Blessed Sacrament reserved. And we help him in the church. The sacristan is a nun, one of the Sisters. We help him. The organist is a Sister – myself, and we help in the town. We do visiting of the people, which is part of our life – looking after others. We help in any work that he's doing, fund-raising efforts as well. We work with him, with the parish priest. We wouldn't go out and do anything in the town without his approval. Our work is set for us. The work that we do now in Wigton we've always done so it doesn't matter who comes as the parish priest, the work will go on. But if we wanted to do anything extra, we would get the approval of the parish priest to do it.

We had one boy within recent years who went from our school into the priesthood. Father Brendan Carrick, a native of Wigton; he was ordained two years ago. He went to the Austin Friars' school in Carlisle. He was brought up with us first of all, then he went on to Austin Friars, so he's an Augustinian – a religious priest. He's working down in London. And there have been two or three girls who left Wigton to become nuns. And they're doing very well. They haven't joined the Sisters of Mercy. I'm quite amazed. We're the largest order in the Church. I used to think we were the second. But I was reading up a Centenary book of the Sisters of Mercy just the other day and I find that we are now the largest order in the Church – in the Catholic Church. The Sisters of Mercy. We go into the thousands – thirty thousand nuns. And we are all over the English-speaking countries.

There haven't been many changes in the order in my time at all, because our Mother Founder, Mother McCauley, she was a – well, as they say about Sir Thomas More, he was a man for all times, and we feel that Mother McCauley was a woman for all times. She was a wonderful person and she founded this order to look after the poor. She was a native of Dublin. To educate the poor – those who couldn't be educated or looked after. And we feel that her approach was very modern. She would have been as much at home today as she was in her day. We have changed the habit but not very much really. In the old days we had a train and our Mother Founder looked upon us as ladies of the court of God of Heaven, just like ladies of the court of the King or the Queen. And we were – yes, well there have been changes now that I recollect.

We had Lay Sisters in the old days and we were Choir Sisters and the Choir Sisters wore the train so when we went into the chapel we always allowed the train to go down, very stylish indeed. Now we have cut the train off. And the front appearance, we had a wide gamp in front. We were very much closed in round the face, that has all been changed. We have now returned showing the hair and the habit is cut down very much, but most of us still wear it fairly long. We prefer it that way to the short habit. Once we had starched gamps and coifs, now we just have nylon collars.

I should say there have been many many little changes really, especially since the Second Vatican Council. It's rather difficult to say but perhaps, in the old days, the Mother Superior, she was at the top, the Sisters down in the Community – you felt there was quite a gap. Today that's all changed. The Mother Superior is very much one with the Community and she fits in – she has a much more simple life. There's not all this outward show of respect. There is always respect but shall we say she's more accessible today; that's what it would appear to be. But we seem to have lost a lot of the thrills of the rank and file. We are now all one. We all look the same and in the old days it was Reverend Mother and Mother and Sisters. Today we all are inclined to be Sisters rather than showing rank; especially outside. We are linked up in a federation of the Sisters of Mercy. So many of the England convents have all joined in a federation and we meet once a year every September. And during the past year we have been revising our rule and constitution so instead of the old, very thick book on the rules and customs we have simplified it quite a lot. We have brought it up to date with present-day trends, shall we say, though the basic rule is still the same – but we have simplified it.

Today, looking after the poor doesn't enter really because, especially here in Wigton where most families are able to cater for themselves today – they've Social Security, it's a great help. But wherever there is need we are always prepared to help. We still help those who come to us from, say travellers along the road and anybody who comes and has a problem we are prepared to help them. We do help, from time to time, people in Wigton who need our help. We visit the sick quite regular. We visit the old people in the town and we always have helped the widows through the years, and we still keep up that little custom of giving the widows a little help three times a year. If we know of anyone who is in need, we are prepared to help them.

I can quite honestly say that our life has become anything but easier. We have taken on extra work if anything. We seem to go non-stop from early morning till late at night. In the old days, you didn't do anything in the evening. You were in the Convent. Today we are out doing youth work or even visiting in the town till late evening, but especially in the youth club – we're over there till ten o'clock, sometimes much later if there's a dance on. Now, we teach – and teaching takes up the best part of your day. We have to fit in our spiritual exercises and we do this evening work as well, so I wouldn't say life was easier. We give so much time to meditation and the office and other prayers that we say, the rosary and visits to the chapel and, of course, the night prayers. But the Office is in three parts; it's made up of Lauds, Vespers and Compline and those are said at different times, morning, late afternoon – after school – and then evening for Compline and we meditate in the morning usually. If we cannot fit it in then, we fit it in sometime in the day. And then we have various visits to the chapel in the day as well.

We're very friendly with the vicars of the other churches. We don't meet very often but when we do meet we're very friendly with each other. We have the children of the Vicar of Abbeytown (C. of E.) in St. Ursula's School. We are very linked up with him. We knew Mr. Winder (C. of E.) quite well. We met up with him from time to time at meetings. We would have a chat. We knew Mr. Ford (C. of E.) very well; his children came to St. Ursula's, too. So there's that kind of link. But, yes, we're prepared to be very friendly and we feel very much at home with the vicars in the town. I feel that in Wigton everybody has a sense that there is a God and I wouldn't say they're irreligious but there are sections, just in our community – our Catholic community – we have the percentage who come to church and lead an outward religious life, and then others lead, I suppose, lead a religious life of a sort. Then there are the indifferent ones. But I wouldn't say that Wigton has shut its eyes to religion or to the things that matter.

Working with youth I find that there's quite a lot of indifference to religion among the youth. But I have seldom come across a boy or a girl who will say there is no God – I don't believe in God. Not in Wigton. And recently the youth – well, they always have been – we have discussions in the youth club. It always ends up about religion. It doesn't matter what you start off about. They just evidently like to bring religion in and to discuss it, and now today with all this superstar business – Jesus Christ Superstar – you feel that they seem to be getting a feel again for what concerns God. But I think basically the youth in Wigton are very good at heart. Yet they don't seem to – I don't know – they appear not to sense that they are doing something that's not right by not attending Mass on Sunday. Because, you

434

see, the Third Commandment says, Keep Holy the Sabbath Day. And our Church, the Catholic Church, we also have the Six Commandments of the Catholic Church, and one says, To keep Holy the Sabbath Day you must hear Mass and rest from Servile Works. Now that has not been changed. If we do not hear Mass on Sunday we are breaking a commandment of the Church. Now it's only God who can judge us so therefore we say that if a person misses Mass on Sunday, you cannot say that person has committed a mortal sin because only God can judge. In the old days anyone who missed Mass they were looked upon . . ."

Noel Sharp is about my age. He lives in a small private house on a neat estate built recently near the middle of the town, on the site of a market garden. The market garden – Fearon's – has moved further out of the town to become a mini-industry.

It seems to me that Noel Sharp represents a great deal of the part religion can play in someone's life. He began in a factory: he became a monk: now he is a teacher. I have set out his story at length to show how the religion came into the life.

"I was born in Wigton, in Proctor's Square, just beside the English church. There were three of us. Father used to work at the tanyards as a labourer. He is a tanner really by trade but they closed up. There was a fire. It was pretty spectacular. There was, let's see now, it was like a big supermarket at the time, you know, it was quite a big place. And Dad used to take us in there to see it – where they used to take the skins and where they used to dip them. In fact, it was pretty dangerous at times because they'd to walk round the big baths where the dyes were with the skins of the sheep, and there was a chap fell in there at one time and he drank some of the water and died. It was pretty poisonous water. But the fire itself, well, it gutted the place completely and just left the mere shell and twisted iron and petrol pumps and things like that were all twisted. We used to play in them on the way back from school. We came through Bird Cage Walk.

We had two rooms, one room above another, and we left there when I was about two, I think. About the time when Grandmother was killed, in King Street. And then we moved to, I think it was, East End, which is another sort of backyard effort – toilet outside and that sort of thing. After that we moved to Brindlefield. Actually about

435

two or three doors from Joan, my wife. I didn't know her then. I think things were pretty tough then but quite honestly I can't remember being ever deprived or anything. Except during the war, of course, but it was different because you couldn't even get sweets and there wasn't a thing in the shops at the time. Not even a nippet.

Mother didn't go out to work. She's pretty astute and pretty proud as well. I think just making do with what we'd got and repatching any clothes. I can't really remember how we made do because we weren't deprived of anything in any way. We used to get eggs from the farm and things like that. But during the war I don't think it was so grand and Dad was away for about seven years. So my mother had more or less to bring us all up. Like during those seven years. So when my dad came back, with me being older – I'd be about six when he went away – you more or less had to get to know him again. My younger brother, Donald, of course, he'd have to get to know him from then on. I was six years ahead of him.

But I remember going to Brindle when we got the first council house; when we got the first bath and hot and cold water and living in the room with electric plugs and things. We used to have an old gramophone that you used to wind up. It was quite a nice one though, I suppose it was a nice bit of furniture. I often used to try to climb up it to find out where the music came from. I was that small. I used to climb up to try and find out how on earth it worked. It was really good in the new council house and you felt really elated. You felt that you'd really got something. And clean walls – well, we were the first tenants. We'd front and back gardens which we'd to work pretty hard to get into shape. I remember that. You felt as though you'd more room, to breathe. We were pretty chuffed with ourselves at the time. Mother missed the backyard. She was always fond of the back-yard. She always likes privacy as well and, of course, that went to the wind because once you live on a council estate you've no privacy whatsoever. Your whole life is in front of everybody else. If you are in a council area you have got to have a common path. You've got adjoining gardens, you tend to brush up with neighbours more. And, of course, they tend to have more children because that's why they are there in the first place. For us, as children, it was great because I mean you'd more to play with but for grown-ups sometimes there would be friction. Getting used to neighbours and one thing and another like. And I suppose you've to take the rough with the smooth. Sometimes you are lucky. We were very lucky; we'd good neighbours. But further up they were real boyos.

I mean, it must be terrible for, say, a proud family in the nicest way, you know, that want to try and keep themselves clean and tidy, and, I mean, not swearing either and things like that or drunkenness. You get a lot of that; at least, you did then, but now you don't. I don't find that now but it was a terrible place at one time. I mean, you hardly dare mention that you came from Brindlefield from here to Carlisle: you were automatically condemned. There was a lot of people in trouble with the law up there. Their children used to do some terrible bad things in the gardens, pulling up roses and stuff like that, and pulling gates off. I don't know whether there was any people in debt or anything like that but it was a pretty boisterous sort of time, you know. We used to have brick fights, and then Brindlefield used to take Union Street at brick fighting on the tip. We used to make arrangements to meet them and get Brindlefield on this side of the tip and then Union Street on that side, and we used to get buckets and knock the bottoms out and get inner tubes off bicycles, you know – tie each side and pull it through the middle. And you'd have a pile of stones each, and you just shot them at one another. Oh, it was really serious at one time. We made a catapult with the inner tube. You see, you held the bucket like that, you put the inner tube through – with the bottom out – and pulled the inner tube through, put the stone on and pulled it back and shot it through the bucket, you see. Or, another thing you used to do – you used to get bottles and put carbide in, you know, from the old carbide-lights, bicycle-lights, you know, put water in and shake them up and then throw them. Sometimes they used to explode in the air and sometimes on impact. Things like that. You'd get cut heads and that from stones and stuff like that but I never heard of anybody being seriously hurt, no.

There was drunkenness, you know, often fights with neighbours (this is in the Forties). I mean, I was too young at the time to realise but I've often heard couples fighting and one of them landing out onto the road and then the next minute they've come back. A lot of that seemed to go on at the time but being a lad I suppose I just over-looked all these things.

I took part in those fights but I didn't often come out the best, you know, in any fight, except sometimes – it just depends, I suppose. I remember once, tatie-picking times, the twins, the Coulthard twins, they used to terrorise the place and I used to take a lot of punishment from those two beggars. But then one day I suppose I just took the bit between the teeth and got stuck into them and I found I come off alright. That was about the only time really but mainly we used to go round in big gangs. Much more aggressive gangs than they are

437

today. Today they are peculiar sort of gangs today. I haven't really studied them but I think they are a bit different. We used to be more or less concentrating on stealing apples, you know, and that sort of thing, or going into areas where you shouldn't go – farm land and things like that rather than being destructive against people. It was more against things, I think, then. I suppose for excitement. There was a big group of us went out to Moorside Loch, couple of miles away, up to the tarn there. And there was a boathouse. Well, we sneaked in there one day and got the boat out and we were playing pirates, tearing bits of branches from one part to another to build a camp. And when we got to the other side there was a policeman and a dog and the farmer waiting for us. We'd only about four bicycles between, I think, ten of us; three to a bicycle I think it was. So we were really in the soup. We had to apologise and one thing and another and the farmer was pretty decent and all and just gave us a good telling off and that was that. We didn't destroy anything but we availed ourselves of the boat.

I think that in our day they used to face the thing and you used to take your punishment fair and square. Today there seems to be a subtlety when they attack anybody. You know, I mean, if you think about these muggings and things, I mean, they just weren't on. There wasn't that sort of sneaky fighting. You tended to face what you had to face and you took for better or worse, one way or another. We seemed to forget it quicker as well. You know, I mean, one street would fight another and then they'd be the best of friends the next day; that sort of thing, you know. It was all finished with. I remember one lad – talk about *High Noon,* he came out of a pub, walked down the middle of the street, faced another chap on the way up, they tussled one another as if they were hugging one another and one took out a bottle, hit him on the head, threw it down, and then walked up Water Street as calm as a cucumber. As simple as that. No bother at all. Always Water Street, mind, was a pretty tough place but not necessarily in my day but I suppose in my dad's day it would be tougher still. Oh, definitely tougher then. It always had the name of being tough, I think. Even when you used to go to dances at Maryport and Aspatria you used to go in big groups, taxi-loads. And wherever you went you seemed as though if you were from Wigton, well, there's going to be trouble. Or anybody come to Wigton, you were very lucky if you went away unscathed, you know. They didn't seem to take very kindly to anybody at all coming into the town. I should imagine it wouldn't be very good for business either, now that I think about it, then. But there's always been groups of some kind of another. I don't really know what they do in Wigton. I'm not very often down town, really.

I left school when I was fifteen. In 1948. I wanted to go to the Fleet Air Arm but I made a real blunder there because I went in and I was told that you'd to have a decent chest measurement. So at the examination I inflated my chest, naturally, when he was measuring it. Then he got me to breathe in. Well, when I couldn't breathe in he thought there was something wrong with me lungs because it didn't expand any so he thought there was something the matter with me. I came out and had a good cry. As a matter of fact it was almost without the consent of my parents at the time so it was just as well, anyway. I'd visions of being in the Royal Navy and writing home to say I'm here, that sort of thing, you know. However, it didn't happen. I used to be a paper boy for Maria and then I got a job in the shop, Redmayne's. Designing windows. I stayed there about a year, the pay wasn't so good, it was only about twenty-five shillings a week. I heard that they were getting better money in the cutting department in the factory (Redmayne's) so I got a job in there. I think it was about three pounds a week. I would be about seventeen then. I was an apprentice cutter. It was just putting different parts of the suit together, you know; making sure they were all together before being sent to the next department, and cutting out suits. And, of course, eventually you do a lot of studying at home to study design, but that was purely off your own bat. But then afterward I went down to the factory, the Rayophane, British Rayophane, it's Sidac now, and they said there was only labouring jobs available at the time. I said I would take a labouring job so I went down and they put me in the finishing department. They used to call it the finishing because that's where the end product is, the packing.

You see, in the cutting room at Redmayne's I got to thinking that there wasn't much future unless you were prepared to move to say Leeds or somewhere like that. You'd have to move if you wanted to get on and that time I couldn't see any prospect in being in Redmayne's all my life. I thought it was quite a dead thing to do. I didn't see any prospect whatsoever, and I looked round and saw some of the old men that had spent their life there, you know – it just wasn't good enough. It just couldn't be. Just by looking around and looking at the people who had been there all their lives. It was quite an old establishment and they had seniority complex sort of, you know. One man moves out and another man moves in, that sort of thing – an impossibility. And that's really why I moved out. It wasn't for the money, although you didn't get much. I just moved

439

out, I think, because I didn't see any prospects whatsoever. I wanted to be something. I didn't know exactly what but I knew that wasn't going to take me there. At the factory, Edwin Routledge, I think, was the labour manager at the time and he took me into the finishing room.

There was a man called Robson who was in charge of the finishing room – he's since died – and his under foreman at the time was a man called Broody. I can't remember his first name. I just spent my time pulling Collis trucks about, that's metal trucks with paper on and stuff, and baling it up in a baler for it to be taken away. A real drudge it was. An unimaginative sort of a job, you know. You were in overalls and you were mucked up to the eyelids. Conditions weren't thought of as very bad: they were pretty standard for the time. You'd to go round collecting all the rayophane off the floor and stuff like that. And you maybe got odd jobs to do in and around the place which could be dirty, it just depended on what type it was. But it was then I realised. I was working with two other lads at the time and I could see that there was something better to be got in life than just this wandering about aimlessly, doing this really boring job, because at Redmayne's I'd had to think about what I was doing where here I could just be Hello, boy; there was no thinking at all to be done. I'd got to use my mind, you see, to get any satisfaction. So I asked Robson if he had any other job available that I could take on, because I told him that I was bored to tears at this terrible job. And he said that he would see Mr. Porritt – do you know Mr. Porritt? And Mr. Porritt at that very moment happened to walk in the finishing room and he said to me, Oh, you are not satisfied with your job, they say. Well, what can you do? Well, I said, what do you mean? Well, obviously, he said, what are you interested in? What do you do at home? I said, Sometimes I draw – try to scratch on to something. Oh, you do, do you? So that was the last I heard of him then that day. The following day Mr. Mumdio (the manager) asked me to come into the office and he sat me down in the chair and Mr. Routledge was in at the time. And Mr. Mumdio said, I understand that you are interested in drawing. I was scared stiff, of course; you know what he was, he was close on seven feet, rather than six. Well, I said, yes, I am. Bring me down some, will you? So I brought them down next day and he saw some of my sketches and he said, Mm, mm, I think then, would you like to start in the office next week? Ooh, I said, would I? And Mr. Routledge pointed out to him that this job that he was offering was needing G.C.E.s. Oh, Mumdio said, Never mind – we'll give the boy a try, he said. So the following

440

week I started in there; a nice clean suit and everything – in the drawing office.

Well it was like, let's see, I used to start at eight, I'd overalls and things like that ... I was just, I had to have a smoke in the toilets like everybody else, you know, that sort of thing. Now it meant coming in with a nice suit and starting at nine. It meant having your coffee brought to you by the secretary, like the boss. It meant quite a lot. It meant you could smoke in the office and all that sort of thing. You didn't get dirty. It meant complete freedom, walk round the whole factory. It gave you full right of admission to anywhere at all and also you saw the plans of future developments and things like that. Because they put me on tracing from the beginning and it was then that I had to be serious about study because I had to go to the technical college. Sometimes you used to go to the pictures, it just depends. You know. It wasn't the right thing to do, mind, because I remember the lads at Technical college they took quite an interest in English and maths and things and they were quite fair really, I thought they were good men. It's a pity I let them down in that way. I should have attended classes more rather than using the firm's time to dodge. I was pretty serious about the exams though when they came round. I did try to do my best and I didn't do so badly. We had to do our Higher Nationals later on but we never got that far. But they were pretty good fellows, and I've met them since and they are still working in the Technical college but they're a lot better off now. That was in Tullie House when we used to go, you know, then. It wasn't the Technical college as it was now. And then later on the draughtsman's life was beginning to be slow, I was smoking a lot, too much time to myself.

I was about nineteen. Mr. Wolseley was alive then. I remember Wolseley was very amused when we had to show him how to bend six-inch nails and things like that as we were pretty fanatical with weight-lifting at that time. I sent away for a set of weights and that. The interest started at the factory when I met some of these men who were really interested in weight lifting. I can't remember their names because they came from the west somewhere but they used to take weight-lifting pretty serious, and there was a lot of a hundred and fifty-six pounds weight and things like that, you know, for holding big doors and they used to just pick them up like that and lift them, you see. Well, I tried it one day and I couldn't. I couldn't move the thing. And this chap said to me. You know you do things gradually, he said, you'll be surprised. So I sent away for a set of weights and everything and I remember they came to Market Hill which used to be the bus terminus at the time and they dumped these weights. I dragged them all the way up from Market Hill to Kirkland Avenue. We'd moved from Brindlefield. Kirkland was another council estate. I used to just practise and I'll tell you who really used to be a fanatic at it, and really good as well, Ian Thwaites. Really good. He had a real marvellous body on him. Sometimes I used to go to his garage and we used to do a bit of press-ups and things like that and then it was from there we used to bend six-inch nails and do all sorts of things that you didn't think you could do. And we could lift these weights after a bit, strange enough, with a bit of technique plus with a bit of extra strength. It's surprising. Ian keeps it up, yes. I think his wife does it with him. She's pretty good at it. Well, you see, Ian has got the sort of body that if he doesn't keep at it he'll go fat and he reached a good peak and it would be a shame if he let it go. I didn't keep it up. Other things took my interest, one way or another.

At the factory I asked to be put in the workshop amongst the lads. To be a fitter – welding and one thing and another. I really enjoyed that because it was practical and I'd a good chap there; he taught me a lot and he wasn't frightened to give me a chance to work. So many times I was given a job where I'd to use my own initiative. I was getting on quite well and I really enjoyed it until, somehow or other, I realised that, you know, when sometimes you sit down and you think about life in general, there doesn't seem to be any purpose to it, there doesn't seem to be any satisfaction – or where is everybody going and what for? And it was from then on that I thought I should do something. Now at that time I was very friendly with a nun, Sister Bridget Magnolia. She was a headmistress. She died yesterday. I suppose I'd just taken the Church for granted. But not – I mean, what should I say? A church-goer, I think. Full stop, you know. I don't think it went beyond that although I was pretty sincere about the rights and wrongs of things and if I did anything wrong I suppose my conscience would play hell one way or the other. You know, I never let myself off light if I'd been doing something wrong. My conscience would just overshadow anything. I think I was pretty serious, if that's the word. I was serious about life, serious about the purpose of life, the meaning of life; trying to find some answer. And there wasn't any answer at that time. Not to what I was battling with, somehow or other. And then I thought, well, perhaps if I went into an Order I would get some reason. In my mind when I thought about an Order I thought about bare feet, wearing a habit and being really strict. It was going to be really tough. And when I chose this one, the De la Salle, I chose it because I liked the picture.

One of their members that had died called Miguel, they call him Blessed Miguel now, and I also liked the tone of the letter which I received. It was written by hand which meant that the person had taken trouble. The others were typed and in bad form, so I chose that one. So I packed my bags and left home with all sorts of misgivings and wonderment and more or less wondering what the end of the track was going to be.

I talked to Canon McNarney, I remember, at the time and he tried to give me the gist of it and I thought, well, I'm not fit to be any priest. I mean, that's just one dignity that I was going to pass by. But I said a monk of some sort, maybe; I could maybe make that grade. I said, Whether I'm fit for that I couldn't say, and then Sister Bridget, of course, often used to talk, wondering whether I could make my mind up what to do and what Order. But nobody actually helped me to choose. My decision was completely and always has been in everything I do mine, I always choose, you know, ultimately. Of course, my parents couldn't believe it, naturally. Mother was pleased but Dad, of course, he said he'd give me six months. He said that We'll have you working on the roads, he said, and then he said, You might have the strength to pick up a pick but you won't have the strength to put it down by the time you've finished. And I left home and I was away eleven years. I met some fine men there.

When I got there I got off at Newbury and I had to get another train for Hungerford, then I had to walk from Hungerford which is about two or three miles, I think. Then I walked to this big lonely place where they breed racehorses nearby. It was a Scholasticate actually – a study house. There would be about in all, about sixty there. But it was divided into two. There was the Novitiate and there was a Scholasticate. Well, the Novitiate used to spend eighteen months in virtually utter silence. And study, and prayer, and more study and more prayer and work. Those three things. Work, Study and Prayer. In the hardest possible way. And to show you how much is spoken there, in eighteen months when I came out I'd a sore throat for the first time, just from speaking.

When I first went down I couldn't understand the silence for a start. I could accept it, but I couldn't understand it. They were rather a good few odd characters because it was the sort of weeding-out place. And a lot of them, you learn people, the closeness of people, you learn how to distinguish very quickly the sensitivity of people's nature, one way or the other. You get deeper into people's lives with the closeness, even though you have never known them, all your life you are close with them. You work with them, you study

443

with them, you sleep in the dormitories with them and you learn a lot about people. You are given jobs like sweeping up acres of leaves and wheeling them away, endless boring jobs. All sorts of things to try your patience one way and another. You are very seldom given praise, very seldom, just sometimes.

If you were taking the Novitiate you would get up in the morning at half past five on the stroke of the bell. You then had to make your way to the washroom, take pot luck there if you happened to be first; if you weren't, you'd to wait your time. Then you got back and dressed quickly and went downstairs to chapel before quarter to six. So you'd fifteen minutes to shave and anything else you wanted to do. Then at six o'clock another bell rang and then there was morning prayers which lasted for fifteen minutes and Commune because the monks would be coming from all over the place then. And then after that time a bell used to go and you had an hour's meditation. And the meditation was set on strict rules. Three main hours – it's rather complicated really but it was divided into nine divisions. Then on Sundays we used to learn the scriptures. You would take a passage of scripture and say maybe half a chapter or something and you had to almost give it verbatim. Things like that. It was good for memory and good for forcing your mind to learn things completely. Very good indeed. I didn't take easy to it because I mean I gave up study at fifteen and I would be, what nineteen then and I found it pretty hard to do. I could only learn maybe six out of ten at a time, and I couldn't understand why these other chaps could learn more at one go. But I found they were grammar-school lads and had never stopped studying, and they found studying pretty easy anyway. All pretty brainy fellows.

Sometimes we'd to go down to the canal which was about a couple of miles away across the fields. And that was a marvellous thing, being able to walk across the fields with a costume and have a swim. We used to play cricket a lot, football, mainly football, cricket and swimming. Oh, and tennis.

A novitiate was just, well, mere novices. If you were caught talking to any of the Scholasticate you were really put on the carpet, you know. You were told off in no uncertain terms. But in the Scholasticate now they say to you seriously, What is it you want to do? Well, when he asked me what I wanted to do I said, Don't know. He said, Have you ever done any study? Well I said, I have and I haven't, sort of. And he said, Well, What are you good at? I tried to tell him and then they go through, just as you are doing now, what did you do before, what did you do before that, how did you do at that, and so on. And from that they work out your capabilities. Well, when I was finished I would have been happy to go on a farm, because they had a big farm there, you see, and we used to work the farm every weekend. I was as happy as life out in the fields, driving the tractor and that, oh, I really enjoyed that. That's how I learned to drive, more or less, and then I said to them, Well, I'll go on the farm, is that alright? He said, You'll not go on the farm, my lad, you are going to study. So I took him at his word and they gave me my books and I started to study. And after that I never looked back. In fact, they had to take the books off me at one time because I realised there was things with books that I had never seen before and I was really learning.

Geography, anything. I used to read anything. I met a fine chap in there called Raymond, Raymond Clive. He's a writer an' all. He actually writes music now though and I got friendly with him. And he said to write an article for the Scholastic magazine. So I said, Everybody is trying so I might as well. So I wrote one about a boy and it was more or less to do with factory work, the engineering and things like that, you see. So I had something to give to that magazine, so I wasn't half surprised to see it in when I opened up the magazine. I really was surprised. I looked at it and to see something in print that you have written for the first time, you know what the feeling is like, and your name at the bottom like. So he said, Have you written much? Well, I said, to tell you the truth, not really. As a matter of fact I don't think I've read a book right through. And I hadn't. And he said, Well, have you never read Dickens, Arnold Bennett? Never even heard of him – like I'd heard of Dickens but Arnold Bennett and a few others which he mentioned I'd never heard of. Oh, he said, I'll tell you what I'm going to do with you. I'm not letting you study for the certificates, G.C.E.s and that, I'm going to give you a year on reading. So he fed me books for a year and he said that When you've finished that one – he gave me one of Thomas Hardy's books, *Mayor of Casterbridge*. Well, I sat down and I started to read. Well, it used to be very hard for me to concentrate, reading a book, but he said, Now get on to the first fifty pages at one sitting, which I did, and I found I read the book in one day. I really enjoyed it. Oh, I said, it was terrific, that. Oh, he said, here's another then. So he gave me another and then another and I sat reading Newman and Arnold Bennett, as I say, and Dickens, Shakespeare, Shaw, like I was really reading these men and I really enjoyed them. Wherever I was, I was with a book. You never see me without a book, never. Even when we had free time. Even if we could do what we liked I

445

was under a bush with a book, you know. I remember the big chief walking by one day and said, What's he doing? and he said, Does he know it's a day off? I said, Well – I was reading a book about North America at the time – and I said Well, and he said, What are you reading anyway? I said, I'm reading about North America. He said, It's a day off; you should be enjoying yourself. Oh, I said, I'm enjoying this and I just kept under the bush, reading it, you know. I remember that. So it was then that they used to take the books off me and be more active. Which was fair enough I mean, I think I was getting a bit more, getting too bookwormish or whatever you call it. I spent about four years in the Scholasticate.

When I saw my mother for the first time – five years later – she looked a bit older, and so was my dad, and it was then that I realised the deep guttural type of accent from where I came from, and the strangeness. Because most of those chaps, you know, spoke rather posh, you know, so when I came home I really recognised the accent for the first time, it really stood out which I've lost now. My ear has lost that sound because I've got back into it again. Other than that I don't think there was anything else different.

Now in the De la Salle Order they had Approved schools, a good number. And then they asked me what type of school I would like to teach in, I chose Approved schools, and they asked me why? I said I thought maybe I could do a bit of good work in those schools, you know, because I felt that is where help is most needed. Well, in my opinion I thought it was there, you see. Now I'd been to see some of these grammar schools, well, most of them they paid, you see, and they were pretty well off. So I thought, well, those fellows don't need any help anyway, except studywise. Mind, I've learned since. I've learned since a different philosophy. And they sent me then to Scotland to Tralient near Edinburgh where I spent three years. An Approved school. From my experience of visiting different schools on different occasions, for different things, I found that where there was some type of religion there was less bother, less trouble. Now whether it was due to this or not I don't know. But I've visited some pretty poor schools, the state Approved schools, where the lads were pretty miserable and where doors were locked, where their freedom was really restricted to a limited amount, you know, and to me it just didn't work out. You see, you get a sort of feeling for these lads, you know, and there's another thing that when you work amongst them, they know if you like them a lot. I mean, they know if you are interested in them. I don't mean you don't have to punish them and I don't mean that you used to let them get away with things

446

that were naughty and were bad things, but somehow or other they accepted being admonished from some but not from others. I mean, I have known lads from Liverpool gang up on a teacher and walk in an arc across the yard and force him right off the playground just because they didn't like him. But I really liked those lads, and I really liked working with them. And if I was asked now who I'd like to teach, well, I'd like to teach these lads. Mind you, they let you down often but there's one thing that they liked and respected and that was no matter how many times you caught them doing things wrong, you didn't add that to the next time you caught them. They respected being punished for the thing they were caught for but they resent old sores being opened you know, and I think that's what some of the unpopular ones used to do. They used to boast about how much they knew about them, how much they knew about their fathers, etcetera – well, of course, this is just needling them all the time and this is wrong.

I mean, many times we used to spend hours in the Gorbals looking for lads who'd run off. That's the sort of job and I'm used to it. You knocked on the door for one boy and we'd actually seen him go through that door, but you'd have a hole through a wall into another house where he'd get out through the back and into somewhere else. Like there's some lads I'll know that's probably there now in that prison. There's a senior school over at Glasgow where they stayed until they were nineteen, and they, well, for example, the school I was in, as I say, was intermediate – now if they continue to, continue being criminals, they are then caught at eighteen and sent to Glasgow, Bishopriggs. And I remember going over there one day and I walked over the yard, I was coming to talk to the teachers or something, oh and one would say, Hello, sir, Hello, sir – some of the old ones, you know, that had passed on. I'd say, I see you've graduated, and they'd say, Aye, and the others would say, Aye. I'd say, Been up to the old larks again? And they'd say, I've been doing this . . . and they'd tell you what they used to do. They never learn. After a bit, when they get to nineteen, they just send them to factories and they gradually try to eke them out to get them used to society again.

Aye, there was one time though – you know, it's funny really, they are funny, kids, really. I remember telling Joan [his wife] – there was two real tough nuts, you know, they ran across the fields. And one of the lads said, Please, sir, there's two away yonder. You see, so I took me habit off, you see, and I ran after them across the field. So I came up to the first one who was the last and I was passing him, so naturally I goes onto the farthest. And at that time there was a little

447

girl, Catherine her name was, Catherine Glynn, and she always used to come over to see us, you know – to mend her bicycle, or I would go down to the seashore with her and give her a ride with her and that. She used to pack little lunches, you know, she was a cute little lass. And she was running after them with me, you see, to help us. And she fell and hurt her knee. So when I caught up with this lad who was last I looked round. Aye, I said, Tom, take her back, will you, she's hurt her knee. Righto, sir, he says. Bends down, picks the lass up and brings her back to sick bay and decided not to bother running away. Which gave me time to run after this other fellow. And he went over the railway bridge, under the bridge and everywhere. I didn't get him, he got mixed up in the shunting wagons and things, and the police caught him the next morning with his feet frozen, you know, because he had been hiding under the bridges. I just forget the name of the lad now, but a very big lad for his age. What he had done, he'd taken his shoes off to run faster down the line and I'm afraid he was over those shunting wagons before I could ever go. And it was very dangerous as well, I remember, at the time. So I decided to come home. They brought him in next morning and he'd been sleeping out the night before.

In my opinion, we were educating them a little bit too high. After they had been well clothed, well taught, I might add, they were having to go back into their environment again, and their environment wasn't very good. You see, they came from areas where they had to belong to a gang, and they just could not, under any circumstances whatever, disassociate themselves from any type of gang, they had to belong to a gang. Now when they got to go back into the gang again, it was very, very hard not to go back to their old ways again. But the only trouble is they went back into their old ways, some of them, with enlightenment – shall we say, which made it harder for them. You know. Because their commandment was like Thou shalt not be caught. That was it. But while they were with you they were, you see, there is such a mixture – I mean, you had even male prostitutes there as well. Now this I didn't agree with. I didn't like this at all because I thought that these should be in a different wing altogether, different area. And these particular boys were always good-looking boys and very plausible, very well mannered, in fact, they didn't steal in the normal sense of the word, you know, but very dangerous. Like a rattlesnake. They'd all the gifts and these were more dangerous, I thought. But at that time they hadn't them separated, I don't know whether they have now. But that's one thing that I would do definitely for the good of the others. They have their own way of dealing with things and you get the ones that hate them. But you get to know the types, you know, the ones that would associate and the ones that wouldn't. I don't know. You see, I was in four Approved schools at different times and different ages and they can do a lot for you, and a lot with you.

I remember once, oh real tough guys – they were playing football for us one day and I came out and was upbraiding them for the way they were playing – I could be rather vehement in a way because I wanted them to win, you see. Well, they came over to me after the game, they won anyway which was fair enough, but they came over to me after the game and they said, Oh, I tried me best, I really did. And they were really hurt to the core because I was telling them off, you know. And I remember two days later they bought me a box of chocolates out of their pocket money. As an offering of some sort, you know. Well, it kind of made me think that even these lads have got their feelings. There was one lad, there's times, you know, you've got to do some things – I remember walking along the corridor one day and I met a lad coming along and I said, Where have you been? I said, You've been coming from the kitchen, I said. You've been up to something, I said. What's in your jerkin? Nothing, he says. I said, Open your jerkin. So he opened up his jerkin and he'd piles of food and all what not and he was going to stash it away for the night so that he could run off. Now one boy came down the corridor and he said, Leave him alone, he says, you see – a real tough boy. I said, Oh aye, leave him alone. So you know how they brush up against you as if to menace you. So I thought there was a situation which called for drastic measures. So, of course, I landed one on him good and hard. Now this is all against the code of education, you know what I mean, this was dealing with the situation in the human way. That was that – it was finished with then. So the headmaster called me in, who has since died, and he said, That laddie, he said, that you'd to deal with, he said. You know, he wouldn't have a word said against you. And he said, I'm not going to upbraid you for what you did. Only thing is he's worried about is whether he's going to lose his teeth. Oh, I said, thank goodness for that. So I went down into the hall, looked at the lad. Oh, I said, I think they are going to be alright. And he'd a kind of squint in his eye, you know. I said, I think they are going to be alright. He said, Aye, I think so. He said, Ee. I said, You're a bit of a laddo, eh? He said, Aye, aye, I was a bit of a fool, he said and just walked away. Now some others in that school had done the same thing and they had a terrible life, you know.

449

Well, I think after working at those schools so long I was getting pretty immersed in the type of lad, you see. I mean, we'd to go camping with the lads, we'd pick strawberries in Forford, have six weeks up there. And sometimes you had to really rough it. And I got to thinking, well, I could be doing this job as well and still have my own freedom of decision, which I hadn't then because I was always dependent on somebody else. And I've always had a sort of independent mind to think things out for myself. And many a time you were told to do things which you didn't agree with, which you probably thought was downright stupid. And I thought, well, I may as well – I can work outside just as easy and do the same work, with the same amount of intensity and all seriousness. So I had to come out of the Order.

It isn't straightforward because, when I was travelling from the south to the north, I remember coming up to begin my first job, well, my whole stomach turned over as if to say, well, what have I done? But I wanted a family and a house. Something to call my own because, for eleven years, nothing was mine – the only thing that I owned was a New Testament and a pair of rosary, that was the only thing I could call mine. Everything else belonged to somebody else, everything I wanted I'd to ask for. If I wanted to go from one town to another, I'd to ask permission. If I wanted to do something, I'd to ask for the fare. I was completely dependent on others. In every way, therefore, when you got a director who was not so good, it was very hard – who was not human, in my eyes, and who was tight and trying to keep to the letter of the law without bending it, that made it hard. Because I went down to a place in Yorkshire, Market Wheaton, another Approved school, and that director I did not like, he was positively bad. Because I saw him, as a headmaster, take a dislike to one boy – and these boys were seventeen – walk up to him and crack him straight in the face. Well that, to me, for a man who was supposed to be bringing justice and fairness and preaching God, that to me was a real sort of a turning-point, I think. I thought that was pretty bad and I didn't like that bloke at all. In fact, I sort of not turned against him but I spoke out to him which, of course, was unheard of because he was a real demigod, you know. See, he was one of these chaps, he was in a very high position, he used to go out golfing – he'd golfing friends – he was a monk, yes, and he had golfing friends and mixed with higher society. He would get his deputy to ring him up at some club or something to bring him back, which was a sort of dodge in order, if he didn't like it, he could come away. You know, the usual dodge – and if he liked it, of course, he'd say, Well it's alright, I'll stay on. He had his car, he used to smoke. Now all this time I wasn't allowed to smoke and you had to get permission to smoke. All the time I was asking for permission to smoke I was denied it, yet he was smoking in front of me, the same man who had the same standing as myself, you see. This I just couldn't stomach. This was all wrong.

Now I met it once or twice throughout the place and the Visitor at the time, who was quite a fair man, he knew I was getting dissatisfied but you see you dare not tell them really what your grouse was because you could get into trouble. I mean, this chap could really make it hard for you because you were a nobody. You know. They could shove you aside, they could put you into some place where you maybe wouldn't be happy. But the Visitor at the time said to me, How would you like to go to France for a bit? I said, I wouldn't mind at all. So they sent me to France, you see, where I spent a while. He gave me six weeks and he said, You can have a bit browse round there. So I went and we visited schools out there where they teach the dumb children and that to speak. They had various devices and that, and I met some Algerians – it was the time when Algeria was sending a lot over to France and that, and they were living in the hills in old châteaux at the time, and then we went camping in the Alps and that. I really enjoyed it – it was really good. So when I came back, he said, Tell you what; I'll give you a bit of a rest after the Approved schools. So he sent me to a grammar school and I went to Manchester and I'd one year in Manchester.

Now the contrast between the grammar school and others and the Approved school was the difference in money-wise. Now in the grammar school you were mixing with a better type of parent, with the result they had a better type of privilege and a more sophisticated type of life. And, you know, you got a sherry every day – a chap would say, Oh, I'll meet you on the golf course on Saturday, or, I'll see that you get a caddy or something, or something like that. And then, of course, it was a great privilege if you got out with the boss on Manchester Golf Course, and they were really living it up. Pretty big men, you see. And I taught English, scriptures and French there and I really enjoyed it. And I used to take the Fifth Form for scripture and they were good lads an' all and you could have good conversations with them, you know, and they used to ask questions straight through and straight to the point. You used to get on with it and I enjoyed that. It was hard work like because they had plenty of homework and you'd be marking books and things like that. But I liked those lads and I started a swimming club there.

Well, the Visitor at the time I left was a good, progressive Visitor and rather good and younger, and I got on very well with him. And I got onto him and I said, It's no good, I want to leave, I really do. And he put me off and he put me off, I would say, for a twelve-month really, if the truth was known, until finally he said, Oh well, alright. So it was then that I had to go to Manchester to get myself a suit and one thing and another. You have quite a struggle – I mean, let's say, eleven years – you tend to get into a routine of life.

I was a real greenhorn when I came back into civvy street. A real greenhorn. I mean, I just didn't know about anything. The first thing I did when I came home was to go up to Nelson School, no, not Nelson school, the secondary modern school, walk into the office and say, Have you got a job? You know, something simple like that. Like, to me now, I laugh my head off when I think of it. They must have thought I was crazy. You know, here's a teacher just walking in off the road – Have you got a job? Well, I don't know who the headmaster was but I am sure he thought I was crazy. He sat me down and he said, Well, we've nothing at the moment, I'm afraid. I got out of there somehow but what he would do as soon as I got out, he would probably ring the office in Carlisle and say, By the way, have you got a chap on your books, or did you send such and such . . . ? So, I mean, I was without a job for a month because I just did not know what to do. Or where to go. Because when I left I didn't think of practicalities. I just didn't think of it. And they probably would think I knew what to do, you see, but it failed me completely actually. So when I got on the train at Manchester I was so pleased with myself and elated with this freedom, I felt like a bird just out of a cage. You know, I felt, well, all my shackles and everything in the world were just completely off my shoulders, and I felt like flying. I felt I could walk the streets like everybody else. I was the same as them. In Manchester, when I got on the train, I was able to sit and talk to people, ordinary, you know. I don't know – it's hard to explain really. I just felt ordinary, you know, and I really liked that. I enjoyed it. I don't know. I mean, we had Bishops and goodness knows what and somehow or other I just felt better. And when I got home, of course, I spent some time at home just staying in. I really didn't know what to do.

But I had to make some money. I mean, I had to live, so I took a job at Cleator Moor (twenty-four miles away) on the understanding that if I got a job nearer home I would take it, which was fair enough. So when I went there, there was a Mr. Nolan, he said, Would you organise the religion? So I thought, religion again. So

I started to organise that. I did art and English. I was doing alright but I had to mark books coming on the bus backwards and forwards, you see. And later on I heard of a job in Carlisle in Rydal Street, a junior school. I had never taught in a junior school before then and I'd never been used to young ones. So I got in touch with this Mr. Lett and he said there was a job there if I was interested. And I told the boss at the other school and he took a terrible turn for the worse. I never realised, you know. Apparently since we'd got things organised in the school he thought more or less everything was sorted, you see. Well, I told him that I was only there temporary until I got one nearer, and I hadn't signed any papers or anything. So he was really angry. He wouldn't shake hands with me when I left. He said, You'll never get back into the County and you'll never this that and the other. He was threatening this, that and the Education Authorities, you know. Like, to me, it was ludicrous, I just couldn't understand what he was at. However, the chap in Carlisle said, Look, he said, just tell him you are leaving and that's it. Which I did.

I went to Carlisle and I was with him for seven years. Then I was thrown right into the deep end. I was given a progress class of the dimmest children you could ever have and for eighteen months I had those children. They were the worst conditions I've ever been in. This is 1964. In Carlisle.

I went into the pubs once or twice. But I thought the conversation was a bit rough, you know, and I thought it was very hard to talk to somebody on a particular level. I found it hard because, you see, there was many things we were taught; for example, choose a topic and we would discuss it. And sometimes they were hypothetical and things like that. I really enjoyed this way of talking. And then you see, for example, let's take yourself. I've met some brilliant men, I mean really brilliant, and when you are talking to them their minds seem to be elevated to a different plane altogether and you tend to lift yourself up towards them. Now if you get, say, to a certain level of a different type you tend perhaps to come down to that level in conversation. I mean, some have the power of lifting a conversation and some have the power of bringing it down. When you are amongst people who are studying and learning you tend to study them as well. If you are amongst people who are layabouts and talk about certain topics, you tend to slide downhill, you know. That's what I think anyway, that's my opinion of people. You can be better amongst good people and you could be worse amongst bad people. It's funny the power of a group, what it has on you, subconsciously even.

For example, small things. I found a lot of people were interested in small things like, What was the winner today? What won this race? How is somebody's pigeons doing? How's this footballer? To me this was small stuff. You know, it was a sort of petty conversation which you have got to learn, as I say, yourself; you've got to talk to people in their own language, not their dialect, I mean their plane of thinking. You have to learn that, I mean, particularly in your job. And if you go beyond their plane of thinking then you've got to get back down again because you want the information and otherwise you won't get it."

We cannot leave out the Church of England. Most people belong to it. James Hodgson left school at fourteen and took no jobs. Now almost seventy, he continues to live in the terraced house bequeathed him by his parents, doing a part-time job at the petrol pumps – evenings – taking photographs, helping people, above all helping in the church, which has been central to his life. His father had wanted to be be a priest, but became instead an ironmonger.

"I love the old stone buildings, nice Gothic arches and decorated windows and lintels and that. Old abbeys, like Abbeytown and places like that. That's a greatly improved place.

I've been the sacrist at St. Mary's for nearly forty years. Since Father Doig's E. T. Doig's, time. Well, for the service, he prepares everything for the Holy Communion. He gets the chalice out and whatever the furnishings of the day are; red or green or violet or white for the festival. You get all these ready and the alb and the amice and everything is ready for the priest to put on. And you prepare the chalice ready, you put the chalice on the burse, that's a square piece of material like a little envelope packet, and there's a white cloth for putting on the altar. You prepare all this. You have the wine fluids ready and the ciborium which holds them wafers, say for eighty people or seventy people. You count the wafers and put them in. You usually put a small slip of paper in to say twenty or thirty. You look after all the altar linen. I don't do the choir vestments, the choir surplices, because I think that should be a lady's job and I don't do it. They have a lady who does bits of minor repairs like, mending bits of garments. You just pretty generally see to the registers, get them out for marriages or baptisms or you could be having to fill baptism cards in. Just general duties and, if you can, you are at each service, say seven o'clock or eight o'clock, mainly for the Holy Communion service or the sung Eucharist. That's what it entails. It isn't a thing you can play about with. I think it is sort of a gift that you must have as such. It could be very boring to some people. I enjoy it, I enjoy doing it."

CHAPTER NINETEEN
Joseph Graham

What needs to be stressed here, I think, is in how short a time things have changed so much for ordinary people: "things" – their conditions of life. It has changed the nature and character of this country so much that people still do not know quite where or who or what they are. The "masses" have, it would seem to any elderly middle-class person, all of a sudden asserted themselves, enriched themselves and got above their former selves. This gossipy generalisation omits mention of those areas of poverty, lack of attention and distress which still persist here as everywhere else – but as a generalisation it has truth. And now and then you meet someone who in one bound has come out of a world which would have been familiar to those of one, two, even three centuries ago in its confusions and tone, landed in the middle of the twentieth century and set himself up for the twenty-first.

Joseph Graham was born in the 1930s in Water Street and lived his childhood there in conditions which he would now consider intolerable and housing inspectors would catalogue as uninhabitable. Yet houses like these, worse than these, much worse, have been lived in by large families for centuries. Airless, cramped, few windows, no gardens, no amenities. Only now do they seem appalling: once they were as welcome as new.

The culture-gap, though, bridged in the mid-century by those born before the turn of it, has often been enormous. Some idea of this, I think, comes from the life of Joseph Graham. We spoke in the sitting-room of his house: he had just sold it and with his brothers he was building a house for himself and his family a couple of miles away, in the country. He's an engaging man, looks as if he has suffered a great deal but speaks with positive optimism – an increasingly heavy body on a thin, bony, even gaunt frame.

"I was born in Water Street in 1932. I was born at me grandmother's.

456

My grandmother seemed to be the most important person in them days. Now, if we go back to me grandmother, she was a member of a large family – I can't say how many; eight or nine anyway. I'm not so sure about my grandfather's side. I can remember him as well, but they were just ordinary people. Me grandfather just laboured about the place and got jobs where they could, the same as anybody else in those days, just took what you could get, and they had a large family, also, again, I should say about nine. A couple died when they were babies, the rest, most of them are still alive. And getting back from my father's side, my mother was the second youngest of the family. She has a younger sister – I believe one of the ones that died was a bit younger, Richard I think they called him – he was the youngest of the lot. I think they lived in me grandmother's house which would comprise of a cellar and above that there was the kitchen, then a bedroom and an attic, and maybe ten or twelve of them would live in there, along with various other relations who had nowhere to live, like sort of cousins and fatherless people who came along. There was always about a dozen people knocking about, in or out, especially at the weekend. You see, me grandmother lived on the front in Water Street in a house which was the two cellars, sort of kitchen, bedroom and a large attic. Now my mother lived at the back which was the same again but no cellar. But they joined them together when I was about six or seven. They made it into one house, so it wasn't so bad after that. But it never bothered us much. We just all got together. We didn't feel cramped or anything like that. We would now but, as I say, there was my grandfather and my grandmother and, you know, as the kids got older they went away. There wouldn't be twelve all together all the time. There might have been seven or eight people really.

My father, actually he was born in Kingstown, Carlisle, in a pub there – Wagon and Horses, I think they called it – and he had a bit of a rough life when he was a kid. He went to stay with his uncle, they had a farm, Blackford, and he was chased off with a shotgun after a bit. He couldn't settle anywhere and he finished up coming to his grandmother's at Wigton. He was chased all over the place. Nobody wanted to look after him. His mother didn't really look after him. She lives in Wigton now. She's still alive. And the grandmother, she's about eighty-six or eighty-eight. They seem to all live to a ripe old age just about. Most of them anyway. So my father really was born at Carlisle, but he was brought up at Wigton. He wasn't really a Wigtonian as such. He's virtually adopted as a Wigtonian – everybody would say he was a Wigton fellow – but he came when he was about five or six years old. And the first thing he did was have a scrap with Moosie Gray, first thing that happened to him, he always said that. He married his sister, you know – that's me mother – Moosie's sister, years afterwards. So I say, he was just an ordinary fellow who came to Wigton. I think his family were quite well off but I think his mother, Millicent, she was maybe the black sheep of the family in a way – sort of went her own way. She's still alive, as I say. She lives down Green-acres with Charlie Mitchison, that's my aunt as well, Gladys. But anyways, he finished up at Wigton and was fetched up by his grand-mother, I believe, or a body reputed to be his grandmother. And he went to the Catholic school, of course. It seems to me that in Wigton there's a certain tradition; it doesn't matter whether you're Catholic or a Protestant, if your father went to that school, they sent you there. I mean, I'm not a Catholic – none of us are, we're all Church of England – but we all had to go to the Catholic school somehow. Don't ask me why, but we went. It's a confused place. But anyway, after that confusion I've just spouted out, there's my father who was, as I say, just an ordinary fellow. His family had quite a bit of money, farmers out on the Bowness side, tailor's shops I think they have about Annan and such places, but my mother there – just ordinary sort of people, sort of farm-working stock. My grandmother was born some-where about Alduth or somewhere like that, and I don't know where my grandfather was born. I think he was born in Wigton – on my mother's side.

My father, they reckoned when he was about twelve that he was a fairly brainy sort of a fellow. He was just wasting his time. They hadn't the teachers to take him any further and he got a bit sick. Anyway he left school at twelve and he went to serve his time in the tan yard. It was at Wigton in those days, round where Tennants has his shop. And he was serving his time to be a tanner, and the fellows used to just go out on the booze and get drunk and leave him to do all the work. So when he was about nineteen he took off to the Army. He joined the Army and went to Malta and the Sudan and China and all these sort of places for about eight years. And he came back in 1928, I think it was, and he met my mother about that time or shortly afterwards. I think it was about 1931 when they got married. They just happened to meet the same as most people do, at dances in those days, and got married.

But my mother now, when she met me father she was working at Carr's Biscuit Works. Like yours. Mine used to solder these biscuit tins – lids on the tins – and she used to bike to work. I used to do that myself, as well, even in my days. But she was a flying machine on a bike. She would bike to Carlisle in twenty-five minutes, she tells me – eleven miles – and I say, well I've only done it once faster than that – twenty-four minutes. And the roads in those days were a lot worse than when I was biking so she must have been a flying machine. They reckon she could really cycle. Of course in those days I mean going to work and coming back was a bit of an adventure. Nowadays you just want to get there and back, don't you. Twenty-four minutes – it's a fair speed like. Johnny Middleham reckoned he had the record for Wigton (there used to be a Wigton Cycling Club) for twenty-four minutes for ten miles. So I think if he was a racing cyclist she must have been doing pretty well. Of course it might be one way with the wind behind you and I suppose on a time trial you might have to go in a bit of a circle and you might be against the wind half the way. Still, it's a fair speed.

She's never worked since I was born. She did get a job once during the war in Hackneys Ammunition Box Factory, but my father came on leave and he went off the deep end, she reckoned. He didn't believe, same as I don't, that women should work. I'm changing me mind a bit now I think they should have something to occupy their minds. I think they must get bored sitting at home. In those days they didn't seem to mind. I think they had more work to do really. When they washed on a Monday – it was always wash day on a Monday – and they used to do the whole wash for everybody on that day, it was really hard labour. Nowadays with washing-machines and launderettes you can do it in no time. I know my wife doesn't like going to the launderette; she would rather wash them in her own washing-machine. She sort of washes clothes every day and it doesn't take as long. I think they have more time really. They could do with some interest anyway to keep their minds occupied and stop them getting bored. But anyways, he wouldn't let her work. He thought that she should be looking after us so he made her pack it in. That's the only time she ever had a job until, of course, the last ten years or so she's had a job. But she never went back to work when we were young. It wasn't the sort of thing before those days. Nowadays she has a sort of job, going out. Maybe cleaning or now she works at Redmayne's on sort of a part-time job, just to make a bit of money, and to see people as well. She's done a few sort of odd jobs like cleaning. I think she worked at a factory in Carlisle for a bit there. But just since my father died, the last eight or ten years.

The person I can remember most, apart from my mother and I think even more than my mother, was my grandmother. And she definitely was the sort of person – well, you know, in Wigton you always called your grandmother your mother and your mother your mam, I don't know why that is – she was always the one that sort of, in my family and I think in lots of others, she was virtually the boss of the house. Perhaps that was since my grandfather died; he died in 1940 but I can remember him. Not very well but I can remember certain things about him.

I can always remember being a small kid and he would come from work and my grandmother would go down to the Vic, you know, before he came with a jug, for a jug full of ale to go with his tea. And he would eat his tea and have the jug and he used to kid me on. I just used to pinch the jug off the table and what was left and get under the table and have a drink. And he used to be asking, Where's that jug gone? And I can just remember in those days I thought I was being that crafty, having a sup of ale out of this jug. And of course they were just egging me on. I can remember things like that. And things like he used to have a marvellous allotment covered in strawberries and goodness knows what. His allotment was on the rubbish tip down East End. Well, they've just recently taken that allotment off them.

Poverty in the Thirties? I can't say that I noticed it very much. If you haven't got a lot of money and everybody else hasn't you don't notice it so much. It's just relative. If everybody's sort of hard up, you don't notice it. And if everybody's rich you perhaps don't notice it, being a rich man among rich people. I suppose we didn't have a lot but I can't say we were ever hungry or had no clothes. Now there were, of course, other people who, we would say, didn't look after their kids properly and you would say they were poor and they weren't very well off. But you would tend to think that was because they spent their money on drink or something. What little money they had. You never thought, oh well, it's the Government that's making us poor, or they're not doing things right, or it's the rich that's oppressing us or anything like that. You just said, Oh well, we haven't got much money but we've got enough to keep us fairly reasonably fed, and clothed. But anybody that didn't do it, you would blame their parents more than anybody else. You wouldn't blame any outside influence. I think people would accept that if there wasn't any jobs, well, there just wasn't any jobs, and we were sort of battered down, I think. I won't say that we were sort of socially well off, or well up in the social line in this town or anything like that, but we were always well looked after. I think better looked after than the vast majority of the kids round about. Of course, there were people who were better looked after than us, people with a bit more money like

Pearsons – they had a shop, and one or two people had bits of shops and things, and they had a bit more money, of course. Well, they maybe had a few more suits or they got a new bike where you got a second-hand one but you just sort of thought, oh well, I've just got an old bike and he's got a good un. Thought nothing about it. But there were people, as I say, who were a bit roughly brought up but we always put it down to the fact that their parents didn't look after them properly or something like that.

Perhaps when you look at it now, perhaps you didn't have much money. But I don't think there was a lot of what you might call poverty. We would call it poverty now. You just didn't have a lot of money, that was all. You spent it on things like food and clothes rather than drink. I suppose if you asked a man about it at the same time, he would say Yes, because you don't realise what sacrifices your parents might have been making just so you could have enough food and a new pair of shoes. I always felt as if I was one of the poor boys of the school or the town. I had to wear a pair of corduroy trousers which I didn't like, and I didn't like this. And I had to wear clogs. My mother would insist when I went to school I had to put clogs on which I used to hate at the time. But, you see, my kids now, they're just the same. It doesn't matter what you give them, they don't like it. They have certain likes and dislikes but they might think, oh well, I don't like that because somebody else has got one of these and you might think, well, why should I wear clogs when he's got boots? I think we can't have had very much money but we weren't physically ill-treated. It was mainly sort of from the point of view of feeling that you might look a bit poorer. You always had a bit of pride, I suppose. If everybody had shoes on and you were the only one with clogs you would stand out sort of thing. Course, you didn't wear clogs all the time, just for mucking about in. Now they'll say, you put your old shoes on and they don't want them on. But there was always one or two people better off and one or two people worse off but I don't think there was anybody really starving. But they would be not very well off. I mean, I suppose if they transported us back now we would be saying, Hell, how did we put up with this?

Kids today, I think they definitely eat more. We would be satisfied with a lot less when we were kids. They don't always eat but, when they do, they eat. They're better fed and better looked after in that respect. But we didn't notice it in those days. I'm not saying they're going to be healthier because they'll be too fat, I think. Mine's not so bad because they're all pretty slim except for the eldest one who tends to be a bit fat. But I think they just eat too much nowadays.

461

You would say that's a bad thing anyways. They might have more money but I think they eat too much. But they certainly have a life which to me might be more important and this is that people think more about children, at least I think they do. Perhaps I'm wrong again. You can't remember when you were a kid what grown-ups were thinking but I think people have more respect for children – what they're thinking – nowadays. We don't just say, unless we lose our temper, Oh, you'll do as I say. You tend more to talk to them, like grown-ups, whereas when we were kids if you didn't do as you were told you got a cuff across the lug and chucked out and upstairs or something. And you had to do as you were told.

Games are different. In my time there was no sitting watching the television. Our kids now they'll spend more time at home, partly I suppose because their homes are more comfortable. In those days, as I say, homes were so small you had to sort of get outside or your mother would chuck you out anyway and say, Oh away and play. Or you wanted to get out of the way in case you got a job. Kids have a different life. My mother would say to me, Go to the Co-operative for the rations. You went once a week – everything was once a week in those days – you didn't go in dribs and drabs. You were organised. You would stand in the Co-operative from maybe nine o'clock and not come out till half past twelve, with two big bags full of groceries. And all the grown-ups that came in, mainly women, they would get served before you. Our children wouldn't go to the street corner for you unless you paid them. But games, ours do play games but they don't play the same games. We used to play old games like 'You can't cross the golden river'. Now hoppie was another game – that was a popular game, hopscotch, as they called it in Scotland. You draw a thing like a double-wing aeroplane and there's also a big square one – that wasn't as popular as the other. But I think the most popular game with us was chessy. One boy chasing all the others: had to touch them to catch them and enrol them. Tiggy was a good game but chessy ... it's one, two, three on the head. You would be a big gang of lads and you would all stand in a line and you would have a dip, as all games did, to find out who was it. Dip dip dip my blue ship, and one potato, two potato. Our kids still say those things now, you know. You used to get the mug on the end and shuffle them about. But chessy was a game where you could run and use a bit of craft, slyness, because you would set off maybe twenty or thirty kids. They would just disappear and muggins would be left counting; they all got away ... hiding his face and counting up to a hundred. You'd be all round the streets – you know what the streets were like in

Wigton; Church Street, Market Hill, Water Street; there were all sorts of twisty lanes and cul de sacs.

It was such a marvellous place. You talk about an adventure playground but you had your own adventure playground. You've got the Crofts. Here's Norman Fell talking about we're going to clear a road through the Crofts and that's about the only place in Wigton where you can walk without getting knocked down. That lane at the back. They've knocked half of it down. But we used to run up all these cuts, through the fields, over the tips, over the sand walls – you know, this was a marvellous game of chessy because, if nobody was after you, you used to start doing something else. You would go and start doing another game and then you would just see him coming. The fellow – he'd see them coming and you'd wonder, well, I wonder if he's been caught, and you would all be watching. It might last for six or eight hours, from the afternoon till ten o'clock at night, even till dark, and you would have a good run. And you thought it was marvellous if you could run from here to East End and back round Tenters; you'd think, what a runner I am! It was a challenge all the time. But there was that, and baa, baa – hide and seek you might call it in other places, but our kids still play that. They don't play things like chessy. I think they call it leo at Carlisle but they play hide and seek just exactly the same. Baa, baa. We spent most of our time in these old broken-down houses. Tear the floorboards up for firewood and make sledges and things like that, depending on what the season was.

We used to run plays in the old houses in Water Street that were condemned and empty. We used to put plays on and things like that. Down the cellars – and charge the kids halfpence to get in. We used to dress up and everything. We had a heck of a time in those old houses. I suppose in bigger towns they would be bomb sites. But it was dangerous. We went through some dangerous things. You often think whether the people who were actually injured were unlucky while we were performing these games and things or whether they weren't just as wiry as the ones that didn't get hurt. Because Ronnie Miller – you know, behind where we lived in Water Street there was a house behind with slates all down the front and bull's eye windows, you know? Well, they used to have horse-drawn vehicles and horse-drawn hearse and all this sort of stuff, and it still has the galvanised roof. Then there was another bit of a shed on the end. Well, this Ronnie Miller he – we would all climb over these roofs, many a time we used to go over them – and he happened to go through this galvanised iron roof, it was rotten. Oh, he was a hell of a mess. His legs were cut from – you know, right up here and zig-zagged, and I don't know how many hundred stiches he didn't have in. Then there was various other lads like had finger-ends off. They were always getting cut on barbed wire. We lived dangerously. When you look at kids now you say, Stay down off there and don't go up there. You think, well, what the hell am I worried about? We used to go and play on the tip. Like get an old tin tray and scuttle down the tip for hours, and you didn't think of anything – you never thought of germs and things like that. You just carried on.

You see, we didn't only play games. We used to go out and collect jam jars, especially when the war was on, and beer bottles. Beer bottles not so much, lemonade bottles, but mainly jam jars; one pound and two pound. I think it was a halfpenny for a pound and a penny for the two pound at the Co-operative. You'd go all round all the houses and then onto the tip and pick them all up, and gan to the well, tip all the ashes out, wash them, scrape the labels off, pile them up in a barrow and wheel them up to the Co-operative. Get yourself a couple of bob or something. A day's work, sort of thing, collecting a few jam jars at the tip. And we went for what we call brummels and mushrooms, blackberries as they call them now. We did that, yes. I'm saying raspberries; there wasn't a lot of raspberries but brummels as we called them – they're really blackberries. Yes, we used to collect them and stand them in the beck for half an hour to see if they'd weigh any more and take them to Dickie Thornton's, see if we could get a bit extra weight out of them, standing them in the beck. And mushrooms, we collected mushrooms.

I think you were brought up more, when you think of it, to go and do a bit of work. You had to sort of to get some money. I didn't realise; money didn't figure much in my way of thinking, when I was a kid. You know, some people might be more mercenary than others but I wasn't really concerned much with money. But I suppose if you could get a few jam jars and a few mushrooms and get yourself to the pictures you were happy. But I don't think we were really too concerned with the money as with the making of it.

My life was cut into a couple of sections. My brothers weren't born until I was about five and a half and I'm not going to say I was spoiled. This is why I keep saying that I don't think, I didn't feel much hardship. I think being the sort of, well, one of the only grandchildren – the only one sort of living close to Wigton – and having a lot of grown-ups in the family, you know, uncles and things like that and cousins, I was fairly well looked after. You know what I mean. Until I was five I can remember having – oh, one Christmas I can remember, you know these old dressing-tables with like tiles on them – they used to stand a jug and a bowl on them with water in. One Christmas I woke up and I can't have had any brothers or sisters and I can remember it quite clearly, I got up and my father and mother – pulled my leg – I couldn't see anything for the Christmas presents. And they had moved the bed out and put this thing behind the bed, this dressing-table, and I can remember clearly to this day it was filled up. You know, when I first woke up I thought, Oh, I've got nothing. And they would say, Has Father Christmas not been? And then, I don't know whether they told me to turn round, and I turned round and I looked behind the head of the bed. And this dressing-table, it was three or four boxes deep with soldiers and a castle and all that.

But as soon as about 1938 I had brothers and they were a bit more to look after. And the war broke out; it would be a different thing, a treat. We used to go on the Sunday School treat, I think it was years before we went to Silloth again; I think it was well near the end of the war before you got to Silloth. That was your treat – Lightfoot's field for a picnic. There seemed to be – I don't know whether, as I say, it was because we had a bigger family or whether it was the war or whether it was a combination of both, all this going to Morecambe and all this stopped, of course. And these places, like people going out to Castle Douglas and things . . . So the treats then were not quite as extravagant. As I say, you went up to Billy Lightfoot's field for your Old Armoury school picnic once a year and played a few games. And it was usually on a field that had had corn or something. It was stubble and it was hellish – you know, the place to have a picnic and races, but we enjoyed it. I can remember the day war broke out. But we were going along West Street and the Drill Hall, as it was then – it's the Legion Club now (British Legion) – it had the wall right down to the road, hadn't it? And I can remember it was a sunny day and we were walking up and down and Alec Barnes (do you know Alec Barnes? – anyway, you've heard of him – and there's Alec), he was marching up and down outside the Drill Hall with his uniform on and his rifle. The place had only been up about twelve months as well, hadn't it? And we were saying, What's he marching up and down with a gun for? And they said, the war's broke out. We'll have a war with Germany. I can't remember any of this eleven o'clock message on the wireless like some lads can remember that – you know, this radio message that came over at eleven o'clock – I can't remember that, but I can remember Alec Barnes marching up and down outside.

I don't think the war really affected us much up here except from the point of view there's always a lot of soldiers about and there's a lot of aerodromes, M.U.s and things. I can remember the evacuees coming to Wigton. All Wigton was out on the streets, waiting for them coming off the train. And they came walking up New Street and Station Road. When you saw them – you were saying about poverty – they were all, perhaps they had their best clothes on, I don't know, but they seemed a bit better off than us local rabble. When you saw them coming from Newcastle and that, and they had these smart uniforms on and hats and bags and cases. And I suppose, when you think back, they must have had a bit more money than we had. Perhaps they were people with a bit more money who were sending them over. But I can remember two girls coming round the corner out of New Street and stopping outside what is now Noel Carrick's and saying, This must be the High Street – it's King Street actually, but she thought this must be the High Street. I can always remember that remark. Why, I don't know. I think it must be because it was the first words one of them said.

But another thing I can remember about the start of the war was going to get gas masks. We all got a gas mask. I think it was just a normal type of gas mask, and me brothers had one with a big nose on – a big red thing – they looked like Mickey Mouse. And then we had one for Margaret, the baby. You just sort of put her inside it and just zipped it up. But to us it was just a load of fun because we used to run up and down the streets with them on. It was just a game to us. There was one or two bombers came over us – bombed the Freemasons' meeting at Gretna or something and killed half of them – well, most of them. Somebody opened the door they reckon and the light shone out and somebody had been floating over them. He hadn't dropped his bombs on the target so he just saw this light and dropped it on the hall. And killed them all. I believe there was one dropped on the cemetery at Silloth and blew all the cemetery to bits. But that's the nearest thing we got to seeing any violence.

There was a lot of soldiers about, and Air Force people and Navy people. And also a lot of prisoners – Italian prisoners – but they just used to wander around Wigton as if they belonged here. They just had these brown uniforms with patches on the knees and on the back for a fellow to shoot at. They had patches on for if they escaped they would shoot them. They were at Moota, of course, and then they were replaced by these D.P.s – Displaced Persons – as they call them, and the Ukrainians and what not. We used to play them at soccer, the Ukrainians – that was our first taste of this Continental soccer. We had it long before they had it down the south. They could play football an' all. They had some classy players.

As I said, I went to the Catholic school, and I think I was rather more intelligent than most. In fact, I was always tops in maths and English and things like that, drawing and stuff like that. I think I should have passed a scholarship. I think what brought us down was being very nervous.

There were three of us should have passed eleven-plus, and I'm not looking for excuses, but I think in my case, having a hell of imagination – and I remember sitting in the class and I hadn't been in half an hour and I was used to being not very confident. And being in a strange school for the first time I was working things out on the blotting paper before I wrote them down. Whereas now I would just write every rubbish down and, if I was doing an exam, I would just write it down the side. I can always remember this lad from Kirkbride turning round and saying to the teacher – This fellow's got some paper in here. And the teacher came over and whoever it was who was supervising he just looked and he went away. Well, that upset me even further and my mind just went a blank. I can remember throwing him down the steps at half-time. You know, those stone steps going down out of the National School, getting him in the toilet and giving him a good thumping. Course that didn't help me – it didn't help him much either. But that was it.

To me education is still the greatest thing there is. But again, if you get too highly qualified, people sort of tend to pigeon-hole you again. If you want to make money today you don't need education at all. You just need a bit of gumption and take risks. I'm inclined to learning more than earning money. You've got to have money, obviously, but I think you've got to strike a balance.

So I said to my father, after all this fuss about leaving school, Well, I'm going to get a job. If I see one in the paper, I'm off. And they just let me do what I wanted after that. After I left school they just let me go my own sweet way. I think they did mainly all my life. We've just done what we wanted, to an extent, but even more so since we left school. We've never been sort of put strict rules on or anything. So when I started there I thought, Well, I'm going to go to night classes. So I went to night classes for three years really, studying on the job. Got up till about the S.3 and then I got a bit sick and then I packed it in. And then I started and did it again. Metal-plate work, it was. I served me time to a sheet-metal worker and just the usual S.1, S.2, S.3, Northern Counties thing. So I got into the third year and then, I say, I got a bit fed up with it. I stopped going half-way through. Playing football and that. You just stand to get a bit sick and you really had to go if you wanted to get deferred as well

467

from going into the Forces when you were eighteen. Not that it made much difference. It just meant when you came out you had to do two or three extra years on your own.

This was at Edgar's and Bendall's at Carlisle. I finished up at Bendall's. Of course, you had to travel, I travelled to Carlisle. You had to get a job to serve your time. I liked working at Edgar's, they were very nice. The took you on. They even gave us a rise to cover me bus fare. I always remember that; thirty shilling they gave us instead of twenty-five. But I carried on, you know, me saying you should get an education, improve your knowledge, broaden your mind and things like that. But I went into the R.A.F. after five years. Anyways, I started studying again in the R.A.F. but the teachers weren't up to much. The English teacher wasn't too bad; anything else you wanted to study you virtually had to study it yourself. They had a few classes on the camp. I passed the trade test when I went in. I think it was the highest fellow they'd ever had at Cardington. They couldn't believe it. I think I'd answered forty-four questions out of forty-five in fifteen minutes or something. They give you three-quarters of an hour to do it. Maybe just a sort of a paper and that then they give you a trade test. I think they were a bit dubious but with having served me time at Bendall's, it's quite a wide variety of things, and working round this part of the world you seem to learn a lot about other things. You're not sort of specialised into one thing. I think that's what foxed them a bit. Anyways I got passed in as an S.A.E. or something which was about three steps up the ladder and I was there all the time I was in. So I did quite well like and it was money. It was a few bob extra weekly. And I got that from the beginning. Well, as I say, we took a few education tests as well and passed them and thought, well, I'll sit a few more and then maybe sit a few of these O-levels. But I never got round to it.

But when I came out of the R.A.F. I thought, well, I'll just go back to classes. In those days if you passed your National Certificate like it was sort of one of the hardest things there was, you know what I mean? I'm talking about fifteen years ago, maybe more. And I thought, I'll sit that. Now I filled the form in and they were a bit taken aback again. They said, Why do you want to go into S.1 when you passed S.3 and the other classes? Well, I said, I want to start at the beginning again. So I went through that and passed and got my Higher National; that was in mechanical engineering. I was still at Carlisle and I started at Porter's then. Actually, when I came out of the R.A.F. I went back to Bendall's and I jacked my job in. I thought I'm sick here. Nobody liked it. It was a hard place to work and it was heavy work. It'll have changed a little now but, you know, firms round here, they're not very go-ahead, are they really, as regards welfare and things like that? I mean, they just have old broken-down bogs, rough and ready washbasins, and there was no amenities or anything like a canteen or anything. But it was a job. People round here were just glad to get money. I worked at Bendall's after I come out of the R.A.F. and then I said, Oh, I'm going to get out of here. So what could I do? So I got myself a job selling books for about six weeks – that was just to get out. So you couldn't leave a place round here and go to a similar place because they ring up and they tell them you've been for a job and they say, Oh, well, don't give him a start. They do this like. They do it in other places, I believe. They don't believe in stealing people's workers. It's wrong really but they seem to have a thing about it, these local firms. They don't like people going – you know, they won't take each other's people. I think it's just to keep them down really. I got this job. I sold a few encyclopaedias like but I thought, well this is a bloody reet racket, so I got out of that. I didn't believe in twisting people. Then I got myself a job in a tailor's shop for three months, selling clothes. I didn't really like that much, but it was a bit of experience.

Then I went to Porter's. That was another place I enjoyed. That's when I started going to classes again. That's an engineering works. And I worked there for twelve months, then I went to Spadeadam and I worked in there as a metal worker for about nine months and then it sort of collapsed. Blue Streak. It was just starting to get on its feet when the government decided to pack it in. Not pack it in but not to use it as a missile for defence. You know, they reckoned that the Russians could pick it off anywhere. Blue Streak, yes. But that was really my first taste of what it was like to work for a firm that wasn't a local firm. Once you went to Rolls-Royce at Spadeadam it was something like being in the Forces. It was an institution. And they really looked after you. You had a bit of an argument. I can remember once having an argument 'cos I couldn't have a new duffle coat. But they were a bit tight in some ways, but I mean really the organisation of it and the welfare, it was different to what we had known. It was a different world altogether. You were treated as a different person altogether. You know, you were treated more like a human being, and it really was a family firm but it's a gigantic family. This is 1959.

I don't know whether that's all big firms but I think firms like I.C.I. are very similar. I think that we thought, and which is true as well, that we were better tradesmen than the ones that had come from

Rolls-Royce in Derby, as regarding trades like metalwork and welding, blacksmiths, plumbers. Turners and machine people were quite good but there was a lot of people who didn't work for Rolls, who came from the North East. And they had people, of course, from Rolls factories at Barnoldswick and different places. But whether it was because it was sort of a government undertaking as well, that might have made it different, you know, more like working for the civil service or something, but definitely the attitude of the bosses was better. I think the main thing was there was a sort of welfare officer – things like this that you'd never known. And you could get a house if you'd wanted one. And when it sort of half packed up there was fellows – you could get a job, they weren't going to pay you off, they were going to take you to another place altogether. Do anything they could for you, lend you money, even a deposit on a house. Well, I mean, we know nothing of that round here. It was entirely different. But they said, They want some people down at Wetheral, at the drawing office. They have a drawing office down there. And I thought, well, I'll have a go at that. I'd had a chance to get in the drawing office at Porter's and I didn't like it, I didn't fancy it. But I said, Oh well, I needn't go away then. I've just sort of got settled in this house in Carlisle, I'll go down there. And they said, Oh well, maybe you haven't passed enough exams and all this that and the other. But then I just got a phone call and they said, Oh, you've got to go down and see this fellow. Well then again I had an interview on the site upstairs in one of the offices and there again it was a piece of bloody cake. I only failed to answer about two questions on that and I got a job there. It was a Rolls-Royce drawing school really. Supposed to go to Derby for six months but they did it at Wetheral. About six miles from Carlisle. We did six months' training.

It just coincided with getting married and finding somewhere to live. So why not find rooms in Carlisle? You've got to find somewhere to live. You might as well live near where you work. Shifted in there 1958 till we went to stay with a bloke down Lismore Place; they called him Coiley. He's a big fisherman but he didn't just want us to live there, like, in rooms – he wanted us sort of to look after him as well, and pay. So we only stayed there about three weeks and we found another old lady up Wigton Road. It's a funny thing happened there. I got married on 5th April so I got a rebate, of course. And there was a couple staying there and I didn't care much for this couple. And they had a daughter or two. Also staying at this house – it was a fairly big house – there were some relatives of this fellow Coiley. He still knocks about. He used to go fishing; stand in the river with his big waders on. He was a real keen fisherman. He had a bad back. He used to strap himself up. And this fellow used to be in the house, and he was a shifty-looking character. He come from Wigton, like you can smell them out. But the wife had left her engagement ring on the draining board, and it was still there. This shifty character that was staying there with his wife, he pointed it out. And I thought, well, he can't be so shifty; he hasn't pinched her ring. But in the meantime he had pinched me bloody income tax rebate! I never saw that. I kept saying, I wonder why it hasn't come? And I went and saw about it. And before I knew where I was at, I was in front of the income tax and they were trying to convince me I'd had it and spent it. Anyway they found this fellow after about nine months and the police said to me, I knew the policeman as well, he says, Why the hell didn't you come and see us? We'd have picked him up in a week – he had a record, this fellow. So I had to wait nearly twelve months for my income tax rebate. Anyways, that's by the by. But when we shifted from there we managed to get a little house down at the end of Fusehill Street. 99 Charles Street. A mate of mine lived in it and he was shifting into another area, so we managed to get into that one.

At the drawing office it was easy because, as I say, I was good at drawing and geometry and I had done it at the Technical college anyway. Smashing.

I worked there for six years, I should think. I think what was really getting on people was the uncertainty of what was going to happen. One day everything was booming and, oh, we're going to have these rocket engines and what nots, and the rocket was coming and they would test that and they were going to fire it from Woomera and everything was great. And then the next thing you know it's fizzling out, and then E.L.D.O. was on. We want some money. It seemed to be forever a battle. Somebody was going to give some money and then things would die off, and then we started doing aircraft engine work. Some Allison Corporation work in America. We had to do a load of drawings for them. Then that was scrapped. That fell through. And then something else came on and that sort of died a death. This E.L.D.O. thing, if you remember, staggered on for years. Then when they got going we were going to do the German end of it, I think. A gas generator and propulsion unit and then that again fell through. Well, people were getting a bit sick of this not knowing. It's still the same now. The country's the same. You never know where it's going to go. I think it's propaganda really that spoils it, that makes people uneasy. But so, anyways, I finally got a job at the factory in Wigton. I don't know whether I was doing right but I've been there about six years now.

It's entirely different from working at Rolls-Royce. There you more specialise in things whereas here you've got to do everything. You've got to sort of do it. You don't do much drawing really. People think a draughtsman does a lot of drawing; well, he doesn't really. You can do a lot if you're just doing draughting work. But we tend to get a job and we've got to sort it out, say, Well, what are we going to do? and order the stuff and design it up, and order it. Draw, if there's any drawing. It might be a machine, it might be a chemical plant, might be anything. You've got to sort of follow it through, from start to finish. Now maybe if you had people who were specialising in bits you would get it better organised perhaps. You can't do everything really. But you enjoy it. You order the stuff and you argue about it. You do it from start to finish. For instance, the biggest one we've put in lately is the boiler house. We've built a new boiler. I mean, it might have cost three or four thousand pounds altogether. It's a natural gas boiler and you have to have a water treatment plant. Well, we started off along with the chief engineer and the assistant chief and Billy Lowther was on it as well at the very beginning. But of course he went away and worked over at Sidac's (the new factory) after that. Well, we had to sort of find a place to put it where it was most convenient. And then we had to have new steam mains and a plant for treating the water and storage tanks. And then there's another lad got on making a control panel for it to make it work and operate and tell you when there's something wrong. Then you've got to put the building of ground down. You've got to see everything going in, this sort of thing. You actually engineer it from the start to the finish.

The old factory wouldn't be much different, really, from my father's time. In fact, some people say that for anybody that's on the staff I think a lot of things might have tended to have got worse. I happen to be still in the finishing rooms ... that might be a bit better, wages-wise. And maybe you might get a bit more advantage in the conditions. But it's the same place. You see, they might have a few more things like protective clothing, shorter hours, but of course you can't knock them out of work, some people. They want overtime. I think the country's being spoiled by this overtime thing. They've convinced people it's necessary to work all the hours that God sends, especially in this part of the world where perhaps people haven't been used to high wages, they've made up their wages by working overtime. They might have a slightly higher wage now, the working people, but as regards conditions I don't think they're a lot different. They're getting a bit better this last few years since I went there. But when I went back there were still the same old rows of lavatories and wash-up places. Still washing up in the same place, the fitting shops virtually the same. It's been altered round a bit now but I think conditions, the actual conditions in the factory, they'll be a lot better maybe for working. But for things like toilets and canteens – the same old canteen – it's even worse. The new factory, of course, I think that's a lot different. I've not really worked in it but I think it has progressed. I think the conditions there are better. But I think in this other side they've sort of given people the money. They've always said, Oh well, if we don't kill the job we'll always have a job. It's the only place at Wigton. We've got to keep going. They might have played on that a bit. It's maybe not as bad now. I think they have progressed this last few years, especially in money.

They've very weak unions round this part of the world. It's not the unions, it's the people. They very rarely go on strike, whether that's a good thing. It might be that they're able to argue things out better. They maybe have a more reasonable approach to things. But I should think they'll be stronger than they used to be. They seem to get their way quite a lot anyway. I mean, when that short time was on with the electricity there were some chaps, they'd been out of work a certain length of time and they had to be out a bit longer to get their full money, but they went back to work before that. Now one fellow, who was a shop steward, says, Oh, we're going back to work tomorrow. It's great, isn't it – get back and get working again? He's a good shop steward, and he gives them some stick, but he thought it was better to be back at work than to be hanging about waiting another three or four days just to get a few more quid. The money they could earn waiting would be better than just waiting for it off the Social Security. The other fellows were saying, Oh, why can't we be off till Monday and get a lot of money? Just different.

I've always been interested in politics. I was the treasurer in the Labour League of Youth. I can rememer that starting.

When I was at school I can always remember one of the Sisters, the nuns, saying that you must never – maybe I shouldn't say this really but this is what she said – she said, you must never vote for the Socialists. Now I don't think she said Communists because I'd never heard of Communists when I was that age. The Socialists were wicked men anyway – you shouldn't support them. She didn't say that the Conservatives were good or anything like that – she just said Socialists were bad. Now whether that was because of this religious thing with Communism, not believing in religion and all that sort of thing, you know, in those days like they did away with the church and everything like that. I don't know whether that being as I am or – immediately do the other thing if anybody said that to me. But, you know, I think that you were fetched up – you weren't sort of told that you should be Tories or anything. I think I've just thought that the Socialist way was best, when I was younger. But the people that you argue with mainly, I would say, the ones who profess to be Tories, are really just working people. I think shopkeepers, but there seemed to be a lot of people among the so-called business people who believed in the Tory way. I'm not saying that they go and support the Tory party and everything, but they definitely believe the Tory methods are the best. Now I disagree with them, but I disagree with the Socialists – I think that the Socialists are a load of rubbish now anyways. I flick from one thing to the other. I sometimes say – Them Tories, that's a good idea. You know, I try to see what good can come out of both things.

Back to earth. We're moving in a month or two. We used to have a garden and they're always crying on about gardens, the kids. Now I just had a chance of getting a bit of land so I think I'll take it. I'll buy it. I've got building permission. I think in a way there are several reasons. I'm not being a bit of a capitalist now like but you see you've got money and to me I've saved up and saved up wherever I can. I always believe in saving up and paying for a thing. I'm not saying I haven't bought anything on the never-never because I have. It would be impossible for people to do without it. That's why the standard of living has gone up so much. But I thought, well, I'll save up. And then I saved up. Then when the Labour Party got in the last time, I thought – well, the country seems to be going through a bit of a period anyway since about 1960 – I said, I bet you before long they'll devalue the blooming pound. I had a few hundred quid saved up – well, it was more than a few hundred. I wasn't bothered about money; I was just saving it up. It was just that I had more than what we were spending. We didn't set out to do anything. Well, my wife's always on about, Well, we might as well buy our own house, and I thought, I don't like this idea. I think that houses should be nationalised and all this. Then I thought, well, we lived down Greenacres when we shifted back to Wigton and it was hellish. I'm not kidding you. More arguments and fights. That's the worst about these housing estates. So it was getting my wife down actually. Waver End Lane. Kids scrapping and women arguing with each other over our kids and everything. The funny thing with people is that's it's alright for their kids to be knocking hell out of yours but when yours turn round it's all wrong somehow, this sort of thing. But we weren't very happy there. We settled down after a bit. People got a bit more reasonable.

Anyway my wife had been seeing these two houses, my mother was pressurising us a bit about she didn't like living up Brackenlands. She said I'll stay next door if you get these two houses we're in now. Well, we got them anyway. It was against my better judgment really but we were going to have another kiddie and we thought, well, it'll be handier for the town. Well, my mother's gone and got herself a bungalow now, so really the place is a bit too big for us, really, if it was knocked into one. So we said, How do we get out of this? Well, I got a bit of money saved up so I've always wanted to build a house. Because I've got a brother who's a bricklayer, and the other one's a joiner. They've always wanted to see if we could build one. I think everybody should own their own house. Either that or they should be nationalised, so you can move about.

I think living on a street is better than living on an estate and where I'm going there's houses but it isn't a street. But it's – you can't live in a street and have gardens. A garden's a lot of work but you've got to have a bit of room and I like to have a place that I've planned out and kind of organised for the minimum of work. And if you're buying another house, an older house, it might not be quite to your liking – it might be smashing, but what we want to do is to try and build a house and get it so there's nothing much to do. This is the way I want then I can go on with the business of doing things like enjoying myself. I think I've busied myself with things too much, over the period of time. But there'll always be something to do. I like playing golf; well, you can't get time. You're always paperhanging or taking the kids out.

I took up golf – it must be about seven or eight years ago. You see, my father always wanted me to play golf, so I was always interested. I even had bits of golf tackle when I was a kid. Putters and sticks and that. But it just so happens that the golf courses, or what there was in Wigton years ago, had collapsed. And people round here keep saying it's a snobs' game but it isn't really. Not round here it isn't anyways. I don't think it is anywhere. There might be snobs play golf but, I mean, it's the greatest game I've ever played. It's the hardest. It's satisfying if you get time to practise at it and do it right. And I think maybe if you'd been young and started up I think it would have been a good living. It would have been ideal for me – professional sport. I would have done that. I would have loved to have been a professional sportsman. I had the chance of being a footballer once over, but I was too shy in those days. My uncle used to take us down when Bill Shankly was manager at Carlisle for training and trials. But, I say, I've always been a shy, sensitive sort of chap. I'm not now like. I've got a hard skin round us now."

CHAPTER TWENTY

Postscript

Obvious things are always easy to overlook, and always important. In the time span of this book there have been great changes in the texture of daily life. If my great grandfather could come out of the grave and look around at the state of England entering the fourth quarter of the twentieth century, he would hardly be able to believe his eyes. The overwhelming majority of people are enormously better housed, dressed, heated, fed, employed, entertained and informed. The change for the greater comfort of the greater number is far and away the most striking fact of all and to ignore it might be to ignore the decisive expression on the domestic portrait of this century – which could be lost. The age of material advancement for the majority could be marooned in history. It is not predetermined that it goes on and on and yet we have very quickly built it into our expectations. More has led to the universal demand for more. That's no surprise. Nor is it particularly worrying unless you enjoy romantic nightmares about the polluting effects of capitalism. It is like the man said when someone complained of the smell from the factory chimney in Wigton, "That's the smell of our wages." And, after some prodding, the smell has been carried away; the wages remain.

No, it is understandable to fear the accretion of wants, to fear the seas as stagnant oceans of dead fish, the land wilting under layers of insecticides, the atmosphere muggy with technological fall-out, but for the majority, the dangers there are worth living with – there is an optimism about the possibility of improvement which is still widely held to. The chimney smell *was* dealt with.

What else would instantly strike the nineteenth-century time-traveller? Well – the place is literally three or four times as big as it was – though the population is only 25% up. The council estates spread out in all directions. Cars instead of horses, the labour gone out of farming, schools vastly extended and richly equipped, churches still there, still attended though by fewer people, the Sabbath becoming the day of recreation rather than the day of rest. Money – perhaps the biggest change. In 1900 a shilling could be lived on, as Joseph Johnston said, in fact less than a shilling could get food for a week. Now that same sum will buy one chocolate biscuit. Middle-aged people, whose parents paid rent of two or three shillings a week in the early years of the century for privately owned accommodation, now live in council houses and pay a real rent of average eight or nine pounds a week, in cash terms four or five hundred times as much: or they are buying a house for eight or nine thousand pounds – the wealth of the Orient to most people in Victorian England. These equations would baffle them.

But though it is bigger and less cosy and less "charming", I expect he would be impressed by the general cleanliness of the place, the houses, the roads, the well-lit streets, the hum of electricity on the farms, well-drained fields, new barns, the important buildings still there though their function is changed. The people too would be found to be bigger, heavier, in a social sense less cosy with the Continent just a package tour away and even sons in Canada and Australia reachable for holidays.

What emerges most strongly, in my opinion, from the records here presented, is the richness of character and interest within this cross-section of people, chosen pretty much at random in a small town which would not claim to be much out of the ordinary. Yet within the group there is a remarkable divergence of intelligence, talent, beliefs, attitudes and skills.

The only propaganda that this book aims at is to demonstrate my conviction that everyone repays attention, that the most surprising lives come out of the most unexpected places and that the generalisations of most affluent intellectuals, at each end of the political spectrum, about "the masses" or "the workers" or even "the people" – that any such herd-like descriptions are worthless. I am absolutely certain that if I had represented those whom, for reasons of space, I had to omit, the overall impression, of individuality, of the quality of life experienced, would be the same.

The social changes which have taken place are implicit and need no underlining here. Nor do the changes in attitude to religion or leisure or work. But perhaps there is one point which should be made.

At the moment England seems threatened by itself. According to some newspapers and politicians and commentators the unions are behaving like medieval barons, according to others, the employers are still behaving like careless profiteers; every day we read and hear sensible people on letter pages, in newspaper columns, on radio, and on television, warning us of crisis, chaos and swift disintegration or, at best, a painful ossification of this country. In the Western world we alone cannot seem to rediscover the basic rules of economic security. The picture presented on all sides is of a house divided against itself and about to fall.

What the burden of these interviews shows, I believe, is that the safety net is sound. It is also newly made each generation. The feeling and certainty which comes from these interviews is so much more confident and fertile in hope and possibilities than the threadbare whining of the headlines that there could be two different worlds. Those I spoke to were worried about inflation, about unemployment, about recessions and disruptions – but the more we spoke the more clearly the lives revealed themselves to be fully capable of taking care of those worries, even of the breakdown, should it come. Because there are still, as Disraeli said, two nations and the division now, I think, is between the past and the future. The future lies in what is said and done and felt in these interviews. The past is in those who rule and write over us at the moment.

For, what most of all comes off the wearying succession of alarums and excursions which paddle across the headlines daily is the certainty that these are men imitating a sort of England which no longer exists. There is clearly no hope at all in making a society which apes the society which was served by an advanced industrial revolution, a secure defence system and the largest empire the world has ever known – that is, England of a hundred years ago. That is gone.

Yet the danger is that this past, this old England, this Imperial Hangover will not retreat into history or art or nostalgia but insist on poking its nose into the present. The "Gentleman" has had his day. If he insists on hanging around, on making social structures akin to the old establishment; if he manoeuvres society for the purpose of perpetuating old privileges, then we, like Spain in the seventeenth century, will sink sadly in the West. But within England now there is, as there has been for centuries, a mass of energy; for it to be released, apart from re-organisations and reforms and the grind of steady work, there needs to be a general recognition that by taking people as they are *now*, as they have found themselves, in a tough but progress-packed century, England will be restored.

So what do we want of the future? Our "glorious past" is always with us, even if it has vanished. And it is not much comfort to rehearse

479

the obvious here. To say that we have gone through two world wars, the loss of immense overseas possessions, the loss of privilege which always accompanies the loss of power – and all this in about sixty years – is not enough, it appears. Nor are we, as a nation talking to itself at the moment, very likely to be persuaded that the massive improvements in domestic living, social services and securities, educational and vocational opportunities, are much value as assets in the twentieth-century bank – more likely to find us complaining about the inadequacies and shortcomings of this or that – the Health Service, schools, libraries – the "roast beef of old England" has changed into the endless beef of all England, judging from the press. And though complaining is a comfortable pastime, even a necessary metaphor to relieve the profounder fears and pains which civilisation – and none more than ours – has ever determined to sink out of the sight of daily life – the fact is that few would hope for the seeds of the future to be found in these particular achievements of the present. Indeed the fear now grows that we have over-organised, over-secured, over-stretched our society; as I write now, in December 1975, this is the latest bogey. There is a nightmare vision of a country gorged fat with bureaucracy – which is the spiders growing bigger every day and the flies, who feed them, becoming fewer. There is a nightmare that the hundreds of thousands of teachers, the hundreds of thousands of people in the National Health Service, the hundreds of thousands in the police force, the hundreds of thousands in the armed forces, the hundreds of thousands in the Civil Service, the hundreds of thousands in Local Authorities, the hundreds of thousands in educational administration, the hundreds of thousands in Social Services – fire services, prisons, probation, borstals – the hundreds of thousands in the law and in Customs and Excise, and the further millions, millions of State-inflation and index-proofed pensioners, the millions of old age pensioners, the million and a half unemployed, the millions drawing supplementary benefits from the State, the tax collectors, the Vatmen, the Lollipop men, the canteen ladies, the territorials, the politicians – that all these are leeches on the body of the State, sucking blood daily, blood which others have to supply, ever hindering the others, growing larger, fatter, less efficient because more impossibly utopian in standards and demands, battening on that free body which makes and sells and inexorably weakening it to a corpse. This latest anxiety sees an England whose fame and fortune came from its freelances, freebooters, pirates, pleasure-seekers, liberty-lovers, independents, awkward customers, eccentrics, pragmatists, opportunists, adventurers – now coddling and constricting these men, their firms, their powers, their chances, and driving them either abroad, into cynicism, or into submission in the security-lined employment of the state. Leading editorials now point out that it was not overmuch sex that sank the Roman Empire, but too many officials – and the empires of Egypt, Byzantium and Spain step up smartly with corroborating evidence.

What, in my opinion, though, most prevents us as a country at this present moment from having much stake in the future are the three overwhelming facts which threaten our existence in the present: local in time, local in interest they may seem in the grander sweep of future historians, but just as the interviews in this book represent what I believe is the truest current of experience in publishable public historical form – so a modest appreciation of the obvious problems currently perturbing both governors and governed might provide the beginnings of release. For that, without any doubt – to my mind – is what we need: some release, some way into a new epoch, the key questions for the answers which will surely be there.

Most people on this Sunday in December, reading the papers, listening to the radio or watching television, would be told yet again of the three-pronged trident pointing at our bowels:

(1) Irish terrorists uncontrollable: solution to Irish problem apparently impossible: worsening of bombings only too likely: urban, civil, war.

(2) Inflation still far too high, prices up, productivity down: investment in industry low, foreign competition tougher: British manufacturing will and methods losing ground and confidence weekly: *and* unemployment, persisting, growing.

(3) Divisions in society seemingly growing not lessening, though harmony easier at local social levels: unions against management, bureaucrats against businessmen, devolutionists against those who want to retain an integrated and united Kingdom: and within medicine and education, the fight between private practice/privilege and public/state hegemony. On all sides people beginning to think that the more extreme the action or statement then the more likely it will be listened to.

This, then, is the backdrop to a normal morning's newsprint for Englishmen – and behind all that the world news forever gliding about sinuously down below the headlines, only occasionally breaking the surface of our press's consciousness, as hidden and portentous as Polaris submarines. Southern Africa. The Third World. Arab-Israel. Russian tyranny.

The three points have this in common: they are undoubtedly real and serious problems; there is no clear leadership; no one man can offer

481

an acceptable solution which leads many to despair of there being one. It would not be too much to propose that as a nation, most of us are, on this day, shutting our eyes tight, burying our heads in the instant and hoping that all our troubles will blow away: scarcely the picture of a society about to break its way into contemporary life.

Why, though, in a nation which has been prolific with leading figures, with men who have made things, decisions, events, for centuries, should we just at this moment be stymied for leadership? The present calibre of politicians and others may not be high, but it has been lower in the past without appearing, as it now does, to jeopardise our will to rediscover ourselves. Why will no one, except extremists, stand up to be counted? Because, we suspect, no one knows what to say or do.

Perhaps behind the lack of decisiveness is a failed belief in the virtues of authoritative solutions. After all, our fathers, grandfathers and their fathers were full of commandments – as they say in their memoirs and wise saws on the radio, in their speeches, blubber-full of nostalgia for the days of Right and Wrong, Black and White, Empire Red and Tory Blue. But we reject the brutalities and intolerance of those ages, the private nastiness, the public injustice, the heartlessness and the cruelty. We do not want their like to rule again. Yet have we thrown out the child with the rod? In the denial of the forces of destruction – a denial which we have practised boldly and on the whole successfully on the domestic scene for thirty years – have we emasculated those dark gods, the impulses to domination, the ferocity of ambition, the necessary ruthlessness of victory without which a country is castrated, able to sing but unable to breed? Having bled from the loss and wounds of the bravest of two generations already this century, have we in fact over-compensated by fattening up the present generation and turned a tradition of fortitude into an assumption of ease? And in the process lost the urge to fight to be what we could be, to go into whatever it is with two great aids – but each infinitely flexible to taste, strength and ability – a reliance on the achievements of the past and a real hope of coming through into a future made different by the passage undertaken. But we feel small beside our past, inadequate: it is not even a burden which will force us to make the effort to shake it off and by that very activity get us going; it's an embarrassment, too big, too grand, too much. And as for the real hope of coming through into a future – where? No one in England today speaks out with a vision of the future which is not dark or, at the very best, dim. So why undertake any journey? And as for changing society by what you do, that too, that essential boost to the crucial egotism within all who make for change, has somehow been ambushed – loans, debts, mortgages, broken political promises, bankrupt political creeds, abandoned religious dogmas, suspect social virtues – what future?

And so what do we want to be? Those I've interviewed have spoken for themselves, with my job basically the fitting and joining, the making of introductions and the carrying of messages, joinery work which was a pleasure to perform. But having lived with these and as many others many times over, and having, over these years, re-bedded myself into the deep north of England and remarried, what are my conclusions? I'm half-way, an intermediary, with axes to sharpen perhaps but none to grind; at thirty-six, about half-way through a reasonable expectation, barring accidents and catastrophes; having lived the first half of those thirty-six years here among the people I interviewed and the following eighteen largely in London where, through working in television, there has been the opportunity to see the superficial and active centre of things, to watch and work in with the comings and doings of politicians, writers, men of affairs, those whose temporary eminence appears from the vantage point of Cumbria to be so very important and influential – yes, a few conclusions are called for if only to round off the book as I began it, on a personal note, to come full circle, and to declare an interest alongside those whose interests I have tried throughout the rest of the book to serve.

Again we are in this peculiar zone which could be called twilight or dawn. I am fairly clear what I want for myself and family and friends, and it is all very local; equally I am not at a great loss when it comes to vote on or debate the large political issues of the day. Where the zone of twilight and dawn casts its spell or its mantle is in the area most central to this book, the area of life commonly and accurately called social life: that part where we are in regular and mutually beneficial contact with others and depend on them for the quality of what happens, life outside the very closest relationships and outside the most mathematical (one man: one vote) relationships. What is there to look for there?

For some of the time, it must be confessed, hedonism appears to offer a real alternative to the puritanical faiths of church, work and social hierarchy which dominated my early life. The gods of Christ, the Working Ethic and the English Class System were a tyrannous trinity: to see the pursuit of pleasure merely as a way in which to undermine them was at one stage justification enough, apart from the logical and sensual certainty there appeared to be in tasting and taking the joys available, without harm to others. But there is cost to oneself and the cost is not debauchery or degeneration or a loosening to licence of proper decent codes of social behaviour; the cost is the neglect of other parts of life through lack of time, energy and availability. And so to propose that we must as a nation race after pleasure solely would be to advise where I would not follow; though a blessing of the times must surely be the reintroduction to large numbers in an open manner of the fact that pleasures of the flesh as of the mind can be cultivated without guilt and shame killing them off.

Besides, the basis of pleasure must be selfish and self-centred and so it is impossible to make hay of it: who knows on whom the sun shines or for how long or when? No, looking for a fertile imagining of that which can be discovered and nourished in this country now, we will find in hedonism a welcome resting-place, a hotel for the night, a spa, a resort, a permanent weekend to loop and loop again about our weeks, but no diet for the days. Hedonism should be kept for private practice; as a public principle it would become mere gluttony for want of the refinements each person needs to develop in order to get what he or she desires.

What, then, do we want to be as a society? Perhaps at this time of worries and alarums we look back on the publicly declared (though often privately derided and ignored) virtues of Victorian, Edwardian and twentieth-century Georgian life, thrift, hard work, unquestioning loyalty, submissiveness – but no, you can't go back. Women cannot creep back into the kitchen – not without being forced there by a series of major disasters – they want to come out and work as well; and men and women equally want a say in their work; and life has moved on.

Why is it so difficult to point an honest way forward now? Why, even in the writing here is there so much reluctance? After all, I had a good home, won scholarships to Oxford, worked for an excellent organisation, the B.B.C., and then left to fulfil a wish that I'd been given the time and the training to cultivate into a possible way of life: I am doing what I most want – a rare enough thing for one to be thankful frequently – and yet I find it difficult to be positive about any present projection. Thus the implacable fact, or thus the infection – which?

We have been battered, drained and badly led but now we wallow when we should be rising to meet the present challenges: on our knees we may be, but surely we should be getting up, not wilting?

What affects us now is an infection of the will at the top: the foundation, as these interviews show, I believe, is sound, full of humour, hope, triumphs, courage, stoicism, full of life-giving qualities and life-enriching virtues. The pen is stubbed by these rotund phrases – but if we are to cease this sickly pawing over sores and scars, what else is there?) An infection because when you have the sense to look at other countries in a fuller perspective than the crude measurement by Gross National Product, you see how many layers of life there still are here and how fertile they could be.

If only this, I suggest. Inside all the greatness of this country which has rightly commanded the fullest respect abroad over the past few hundred years has been the idea of liberty. Now more than ever it seems to me is the time for us re-assert, re-define and re-impose the belief in liberties and the quest for liberties and the championship of liberties in our lives. To resist encroachments at home and protest against tyrannies abroad; to extend liberties around us and help others feel the fibre of them. For though empires come and go, though geniuses cannot be manufactured, ideas, once established in societies, can be rediscovered, reinvented and used to guide an ailing society to health.

The cultivation of ideas of liberty and their implementation inside society is a great gift which we have found and can take up again and pass on. Asserting a belief in that, finding in that the will to see the country represented abroad by the idea of liberties tested at home, would begin to banish the shades of dread which creep about any full expression of ourselves now.

Perhaps in the end we are afraid that we have nothing left to give anyone else or each other. Perhaps that is the greatest of all fears – that we are empty, unable to seed for the future. But in this notion of liberty, individual and social, forever reaching out for more areas to claim in which independent men can lead free lives, there is everything to give, and everywhere the gift is needed.

For one fact appears to be over-ridingly certain and important: whether you live under the Russian tyranny or within the corporate capitalist states of America, whether you work in semi-socialist countries like ours or the primitive capitalist/revolutionist countries of the third world, the *Thems* are getting bigger, the *Us*, smaller. Decisions are being made for us – always, of course, "for our own good" and always by people who are "better informed", but these decisions increasingly affect and contain our lives. I used to think that the visions of "grey men", of "ciphers", of 1984 bland drab uniformity were no more than panic-inspired notions of a secular hell (and I still do) but the pressure to "look after you" is certainly on and, in my own experience, the screws are tightening. This house, for example, in which I am concluding the book, has been extended over the past year or two, and at every stage, various authorities have been able to force me to comply with rules – just like everyone else, of course – which were always for my own good. Well, most of them were. But in the end,

485

when unknown officials can walk into your house and tell you to enlarge a window here, put a banister there, widen a path there, it's merely a pointer, a small indicator, but typical of the scores, hundreds of ways in which ministries, governments, corporations, unions, the Big Guys impose Their patterns, Their solutions and conclusions, Their *will* on individuals. They have to be resisted.

And yet if one point struck me more than any other about those I interviewed, it would be their differences from each other and the evidence of a wish to be distinctive and have freedom to do what pleased them and what impressed them as the best thing to do. In short there is, definitely, love of liberty all around and it is the re-instating of that passion which could re-establish England as a place where life was added unto. Power to the people indeed.

If this seems a grandiose claim – then look back on some of the matters revealed in this book. Modest, perhaps; unheroic, possibly, but again and again we met with that stubborn resistance to the arbitrary imposition of authority which has been the best boast of the England that rose and can rise again. Mr Postlethwaite, firm disciplinarian, adamant that "kids would not accept injustice"; Harry Watson printing what he thought ought to be printed; Henry Fell "not being pushed around" in World War One; Norman Fell sticking up for his rights in World War Two; Edwin Routledge resisting pressures first from management and then from workers; Kenneth Wallace refusing to be "a servant"; Noel Sharp's entire life; small they may seem on incidents and small they may be – but so was John Hampden's initial gesture when he took the action which eventually led to the Civil War and end of the idea of the Divine Right of Kings three and a half centuries ago. In almost every contribution there is an idea of self-dependence and an ambition for independence – something inherited, embraced and cherished and something which, at this moment in world history, could not be more valuable. For ideas of liberty, like all ideas, can fade and die if they are not nourished. And inside the grand notions of freedom and liberty which come from this country and can still come from this country, there is the simple stubbornness and fair-mindedness of the individual English man or woman. Not to be "put on", not to be "used", not to be "pushed around" – these are the colloquial expressions which are the foundations of those large ideas of free man in a free society which need re-stating now as loudly and firmly as ever. In this, I believe we are unique as a country. It is not fashionable and it is not headline news – but it is vital and can only be increasingly important as the world seems to swing to authoritarian

solutions of the Left, of the Right and of the Big. If we have a rôle –
then that is it – not only the guardians of Liberty but the spokesmen
for it and fighters for it. The need may be greater than ever.

London and Cumberland, 1971–1976

APPENDIX I

The People

This section is written at the suggestion and with the encouragement of Dr. Paul Thompson of Essex University. He has been kind enough to take an interest in the book from the beginning and, though he appreciated that my ambition was to write a general book for the general reader, he pointed out, having read some of the interview material, that it might also have a useful academic life if some such appendix as this were included.

Dr. Thompson worked out a questionnaire and this has been filled in by more than 95 percent of those interviewed. The gaps occur because of the death of the person between the interview – in some cases three or four years ago, in most about two – and the sending out of those questionnaires which were kept back until the end when I finally knew who was to be included. And in two cases, those concerned preferred not to fill in the forms.

Two points before the information. Firstly, once again thanks to those who helped – to those who appear in these pages and to those who were equally generous but who do not appear, simply for reasons of space, cost and manageability. Secondly, I would like to set down here how much the help of my parents in the most practical ways has been an asset in the compiling and writing of this book. Not only were many interviews arranged by them and many qualms stilled by them; many forms were taken out, phone calls made, explanations offered and persistent understanding given to the author by them whose life in Wigton was the true enabling factor in the making of this book.

People are listed in order of appearance. The key to the simple code used is as follows:

b.	Place and date of birth	*e.*	Education
br.	Number of brothers	*r.*	Religion
s.	Number of sisters	*p.*	Politics
pl.	Places lived in	*m.*	Marital status
f.j.	Father's job	*ch.*	Number of children
o.j.	Own job		

page

9 Mrs. CARRICK (died 1973; details gathered from friends) *b.* Wigton *c.* 1890 *br.* and *s.* None *pl.* Wigton, chiefly around George Street *o.j.* Housewife *e.* Private kindergarten and then Thomlinson Girls' School *r.* C.E. *p.* Unknown *m.* Married to William Carrick, Clerk to the Council and local historian *ch.* None

488

12 AGNES JOAN PARKER MOORE (*née* ROUTLEDGE) *b.* Abbeytown 29th May 1903 *br.* None *s.* Two *pl.* Abbeytown, Blennerhasset, Wigton *f.j.* Self-employed – carting, fruit-selling, laid greens, small shop *o.j.* Housework and housewife *e.* Abbeytown Elementary School *r.* Protestant *p.* Liberal *m.* Married *ch.* Two

13 Miss SNAITH *b.* Florence Jane Snaith, Wigton 5th April 1889 *br.* None *s.* Three *pl.* Wigton always *f.j.* Watchmaker and jeweller *o.j.* Retired jeweller *e.* Wigton National and private schools, left at 17 *r.* C.E. *p.* Conservative *m.* Single

20 WILLIAM JOHNSTON *b.* 59 High Street, Wigton 1904 *br.* One *s.* Four *pl.* One move – to 2 Hill Terrace, Market Hill, Wigton *f.j.* Grocer and pork butcher *o.j.* Group secretary N.F.U.; previous to that, chemist's shop assistant, clerk, pork butcher, all in Wigton *e.* Wigton National and Nelson, left at 15 *r.* C.E. *p.* Conservative *m.* Married *ch.* One (Died 1974)

24 Dr. DOLAN (died 1973; details gathered from friends) *b.* Wigton *c.* 1910 *pl.* Wigton, Edinburgh (university), Switzerland (convalescence in youth), Wigton *f.j.* Doctor *o.j.* General practitioner – doctor *e.* St Cuthbert's, Wigton, public school, Edinburgh University *r.* R.C. *p.* Unknown *m.* Married *ch.* Two

26 WILLIAM LOWTHER *b.* Ireby 1939 *pl.* Wigton – always around Station Hill area *br.* One *f.j.* Factory worker *o.j.* Site manager *e.* Wigton National and Secondary Modern Schools, night classes Carlisle from 15 to 21 *p.* Unknown *m.* Married *ch.* One

28 Mrs. SCOTT (details supplied by friends) *b.* Caldbeck *c.* 1900 *pl.* Around Caldbeck and in Wigton *f.j.* Farmer *o.j.* Farmer's wife, housewife *e.* Caldbeck School, left at 14 *p.* Unknown *m.* Married

30 SAMUEL TATE *b.* Fletchertown in the parish of Allhallows 23rd September 1891 *br.* Three *s.* Five *pl.* Lancashire (H.M. Forces), Fletchertown, Aspatria, Wigton *f.j.* Draper *o.j.* Retired hardware, seedsman, etc. – began as a coal-miner, Allhallows colliery *e.* Allhallows C.E. School, left at 14, later learned script-shorthand at local night-school *r.* Methodist *p.* Liberal *m.* Now widower *ch.* Three

30 JOSEPH WILLIAM BARNES *b.* Abbeytown 6th April 1902 *s.* One *pl.* Micklethwaite 1904, Wigton 1929 *f.j.* Agricultural worker *o.j.* Painter and decorator *e.* Wiggonby School, left at 14 *r.* C.E. *p.* Varied *m.* Single

32 KATHLEEN DIXON *b.* Wigton 29th December 1903 *br.* Three *s.* Six *pl.* Wigton always *f.j.* Railway foreman *o.j.* Housewife, previously nurse-maid *e.* St. Cuthbert's R.C. School, Wigton, left 14 *r.* C.E. *p.* Conservative *m.* Widow *ch.* Two

38 HANNAH ELIZABETH BRAGG (*née* ARMSTRONG) *b.* Aspatria 25th February 1898 *br.* Four *s.* Four *pl.* East End Farm, Hayton 1912, Westnewton Hall 1913 – both around Aspatria; Westfield House, Wigton 1914, Moorhouse, Wigton 1916, Garshileds, Gilsland, Northumberland 1920, Brookfield School, Wigton 1921, Orton Park, Carlisle 1921, Flimby 1921; then three different houses in Wigton Park, Wiza Avenue, finally Highmoor *f.j.* Mining engineer *o.j.* Housewife, previously farm labourer and cook *e.* Aspatria School, left 14 *r.* C.E. *p.* Labour *m.* Married *ch.* Five and four step-children

63 EDWIN ROUTLEDGE *b.* Aspatria 24th October 1898 *br.* Five *s.* Two *pl.* Forres 1915, Darfield, Yorkshire 1924, Aspatria 1928, Wigton 1929 *f.j.*

Butcher *o.j.* Retired (Justice of the Peace 1945–), previously Personnel Manager British Sidac Ltd 1946–64, machine minder British Sidac Ltd 1933–46, coal-miner 1912–28 *e.* Aspatria County School, left at 14, night school – learned book-keeping, English shorthand, social problems, self-taught *r.* None *p.* Socialist beliefs *m.* Widower *ch.* Three. (M.B.E. 1976)

68 WILLIAM STUART FELL *b.* Wigton 22nd December 1889 *br.* Four *s.* Four *f.j.* Slater *o.j.* Woodcutter *pl.* Wigton always except in First World War *e.* St. Cuthbert's, left at 14 *r.* C.E. *p.* Conservative *m.* Married *ch.* Six

74 HENRY FELL *b.* Wigton 5th August 1892 *br.* Four *s.* Four *pl.* Wigton *f.j.* Slater *o.j.* O.A.P., previously on fire tender Kirkbride aerodrome 1939–60, postman before that starting as a messenger boy aged 14 *e.* St. Cuthbert's, left at 14 *r.* C.E. *p.* Liberal *m.* Married *ch.* Three

79 GEORGE ARNOLD MILLER *b.* Wigton 31st July 1898 *br.* None *s.* One *pl.* All within Wigton *f.j.* coal-miner *o.j.* Tailor's cutter 1912–64, except for First World War *e.* Wigton National School, later postal tuition *r.* C.E. *p.* Unknown *m.* Married *ch.* One

88 RICHARD IRVING LOWTHER *b.* Wigton 8th June 1917 *br.* Four *s.* One *pl.* Northampton 1934, Cottesbrook Hall, Northampton 1935, Ascot and London 1936–9, Naworth Castle, Brampton, Cumbria 1939–42, Wigton 1942 *f.j.* Tanner *o.j.* Leading storeman, previously valet *e.* St. Cuthbert's until 15 *r.* R.C. *p.* Labour *m.* Married *ch.* None

117 Mrs. RHODA FELL *b.* Dearham, near Maryport, 22nd January 1898 *br.* One *s.* None *pl.* Local farms – Aspatria, Abbeytown, Wigton – 1913, 1914, 1916, 1918, Mains Farm, Wigton, plus house in Wigton 1923 *o.j.* Farm servant, also school cleaner *e.* Left local school at 14 *r.* C.E. *m.* Married *ch.* Three daughters

119 WILLIAM HENRY FELL (Jr) *b.* Wigton 12 April 1915 *br.* Three *s.* Two *pl.* Wigton always – various moves *f.j.* Woodcutter *o.j.* Inspector of Postmen, postman, telegraph boy, soldier Second World War *e.* Wigton National, left at 14 *r.* C.E. *p.* Socialist *m.* Widower *ch.* None

129 MARGARET COOK *b.* Carlisle 1st January 1907 *br.* Two *s.* Four *pl.* Wigton since 1911 *f.j.* Blacksmith *o.j.* Housewife, previously tailoress at Redmayne's *e.* St. Cuthbert's R.C. until 14 *r.* C.E. *p.* Conservative *m.* Married *ch.* Two

130 JEAN MORRISON *b.* Wigton 18th August 1919 *br.* One *s.* One *pl.* "Wentbridge", Wigton since 1940 *f.j.* Boot and shoe retailer *o.j.* Housewife, previously shop assistant in father's business *e.* Wigton National School to 14, further education classes later *r.* C.E. *p.* Liberal *m.* Married *ch.* Two

132 Miss BARBARA WILSON (available information in the text)

135 JOHN JOHNSTON *b.* Wigton 18th March 1922 *br.* None *s.* Two *pl.* Wigton *f.j.* Shopkeeper *o.j.* Schoolmaster, R.A.F. navigator in Second World War *e.* Nelson School until 18, teacher training college *r.* C.E. *p.* Labour *m.* Married *ch.* Four

137 MARY TERESA REEVES (*née* CHARTERS) *b.* Wigton 27th July 1927 *br.* Four *s.* Two *pl.* Arbroath (Scotland) 1951, Portsmouth 1957, Wigton 1963 *f.j.* Clerk *o.j.* Housewife, previously canteen manageress *e.* St. Cuthbert's R.C. School until 14 *r.* R.C. *p.* Labour *m.* Married *ch.* None

144 EDNA CARRUTHERS (*née* STAMPER) *b.* Wigton 8th December 1919 *br.* One *s.* None *pl.* Wigton always *f.j.* Steam-roller driver *o.j.* Housewife, pre-

viously tailoress, Redmayne's *e.* St. Cuthbert's R.C. until 14 *r.* C.E. *p.* Labour *m.* Married *ch.* Three

147 J. J. JOHNSTON *b.* Wigton *c.* 1910 *s.* One *pl.* Wigton always *f.j.* Master baker *o.j.* Master baker, previously cook in R.A.F. *e.* Wigton National School until 14 *r.* C.E. *p.* Undeclared *m.* Married *ch.* One

152 NORMAN FELL *b.* Wigton 12th May 1918 *br.* Three *s.* Two *pl.* Wigton, moves 1920, 1934, 1939, 1951, 1955, service abroad Second World War *f.j.* Woodcutter *o.j.* Plumber and pipefitter *e.* Wigton National until 14, self-taught local government *r.* C.E. *p.* Labour *m.* Married *ch.* Two

160 JOSEPH WILLIAM PARKIN LIGHTFOOT *b.* Bolton Low Houses 13th December 1908 *br.* Two *s.* Two *pl.* Fletchertown 1938, Kirkland 1942, Wigton 1954 *f.j.* Coal-miner *o.j.* Retired, previously coal-miner 1922, farm labourer 1924, labourer on pipe-tracks, part-time gardener 1930s, driver Cumberland Motor Services 1942–68, own shop in 1950s *e.* Bolton Low Houses until 14 *r.* Methodist *p.* Labour *m.* Married *ch.* Two

177 MARION R. M. KERR *b.* Woodhouse, Whitehaven 26th July 1904 *br.* Two *s.* One *pl.* Hiswall 1911, Whelpside 1925, Red Hall 1928 *f.j.* Mining engineer *o.j.* Housewife *e.* Miss Strathern's school and Sedbergh until 17½ *r.* Presbyterian *p.* Conservative *m.* Married *ch.* Three

184 ROBERT EDWIN STEPHENS *b.* Asby 11th March 1904 *br.* Two half-brothers *pl.* Cleator Moor, Egremont, Lamplugh, Wigton, Lorton, Asby, Wiggonby, Lorton, Corlatton Mill, Risley, Woodhouses, Great Orton, Hesket-New-Market, Kirkland, Lamplugh *f.j.* Not known *o.j.* Retired, previously farm worker 1917–22, coal-miner, farm worker, timber-feller 1951–68, quarry man *e.* Arlecdon Council School until 13½ *r.* Protestant *p.* Labour *m.* Married *ch.* Three

187 MARGARET ELLIS *b.* Wellrash, Bolton Gate 25th November 1931 *br.* One *s.* Two *pl.* Lees Rigg 1932, Church Rigg 1942, Wigton 1952 *f.j.* Farmer *o.j.* Shopkeeper – self-employed *e.* Thomlinson School *r.* C.E. *p.* Conservative *m.* Married (twice – first husband deceased) *ch.* One

189 JOHN DIXON *b.* Thursby 23rd March 1906 *br.* Three *s.* Four *pl.* Thursby always *f.j.* Farmer *o.j.* Farmer and horse-trainer *e.* Thursby until 14 *r.* C.E. *p.* Conservative *m.* Married *ch.* Two

190 JOSEPH BENSON *b.* Maryport 8th July 1924 *br.* Two *pl.* Risley 1950, Dumfries 1960, Wigton 1970, excluding war-service *f.j.* Sea captain *o.j.* Auctioneer *e.* Wigton National and Brookfield until 16 *r.* C.E. *p.* Conservative *m.* Married *ch.* Three

193 LLEWELLYN THOMPSON EVANS *b.* Goody Hills, Mowbray 7th November 1939 *br.* Five *s.* Seven *pl.* Angerton, Kirkbride 1944, Meadsgate 1964–5, Wigton 1965 *f.j.* Farmer *o.j.* Factory charge hand, previously farming *e.* Kirkbride and Wigton Secondary until 15 *r.* C.E. *p.* Conservative *m.* Married *ch.* Two

196 KENNETH WALLACE *b.* Wigton 20th April 1921 *br.* Two *s.* Two *pl.* Lancashire 1935, Berwickshire 1936, Yorkshire 1938, Wigton 1939, Services 1941–6, Wigtown, Galloway 1947, Oulton, Cumbria 1948 *f.j.* Carpenter *o.j.* Machinist, previously groom *e.* Wigton National School until 14 *r.* C.E. *p.* Labour *m.* Married *ch.* Three

219 JOHN FEARON MORRISON *b.* Grassloe, Maryport 6th August 1901 *br.* None *s.* Two *pl.* Flimby 1911, Wigton 1932 *f.j.* Coal-minder (overman) *o.j.* Engineer, previously marine engineer Hong Kong, New York,

Vladivostok, Vancouver, etc *e*. Higher Top School, Maryport until 14, Workington Technical College *r*. C.E. *p*. Liberal *m*. Married *ch*. Two

267 JOHN RAYMOND HUNTINGDON *b*. Dearham 11th November 1929 *br*. Two *s*. One *pl*. Frimby 1930, Wigton 1933 *f.j*. Insurance agent *o.j*. Committee Clerk local government, previously other grades in local government *e*. Nelson School, Wigton until 18, Carlisle Technical College *r*. C.E. *p*. Labour *m*. Married *ch*. Two

273 Miss BELL (died 1964; details gathered from friends) *b*. Wigton 1893 *s*. One *pl*. Wigton always *f.j*. Coach-builder *o.j*. Schoolteacher *e*. Locally *r*. C.E. *m*. Single

275 GLENVILLE FORESTER RITSON *b*. Wigton 3rd July 1922 *br*. None *s*. None *pl*. Wigton always or outskirts *f.j*. Solicitor *o.j*. Solicitor *e*. Nelson School until 14, St. Bees *r*. C.E. *p*. Conservative *m*. Married *ch*. One

282 ANDREW SAVAGE (died 1973; details gathered from friends) *b*. Near Wigton 1912 *pl*. All over Cumberland in early youth – hired, Wigton late 1930s *f.j*. Unknown *o.j*. Factory worker *e*. Local village schools until 14 *r*. C.E. *p*. Labour *m*. Single

282 FRANCIS BROWN MOFFAT *b*. Wigton 27th March 1927 *br*. None *s*. One *pl*. Wigton always *f.j*. Solicitor's managing clerk *o.j*. Solicitor *e*. Nelson School until 16, King's College, Newcastle-upon-Tyne, Metropolitan College of Law, St. Alban's *r*. C.E. *p*. Liberal (inclined to the right!) *m*. Married *ch*. Three

291 HARRY F. WATSON *b*. Wigton 20th July 1918 *br*. One *s*. Two *pl*. Three years in Warrington and three years in India while in R.A.F. 1940–6, otherwise Wigton always *f.j*. Transport (own business) and Cumberland Motor Services *o.j*. Journalist *e*. C.E. School, Wigton to 14, night school at Carlisle Technical College for four years *r*. Methodist *m*. Married *ch*. Two

309 ROBERT POSTLETHWAITE *b*. Egremont, Cumberland 2nd May 1910 *br*. Two *pl*. Dudley, Worcestershire 1929, Seaton, Cumberland 1931, Wigton 1933 *f.j*. Insurance agent *o.j*. Schoolmaster *e*. Egremont Infants, Egremont Bookwell Boys', Whitehaven (Sec) Grammar School until 18, teacher training college *r*. C.E. *p*. Conservative *m*. Married *ch*. Three

323 THOMAS CHARLES ALLARDYCE *b*. Wigton 6th August 1925 *s*. One *pl*. Wigton always *f.j*. Coachman, *o.j*. Factory supervisor, previously fish-monger Wigton 1941–54 *e*. National School until 15 *r*. C.E. *p*. Conservative *m*. Married *ch*. Two step-sons

325 LEONARD IVAN STOWE *b*. Greenock, Renfrewshire 18th February 1916 *br*. Two *s*. Two *pl*. Berwick-upon-Tweed, Northumberland 1916–24, Hartlepool, Durham 1924–7, Aspatria, Cumberland 1927–33, Alston, Cumberland 1933–5, Silchester, Hampshire 1938–40, Brighton, Sussex 1946–7, Devon 1947–8, Oxford 1948–9, Bridlington, Yorkshire 1949–52, Wigton 1953–71, Anshorn, Cumberland 1971 *f.j*. Methodist minister *o.j*. Headmaster, always in teaching except for Second World War *e*. Berwick, Hartlepool, Wigton, Alston, Grammar Schools until 18, then Oxford *r*. Methodist *p*. No firm commitment *m*. Married *ch*. Two

333 THOMAS JACKSON "Letter" – information in text

352 COLIN GRAHAM *b*. Aspatria 12th July 1913 *s*. One *pl*. Wigton 1941, Penrith 1975 *f.j*. Drapery manager *o.j*. Local government officer *e*. National School, Aspatria, Nelson Grammar School, Wigton, night

492

school later *r.* C.E. *p.* Undeclared *m.* Married *ch.* None

367 DAVID PEARSON *b.* Wigton 27th November 1937 *br.* One *pl.* Hampshire, Surrey, Berkshire during National Service 1955–7, Sheffield (college) 1957–9, Cardiff 1959–60, Waverbridge, Wigton 1960 *f.j.* Joiner and undertaker *o.j.* Teacher; vacation jobs have included timber worker, building-site worker, demolition labourer, dam construction, pipe layer, own house builder *e.* Friends' School, Brookfield, Wigton until 17, City of Sheffield and Cardiff colleges *r.* C.E. *p.* Conservative *m.* Married *ch.* Three

381 JEFFREY BELL *b.* Wigton *c.* 1908 *br.* One *pl.* Wigton always *f.j.* Licensee *o.j.* Shop manager *e.* National School until 14 *r.* C.E. *p.* Liberal *m.* Single

390 AGNES MOFFAT SINTON *b.* Wigton 5th August 1933 *s.* One *pl.* Carlisle 1955, Workington 1959, Hawera, New Zealand 1961, Wigton 1965 *f.j.* Chemical plumber, publican *o.j.* Housewife, part-time assistant librarian, previously confectioner *e.* Wigton National School until 15 *r.* C.E. *p.* Socialist *m.* Married *ch.* Two

393 WILLIAM LIGHTFOOT *b.* Reathwaite, Brocklebank, Wigton 23rd August 1910 *br.* One *pl.* Wigton always *f.j.* Farmer *o.j.* Farmer *e.* Bolton Low Houses School until 14 *r.* C.E. *p.* None *m.* Married *ch.* Six

401 SUSAN MARGARET ALLEN *b.* Wigton 28th June 1952 *br.* One *pl.* Trent Park College, Middlesex 1970, Scalesby, Carlisle 1975 *f.j.* Sales representative *o.j.* Teacher *e.* Nelson Thomlinson School, Wigton until 18, College of Education *r.* C.E. *p.* None *m.* Single

407 GEORGE JOHNSTON *b.* Aspatria 28th February 1937 *pl.* Wigton always, same house *f.j.* Boot and shoe retailer *o.j.* Boot and shoe retailer, except for two years' National Service in Germany 1953–5 *e.* Wigton Primary and Secondary Schools, St. Ursula's High School until 16, attended French language classes, night school *r.* C.E. *p.* Unimpressed by all *m.* Married *ch.* One.

428 MOTHER PHILOMENA (information in text)

435 NOEL CHRISTOPHER SHARP *b.* Wigton 24th December 1933 *br.* One *s.* One *pl.* Berkshire 1953, Lancashire 1957, Scotland 1959, Lancashire 1962, Yorkshire 1963, Wigton 1964 *f.j.* Tanner *o.j.* Teacher, previously trainee cutter, factory worker, trainee draughtsman, monk *e.* St. Cuthbert's, Wigton until 15, teacher training college plus five years in private scholasticate *r.* R.C. *p.* Conservative *m.* Married *ch.* Two

454 JOHN JAMES HODGSON *b.* Carlisle 1911 *pl.* Carlisle 1911, Wigton 1912 *f.j.* Ironmonger, manager *o.j.* Part-time shop assistant in garage *e.* National School until 16, plus self-taught with the help of a Catholic priest *r.* C.E. *p.* Liberal *m.* Single

456 JOSEPH GRAHAM *b.* Wigton 1932 *br.* Two *pl.* Carlisle, Wigton *f.j.* Boiler fireman *o.j.* Engineer *e.* R.C. school, Wigton, Carlisle Technical College, night school *r.* C.E. *p.* Democratic Socialist *m.* Married *ch.* Four

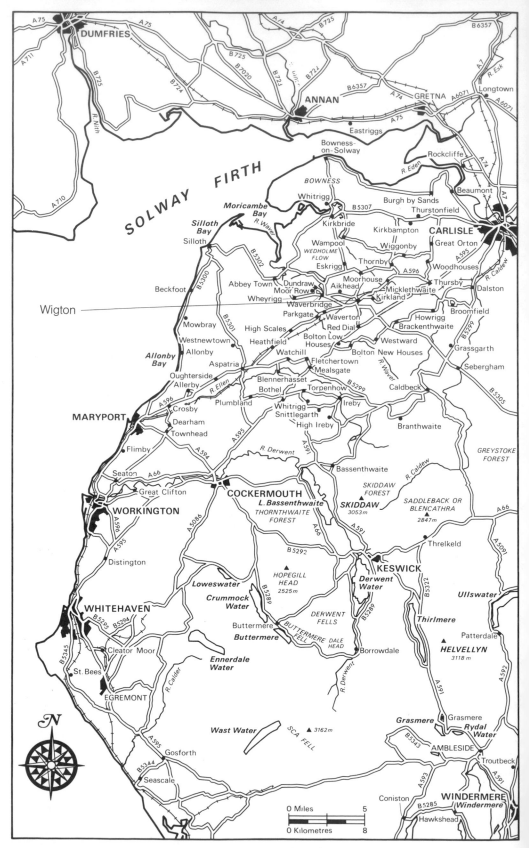

Wigton and the North-East

APPENDIX II

The Place

Although this is for the general reader and deliberately makes no attempt to discover or follow up facts and features of local history, there would undoubtedly be a sense of incompleteness were there not to be a brief outline of certain useful information about Wigton. For though there is, I believe, a representative collation of views and experiences, it is bound together, in one way, by the fact that all the contributors come from and live in the same area.

Besides this, just as in the previous appendix there was an intention to make the book of some proper academic value, with these details of the people and the place, those interested in using the book for their own future studies ought, I'm told, to have the statistical substructure they need.

For all of this appendix I am greatly indebted to John Higham, the head of the History Department at the Nelson Thomlinson Comprehensive School. He has recently produced a seven-thousand-word Guide to Wigton and his help has been most generously extended to my own project. Some of the information in this part was collected by his pupils and I would like to record my thanks to them, too. The bulk of the work, though, was done by John Higham himself and it is a pleasure to acknowledge this publicly.

(a) *General Introduction*

The original village of Wigton was probably of Anglian origin, seventh century, built on a well-drained ridge of land between two small stream valleys a mile south of the Roman cavalry fort of Olenacum, popularly known as "Old Carlisle". It is centrally placed on the Solway Plain.

In 1100 it became the centre of a Norman barony; in 1262 it obtained its market charter; evidence of the strength of the medieval town can still be seen today in the centre of Wigton which retains the main features of the medieval street plan – especially in its small, scattered market places.

The industrial revolution of the eighteenth and nineteenth centuries brought prosperity: Wigton became a centre for flax, cotton and woollen manufacture using water power and handloom weavers. There were associated dye works, and calico printing works. There were blacksmiths, gunsmiths, clock-makers, nail-makers, tanners, coopers and tool-makers. Between 1801 and 1831 the population doubled. Industry declined somewhat as the century went on–

textiles slowly, the printworks dramatically (by fire: 1845), cotton unhappily in the 1860's cotton famine.

While it lasted, the prosperity made possible a rebuilding of Wigton – sandstone replaced clay dabbin thatched cottages – predominantly in Georgian style – still in existence, most of these houses and buildings bringing a pleasant uniformity to the town centre.

Gate's *History and Topography of Wigton 1894* brings us to our starting point with all the self-confidence and self-congratulation of official Victorian England. He writes of "our substantial imposing public buildings, spacious shops, clean-kept streets, our handsome villa residences, the charming gardens of our suburbs, the mansions, farms and cultivated fields and grazing ground and splendid stock pasturing there . . ."

(b) *Local Government 1900 and 1975*

    (i) *1900*

Local Government Act adopted 1875 and Parish Councils Act 1894. Main concern seems to have been to save ratepayers money.

In 1894, Gate recorded with pride that the Poor Law Guardians did not waste money by giving unnecessary relief. The workhouse (built 1841 for 250 people) held 22 men and 9 women in 1900 costing 3s. 6d. per week per head, including clothing.

In 1901 the Council refused Edwin Banks' (of Highmoor Mansion) gift of the swimming bath lest it become a burden on the rates. He rented it to them for a shilling.

The amenities of 1900 included the Gasworks (1831), Waterworks (1866), Public Sewerage (1882), Market Hall (1882), Market House Co. – now Hope's Auction Co. – (1870), Highways Authority (1867), Fire Brigade and Post Office with eight "rural post messengers" and two "town letter carriers".

The County Court met annually in the town.

    (ii) *1975*

Wigton Rural District Council with its 1964–5 council offices at Southend now merged into Allerdale District Council in local Government Reorganisation of 1974.

The chief concern of the present council, I can report, ruefully, seems to be to spend as much of the ratepayers' money as possible.

The amenities of 1975 include water and sewerage, electricity, streets and dustbins, roads and footpaths, public park – with bowls, tennis, putting green and children's playground – swimming baths (still Banks' old baths, bought by the town in 1910 when he went bankrupt), public library (new building, opened 1975), fire brigade.

The gasworks was demolished in 1968. There is now only a sub-post office.

(c) *Population and Housing 1900 and 1975*

    (i) Wigton-cum-Woodside Parish 1901 – 3,692

                                     1971 – 4,720

    (ii) *Housing c. 1900*

1891: 980 inhabited and 149 uninhabited houses.

Most people lived in the centre of the town: Church Street, Water Street, Union Street, various courts, lanes, alleys, backyards. East End was still thought of as a "poorer and tougher" area.

Middle-class parts were: Station Hill (large Victorian villas), Standingtone, South End of High Street, Longthwaite Road, Park Square. (There was a Wigton and District Economic and Building Society which undoubtedly funded some of these houses.)

Some large mansions on the outskirts of the town:

Highmoor was easily the most important in 1900. Residence of Edwin Banks, whose inherited fortune was built on cloth exports to Australia. He renovated the parish church at his own expense, built the Kildare for the Conservative Club (they couldn't afford it: it became an hotel). He built the Baths for the town and other projects were undertaken. He owned over 1,000 acres locally, bred racehorses, collected antiques, ornamental trees, exotic waterfowl, park animals (deer, wallabies and llamas), and kept "open grounds" for the towns-people in a hundred-acre park.

His passion was campanology. In his belltower (1884) was a large striking bell (Big Tom: 7 tons) with a "range" of twelve miles and a tuned set of eight bells which rang Westminster chimes and played variations on 36 pre-set tunes at 9 a.m., 12 noon, 3 p.m. and 6 p.m. The tunes changed daily: on Sunday they were hymns.

In 1908–9 he was made bankrupt. Died 1917, buried in the local cemetery.

Wigton Hall – mock gothic, built on the profits of East India Company Trade – was occupied in 1900 by Mrs Kentish.

Greenhill had just been purchased by successful solicitor H. A. Dudding from the estate of one of his clients Joseph Nelson. (The Nelson School founded by Dudding from this Estate.)

Westmorland House – just taken over for the Thomlinson Girls' Grammar School.

Floshfield House – just taken over for the Nelson School.

(iii) *Housing in 1975*

1,815 houscholds registered in 1971 census.

Some people still live in the centre – chiefly above shops/pubs. Most of Church Street and Water Street and the interconnecting alleys, etc., was demolished 1968–73: now there is a car park.

Council Housing: gradual proliferation: small Skiddaw View Estate (1919); Brackenlands (1924); Bridlefield (1938) – 80 houses; Green-acres – 490 houses; Kirklands (post-World War Two).

Private House-building: Cross Grove (Station Hill: later 50s–early 60s – 19 houses); Mount Pleasant Gardens (Southend *c.* 1959 – 37 houses); Highmoor Park (1969 – 63 houses); Deer Park (1971 – 23 houses); Springfields (1973 – *c.* 80 houses). These last three estates are near or around the old Highmoor Mansion (all put up by Border Engineering). Some smaller estates of 6 to 10 houses and private, individual development, e.g. along Lowmoor Road.

There is also Howrigg Bank, built 1939–40 for R.A.F. civilian workers at Kirkbride Airfield, now 31 private houses, 19 council.

Old People's Housing: Highfield House (the nineteenth-century workhouse – 56 beds) operates as Old People's Home, along with Grange Bank (19 residents, 7 day-care) and Inglewood (built 1967 –

497

38 residents and 28 day-care).

Children's Home: transferred from Greenhill by Allerdale 1970. Ten boys and five girls between 4 and 16.

Middle class/exclusive/more expensive/"posher" areas: Station Hill, West Road (built up between the wars), and the South side of the town.

The Mansions: *Wigton Hall* is now 6 maisonettes.

Highmoor Mansions is now 14 luxury flats.

Greenhill is an hotel.

(d) *Where People Work. 1900 and 1975*

    (i) *1900* Satisfactory information difficult to come by. Textile and metal trades had declined. Gate (1894) – main textiles were "checks, ginghams and winsey". Kelly's Directories (1894 and 1897) repeats this, plus names two "factories" J. Pattinson and Co. Ltd. (woollen manufacturers) and "Lenim and Pattinson" (woollen, linen and cotton manufacturers) – both of Brookside Works.

Other industries in 1894 include tanning, brewing, spade and shovel handles. Bulmer's Directory (1901) mentions the jam factory and the three tailors and clothing manufacturers (including Redmayne's).

In 1900 trade appears to have been depressed, judging, for example, by the number of uninhabited houses in the 1891 census.

    (ii) *1975*

Sidac/ICI – manufactures polypropylene and transparent packaging material – workforce of *c.* 1,000 drawn from wide area – using special buses to bring in workers.

Redmayne's – clothing factory with its own shops and large mail order business – family firm, workforce of about 130.

Nelson Thomlinson School – including teachers and full-time and part-time ancillary staff (cooks, cleaners, caretakers, administrators) *c.* 120.

There is then a sudden drop to about 20–30 which are in other schools, local government, Cumberland farmers and Armisons.

An unknown but increasing number live in Wigton and work elsewhere, especially in Carlisle and Cockermouth. Some (mainly teachers and civil servants) travel in from considerable distances daily (15 miles or more).

A book like this must of course engender a good deal of sentimentality in the writer. In the general text and the appendices this, I trust, has been kept to a minimum: certainly I've tried to guard against it. However, just as I could not write the previous section without a reference to my parents, so I cannot finally quit this book without mentioning and thanking S. R. James, now deputy headmaster of the school in which he taught me not only history but a love for history.